ISBN 978-1-330-39723-7
PIBN 10051206

V. B. Yeoman
Nov '908

THE

PARKS AND GARDENS

OF

PARIS.

TREES AND BUILDINGS
In the small Garden in the Place du Carrousel.

THE

PARKS AND GARDENS

OF

PARIS

CONSIDERED IN

RELATION TO THE WANTS OF OTHER CITIES AND OF
PUBLIC AND PRIVATE GARDENS;

Being Notes on a Study of Paris Gardens.

By W. ROBINSON, F.L.S.

SECOND EDITION REVISED, SEVENTH THOUSAND.

ILLUSTRATED.

London:

MACMILLAN AND CO.

1878.

LONDON:
PRINTED BY WILLIAM CLOWES AND SONS,
STAMFORD STREET AND CHARING CROSS.

TO

VERNON LUSHINGTON, Q.C.,

THIS BOOK IS DEDICATED

BY

THE AUTHOR.

INTRODUCTION.

——◦◦◦——

"And let it appeare that he doth not change his Country Manners for those of Forraigne Parts: But only prick in some Flowers of that he hath Learned abroad into the Customes of his own country."—BACON's *Essay on Travel*.

THIS book originated as follows: when some years ago the author first went to Paris, he was privileged to note in the *Times* anything of importance with reference to horticulture that might be observed in that city and its neighbourhood interesting from an English point of view. Upon some of the points noted a lengthy correspondence arose, which (like most discussions) not being calculated to point to any definite conclusions, he was led to embody his notes upon the various subjects in the form of a book. At first the questions discussed were of purely horticultural interest, such as the extensive and skilful cultivation of hardy fruit-trees in France which has made fruit so good and plentiful in that country and led to its being so largely exported; the remarkable culture of Asparagus round Paris; the system by which in a harsh climate the French growers supply so well not only their own markets but those of many other cities with excellent salads throughout the winter and spring; the cultivation in the market-gardens round Paris, in which at least threefold more produce is gathered than from similar extent of garden-ground elsewhere; the very curious growth of Mushrooms beneath Paris, which had, till then, not been described or illustrated. With the idea of the book, however, came a feeling that the great system of public gardens formed of recent years in Paris, the many squares, the vast series of tree-planted streets and avenues, and generally that public gardening which has made New Paris, might be discussed with profit at a time when our own cities are so much in need of change. And I wished not only to record and illustrate what is good in them, but also to point out what is harmful.

It is scarcely necessary to show that a clean and ordered city is better than an ugly and filthy one, but it may be well to consider that from the lowest point of view it is the interest of even the poorest tradesman in London to help forward bold measures for its improvement. Whatever the fortunes of our country in the future, nobody can doubt that the English race will form the most numerous of civilised peoples, nor that the city where Shakespeare and Milton wrote will be holiday-ground to millions of English-speaking people besides those that inhabit it. The attractions of London to strangers are really greater than those of any other city that exists, but our total want of plan, or of any wise provision calculated to make locomotion pleasant or even possible throughout London, and the filthy and depressing aspect of the narrow streets, effectually drive away thousands of people from America and our vast colonies only too anxious to stay in London were it made possible to them. It is a common occurrence for Americans to run the gauntlet of Fleet Street and the Strand, and judging the whole town by their experience of a few narrow and greasy thoroughfares, to escape with all speed to pleasanter places. In Paris superb avenues may be seen often leading to nothing; in London many important points of interest are practically unapproachable even to those who know the town. Of course we cannot cut down our Fleet Streets or our Strands, but we could at much less cost than that of similar improvements in Paris drive a series of noble roads through the wretched shanties that cover a good half of London, so that it would be possible to get some clear and comprehensive idea of its plan, its suburbs, its parks—its noblest treasure of all, its ship-cities, the river below the bridges, its buildings, and its commerce.

The recent very remarkable improvements in Paris, such as the opening of the stately Boulevard de Saint-Germain running through and opening up to sun and air and trees the whole of the south of the city, and the new Avenue between the new Opera House and the Rue de Rivoli, have not only been made without cost to the town, but even with a balance on the right side, the vastly-increased value of sites for business premises in these new and noble streets having more than repaid the cost of their formation and the removal of the old houses through which they were driven. Abroad, every little capital possessing enough interest to occupy one for two hours, is furbishing-up its attractions, while we in London are neglecting advantages the like of which are not possessed by any other city in Europe. The river, the bridges, the suburbs, the surroundings, are infinitely superior to Paris, but owing to stupid absence of plan many of the good points are lost, many of the best suburbs being unknown ground even to thousands of Londoners, owing to the impossibility of reaching them without struggling through narrow and mean streets and roads. The finest city avenue in Europe is the Champs Elysées in Paris, and probably few would think it possible that a site with equal capacities lies wholly unused in the heart of London. Yet there it is in the Regent's Park, barred up by the railing of Park Crescent, and frittered away recently by narrow strips of geometrical gardening. I have said as good a site as the Champs Elysées, but it is really much better, the wide expanse of beautiful ground which may be seen from the top of the Broad Walk being entirely in the hands of the State. It has thus the advantage of being freely open to noble improvement without the enormous cost for removing massive, lofty, densely-packed houses which had so often to be incurred in Paris. In many other cases in like manner great opportunities are frequently unnoticed from dead walls or narrow streets or miserable railings stopping the view.

All this is not only sad, from its depriving us of so much beauty that London might possess, but also from its far more serious evil in the depreciation of property. I think it is very clear that many quarters of London, beautiful in themselves, are greatly lowered in value owing to bad approaches. A good and simple system of broad tree-planted roads, radiating from the centre to the suburbs, and connected by outer circular roads, would tend to make all parts of the town of more equal value, and would go far to prevent that terrible isolation of the poor in various parts of the city the misery of which is at present a by-word throughout the world. The real want is a want of plan, and this it is to be hoped Parliament will some day give us power to obtain. At present this want is glaringly apparent, not only in the central and more crowded parts, but all round London, where

ments than they are? My object is to point out in what way we may learn from the French. That they, in turn, may learn from us will be apparent when it is stated that intelligent Frenchmen have in botanic gardens pointed doubtfully at plants of Rhubarb and Seakale and asked me if it were true that we eat them in England! The general introduction into France of these two hardy easily-grown vegetables would be a material addition to the riches and food-supplies of that country.

Of the practices which we may with advantage, and which indeed we must, adopt from the French, those of fruit-culture command our first attention, because good fruit-culture combines the beautiful and the useful in a very high degree. There are at least six important ways in which we may highly improve and enrich our fruit-gardens and fruit-stores.

First, by planting against walls the very finest kinds of Winter Pears—the Pears that keep long, the Pears that bring a good return, the Pears of which the French now send us many thousands of pounds' worth annually. Varieties of Winter Pears are frequently planted in the open, in all parts of these islands, that an experienced fruit-grower in the neighbourhood of Paris or even further south would never plant away from a wall, knowing well that it would be sheer loss to do so. Sir H. Scudamore Stanhope has proved in his garden at Holme Lacy (p. 299) that improved wall-culture of the finer Winter Pears is as possible in England as in France.

Secondly, by the general adoption of the cordon system of Apple-growing in gardens. This will enable us to produce a finer class of fruit than that grown in orchards. It may be carried out in spots hitherto useless or unemployed, and will enable us to do away with the big Apple-trees that now shade our gardens. It should be distinctly understood, however, that *I do not recommend this system for orchard-culture, or for the production of the kinds and qualities of fruits that may be gathered in profusion from naturally-developed standard trees.*

Thirdly, by the general introduction of the true French Paradise stock into the gardens of the British Isles. Its merits are that it is dwarfer in growth than any other, and that in wet, cold or stiff soils it keeps its roots in a wig-like tuft near the surface —a most valuable quality on such soils. When well known, it will be found an immense gain in every class of garden except those on dry and poor sandy or gravelly soils, remarkable as it is in inducing early fertility, and affording a better result without root-pruning than either the Crab or English Paradise does with that attention. The knowledge that the Doucin of the French is an admirable stock for all forms of tree between the standard of the orchard and the very dwarf cordon or bush, will also be useful. The Apple should not be worked on the Crab unless it is desired to form standard trees in orchards—by far the best method, if properly carried out, for market and general supplies.

Fourthly, by the adoption in Peach-culture of some of the smaller forms of tree that may be observed in French gardens, as they will enable us to cover our walls with fruitful handsome trees in a few seasons instead of waiting many years, as hitherto, only perhaps to see them partially covered after all. These forms, the cordon, U or double U forms figured in this book, are particularly desirable where the soil is too light and poor for the health and full development of large wide-spreading trees.

Fifthly, by adopting for every kind of fruit-tree grown against walls a more efficient and simple mode of protection than we now use. In speaking of fruit-culture, nothing is more common than to hear our climate spoken of as the cause of all our deficiencies— the " fine " climate of Northern France being supposed to do everything for the cultivator. The error of this view of the case is well illustrated by the fact that the fruit-growers about Paris take care to protect their fruit-walls in spring by means of wide temporary copings. In this country I have never anywhere seen a really efficient temporary coping, though endless time is wasted in applying boughs, nets, etc., none of which are in the least effective in protecting the trees from the cold sleety rains, which, if they do not always destroy the fertilising power of the blossoms, prepare them to become an easy prey to frost.*

Sixthly, by the acquirement and diffusion among every class of gardeners of a knowledge of budding, grafting, pruning, and training equal to that now possessed by the French. Many of the illustrations in this book show the mastery they possess over each detail of training—the branches of every kind of tree being con-

* Since writing the above, various persons have introduced useful wide temporary and permanent copings, and with excellent results.

ducted in any way the trainer may desire, and with the greatest case. This knowledge is quite common amongst amateurs and workmen whose fellows in this country know nothing of such subjects. There are numerous professors who teach it in France; in this country, where it is really of far greater importance it is not taught at all or only in the most imperfect manner. It is a common thing in France to see a professor of fruit-culture and his class assembled round a tree pruning it and discussing every operation as it goes on. We require walls for our fruit-trees more than the French do, and there is no way in which we need improvement more than in the matter of the proper covering of fruit-walls and development of wall-trees. With standard trees, pruning may be dispensed with to some extent; but so long as we are obliged to devote walls to the production of our finer fruits, such knowledge as is now possessed by French fruit-growers would prove a great aid.

In the vegetable department we have also several important things to learn from the French, and not the least among these is the winter and spring culture of Salads. Enormous quantities of these are sent from Paris to our and other markets during the spring months. As I write this (April 19th) the market-gardens near London are faintly traced with light green lines of weak young Lettuce-plants, that have been for weeks barely existing under the influences of our harsh spring. Around Paris at the same season and for months before, in consequence of the adoption of the cloche and a most skilful system of culture, it is a pleasure to see the size and perfect health of the Lettuces—the difference in culture, and not the imaginary difference in climate, solely producing the result. By adopting the French system they may be grown to fully as great perfection near London and in the home counties as near Paris. The fact that we have to be supplied by our neighbours with articles that could be so easily produced in this country is a standing reproach. The French system will have the first difficulty to get over—that of people becoming used to it, and slightly changing their modes of culture to accommodate it; but it must some day be universally adopted by us, and with the certain result of a great benefit being reaped from it by the horticulturists of the United Kingdom. This culture is, in all its stages, so distinct from what is done elsewhere, that it is not surprising that growers do not even know how to begin. No doubt many still suppose that the tender Lettuces sent in such abundance to our markets in winter and spring come from some paradise in the south; these all the while being the result, in a harsh northern clime, of the most skilful cultivation I have ever seen adapted to the growth of a vegetable.

The French are also far before us in the culture and use of Asparagus, pursuing a system quite distinct from ours and growing it so abundantly that for many weeks in spring it is an article of popular consumption. Some among us affect to ridicule French Asparagus in consequence of its being blanched nearly to the top of the shoot; but to avoid this imperfection, if it be one, the grower has merely to adopt the superior mode of culture pursued by the French, but without blanching the shoot. But real students of Asparagus who have had much experience of its use both in France and England, and in its best state in both countries, will probably agree that he has but a very one-sided knowledge of Asparagus who prefers to eat it green. The experience of persons who abuse French Asparagus is frequently limited to samples that may have been cut in France a fortnight before they reach the table in England, having passed the intermediate time in travelling and losing quality in market or shop. However, nobody will deny that it ought to be more abundantly and better grown in this country. Parisian Mushroom-culture is interesting and curious in a degree of which few have any conception, as will be seen by a perusal of the chapter devoted to it. The sketches and plan that illustrate it will help the reader to obtain a fair idea of places that have been seen by very few people beyond the cultivators.

Among my own I have given illustrations from trustworthy French sources, such as Dubreuil's 'Arbres Fruitiers,' Decaisne and Naudin's 'Manuel de l'Amateur des Jardins;' from the collections of engravings belonging to Messrs. Vilmorin, Messrs. Hachette, from Mangin's 'Les Jardins,' the 'Revue Horticole,' and 'La Culture du Chasselas,' but these, as a rule, only when they were as useful in their way as if made specially for the book. Such illustrations have been used for the most part in discussing modes of culture at once good and different from those employed by us, and which have naturally been treated of by

French authors.   The main source of such ideas as are expressed
in the book is personal observation in the gardens of Paris of
every kind, at various seasons and for a considerable length of
time.

  Since the first edition of the work was published, a variety of
trials have been made concerning certain modes of culture described in it.   Of improvements then advocated the preservation
of Grapes without letting them hang on the Vines, has been
adopted by most good Grape-growers throughout the land;
Asparagus on the distinct and wholly superior French plan has
been tried with exactly the same excellent result as in the
neighbourhood of Paris; the true Paradise stock has been tried
in various districts and found quite hardy and excellent on moist
and stiff soils; the cordon system for choice Apples and late-keeping
Pears grown on walls has been proved to be a great success; the
light, neat system of wiring garden-walls, forming espaliers and
supports for fruit-trees, has been carried out in numerous gardens,
and a great quantity of wide and effective coping for wall-trees
has been erected throughout the country with very good results.

                                                    W. R.

April, 1878.

CONTENTS.

b

CONTENTS.

LIST OF ILLUSTRATIONS.

THE

PARKS AND GARDENS OF PARIS.

CHAPTER I.

THE BOIS DE BOULOGNE.

IF there be any aim more worthy of a national botanic garden than another, it is surely the expression of the beauty of the vegetable world; but the botanists at the Jardin des Plantes have so arranged matters there that all who visit it in the hope of seeing a fair garden will be disappointed. So we had better follow the world to the Bois de Boulogne. There we break quite away from the old and dismal style of French gardening, with its clipped trees and unendurable monotony, and from the sad results of the open-air pedantry of the botanist. The Bois is in many ways a garden such as a great city like Paris should possess; a noble system of roads, ample space, and fine sheets of water contributing to render it deserving of a visit from all for whom gardens possess an interest.

Pains are taken to make the vegetation along the banks of the artificial water diversified in character, so that at one place we meet with conifers, at another rock-shrubs, at another Magnolias,

B

and so on ; without the eternal repetition of common things which one too often sees.

The islands seen from the margin of the lakes are beautiful, in consequence of the presence of a varied collection of the finest shrubs and trees. They show at a glance the superiority of permanent embellishment over fleeting annual display. The planting of these islands was expensive at first, and required a good knowledge of trees and shrubs, besides a large amount of taste in the designer ; but it is so done that were the hand of man withheld from them for half a century they would not suffer in the least. Nothing could be easier than to find examples of gardens quite as costly in the first instance which, while involving a yearly expenditure, would be ruined by a year's neglect. In spring the scene is animated by the cheerful flush of bloom of the many shrubs that burst into blossom with the strengthening sun, and while the Oaks are yet leafless the large, swollen flower-buds of the splendid deciduous Magnolias may be seen conspicuous at long distances through the other trees. In summer, along the margins of these islands the fresh pyramids of the deciduous Cypress start from graceful surroundings of hardy Bamboos and Pampas grass, and far beyond is a group of bright silvery Negundo in the midst of green vegetation, with an infinite variety of tree-form around. In autumn the number and richness of the tints of the foliage afford a varied picture from week to week ; and in winter the many graceful forms of the deciduous trees among the evergreen shrubs and Pines offer as much to interest an observant eye as at any other season.

Looking deeper than the immediate results, we may see how the adoption of the system of careful permanent planting enables us to secure what is the most important point in the whole art of gardening—variety, and that of the noblest kind. We are told that " change or variety is as much a necessity to the human heart in buildings as in books ; that there is no merit, though there is some occasional use, in monotony ; and that we must no more expect to derive either pleasure or profit from an architecture whose ornaments are of one pattern and whose pillars are of one proportion than we should out of a universe in which the clouds were all of one shape and the trees all of one size." All this applies to public gardens with even greater force. In them we need not be tied by

the formalism which convenience and economy require the architect to bear in mind, no matter how widely he diverges from the
commonplace in general design. In garden or in park there is
practically no limit to variety; in buildings there are many.
Vegetation varies every day in the year, but buildings bear the
stamp of unchangeableness. In the tree and plant world we deal
with things by no means remotely allied to ourselves : their lives,

LAKE AND ISLAND VIEW

An absurd kiosk-like structure on this point of the island has been omitted in the sketch.

from the unfolding bud to the tottering trunk, are as the lives of
men.   There is infinite change in the individual, and boundless
variety in species and their forms.   Therefore the opportunity for
variety is beyond comparison greater in gardening than in the
building art, or indeed in any other art whatever. ˙
   As yet we are far from perfection as builders, and the garden
still holds the relation to the building art which is described by

Bacon. There is no indication that any knowledge of the all-important necessity for variety exists in the minds of those who arrange or manage our gardens, public or private. And yet this unrecognised variety is the life and soul of true gardening. If people generally could see this clearly, it would lead to the greatest improvement our gardening has ever witnessed. Considering the wealth of the vegetable kingdom, even in northern countries, and the differences in soil, climate, and position which we can command, it is impossible to doubt that our power to produce variety is unlimited.

The necessity for it is great. What is the broadly marked defect of the gardening of the present day? The want of variety. What is it that causes us to take little more interest in the ordinary displays of " bedding out," which are fostered with so much care, than we do in the bricks that go to make up the face of a house? Simply the want of that variety of beauty which a walk along a flowery lane or over a wild heath shows us may be afforded by even the indigenous vegetation of˘ one spot in a northern and unfavourable clime. But in our parks we can, if we will, have an endless variety of form, from the Fern to the Oak and the Pine—infinite charms of colour and fragrance, from the Alpine plant to the Lilies of Japan and Siberia. And yet out of all these riches the fashion for a long time has been to select a few kinds which have the property of producing dense masses of their particular colours on the ground, to the almost entire neglect of the nobler and hardier vegetation. The expense of the present system is great, and must be renewed annually, while the end obtained is of the poorest kind. To a person with no idea of the rich variety of vegetation the system may prove sufficient, and to the professional gardener it is often so; but to most persons the result attained by the above method is almost a blank. There can be little doubt that numbers are, for this reason unknown to themselves, deterred from taking any interest in the garden; in fact, it is without meaning to them.

Eyes everywhere among us are hungering after beauty; but in our public gardens they, as a rule, look for it in vain; for the presence of a few things with which they are already as familiar as with the texture of a gravel walk must impress them with an opinion that gardening is the most inane of arts. In books

they everywhere find variety and some interest, even if high
merit is rare : the same is the case in painting, in sculpture,
in music, and indeed in most arts; but in that which should
possess it more than any other, and is more capable of it than any
other, there is as a rule little to be found.   This is not merely the
case with the flower-garden and its adjuncts ; it prevails in wood,
grove, shrubbery, and in everything connected with the garden.

ROCKY GROTTOES IN BANKS, CLOTHED WITH IVY.

*These serve for shelter or garden-stores: a suggestion for those who build hideous wooden
structures for such purposes.*

What attempt is made in our parks and pleasure-grounds to give
an idea of the dignity and beauty of our hardy trees ?   How rare
it is to see in any garden a tithe of the beauty afforded by
deciduous shrubs !   Hitherto our gardening has been governed by
two schools—by one of which a few, or comparatively few, plants
are grown ; while by the other, the botanic-garden school, every
obtainable thing is grown, be it ugly or handsome.   What we

want for the ornamental public garden is the mean between these
two : we want the variety of the botanic garden without its so-
called scientific but very unnatural and ugly arrangement; we
want its interest without its weediness and monotony.

There is no way in which the deadening formalism of our
gardens may be more effectually destroyed than by the system of
naturally grouping hardy plants. It may afford the most pleasing
results, and impress on others the beauty of many families now
almost unused. Suppose that in a case where the chief labour
and expense now go for an annual display, or what some might
call an annual muddle, the system is given up for one in which all
the taste and skill and expense go to the making of features that
do not perish with the first frosts. Let us begin, then, with a
carefully selected collection of trees and shrubs distinguished for
their fine foliage—by noble leaf-beauty, selecting a quiet glade
in which to develop it. It would make a feature in itself attractive, and show many that it is not quite necessary to resort to
things that require the climate of Rio before we find marked leaf-
beauty and character. It would teach, too, how valuable such
things would prove for general use. Many kinds of leaf might be
therein developed, from the great simple-leaved species of the
Rhubarb type to the divided ones of Lindley's Spiræa, and the taller
Ailantus, and other noble-leaved trees of Asia and America. The
fringes of such a group might well be lit up with beds of Lilies,
Irises, or any showy flowers; or, better still, by hardy flowering
shrubs. An irregularly and artistically planted group of this kind
would prove at all times a source of interest; it might be improved
and added to from time to time, but the original expense would
be almost the only one.

Pass by this rather sheltered nook, and come to a gentle knoll
in an open spot. Here we will make a group from that wonderful
rosaceous family which does so much to beautify all northern and
temperate climes. And what a glorious bouquet it might be made,
with American and European hawthorns, double-flowered cherries
and peaches, plums, almonds, pears ! While we should here have
a marked family likeness prevailing in the groups, we should
entirely escape the monotony resulting from planting, say, five
or six thousand plants of Rhododendron in one spot, as is the
fashion with some; for each tree would differ considerably from its

neighbour in flower and fruit. Then, having arranged the groups
in a picturesque way, we might finish off with a new feature. It
is the custom to margin our shrubberies and ornamental plantings
with a rather well-marked line. Strong-growing trees come near
the edge as a rule, and many of the prettiest spring-flowering
shrubs of low growth are lost in the shade or crowding of more

Rustic Bridge between Wooded Islands.

robust subjects. They are often overshadowed, often deprived of
food, often injured by the rough digging which people usually
think wholesome for the shrubbery. The best of these should be
planted as neat low groups, or isolated well-grown specimens, not
far from the medium-sized or low trees of the central groupings,
but quite clear of their shade. The result would be that choice
dwarf shrubs would display a perfection to which they are usually
strangers. It would be putting them as far in advance of their
ordinary appearance as the stove and greenhouse plants at the

great flower-shows are to the ordinary stock in a nursery or neglected greenhouse. It would teach people that there are many unnoticed hardy little shrubs which merely want growing in some open spot to appear as beautiful as any tropical or subtropical plant. The system might be varied as much as the plants themselves, while one garden or pleasure-ground need no more resemble another than the clouds of to-day do those of yesterday.

In the rich alluvial soil in level spots, near water or in some open break in a wood, we might have numbers of the fine herbaceous families of Northern Asia, America, and Europe. These, if well selected, would furnish a type of vegetation now very rarely seen in this country, and flourish after once being planted without the slightest attention. On rocky mounds quite free from shade we might well display true Alpine vegetation, selecting dwarf shrubs and the many free-growing, hardy Alpines which flourish everywhere. To turn from the somewhat natural arrangements, occasional plantings might be made as the years rolled on to show in greatest abundance the subjects of greatest novelty or interest at the time of planting. In one select spot, for example, we might enjoy our plantation of Japanese evergreens, many of them valuable in the ornamental garden; in another, the Californian Pines ; in another, a picturesque group of wild Roses; and so on without end. Were this the place to do any more than suggest what may be accomplished in this way in the splendid positions offered by our public gardens and parks, scores of arrangements equal in interest to the above could be mentioned. If the principle of annually planting a portion of a great park or garden of this kind were adopted instead of giving all the same routine attention after the first laying out, it would be found to be the greatest improvement ever introduced into gardening. The embellishment of the islands in the Bois de Boulogne is very successful, but it is merely one of many fine results that artistic planting would secure. Plantations as full of interest and beauty might be made in other portions, and the fact is the vegetable kingdom is so extensive that, although the combination of knowledge and taste necessary to success might not often be found in the designer, the materials for any number of varied pictures could never fail.

More than one view of the river as it glides along one side of
this noble park may serve to show how much may be gained by
arranging the ground and planting so that the beauty of the
natural water may be seen.   In the park various artificial lakes
have been made, while, for the most part, the fine opportunities
offered by the river have not been taken advantage of.   Wherever
a garden or park possesses natural advantages of this kind it is

THE " GRAND " CASCADE IN THE BOIS DE BOULOGNE.
Pines, Birch, and Ivy have somewhat concealed its original ugliness.

well to develop them in preference to making pieces of artificial
water.   Lake-like reaches, islets, effective planting, turf-margined
bays, and every feature that makes water, or ground near water,
charming may be secured in such a case far more readily than
with artificial water.

As a combination of wild wood and noble pleasure-garden, the
Bois is magnificent.   As regards size, it is ample, containing more
than two thousand acres, of which nearly half is wood, a quarter

grass, an eighth roads, and more than seventy acres water. In
some spots it has more beauty and finish than any of our London
parks; while in others large spaces are covered with a thick scrub-
like wood, in which there is an abundant growth of wild flowers,
such as are never seen in our prim London inclosures. There are
plenty of wild Cowslips dotted about, even over the best parts of
it, in spring.

From a landscape-gardening point of view, the great drawback
of the Bois is its want of breadth. Except for the roads and
avenues that intersect it, it is, speaking generally, a mass of
dense monotonous wood. There is no open, airy space of any
extent (except the broad roads) for a long distance from the gate
nearest Paris. This of course is stupid in a park of such vast
extent. Even if effect were not taken into consideration, it must,
nevertheless, be remembered that the result of such dense masses
of low wood is to prevent that motion of the air which is so desirable in a great park. It would be difficult to find a city park so
ill-arranged in this respect. It is owing to other things than
design that the parts more distant from Paris are breezy, open,
and pleasant to the eye. The racecourse of Longchamps and the
training-ground necessitated open spaces, and the result is very
satisfactory from a landscape point of view.

Various banks and rocks near the water here are very tastefully
adorned with Ivy and rock-shrubs. The planting of the banks
near artificial water offers an opportunity for securing good effects
which are worth studying. The contrast with the water, and the
certainty that from across the water at least the result of tasteful
planting will be seen and not be obscured by chance or unre-
strained growth or unwise planting, should encourage the planter
to devote his attention to the subject. One happy effect here is
afforded by ivy on the rocky margin of the water, in combination
with rock-shrubs and hardy Cupressus and Junipers. Sheets of
luxuriant Irish Ivy fall over the rocks and carpet the banks. This
is welcome in winter, when it forms such a contrast to the dug
surface on which so many shrubs have to stand through most of
the year. Among the evergreen rock-shrubs and low conifers
suitable for such positions, a few good deciduous early-flowering
shrubs may be placed with charming effect; such, for example,
are the Japan Pyrus (P. japonica) and its varieties, the Forsythias,

the large white Chinese Magnolia (M. conspicua), and other early-flowering shrubs. The attractive Chinese, Japanese, and Ghent Azaleas, and the Rhododendrons, are, of course, admirable for such positions; but there is a peculiar fitness in placing the very early-flowering shrubs on these well-carpeted green banks, where the surroundings are not so winterly as they are often needlessly made in gardens.

Plantations on Banks of Lake; rock-shrubs and small cascades.

There is one feature in the Bois de Boulogne which cannot be too much condemned—the practice of laying down here and there on some of its freshest sweeps of sloping grass enormous beds containing one kind of flower only. In several instances, near the plantations on the islands, may be seen hundreds of one kind of tender plant in a great unmeaning mass, just in the positions where the turf ought to have been left free for a little repose. This is done to secure a sensational effect, but its only result is to spoil some of the prettiest spots.   Let us hope that some winter day, when the great beds are empty, they may be neatly covered with green turf.   It would be a great gain to horticulture if ten out of every twelve "flower-beds" in Europe were blotted out with fresh green grass.

The illustrations in this chapter show some of the beauty of the Bois, in the part that is most essentially a garden.   They show the rocks in the lower lake with their drapery of Ivy and shrubs; the " grand " cascade from its best point of view — it was originally ill-formed and unhappy as regards its surroundings, but

False curves to banks, hard formal margin, and parallel walk ugly and needless.   Compare with two margins to natural water on page 13.

nature has thrown a graceful mantle over it in parts—the island view, which is pretty ; the St. Cloud view, from a point near the training-ground, one of the most charming views in Paris, but which is more the result of accident than design; the bridge with its fringe of creepers and shrubs; and the river view, which tells of the wisdom of developing the natural advantages of a beautiful stream, instead of wasting efforts in creating an artificial lake.

The main defect of the most frequented part of the Bois de Boulogne is that the banks which fall to the water are in some parts too suggestive of a railway embankment, and display but little of that indefiniteness of gradation and outline which we find in the true examples of the " English style " of laying out grounds. This fault is common to almost every example of the "picturesque" garden to be seen about Paris; in most of the walks, mounds, and turnings of the streams may be detected a family likeness and a style of curvature which is certainly never exhibited by Nature, and would never be drawn by an artist who had studied her. The natural style of laying out ground cannot be fairly judged of till we are accustomed to obey in our gardens the same laws by which artists are governed in their work.   An avowedly geometrical

garden with stately and abundant vegetation is often more pleasing
than a so-called naturally designed garden in which the great
lines are laid down by persons who have no knowledge of or
feeling for what is right in the matter.   It must not be supposed
that the right thing is not possible : a good deal of English work

Rocky margin of island in Lago Maggiore.

in this direction is irreproachable.   The gentle and graceful
gradation which would generally recommend itself in our lowland
gardens is indeed easier to form and to keep in order than such
stiff embankments as those by the water here.   These too clearly
bear the impress of the engineer and the navvy.
     More vicious still are the walks which run by the margin of

Water margin in Loch Achray.

the water on all sides, destroying the good effect which turf
running down to clear water generally produces.   These walks are
a fatal error in a scene like this : from many points of view they
are offensive.   There is no surer way of robbing garden-lake
scenery of its charms than by putting formal walks close to and

parallel with the margin. Frequently it may be found desirable
to approach the water edge for the sake of a view, or for other
reasons. In such cases it is right to approach it boldly, and to
let the gravel touch and run into it. Then it should recede again
and leave the margin green, quiet, and artistic in outline and
gradation. It is vexing to notice that these eternal and ever
visible serpentine walks steal all beauty from the margins of
the water.

Forming racecourses in important positions in public parks
is surely a great mistake. France is large enough to accommodate her racing men in the way usual in other countries. The
creation of a new steeplechase-course in the very best position in
the Bois, just beyond the top end of the upper lake, is as vulgar
an error as can well be committed in a public garden! Imagine
the best part of the Regent's Park in London, or the Central
Park, New York, prostituted to the purposes of "suburban
meetings"! And not only is this park thus misused from time to
time, but a large space railed in with a "grand stand" and all
its appurtenances are in permanent occupation of what, three years
ago, was one of the most beautiful spots round Paris. It is unworthy of a city to allow its finest open spaces to be thus violated.
Apart from the incongruity of a great city or state taking such
doubtful gambling business under its care, there is the objection
that the great numbers attracted are likely to do much damage to
the planting, as, indeed, they often have done on crowded days in
this park. The older Longchamps course, almost apart as it is,
might have been excused in a people anxious to naturalise
"meetings" that English people even dread coming near their
houses; but this creation of a second racecourse in the same park
is no credit to the city authorities.

Trees and Avenues in the Bois de Boulogne.—It would be
impossible to find nobler roads and avenues than in the Bois de
Boulogne; but they are bordered by the usual badly grown trees
seen everywhere in Paris. There may be some reason for being
satisfied with mere sticks in narrow streets and in gas-saturated
earth, but not here! Trees are planted everywhere to give shade,
but they are so managed that they never afford any such pleasant
shelter from the sun's rays as may be enjoyed under tall spreading
trees. The shade, forsooth, from these starvelings is not to be

compared to that from stately trees beneath the tall limbs of which the cool air might circulate. It is easy to imagine the effect of really well-grown trees along these superb avenues. They only want room on all sides and freedom from the municipal pruning-knife. For grand avenues trees must have space to grow, and sufficient exposure to winds to cause them to anchor

VIEW BY THE SEINE, *Looking north from near the Bridge of Suresnes.*

Developing views of this kind is better than dabbling in artificial water. This quiet nook of the park has escaped the attention of the landscape-engineer; there are, therefore, no false curves on the banks, no hard straight margin, and no parallel walk. Compare this with margins of artificial water in this same park, and kerbstone to our own Serpentine.

well in the soil on all sides. The lines of young Planes and other trees are often planted at a distance not greater than from nine to twelve feet from the dense, badly grown wood, so that their tops touch; and the trees themselves are often only fifteen feet apart in the lines! It is curious to notice how people persist in wasting money in so planting trees that they can never attain a third of their proper size. The result here deplored is not owing to the soil or any other disadvantages of the site. Many of the trees of Europe and America would attain their full stature and dignity here if not crammed together in the way the engineers seem to have decided that trees should grow.

More noticeable still is the condition of the trees in the wood itself generally. They look as if France wished only to grow coppice-wood for barrel-hoops in this her favourite park! Monotony reigns along all the main drives from this cause. There is nothing to be seen but illimitable and impenetrable forests of sticks and brambles. Why allow the trees to crowd each other to death or starvation? Thousands of Acacias and Oaks are struggling for bare life, while by thinning them out those left would form noble trees in good time. Where a wood of Pines breaks the monotony, it looks like a deserted nursery—the trees as close together as a plantation of saplings, and never thinned! These woods ought not only to be properly thinned, but spaces cleared to give breadth and to relieve the eye. In these spaces various noble aspects of tree-life might be easily developed. There are other and better gardens than those that require the mowing-machine. It is in such wide expanses of ground as this that the tree-gardens of the future will be made, and not in the narrow botanic gardens hitherto formed in Europe. Even all the trees and shrubs native in France planted, not in any formal order, but in ample groves and groups, would form features which would be very beautiful and interesting, while valuable to the country. And instead of bracken beneath and around these trees, why not naturalise everywhere in the grass the beautiful hardy herbaceous plants of France? In such a way we might form gardens requiring no perennial care, and which would soon surpass in beauty the trimmest and most costly.

The Gardens of the Acclimatisation Society.—Nowadays other gardens than those avowedly botanical or horticultural often claim attention from their gardening interest. In our own Zoological Gardens there have for some years past been attractive floral displays both in spring and summer. The warm temperature and light of some of the new houses afforded opportunities for indoor gardening which were taken advantage of. This desirable innovation might be carried out with advantage in many

BOIS DE BOLOGNE : *View towards St. Cloud.*

1.

other cases.   The temperature, moisture, air, etc., given to houses
of exotic plants of various classes would perfectly suit various
forms of animal life difficult to preserve in good health in cold
northern countries.   The interest and beauty of both the animal
and vegetable kingdom might be heightened by such a mixed
arrangement as we speak of, tastefully and judiciously carried
out.   The economy resulting from adapting the same structures
and heating power to the wants of both the animal and vegetable

Weeping Beech on Sloping Bank of Island.

treasures would permit of fuller justice being done to each.   In
cities rich enough to afford first-class separate establishments, this
proposal in its entirety would not so readily commend itself.   But,
however objectionable it might seem to introduce zoological
elements into the botanic garden, there would be no two opinions
as to the good of adding all the charms of vegetation to the
zoological garden.   In small cities with only one zoological or
botanical garden it would be easy so to arrange the two matters

that a happy result might be produced. If these ideas be sound so far as buildings are concerned, they are equally so as regards the open air. The old narrow idea that a small portion of ground in a town suffices to worthily represent vegetation in a public garden—the idea that we see illustrated in so many continental cities, and in some dozen of our own—must be got rid of before we ever see ornamental horticulture properly carried out in any city. Every garden and open space may do as much towards this end as any similar space of the so-called botanic garden. That it should do so two things are mainly requisite—first, that the

BOIS DE BOULOGNE.

Line of Planes near the Mare d'Auteuil, showing scrubby wood and crowded planting.

garden should be laid out on a sensible plan; secondly, that it should not be devoted to imitating what is done everywhere else. Beautiful it might be made with every flower or tree that those who resort to it love; but, in addition, let it show us one or more families of trees, shrubs, plants, or fruits, as completely illustrated as may be. It should, in fact, like a useful type of man, know a little of everything and everything of something. Among modern public gardens, that of the Acclimatisation Society in the Bois de Boulogne shows a fair attempt to make a garden, mainly zoological, satisfactory from a landscape point of view. At one

time it was pleasant, from the judicious planting of a variety of
trees and shrubs.   Recently, however, the zoological element has
predominated so much over the rest that the beauty of the place
is almost destroyed, with, perhaps, the exception of the winter-
garden, which shows a variety of subtropical subjects planted out.
It is suggestive of what lovely scenes may be made by means of
this plan as compared with the tub-and-pot one.   Here masses of
Bambusa gracilis grow up 15 feet high, and with all the elegance
of a weeping Willow, while graceful Palms and Tree-ferns look
quite at home when seen without the usual ugly assemblage of
pots and tubs.

CHAPTER II.

The Parc Monceau.

WHAT first excites the interest of the visitor accustomed to
the monotonous type of garden now so common is the variety,
beauty of form, and refreshing verdure which characterise this
garden—for it is not a park in our sense.   The true garden is a
scene which should be so delightfully varied in all its parts—so
bright, so green, so freely adorned with the majesty of the tree,
the beauty of the shrub, the noble lines of fine-leaved plants, and
the minute beauty of the dwarfish ones ; so perpetually interesting, with vegetation that changes with the days and seasons,
rather than stamping the scene with monotony for months ;
and so stored with new or rare, neglected or forgotten, curious
or interesting plants—that the simplest observer may feel that
indefinable joy which lovers of Nature derive from her charms in
her own fairest gardens.   If any good at all is to be done by
means of flowers and gardens, we must give men a living interest
in them, and some other objects than those which can be taken in
by the eye in a moment.   Numbers are occupied with gardening
as it is at present, but it cannot be doubted that a system with
something like an aim at true art would be sure to attract many
more.   It is patent that there are numbers even among the
educated classes who take little or no interest in the garden,
simply because they can in few places find any real beauty or
character in it.

Here it is that the phase of gardening which is known among
us as the subtropical, and which so much helped to open peeple's
eyes to the drawbacks of the "bedding out" so common a
few years ago, was first practised extensively.   This system

of garden-decoration, which simply means the use in gardens
of plants having large leaves, picturesque habit, or graceful
port, has taught us the value of grace and verdure amid masses
of low, brilliant, and unrelieved flowers, and has reminded us
how far we have diverged from Nature's ways of displaying
the beauty of vegetation. Our love for rude colour led us too
often to ignore the exquisite and inexhaustible way in which
plants are naturally arranged.   In a wild state flowers are usually

SKETCH IN THE PARC MONCEAU.

relieved by a setting of abundant green; and even where mountain and meadow plants of a few kinds produce a wide blaze of
colour at one season, there is intermingled a spray of pointed
grass and other leaves, which tone down the mass and quite separate it from anything shown by what is called the "bedding
system" in gardens. When we come to examine the most pleasing examples of our own indigenous or any other wild vegetation,
we find that their attraction mainly depends on flower and fern,

trailer, shrub, and tree, sheltering, supporting, and relieving each other, so that the whole array has an indefinite charm and mystery of arrangement.

We may be pleased by the wide spread of purple on a heath or mountain, but when we go near and examine it in detail we find that its most exquisite aspect is seen in places where the long Moss cushions itself beside the Ling, and the fronds of the

HARDY BAMBOO (*Bambusa metake*) *in the Parc Monceau.*

Polypody peer forth around little masses of heather. Everywhere we see Nature judicious in the arrangement of her highest effects, setting them in clouds of verdant leafage, so that monotony is rarely produced—a state of things which it is highly desirable to attain as far as possible in the garden. We cannot attempt to reproduce this literally—nor would it be wise or convenient to do so—but assuredly herein will be found the chief source of true beauty and interest in our gardens; and the more we keep this fact before our eyes, the nearer will be our approach to truth and success.

We should compose from Nature, as landscape artists do. We may have in our gardens—and without making wildernesses of

CASTOR-OIL PLANT.
Showing one year's growth in European climate; type of tender plants that make vigorous growth in open air in summer.

them—all the shade, the relief, the grace, the beauty, and nearly all the irregularity of Nature. This bold growth of " fine-foliaged plants " has shown us that one of the greatest mistakes ever made in the garden was the adoption of a few varieties of plants for culture on a vast scale, to the exclusion of interest and variety, and too often of beauty or taste. We have seen how well the pointed, tapering leaves of the Cannas carry the eye upwards; how refreshing it is to cool the eyes in the deep green of those thoroughly tropical Castor-oil plants, with their gigantic leaves; how noble the Wigandia, with its fine texture and massive outline, looks, after we have surveyed brilliant hues and richly

Giant Knotweed (Polygonum sachalinense) in the Parc Monceau, Sept. 1877.

painted leaves; how too the bold tropical palm-leaves beautify the garden. In a word, the system has shown us the difference between the gardening that interests and delights all beholders, and not the horticulturist only, and that which is too often offensive to the eye of taste, and pernicious to every true interest of what has been called the " purest of humane pleasures."

But are we to adopt this system in its purity—as shown, for

example, by Mr. Gibson when superintendent of Battersea Park? It is evident that to accommodate it to private gardens an expense and a revolution of appliances would be necessary, which are in nearly all cases quite impossible, and if possible hardly desirable.   We can, however, introduce into our gardens most of its better features; we can vary their contents, and render them more interesting by a better and nobler system.   The use of all

Tropical Arum (after a storm), Parc Monceau.

plants without any particular and striking habit or foliage or other desirable peculiarity, merely because they are natives of very hot countries, is unwise and generally impossible.   Selection of the most beautiful and useful from the great mass of plants known is the good gardener's pride, and in no branch must he exercise it more thoroughly than in this.   Some of the plants used are indispensable—the different kinds of Ricinus, Canna in great variety, Polymnia, Colocasia, Uhdea, Wigandia, Ferdinanda, Palms, Yuccas, Dracænas, and many fine-leaved plants. A few specimens of these may be accommodated in many gardens; they will embellish the houses in winter, and may be transferred to the open garden in summer. Some Palms, like Seaforthia, may be used with the best effect for the winter decoration of the conservatory, and be placed out with a good result, and without danger, in summer. Many fine kinds of Dracænas, Yuccas, Agaves, etc., are adapted for standing out in summer, and are in fact benefited by it. So with

MONTAGNÆA HERACLEIFOLIA.

some Cycads and other plants of distinct habit—the very things best fitted to add to the attractions of the flower-garden.

Thus we may, in all but the smallest gardens, enjoy all the charms of this style of gardening, without creating any special arrangements for it. But what of those who have no conservatory, no hothouses, no means for preserving large tender plants in winter? They too may enjoy the beauty which plants of fine form afford. A better effect than any yet seen in an English

MUSA ENSETE, IN THE PARC MONCEAU, 1868.
(*The artist is responsible for the liberties taken with the "formalities" around.*)

garden from tender plants may be obtained by planting hardy ones only! There is the Pampas grass, which when well-grown is unsurpassed by anything that requires protection. There are the Yuccas, noble and graceful in outline, and hardy. There are Arundo conspicua and Donax, and there are noble hardy herbaceous plants like Crambe cordifolia, the giant Japanese Polygonums, Rheum Emodi, Ferulas, and various graceful umbelliferous plants that will furnish effects equal to any we can produce by using the tenderest exotics. Acanthuses too, when well-grown, are very suitable for this use. Then we have a hardy Palm, that has preserved its health and greenness, in sheltered positions where its leaves could not be torn to shreds by storms, through many hard winters.

And when we have obtained these, and many like subjects, we may associate them with not a few things of much beauty among trees and shrubs—with elegant young Pines; not of necessity bringing the larger plants into close or awkward association with the humbler and dwarfer subjects, but sufficiently so to carry the eye from the minute and pretty to the higher and more dignified forms of vegetation. By a judicious selection from the vast number of hardy plants now obtainable in this country, and by associating with them, where it is convenient, house plants that may be placed out for the summer, we may arrange and enjoy charms in the flower-garden to which we are as yet strangers, because we have not utilised the vast amount of plant loveliness now in our garden-flora.

In dealing with the tenderer subjects, we must choose such as will make a healthy growth in sheltered places. In all parts the kinds with permanent foliage, such as the New Zealand Flax and the hardier Dracænas, will be found as effective as around London and Paris; and to such the northern gardener should turn his attention. Even if it were possible to cultivate the softer-growing kinds, like the Ferdinandas, to the same perfection in all parts as in the south of England, it would by no means be everywhere desirable, and especially where expense is a consideration, as these kinds are not capable of being used indoors in winter. The many fine permanent-leaved subjects that stand out in summer without the least injury, and may be transferred to the conservatory in autumn, there to produce as fine an effect all through the cold months as they do in the flower-garden in summer, are the best generally.

But of infinitely greater importance are the hardy plants; for however few can indulge in the luxury of rich displays of tender plants, or however rare the spots in which they may be ventured out with confidence, all may enjoy those that are hardy, and that too with infinitely less trouble than is required by the tender ones. Those noble masses of fine foliage displayed to us by tender plants have done much towards correcting a false taste. In whatever part of these islands one may live, one need not despair of producing sufficient similar effect to vary the flower-

BEAUTY OF FORM FROM HARDY PLANTS.

All the plants shown are, with two exceptions, hardy.   (Drawn by Alfred Dawson.)

garden or pleasure-ground beautifully by the use of hardy plants alone. The noble lines of a well-grown Yucca recurva, or the finely chiselled yet fern-like spray of a graceful young conifer, will aid him as much in this direction as anything that requires either tropical or subtropical temperature.

The fault of this "subtropical gardening," as hitherto seen, is its lumpish monotony and the neglect of graceful combinations. The subjects are not used to contrast with or relieve others of less attractive port and brilliant colour, but are generally set down in large masses. Here we meet a troop of Cannas, numbering 500, in one long formal bed; next there is a circle of Aralias,

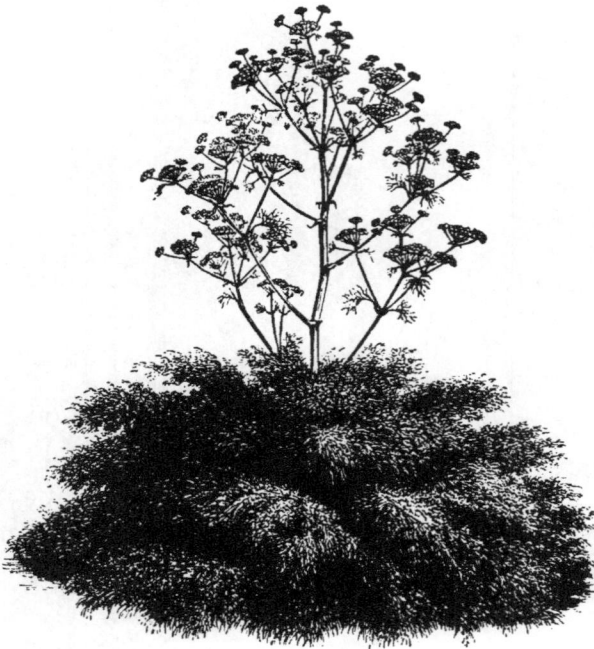

Isolated Feru'a, on Grass (Decaisne and Naudin).

or an oval of Ficus, in which hundreds of plants are so densely packed that their tops form a dead level. Isolated from everything else, as a rule these masses fail to throw any natural grace into the garden, but, on the other hand, go a long way towards spoiling the character of the subjects of which they are composed. For it is manifest that we get a far superior effect from a group of such a plant as the Gunnera, the Polymnia, or the Castor-oil plant, properly associated with other subjects of entirely diverse character, than when the masses of such as these become so large that there is no relieving point within reach of the eye. A single specimen or small group of a fine Canna forms one of the most graceful objects the eye can see. Plant a rood of it, and it soon becomes as attractive as so much maize or wheat.

The fact is, we do not want purely "subtropical gardens" or "leaf gardens" or "colour gardens," but such gardens as, by happy combinations of the materials at our disposal, shall be delightful, ever-changing museums of beautiful life. For it is

Rhus glabra lacinlata.   Hardy shrub, cut down annually to secure fine foliage.

quite a mistake to assume that because people, ignorant of the inexhaustible stores of the vegetable kingdom, admire the showy glares of colour now so often seen in our gardens, they would be incapable of enjoying scenes displaying some traces of natural beauty and variety if they could see them.

The fine-leaved plants have not yet been associated immediately with the flowers : hence also a fault. Till they are so treated we can hardly see the great value of such in ornamental garden-ing. Avoid unmeaning masses, and associate more intimately the fine-leaved plants with the brilliant flowers. A quiet mass of green might be desirable in some positions, but even that could be varied most effectively as regards form. The combinations of this kind that may be made are innumerable, and there is no reason why flower-beds should not be as graceful as bouquets well and simply made.

Fine effects may be secured, from the simplest and most easily obtained materials, by using some of our hardy trees and

Aralia japonica (Hort.). Hardy shrub with fine leaves.

shrubs in the picturesque garden. Our object generally is to secure large and handsome types of leaves; and for this purpose we usually place in the open air young plants of exotic trees, taking them in again in autumn. As we usually see them in a diminutive state, we often forget that, when branched into a large head in their native countries, they are not a whit more remarkable in foliage than many of the trees of our pleasure-grounds. Thus, if the well-known Paulownia im-

perialis were too tender to stand our winters, and if we were
accustomed to see it only in a young and simple-stemmed
condition and with large leaves, we should doubtless plant it
out every summer as we do Ferdinanda.   There is no occasion
whatever to resort to exotic subjects, while we can so easily
obtain fine hardy plants—which, moreover, may be grown
by everybody and everywhere.   By annually cutting down

AILANTUS AND CANNAS.

Suggesting the effects to be obtained from certain young trees cut down annually.

young plants of various hardy trees and shrubs, and letting
them make a simple-stemmed growth every year, we shall, as
a rule, obtain finer effects than can be got from tender ones.
The Ailantus, for example, treated in this way, gives us as
fine a type of pinnate leaf as can be desired.   Nor need we
place Astrapæa Wallichii in the open air, so long as a simple-
stemmed young plant of the Paulownia makes a column of
superb leaves.   The delicately cut leaves of the Gleditschias,

D

borne on strong young stems, would be as pretty as those of any Fern; and so in the case of various other hardy trees and shrubs. Persons in the least favourable parts of the country need not doubt of being able to obtain as fine types of foliage as they can desire, by selecting a dozen kinds of hardy trees and treating them in this way.

Pretty are the results obtained in this Park by carpeting the ground beneath masses of tender subtropical plants with quick-growing ornamental annuals and bedding plants, which will bloom before the larger subjects have put forth their strength and beauty of leaf. If all interested in flower-gardening had an opportunity of seeing the charming effects produced by judiciously intermingling fine-leaved plants with brilliant flowers, there would be an immediate improvement in our flower-gardening, and verdant grace and beauty of form would be introduced, while all the brilliancy of colour that could be desired might be seen at the same time. Here is a bed of Erythrinas not yet in flower: but there is a brilliant mass of colour beneath them. It is a mixture of Lobelia speciosa with variously coloured Portulacas. The beautiful surfacings that may thus be made with annual, biennial, or ordinary bedding plants, from Mignonette to Petunias and Nierembergias, are almost innumerable.

The bare earth is covered quickly with the free-growing dwarfs; there is an immediate and a charming contrast between the dwarf-flowering and the fine-foliaged plants; and should the former at any time put their heads too high for the more valuable things above them, they can be cut in for a second bloom. In the case of using foliage-plants that are eventually to cover the bed completely, annuals may be sown, and they in many cases will pass out of bloom and may be cleared away just as the large leaves begin to cover the ground. Where this is not the case, and the larger plants are placed thin enough to allow of the lower ones always being seen, two or even more kinds of dwarf plants may be employed, so that one may succeed the other, and that there may be a mingling of bloom. It may be thought that this kind of mixture would interfere with what is called the unity of effect that we attempt to attain in our flower-gardens. This need not be so by any means; the system could be used effectively in the most formal of gardens.

One of the most useful and natural ways of diversifying a garden, and one that we rarely or never take advantage of, consists in placing really distinct and handsome plants alone and in groups upon the grass, to break the monotony of clump margins. To follow this plan is necessary wherever great variety and the highest beauty are desired in the ornamental garden. Plants may be placed singly or in open groups near the margins of a bold clump of shrubs or in the open grass : the system is applicable to all kinds of hardy ornamental subjects, from trees downwards, though in our case the want is for the fine-leaved plants and the more distinct hardy subjects. Nothing, for instance, can look better than a well-developed tuft of the broad-leaved Acanthus latifolius, springing from the turf not far from the margin of a walk or shrubbery; and the same is true of the Yuccas, Tritomas, and other things of like character and hardiness. We may make attractive groups of one family, as the hardiest Yuccas; or varied groups of one species, like the Pampas grass—not by any means repeating the individual, for there are about twenty varieties of this plant known on the Continent, and from these half a dozen really distinct

Group and single specimens of plants isolated on the grass.

and charming kinds might be selected to form a group. The same applies to the Tritomas, which we usually manage to drill into straight lines: in an isolated group in a verdant glade they are for the first time seen to best advantage. And what might not be done with these and the like by making mixed groups, or letting each plant stand distinct upon the grass, perfectly isolated in its beauty !

Let us again try to illustrate the idea simply. Take an important spot in a pleasure-ground—a sweep of grass in face of a shrubbery—and see what can be done with it by means of these isolated plants. If, instead of leaving it in the bald state in which it is often found, we place distinct things isolated here and there upon the grass, the margin of shrubbery may be made as free as the fringe of a copse on the side of a mountain. If one who knew many plants were to arrange them in this way, he might produce numberless fine effects. In the case of the smaller plants,

D 2

such as the Yucca and variegated Arundo, groups of four or five good plants should be used to form one. In addition to such arrangements, two or three individuals of a species might be placed here and there upon the grass with the best effect. For example, there is at present in our nurseries a great Japanese Polygonum (P. Sieboldi), which has seldom yet been used with much effect in the garden. If anybody will select some open grassy spot in a pleasure-garden, or grassy glade near a wood—some spot considered unworthy of attention as regards ornamenting it— and plant a group of three plants of this Polygonum, leaving fifteen feet or so between the stools, a distinct aspect of vegetation will be the result. It is needless to multiply examples ; the plan is capable of endless variation, and on that account alone should be welcome to all lovers of gardens.

Portion of plan showing Yuccas, Pampas grass, Tritomas, Retinospora, Acanthus latifolius, Arundo Donax variegata, etc., irregularly isolated on the grass.

But many will only see in it an interference with the mowing machine or the formal margin. The progress of improvement in our gardens is much retarded by the habit of looking from the housemaid's point of view at any suggested innovation. Very often the question is not, " Is the alteration a desirable one ?" but " How will it interfere with the progress of the garden dusters ?" If one suggests the very obvious improvement that might be wrought by breaking up and arranging in a perfectly easy, varied, and broken manner the margin of a mass of choice shrubs—formal even to ugliness—the reply will probably be, " How could we get the mowing machine to work ?" Need it be said that gardens are not made for the mowing-machine, the broom, or the edging-iron, but for the highest expression of the beauty of the vegetable kingdom, and for the enjoyment and instruction of men and women ? The gardener should be relieved of much of the needless, fruitless drudgery that he now has to endure. The whole course of his existence at present is a weary repetition of the same endless routine. Not in one place out of twenty are the gardener's labours devoted to the formation of features which take care of themselves after planting, and improve year by year. To be told in the face of this, in an age when people go to the trouble of scratching over and replanting the same flower-gardens year after year, that any attempt at a purer system of gardening is likely to interfere with the progress of the mower or the straight run of the edging-iron is really too much. Certainly it is a little easier to mow and rake, if raking be permitted, a long, straight, and, it may probably be, bare margin to a belt of plantation or mass of choice shrubs, than it is to give the necessary attention

Nook in Parc Monceau.

to a border fringed as some of the shrub borders in Battersea Park have been recently. But the difference in aspect is so great that the small additional care required in mowing, etc., should never be named against it, especially at a time when the whole of the resources of most gardens go to produce costly displays which endure but a few short months, leaving the ground ready for fresh labours.

One kind of arrangement needs to be particularly guarded against—the geometro-picturesque one seen in some places combined with much showy gardening. The plants are often of the finest kinds and in the most robust health, all the materials for the best results are abundant, and yet the scene fails to satisfy the eye, from the needless formality of many of the beds, produced by the heaping together of a great number of species of one kind in long, straight or twisting beds with high raised edges frequently of hard-beaten soil. Too many such examples are found. The formality of the true geometrical garden is charming to many to whom this style is offensive; and there is not the slightest reason why the most beautiful combinations of fine-leaved and fine-flowered plants should not be made in any kind of geometrical garden.

But in the purely picturesque garden it is as needless as it is false in taste to follow the course here objected to. Hardy plants may be isolated on the turf, and may be arranged in beautiful irregular groups, with the turf or some graceful spray of hardy trailing plants for a carpet. Flower-beds may be readily placed so that no objectionable stage-like results will be seen : tender plants may be grouped as freely as may be desired— a formal edge avoided by the turf being allowed to play irregularly under and along the margins, while the remaining bare ground beneath the tall plants may be quickly covered with some fast-growing low plants. Choice tender specimens of Tree-ferns, etc., placed in dark shady dells, may be plunged to the rims of the pots in the turf or earth, and some graceful or bold trailing herb placed round the cavity so as to conceal it; and in these and various ways we may have every loveliness of the plant world free from all geometry. The day will come when we shall be as anxious to avoid all formal twirlings in our gardens as we now are to have such twistings perpetrated by landscape-gardeners of great repute for applying wall-paper or fire-shovel patterns to the surface of the reluctant earth, and when we shall cease to tolerate in our gardens such scenes as no landscape-artist would endure in a sketch.

The old landscape-gardening dogma,* which tells us we cannot

---

* "In gardening, the materials of the scene are few, and those few unwieldy, and the artist must often content himself with the reflection that he has given the best disposition in his power to the scanty and intractable materials of nature." —Allison. (This is only one of many statements, equally untrue, made by persons who had no idea of the extent of the plant world.)

have all the wild beauty of nature in our gardens, and may as
well resign ourselves to the compass and the level, the defined
daub of colour and pudding-like heaps of shrubs, had some faint
force when our materials for gardening were few ; but considering
our present rich and, to a great extent, unused stores from every
clime, and from almost every important section of the vegetable
kingdom, it is demonstrably false and foolish.

There is a graceful way of using hardy climbers here which,
improved and modified, deserves to be generally practised. The
numerous cultivated hardy climbers are rarely seen to advantage,
owing to their being stiffly trained against walls. The greater

Japanese Honeysuckle on Stem of Birch-tree, Parc Monceau.

number of hardy climbers have gone out of cultivation, owing to
their being generally ill-placed and ill-treated. One of the
happiest of all ways of using them is that of training them in a
free manner against trees ; by this means many beautiful effects
may be secured. The trees must not, as a rule, be those crowded
in shrubberies. They must stand free on the turf. Established
trees have usually somewhat exhausted the ground near their base,
which may, however, afford nutriment to a hardy climbing shrub.
In some low trees the graceful companion may garland their
heads ; in tall ones the stem only may at first be adorned. But
some vigorous climbers could in time ascend the tallest trees, and

we can conceive nothing more beautiful than a veil of such a one as Clematis montana suspended from the branch of a tall tree. A whole host of lovely plants may be grown in this way, apart from the well-known and popular climbing plants. There are, for example, many species of Clematis which have never come into cultivation, but which are quite as beautiful as climbers can be. The same may be said of the Honeysuckles, wild Vines, and various other families the names of which may be found in catalogues. In consequence, however, of the fact that no system of growing these plants to advantage has ever been carried out in our gardens, nurseries are by no means so rich in them as could be desired. Much of the northern tree and shrub world is garlanded with creepers, which may be grown in the way suggested and in similar ones, as, for example, on banks and in hedgerows. The naked stems of the trees in our pleasure-grounds, however, have the first claim on our attention in planting garlands. There would seldom be reason to fear injury to established trees.

The view showing the effect of Clematis on trees is drawn and engraved from a photograph taken in May, showing an old and vigorous plant of the handsome and hardy Clematis montana allowed to have its own way to some extent. This climbing shrub, of which the large-flowered variety called grandiflora is grown here and there on walls, is most precious for those who wish to garland trees and stumps and hedges with lovely flowers. It is as hardy and free as the common English Clematis vitalba. The sketch will also suggest to many various ways in which hardy climbers may be used to produce similar beautiful effects. Other families of climbers might be named as equally useful, but the Clematises are so numerous, so hardy, so beautiful in flower, and so singularly varied in the colour and form of their blossoms, that whole wild gardens of beauty may be formed of them alone.

After the great central blemish of monotony in gardens, few of the secondary ones call for censure more loudly than needless ugly structures. No doubt the majority of these unfortunate erections have some reason to be: they are simply in the wrong position. A good, honest black saucepan in the middle of the dining-room table would not be more incongruous than a tool-shed is in the middle of Cavendish Square. In the Parc Monceau there are several

villanously ugly and wholly needless buildings which are quite
out of place, and tend to confuse and limit the garden.   There is
about the most absurd of bridges stuck over an unclean pool of
water, with a hard, black asphalte margin—proper enough in a

CLEMATIS ON TREES IN MAY, *Parc Monceau.*

tanyard no doubt, but not in a fair garden.   Such puerile structures are figured with the most elaborate detail in illustrated
works, as if they were as worthy of admiration as a Roman arch.
A man who really knew their value and had power to treat them

accordingly would shovel them out of the way as rubbish—more offensive than the biggest weeds.

But the greatest drawback to the beauty of this garden is a dirty and formal pool dignified by the name of a lake, and by the side of which is one of the meanest of all shams—the sham ruin. There are few greater mistakes made in gardens than placing small sheets of artificial water in them. There is, however, one virtue in artificial waters seen abroad—they are rarely deep or large enough to drown the children, though ugly enough to irritate sensitive adults. With us the artificial water generally assumes the form of a duck-pond; in France it is much nearer to a hand-basin. There, if the "lawn" be only as large as a table-cloth, a tub in cement is sure to find a place on it. Happily in

Ugly and needless Structures in the Parc Monceau.

our small gardens water is less frequently seen. The effect of still water is only pleasant where it sparkles in the sun in broad masses. Nothing can be much more offensive than small pools of stagnant water. Near a dwelling-house they are objectionable for many reasons; besides, the space they occupy is precious for better things. Good design in other ways will not in these cases compensate for the error of forming artificial water where there is not abundant room for it. It is enough to have half the little gardens about Paris spoiled with cemented tubs without disfiguring this small park with a "lake" of soup-like water. No doubt when the gardens of Paris are delivered from the engineer and the architect and placed in the hands of trained garden-artists we shall see an end of these sham ruins, sham pools, sham pyramids, toy bridges.

This park might readily have been made an earthly paradise of a town garden by not slashing it into four pieces by needless roads. To form short cuts for man or horse is not usually reckoned among the objects for which town gardens are formed. Yet they are often spoiled in the effort. A road round this would have been the right thing, if any were really required. However, so long as we have

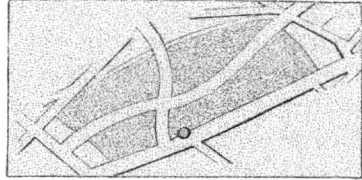

Roads in the Parc Monceau. How to spoil a garden.

engineers for landscape-gardeners, so long shall we have stones and cement where turf and flowers ought to be. Instead of making such places too facile by roads, the designer might be pardoned for following an opposite course and allowing nothing in the way of needless roads to rob the garden of its most valuable spaces.

A hideous blotch, from an artistic point of view, is the prodigious oval of the white-leaved Maple in the centre of the park. This clump consists of hundreds of trees graduated from edge to centre so as to form an enormous pudding-like mass. The value and beauty of the trees themselves are quite lost through their being thus thickly massed together, in addition to which the general effect of the park is spoilt. The

Cocked-up flower-bed in the Parc Monceau.

true way to enhance the value of trees with variegated leaves is to plant them in clumps of two or three, but when planted in masses or lines their real worth is lost. Some people would pave the streets with diamonds, and expect diamonds to become more admired in consequence.

The Parc Monceau also contains some of the least agreeable features of our modern flower-garden in the form of beds on the top of small embankments. The fashion first came to us from Paris. It was once employed to secure a greater degree of heat to the more tender plants. But now beds of the freest-growing flowers may be seen fortified with these ugly banks, though no

more in want of their assistance than a nettle. In any garden
well laid out the shape of the beds must not be obtrusive. In
the gardening of the future, the plants, not the beds, will be
what meets the sight. Over the whole of this large garden the
impudent bed shown in the woodcut preceding stares at one,
not only when it is filled, be it observed, but when it is bare of plants.
The plan is as needless as it is offensive. Given a good warm soil
and good drainage, there is no need for this awkward elevation of
the bed ! On the contrary, there is often decided advantage in
having the roots in a cool medium, not more exposed to evaporation than need be. The gentle rise towards the centre of a bed
that is sometimes desirable is easily secured without raising the
edge above the turf, from which all flowers should spring.

CHAPTER III.

THE GARDEN OF PLANTS.

THIS garden, the botanic garden of Paris, and one of the most famous in the world, is the type of all that is stupid and harmful to horticulture in the botanic gardens of Europe. It is pedantry in the full sun—mismanagement posing as science. We must not seek here for much of the beauty of the vegetable kingdom: the systems adopted steal that away. Clipped lines of wretched trees; wide, needless walks; wretched culture; overcrowding of plants in the houses; overcrowding of trees from the endeavour to squeeze them into narrow beds to illustrate classification; absence of all design calculated to allow the garden to retain any beauty of grove or lawn or spring; in a word, every depressing feature of the worst-managed botanic gardens is seen here. It is the natural result of placing at the head of such an establishment a person with no knowledge of or sympathy with the art he is supposed to cultivate; while under him are placed men whose efforts under the system are powerless for good.

Shall our public gardens be managed by men thoroughly conversant with the art of gardening, or by those who frequently have no knowledge whatever of it, and whose work is in other fields? Horticulture is an art embodying so many branches that it is difficult to find any one person who possesses a good general knowledge of the whole. Men spend their lives in studying orchid culture or arboriculture, and yet these are but departments of the art. Difficult, however, as it is to secure a man with a good general knowledge of horticulture, we happily have in various countries examples of brilliant success in this way— men who might be named as having as nearly perfect a know-

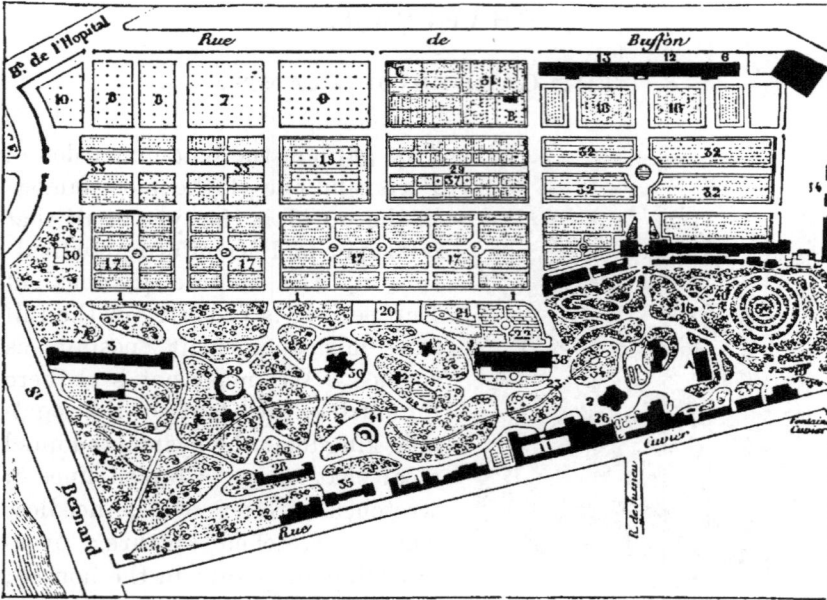

PLAN OF THE JARDIN DES PLANTES. *How not to lay out a botanic garden.*

1. *Promenade.* 2. *Amphitheatre.* 3. *Beasts of Prey.* 4, 19. *Fountain.* 6. *Library.* 7, 8, 9, 10, 18, 29. *Mixed plantations and nurseries.* 11, 12, 13, 14. *Museums of Anatomy, Botany, Mineralogy, and Zoology.* 15. *Parterre.* 16. *Cedar.* 17. *School of Botany.* 20. *Bears.* 21, 22, 23. *Nurseries, &c.* 24, 25. *Labyrinths.* 26. *Cuvier's house.* 27, 28. *Birds.* 30, 31, 32, 33, 34. *Aquatic, Edible, Herbaceous, Officinal, and Tropical Plants.* 35. *Reptiles.* 36, 37, 39. *Animals.* 38. *Glass-houses.* 40. *Monument to Daubenton.* A. B. C. *Offices.*

ledge of the art of gardening as it is possible to attain. Yet by our present system, we paralyse the efforts of such men by placing them under the control of a person who is, as a rule, without knowledge of horticulture.

What should we think of people who placed the designing and building of important architectural works in the hands or under the control of a geologist who had spent his life in gathering and examining stones and had never taken the least interest in the building art?   And yet such a plan is precisely analogous to that followed in a good many public gardens.   And what is the result of this course?   That all gardens not actually or virtually managed by real gardeners are generally in a poor, sometimes in a wretched, condition.   The best collections of plants and the best grown are in gardens where they are cultivated for their beauty,

OLD JUDAS TREE,   *Garden of Plants.*

and not to illustrate their place in this or that system.   Where is what is called our " scientific " horticulture, to adopt the weak phrase of the day, or, in plain English, where is our best and most advanced gardening?   In the same hands.   And who are the pioneers — who are they who discover for us paths and pleasures new in our always delightful gardens?   Our gardeners only, and in that term are included all who love the art.

The best managers of botanic gardens are invariably such as have had a thorough garden training—men who have lived all their days among large collections of living plants in gardens. It by no means follows that such men, because first of all excellent gardeners, may not also be good botanists. It is almost impossible that they can be otherwise; but the botany comes to them through life-long association with living garden plants. Such gardeners may be compared to architects and builders who build nobly, but whose practice and intelligence lead them to understand the classification of the stones they use.

It may be objected that when a botanic garden is wholly under the charge of a horticulturist, the general collections might suffer from his partiality for a few common types. The answer is that by far the most complete and rare collections and the best grown are those in the possession of amateurs, gardeners, and nursery-men. The real danger lies in the opposite direction—that is, when a botanist has sole control. He may select a cultivator only, instead of a really accomplished botanic gardener. Now we want good cultivators in all our botanic gardens; but in a first-rate curator that skill should be accompanied by a wide knowledge of every type of vegetation as grown in gardens. Hence to select a man merely because he happens to grow well some one or two classes of plants is a mistake. It should never be forgotten that the trees and plants which are of the highest value in a botanic garden in any country are such as are quite hardy in the open air in that country, and that one may quickly acquire a reputation as a cultivator of indoor plants, without knowing or caring for any hardy subjects. Hence the necessity of selecting a director or curator possessing a general knowledge and love of every family of the garden flora. It should also be borne in mind that when a botanist holds the appointment of the curator of a garden, he is, as a rule, not apt to select a first-rate man. Many professional gardeners know living cultivated plants, that is to say, know the flora of botanic gardens far better than botanists. Obviously, except in the case of a noble nature, the botanist is therefore not likely to select a man who knows more than he does himself about the plants in the garden—the only things that either the visitors, or supporters of such places care about.

It is not only want of knowledge of good gardening that

causes this state of things, but certain botanists have got a fixed idea that it is even wrong to arrange a scientific garden so that it should be beautiful!—that is to say, that having rich and varied collections of plants from many countries is necessarily antago- nistic to disposing the garden in a picturesque and agreeable

NEW WEEPING HONEY LOCUST (*Gleditschia Bojoti*)—*Garden of Plants.*

manner. Probably some may remember to have heard this view laid down as regards our most important gardens. Nothing can be more untrue, and nothing more harmful to every interest of the garden. Anybody really acquainted with horticulture knows that the best collections very often are found in the gardens most beautifully disposed. For example, it is well known that by far

E

the richest and best collection of alpine plants existing is to be found in the garden which is also the most beautifully arranged for their reception.   So, again, some of the most lovely collections of Ferns ever got together are arranged in a manner in which one can enjoy to the fullest their beauty and variety.   Many other instances could be given.

The botanist should have no more to do with the cultivation or arrangement of the living plants than the gardener has with the herbarium.   Progress is sure some day to break up this unnatural subjection of the garden to the botanist, and the sooner the better. The botanist has his collections, and the wide earth in which to gather them.   His is a beautiful and vast science, but it is wholly apart from horticulture.

It is assumed by the ordinary type of the grammarian of " science" that he is a " scientific man"—the horticulturist or agriculturist not even being thought worthy of the name. Few will be inclined to dispute the usefulness of the classifiers, or that they are in their degree men of science ; but when, if their position be named in the same breath with that of the horticulturist, they bristle up with disdain, people are led to put the question to themselves—Is the mere finder of names for things a more important person than he who modifies, combines, and improves those things so as to make them more useful and more beautiful ?   In literature, for instance, is the higher place to be given to grammarians, rhetoricians, and lexicon-makers ? Even the adventurous explorer who brings us, at the risk of his life, beautiful things from distant parts of the world is often excluded from his hard-earned honour by narrow considerations of this kind.   But really high-minded and able men in any branch of human knowledge are more liberal and just.

One of the first things done by our greatest thinkers, in clearing the ground for the study of the highest philosophical problems, is to prove the identity in kind of the ordinary and the " scientific" methods of observation, and the oneness, so to speak, of " theory" and " practice."   It may be urged by the botanist that his knowledge is capable of more accurate demon-stration than the gardener's ; but this is not the case, except as regards descriptions of plants.   Such a book, for example, as Lindley's ' Theory of Horticulture ' would be called a scientific book, while one of Loudon's might not be considered worthy of that distinction. Yet it has been demonstrated that the 'Theory of Horticulture' embodies many erroneous propositions, and more important errors than will probably ever find their way into a gardening book.

ALGERIAN IVY.—*Garden of Plants*

It should be clearly understood that all knowledge is the same in kind; that there is no real difference between "science" and practice; and that what is sound in theory must be sound also in practice, and *vice versâ*. There is no real difference. The old meaning of the word *science* is *knowledge*; the modern meaning

E 2

is the same. It has been shown over and over again by eminent
men that the methods of investigation applied to the most
difficult problems that have yet engaged the attention of man
differ in no essential respect from those used by the humblest
observant cultivator. What is true scientifically must be true
also in practice. Such an expression as " It is right enough in
theory but wrong in practice " is nonsense. Nothing can be
" right in theory and wrong in practice."

Who is to blame for this state of things? Chiefly the class of
botanists and " scientific " men who do not rise higher in the
study of the vegetable kingdom than the stage of mere techni-
calities and their application. We might suppose that the
Royal Horticultural Society of London would not propagate
errors of this kind. But this is precisely what it does, and at
its meeting at Birmingham there were a " scientific " and a
" practical " congress. Addresses were also given on separate
days on " recent progress in scientific " and " recent progress in
practical " horticulture ; as if these terms did not mean one and
the same thing. Thus a society for the encouragement of
gardening says, in effect, to gardeners : Your labours and
observations have nothing to do with science (knowledge), and
we will take care that there is no mingling of such different
classes. Your " practical " notions are of some slight account ;
we will devote a day to them as soon as we have completed
our " scientific " labours. And thus a puerile distinction is
maintained by the very body whose true work it should be to
counteract the effects of a use of language false in itself and
hurtful to horticulture.

Looking round on all the miserable ugliness and mismanagement in this unfortunate Garden of Plants, I thought of the kind
of national botanic garden that would be worthy of France. The
objects of a national garden should be threefold—to show living
examples of the vegetation of the country in which it occurs ; to
grow in the open air plants from other countries likely to be of
value for use or ornament in that country ; and also to display as
far as possible the vegetation of distant and very different
countries. We will leave this last question entirely out of sight,
and think only of France, its vegetation and its improvements, in
garden and in farm, in orchard and in forest.

First we think of the flora of France, beautiful exceedingly in many parts, rich and varied beyond description or remembrance We have the France of the blue warm sea, with its lavender- and rosemary-clad hills, Anemones and Narcissi in its winter fields, and woods fragrant with Myrtle and aromatic herbs.

CEDRELA SINENSIS (*New Tree*)—*Garden of Plants.*

Colder and later than the maritime Alps, we have those of Savoy, with a glorious alpine flora; the Ardennes and the Vosges; the Alps of Dauphiny; and the wide area of the Pyrenean slopes and meadows and valleys.   And we have the France of the lower hills and plains, with their wild Roses and Harebells, and the flora of the western sea-shores, and of Brittany and of Normandy—

in all a lovely and wonderful host which certainly deserve some
better illustration in a national garden than they have already
had at the hands of the classifier.   But when we come to think of
the extent and the wants of this varied country, the taste of its
people for the more refined branches of cultivation, and the vast
improvement that has in many districts to be wrought before the
land can enjoy in all its parts a full expression of the wealth and
happiness it is capable of producing, then we may see more fully
the great aid which a really worthy national garden would afford
to France.   Her now bare northern fields have to be made
beautiful and fertile ; her mountains have to be replanted.   Here
is a reason, even if there were not twenty others as cogent, for a
worthy national arboretum.   The gardens and orchards of France
have to be replenished ; the planting in her cities and towns made
more beautiful and varied ; the pure and invigorating pleasures
and material benefits of good gardening have to be brought to the
doors of every owner of a rood of land ; and in short there are
many objects of national importance which a Garden of Plants
worthy of Paris and of France could materially aid.   But these
squares and these rows of clipped Limes, and narrow beds for trees
and shrubs, and railed-in compartments contrasted with bear-pits,
and the general aspect of barren formality, demean and ridicule
and blight the whole beautiful art of gardening and all that it
concerns.   Let it not be supposed from the silence in France
on mismanagement of this kind that the evil effects noted are
only evil to the few who notice them.   Those who see the errors
know how to avoid them.   It is the public who visit places of
this kind, and naturally take them to be models of their kind,
who insensibly imbibe a harmful influence—harmful to an
incalculable extent.

Therefore, for many reasons there is no nobler work before the
municipality of Paris than the creation of a Garden of Plants
worthy of the name.   The old one is a fitting site for museums,
for herbariums, for the skeletons of whales and the pits of bears,
or even for big glass sheds filled with sickly over-crowded plants,
but a fair garden it can never be made.

A Garden of Plants worthy of France should not be much less
than a thousand acres in extent.   If much larger spaces are
devoted to mere parks with a small variety of vegetation, and for

the sole object of their air and space and drives, why should not an equally large one be devoted to this national purpose, considering that a botanical garden of the nobler type would have more than the charms of the park, even in the objects for which that is avowedly created.   A Garden of Plants worthy of France

THE JUJUBE TREE (*Zizyphus jujuba*).—*Garden of Plants.*

should be arranged in a natural manner, showing in its very disposition that all known of the art of pure garden-design had been considered. It should be roomy enough for the full and natural development of every tree or shrub or flower, native or hardy, in France. It should group the largest of these, not merely as isolated specimens, but also in groves, so as to show the full expression of their beauty in the various ways in which they might be used.

The principles on which vegetation is arranged to express the highest amount of beauty and give the greatest charm having been settled from the beginning of the world, no professor should be allowed to plant it to illustrate his notion of classification. The place for his work, it cannot be too clearly understood, is the herbarium or the museum. Such a garden should illustrate the flora of France nobly and naturally, as far as possible without burying it under a nightmare of long names; it should have open lawns, if only to let people see the beauty of the many treasures of the garden at varying distances, though there are many other reasons; it should have few glass houses, and these not in prominent positions. Those who are really interested in tropical vegetation can now see it in a few weeks, whereas a few generations ago it was problematical if it could be seen at all. Even those who imagine they can illustrate the vegetation of the tropics in a glass shed will probably admit that we had better leave the building of the glass sheds till we have done justice to the treasures of the vegetable kingdom hardy in our climate, and which we may arrange under the dome of the sky. It is hardly necessary to add that it should not be a place for exhibiting geometrical tracings on the ground, and various other and more costly puerilities of which gardens are frequently made the scene.

We have nothing in England like the Garden of Plants—half zoological, half botanical, and nearly surrounded by museums containing vast zoological, botanical, and mineralogical collections. The portion entirely devoted to botany is laid out in the straight, regular style, while other parts have winding walks, and some trifling diversity here and there. The place is really an important school of botany, and as such it is useful, though with nothing to charm. Here Buffon, Cuvier, Jussieu, and other great men have worked; and here at the present day, even in minor departments, are many men of well-known ability.

Although the Garden of Plants is quite inferior in point of beauty to any of our large British botanic gardens, it contains some features which might be introduced into them with advantage. Its chief merits are that its plants are better named than in any British garden; it possesses several arrangements which enable the student to see conveniently all obtainable useful plants better than in any British botanic garden. Its chief faults are that it has a bad position in an out-of-the-way part of the town; the greater part of its surface is covered with plants systematically disposed; the houses are poor and badly arranged compared to those in our own good botanic gardens; and there is no green turf to be seen in its open parts. It has, in addition, a very bad atmosphere for evergreens, and a ridiculous maze.

There is one admirable feature which must not be forgotten, and that is the fine collection of fruit-trees. This was established by the National Conven-tion by a decree dated June 1793: "So as to estab-lish the uniformity of nomenclature necessary for all parts of the re-public." The col-lection dates from

Clipped Trees in the Garden of Plants. (Hachette.) Compare with illustrations on pp. 3, 5, 22, 29, 37, and others in this book.

the year 1792, when the fruit-garden of the Chartreux of Paris was broken up, and two trees of each variety transported to the Garden of Plants. In 1793 it contained 185 varieties. In 1824, when Thouin died, there were in it 265 varieties of pears alone; it has now more than 1400 varieties of this fruit. It is interesting and important to know that the collection still preserves the greater portion of the very types described a century ago by Duhamel.

A large division is devoted to the culture of plants used as food, and in commerce. It is at once successful, useful, and complete. The chief varieties of all garden crops are to be seen; the various species of Rhubarb, all important varieties of Lettuce—in a word, everything that the learner could desire to see in this way. It is not merely the plan of the thing, but the manner in which it is carried out, that is good. Such arrangements, well planned and cut off by judicious planting from the general verdure and chief area of any of our great public gardens, would be of the greatest service.

Near the river end of the garden there is another very interesting division. It is chiefly devoted to medicinal and useful plants of all kinds, arranged in a distinct way. First we have the Sorghums, Millets, Wheats, and cereals generally — all plants cultivated for grain. Then come plants cultivated for their stems, from Polymnia edulis to Ullucus tuberosus. Next we have the chief species and varieties of Onion; such plants as Urtica utilis, the Dalmatian Pyrethrum rigidum, and almost everything likely to interest in this way, from Lactuca perennis to the esculent Hibiscus. Here again the plants are well named and kept clear and distinct, each having full room for development, the general space devoted to the subject being sufficiently large; and the practice of giving each plant a portion of the whole breadth of each bed to itself is better than the more crowded arrangements adopted in our British botanic gardens.

Effect of large umbelliferous Plant.—Garden of Plants.

The " school of botany " is simply a department planted on the natural system, remarkable for the correctness of the nomenclature and the richness of its collection. Here again everything is well taken care of and kept distinct; the aquatics are furnished with cemented troughs, in which they grow luxuriantly, one of the singular and handsome Sacred Beans (Nelumbium) growing in the open air. The whole is most satisfactory, with one exception —that the director places out the greenhouse and stove plants in summer to complete the natural orders in the beds. These poor plants are stored pell-mell in winter in a great orangery, from which they are taken out in early summer literally more dead than alive. They make a few leaves during the summer, and are again put into their den to sicken or die.

Here among the herbaceous plants growing on a rough old stake is a beautiful plant of Ivy, trained in a way suggestive of what may be done with other Ivies in similar ways. Placed in a narrow bed here in the botanical arrangement there was no attempt whatever at making it "ornamental," and yet the result, as will be seen by the woodcut (p. 51), is more beautiful than if planted or trained on a wall. The noble leaves clothed the stake, and the shoots about the bottom began to wander over the ground in the most charming way, even here among these stiff and narrow beds, which seemed designed to destroy all beauty and individuality in plants. On a lawn it may be imagined how much prettier it would be. This is probably

Sacred Bean in the open air. (*Vilmorin.*)

the best way of growing the finer kinds of Ivy. It would be difficult to imagine anything more beautiful than a group of pyramids, each of a different kind of Ivy, springing from the turf in some quiet corner of the garden.

There is a Cedar of Lebanon, planted by Jussieu, to whom it was given by the English botanist Collinson. It is the first Cedar ever planted in France. Beyond this there is not much tree-beauty in the garden, though there are several new or rare hardy trees, some of which have been drawn and engraved for this book; among them being Cedrela sinensis and Gleditschia Bojoti, the last a lovely light-leaved weeping tree.

An interesting object is all that now remains of a somewhat remarkable tree which has stood for nearly three hundred years

in the gardens of the Museum.   The seed from which this tree
sprang was received amongst others from North America in the
year 1601, by Jean Robin, Professor of Botany at the Garden of
Plants, and, thirty-five years later, it was planted here by Ves-
pasien Robin, so that it is now probably two hundred and seventy-
six years old.   The top of the tree, having gradually decayed, was
cut off many years since, and the stump which remains is about
nine feet high, and three feet three inches in diameter at the
base.   The branches, however, which still continue alive, exhibit
a considerable amount of vigour, which promises a prolongation
of existence for many years to come, though its beauty is gone.
This venerable tree is considered to be the parent of all the
varieties of Robinia which are now so extensively spread over
Europe.

M. Carrière, one of the heads of departments here, among other
services to horticulture, has long been an acute observer of those
sports or differences among plants which, when preserved and
increased, often prove of great value.   Frequently it happens that
what may be called, from a botanical point of view, a mere
variety is of as great importance for our gardens as the most
distinct of species.   In gardening the question of form is second
to no other, and frequently valuable deviations from ordinary
forms characterise what are called mere varieties.   Thus such
varieties of hardy native trees as the weeping wych Elm and the
weeping Beech are more precious for the garden landscape than
most new species of hardy trees; this must be evident to all who
have seen these varieties in a mature state.   We are, indeed,
only in the beginning of our due appreciation of the value of the
varieties as distinguished from the original forms of hardy trees.
All interested in trees would do well to observe accidental
deviations from the normal type in gardens under their care, as
they may find something of high importance to our gardens.
A stray shoot or sucker showing a habit different from the
type may, if separated and increased, perpetuate constantly
its peculiarity.   He who observes and increases it may render
as great a service to the gardens of Europe as was rendered
by those who secured for us the upright Yew or the weeping
Ash.

In a collection of the genus Asparagus, one, A. Broussonetii, is remarkable for its great vigour and rapidity of growth—it quickly runs up with dense vigour to a height of ten feet in spring, its foliage is glossy and dense, and it might be used with success as a covering for bowers or to make pyramids in a diversified garden of hardy plants.   Asparagus tenuifolius is as graceful and elegant as the one before named is vigorous.   It is probable that a variety of forms of this family will be found to possess some merit for our outdoor gardens.

Among the hardy plants here one is often struck during the various seasons, particularly in the spring and early summer, with the beauty of the fine Umbelliferæ, one of which (Molopospermum) is illustrated in this chapter.   These plants have hitherto been left too much in the botanic garden, whereas they have rare merits as decorative plants for the choicest hardy collections. There is a deep green and fern-like beauty displayed by them, which one does not meet in any other plants.   Some of them, while very beautiful in very early spring, like the Ferulas, die down in early summer ; but the one here illustrated lasts longer into the season.   The illustration is to show the effect of this type of plant rather than the

Climbing Hardy Asparagus.—Garden of Plants.

botanical details.   Not only are a great variety of umbelliferous plants beautiful in themselves, but from their absolute distinctness from any types common in gardens they impart wholly new features to the garden.   Of course they should be very carefully placed, so that while their beauty may have full effect on the garden landscape in winter and early in the year, when their large and delicate plumes spring up—there may not when

these die down be awkward blanks left.   By placing them singly
or in groups on the grass this would not occur.

For the information of those taking a botanical interest in
curious plants, I may state that Cuscuta major is luxuriantly
grown here upon the Nettle, C. Epithymum upon Calliopsis
tinctoria, C. Engelmanii upon a Solidago, and Orobanche grows
upon Hemp. O. minor has been grown upon perennial Clovers,
and O. Hederæ upon Ivy at the bottom of a wall; so that
there ought not to be the difficulty which botanic gardeners
find in growing these curious plants.   Orobanche ramosa is
also grown here upon Calliopsis tinctoria. The best way with
the Orobanches is to scrape the soil away to near the root of
the plant on which it is intended to be parasitical, and then
sow the seed.   A very old and fine pair of dwarf Fan-palms, given
to Louis XIV. by Charles William, Margrave of Baden-Durlach,
are usually placed in summer one at each side of the entrance of
the amphitheatre.   They have straight clean stems, and are more
than twenty feet high.   They escape the notice of many visitors,
but are well worth seeing by all plant-lovers, both on account of
their age and their exceptional height.

Should any visitor to the Garden of Plants wonder at the
poor external aspect of its glass-houses and various other
departments as compared with those at Kew, he would do
well to bear in mind that money has a good deal to do with
such things ; and that the grant for museums, lecturers (the
lectures are free), the expensive collection of animals, and everything else in the Garden of Plants, is miserably small.   On the
other hand, the gardens and plants of the city are plentifully
provided with means, the municipality of Paris often spending
prodigious sums for the purchase of plants, and even for the
plant decoration of a single ball.   One ball at the Hôtel de Ville
during the festivities of 1867 cost considerably over £30,000,
while the Garden of Plants gets from the state not more than
one-third of that sum for a whole year for museums and all.

Although the Garden of Plants is the very opposite of a model
of what a garden ought to be, it may be noticed that the public
have free access to it at all hours of the day.   This is a rule very
much to be desired in all such cases.   There are one or two small
departments in this garden shut off from the public except at certain

hours, though it is by no means wise or necessary to do so. But even these partially closed departments are only surrounded by low open railings, so that their contents can be viewed and enjoyed

OLD ACACIA TREE.   *Garden of Plants (Revue Horticole).*

to a great extent from the parts always open. This suggests comparison with the state of things at Kew, which is only open to the public in the afternoon. For some time past there has been a growing desire that the Kew Gardens should be opened at an earlier hour. The speakers of the various deputations to the First Commissioner of Public Works have expressed this desire with far too much diffidence. From official utterances and their repetition, some persons have become impressed with an idea that "science" and botanical research require the gardens to be closed for half the day, and even some members of the deputations seem to have accepted this nonsense in its entirety, and said they did not want the botanic part of the gardens to be open at all, except at the hours at which they are now open. But this is not fighting half the battle. Setting aside local interest, from the point of view of horticulturists and botanists of England and throughout the world, it is an injustice to keep the gardens shut up during the best hours of the day. Even in the case of local residents, if they enter the gardens the moment they are opened there is very little time in the short winter days to see anything. Throughout the whole of the winter and spring the most agreeable time to visit Kew is the morning and noon; in summer, too, it would be, to persons visiting London, far preferable to go out to Kew in the early morning.

Numbers of persons come from our colonies and America to London to whom one visit or frequent visits to Kew are important; and the time and arrangements of these people are very often interfered with by the absurd rules that exist there. Then, taking the case of anybody in London wanting to see a certain plant in flower at Kew, or to look up any other question there, is it not ridiculous that this cannot be done without encountering difficulties as to hours? Of late years the plants put out in the various parts of the London parks are even more choice and costly than those at Kew, as, for example, in various parts of Hyde, Battersea, and Victoria Parks. Yet there is no reason for keeping the public out at any time. People may be seen there enjoying the flowers in the morning sun. Surely if this be possible in London itself, with its vast and varied population, it is no less possible at Kew. To those who know anything of botanic gardens and their management, the "scientific purpose" objection to their being thrown open early would be amusing if it were not so untrue and so puerile. On the contrary, this very purpose is a reason for their being open throughout the day. How have "scientific purposes" suffered in Edinburgh and Dublin and Paris by the opening of scientific gardens at an earlier hour?

There never was a more reasonable demand, and it must be granted sooner or later. The question of expense is no sufficient excuse. Surely the first and most legitimate object for expenditure in such a garden is that it may be enjoyed by those who pay for it. It is, however, very doubtful if early opening would increase the expense in any material way; but assuming for a moment that it would, the answer is—save the money needed, by reducing expenditure on things less essential than the opening of the Gardens. The hours in public gardens should be from six o'clock until dusk throughout the summer, and in winter from nine o'clock till dusk.

CHAPTER IV.

THE PARC DES BUTTES CHAUMONT.

THIS is, as regards garden-design, the most distinct and interesting garden in Paris. After Versailles and the Garden of Plants and the Champs Elysées, and even the varied beauty of the Parc Monceau, no one is prepared for the striking difference shown by this garden. There are beautiful open lawns with tasteful fringes of shrubs and groups of trees; and in many parts an airiness and breadth which are admirable. It is the boldest attempt at what is called the picturesque style that has been made in any Paris or London gardens. It is hardly wise to attempt expensive and extraordinary works in places of this sort, but in this instance an unusual effort was to some extent invited by the peculiar nature of the ground. The whole park may be described as a diversified Primrose Hill with two or three "peaks and valleys," and immense masses of rock.

Old quarries, enormous in size, and surrounded by acres of rubbish, once occupied this spot. It was by cutting away the ground around three sides of these, and leaving the highest and most picturesque side intact, that the present results were brought about. A very extensive and imposing cliff rises to a height of over one hundred and sixty feet, half surrounded by an artificial lake. Hard by, enormous stalactite caves, sixty feet in height from floor to ceiling, have been constructed. These last are well formed and striking, though hardly the kind of thing to be recommended for a public garden. It is better to leave the eccentricities of the cave-makers out of the question till we have provided for the population of great towns green lawns, trees, and wide open streets and ways, with their consequence, purer air.

Through the top of one of the great caves a stream dashes in, and as its course, as it tumbles down the steep above the aperture, is gracefully planted, the effect is very pretty.

Planting of Stream above Stalactite Cave.—Parc des Buttes Chaumont.

The streamlets in this park are arranged and planted in a tasteful way, their beds being sometimes rocky; and by taking advantage of their twinings and tiny cascades, positions have been formed for a great variety of hardy plants which are grouped along the sides. Among these the free-flowering Yuccas, Y. filamentosa and Y. flaccida, occur in groups and masses, and are very effective when in bloom. Such handsome evergreens are well introduced in places which are generally left to common water-weeds only. By the side of these streamlets alpine plants are sometimes placed, to grow here and there in little beds along their course, associated with lowland marsh-plants; but alpine

plants can never be grown thus. With the supply of water that
these parks command, nothing could be easier than the creation
of healthfully covered rocky mounds with true alpine plants,
even if the great rocky cliffs did not invite this type of vegetation.

One of the most beautiful features ever seen in such a place
is afforded by enormous curtains of Ivy, which drape the great
rock walls with the most refreshing verdure at all seasons.   Here
and there towards the base of these ivy-clad rocks spring flowering shrubs, like the Japan Pear and the Forsythia, sparkling with
blossom in early spring.   The effect of these among the Ivy is
very suggestive, especially to those weary of the prim bareness
which flowering shrubs too often display in dug borders.   Along
the crest of the cliffs in many places where the turf of the high
lawns meets the Ivy, a hardy flower, the common red Valerian,
comes in to play a very useful part.   This bright old border
flower, which like the Wallflower adorns many ruins and bridges,
has established itself in groups among the upper part of the
Ivy, and its effect in summer growing above sheets of Ivy
forty or fifty feet high is very charming.

Here and there in this garden may be noticed unshorn fringes
of shrubs instead of the mutilated objects and frequently dug
borders too often seen.   In nature, especially on mountains,
nothing is more delightful than the way the shrubs and low trees
nestle themselves in little colonies and groups on the grass.   Our
gardens will never be worthy of intelligent beings so long as all
the flowering shrubs and like plants are primly placed on bare
dug borders, margined by a stiff formal line.   The effect is all
the worse when a line of some showy flower forms a belt,
making the whole thing as glaring and changeless as possible.
What calls for this hideous and unnatural nakedness?   It is only
the convenience of the mowing-machine that is consulted.   It
is sad to think of the miles of shrubbery in London parks and
in gardens elsewhere so mutilated annually that either individual beauty or good effect of the whole is impossible.

Unhappily the great central cliff is so high that it cannot be
veiled like the minor ones with Ivy, and it is so formed that it
presents only an arid mass, on closely examining which one may
see ugly seams of plaster bulging out.   There never was in a

IVY-CLAD ROCKS AND HIGH LAWNS IN PARC DES BUTTES CHAUMONT

garden such a chance of having walls of rock-plants almost as interesting as those one meets with on an Alpine pass, and yet it is entirely lost.   By leaving chinks here and there and filling them with turf; by leaving the face of the high rock sloping in places, so that they would be well exposed to the rain; by having little streamlets trickling over the face of the cliffs here and there; by scattering a few packets of seeds over the surface in spring, a rock vegetation of great beauty could soon be obtained. The great silvery Saxifrages of the Pyrenees and the Alps might have spread forth their rosettes here, while little Harebells, Thymes, Rock-brooms, Stone-creps, Houseleeks of many kinds,

Unmutilated Shrubs on Turf.—Parc des Buttes Chaumont.

with hundreds of the prettiest plants of northern and temperate climes, might also have been grown.   Now all is daubed over and plantless, save a bit of wiry grass in some few spots; and the face of the high rocks is only suggestive of danger.

This results from leaving the face of the higher part of the rocks almost vertical, so depriving vegetation of all chance of foothold.   But the system of plastering, instead of having broken isolated clumps of rock, is still more to blame for the crater-like bareness of this enormous mass.   With plastered rock, and a hole left here and there in which a plant may dwindle or perish, there is no chance of any but a stone-yard effect—one-fourth the quantity of natural blocks of stone, visible through a rising mass of rock-shrubs, would have been far better. By this means one could get the necessary elevation, concealing the basis of the stones with evergreens and trailing plants, and not sealing up with cement in any part. A mistake has been made in placing a café on the edge of the rock, occupying one of the finest central sites in the park. There are plenty of less prominent positions in which such houses might be placed, if they were thought necessary, but in so small a park as this, surrounded as it is by houses or sites accessible in a few moments, such buildings ought not to be tolerated. Besides, they add very seriously to the cost of public gardens. The restaurants here, and a few other buildings wholly needless in the garden, have cost not less than £20,000, a sum that wisely laid out would suffice to form a large public garden.

A marked defect in many French gardens is having too many walks. The way these are wound about in symmetrical twirlings is quite ridiculous. In these cases the garden is made for the walks, not the walks for the garden. In gardens otherwise charming, with plenty of turf and groups of handsome plants in great variety, and a command of good views, one sometimes sees five times as many walks as are necessary. In the plans of the modern French landscape-gardeners, all of whom delight in forming "English gardens," a series of walks like so many sections of eggs are crowded over the surface without reference to the wants of the place or the formation of the ground, and evidently without thought of the hideous effects they produce in the garden landscape. It is hardly necessary to state that to secure a good and quiet effect in gardens not one inch of walk should be made or exposed more than is needed for convenience. One walk, concealed or half hidden in parts where the formation of the ground or the planting permitted, might often well replace a round dozen of the senseless intercrossing windings complained of.

One can scarcely carefully examine this park without being struck by the power of garden-design to beautify unpromising sites in town or country. A more unlikely position for a garden could hardly be found, and yet there are now parts of it almost as lovely as the little open lawns that here and there spread out among the rocks and trees of the fairest mountain region.

It is sad to reflect that an art capable of so much should be left to the control of persons ignorant of it, often by men belonging to other professions, whose education unfits them for such work. Here, for example, the too-abundant walks and roads, the absurdly stiff tank-like curve and margin to the water, the unnecessary bridges, the restaurant impudently placed in one of the best sites in the park, the badly formed artificial rock, and the other disfigurements of this noble garden are mainly owing to the influence of the engineer element in the direction. The engineer, the architect, even the botanist naturally enough

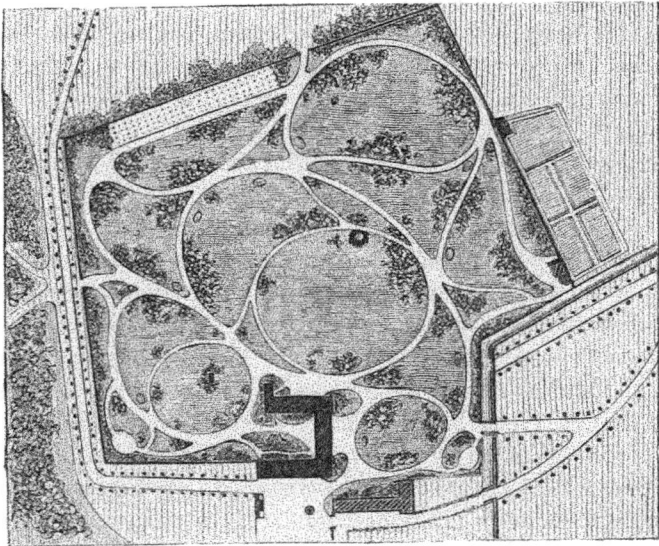

Type of Modern French Garden Plan. (Ernouf, 'L'art des jardins.')

thinks mainly of his own profession, and regards the horticultural portion of his duties as being an affair which may be deputed to any sufficiently pliant creature. But we shall never have beautiful, and in all ways instructive and useful, national gardens so long as we confide their direction to men to whom gardening is quite a secondary matter. Unhappily there is too much of the evil result of this seen, not only here but in all countries. In England we are at present without means to remedy this state of things. While our Royal Horticultural Society had still some vigour, it endowed a professorship of botany, but the creation of a professorship of any of the important branches of horticulture never entered into its scheme. In France it is somewhat different. There the state and the municipal authorities teach the useful arts betimes. And Paris would greatly help progress in horticulture by founding a school of gardening, through which she might eventually obtain garden-artists who would adorn and not deface her gardens. With true art and good examples in the national gardens, every private garden, even to the smallest, would benefit greatly ; just as now nearly every blemish may be traced to the expensive puerilities of Versailles, the ugliness of the Garden of Plants, and the stony dreariness of many other national gardens. Numbers of persons interested in horticulture, especially those who have not travelled or gained experience, look to public gardens as models of all that is worth imitation. It is most unfortunate that with us this influence can rarely be anything but injurious to all the true interests of garden-design. Most of our public gardens and parks are planned in direct violation of the very essentials of the art of laying out grounds ; many of them show precisely what to avoid, and though this merit is not alluded to in their guide-books, it may, to one who rightly uses it, be of greater importance than any other feature. Kew, for example, in some respects superior to any botanic garden or botanical establishment in the world, is in point of design no higher than a chess-board. That breadth—i.e., an open spread of lawn here and there—is the most essential principle in garden-design one would think known to anybody arranging or planting a public garden or park. Without this we cannot get anything but a confused effect—we cannot see the beauty and dignity of our now rich arboreal flora ; without this we may have a thousand kinds of noble trees, and get little better effect than in an unthinned plantation. It is, in fact, as impossible to make a really beautiful garden or park without open turfy lawns as it is to make a lake without water. At Kew, both in general design and in the arrangement of details, this principle is completely ignored, and the good old one adopted of putting in a tree wherever there is room for it. The result is that the largest botanic garden in the world is devoid of any picturesque beauty. As to the Paris botanic garden it is infinitely worse ; there not only is there no breadth, but even the very turf has disappeared.

Take, again, the Royal Horticultural Society's garden at South Kensington, and, leaving out of view entirely the question of style, assume that the geometrical is the only one. This garden was specially designed for flower-shows and for the reception of crowds. Now, if there has been any one thing taught by all previous experience of large flower-shows and the gardens in which they have been held, it has been that the happiest effect is only obtained where there is a quiet open lawn for walking,

View from Central Cliff towards Stalactite Caves.—Parc des Buttes Chaumont.

and giving easy access to the various points of interest in the garden. And what has been done to meet this want? The design is the most complicated ever seen, even for a geometrical garden. Every spot where the turf might have spread out to form a foreground, or a setting for the different objects which a garden should contain, is frittered away—here a maze (what an idiotic adjunct to any public garden ranking above that of a tea-house!); there a short avenue of Lombardy Poplars cutting off the view, for no evident reason; beyond, placed on a bank, lest its lovely effect should be lost, a fire-shovel pattern wrought on the earth, with all the beds filled with broken stone-rubbish of various colours! In short, there is no room anywhere except on parched and wearying gravel walks. At every step a sensitive person who visits the garden in the hope of seeing trees or plants or flowers is offended by a sickly low-clipped yew-hedge, a dead wall, a flight of steps, or a ghastly corridor. If a prize had been offered for the very worst kind of garden in which to enjoy a flower-show or plants or trees of any kind, a garden more fitted to win it could scarcely have been designed. It is true that of late improvements have been carried out by the simple removal of some of the features alluded to. Every step in removing hedges or mazes or gravelled panels is accompanied by an immediate improvement in the general aspect of the garden. These are some of the results we get by employing men to plan or direct our national gardens who are not, in the true sense of the word, landscape-gardeners.

There is nothing so dangerous to the beautiful but as yet undeveloped art of landscape-gardening as its practice by men into whose life the love and knowledge of it has not been interwoven by long practice and devotion. Thus, if we have an architect who does us the honour to add the term gardener to that of his own profession, we are very likely to see stones where we asked for grass and flowers and trees. His heart is in buildings, and accordingly he is not always content to limit architecture to its legitimate use, but brings it into the garden to the invariable ruin of the latter. Hence a thousand things that men will cart away as abominations, ugly, costly, and in all ways hateful, as soon as they understand what pure landscape-gardening might do towards the adornment of the willing earth; hence the gardens at Versailles, mouldering, slimy, dead as the state of things that gave them birth—a garden tomb, in fact; hence the fountains and geometrical desert at the Crystal Palace, acres of unclean water-basins, horizons of dead walls, decay of stone, gigantic water-spouting apparatus; hence such unmeaning wastes as those of Trafalgar Square and that at the Bayswater end of the Serpentine: these constitute a little of what we get by having an architect to carry out that which should be entrusted to an artist gardener. To a painter we are actually indebted for the revival

of the absurd practice of using coloured gravels. It is needful
to bear in mind that our benefactors in the above way are not
wittingly unkind, but simply give us the best they know. If
they knew the many " leaf-builders," they would not build where
building is out of place, and then cut the lime-trees into shapes
to " harmonise " with the stony dreariness thereby created, as is
often the case in France. This brings us to the subject—what
the landscape-gardener of the future should know. He should be
in the most complete sense a gardener. He should know all
about gardening, whatever he did not know. He should know

Rock-shrubs and trailing evergreens.

the trees after their kind, from the stateliest forest trees to the
lowliest flowering trees—know as far as possible their aspect in
age as well as in youth—know the circumstances suited to each
as regards soil and position—know their value in the landscape,
singly or in groups or groves—know their character in all
seasons, whether of spring blossoms, summer green, or autumn
glory.
    Then there is the important question of floral embellishment.
Is it to be artistic and natural, of materials which we can grow in
the open air? The mountains and hills and plains of northern
and temperate countries must ever be the main source of interest

in the gardens of such countries. These must be our storehouse
for material; these, in a sense, the spring of our right feeling as
regards arrangement. Therefore no man can be a true landscape-
gardener unless he has a fair knowledge of the flora of these
countries—the plant-inhabitants of wood and copse, of rock and
meadow. Not less needful for him is a certain amount of educational travel : as his highest duty and pleasure must ever be the
planting of beautiful trees so as to allow them to attain fullest
vigour and express their highest beauty, he must study them in
their own homes to do them justice in our gardens. The character and associations of a tree are not easily understood by
those who have not seen it in its native country; therefore every
landscape-gardener should see the natural mountain woods of
Europe, as well as her forests; should see the rich and varied
treasures of the woods in Eastern America, the giant Pines on
the great western ranges, and take advantage of every opportunity to see the natural forest and copse vegetation of the
northern world. To travel southward would be a benefit, too,
but it is not essential. If only as the best way of noting beautiful
or suggestive scenes observed in his travels, the power of sketching faithfully and rapidly should be possessed by every landscape-
gardener. It is, however, otherwise essential in his profession.
Beyond sketching, his artistic ambition should not soar ; it is his
privilege to make ever-changing pictures out of Nature's own
materials—sky and trees, and water and flowers and grass. If
he would not prefer this to painting in pigments, he has no
business to be a landscape-gardener. But most essential of all
for him is garden-travel. He ought to know fairly well what
others have done and are doing in landscape-gardening. Years
might be profitably employed in visiting gardens, not one of
them without some feature instructive for the garden-artist. Yet
bad design has been so much the rule that good models are most
rare. At present it is absolutely necessary to see hundreds of
gardens before one gets a clear all-round idea of what good
design actually is. Many places for years praised as models are
really examples of what to avoid. But we have to thank accident,
diversity of surface, peculiar individual taste, and sometimes what
is called neglect, for so neutralising the efforts of the geometrical
designer, for centuries, that it is yet possible for the independent

mind to distinguish the right from the wrong path.   Every visit
paid to a garden should make the path of future effort clearer.
Artists and writers throw false glories round places famous for
size only, or for miles of clipped trees, or for mere extravagance
of expenditure—a personal visit may give the young observer a
wholesome antidote.   A good engraving or picture may, by the
introduction of artistic touches and variety, give a pleasant impression of a place really devoid of beauty of any kind, as a visit

GROUP OF ROCKS.—*Parc des Buttes Chaumont.*

to many Italian gardens would show.   Surely the old French
styles, as witnessed at Sceaux, at the Grand Trianon, at St. Cloud,
or what remains of it, and at Fontainebleau, only require to be
seen to be for ever laughed at as examples of garden-design.
But some modern gardens in France, such as parts of Vincennes,
the English garden in the Little Trianon, and many other gardens
on the Continent, deserve to be seen.   Then again some of the
public gardens and cemeteries in America should be visited.

Nothing will profit more. In each country also travel is needed as a guide to judicious planting. Even in a small country like Britain there is an immense amount of wasted energy, owing to ignorance of the trees that will thrive in any given district. No fairly instructed landscape-gardener would, for example, plant trees where they are certain never to attain maturity—a common error, however.

In teaching the art of garden-design all has yet to be done. What we want is a body of trained garden-artists imbued with sympathy with nature and love for the work. Such a training as that above mentioned would give us men who would add to our healthy pleasures, and to the beauty of country and town. Gardening is now, even with the most civilised nations, in the same state as that in which art is among the Pawnees, who daub diagrams of a few horses and men on their blankets. We leave all the pictures to those who make them in oil, when we could make living pictures. Garden-artists will, it is to be hoped, be a part of the working force of the coming time.

CHAPTER V.

THE GARDENS OF THE LOUVRE, THE TUILERIES, AND THE ÉLYSÉE.

The Gardens of the Louvre.

THE Place du Carrousel, stretching between the Palaces of the Louvre and the Tuileries, a large open paved square, at its eastern end merges into a narrower space, to which I wish more particularly to direct attention. On one side the Place is perfectly bare and without ornament; but on the other the eye is refreshed by two little gardens which embellish the smaller space referred to, and form veritable oases in a desert of paving-stone. There is perhaps no spot more capable of teaching a valuable lesson in city-gardening.

Viewed externally from their immediate surroundings, the gardens have a pretty effect, and show at once the utility of such near buildings. On the one hand there is a space as devoid of vegetation as the desert—ou the other, by the creation of the simplest type of garden, the sculptor's work in stone and the changeless lines of the great buildings are relieved by the living grace of vegetation, so as to make a garden-picture of the most charming kind, and all by merely encroaching a little on the space that would otherwise be monopolised by paving-stones. The view from inside the gardens, however, shows their good effect with still greater force. The gardens are very small and most simple in plan, a circle of grass, a walk, and a belt of hardy trees and shrubs around the whole, with an edging of Ivy. No gaudy colouring of the ground—no expensive temporary decoration with tender costly flowers, but all green and quiet.

It has been the rule amongst landscape-gardeners and others

to accept as a law that when a garden is made very near to
any kind of ornamental building it is indispensable to make it
"associate" with the buildings—to carry the lines of stone as
much as possible into the garden, to make it as angular and,
it may be, as brick-dusty as possible, like some recent examples
with us.   These gardens, among many others, prove the fallacy
of this.   There are numbers of men professing taste in designing
gardens who would never think of putting anything in this

Little Gardens within the Louvre, exterior view.   (Hachette.)

position but expensive gewgaws in the shape of trees in tubs,
squirting water, vases, coloured and broken gravels—things which
in their opinion would "harmonise" with the work of the
architect.   But unaided by these, and at a tenth of the cost, from
the simplest natural materials, far better results are obtained.
It is well worth while walking round the little lawn in each of
these gardens to notice the various happy effects resulting from
the contrast of the buildings with the trees, one of which is
shown in the page illustration.   The small patches of grass in

LITTLE GARDEN WITHIN THE LOUVRE.
View from the interior.

these little gardens, like grass everywhere in Paris, are green and fresh at all seasons. The secret of this is, repeated waterings whenever the natural rainfall does not serve to keep it as fresh as June leaves.

Passing through the great court of the Louvre, and out at the eastern side, we see the garden of the Louvre, which is simply a railed-in space, laid out with the usual well-kept grass, round-headed bushes of Lilac, Ivy edgings, evergreen shrubs here and there, and flowers, at all seasons. Much of this garden was once covered with old buildings and streets—even the great square just spoken of was once packed with alleys : improvements have, however, swept all those things away, and on every side the buildings stand free—very unlike some public edifices in London, which are not easily to be found.

In the gardens of the Louvre, the system of planting shrubs and flowers is the monotonous one of repeating the same thing everywhere—Lilac-bushes, flowers and all—without any effort at variety. In short, it is a successful attempt at making living things as interesting as the slates on a roof. It is as if all the pictures in the Louvre consisted of copies of a few popular works. It would be easy to pursue a very different system ; to make the plants and shrubs out of-doors as varied as the pictures indoors, added to which the plants would possess life and change. But while men have learnt to use pigments to a good end in art, few think as yet of using the living plants or shrubs in any but a formal inartistic manner.

The Tuileries Gardens.

In this, one of the most famous of gardens, the stupidity of the Le Nôtre or Versailles style of laying out grounds is more apparent than in perhaps any other : Orange-trees in ugly tubs, clipped trees, broad wastes of gravel, dying over-crowded trees, gigantic water-basins, are some of the most evident vices of the system pursued here.

There are many ways of wasting money in gardens, but few worse than growing trees in tubs. Consider the enormous expense incurred by those lines of old Orange-trees in the gardens of the

Tuileries, at Versailles, the Luxembourg, and in other gardens, public and private! Every one of them has cost hundreds of pounds to rear it to a condition that is presentable, and only to produce a deep round tuft of not very healthy green leaves at the end of some seven feet of black stem. Costly tubs that rot; costly storing in large conservatories in winter; costly carriage from house to open garden, and from open garden to house, and all to no good purpose whatever. The foliage differs not at all, or in but a trifling degree, from that of evergreens common in our shrubberies; the clipped head of green is far inferior to that afforded by the hardy and elegant spineless Robinia: the flowers are few or none. The whole thing is a relic of barbarism, and as such should be excluded from any well-arranged garden. The

The Survival of the most Unfit: Trees in Tubs.

kind of effect they produce, if desirable, might be afforded in a far higher degree by perfectly hardy subjects requiring no tubs. They were all very well in an age when exotics were rare, and glass-houses unknown; but now, when we have exotics in profusion, and among them hardy evergreens handsomer than these, and in days too when there are beautiful Orange and Lemon groves in Southern France within twenty-four hours of Paris, such an expensive and inartistic mode of garden-embellishment should be among the things of the past.

It is considered "correct taste" to use trees in tubs in geometrically-laid-out terrace gardens, but there are many terraces where their absence is no blemish. A row of trees in tubs is no more necessary to the good effect of the terrace garden than a row of

balloons.   The culture of Orange, Bay, and other trees in tubs is
a custom more justifiable in those parts of Northern Europe where
but few evergreens can be grown in the open air, than in France
or Britain.   Although now we often see handsome specimens of
hardy evergreens grown in tubs, tender subjects alone were thus
kept when the system originated.   It was found that the Oleander
and Orange trees could be grown very well by storing them in any
sort of half-lighted, frost-proof structure in winter, and placing
them in the open air in summer; and hence these plants became
very popular for that purpose.   But the conditions are now wholly
altered in the garden, and growing trees in tubs is foolish work.

In the Inner Garden, Tuileries.

Uglier still than the Orange-trees in tubs, which after all are
not altogether devoid of a sort of picturesque effect, are the wide
saharas of gravel and the enormous meaningless water-basins,
which interrupt the course of the great central spread of gravel
here and have no good effect or use.   No doubt the providing of
space for the crowds that frequent such a garden must not be
neglected; but that could be done without sacrificing the garden
to boulevards of gravel and stone-encircled ponds.   The beauty
or the use of these ponds it is difficult to see.   The walks
are far more capacious than they need be for ordinary use,

while space for crowds could be provided to any extent upon
gravelled surfaces under groves of trees. The trees here are
for the most part in miserable health, and the new planting
exhibits examples of the most vicious work possible with trees,
young or old. Instead of clearing a portion of the ground and
thoroughly preparing and replanting it, young trees are planted
among old ones. They are planted in pits, the fresh soil of
which the old roots soon afterwards enter and exhaust, so
that neither in the air nor in the ground have the young trees
a chance. The result is that
there is scarcely a fine tree in
the place.

Vicious mode of Tree-planting.

The general effect of the few
flower-borders in the gardens, seen
across the wide areas of gravel
before alluded to, and mixed up
with tubs, statues, chairs, railings,
and what-not, is from most points
of view deplorable. The whole
of the outer and larger portions
of the gardens show us, in fact,
the most lifeless and hopeless style
of gardening possible under stereo-
typed management that success-
fully conserves all the blemishes from generation to generation.
Much better is the portion near the Tuileries ruin, which used
to be known as the private gardens. Here, without close-crowd-
ing, are shrubs which are allowed to grow untortured; graceful
Ivy edgings garlanding the borders of flowers; some green grass,
and fine-leaved plants.

Stiff as this part near the site of the Palace is, in consequence
mainly of its wide straight walks, it owes none of this stiffness
to elaborate geometrical display of beds, or to coloured gravels
and the like. Vegetation, as in any Italian garden which produces a good impression, predominates and relieves the effect of
the statuary or stonework introduced. There are mixed borders
of effective plants along most of the walks, while the squares
have open carpets of turf in the central parts. The mixed
borders include Lilac-bushes, dwarfed by close annual cutting,

Cannas, Roses, Honeysuckles, and herbaceous plants.   In autumn they are planted with flowers which bloom in early spring, and blossom on till about the time of Lilac-bloom, when the summer plants replace them.   The practice of relieving the stony glare from pedestals, statues, &c., by rich bands of Ivy and graceful mixed borders, produces some happy effects.   But, notwithstanding the means taken to tone them down, there are too many huge vases, statues, &c., in these gardens to permit of that repose which is a garden's greatest charm.

The stone seats in this and other gardens, among other advantages which they have over wooden ones, are much easier to make in simple and good forms, not so easily damaged, and do away with the disagreeable need of painting.

Marble Seat, Tuileries Garden

The Garden of the Elysée.

This, a state garden, is typical of a large class of Parisian private gardens. The too-frequently accepted notion is that, given a small garden in a city, it should be geometrical in design. In the neighbourhood of this garden we have streets, high walls, houses and all the other impediments to good effect in landscape-gardening, and yet a quiet, picturesque result is produced. It is always easy, by judicious planting, to hide objectionable surroundings, and, both in Paris and London, noble deciduous trees attain almost as grand proportions as in their native forests. Then in these French city private gardens they cover objectionable wall-surfaces with a lovely mantle of Ivy, so carefully pinched and tended that in winter or summer it forms a level sheet of green. In this way trellises, high railings surmounting walls, gates, &c., are not only rendered inoffensive to the eye, but made to add to the beauty of the garden by the extent of rich glossy verdure which they support. There are cool shady walks here, too, quite as refreshing in their way as many away from cities; there is grass kept green with abundance of water; and there is a pleasant and open lawn—though a small one. Without the little open lawn as a foreground, so to speak, the garden picture would be, to a great extent, lost. It is instructive to compare the sketch with one of the old Dutch or other geometrical gardens frequently represented in old engravings, or with some modern English geometrical gardens, sometimes supposed to be "original" in design, but which are simply reproductions from times when people had not half a dozen kinds of evergreens—when simple conventional figures were sufficiently appreciated to be thought worth delineating on the ground.

In French gardens of this type it is unusual to have any regular or formal set of beds, and this is a great improvement. One half the miserable formalities existing in our gardens arise from the presence of a series of formal "figures," or beds, which have to be filled once or twice a year, in the hope of making them look somewhat presentable—a result seldom obtained. Anything artistic in effect can never be produced through or near them.

In the Garden of the Elysée. (Mangin, Les Jardins.)

If one desires to place some favourite plant in one of these beds, the chances are that it must not be done for fear of violating the " unity " of character which the whole should, we are told, possess. A beautiful garden may be made without a set of formal figures of any kind, and by the adoption of one or more simple forms of beds, such as circles and ovals, placed here and there either singly or in groups in the spots we desire to embellish with flowers. This is the way now common in many recent French gardens. The very general mistake of forming small pools of water near a house exists in French gardens as in our own; and usually the margin is stiff in outline, and not by any means an addition to the charms of the garden. The wise landscape-gardener will not attempt that which he cannot do well. In a small garden no satisfactory effect can be produced from water, except in the form of a clear rivulet.

CHAPTER VI.

THE LUXEMBOURG GARDEN.

THE garden here is under the sole control of an architect, in whose education horticulture has, naturally, formed no part. There have been able horticulturists at the Luxembourg, but their powers for the improvement of the gardens may be estimated by the fact that a dozen flower-pots could not be purchased by them without first obtaining permission from the architect. No change for good is possible under such a system. Horticulture is an art which more than any other is concerned with living things in infinite variety. Without long acquaintance with numbers of these living things under various conditions, no man can intelligently know their wants and arrange them so that we may enjoy them. The profession of an architect has no one thing in common with that of horticulturist. Being wholly concerned with inorganic matter, it is impossible that he could, if really an architect, ever give the study necessary to master even one phase of horticulture. It must surely be obvious that, if our object is to have beautiful gardens, no more serious error can be made than by committing the charge of a garden wholly to the care of men who know, and still worse care, nothing about the art. If we are content with stones and walls where there is no need for them; with a posing ground for the refuse of the studios; with diseased and melancholy trees in formal lines; with flowers drilled into set forms, with false curves and railway-like slopes, with a leprosy of vases and broken gravel instead of flowers and grass, then let us hold to the engineer, the architect, or anyone else who bars the way. This system also secures for us a garden as changeful in aspect from year to year, as a piece of oilcloth. The cause is not difficult to

seek. The director not knowing how to lead the way himself,
will not let anyone else move. Few men who love their work can
endure the dull rule resulting from so harmful a system.

The curiously bad system of planting young trees beneath the
old ones, mentioned and illustrated in connection with the
Tuileries gardens, may also be seen here, the general tree-mis-
management resulting in overcrowded trees, without natural
dignity or size.

Flowers in Hollow Wall.

Among the more instructive features of the garden may be
mentioned the fountain of Jacques Debrosse and its surroundings.
Stretching from the foot of this fountain there is a long water-
basin, with a walk on each side bordered with Plane-trees, which,
meeting overhead, make a long, leafy arch, the effect of the
fountain-group at the end being good. It is, of course, heightened
by the leafy canopy of Planes, but very much more so by the use
made of Ivy and Virginian Creeper. Between the trees the Irish
Ivy is planted, and then trained up in rich, thick, but graceful

wreaths, so as to join the stems at about eight feet from the
ground.   At about a foot or so above the Ivy, another and almost
straight wreath of Virginian Creeper is placed, and the effect of
these two simple wreaths from tree to tree is excellent.   They
seem to fall from the pillar-like stems of the Planes, the bottom
of the lower wreath resting on the earth.   An adoption of such a
plan would add verdure and grace to many a formal grove, now
bare about the base of the trees.

A little pavilion here has a hollow wall with a space for plants
in it, reminding one of a
way of growing flowers
in various countries
which deserves more
attention than it has re-
ceived from us.   It con-
sists in leaving hollow
the upper portion of
a terrace or other wall,
and using this for
flowers.   The crest of
the wall is, in fact, a
flower-border from one
to two feet in breadth ;
but, though narrow, it
has a depth of from
two to three feet for
soil, thus giving ample
root-room for the pro-
duction of a vigorous
and graceful vegetation.
The architect or builder

Climbing Rose isolated on Grass.

can easily arrange for such wall-vases.   One may often see very
charming effects produced in this way on the Continent, even in
poor houses where little evidence of other beauty is to be seen.
By adopting the principle of variety instead of repetition in such
cases, a beautiful garden of flowers might be grown on the crest
of many a barren wall near, or part of, a town house.

In one of the small side gardens here is a climbing Rose,
allowed to grow free on the grass unstaked and untrimmed.

There are remedies for some of our garden-troubles if people
will only try to find them out.   There are few more unprofitable
and tedious labours than that of continually pruning and training
climbing plants.   In many positions we can only partially avoid
this; in others we can avoid it altogether, and obtain a much
more beautiful result.   For example, many vigorous trailers and
climbers are more beautiful planted out on banks of turf and let
alone than under the most careful training.   Such effects are, of

WREATHS ON TREES.—*Luxembourg Gardens.*

course, most suitable for the wilder and more picturesque spots,
but in some degree they may be carried out in any part of the
garden.   That is to say, climbing Roses might be allowed to grow
naturally, and be at the same time so thinned out and otherwise
attended to that they would not become weak in flower or growth.
There are also here some edgings of pegged-down Roses which
form very beautiful margins to masses of flowering shrubs and the
like.   It is one of the ways in which the Rose, so often grown on

FOUNTAIN IN THE GARDEN OF THE LUXEMBOURG

the end of a stick, may be shown to best advantage, its foliage springing from the turf.

Usually in geometrical gardens the portion nearest the building is a terrace commanding the surroundings—here, on the contrary, the part nearest the palace is a basin flanked by balustraded terraces. The grass banks that rise from the lower garden to the balustrade are not left naked, but planted with two lines of dwarf Rose-bushes. There seems no reason why such spots should be left bare. Continuous borders, not beds, run round the plots of grass in the flower-garden here, and from spring to the end of autumn these are never flowerless. The system adopted is one of "bedding" plants and herbaceous plants mixed, but all are changed every year. A spring flower this week is replaced by a summer flowering plant next week, and so on as the season requires. Stocks of plants are always kept on hand to carry this system out, and the placing of the herbaceous plants into fresh ground every year causes them to flower as freely as the tender bedding plants.

But these borders also contain permanent bushes—Lilacs, Roses, &c., which give a line of verdure throughout the centre, and prevent it from being overdone with flowers. Among these woody plants are others very sweet for many weeks through the better part of the season. These are low standard bushes of the common Honeysuckle. Alternating between a Rose and a Lilac, or other bush, and throwing down a head of flowering shoots, few exotic subjects are more welcome in the flower-garden than these Honeysuckle-standards. There are also mixed beds of Ferns in the open air, isolated specimens of Tree-ferns and graceful Woodwardias elevated on moss-covered stands, which add a touch of novelty to the garden as compared with others in Paris.

Many large trees—Planes and Chestnuts—have been moved in full leaf in this garden in midsummer. They are taken up with great "balls" of earth, by powerful machinery, and very successfully; but though it may be very desirable in Paris to move common trees of large size to complete and re-arrange straight avenues here and there, the plan, generally, is not worth the expense.

Before the alterations that took place here some years ago there was a good botanic garden, an irregular sort of English garden, which the French call the "never-to-be-forgotten nursery," and many matters of interest now passed away. The garden used to be famed for its Roses, and for perhaps the largest collection of Vines ever brought together. The Vines were removed bodily to the Jardin d'Acclimatation, in the Bois de Boulogne, and thus it lost some of its most important treasures.

Those taking interest in fruit-gardens should see the little one here. Although small, it is a model of its kind, and very in_structive in much that relates to the training and culture of fruit_trees. The glass-house department retains most of its former

English part of Luxembourg Gardens.

attractions, and to the horticultural visitor will present a good deal of interest. It contains the best collection of Orchids in any public garden about Paris, Camellia-houses in which the specimens attain great size, and good miscellaneous collections.

Free lectures are delivered here, which are thoroughly practical, and illustrated by the aid of living specimens and all the necessary material. The lecturer usually addresses a large and attentive class, consisting of several hundred persons, and elucidates the

H

subject in a way which cannot fail to benefit the numerous amateurs who attend.   As botanical professors lead their pupils on occasional excursions over meadow and hill, so the lecturer takes his classes to famous horticultural establishments from time to time,—to Montreuil, famous for its Peaches; Thomery, for its Vines, and so on.   The custom of lecturing on pure gardening, as distinguished from botany, is common in France, and in many cases a source of much good.   It has, in fact, been a main cause of the knowledge of fruit-trees, grafting, &c., so widely spread in France, the lecturers being always men knowing the subject thoroughly.   Here we leave all the garden-lecturing to the botanists, who, of course, never discourse on horticulture.   This is a pity when we consider how few of the sciences commonly so called are so important for the well-being of a country, and for its beauty, as that of horticulture.

Visitors to the Continent in the summer months can hardly fail to be struck with the growth in tubs or boxes of certain plants of which we in this country make comparatively little use. Some may remember the beautiful effect produced on a quay fronting the Lake of Lucerne by a number of standards, includ- ing Orange-trees, Portugal Laurels, Pomegranates, Pittosporums, Yellow Jasmines, Evergreen Oaks, Euonymus, Aucubas, and Figs. At Vienna a similar assortment may be seen in front of some of the principal cafés, where one may sit in the open street under the shadow of the Oleander and the Pomegranate.   The Oleander is, with the Myrtle and the Pomegranate, a great favourite of the Parisians.   The reasons for this are obvious—its elegant habit, glossy foliage, profusion of bright rosy or white flowers, endowed, moreover, with an agreeable almond-like perfume, offer recom- mendations hardly to be exceeded by those of other plants.   The culture, moreover, is easy.   Indifferent as to the treatment it receives in winter, it may be kept in cellars or passages ; hence its frequency abroad in the windows of the artizan and at the doors of the merchant's office.

Much as one may dislike the culture of trees in tubs, it is impossible not to admire the superb specimens of Oleanders in large tubs which may be seen in the Luxembourg Gardens in summer, often so profusely covered with flowers that the upper part of each bush looks like a bed of flowers.   They are treated somewhat like Orange-trees in tubs, carried like them into the open air in summer, and stored in half-lighted buildings in winter. Probably the complete winter's rest that the plants get in an orangery, and the making of all their growth out-of-doors in the full light and free air, are more conducive to their well-being than the culture they receive in glass-houses.   The treatment given it on the Continent insures the plant a perfect rest in winter : as it cannot grow in the cellars, caves, and dark orangeries in which

The Gardens and Palace of the Luxembourg. (Hachette.)

it is then placed. Therefore, when put in the open air, the growth of the plant pushes equably and immediately : the shoots, being produced in the open air, are indifferent to any changes therein, and the plants enjoy the full sun and uninterrupted light.

It may be noticed in two different conditions about Paris—in the large specimen form in tubs of various sizes, and as small neat plants in six-inch pots.   These last are sold in great numbers in the markets, and flower as abundantly as the best managed of the

large specimens.   The finest examples of large specimens I have
ever seen are those in the garden of the Luxembourg Palace.
Judging by the habit of the Oleander, as generally seen with us,
it might be supposed that it would not make an ornamental tree
for a terrace, but nothing can be finer than the immense specimens
seen in these gardens, the heads being round, dense, and sometimes as much as ten feet through, resembling when in flower
a bed of Roses.   They are certainly far handsomer objects than
Orange-trees, grow equally well or better in tubs, and are more
worthy of culture in this way.   The following account of their
culture was given to me by M. Rivière fils, late of the Luxembourg Gardens.

"This beautiful shrub is a native of North Africa and the south of Europe. In
a state of nature, it prefers damp and fresh soil; it is consequently found in
abundance on the banks of rivers and the edges of marshes. In the wild state it
rarely reaches the height of more than from three to five feet, but under cultivation it may grow even to nine or ten feet. Its flowers are of a delicate rose
colour, and from seed horticulturists have succeeded in obtaining yellow, white,
and double-flowering varieties, which form some of the most beautiful ornaments
of our gardens. The sap is very poisonous, and it is therefore advisable never to
put any of the flowers in the mouth, and to take care that no children should be
allowed near the plants. The hotter the district in which the plant is grown,
the more poisonous is the sap.

"The Oleander puts forth its flowering branches a year before blooming and
then blossoms for two consecutive years, so it is well not to cut them down in
the autumn after the first time of flowering. The beautiful specimens so much
admired in the Gardens of the Luxembourg are from sixty to one hundred years
old. They are grown in tubs three or four feet square, and in a compost of peat
and loam well enriched. The operation of re-potting should be performed every
five years, about the month of May. The sides of the tubs being movable, the
earth is taken away from the roots of the tree, which is itself lifted up about three
inches, so as to remove the soil all round it; it is then lowered into its former
place and potted up with the compost just described.

"The Oleander is generally placed out of doors about the 10th of May, and as
it grows naturally under a burning sky, it is advisable to give it as much sun as
possible. A few days after it is put out, the surface of the soil in the tubs should
be mulched with manure, and during the whole of the summer season they should
be copiously watered at least three times a week. As soon as October comes, the
waterings are diminished, and the top portions of the mulching being taken away,
the surface is stirred up with a pointed stick to render it more permeable. The
Oleander being extremely sensitive to cold, the plants should be taken under
cover once more about the 15th of October, where they must remain until the 10th
of May, being watered in the meantime not more than three or four times every

month.   In France the Oleander-tree is attacked by a parasite called the Chermes Nerii, which does it a great deal of injury. While in the greenhouse no pains should be spared to deliver it from its enemy by means of a stiff dry brush.   The mischief caused by this insect will often kill the tree ; prompt means must therefore be taken as soon as it makes its appearance.   If, in spite of all care, the Chermes still keeps up its depredations, all the old wood that is attacked must be pruned out.   By this means the evil may be entirely remedied, a new set of shoots appearing and bearing flowers the following year."

The groves of stunted and crowded trees, the great expanse of gravel, and the stiff borders are somewhat relieved in the Luxembourg garden by a considerable extent of ground disposed in a more easy and natural manner, which, as usual, is called the "English garden."   Here there is some repose from wide carpets of turf on which are dotted Pillar-roses, Yuccas, groups of fine foliage plants, masses of Roses, with a result that in this part the effect is much better than in the older quarters.   The Papyrus of the ancients, Papyrus antiquorum, has here been for years a striking object, planted out in summer in masses.

Border of Roses.—Luxembourg Gardens.

Streamlet issuing from Ivy-clad Rock.

CHAPTER VII.

THE BOIS DE VINCENNES.

THE Bois de Vincennes may be briefly described as a vast training ground, but it is also, in parts, a beautiful public garden. It is much broader in effect than the Bois de Boulogne, and has really fine open airy spaces such as all large public parks should have; but this we mainly owe to the drill-master. Here, as in the Bois de Boulogne, the plantations are far too dense, and the trees starved for want of space. Still there are pleasant openings and graceful evergreen trees and sparkling water, and altogether it would be difficult to find a nobler advance on the old dismal French garden with its shorn trees and hideous formalism. A glance along some parts of the lakes here is more instructive and satisfying than a study of all the geometrical gardening in France.

Across the little Lake S. Mandé is a good view of the old Donjon of Vincennes. On the islet in the lake there is a large interesting group of trees showing weeping and columnar trees in juxtaposition. The effect of these—Lombardy and other Poplars, and the weeping Willow—is shown in the illustration of the small lake. The state in which water becomes a vital element in garden scenery is seen here in the large lake that sparkles in the sun and gives pleasant distance to the plantations. A temple on a knoll over the water has a certain beauty in the landscape; but such structures are mere affectations in modern gardens. If we must have buildings, let them be such as have relation to modern wants. In the neighbourhood of this temple there is some pretty planting with glossy evergreens by the rocks near the water, tufts of the Giant Arundo and rock-trailers.

The most instructive and beautiful thing in the park is this larger lake near the entrance from the Avenue Daumesnil. This is right in various ways—in size, variety of meadow and wood on the shores, islands, rocky islets, judicious planting and not

Small Lake with Chateau in distance; weeping and erect Trees on Islet.

offensive rock-gardens. The bridge connecting two of the islands is a doubtful feature ; if it be necessary at all, it is certainly placed in too conspicuous a position.

One of the charms of the park is the commanding view it gives on one elevated spot of a sweep of country outside the park and beyond the fortifications, the district of the confluence of the Seine and Marne. The Marne is at our feet ; a glimpse of the Seine may be seen in the distance, and the wide and beautiful

view of the country well illustrates the importance of arranging
public gardens in relation to their surroundings. There are too
many examples of the neglect of this in private as well as public
gardens. In towns we are frequently obliged to plant to hide
ugly things. In the country plantations often conceal beautiful
scenes. The whole system of dead walls, useless fences, and the
like, deserves to be reconsidered ; and as regards such treasures
of park or garden landscape as are enclosed by our own hedges
and ditches, whether we are justified in always shutting them out

View across larger Lake.

from the rest of the world is a point that may well be weighed in
the future by many. At present there is too much of the art of
fortification in planting.

In Vincennes, as elsewhere in the public gardens of Paris,
false curves and steep abrupt slopes abound ; and, as usual, some
of the prettiest parts are marred by the walks and roads. It is
indeed difficult to find a bit of green margin to the water
unspoilt by needlessly offensive walks.

In contrast with these hard margins round the Lac des
Minimes are some little rocky streamlets which are, on the

other hand, naturally and gracefully disposed. The grass meets
the margin of the water as gently as it often does in natural
streams.   Little rocks stand in the bed, sometimes clad with
plants, while Yuccas, trailing shrubs and marsh plants crowd
along the banks.   One of these streamlets issues from an Ivy-clad
rock, of which an illustration is given. Where the streamlets
cross the walks they are conveniently bridged by stepping-stones
and rocks, round which the water-plants cluster. The sketch of
the rocky streamlet in this wood shows a successful attempt
to ornament the mouth of a rivulet as it joins a piece of water.

Near where a streamlet enters the larger lake, there is a group
of little islets dotting the water, as shown in the engraving of the

Rocky Streamlet with Yuccas and trailing Shrubs.

view across the lake.   Islets of this kind artistically formed are a
pleasing feature in good water, and they have a use of which some
of their designers never thought, in the culture and preservation
of a variety of hardy flowers, quite at home in such places.   It
is often possible in such situations to establish little colonies
of bog, or marsh, or rock plants, which could not so easily be
grown elsewhere.   The safety from encroachment by coarser
plants, the complete exposure with at the same time abundant
moisture, and the power of isolating a species or a family where
that seems desirable, make it clear that such spots might be made

much better use of than leaving them to briars and weeds, though
even with these they are charming. The margin of the larger
lake near these little rocks, and indeed in many other parts,
compares favourably with the more abrupt and stiff lines of the
Lac des Minimes.

A restaurant near the Lac des Minimes well shows how such
conveniences may be introduced into public parks without rendering them objectionable. It commands good views of the park and
water from the groups of trees by which it is partially hidden
It would be well if like care were always taken to veil such
structures. In this park are the City Nursery for herbaceous
plants, and the Fruit Garden of the City, descriptions of which
are given in another chapter. The first is an excellent establishment for the supply of a large city.

The system of planting the same subjects in the same proportions, that now obtains in nearly all gardens public and private
throughout Europe, makes them nearly all alike in details; and
this park, instead of offering an absolute change in details
from others, simply repeats the same things. Under this system,
public parks do not represent a tithe of the beauty and interest
of the vegetable kingdom of which they are capable, taking into
consideration their extent, their variety in soil and surface, and
the large sums spent upon them. Everywhere in them we see
vast surfaces almost totally neglected, or only garnished with a
few commonplace trees : everywhere evidence that no thought is
given to the production of noble and permanent features. Sometimes, indeed, one or two spots are embellished at great expense
during the summer months with tender plants, while the remainder of the surface is usually wholly uncared for. This is like
decorating a man clad in fluttering rags with a costly button-
hole bouquet. But the radical fault, everywhere strikingly
apparent, is monotony in the materials used. A tree or a shrub
becomes popular, and is planted everywhere in about the same
proportion. Thus we invariably find similar types of vegetation
everywhere, while the capabilities of city parks as instructive
national gardens are quite undeveloped.

The system best calculated to give us the noblest series of
public gardens the world has ever seen, is to treat them as a whole,
and to establish in each a distinct type of vegetation. For example,

we might devote one city park chiefly to large deciduous trees; another, say a suburban one, as Richmond, mainly to evergreen forest trees; a third to the almost countless flowering deciduous trees and shrubs that are the glory of the grove and copse in all northern and temperate countries; and so on. Or we might treat the subject geographically, and have one small park of French or British trees, shrubs, and plants; another of European, a third of American. a fourth of Siberian, and so on. This plan

Streamlet entering Lake.

does not involve the rejection of other types of vegetation. On the contrary, their presence would often be necessary to contrast with those to which a park or garden might be chiefly devoted. But even if it were determined to devote a park exclusively to the vegetation of one country, no one need doubt that the highest effects could be produced by it alone who remembers what we find in our lanes and woodlands from the association of a few kinds of native plants. We could, by the adoption of this system, define for each manager of a public garden, in what direction his efforts should chiefly tend; give each a distinct aim, and thereby free him from puerile rivalry with his fellows in the matter of " bedding plants." He could then take up a Family, Order, or Flora, and develop its beauty and variety to the completest extent. In the vast expanse of our public gardens, there is not one interesting and important branch of arboriculture or horticulture which could not be developed in a way hitherto quite unexampled. On our botanic gardens already in existence—of which many of the older ones are not large enough for the proper grouping and arrangement of one single family of trees —the system would have the best results. It would relieve the botanic gardens of the necessity of cramming every available plant or tree into a small space, and permit their managers to devote most of their attention to the many tribes of plants which require special and continual care or renewal.

Margin of Lake near Temple, with tuft of Giant Arundo.

Generally our national gardens give no more idea of the beauty of vegetation, than the fountain-basin does of the sea. No botanic garden in existence gives any worthy expression of the vegetation of even the cold and temperate climes of Europe alone! What do we see of the beauty and character of any one large family of trees by planting them all at regular intervals over a plot, or in the various ways they are at present arranged in botanic gardens?

This plan might be continued, if we have no higher object than to procure specimens to illustrate the scientific names that men have given plants.   But if our aim be to show the inexhaustible beauty and dignity of the vegetable kingdom, we must disentangle ourselves from such limitations.   And, clearly, the way to do this is to treat each city's series of gardens (both botanic gardens and parks) as a whole, developing in each some distinguishing feature —from the smallest square with a complete collection of Ivies or Hawthorns, to the noblest park adorned with the trees of a hundred hills.

Finally, though the subject suggests other points of interest, let it be considered what a noble school of instruction the parks of Paris or London, New York, or any other great city, might in this way become.   The whole would thus be made a great experimental garden, in which every question in connection with arboriculture might be thoroughly tested.   In every direction distinct types of vegetation would be met with, instead of the " universal mixture " now everywhere seen, and which so soon and so thoroughly trains the eye to take no more notice of trees or plants than of the railing-spikes round a square.   The contents of no botanic garden now in existence would be worthy of mention compared with the good results we could obtain in this way.   It is not, like many of the changes we long for in towns, impossible to carry out from want of means. The adoption of it would at once tend to make the expenditure of every shilling in our public gardens go toward definite and precious results, and by it we should soon have national gardens worthier of the name than any hitherto in existence.

Near Lac des Minimes, showing bad effect of Road and Walk parallel with Margin.

In the Square des Batignolles.

CHAPTER VIII.

SQUARES.

It would perhaps be difficult to find a greater contrast than that presented by the London and the Paris squares, both as regards their arrangement and management. Most people are familiar enough with the aspects of squares in London, their ill-keeping, melancholy and deserted air, well though the scraggy hedges of miserable Privet conceal their interior. Indeed they are so carefully hedged in and locked up that of them might well be written the motto, "Thieves without, and nothing to steal within."

If we glance at the state of a few of the best-known squares in Paris before entering on the general question of the management of city squares, we shall be able to get a general idea of the very different system pursued in that city, and of its value as a guide

to us in dealing with such important open spaces in large towns,
The Square and Tour St. Jacques well illustrate judicious city
improvements. This tower, originally part of an old church, and
hidden from view by tall, narrow, dirty streets which crowded
around it, is now one of the most striking objects in Paris ; while
the garden is a source of much pleasure and benefit to the people
in this central neighbourhood.

The first thing that strikes the visitor in this square is its
freshness, perfect keeping, and the numbers of people in it, reading,
working, or playing. " The same reason," it is said in ' Guesses
at Truth,' " which calls for the restoration of our village greens,
calls no less imperatively in London for the throwing open of the
gardens in all the squares. What bright refreshing spots would
these be in the midst of our huge brick and stone labyrinths, if we
saw them crowded on summer evenings with the tradespeople and
mechanics from the neighbouring streets, and if the poor children
who now grow up amid the filth and impurities of the alleys and
courts, were allowed to run about these playgrounds, so much
healthier both for the body and the mind! We have them all
ready, a word may open them. At present the gardens in our
squares are painful mementoes of exclusiveness. They who need
them the least, monopolize them. All the fences and walls by
which this exclusiveness bars itself out from
the sympathies of common humanity must
be cast down." The aspect of this square
with its wide walks thronged by people,
would have well realized that writer's ideal
of what a square should be. No gardens
contain more beautiful or diverse objects
than are here for all who will enjoy them.

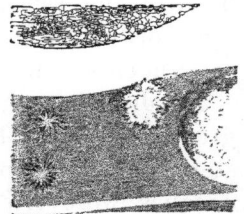

Portion of Margin of a Paris Square, not hedged in.

It is almost as attractive to the passer-by as
to those inside, for instead of a clump of shrubs of commonplace
character cutting it off from view, there is a belt of grass of
varying width, kept perfectly fresh and green, and on it here and
there large beds and groups usually distinct from each other.
Now it is a fine bed of the dwarf Fan-palm, as easily seen from
the street as in the square ; now a group of shade-giving hardy
trees, furnished beneath with evergreens, and finished off with
flowers ; next, a mixed bed of Dahlias and other tall autumn

flowers, and so on. On the carpets of fresh grass between these various clumps there are isolated trees to give the necessary shade and dignity, and to flower in their season. In nearly every case the stems of these are clothed with climbers, generally Ivy, occasionally Aristolochia and Clematis. But the grassy carpet is also ornamented by smaller, though not less beautiful things than the large trees just mentioned. It is sparsely dotted with plants having fine leaves, or distinct character, as Acanthuses, large grasses, and Yuccas.

Between the walk and the tower there is a little lawn, and in one bay of its green carpet, sheltered on three sides, but coming boldly into view from the greater part of the square, is a specimen of the noblest of fine-leaved plants, the great Abyssinian Musa. It is about twelve feet high; the base appears quite two feet in diameter; the young leaves made during the season are intact, each of them eight feet long, with a great red tapering midrib, like a huge billiard cue, running from base to point. Relieved by the foliage of the trees of our own latitude, it forms a fine object. In the immediate foreground there is a mass of a scarcely less striking plant, the edible Caladium, which springs from a groundwork of Mignonette. In like manner are scattered over the green (the central parts being kept clear to secure a little breadth and repose) striking specimens or groups of specimens, some of which it would repay the city to grow, if only to give art students living specimens of the finest leaf-forms.

Amidst the whole stands the famous old tower, its beauty greatly enhanced by being set in a pleasant garden. At every step the square presents a new charm. About this Tour St. Jacques were tried for the first time the Wigandias, now the admiration of so many in both French and English gardens, the Cannas, the Musas, Palms, Ficuses, and others of the better kinds of what may be termed the flora of Parisian gardens. What a change from the filth and consequent unwholesomeness of its old state! How different from the small squares around our churches and monuments!

Although our island is in good repute for its natural verdure, there are few of us who would not be persuaded of the necessity of more efficient watering in our public gardens if they had seen the Square Montrouge during the last days of August. To say it was green would be to give the faintest idea of the glistening verdure displayed by everything in it, from the trees to the grass. It is a very small place, but quite a gem in its way. It is laid out with belts of low trees and shrubs; the centre of the little lawn left unadorned, while all around its edges really distinct plants are dotted about. A handsome specimen of Bambusa aurea, planted alone on the grass, helps to show what may be expected of these tall, shrub-like grasses in the time to come:

In the Square Montrouge, evening—(a wretched statue is omitted).

they will impart to our gardens an entirely new aspect, and that of the most desirable sort. The one we suppose to be the hardiest of all is tenderer than several other species grown in Parisian gardens. This little Square Montrouge has lately been marred of much of its beauty by an attempt to adorn it with statuary, one wretched thing in the centre indeed taking away almost all its grace. The remarks on statuary in the chapter on Versailles apply with greater force to statuary in small squares.

The Square des Batignolles is one of the largest in Paris. Entering from its lower side, the general scheme is seen to be

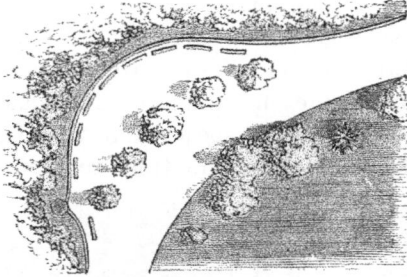

Showing widening of Walk for Playground, with Seats and Shade-giving Trees.

that of a little vale, down which meanders a streamlet, ending in a small round piece of water. The rich grassy sides of the streamlet slope up till they end in dense plantations, so well planted and watered that they look as fresh as if growing far from a large city. The walk round the grass expands from a breadth of ten or a dozen feet to forty, in the first corner of the square, so that the children find little playgrounds without going on the grass. The Plane-trees have Honeysuckles trained up their stems here—a pretty mode of training them.

Here is a profuse variety of the very best shrubs, flowering and otherwise; all these groups of shrubs being edged with flowers. Indeed, it is these margins that afford the floral display; and the absence of all attempt to make a garden of the coloured-cotton-handkerchief pattern makes it almost as free from gaudiness as a ferny dell in a forest. The keeping is perfect, and there is no fence between the public and the flowers but an edging of rustic iron, which rises about five inches above the gravel, and is placed about two inches outside the grass.

The streamlet is tastefully margined with tufts of water-plants, but a novel feature is added. At some distance from the margin —from four to ten feet—are planted here and there single specimens of plants which, while not absolutely aquatic, associate well with such plants; for instance, hardy Bamboos, Yuccas, Erianthus, and other large grasses, some fine Acanthus latifolius, the Pampas grass, and Tamarix.

The square or garden around the Hôtel Cluny and Palais des Thermes is quite distinct from all its fellows, and rightly so. Inclosing ruins and a museum of antiquities, the character of both has been imparted to it by arranging some of the rougher and more enduring objects in it; and being green and shady, the effect of the whole is quiet and good, though situated alongside the busy Boulevard St. Michel. As in many cities there are old ruins and buildings bearing some resemblance to those in this garden, it may not be amiss to say that they are always greatly enhanced by being surrounded with the simplest kind of garden. Ivy, grass, and a few hardy trees and shrubs are sufficient to change their aspect from grimness, hardness, and

Streamlet in Paris Square with Yuccas and Water-side Plants.

decay to great beauty. A few seeds of Alpine plants shaken in the tufts of moss or cracks of mortar would give rise to a dwarf vegetation interesting in itself, and also as illustrating the ceaseless spring of life even in the most unlikely places. For the embellishment of gardens round old buildings, abbeys, &c., there

I 2

are usually *disjecta membra,* not of importance enough to be preserved indoors, in sufficient abundance, and if arranged somewhat
as they are here, the result will prove satisfactory.   The grounds
of the museum at York afford an admirable example of good taste
in this kind of garden.

Although so far in advance of our own squares in every way, it
may be noted that the idea was first taken from London; but
while we Londoners still persist in keeping the squares exclusively
for the few overlooking residents, and usually without a trace of
any but the poorest plant ornament, the French make them as
open as our parks, and decorate them with a charming variety of
trees and plants.

"It has been often remarked," says M. Robert Mitchell of
Paris, "and with great reason, that the English have carried
their material civilization further than we have.   Comparisons
have frequently been made between Paris and London that were
not at all to our advantage, and we are obliged to allow that the
sort of accusation brought against us was not wanting in justice.
It is not many years since the boundaries of Paris inclosed an old
city that was a disgrace to our civilization; streets, or rather
fissures, without ventilation, and unhealthy districts where an
entire population of poor people were languishing and dying.
Now, however—thanks to the useful and important works that
have been lately carried out—the sun shines everywhere; streets
have been enlarged, and every one has sufficient air to breathe.
Paris contains but few unhealthy alleys, whilst in London the
existence of such localities as Bermondsey, Soho, St. Giles's,
Spitalfields, Whitechapel, &c., &c., is still to be deplored.

"We are far from forgetting the immense development of
material civilization in England.   We simply mean to say that
our neighbours frequently invent for the sake of privilege, and
that when their ideas are good we take advantage of them and
popularize them.   We will take a single example: every one
knows how justly the English pride themselves on their gardens
called squares, which are the admiration of every foreigner.   Our
unfortunate public places that the pedestrian cannot cross in
summer without being grilled by the sun or blinded by the dust,
only serve as examples of our inferiority in this respect.   The
square, that is to say, a garden surrounded by a railing, is at

once the representation of a question of health, a question of morality, and perhaps even of national self-respect. We certainly could boast of the Place Royale, which, however, much more closely resembled an unsuccessful attempt than the first step in a happy direction. At present, however, Paris need envy London for nothing. The Squares of St. Jacques, La Boucherie, St. Clothilde, the Temple, Louvois, des Arts et Métiers, and the Parc Monceau are worthy of our city. These masses of vegetation widely distributed amongst the most populous neighbourhoods, cleanse the air by absorbing the miasmatic exhalations, thus enabling everyone to breathe freely.

" Before the establishment of the Paris squares, the existence of a great number of children was passed in confined and unwholesome districts The fresh air for them was only the threshold of a vitiated atmosphere. They were obliged to walk far before they could find a patch of verdure or a bit of country. The children went out but little ; it was thought useless to dress them or make them clean, because they never went out of their own neighbourhood, and in this way their early years passed away. How many times have we not noticed with painful emotion these little, ragged, pale creatures, who never apparently thought of the filth in which they were obliged to live !

" Now, thank God, this dark picture has become bright. Within a couple of steps of the poor man's house there are trees, flowers, and gravel-walks where his children can run about, and seats where their parents may sit together and talk. Family ties are strengthened, and the workman soon understands that there are calmer and more moral pleasures than those in the wine-shop. Again, the different degrees of the members of the working-classes meet together on common ground, and parental feeling is developed by emulation. A child must not be allowed to be ragged for fear of its being remarked, and we will answer for it that a woman in whose breast maternal instinct has not been entirely smothered will never take her child into a public place without first paying attention to the cleanliness which is the ornament of the poor. Some time ago, while walking through the Square du Temple, where hundreds of children were running and jumping and filling their lungs with the country air that has thus been brought into

Paris, we could not help saying to ourselves that, strengthened and developed by continual exercise, these youngsters would one day form a true race of men, which would give the State excellent soldiers, good labourers for our farms, and strong artisans for our factories.

" It has already been stated that the English originate privileges, and that we popularize and perfect their ideas. We shall prove what we advance by comparison. The Parisian Ædiles have made squares wherever a too-crowded population threatened to contaminate the atmosphere, and in all the parts of the city farthest from the Tuileries, the Luxembourg, or the Bois de Boulogne, so that those living in the neighbourhood might be able to get to them easily. In London, on the contrary, with but few exceptions, there are no squares worthy of the name, except in rich and open neighbourhoods. The largest and most beautiful gardens are found at the West-end in Belgravia, or at Brompton, that is to say, at the very gates of Hyde Park. With us trees are planted for sanitary reasons, and the squares have been established more especially in those neighbourhoods where the atmosphere most required to be constantly purified, and to this end trees of a particular sort were chosen for their power of absorption.

" In London they appear to have been above everything anxious about the health of the trees ; a healthy and warm climate was chosen for them in open neighbourhoods close to the parks, so that they should not suffer too much from home sickness. We do not mean to say that the city, for instance, or the other parts of the town are completely provided with squares, but simply that they are so small and mean that they give one the idea of having been blown into their position by the wind. But the headquarters of misery that we spoke of a short time ago—those masses of crumbling houses--those networks of dark alleys—in a word, all that most need pure air and daylight—have been forgotten, or rather neglected, while the richer parts have been improved. In Paris the squares are open to everyone : in England they are locked up, surrounded by a railing surmounted with spikes, and planted with bushes so as to impede the view of all that is going on inside. By the payment of a small sum, generally a pound a year, each inhabitant of the houses forming the four sides of the square has the right to a key of the gate. So that for a poor man to walk with his family in any of these gardens, he must first live in a square and pay a high rent for the privilege, and then contribute a pound a year towards the expense of maintaining it. Practically these squares are useless, and nearly always deserted. In London the squares are private property with which the State cannot meddle. With us, on the contrary, it is the Government that takes the initiative in these municipal improvements. It is to the city of Paris that we owe their construction; they have cost a great deal, and the idea has to be yet further carried out.

Acanthus on Turf in Paris Square.

"It is only necessary to walk in the neighbourhood of any of the squares of Paris towards the middle of the day to see with what pleasing readiness they are frequented by the working-classes. To give only an example, the Square des Arts et Métiers is so crowded with people after four o'clock that it is impossible to pass through it. It was at one time said that the establishment of a public garden was an idea that was perfectly practical in London, but not in Paris, where the inhabitants were so turbulent and revolutionary that they would soon pull down the trees, pluck the flowers, and pull up the plants by the roots. Experience, how-

ever, has shown how utterly this opinion was devoid of foundation. At the inauguration of the Parc Monceau all the gates
were thrown open to the crowd. No surveillance was exercised
over the fifty thousand persons who crowded the walks. At the
end of the day the total amount of damage done only amounted to
some thirty-five shillings for a few turf borders that had been
trampled upon. The fact is perfectly conclusive. Besides, the
squares have now been opened for a long time, and the numberless
frequenters of them have conducted themselves with admirable
order and decency. The people evidently understand that they
are at home; that it is for their especial behoof that the gardens
have been constructed; they know that in pulling up a flower it
is their own property they are destroying; and, moreover, they
evince a respectful gratitude for the hands that have given them
these pleasant places of resort. The establishment of public
squares in Paris is an eminently social idea. We repeat it tends
to regenerate the human race by the development of the physical
forces; by exercise in the open air it improves the morals of the
people, by allowing the working-man to change the dirty wine-
shop for a pleasant walk and an agreeable resting-place; and,
lastly, it proves our readiness to adopt in our own country whatever appears good and useful to our neighbours."

It is to be hoped that we in our turn shall show an equal
readiness to profit by the excellent example shown us in city
squares. There are many private squares in London which
merely occupy space that otherwise would be devoted to the
gardens of the houses around; but, on the other hand, there are
not a few which seem to invite a trial of the system found to work
so well in Paris.

Whatever the condition of the squares of London now, we should
be thankful that we have them. The haunts of disease are
weakened by these islets in our desert of slate, brick, and mud.
In them the sun shines—dimly, no doubt, from our smoke-plague
—the air seems to attain a little more freedom, and trees persist
in growing, no matter how badly they are treated.. We have
many squares in London, but assuredly not half so many as its
colossal expanse requires. In the suburbs, unhappily, they do
not seem fashionable with the cheap builders nowadays. If
matters were arranged as in Paris, the square and the wide airy

road would be laid down long before the builder came to arrange the ground as seemed best to him. There they say to him : Here you may build, but do not encroach on the space necessary for public convenience; and thus avoid the tortuous, close, and often dirty suburban roads which tend to make many districts round London unvisited by and unknown to all but their immediate inhabitants. A broad and pleasant tree-planted road through such a district would, by opening it up. and making it attractive to the inhabitants of London generally, prove as beneficial from a commercial as from a sanitary and an æsthetic point of view.

And if such roads as convenience and good taste demand existed in a city the size of London, squares would be of less importance. Our Thames Embankment, for example, is better than a score of squares.

" Thieves without and nothing to steal within."
Margin of a London Square, with Edge of Plantation designed to cut off the View (Park Crescent).

It can hardly be necessary to point out the benefits that a square confers on the district immediately around it. All, or nearly all, our present expenditure for public gardening is on the vast parks of which London is happily the possessor. As, however, many of the parks are separated by miles from each other, the squares or any open space is of the highest importance. Parks for play and exercise, and beautiful garden scenery, let us have by all means; but our great want is the smaller open spaces called squares, and wide roads planted with trees. We have in London squares of various degrees of magnitude and keeping, from the West Central squares, with their fine old trees, to the new ones at Brompton; from the wide West-end square to the small dark grimy ones in Soho or the City; but even the best of them are badly kept, and unworthy of London. No clear idea of what a square should be seems to have been possessed by those who designed them. The chief feature they have in common is a dirty and ugly crowded bank of Lilac and other common shrubs just within the margin, to prevent a view into them.

There is nothing in any of our parks, there is no feature in any of our public gardens, more beautiful and effective than even our small squares could be made; but little can be done so long as the absurd system of cutting off the scene from public view, and from the view of the persons who inhabit the square, prevails. There are squares in London in which views, almost Arcadian in their beauty, could be made; yet, except from the windows of the houses that surround them, one can see nothing but a struggle between Privet and Lilac. Two of the finest weeping Ash-trees in London are near the margin of Brunswick Square, but they are so surrounded by the usual mean scrub that they are rarely recognized by the passer-by. Cleared around and surrounded by well-kept turf, they would prove ornaments to the whole district. But it may be urged that the squares are private property, and that their owners have a perfect right to keep them shut out from public view, if so disposed. Even so, it is quite possible to do this without making the margin inviting as a receptacle for miscellaneous rubbish, and without concealing the finest objects the squares contain.

By allowing the grass to venture near the railing here and there, and dotting it with flowers and isolated shrubs, so as to permit of pleasant peeps into the interior, quite a new aspect would be given to our now gloomy squares, and the change would not by any means destroy privacy. No conceivable harm could come of making these little gardens attractive to the public, and in doing so, to those having "vested rights" also. There can be little doubt that if we could drop the Square Montrouge into our West Central district, there would soon be a general desire on the part of the owners of our squares that they should be disposed in like manner. In that small, much-frequented square, may be seen plants in masses in the open air as valuable as those exposed in our great public gardens here, and that without the least danger, though crowds frequent the place from morning till after dusk.

Another important feature of the arrangement of our squares, and one which, like the filthy and crowded marginal shrubbery, is common to nearly all of them, is the disposition of the central portion. The ground is usually so small that it is desirable to make the most of it. The best way to make it look mean and contracted is to build a structure varying in appearance from a wooden fowl-house to a bathing-machine. Yet this is what is done in the majority of the " best " London squares. The eye is thus fixed on the contemptible objects in the centre, an agreeable spread of turf is made impossible, and the beauty of the trees or shrubs cannot be felt. It is unwise to desire uniformity in any art, but one principle deserves being engraved on the mind of every person who has the care of squares, which is that the best way to obtain an excellent effect is by keeping the centre open and grassy, untortured by walks, hedges, or beds.

The gardening in our squares is of a peculiarly lugubrious description, and of a style quite apart. Hardy subjects are not made a study of, and the bedding plants with which the country is ablaze in many parts are rarely seen. Year after year the same tone of slimy melancholy is assiduously preserved. The trees crowd upon each other, and even those that tower above all, and assert their dignity in spite of neglect, are not seen to advantage. Any flowers planted usually soon perish in the dismal shade.

Structure in centre of a London Square.

The walks, generally designed so as to cut through and destroy the prettiest spots in the square, appear to receive most attention, but it is sometimes shared by the ugly, high, and elaborate seats piled round the bases of the beautiful trees so as to cut short the effect of their stems as seen across the lawn. All the necessary seats, as well as tool-houses and arbours, should be placed near or towards the sides, where they would be useful without being obtrusive. It is quite easy to so place such objectionable features that while convenient for shade and comfort, they shall not be objectionable from any point of view.

The best feature of the London squares is their trees. In the West-Central districts are frequently seen Planes which would command admiration in their native forests. Huddled together, at first, with a number of miscellaneous trees, they, thanks to their constitutions and stature, now tower above the masses of overcrowded shrubs around them, and spread forth their boughs

so freely that each tree seems as if it tried to fill up the square.
When the multitudinous fires are active around them in winter,
these trees give us in the dreary wastes of London a glimpse of
the beauty of the wild woods. And let it not be thought that
the Plane is the only tree that would thrive perfectly in our
squares, even in the most smoky and crowded parts. It would
take a long list to enumerate all the beautiful deciduous trees
and shrubs that grow in the temperate and colder regions of
the world, and the great majority of which would do perfectly
well in our London squares, if properly planted and attended to.
It would be perfectly easy, even with our present knowledge,
to select as many beautiful trees that would thrive in the squares
of London, as would represent in them the brake and forest
beauty of every important cold region in America, Europe or
Asia. To select such trees and shrubs, and plant them so as to
secure to each a due amount of light and air for its development, should be the aim of those responsible for the squares of
London.

One way of encouraging desirable variety would be the devoting
of one square to the trees and shrubs of a particular country;
one, for example, might have British trees and shrubs alone,
another American trees, another Chinese and Japanese trees and
shrubs, and so on. It would be permanent, too; and permanence
in these matters simply means saving of constant trouble and
expense. But there is no reason whatever why the squares
should be devoted to hardy trees and shrubs alone. On the
contrary, the best way would be to allow much latitude, so as to
secure variety. When people begin to understand the management
of city gardens, one of the first principles they will discover is
that each square and small garden should differ as much as
possible from its neighbours. Some of the suburban squares
might be devoted to that evergreen vegetation which cannot be
grown in the central parts; some in all parts might be gaily
decorated with flowers and fine-foliaged plants; others chiefly
with hardy flowers and shrubs, and so on. But little of this
kind could be well done unless all or most of the squares were
under one responsible head, who could determine what was best
to do in each case and prevent imitation and paltry rivalry.

Private interests and public prejudice may be against the

opening of most of our squares to the public now, and may long
continue so, but in the interest of all it is the true plan, and
will yet, it is to be hoped, be the rule in all parts of London.
The advantages enjoyed by those who " possess keys " are surely
not such as need prevent their offering the boon in question to
the poorer inhabitants, many of whom, perhaps, seldom have an
opportunity of seeing more of nature than is visible in the streets
of London.   Once devoted to public use, and under intelligent
supervision, a modest allowance from the public purse would
suffice to convert the squares into beautiful gardens.   They
would save some from the attractions of the public-house, and
keep the world of London children from the gutter.

A Town Square opened up.

An important subject in connection with squares and city
gardens is that of playgrounds.   These small spaces, provided for
play and rest, form a commendable feature in the Paris squares.
They are usually formed by widening the outer walk of the
square at each corner, where trees are generally planted so as to
afford shade.   Here the children play and their nurses work.   It
is one of the pleasantest sights in Paris to see these playing-
places with crowds of happy children on fine days.   No system
of city-gardening can be good which does not meet this want.   It
is not enough to have open spaces or beautiful little gardens; we
should keep the children from the filth and dangers of the
crowded streets.   The best way, in the case of all large cities, is

to have, as far as possible, squares or open spaces arranged as playgrounds alone. These should be planted with large trees, which, while affording ample shade, would not suffer from the crowds beneath. The smaller class of square would do best as playgrounds, and there are not unfrequently in large cities open spaces which, at a trifling expense, might be made into useful recreation-grounds of this kind. The only requirements are hardy trees, gravelled spaces, and seats. In these cases the whole surface should be gravelled over after thorough preparation has been made for the trees. The reason of the superiority of trees alone for such places is that the whole of the space beneath them is free as a playground, while overhead their leaves and flowers and forms may do as much to adorn the neighbourhood as an elaborate garden. In several of the small spaces and squares opened of late in London, an opposite plan has been adopted—that of flower-beds and elaborate gardening; hence their use as playgrounds is interfered with. Of course garden-squares are needed as well as playing-squares; but in most districts the playground is the greater want.

The recent improvements in Leicester Square invite a word here. A garden of any kind, in lieu of the nuisance of Leicester Square, with its decaying and not inodorous rubbish of various kinds, is a boon to the district, and the most notorious eyesore in London is now to be seen no more. But we have scores of squares needing like changes; and the manner in which this transformation has been done being likely to influence future work in the same direction, it is desirable that the points in which the design of Leicester Square is deficient should be made known to all interested in such improvements. The first and chief defect in the plan is that it is too much "cut up." There is a broad walk immediately encircling the fountain, and another walk all round, between that and the enclosure, and then there are four other walks, one from each of the four entrances, intersecting the external walk, and leading directly to the one round the fountain. This needless prevalence of gravel instead of turf, is a radical mistake: it is a repetition of the tones of the surrounding houses; it wearies the eye, and destroys all repose. The fountain is too big for the space, while the lesser pieces of sculpture.dotted about would be better away. There is far too

CORNER FOR PLAY IN THE SQUARE MONTROUGE.

much of the architect and sculptor, and too little of the gardener. This is a very common defect in the embellishment of town-gardens. In the centre, where there ought to be repose, there is nothing but stone, chairs, gravel—and confusion. As for the planting, much is wrong, both as to the kind of trees selected, and

The Square and Fountain des Innocents

their disposal as to position. It is curious that in spite of all the experience of the constant failure of evergreens in the London squares, few deciduous trees have been employed in the planting of Leicester Square ; Rhododendrons and Portugal Laurels are the plants chiefly made use of, though a moment's thought, with all

the experience that our town-plantations furnish, would have
shown that trees which do not shed their leaves annually, become
so encrusted with soot after a single winter in the midst of
London smoke, that they soon dwindle into miserable dying
objects.

As the freshness and texture of the lawns in Paris gardens is a frequent subject
of remark, we have thought it well to translate the following account of how they
are formed. Nothing can surpass the beauty and texture of our own garden-
carpets; but the Paris system may be worth trying in countries drier than ours.
In any case, the information conveyed by M. Rafarin to the ' Revue Horticole'
is worth repeating. In order to obtain the best results in forming a lawn, three
points must not be lost sight of :—1st. Preparation of the Soil; 2nd. Choice of
Grass-seed ; 3rd. Maintenance.

1. *Preparation of the Soil.*—In the first place, it must be well drained, that
is, if it be too damp, swampy, or if it rests upon an impenetrable sub-soil.
Secondly, light dry soils must be enriched by means of manure, as must also
clayey, damp, or cold soils. Thirdly, the soil should be mellowed by repeated
ploughings and harrowings, taking care, during each operation, to break the clods,
and to extract the stones and roots of weeds. Fourthly, it must be made even
by levelling a fortnight after it has been ploughed ; then roll it, break the clods
afresh, and finally sow the seed.

2. *Choice of Seeds.*—It is indispensable that the seeds used be of the best
quality. Having chosen the seeds, mix together those that resemble each other
in size, form, and weight, taking care that they are suitable for the nature of the
soil on which they are to be sown. The following are four mixtures that are
very commonly used in France; they should, however, only be considered as
examples, and may be modified according to circumstances.

FIRST MIXTURE—FOR A FRESH SOIL, IMPROVED AND PREPARED AS JUST DIRECTED.

	lbs.		lbs.
Agrostis stolonifera . . .	22	Poa trivialis	11
Bromus pratensis	11	„ pratensis	22
Cynosurus cristatus . . .	19¾	Lolium perenne . . · .	66
Festuca tenuifolia	22	Trifolium repens	2¼
„ rubra	33		
Anthoxanthum odoratum .	11		220

The amount will suffice for an area of rather more than two acres. For smaller
pieces of land and for borders a larger proportion must be used.

SECOND MIXTURE.

	lbs.		lbs.
Agrostis vulgaris	11	Cynosurus cristatus . . .	8¾
Avena flavescens	11	Festuca tenuifolia	11
Bromus pratensis	11	„ heterophylla . . .	11

	lbs.		lbs.
Festuca ovina	22	Poa nemoralis	11
„ rubra	11	Lolium perenne	77
Anthoxanthum odoratum	11	Trifolium repens	2¼
Poa trivialis	11		——
„ pratensis	11		220

THIRD MIXTURE—FOR SHADY GROUND, AS, FOR EXAMPLE, THAT BENEATH TREES.

	lbs.		lbs.
Aira elatior	22	Poa trivialis	8¾
„ flexuosa	22	„ pratensis	11
Festuca elatior	22	„ nemoralis	11
„ tenuifolia	11	Lolium perenne	44
„ heterophylla	22	Trifolium repens	2¼
„ rubra	22		——
Anthoxanthum odoratum	11		220
Holcus lanatus	11		

For small patches, an increase of 20 to 50 per cent. is required.

FOURTH MIXTURE—FOR CALCAREOUS SOILS.

	lbs.		lbs.
Agrostis stolonifera	11	Anthoxanthum odoratum	19¾
„ vulgaris	11	Poa trivialis	11
Bromus pratensis	33	Lolium perenne	88
Cynosurus cristatus	11	Trifolium repens	2¼
Festuca ovina	11		——
„ rubra	22		220

For borders and small plots, from 20 to 50 per cent. more should be used. Sowing should take place in the spring in the case of stiff, damp, or cold soils, and in autumn in soils that are light, dry, or scorched, and, as far as possible, when the weather is calm, and the earth cool without being damp. Each variety of seed, of which the mixture is composed, should be sown separately, commencing with that of which there is the largest quantity, and which requires to be buried at a greater depth in the soil than the others; and finishing with that of which there is the smallest proportion. After each sowing, harrow with an implement of a power proportionate to the depth which each kind of seed should reach. Then beat down the earth (especially if it be light), and scatter a layer of mould to the depth of an inch or so. Finally, water when the soil has become dry to hasten germination, which will take place in from eight to forty-five days according to the variety.

3. *Maintenance.*—The old popular saying—" Water makes the Grass," proves the importance of frequent waterings for maintaining turf in perfect order. It is necessary to water after each cutting and whenever the ground becomes too dry. Each year in autumn and during cool but not damp weather in spring, after having given the turf a vigorous harrowing, and, above all, those parts which are covered with Moss, first remove the Moss and noxious weeds—an operation which

K

is indispensable, though too often neglected, and which it is necessary to repeat during the course of the year, whenever they make their appearance; secondly, sow the seed over all parts which are bare; thirdly, scatter upon the surface a layer of good soil, using guano if the ground requires enriching; fourthly, roll with a roller, the weight of which is adapted to the nature of the soil. Lawns should be mown with the scythe once or twice a month in spring, three times a month during the summer, ceasing towards the end of October, so that the Grass may grow again before the winter frosts set in.

Within the past few years there have been signs of slight change for the better in some squares in London. Some of the ugliest structures in the centre, and the most puerile features have in various cases been removed; but much remains yet to be done. The best recent work in London is in Bedford Square, which has been very much improved by Mr. Meston for the Duke of Bedford. The dwindling, mean, undershrub vegetation has been swept away, root and branch, from beneath the fine old Planes, which now stand out grandly over the smaller trees. Unsuitable and decaying trees have been cut down, and the soil renewed on the surface, so that since then the trees that remain have grown well, and there has been fresh green turf throughout the summer. The effect from the streets, but more particularly from the windows of the surrounding houses, is greatly improved. It is to be hoped that this step of the Duke of Bedford's may happily inaugurate a general adoption of such improvements. The capabilities, so to speak, of many of the older London squares are so remarkable, that a little good taste and good gardening are all that are required to make them beautiful gardens and a credit to the nation.

Tuft of large grass (Sorghum) in Paris square

CHAPTER IX.

AVENUES AND BOULEVARDS.

PARKS and gardens are excellent in their way, but they effect
only a partial good if vast areas of densely-packed streets are
unrelieved by green or open spots where the air may obtain a
vantage ground in its work of removing impurities. The slight
good effected by fine parks placed here and there in or towards
the outskirts of a city is as nothing compared with what may be
carried out by so planning and planting streets and roads that
the air might be comparatively pure and free, and the eye
refreshed with green at almost every point. What would the
new boulevards of white stone be without the softening and
refreshing aid of those long lines of trees that everywhere rise
around the buildings, helping them somewhat as the grass does
the buttercups? The makers of new Paris—who deserve the
thanks of the inhabitants of all the filthy cities of the world
for setting such an example—answer these questions for us by
pulling down close and noisome quarters, where the influence of
fresh air and trees was not felt; by piercing the city with long
wide streets, flanked with rows of trees; and by relieving in
every possible direction man's work in stone with the changeful
beauty of tree-life. It is pleasant to add that these improvements
of Paris were not part of the scheme of one government only.
Since the Empire the good work has gone on more vigorously,
and certainly more economically than before. Only lately, two
of the most striking improvements ever effected in Paris—the
avenue from the Opera to the Rue de Rivoli, and the Boulevard
St. Germain, have been completed.

Paris shows the most praiseworthy attempts yet seen to render
an originally close and dirty city healthy and pleasant; and this

has been chiefly effected by her vast system of wide streets and roads bordered with trees, and with footways as wide as many of the old streets. These streets do not merely pass through the city in a few important lines, but pierce it in every direction, and are designed upon a far-seeing and systematic plan. Many visitors who walk along the crowded boulevards of central Paris, who see those extending in all directions from the Arc de Triomphe and offering bold approaches to every important position, may yet have but a meagre idea of their vast extent in the outward and less-known regions of the city. The elm-bordered Boulevards Sébastopol and St. Michel cut through Paris from north to south in a straight line, and on their way effectually open up the old Latin quarter and many others as bad; while beyond their outer extremities and between the fortifications and the central districts still larger boulevards sweep round, wide enough to be planted with groves of trees, and to prevent overcrowding for all time. Immediately within the fortifications there is a wide boulevard running round the city under various names for many miles, while from every circular open space—like the Place du Trône, Place du Trocadéro, Place d'Italie, or Place de l'Etoile—broad tree-planted streets radiate. In fact the whole of the space within the fortifications is netted over by them, and the outer and less-frequented boulevards are often much wider than the central ones. - In many instances these outer boulevards pass through parts but thinly or not at all populated, so that the buildings of the future cannot encroach upon the space necessary for free circulation, air, and trees.

How backward we are in England, those can tell who know what has been done of late years in such cities as Rouen, Lyons, and Paris, and are also acquainted with our own sooty, packed, and cheerless cities. Are our cities and towns to remain a mere agglomeration of ruts which form such an excellent contrivance for preventing foul vapours to escape from the town? At first sight there does not seem any reason why the places where men most congregate should be those from which all who can afford it, escape as often as possible; though, doubtless, in a country where the laws of supply and demand regulate everything and everybody in such a satisfactory way, one would not have far to travel for reasons why things are right as they are. Nevertheless, it cannot be denied that the disposition of our cities is a disgrace to any civilized race. Why, without touching at all upon the most crowded and filthy parts of London, one may see in a walk from the Strand to the Regent's Park such a reeking mass of mismanagement as may be found in no other European capital ; and yet London is the " richest city in the world ! "

It is a city of commerce, and we cannot afford space or money to remodel it, say some ; but apart altogether from questions of salubrity and appearance, it is worth considering how much material loss occurs from mere want of room even in our leading thoroughfares. In many cases they are almost impassable except to those compelled to force their way through them. All real improvements would result in a clear gain to the business of the city ! But the space ? " Land is too dear ! " This is really not a great difficulty in London. There is no city which could be pierced with free, open roads and boulevards more cheaply and readily. In its very centre there are acres covered by shallow brick buildings, which have not cost nearly so much as closely-packed, tall, stone houses in interior parts of Paris, that are cut through every day almost as freely as if they were made of pasteboard. Whole regions of London, most important and well situated for business purposes, are covered by the veriest shanties. In such places houses to accommodate thrice the number of persons might be built, while the streets might be as wide again, and therefore have purer air and more light. Wide tree-planted avenues might lead from the embankment out towards the suburbs, and would act as veins of salubrity to the regions they traversed. The increase in the value of property along such main arteries would repay for the outlay. If land be so valuable, why occupy it with such trifling and unprofitable buildings? The fact is, the objection as to space, which is usually urged as the greatest, is a groundless one. Half occupied and sometimes waste ground without the margin of the city, and square miles almost worse than waste within, attest this.

A change for the better would probably involve the adoption of the " flat " system, which, some say, our people have a great objection to. In houses constructed well in this way, and with many modern improvements never to be found in the miserable and fragile structures now everywhere to be seen, the

additional warmth and dryness could hardly fail to have a beneficial effect on the health of the inmates, besides other manifest
advantages which such buildings possess.   Our narrow streets, and
flimsy houses, and the want of anything like a generally recognised
plan, are worthy only of a period when men first herded together
within walls for security, not of the Victorian era.   No sprinkling
about of disinfecting agents when danger becomes imminent, or
pulling down of a few shops that have protruded themselves so
far into the narrow street that they have become intolerable even
to those accustomed to dodge through the streets of London, will
touch more than the surface-roots of the evil.   We want a plan .
with the Thames Embankment for its backbone.   There is nothing
to prevent us having the embellishments seen in Continental
cities, minus their trees in tubs and paltrier features.   But to
have them it is indispensable that we first have breadth and room,
that the street-traffic may circulate freely.   Footways and roads,
wide and open, are the first and greatest necessaries, and they ought
to be planted with trees, which thrive better in London than in
Paris.   No fancy-gardening, no stone work, vases, griffins, expensive
fountains, and fountain-basins—nothing whatever of that type
—should be tolerated until free air be enabled to penetrate
into the heart of the town, through open verdure-bordered roads;
which indeed would induce it to ignore the boundary line that
now so widely marks the difference between town and country.
Pure air and light are naturally the property of all; but
civilized man repels them by his stupid arrangement of our cities.
To make them once more, even in cities, the property of all should
be the aim of all.

The conditions complained of do not simply occur in central
parts of London where land is very dear: far beyond the radius
of the parks, the arrangements of streets are frequently quite as
bad as in the more central districts, and capital preparations are
being made to secure a dozen years hence a suburban cordon of
districts like St. Giles's.   To experience the truth of this the
reader has merely to go from Kensington Gardens to Kew—not
the most unpleasant stroll that could be selected in suburban
London.   In the course of his journey he will find in the least-
populated parts pleasant open roads, in some cases wider than a
boulevard, and with useless spaces railed off, and gravelled spaces,

wide as an avenue, before some public-house; but the moment he
arrives at a densely-populated part, the dead rabbits, sheep, &c.,
thrust out from the shops into the few feet of crowded footway,
oblige him to dodge so often among the manure-carts and
omnibuses of the narrow crowded street that, if he has ever
seen anything like a decently-arranged city, he will be forced to
admit that suburbs of London, miles in extent, have received less
attention as to design than a cottager bestows upon his little
garden, or a designer of wall-paper on his rudest patterns. From
a like, or even a worse, condition our neighbours have by spirited
improvements been delivered, and in a very short time.

The boulevards of Paris are, generally speaking, so very much
alike that to describe them in detail is needless. From house to
house they are usually, in the most-frequented parts, over 100
feet wide, occasionally reaching between 130 and 140 feet, and
even much wider than this in the outer boulevards, which are
sometimes large enough for half a dozen lines of trees, in addition
to very wide footways, and perhaps two minor side roads, besides a
broad central one, as in the Avenue de la Grande Armée. The
footways of the most-frequented boulevards are about twenty-six
feet wide on each side, and sometimes more. But, notwithstanding their general similarity, there are a few distinctive
enough for special mention, and among these none more so than
the Boulevard Richard Lenoir, which runs from the Place de la
Bastille to the Rue du Faubourg du Temple. This often escapes
observation from visitors, as the Boulevard Beaumarchais drains
most of the traffic from the Bastille to the fashionable boulevards;
but it is one of the most remarkable in Paris, and more than
usually ornamental. It is nearly 2000 yards long, and is in
great part built over a canal. It was thought desirable to cover
a large portion of the canal, and to make a wide boulevard over
this huge bridge, in order to facilitate the traffic and improve the
appearance of the district. It became necessary to have ventilating and lighting shafts for the canal, and eighteen pairs of these
openings occur in the course of its length. These have been
ingeniously and tastefully hidden by eighteen little railed-in
parterres. In these the openings, which are wired over, are
surrounded by a thick low hedge of Euonymus or some close
evergreen, so that no opening of any kind is exposed to the

passing observer.   In the centre of each garden there is a long basin and a fountain, the whole being connected and surrounded by flowers and grass.   Then on each side of these parterres there is a very wide avenue footway, shaded by two lines of Plane-trees— a road being on each side of the parterres and tree-avenues.   For a considerable distance from the Château d'Eau, the flower-market that has its head-quarters held there extends down amongst the little railed-in parterres, and the effect is altogether unique.

Of avenues, the largest and most picturesque is the Avenue du Bois de Boulogne, leading from the Arc de Triomphe to the Bois de Boulogne.   The beauty of which avenue-gardening is capable, even in cities, is fairly shown in the engraving of this avenue. The effect is from various points of view very free and graceful, there being considerable variety in the vegetation and ample room in the well-formed footways and roads.   There is also considerable breadth—a notable fact in days when large gardens have none ; indeed, the most pleasing feature to anyone caring about garden-design is the ample turf that forms a carpet for the groups and masses of shrubs.   Most large cities have opportunities for the formation of avenue-gardens which have hitherto seldom been taken advantage of.

This handsome avenue was formed in order to put the centre of Paris in communication with the Bois de Boulogne by means of a wide direct road.   Half the expense was borne by the State, under the conditions that an iron railing of uniform design was to be constructed along the whole length of the road, that a strip of eleven yards in breadth be left for a garden between this railing and the houses on each side, and further, that no kind of trade or manufacture should be carried on in the houses adjoining.   The avenue was made entirely through private lands which were required for the purpose.   Its total length is 1300 yards; the width 130 yards.   It consists of a central drive, seventeen yards wide, of two large side walks, each measuring thirteen yards wide, and of two long pieces of grass with shrubs and flowers.

The Champs Elysées, the great central avenue of Paris, happily combines the grand avenue and the public garden; the wide belts of varied shrubs are encircled with the choicest flowers ; the grass spreads out widely here and there ; great clumps of Rhododendrons and trees shroud buildings, not completely to hide

A C IX AVENUE GARDEN: *Side View in the Avenue du Bois de Boulogne, looking toward Paris.*

them, but to prevent them from staring forth nakedly in the midst of the quiet of the garden. These buildings are chiefly for concerts, cafés, etc., and are wholly out of place in such a position ; this noble avenue is in fact blighted by a crowd of petty theatres, etc., which should have no place therein. Were the avenue at some distance from the streets, there might be some reason to give place in it to a number of insignificant buildings, but as matters are there is none whatever. This system of introducing paltry structures, statues, fountain-basins and water-spouting apparatus in the public gardens and parks ought to be jealously watched by those who care more for the garden than for stones or slates. It would be easy to point out places already much defaced in this way.

It was only in 1860 that the garden of the Champs Elysées was laid out, and yet it looks long-established, has many good specimens of Conifers, Magnolias, etc., numerous large and well-made banks and beds of Rhododendrons, Azaleas, Hollies, and the best shrubs and trees generally, with abundant room for planting summer-flowers, chiefly, however, as margins to the clumps of shrubs. The gardens finish at the Rond Point, a circular open space, in which there are large beds for flowers, fountains, etc., disfigured, however, by the undulations which some poor little bits of grass are made to assume. Useless and unnatural diversification of the ground in some small spaces, and the grouping together of too many things in one mass, are weak points in the gardening of Paris.

The Place de l'Etoile, with its surroundings, is precisely the reverse of our own efforts in like positions—its breadth, dignity, and airiness contrasting strikingly with the narrowness, meanness, and closeness of the arrangements in our so very much larger and busier London.

In contrast to this remarkable city-avenue garden that in the Regent's Park deserves notice, the site being even better than that in Paris. No such opportunity for noble improvement of this kind exists in any city of Europe as in London. And there is not even any such expense required as would be the case if the space were covered with houses. Portland Place is broad enough to allow of planting a line of trees on either side of the roadway, which would give it almost the aspect of a Parisian

boulevard. The carriage-way might, at its northern end, turn
to the right and left, as at present; but in a line with its straight
portion a broad footway of equal width to the straight carriage-
way should be opened through the Park-Crescent gardens into
the Regent's Park. Such an improvement, if worthily carried
out, would be the grandest that could be effected in the park-
ways of London. It would, in some respects, surpass even the
Champs Elysées themselves. Why the direct opening from Portland Place to the Regent's Park should not have been effected
long ago is difficult to understand. Another fine opportunity for
an avenue occurs in Westbourne Terrace. From the Bishop's
Road to Hyde Park, in a direct line, a noble avenue of trees,
springing from a strip of turf, might be established, which would
produce a fine effect—unlike anything else in the metropolis. To
effect this, it would only be necessary to sweep away the paltry
lines of balustrades and the (so-called) shrubberies of mutilated
Lilacs and Privet bushes, and of irregularly-planted trees stunted
by reckless lopping, and establish in their place a stretch of
simple turf, in which detached trees and groups should be
planted. This treatment of the important thoroughfare in question would so greatly add to its apparent spaciousness, and to
its beauty, that the value of the property would be at once greatly
increased.

Naturally the features of the boulevards which command most
attention in this book are the trees that adorn them so well.
The planting in all the London parks is as nothing compared
to the avenue and boulevard planting in and around Paris.
Trained and pruned so as to form a symmetrical straight-ascend-
ing head, with a clean stem, every tree is protected by a slight
cast-iron or stick basket, and is staked when young, and when
old if necessary; nearly every tree being also provided with a
cast-iron grating six feet wide or so, which effectually prevents
the ground from becoming hard about the trees in the most-
frequented thoroughfares, permits of any attention they may
require when young, and of abundance of water being quickly
given in summer. The expense for these strong and wide
gratings must be great, but the result that will be presented by
the trees a few years hence will more than repay for all the outlay by the grateful shade and beauty they will afford. As soon

as a new road or boulevard is made in Paris, it is planted with trees; and every one of the millions is as carefully trained and protected as a pet tree in an English park.

To plant trees so closely as those on the boulevards helps to provide the streets with some shade almost directly; and as the trees are usually trained specially for boulevard-planting, some little effect is obtained at once; but there can be no doubt that it is too close a system of planting, as the trees cannot grow sufficiently when so much crowded. A better way would be to place them further apart, and to plant alternately with the permanent trees some kind that grows very rapidly when young. This would help to furnish the avenue until the trees intended to permanently adorn it have been established a few years. As soon as those of the free-growing, nursing kind become large enough to deprive their neighbours of light, they might be cut in vigorously, and finally removed altogether. Sometimes double ranks of trees are planted, but this is only wise where the boulevards are very wide. It is occasionally practised in avenues—like some of those that radiate from the Arc de Triomphe; but usually it has the effect of darkening the houses too much. They should however be planted wherever, as is often the case in the outer boulevards, there is abundant room for a double or even treble line of trees to develop without disagreeably shading the houses. The trees are usually placed within three and a half or four feet of the edge of the footway, but there can be little doubt that it would be a better plan to keep them a few feet further from the road, and this would admit of giving them a larger body of soil, of which generally they receive too little in Paris.

With the boulevards one naturally associates the quays, planted in every available spot with trees, and in Paris the public swimming-baths are all on the silent boulevard. However, the Seine at Paris is not a noble river, and the ugliest things to be seen from its banks in summer are the floating baths, which in some places half cover its surface. But public bathing is a matter of the highest importance, and it is perhaps better to have floating baths on the river than tolerate the exhibition which may be witnessed on the Serpentine on any fine summer evening. Whatever may be thought upon this point, it is certain that there is no question connected with the healthful exercise of the people that has been more neglected than that of public bathing.

There is no city in which a series of convenient open-air swimming-baths could be so economically made as in London. Abundance of wide-spreading park and garden ground belonging to the public is at hand in which capital sites occur. Our parks are not like those of Paris, outside the town, but for the most part quite surrounded by it, so that swimming-places in them would be most convenient for the inhabitants of the surrounding districts. Consider, for example, what a boon one or more small swimming-lakes in Regent's Park would prove to the districts around it. The land in the possession of the public, the excavation and proper shielding of such lake-baths by belts of varied plantation would be quite easy and inexpensive. Something like a model for an open-air swimming-bath already exists in Victoria Park. Such baths once formed, the expense of maintaining them would be little or no more than would be bestowed on the same piece of ground if kept as a park or garden. Shrouded by shrubbery, they could be used for fourteen hours of the summer day, while, if their disposition were entrusted to a good landscape-gardener, they and their surroundings could be made charming embellishments of our parks, now in many parts bare and unattractive. It is needless to point out how beneficial such a series of baths would prove to the population of London, by placing within reach of all the means of practising in the open air, and in the pleasantest manner, the doubly-useful exercise of swimming. By the Serpentine, the army of the great unwashed is so densely packed that none but those with the least-developed sensibilities could enter the water; indeed, it is not quite agreeable to go near the margin when the crowd is away, for the authorities make no sanitary provision whatever for the crowds, and the place is filthy to a degree not pleasant to see illustrated within a few hundred feet of the most fashionable lounge in Europe. A good suggestion has been made as to bathing-places in the centre of islands in such a piece of water as the Serpentine. More convenient would be little bays opening from the main sheet of water and surrounded by dense plantations.

It would be an excellent plan if roomy bathing-sheds were also erected near the water's edge, near those bathing-places, but slightly thrown back and concealed by vegetation. These might be well utilised in the winter as a working-place for the park-men or other labourers. In all places where a number of work-men are employed in winter, there is generally a difficulty in providing them with work unless there are large sheds to shelter them. They might also be advantageously used as winter store-houses for seats, boats, and the like. But their chief use would be in making it possible for people to bathe at all times. How many summer, spring, and autumn days are there on which bathing would be pleasant, but when showers of rain prevent it in the open air! Those sheds would afford a place where clothes could be kept dry, and then rain, light or heavy, would not make any difference—a swim being as enjoyable in the heaviest of rains as at any other time. Partial bathing, such as that practised in the Serpentine during the mornings and evenings, goes a very short way towards meeting the public wants. There-fore it is in the public interest to be desired that some of the means so liberally granted to the parks should be devoted to the formation of proper bathing-places, judiciously veiled with trees and open throughout the day.

Street Pavements.

The subject of street-pavements is one of such vital importance for health as well as convenience, that municipal authorities ought to be extremely careful in deciding questions as to the material to be adopted.

The number of streets recently laid down with wood-pavement in London, make it desirable to state, as an opinion carefully derived from observation, that wood is the very worst material for such.

The requirements of a city or town thoroughfare are, that the surface shall be (1) firm ; (2) noiseless, clean, and dry ; (3) smooth ; (4) permanent, yet easily removed ; (5) durable, producing a minimum amount of wear and tear ; (6) cheap ; and (7) non-combustible. In the very first of these requirements wood is found to fail, the vibration experienced in passing over a wood-pavement in a vehicle being to many persons more unpleasant than the rougher jarring of the stones.

Vegetable substances, containing within themselves elements of decay and putrefaction, should be rejected from sanitary considerations alone ; but in addition to this, their combustibility, softness of fibre, permeability, and cost are serious obstacles, and experiences on both continents, under varied conditions, have proved wood-pavements failures as to durability.

Wood-pavements have been laid down in New York for thirty years, and are now altogether condemned, the surveyors describing them as " worse than worthless." Thirty years ago it was laid down in Oxford Street, and was generally condemned by the shopkeepers as an offensive nuisance, and it was soon discarded. It is the dirtiest of all pavements, the most expensive, and the most unhealthy. The easy removal of mud, slush, and other accumulations from the surface of the asphalte, is not by any means so attainable on the wood-paving. Owing to the porous character of the material, a large proportion of the refuse soaks in, and in hot weather or during stress of traffic the smell and the offensive particles are given off to add to the impurities of the atmosphere. On the contrary, where the road and footways are properly asphalted, the whole may be so washed with a hose that not even a particle of dust shall be left on a summer's day.

As a matter of health and comfort, then, the wood-pavements are clearly inferior. But besides being by far the most offensive of all forms of street-paving, it is also the most troublesome to put down properly. It also requires more frequent renewals than any other form. Wood was laid in King William Street four years ago. It has since then been entirely relaid, and is moreover in constant repair, no part of it lasting three years at the outside, and some scarcely two years.

Although much improvement may have been introduced in the manner of laying it down, yet its inherent defects will always prevent its forming a perfect roadway. In a state of decay it is both offensive and unhealthy. It is also most costly to repair. The New York surveyor states that the yearly repair for stone in 1874 was £87 per mile, for wood £392 per mile. Are ratepayers prepared to pay a rate for paving four times in excess of that now paid, and that for a bad pavement ?

In times of slight frost the wood-paving is exceedingly dangerous, owing to the continual moisture of the surface of the wood which is quickly iced over, while in similar weather the smooth surface of the asphalte dries immediately and the frost takes no effect. The combustibility of the wood, heightened as it is by the pitch-dressing, is also a strong objection to it. It is frequently supposed that the buildings in Chicago and Boston burnt by the great fires of the past few years, were built of more combustible materials than ours, but to a very large extent this was not the case. They were often of stone, and as massive as any in London; fires of much less intensity would quickly extend to the road-ways, and add new horrors to such calamities.

For park, boulevard and suburban roads, macadam is em-ployed in Paris, frequently adding two side-ways of paving-stone for heavy traffic. These macadamized roads are well formed by the aid of heavy rollers, and are usually excellent. Asphalte has, in addition to macadam, long been used in Paris, and for two reasons: first, shortness in the supply of good paving-stone similar in quality to our York stone, the few quarries which yield it being also some distance from the capital; and secondly, the cheapness and abundance of the peculiar bituminous stone from which the asphalte-pavement is made. Asphalte has proved its superiority over all pavements yet known, especially for a wet climate. Nothing else is so clean, smooth, dry and agreeable in all weathers.

Bad attempts at laying asphalte produce such very disagreeable results that the very name has rendered it dreadful to some people; but in a sloppy climate the advantage of having in all weathers dry, smooth and permanent roads and footways, insteady of cloggy, saturated gravel, wood, or mud, is so great that some account of the best system of laying this material may be useful. Some years ago asphalte produced quite an industrial fever, and pavements were made in all directions in Paris and London, of any material at all resembling it. Gas tar, wood tar, pitch, and all sorts of abominations were ground up with stone, and laid down without proper preparation, the consequence being a large number of failures and (at least in this country) the tabooing of asphalte by many. But asphalte, properly so called, and properly laid down, is, notwithstanding, so far as our present knowledge goes, the very best material for a pavement in a crowded street.

Bituminous limestone occurs naturally in many parts of the world, notably at Val de Travers, in the Canton of Neufchâtel, Switzerland, and at Pyrimont, near Seyssel, a small town in the department of Ain, on the right bank of the Rhone. The asphalte-rock near Pyrimont consists of pure limestone impregnated with about ten per cent. of fossil or natural bitumen. It may be asked how it is that ordinary tar or pitch of good quality mixed with pounded limestone does not answer the purpose of this natural combination; but it is found by experiment that, although natural bitumen differs but slightly in chemical composition from pitch and tar, it is much more elastic and durable. If made with tar, the resulting asphalte is sticky and soft in hot weather; if with pitch, it is too brittle, and soon cracks and splits.

In the natural asphaltic rock the bitumen is so intimately combined with the calcareous matter, that it not only resists the action of the air and water for a considerable time, but even that of some of the strong mineral acids. The ancients were in the constant habit of using natural bitumen instead of mortar. The principal ingredients used in forming the mastic for the pavement is the dark brown bituminous limestone from Pyrimont, just described. The stone is first reduced to fine powder, and then mixed with a certain proportion of mineral bitumen, extracted previously from another portion of it.

When it is intended to be used for covering roofs, lining tanks, etc., no other addition is necessary; but if it is to be used for paving, a certain quantity of sea-grit is added. One specimen analysed by an English chemist yielded 29 of bitumen, 52 of limestone, and 19 of siliceous sand. The ingredients are exposed for some hours to a strong heat in large cauldrons, and kept constantly stirred by machinery. The mastic thus formed is made into blocks, measuring eighteen inches square by six inches deep, and weighing from 112lb. to 130lb. each. In this state they are sold ready for use and are remelted on the spot where the asphalte has to be applied; for which purpose small portable furnaces fitted with cauldrons are employed. A pound weight of mineral bitumen is first put into the cauldron, and when melted 56lb. of the mastic is added, the whole being repeatedly stirred. When fully mixed, another 56lb. of mastic is stirred in, and so on until the cauldron is full. When thoroughly melted—which may be known by the mastic dropping freely off the stirrer, and by jets of light smoke darting out of the mixture—it is conveyed quickly to the spot where it is to be used, in heated iron buckets or ladles. The cauldron ought to be as close to the work as possible, and in covering brick arches it should be hoisted to the top of the building. It must be clearly understood that the only kind of bitumen to be used is that impregnating the limestone itself.

In forming foot or carriage ways it is most important to secure a good foundation by removing or ramming the soft earth, and laying a course of concrete, care being taken to allow the whole to dry before putting down the asphalte. If this precaution is not attended to, the heat will convert the moisture in the concrete into steam, and fill the asphalte full of airholes and bubbles. The thickness of the layer of asphalte may be regulated by slips of wood arranged across the pavement at a distance of 30 inches from each other—a width quite sufficient for one man to work at a time. If two men are employed, double the width may be taken, as it is always better to have as few joints as possible. The work is levelled with a long curved wooden spatula, assisted by a long straight ruler, which stretches across the layer of asphalte, over which it is moved backwards and forwards, the wooden gauges supporting its ends. If the surface is intended to be smooth, a mixture of equal parts of silver-sand and slate-dust or plaster of Paris is sifted over it before it has quite set, and rubbed down with a flat tool of wood. If it is required to be rough, sharp grit is to be beaten in with a heavy wooden block. One portion of the pavement being complete, it is best to proceed to lay the next but one, leaving the intermediate space to be filled up afterwards, when the first layer is firm and cold, so as to insure a good joint.

The thickness of asphalte for footways varies from half an inch to an inch and a quarter, the former being sufficient for common floors and courtyards, the latter for carriage-pavements. A thickness of from half an inch to five-eighths is sufficient for roofs and the coverings of arches, and for lining tanks and ponds, and about half an inch for the ground line of brickwork to prevent the damp from rising. An asphalted surface admits of easy repair. By placing hot mastic on the places requiring it, the faulty part may be cut away and the edges cut square, when the hot material will be found to adhere to them if they are perfectly free from damp or moisture.

The great secret, then, in obtaining a perfect layer of asphalte paving, dry, hard, elastic, warm, and durable, is first to employ only the natural material, such as that from Pyrimont-Seyssel; and secondly, to provide a firm, dry substratum of concrete for it to rest upon.   For pavements, terraces, etc., nothing can be better. It is always warm and elastic to the tread; there are no joints to encourage the accumulation of filth or the growth of weeds; and in case of rain it dries in a few minutes.   As laid down by the Seyssel Asphalte Company, its durability is immense.   The whole of the quadrangle in Trafalgar Square has been laid with asphalte since 1863, and yet there is no sign of wear upon it, in spite of the traffic.

After rain, asphalte (more especially if there is any mud about) becomes disagreeably slippery both for horses and foot-passengers.   Therefore it is necessary to keep it thoroughly clean. For laying between the courses of brickwork to prevent the damp from rising, it is unequalled, a layer, even only one quarter of an inch thick, keeping all damp down most effectually.   It is especially fitted for this purpose in the case of boat-houses built by the sides of rivers or lakes.   For ornamental ponds and banks it is also excellent, but it should be roughened for, say, a foot in depth, so as to hold sufficient soil or mud to grow water-plants and weeds, and so entirely conceal its existence.

. During the last few years the preparation of the asphalte in Paris has been much improved.   Some years ago, when a pavement was to be made with bitumen, a great nuisance was experienced by the public during the operation.   The mastic was liquefied on the spot, and produced a nasty smell and smoke, disagreeable and injurious; but now some of these inconveniences have been done away with by a new system, and asphalte is laid down in the most expeditious manner.   It is prepared first in out-of-the-way places devoted to the purpose, and the material, ready for use and liquefied, may be transported from these places to any parts of the town without the least inconvenience in a semi-cylindrical boiler, closed by iron doors, and moved about on iron wheels as freely as a common cart.   Under the boiler is a fireplace, and the blaze, after having heated the two sides of the boiler, passes out by a chimney placed at the back of the machine. Means to keep the mastic in motion, and prevent its burning by adhering to the sides of the boiler, are secured by a simple mechanism easily worked by the hand. These carriage boilers, full of liquid asphalte, are driven from place to place with the greatest facility. The boiler is emptied by the means of a pipe fixed to its bottom, and the mastic is collected in a pail, and spread on the surface to the thickness of three-quarters of an inch.

If the surface is not perfectly dry, the drying must be accelerated with hot ashes, which are to be taken away afterwards, or with a little spreading of quicklime in powder. These operations are indispensable, as if the mastic were laid on before the surface is dry, the heat of it would dispel in steam the water underneath, and that steam would produce blisters in the asphalte which would crack under the pressure of the feet, and endanger the success of the operation. The workmen place on the platform two iron bars of the same thickness as the asphalte is to be, at equal distance from each other; it is then laid down in a very warm state, and thick enough to require some slight exertion of the operator to make it level. This done, a small quantity of fine gravel must be spread over the asphalte while hot, and slightly beaten down to penetrate into it. This gives a greater hardness and solidity to the footway, and insures its lasting for a very long time.

The roads before spoken of are made of the powdered and not liquid asphalte. The surface of the roadway must be beaten down very hard, and covered with a thickness of about three inches of concrete, well beaten down and dry. If the dryness is very necessary in the making of a pavement, this condition is of a greater importance for the road, as, if the powder were spread on a wet surface, the steam caused by the heat would produce a great number of little fissures, the elasticity would be destroyed, and the road would be useless after a few months' use. The concrete well dried, the powder (hot) must be spread about three inches thick; and then well levelled and beaten. The sides must be done first, and pressed down with a rectangular iron pestle eight or nine inches in length and two or two and a half inches in width. When the sides are done, the middle is proceeded with

L 2

The pestles used in pressing it are of cast-iron, circular, and about eight inches in diameter. The pestles of either form are heated and used quite hot, so as to compress the asphalte into a hard smooth mass.

When the crust of asphalte is brought to the thickness required, and is sufficiently smoothed and beaten hard, a little quantity of very fine powder is spread with a sieve to fill all the unevenness, and the whole is again smoothed with a flat piece of hot iron. The compression is completed by the employment of two cast-iron rollers, one of 4000lb. weight and the other of 3000lb. Sometimes three of these rollers are employed, the intermediate one being about 1500lb. or 1600lb. in weight. This rolling is not always necessary, in many cases the beating down with pestles being sufficient. The roads thus made, completely noiseless and lasting a long time, have been adopted with the greatest success by the city of Paris, and are supplanting the paving-stones, macadamized and other pavements in many narrow streets.

"The city swims in verdure, beautiful
As Venice on the waters, the sea-swan.
What bosky gardens dropped in close-walled courts
Like plums in ladies' laps, who start and laugh!
What miles of streets that run on after trees!"

AURORA LEIGH.

CHAPTER X.

TREES FOR CITIES.

IT is a popular but erroneous notion that trees will not thrive in London. People often see in France streets bordered with rows of handsome young trees, and they naturally compare these verdant avenues with our own streets, where trees are rarely planted, and come to the conclusion that there is "something in the air" which prevents trees thriving in London. The following letter to the 'Pall Mall Gazette' is an example of the ideas often held on the subject. "When people propose to decorate London, the first consideration should be what will suit the climate. It cannot be too often repeated that our city atmosphere is fatally inimical to delicacy of architecture, and quite equally so to delicacy of vegetation. Our skies will rain soot continually, and moisture therewithal to make the soot adhere; the soot will insinuate itself amidst fairy tracery of stone, and clog the pores of beautiful trees and shrubs; and it is an utter waste of art and money to disregard these inevitable conditions of the question. It is very childish to tickle our fancy by providing for a momentary admiration of things which a short time will make hideous, and then, when the inevitable has taken place, contenting ourselves with a shrug of the shoulders and 'what a pity!' Few young trees will really flourish in the climate of our modern London; the case was perhaps different some years ago. But from any general planting of trees in London, especially in leading thoroughfares, I cannot expect agreeable results—MISODENDROS."

These opinions are as erroneous as they are emphatic; the splendid Planes in Berkeley Square, and other places in London, should rid us of the erroneous notion that trees cannot be grown well in London.   It is the custom in Paris and other Continental cities to plant trees with care, to provide them with good soil, to spend a great deal of money in attending to them and watering them, and yet neither in all Paris, nor in any Continental city, can such noble examples as these be found.   But some may say, An open square at the West-end of town may do that which the smoky, densely-packed city will not.   If these persons, who are evidently not yet acquainted with Stationers' Hall Court, will inquire for that narrow enclosure the next time they are passing near St. Paul's, they will find in it a great Plane-tree looking as happy as if it were in its native forest.   Much, however, depends upon the kind of tree selected for the purpose; for even our landscape-gardeners make mistakes, by persisting in planting evergreens, which as a class are totally unfit for town-cultivation.   Even when moderately healthy, these trees are generally so coated with smut that they entirely lack that refreshing verdure which is so characteristic of evergreens grown in fresh and pure air.

Will nobody deliver us from the perils of smoke?   Every year our cities grow vaster, and the great pall of "blacks" is ever widening!   To hope to arouse public attention to the magnitude of the evil, by pointing to the thousands of plants that are always perishing from it, would be vain considering that its pernicious effects on our own lives do not seem to be taken the least notice of.   London and all our large cities are always under its ban; but its most detestable aspects are most apparent on those still, frosty, autumnal and winter days, which in the country are so clear and sunny.   On these, there being no breeze to brush away the outpourings of the innumerable chimneys, the whole settles down in the streets, leaving the sun powerless to shoot a ray through its density.   Not the least curious thing about this great but avoidable plague, is that both foreigners and natives often put it down to the climate.   M. Taine speaks of the woefully-depressing influences of the climate of London.   Doubtless there are many better; but certainly the climate of London is quite as agreeable as that of Paris or

Northern France. The clouds of smoke make the difference. In consequence of being contented to live in a sea of refuse of our fires, we possess the privilege of having our fairest still, winter days turned into foulest nights, in which one is stifled with vapours that would add a new terror to the lower regions. If anybody doubts the true cause of the horrible " climate " of our large cities, let him walk forth at three or four o'clock in the morning into the heart of one of them, in November and December, when the fogs are at their worst. If he has any memories of the fog of the previous evening, he may be surprised to see the street quite free of fog, the buildings not only visible, but perfectly clear in outline; and the air pure! Let him sally forth again at from half-past seven to half-past eight, and he will find a change; the street is filling with a bluish foulness, the buildings losing shape. An hour later, and the smoke, which we fancy would vanish, after passing up the chimney, has fallen down into the street, dimming the sight, and stinging us as we breathe it. It is not the climate that we should blame, but our own complacent stupidity in resting content under an evil which, as half the population of these islands is now gathered in cities, has a hurtful effect on the national health.

It is a difficult problem to solve, but surely there are no pains or expense to which we could be put in the defeat of this smoke-monster, for which we should not be abundantly repaid by its destruction. Lengthened days, or at least some of heaven's light in those we have, and undefiled air, are surely blessings to secure which we might well submit to some inconvenience. If questions were brought forward in the degree of their importance, the smoke-plague of our cities would be one of the first before Parliament.

Notwithstanding this foul state of the atmosphere, the slaughter of the evergreens, through being planted in it, goes on without ceasing. What a pity it is we do not contrive some less-expensive and more-attractive way of destroying the thousands of evergreens planted about London every year, than that of planting them and allowing them to blacken and perish before our eyes from the effects of our smoke-laden air! There perish annually as many beautiful young evergreen shrubs and trees in and near London from smoke, as would suffice to plant a whole county. There are surely few greater evidences of obtusity of mind than is shown by this persistent wasting of precious time and precious energy, and thoughtless destruction of trees and shrubs, which so soon perish in the smoke of London.

It is not so with the deciduous tree or shrub; nor with those beautiful rosaceous bushes and trees which are the glory of the grove in all temperate climes. After their summer-life they enjoy a long winter-rest leafless, and when spring returns and the flues cease vomiting " blacks " they again put forth their leaves in the purer air. The consequence is, they grow nearly as well in London as in the country. No charm of tropical or other climes surpasses the freshness of an English spring, during the period of the leafing and blossoming of these winter-sleeping northern trees. Why, then, should we not take advantage of the fact, by developing chiefly those plants which flourish as well in towns as out of them? It may be noticed that Peaches, Almonds, the double Cherries, and the numerous flowering trees and shrubs allied to them, flourish as well in cities as they do in the country, while beside them valuable evergreens are but the ghosts of what evergreens should be. Supposing for a moment that evergreen trees and shrubs throve as well within city influences as deciduous ones do, it would even then be a questionable practice to use them extensively, because they do not gladden us with that floral and changing beauty which deciduous trees are wont to put on. They do not keep time with our suns and seasons; and they are not so beautiful, because not so changeful, as the deciduous kinds.

Notwithstanding the obvious advantages offered by the many deciduous trees, planting in most of our parks is much neglected —at least, in all its nobler aspects, while great expense and skill are lavished on myriads of plants that live for the summer only. The remedy wanted is the annual planting of a certain portion of ground in each great park. That portion should be thoroughly cleared, prepared, and planted. We should thus secure perpetual growth and vigour, as well as stately beauty in our park-trees. Stealing out a dying tree here and there, and stealing in a young one—often done in Paris and London—is a mistake. Frequently there are open bare spaces left unplanted for years, as, for example, Primrose Hill, which is as bare as a great inverted basin.

The evils that affect the trees in Kensington Gardens—old age, injury from overcrowding or from exhaustion of the ground, or from the trees being in unsuitable positions—are such as would work like results everywhere else. Old trees die at last, and if we fail to raise an annual crop, decay soon begins to be disagreeably conspicuous. The difficulties of planting even in the very heart of London are exaggerated. In Printing-house Square, under the very windows of the 'Times' office, are trees of the American shrubby Trefoil (Ptelea trifoliata) as healthy and as large as we have ever seen them in any collection in this country. Look at the beautiful weeping Ash trees in Brunswick Square and else-where in west-central London, and the excellent Catalpas seen here and there (in the Marylebone Road, for instance), that are covered with handsome blossoms and large shade-giving leaves. Look, also, at the Hawthorns and other trees of the Rosaceous order in the Botanic Gardens, Regent's Park, where the soil is very cold, at the Sumach, Pyruses, Medlars, snowy Mespilus, Bird Cherry, Tulip-tree, Sir Charles Wager's Maple, flowering Ash, and many other trees, which anyone who cares about trees may see thriving in London. Let one-fifth of the means and skill now devoted to the building of glass-houses and the culture of tender plants in London parks be diverted to the systematic and judicious planting of hardy trees; and, in due time, the parks of London will become the finest Arboretum of deciduous trees in the world, for there is no city where they thrive better, no city with anything like the same grand opportunities for planting.

It is a curious fact that there are no big trees in the streets or avenues of Paris! And not only no big trees, but scarcely a medium-sized one! It is not the fault of the poor trees, or the soil, or the air. It is caused by a system of management apparently based on the notion that trees, like soldiers, are best arranged in close order, or like the poor fellows who find a last rest in the Fosse Commune without any earth between the boxes. There is no evidence whatever that any one responsible for the street-trees of Paris has the least idea of the beauty of hardy trees when well developed. At best they are only seen a little better grown than in the nursery-garden. They are everywhere with heads crowded together—starving for want of space above and below. Two or three Planes usually stand where one fairly-developed tree would be sufficient. Often the Planes may be seen running up before the tall houses in the finer streets with a stem before every window. The Plane-trees in our squares are far finer than any in Paris, owing to the fact that they had room to grow and were let alone. Pruning, to throw the strength of a tree or shrub into fruit or flower, or into some shape desired by the cultivator, is a rational process, but nothing of the kind can be said of the pruning of any grown forest or ornamental tree, to prune which is in fact to destroy its beauty, individuality, and dignity. In Paris, pruning into a miserable uniformity is carried out to a deplorable extent. These remarks apply to trees in open spaces as well as in the street, which are, however, often wide enough to admit of fair development. If this system is to go on, it will be wise of the educational powers now doing so much for young France to plant a few acres with native and hardy trees to be allowed to assume their full size and natural development. One does now and then see in the etchings in the shop-windows a portrait of a fine tree, but it is desirable to have living examples. It has been said to the writer that fine trees cannot be grown in Paris; but that this is not the case is proved by the existence of occasional good specimens in courts and small gardens, which the municipal pruners did not visit. Here and there, when "demolitions" are in active progress, a fine old tree may sometimes be seen as the houses are taken down around it. In such positions the conditions are by no means so favourable to tree-growth as in the many open streets and wide avenues. Along the quays, too, where the trees might throw their arms over the water on one side, and over a wide road on the other, they are just as prim and as unlike fine trees as they are anywhere else; no doubt, in some narrow streets very wide-spreading trees are not desirable, but in such cases the right way is to select species and varieties which will suit the position without needless mutilation.

Some Trees for Cities.

The best of all trees for European cities is the Western Plane (Platanus occidentalis). It may be seen in many places in towns, from the heart of the city of London to the shores of the lakes of

Northern Italy; in the towns of cold Central France, in the fine old cities in La Belle Touraine, and in Anjou, where the Camellia and Azalea grow luxuriantly in the open air; in the numerous new boulevards of Paris; under a scorching sun in Naples; and in many other places, thousands of miles from its native home in North America; and everywhere it is by far the noblest city-tree. In no place are there finer individual specimens of it than in London, although receiving no such attention as they do elsewhere.

Planes on Paris Quays.

Fairly and roundly developed specimens of the Plane have in summer almost the grace of a weeping-tree. In winter the branches retain this character, but also present a rugged Gothic picturesqueness, while the pendulous seed-vessels and striking column-like bole add to their beauty in the winter season, when the trees are at rest and safe from smoke.

It is only a few years since the possibility of growing Planes on the Thames Embankment was doubted by many; now we have them not only growing, but thriving as well as anywhere. There is, indeed, good reason to think that they will soon overtake their older Paris relations, and as we (unlike our neighbours) are fortunately not often obliged to boil the soldier's pot or warm the famished citizen with our trees, we may expect them to live long; how long they may live we cannot say, but there is some proof that the Plane is a very long-lived tree even with us. Other trees we have in all stages of decay, but where are the crippled Planes? The oldest and biggest trees in London seem infants as regards freedom from decay. There being such good promise of fine trees, more than ordinary care should be taken to guard against impeding their growth from over-planting or want of timely thinning. The Planes on the Paris quays are not unfrequently too close together; such, we hope, will not be the case here. When timely thinning is not carried out, it is not only that the trees are not allowed to assume their full beauty overhead, but the exhaustion of the soil by the trees to be eventually cut away is an important consideration; therefore we should never wait till the trees crowd each other, but remove them as soon as they come in contact.

Next to the Plane, the Horse-chestnut seems to offer the greatest advantages. It has not indeed the stature and beauty of the Plane, nor does it attain as large a size and as perfect health in cities, but it possesses great claims from its fine foliage, large sweet silvery spikes of bloom, and proved capacity of growing well as a town-tree. While selecting trees for towns that are not liable to suffer from disease or insect-pests, we should encourage variety as much as possible. The Horse-chestnut would be worth growing for the sake of its foliage alone, but when the additional charm of its blossoms is taken into account, there can be no hesitation in placing it among the town-trees.

The common Robinia or Locust-tree has been so long and extensively tried that we need have no more doubt about it. It will never justify the reputation that Cobbett gave it, but no tree maintains such a depth of sweet verdure even in the dustiest roads. No drought seems to affect it; no heat renders it rusty-looking or fatigued. It is worthy of being much more extensively used as a park and square tree; it is also good for street-use, not growing too large, and is the best of all trees for planting in the front of a suburban house or villa, or in any position where a pleasant object is required to refresh the eye at all times.

At first sight there seems little reason why the somewhat despised and roughly-treated Acacia, should come in after such stately and noble trees as the Plane and the Chestnut; but, taking the varieties as well as the original tree into consideration, it is worthy of this rank, being equally well adapted for the smallest town-garden as for the largest public park.

To many rows of suburban houses a thin line of trees is an improvement, and forms the only species of garden-embellishment of which they are capable. The qualities necessary in such trees are hardiness, healthy constitution, and size and habits suited to the positions for which they are destined. No tree combines these better than the spineless round-headed variety of the Robinia (R. inermis).

Perhaps the most beautiful and appropriate city-trees in Europe are those formed by the round-headed Robinias in some of the cities of Northern Italy; their grace, dense and grateful shade, and deep verdure being perfect. I measured several nearly thirty feet in diameter of head, and with a bole a foot or more through, the heads being picturesque and somewhat irregular from age, while preserving their compactness and valuable shading-properties. It would be impossible to find a greater improvement upon the hideous lines of clipped Limes so common in France than is presented by these trees at Novara. But as we have no proof that as good a result could be obtained in our English streets, we must turn to those trees that we have already tested thoroughly.

The bad and not the good qualities of the Lime place it so high in the list; for, while planted more abundantly than any other city-tree, it is by far the worst, and the extensive use of it in our streets is a great mistake. The tall lines of Lime-trees in the Garden of Plants at Paris fall into the sere and yellow leaf before one has time to admire their soft green. In London, at the end of July, the Limes are often the most miserable-looking trees anywhere to be seen. And all this in the midst of the summer. The withered, burnt, insect-covered leaves rustle lifeless upon the trees, hoarsely whispering the coming death of the year in our ears before we have half enjoyed the summer.

It is very unwise to persist in planting such a tree so largely as we do when there are various deciduous trees that will do all that a Lime does at the best of times, and that have none of its drawbacks. Our winter, the period when our deciduous trees must be devoid of leaves, is long enough without making it needlessly so by lining every street with the Lime. In the parks this tree may sometimes be planted, but never in streets, quays, or boulevards. Apart from its presenting a diseased appearance for more than half the time that it ought to be full of green life, the Lime grows much too large for the little front gardens where it is so abundantly employed, and will soon deprive of a large share of light and sun the house it is planted to adorn.

The Elm is a tree much used in the London parks, and sometimes seen of fine dimensions, but occasionally it is much diseased when used as an avenue-tree—for example, in the Mall, in St. James's Park, where the effect of the avenue-planting is as bad as it can be. A few Plane-trees near the Buckingham Palace end of the Mall almost save it from looking absolutely hideous from that point of view. The effect of the Elms in Rotten Row, though much better, is not nearly so good as may be produced in like positions by using other trees. The variety chosen has a good deal to do with it—the long Boulevard St. Michel, in Paris, planted with the large-leaved Elm, is a success.

Paulownia imperialis is a very noble subject for town-gardens, especially so for those on a dry soil like Paris, and where a good shading-medium is wanted. It might well replace some of the miles of poor clipped Elms and Limes about Paris and around numbers of French country-houses. The stems of the trees are straight, and just about the right elevation for a shade-giving tree, and the heads spread out flat, so as to give complete shade without betraying an awkward tendency to rise too high and require clipping to prevent them from keeping the light from the windows. The large leaves are quite fresh in autumn. The Paulownia, the Ailantus, and the Plane seem to preserve freshness and vigour no matter how great the heat or abundant the dust. The forest-trees of our own latitudes do not do this, but become withered while their companions from Japan and America are in the greenest health. It is not easy to imagine a greater improvement than that which would be effected by planting this tree where a low and yet good shade is required. It is also worthy of attention as a town-garden tree, and for similar reasons.

The Ailantus glandulosa is a town-tree of great excellence. When young it is graceful from its long pinnate leaves—when old and well grown it becomes a noble forest-tree. But the qualities that will above all others recommend it to the town-planter are its health and freshness, under all circumstances, in towns. Dust, foul air, or drought seem to have no effect upon it. For parks and avenues it is valuable, as it perfectly retains its foliage long after our own deciduous trees have been scorched by drought and dust. It seems to do equally well on all soils, having a constitution which seems perfectly indifferent to any vicissitude of climate of these latitudes.

Everywhere in cities the Lombardy Poplar retains its health, proving its claims to be far more abundantly used than it is at present. Avenues of this tree would tell as well in some positions in cities as single specimens and groups of it do in the landscape. The drip of trees is sometimes objected to : this erect and close-growing kind would seem to offer itself for rather narrow streets and positions, where a spreading habit or a drip might be an inconvenience at any time. Of other tapering, columnar, or fastigiate trees, the pyramidal variety of the Oak and the tapering variety of the Robinia do particularly well in the parks; and the last is deserving of recommendation for the town-garden.

Of weeping-trees, in addition to the long-proved and indispensable Weeping Willow, we have the Weeping Birch, Ash, Beech, and Elm, in all cases in perfect health in the parks. There is one tree of those above-mentioned which ought to be much more grown—the weeping variety of the large-leaved Elm (Ulmus montana pendula). This is a tree of much beauty and character, and it does not seem in the least to suffer from the atmosphere of London. It is a weeping-tree of the first order : its foliage is massive, shade dense, and outline most picturesque when thickly clothed in summer—the backbone, so to speak, of each wide-spreading branch being seen just glistening above the dense mass of leaves. It is a hardier tree than the weeping Willow, and never grows too high for a London or any other town-garden ; in all courtyards or open gravelled spaces, in little squares wherever a shady tree is desired, it is invaluable.

The numerous free-growing trees of the Rose order, from the Chinese Pear and the Almonds that illuminate our groves with masses of light rosy flowers in earliest spring, to the dwarf double Prunus, all grow healthfully in our parks; and though unfit for street-planting as streets are at present, are worthy of the highest attention both for small gardens in towns, and for squares, public gardens, and parks.

The group near the museum in the Botanic Gardens in the Regent's Park proves that the Hawthorn family will succeed perfectly on the worst kind of soil—the deep bed of clay on the north side of the city. The Hawthorn family furnish a greater number of hardy ornamental dwarf trees than any other known to us. They are not only pretty and fragrant in flower, but the aspect of the fruit in autumn—borne in showers of bright red, yellow, black, and scarlet—is of itself a recommendation which should entitle them to general cultivation, even if the bloom and fragrance were of that obscure type which never attracts the attention of any one but a botanist.

Of tribes that may be associated with the Hawthorns there are the Cotoneasters—the freely flowering and fruiting deciduous species; the Almonds and Peaches, double and single; the various double Cherries and Plums; Amelanchiers (Snowy Mespilus); the Bird Cherry and the Weeping Cherry; the Judas-tree; the Quinces and Medlars (particularly Mespilus Smithii); the varieties of the Scotch and common Laburnums; the Daphnes, the Deutzias, the various kinds of Lilac, and numerous other rather dwarf shrubs for the embellishment of the margins of groups, etc.; the various kinds of Pyrus from the great P. vestita to the handsome Chinese Pear and Japan Quince.

The common Stag's-horn Sumach succeeds so well in the small town-garden that it deserves a word of praise. It does not grow so gross as to require clipping, and retains its verdure without taint long after the Lime; but it is apt to produce suckers too abundantly. Amongst deciduous flowering shrubs, the Althea would seem to be the best. With attention it should form a telling object in all parts where the bottom is dry. By "attention," is meant planting it so as to develop it into a specimen, and not thrusting it promiscuously amongst rough and mixed shrubs, which may obscure it from the sun or tend to rob it of nutriment at the root.

Liriodendron tulipifera, the Tulip-tree, seems perfectly at home in city parks or gardens, and, being a handsome and distinct tree, in every way deserves to be planted largely in such places. Sophora japonica forms on dry soils a grand tree in the neighbourhood of London, and has the valuable property of never seeming to suffer from drought, no matter how dry the soil, retaining its verdure to the end of the season. It therefore merits an important place in all our parks and squares, especially those with a light soil.

The various species of Ash offer many valuable trees for the town planter, of which good evidence may be seen in Kensington Gardens. To enumerate fully all the other deciduous trees that would thrive in cities, would simply mean a catalogue of all the more vigorous species that flourish in the northern world.

Transplanting Large Trees. — Not the least remarkable feature of the public gardening of Paris is the excellent system of transplanting trees there practised. For the following article on this subject I am indebted to my friend M. Edouard André, of Paris :—

" The city of Paris, prior to having formed the large parks and public gardens which she now possesses, had no regular system of transplanting large trees, with the exception of the old-fashioned carts which had been used at Versailles and the other royal parks, and at M. de Rothschild's châteaux at Boulogne and Ferrières, principally for the purpose of removing large Orange-trees in tubs, and occasionally for transplanting old and valuable trees. These carts were designed and constructed in the time of Louis XIV., and it may well be imagined that they were extremely cumbersome and inconvenient. In recent days, however, when the chief gardeners and the city architects were often called upon to extemporize shady avenues in a few days, it became absolutely necessary for them to put their heads together to invent some new machine which would work more easily and with less damage to the lives of the trees. The first apparatus built consisted of a frame bearing two movable wooden rollers, one on the fore-carriage and the other at the back, each provided with holes in which to place the ends of the levers when hoisting up the tree. A round case made of sheet-iron was hung in the centre suspended from the rollers by chains, which, when the tree was raised up by the levers, held the earth-ball and roots.

" We do not intend reviewing all the improved means successively employed before the models now in use were adopted ; we have only to state the way in which the removal of large trees is now managed in Paris.

" We take, for example, a specimen tree, thirty years old, thirty feet in height, the trunk of which has a circumference of three feet at a height of three feet from the ground, its total weight with the earth-ball being nearly two tons. The

M

operation is commenced by staking out, round the stem, the circumference of the
earth-ball, which will be on an average about four feet in diameter for most
species, and larger according to the size of the trees to be removed. A second
concentric circle is then made about two feet outside the first, the space between
which will be the place for the trench to be dug for preparing the tree. The soil
is then removed from this trench to the depth of three feet, and the small and
delicate roots are drawn out of the earth, left hanging, and carefully preserved.
The earth-ball is then undermined to prevent the roots from adhering to the
subsoil ; two thick planks, a foot wide, and a little longer than the ball, are
placed underneath parallel with the width of the cart, so that they sustain the
weight of the earth when the tree is lifted. Privet-branches are now placed
upright, close together, all round the earth-ball, tied round securely with ropes,
so as to prevent the earth from crumbling away, and also to protect the small
roots from the influences of the weather.

"The removal of the tree is then commenced in the following manner :—
Two stout thick planks, strong enough to support the cart with the tree slung in
it, and a little longer than the entire excavation, and having iron guard-plates
about two inches higher than the surface bolted on each side so as to prevent the
wheels from slipping off, are placed parallel to each other across the excavation
of the exact width existing between the wheels. The movable bars at the back
of the cart are then removed, and the cart is backed into the ways until the trunk
of the tree is exactly in the centre of the frame. The movable bars are then put
in their place again so as to strengthen the back of the wheels, which do not run
on an axletree, but are fitted in wrought-iron frames hanging from the upper part
of the cart. The chains attached to the rollers on each side of the cart are now
lowered and passed under the planks before described, which are placed under
the earth-ball. When all is fast, four workmen begin simultaneously to turn the
handles attached to the cast-iron cog-wheels, by which great power is obtained on
the rollers. The tree is raised slowly and steadily until it just swings clear of the
ground, and then nothing is left to be done but to steady the tree before it is
hoisted up to its proper height. For this purpose there is at each corner of the
cart a strong wrought-iron hook, to which is attached a block, through which runs
a strong rope fixed at the other end to a leather collar. These four ropes are
then raised up together and the collar firmly fastened on the stem of the tree
about seven or eight feet from the top of the earth-ball. The tree can now be
easily removed without fear of its falling over.

"The horses are then attached to the cart, which is drawn slowly off the ways,
and the tree can be removed with safety to its future resting-place. If the tree
be vigorous and healthy, a hole a little wider than the one from which it has been
removed should be dug beforehand, the earth being placed carefully on one side
if it should be of a kind to suit the tree about to be planted, and if not, it should
be replaced by suitable soil. The average dimensions for the hole, for an earth-
ball of four feet in diameter, should be about seven feet, so that eighteen inches
are preserved all round the tree to be filled up with good vegetable soil. The
depth should be equal to the height of the earth-ball, or a little more, if the tree
be of a species with tap-roots. The bottom of the excavation should be filled in

with a little good soil, which will allow the top of the earth-ball to be a little higher than the surrounding ground, in accordance with an instinctive notion, which almost invariably induces us to place trees used as isolated specimens in lawns on small hillocks.

" When this is done the planks or ways are placed in position as before described, and the cart is very carefully drawn on them until the earth-ball is exactly in the centre of the hole. The tree is then slowly lowered, and when it touches the ground the guy-ropes from the corners of the cart are pulled tight, so as to have the tree perfectly upright and steady; the chains are unfastened and hoisted up round rollers; the two planks beneath the earth-ball are undermined and removed, and the privet-shoots taken off. They then proceed to fill up the hole, particular attention being paid to the small roots, which are each separately covered in. When this is finished and the tree is considered sufficiently steady, the ropes are removed; the bars are taken out of the back of the cart, which is drawn away, and the bars having been refixed all is ready for another removal.

" An abundant watering, if the removal has been made in the growing-season, will be the end of the operation. The tree must now be protected against the wind, being as yet merely dependent upon its own gravity, as the roots take time to get hold of the ground. This result is obtained by placing at about half-way up the stem of the tree a padding of straw, round which three or four long pieces of wire-rope are attached; these are carried out on all sides of the tree and firmly fastened to strong stakes driven in the ground. We may then bid defiance to the strongest winds that blow.

" If drought is to be feared, the stem and main branches of the tree can be surrounded with plaited straw watered from time to time, or by a coating of clay mixed with cow-dung and covered with rough canvas, which is much about the same colour as the bark. Sometimes in the boulevards of Paris they water trees surrounded in this manner by pouring water through a funnel from the top, between the clay and the trunk of the tree. These auxiliary means for keeping the tree alive may be supplemented by many others, such as covering it entirely on the south side with canvas, to preserve it from the sun and drought if it is of a rare kind; by watering the ground well if it is dry, or by draining the hole with rubbish or drain-pipes if the soil be too damp, etc.

" The ordinary season for transplanting large deciduous trees is from October to April, and from March or April to August for evergreens. But with sufficient care it is quite possible to transplant trees all the year round, provided the weather be suitable, the roots uninjured, the soil good, and that they be kept well sheltered and watered.

" In choosing the tree to be transplanted, its age and species must be duly considered. For instance, it is useless to remove a tree that is sixty or eighty years of age, as it will never produce as fine foliage as it did before its removal, nor will it make any remarkable progress in size. It is better only to remove those not more than fifteen years old and under without any earth-ball at all, taking especial care to preserve all the roots intact. The best age for transplanting larger trees is from twenty to thirty years. The number of species ordinarily removed is limited, as only the more common kinds of trees are subjected to the process, no one caring to run the risk of losing a rare and valuable tree. In Paris, experiments made on various species have given the following results :—

"*Success nearly always certain* : Elms, Planes, white and red Horse-chestnuts, Limes, Ailantus, Catalpa, Paulownia, Celtis, Planera, Sophora, and Willows.

"*Success uncertain, but sometimes satisfactory* : Poplars, Sycamores, Maples, Alders, Mulberries, Beech, Ash, Magnolias, American Walnuts, Cercis, Diospyros.

"*Success very rare* : Robinias, Cratægus, Hawthorns, and nearly all the Rosaceæ, Birch, Laburnum, and many Leguminosæ, Oaks (European and American), Pavias, Elms, and Gleditschias."

With respect to the value of this machine as compared with any in use in England, there can be no doubt that the Paris machine is the best. Trees are there removed daily without the least difficulty or fuss, that, if removed in this country, would probably be honoured with a notice in the local papers. The best of our English machines must be taken to pieces for the removal of every tree: the beams have to be taken off in order to bring the wheels in position, then they have to be replaced in position, as well as the lifting apparatus. Besides, the machines are unwieldy and awkward. The advantage of the French machine is, that by removing the iron rod which connects the hind wheels and the hind cross-beam, the machine is put to the tree without trouble or awkwardness. The lifting power is by means of racks, pinions, and levers. Lately whole boulevards of trees have been moved when half-grown by the aid of these machines. A few years ago only comparatively young trees were tried as a rule. The new Boulevard Henri IV. was planted recently with Planes almost as large as any long-established trees in Paris.

CHAPTER XI.

THE JARDIN FLEURISTE AND OTHER PUBLIC NURSERIES OF THE CITY OF PARIS.

In its public nurseries Paris possesses a very useful aid which we have not in England. With us each park or garden produces or purchases its own supplies; in Paris all the public gardens of the city are furnished from the city-nurseries. There are two sets of public gardens—those of the city comprising the boulevards, squares, parks, and church-gardens, and those of the State, the gardens of the Luxembourg, Tuileries, Louvre, and others. All are equally open to the public—all arranged with a view to its pleasure and convenience; but in the case of the State-gardens each supplies its own stock. What we have to deal with now is the manufactory, so to speak, for the great number of gardens and open spaces made during recent years. At one time the old State-gardens were by far the most important in Paris; now they are surpassed by those created specially for the city and its people. In commencing to improve the public gardens of the city, it was a wise step to begin with central nurseries, from whence all those gardens could be supplied.

The advantage of having public nurseries of this kind to supply the parks, gardens, and squares of a great city is so great, that it is surprising they have not been already adopted by us. Not only could the necessary trees, shrubs, and flowers be procured much more cheaply, but a greater selection of choice subjects would be at the disposal of the planters. By selecting ground favourable to each class of plants, shrubs, or trees, each could· be grown to perfection, and at a cheaper rate than they could be bought; and the necessity of inquiry, selecting and bargaining, would be done away with, the planter having merely to indicate the subjects required. They could be quickly despatched to any given point in vans constructed for the purpose. In addition to these advantages, a small portion of each nursery might be set apart as an experimental ground to test newly-introduced or imperfectly-known plants; and in this respect each would be of valuable aid, not only to the State, but also to the general public. With our parks and crown lands in which to select positions, the establishment of such gardens would not be expensive, and would in a very few years save the first cost of their formation. Our large nurserymen would feel a pleasure in contributing their novelties and rarities, as they now do to our botanic gardens, and a system of exchange might be arranged between them to the advantage of both public, private, and commercial establishments. The adoption of such a system does not do away with the commerce with nurserymen for new or rare plants, but simply secures ample supplies of those in general request.

The present system is too expensive and imperfect to last. We have, in and around London and our other great cities, numerous public parks and gardens, and it is to be hoped their number will go on increasing from year to year. Let us suppose that the superintendent or designer of a new public park or garden wants many thousand trees and shrubs for its embellishment. He has to obtain them wherever he can, and as our nurseries are arranged chiefly or solely for private supply, most probably there will be great difficulty in getting some things even at high prices. For example, a very important item in town-gardening consists of trees for park and avenue planting. If at the present moment we wished to plant an avenue of Plane-trees, of suitable size and properly prepared for the purpose, we should have to send to the Continent for them, as in our own nurseries they are not prepared for street-planting; in which case they would cost much more than if bought in this country, and be in far worse condition for the purpose than if they had been grown at home. The Planes on the Thames Embankment were imported from the Continent, and of course there would not have been the slightest occasion for this if we possessed the kind of establishments described, and of which the necessity must be obvious. In Paris there is a great central establishment at Passy where all the tender plants are raised and reared, and there are nurseries devoted to the production of city-trees and shrubs, in which the most suitable kinds are grown, and grown to the size in which they are best suited for being placed in the streets, parks, or gardens. The cost of each plant or tree is in this case a mere trifle; with us the plantation of even a very small park, or one boulevard, would amount to a very considerable sum. It would, therefore, be wise to establish a large nursery for all hardy subjects, from trees downwards, for the supply of the public parks of London.

Glass-covered Corridor between the Plant-houses in the Jardin Fleuriste.

The Jardin Fleuriste of the city of Paris is situated in the Avenue d'Eylau, close to the Porte de la Muette, leading to the principal promenade of the Bois de Boulogne. It is the depot for all the tender plants used in the decoration of the parks, gardens, and squares of the city. Entering from the Avenue d'Eylau, the first objects of interest that are seen are collections of hardy plants growing in the open air on a small lawn amidst the glass houses with which the place is nearly covered. The most interesting and valuable group planted on this lawn is a number of hardy Bamboos, proving clearly that in our latitudes we may enjoy the peculiar grace and verdure of these giant grasses, and, by planting them, highly improve the appearance of our gardens and pleasure-grounds, especially in places under the mild influences of the sea and in the west and south of England and Ireland.

The interior arrangements made in the glass houses here for the convenience of the workmen and for the preservation of the plants in winter are admirable, and should be adopted in similar instances. We build more hot-houses than any other people, construct them better, and furnish them better; and therefore it is desirable that in disposing them in relation to each other, we should employ the most economical and convenient plan. They are frequently scattered about without any connection with each other, and there is consequent additional expense and trouble. But, even where the errors of the scattering-system are guarded against, there is seldom an effective means of communication from one to the other without going into the open air. All know how disagreeable it is to pass from a hot stove to frosty or damp air; it is dangerous to tender plants; nor can it be otherwise than injurious to the health of those employed in such structures. All these inconveniences are got rid of by the very simple plan adopted in the case of the group of houses, the arrangement of which the woodcut may serve to explain. The plant-houses are ranged on each side of a glass-covered passage, and there is no necessity for taking the plants into the open air in winter, or for the men who work in the houses to undergo any change of temperature for hours at a time. The houses are placed so close together, that heating them becomes much less difficult than when they are separated. The advantages of the plan are so great, that nobody building houses for growing or storing plants should neglect to adopt it. For Graperies with the borders outside, it would not be so suitable; but where good borders are made inside, it would answer well; or the Vineries or Peach-houses might form the outer four houses of each block, leaving the plant-houses and forcing-houses inside.

Plants may be placed in the passage, when narrow, in half-oval groups between each door. In large places where the houses on each side would be filled with ornamental specimen plants, it would be a good plan to make the glass-covered passage as wide as one of the houses. Beds might be placed between the doors, and climbers run up the roof, thus converting the passage into an agreeable winter-garden. With the better kinds of climbers depending from the roof; a few beds of Oranges and Camellias, and some Palms and fine-leaved plants here and there, to lend grace and character to the scene, one can fancy few things more agreeable in the way of winter-garden or conservatory, particularly as the varied contents of the houses on each side could be seen through the glass from the corridor or promenade.

The Cannas and like plants, of which such graceful use is made in Paris gardens, are preserved in a most efficient way in caves in this garden. When the stone is quarried for building purposes, a rough propping column is left here and there, and thus dark

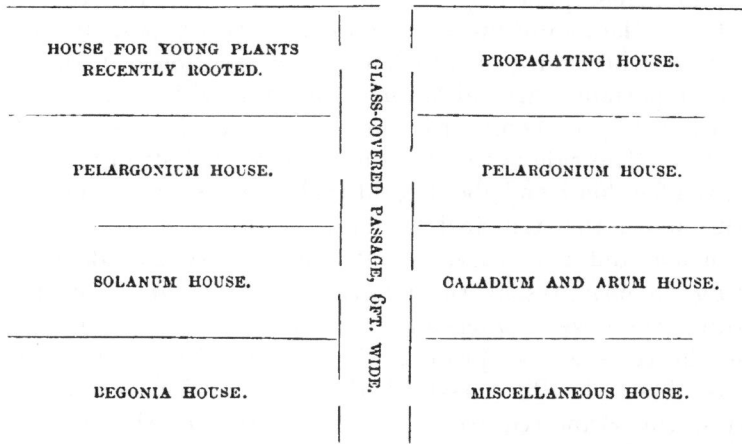

HOUSE FOR YOUNG PLANTS RECENTLY ROOTED.	GLASS-COVERED PASSAGE, 6FT. WIDE.	PROPAGATING HOUSE.
PELARGONIUM HOUSE.		PELARGONIUM HOUSE.
SOLANUM HOUSE.		CALADIUM AND ARUM HOUSE.
BEGONIA HOUSE.		MISCELLANEOUS HOUSE.

Diagram showing the arrangement of a group of Glass Houses in the Jardin Fleuriste.

and spacious caves of equable temperature are left underground. They are in this case about seven feet high, and are used for storing plants that may be well preserved without light in the winter. Here too in masses against the cave walls are arrayed quantities of the Chinese Rice-paper plant, which is so much grown in the gardens. It seems in a perfectly firm and safe condition, growing in the gas-lighted atmosphere, and sending out long blanched leaves of a delicate lemon-colour, which when the plants are placed in the open air in the summer, soon acquire a healthy green.

The nursery for trees for the boulevards is situated at Petit Bry, near Nogent-sur-Marne. It consists of nearly forty-five acres, entirely devoted to the raising of the commoner and more useful kinds of trees for avenue and boulevard planting. On entering, the first thing that strikes the visitor is, that the whole of the surface of the ground is thrown into ridges nearly six feet in width, on the apex of which the trees are planted. This arrangement is adopted in consequence of the ground being occasionally flooded by the river Marne, which is close by, to prevent the trees being injured by the water freezing above the base of their stems. The kinds mostly raised are the Western Plane, the Horse-chestnut, the large-leaved Elm, Ailantus glandulosa, Planeras, and Lombardy Poplars—the last, however, are not used for avenue or street planting. Other kinds used on a smaller scale than these—the Paulownia, for example, are grown at Longchamps. These trees, the names of which are here mentioned in the order of their importance, are all trained with straight stems, and sent from hence to the boulevards for planting as far as possible of equal size. The rule is to send them out with a straight stem of nearly ten feet long, and about eight inches in circumference. The portion above the ten feet of clear stem is not of so much consequence and may vary, but if the trees when taken up for planting do not present the length of "clean" stem considered necessary, the lower branches are cut away till it is attained. Of course the trees are so pruned when young that straightness of stem is obtained. To arrive at the size and fitness for street-planting, the Plane requires about five years, the Horse-chestnut ten, the Ailantus four, the Elm and Planera about five years each. The Elm and Planera are the only trees that require support in training them into the necessary form, for which purpose stakes from fifteen to eighteen feet high are used.

The nursery for shrubs is very pleasantly situated near the racecourse of Longchamps in the Bois de Boulogne, and is some-what more than twelve acres in extent. It is in excellent keeping, and contains a good stock of both well-known and rarely-used subjects. Roses and all kinds of shrubs and hardy climbers are grown here for the city-gardens, as well as nearly every kind of low tree..

The nursery for hardy flowers is situated in the Bois de Vincennes, and consists of nearly twenty acres of sandy ground just outside the fortifications, near the Porte Picpus and Lac

Daumesnil.   The stock of spring flowers is not a varied one, and leaves much to be desired.   Where there is so much ground devoted to a speciality, it ought to be well done ; and it is a matter of regret that with so much improvement in other ways a large stock of all the really ornamental hardy flowers is not formed.   It would be conferring a general benefit if, instead of depending so much on plants requiring expensive stoves and ceaseless trouble for their preservation, the chief gardeners of the city showed what may be done with the hardy plants belonging to our own and similar climates.   At present their collections of

Caves under the Jardin Fleuriste, used for Storing Tender Plants in Winter.

herbaceous plants and spring flowers consist of quantities of ordinary kinds.   A dozen years ago there was a greater number of hardy plants grown in Paris gardens than in London.   But since then a great impetus has been given to the culture of hardy flowers in England, and now our collections are far richer than any to be found in France.

The nursery for the Pines and Rhododendrons is also in the Bois de Boulogne, near Auteuil, and is about the same size as the hardy-flower nursery.   The climate of Paris is not so favourable to the growth of coniferous trees as that of England, and consequently to the English visitor the Auteuil nursery does not look

so attractive as that at Longchamps, but it is well stocked, and
serves its purpose admirably. The American plants are mostly
grown in the slight shade afforded by thin hedges of Arbor vitæ.
The Ivy used for making the edgings, which are so much admired
in the public gardens of Paris, and for every other purpose for
which the plant is employed, is grown here.

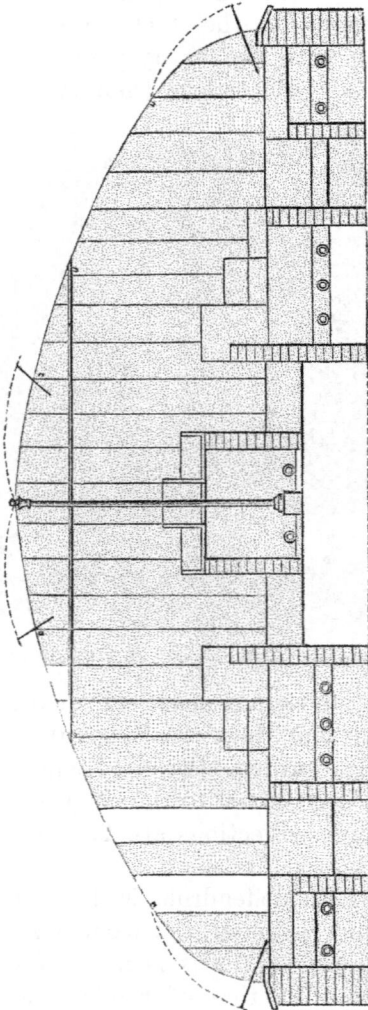

Propagating House in the Jardin Fleuriste.

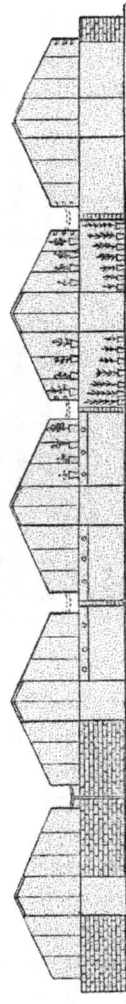

End view of Range of Small-Plant Houses in the Jardin Fleuriste.

CHAPTER XII.

The Cemeteries of Paris.

To anyone accustomed to associate cemeteries with gardens more or less beautiful, the cemeteries of Paris are far from being agreeable. In these human love does not fail in its testimony ; but such are the evils of overcrowding, of still following plans less evidently wrong when the city was much smaller, and of a horrible system of using the same ground for interments many times over—that the best aspects of these cemeteries are painful to anyone who knows what is possible or what has already been accomplished in the formation of decent burial-grounds near large cities. Nothing more agreeable is to be seen than crowded stones and whole acres covered with decaying blackened " immortelles "—the sight being most depressing to anyone accustomed to green churchyards. In the portions devoted to the graves of the rich, or of such as passed on their way to the grave by the paths of fame or glory, a little chapel or a ponderous tomb often prevents, for a time, the dust of individuals from mingling with the common clay of their neighbours, and the earth is not used merely as a deodorising medium, as in other parts of the same cemetery.

Where the poorer people bury their dead in this part of the graveyard may be seen a most revolting mode of sepulture. A very wide trench, or fosse, is cut, broad enough to hold two rows of coffins placed across it, and one hundred yards or so in length. Here they are rapidly stowed in one after another, close together, no earth between the coffins, and wherever the coffins, which are very fragile, happen to be short so that a little space is left between the two rows, those of children are placed in lengthwise between them to economise space ; the whole being done much as a workman would pack bricks together. This is the fosse commune, or grave of the humble class of people, who cannot afford to pay for the ground. The remains of these people thus dishonoured are not even allowed to rest in the grave, such as it is, but after the lapse of a short time their bones are dug up and the ground prepared for another crop. There is thus a very wide difference between "sickle and crown" in Père-la-chaise. .A cutting thirteen or fourteen feet wide, with the earth thrown up in high banks on either side, a priest standing at one part near a slope formed by the slight covering thrown over the buried of that day, and, frequently, a little crowd of mourners and friends, bearing a coffin. They hand it to the man in the bottom of the trench, who packs it beside the others without placing a particle of earth between; the priest says a few words, and sprinkles a few drops of water on the coffin and clay; some of the mourners weep, but are soon moved out by another little crowd, with its dead, and so on till the long and

In a Paris Cemetery in the Nineteenth Century.

wide trench is full. They do not even take the trouble to throw a little earth against the coffins last put in, but simply place a rough board against them for the night. Those places not paid for in perpetuity are completely cleared out, dug up, and used again after a few years. The wooden crosses, little headstones, and countless ornaments are carted away or are thrown together in great heaps, the crosses and consumable parts being generally sent to the hospitals as fuel. The headstones from such a clearance (when not claimed in good time by their owners) go to make the drainage of a drive, or for some similar end. And yet these people, who cannot afford to pay for the ground in perpetuity, go on erecting inscribed headstones, and bringing often their little tokens of love, knowing well that a few years will sweep away these, and that afterwards they cannot even tell where is the dust of those that have been taken from them.   One day, when in the Cemetery of Mont Parnasse, I saw the workmen making a new road, the bottom of which was formed of broken

View in an American Garden-cemetery, 1876.

headstones, many of them bearing a date four years before. These had been placed on ground that had not been paid for in perpetuity, and were consequently grubbed up at the end of a few years when the ground was required again for another series of these disgusting interments, which are needless too so long as there is plenty of cheap land in the environs of Paris.   Let us hope that whatever else may be "taken from the French," we may never imitate them in their cemetery-management.

The Americans are the only people who bury their dead decently and beautifully, that is, so far as the present mode of sepulture will allow them.   For beauty, extent, careful planting, picturesque views and keeping the garden-cemeteries formed within the past generation or so near all the principal American cities are a great advance upon anything of the kind in Europe.   They are in some cases as large as national parks, and as full of trees and flowers as a choice garden.   Many of the larger cities have several of these beautiful large garden-like cemeteries.   There are half-a-dozen or more within driving distance of New York.   Not the least interesting or admirable feature of these American cemeteries is the room allotted to each family and to each grave.   Each family possesses a " lot "—quite a little garden—in which the graves are dotted about, and which is usually neatly kept and well planted.   Thus the repulsive overcrowding of the European city-cemeteries does not exist in America.

The gentleman who first originated these noble American cemeteries, Mr. J. Jay Smith of Germantown, Philadelphia, is yet alive, and only a year or two ago visited London with the view of founding a similar kind of cemetery here, with all recent improvements.   When in America a few years ago, I had the pleasure of seeing with him some of the larger cemeteries of Philadelphia, and was pleasantly surprised at their riches in trees and shrubs, their vast extent, and the beautiful position occupied by the West Laurel Hill Cemetery, on the slopes on both sides of the noble river.   This quiet, impressive resting-place for the dead, which looks more like a great national garden than a cemetery, is situated at such a distance from the city as to preclude any danger of the requirement of the ground for building purposes.   Moreover, it is bounded on the east by the valley and river of the Schuylkill, and on its northern and southern sides by ravines so deep and precipitous as to insure that no engineering skill will ever pierce them with roads or streets.   It consists of a delightfully-undulating plateau, situated on a bluff projecting into the Schuylkill, thus constituting it a promontory bounded on three sides by the deep valleys already mentioned. In America even small country-towns have followed the example of the cities, and instead of the old city graveyard, we see imitations of Greenwood, Laurel Hill, or Mount Auburn, with their drives, walks, and avenues. In many respects the change is a beneficial one, especially in the matter of healthfulness. When nearly forty years ago, the idea of such cemeteries was first broached, it encountered great opposition. Since then no good fashion ever spread so rapidly. I am indebted to Mr. T. L. Olmstead of New York, for the photographs from which the engravings of American cemeteries were made, and also for the following notes upon the Spring Grove cemetery, said to be, in some respects, the best ordered in America, and which may be taken as a typical specimen of its kind. I take pleasure in illustrating these beautiful cemeteries for the sake of comparing them with the ghoul-yards of Paris and other European cities. In Spring Grove an important improvement is effected by a rule which prevents the erection of more than one monument on each family burial-lot. This is placed in the centre, and on a solid foundation not less than six feet deep, the usual depth of graves, so that burials can be made around the monument, and the respective inscriptions be placed on it, thus saving the expense of head and foot stones, which always, more or less, convey the idea of a potter's field, particularly in the case of single interments ; and where people, to all appearance, vie with each other in procuring the tallest headstones and the largest amount of ornament, thus increasing the difficulty of keeping such places in proper order. Wherever grave-marks are necessary, they should project but little above the surface of the ground, and be not much larger than ordinary landmarks to lots, but the base deep enough to be below the action of frost. In some instances lot-holders have planted a tree until a suitable monument can be procured, or sometimes even to remain permanently, which latter course is very desirable on sections where there is already a great abundance of tomb-stones.

To the arboriculturist, in particular, Spring Grove ought to be a place of great interest, as indeed will be many like places. It was the desire of the directorate from the first to introduce a variety of suitable representatives of the vegetable kingdom into the grounds. In this they were considerably assisted by the

N

owners of the lots, the most prominent of them being members of
the Cincinnati Horticultural Society, in which Society originated
the idea of establishing a rural cemetery in this spot. The greater
part of the grounds, when purchased, was densely covered with
native forest-trees. In the lower or southern portion, the Elm,
Sycamore and Ash predominate; the central part is chiefly
covered with Tulip-trees, Sugar-maples, Sassafras, etc., while the
western division is almost exclusively occupied by Beech, Sour-
gum, Red-bud, and Dog-wood. The northern part is adorned with
some of the finest groves of various kinds of Oak, of Nature's own

A Contrast: the Cemetery of Père la Chaise. (After Hachette.)

planting centuries ago. The effect produced by the brilliant
colours which most of these trees and shrubs assume in autumn,
is magnificent. The introduction of varieties of evergreens, whose
perennial verdure is particularly appropriate for ornamenting
places of sepulture, has contributed much to mitigate the bleak
desolation of winter and to render the prospect agreeable at all
times. The area of Spring Grove is considerably over 300 acres
of undulating surface, mostly of sandy subsoil, and abundantly
supplied with water and forest-scenery.
   Although we do not allow the remains of our poor to be treated
with the same disrespect as the French, there is no place where

A CONTRAST: *View in an American Garden Cemetery.*

our backwardness in all that is best and most essential in gardening is more apparent than in the churchyard.   All the advantages that could be desired for a charming garden are sometimes at hand in these places, yet the rule is to see them as bare as a housetop, and much less interesting as regards vegetation than the very ditches by which they are surrounded.   This is true, not so much of churchyards in towns, as in the fairest parts of our fairest counties.   Indeed, in cities and towns trees and shrubs often embellish the space around the church, whereas in some beautiful parts of Kent, or Surrey, or Warwickshire, it is common to see a church without a particle of graceful vegetation on either the walls of the church, the ground, or the low walls that sometimes surround the whole, although no spots are more easily converted into lovely gardens.   In these days of costly church-decorations one may surely not in vain call attention to the wants of the church-garden.   Thousands spent on the most elaborate artistic decorations indoors will never produce such a beautiful and all-satisfying result as a few pounds judiciously spent in converting the churchyard into a church-garden.   There are several reasons why churchyards are more than usually favourable spots for the formation of gardens of the best kind. The site and situation, in the country at least, are frequently favourable and picturesque, the soil is generally suitable, the tree-planter has usually the assurance that what he does will remain for ages, the associations of the spot are such as to awaken the mind to the influences of great natural beauty, the walls of the church usually offer excellent opportunities for the display of the larger hardy climbers, the walls of the churchyard advantages for the development of those of more humble growth; the ground is generally admirably adapted for trees, and the very turf may easily be converted into a garden of spring-flowers.

Of suitable trees the Yew is even more enduring than architecture itself; and it should never be forgotten that gardeners have observed and propagated varieties of this tree which differ greatly from the ordinary type, and are no less beautiful—the Irish Yew, for example, one of the most precious trees in existence, because it is as hardy as it is distinct from all other trees in beauty.   It would be easy to adorn many a churchyard with varieties of the common Yew alone, and of these we should certainly give preference to the green as against the variegated kinds. Although we shall never get any finer trees than our native Yew and its varieties, it must yet be remembered that our gardens now contain many evergreen trees from various countries, and from these a selection may be made; but in that selection there should never be a tender tree. It has long been fashionable to plant quantities of evergreen trees not hardy enough for many districts of the country, and even where they seem so far to be hardy, anybody who knows anything of the quick growth of the trees in their own and in more favourable climes, knows also that they will never attain their natural dignity or beauty in this country. There are, for example, many places where the Deodar, the Wellingtonia, or the Araucaria should not be planted. The church-garden being usually limited in space, for this reason alone only trees certain to be long-lived in the situation should be planted. Evergreens have been mentioned first. Summer-leafing trees should, however, not be neglected, as among these are our most beautiful flowering-trees, and many of them give also refreshing shade and pleasant green foliage long into the autumn, as, for instance, the Locust-tree. Where the space is limited and it is desirable, as it nearly always is, to leave some room between the trees for views, etc., the various pyramidal or tapering trees will be useful. In planting it is essential not to hide the building itself from important points of view. To enhance and not to conceal beauty should be the planter's object, and he can scarcely pay too much attention to points for view both of and from his site.

All who know how readily and simply the walls of churches may be made into charming gardens of evergreen or flowering plants, must regret that so many of them are bare of even Ivy or Virginian Creeper. Many of the finest flowering Roses and climbers could be grown in such positions. Fresh foliage or roseate blooms are never seen to greater advantage than against the worn grey or brown stones of our churches. The several sides of the church may each have its appropriate plants, choice Roses and the least-hardy subjects having the warmer and more sheltered walls. Where Ivy is used it should not be allowed to wholly exclude other and rarer subjects. The low walls often placed round graveyards offer also a desirable position for wall-plants, such as the various Ivies, Clematis, Cotoneaster, etc. Sometimes tombs may offer opportunities here and there for the growth of a plant of similar character ; but there should be no disturbance of any monuments or graves for planting of any kind. Intelligence will be best employed in beautifying, not concealing or obliterating such objects.

.Flower-beds of the common type are quite out of place in a churchyard. A group of Yuccas or of Lilies may be planted, but they do not need formal beds ; the tasteful gardener may make at least one beautiful large bed—the whole of the turf. In this one of the ideas of the " wild garden "—dotting bulbous flowers through the grass—may be most effectively carried out. It is scarcely necessary to state here that many of our fairest spring-flowers are easily naturalised in grass. The surface of the churchyard is often suitable for this, because the grass in it is not mown so early or so primly as that in gardens. There are usually in churchyards little variations in surface or soil which favour the development of a variety of spring-flower life, and the flowers are very welcome among the budding grass in spring. The Scillas and Snowdrops do exceedingly well in turf, and so does the Apennine Anemone. It may be urged that the occasional needful disturbance of the ground would interfere with these plants, but once well established, they would not mind this in the least. Groups of Daffodils of various kinds would look exceedingly well in the turf ; perhaps they would require watching, but they would repay it by their noble blossoms, which seem quite regardless of harsh weather in spring.

In connection with this subject the state of our old London cemeteries invites some notice. They could for the most part be readily converted into oases of trees, and surely they ought to be preserved for ever inviolate—if not as graveyards, yet as gardens. In some places they have commenced rooting up the graveyards, not merely where the tunnelling power of a railway company is brought to bear, but where the thing is done for mere love of "improvement." Tombs and headstones are being cleared out of the way and all obstructions removed, so that a level surface may be obtained on which to set a few hundred evergreens, which have little more chance of flourishing in London with its present atmosphere than if planted in the Salt Lake. To

have the memorials of one's friends disturbed for the ill-digested
schemes of a jobbing gardener is bad enough; but when it is
considered that this sacrilege is performed to plant subjects that
have no chance of thriving, then the wisdom of the change is fully
seen.   It is true the sculpture of these stones in our cemeteries is
anything but Greek, but the rudest tell of love and death "where
human harvests grow," and to all but vulgar minds must be
sacred.   What, then, must. be the feelings of those who have had
the memorials they cherish disturbed for such a purpose?   And it is
the more inexcusable when we reflect that there is not the least
occasion for any mutilation of the kind, and that the most
suitable trees for such places are those that would not require
any alteration of the ground, and would flourish freely in a town-
atmosphere.   The weeping Willow, Birch, Ash, weeping Elm,
and a considerable variety of drooping and other deciduous trees,
are especially suited for this purpose, and might be planted
without interfering with the stones in any way.   Would the
latter look any the worse for being shaded by a beautiful
pendulous tree here and there?   The fact is, town-cemeteries
may be made as beautiful as it is possible to make them with
vegetation, by the use of deciduous trees and shrubs and a few
well-tried evergreens.   Instead of any clearance or levelling being
required for the judicious placing of these, they will look all the
better for being picturesquely grouped among the tombstones and
other irregularities of the surface.   When new gardens are made
in connection with a new church, it matters not of course how the
ground is moved, but it would be a great advantage if the
churchwarden-mind could get rid of the idea that before making
a garden in a graveyard it is necessary to level the space and
make it like any commonplace bit of ground.   Instead of pursuing
such a course they should procure advice from some intelligent
landscape-gardener, and say to him, "Embellish the spot without
destroying its memorials or associations."   If it must be levelled,
mutilated, and planted with a few formal beds and shrubberies,
confide its execution to a navvy.   In such graveyard-gardens much
short-lived flower-gardening should be avoided in consequence
of the ceaseless care it requires, and the attention should be
confined to the hardy and permanent ornaments suitable for such
a spot.

There is no place in which a fresh little garden can be made in better taste than round a city-church ; and in Paris, where the difficulty would be to find an open spot that is not planted, the spaces around churches are of course not neglected.   The view of the Square and Church of St. Clothilde, engraved from a photograph, will serve to show how much the beauty of similar buildings may be enhanced by a little judicious planting.

St. Clothilde.

Ivy in Wreaths and Sheets on Railings of Suburban Gardens (Auteuil).

CHAPTER XIII.

Ivy in Paris.

ANYONE who traverses the streets of the newer parts of Paris may see many evidences of the graceful way in which Ivy is used to embellish the court-yards, railings, walls, and the public and private gardens of that city. It would be difficult to give any adequate idea of the charms it imparts to many surfaces that would otherwise be hard and bare. In any city or town, where the air is not much polluted by smoke, the same effects may be easily produced. In cold districts, where evergreens are liable to suffer, it is all the more desirable to make judicious use of the most valuable of all evergreen climbers for northern countries. To rob the monotonous garden-railings of their nakedness and openness, the French use it most extensively, so that even in the dead of winter it is refreshing to walk along by them. And if it does so much for the street, how much more for the garden ? Instead of the inmates of the house gazing from the windows into the street swarming with dust, or splashing with mud, a wall of verdure encloses the garden ;

privacy is secured ; the effect of any flowers contained in the
garden is heightened ; and lastly, the heavier clouds of dust are
kept out in summer, for so well are the railings covered by
planting the Ivy rather thickly, and giving it some rich light

Ivy on Trees in Champs Elysées

soil to grow in, that a dense screen is soon formed. Ivy-edgings
also make excellent margins to beds on grass-lawns. In this
case one would have thought the verdant carpet of turf sufficient,
and so it is, if the subjects fill the bed properly and come flush

to the margin; but, with the bare earth more conspicuous than the bedding-plants, as is so often the ease early in the summer, the belt of fresh Ivy, rising as it does several inches above the level of the earth, effects great improvement.   Near at hand this is not so evident, but when a little way off, the nakedness of the earth is hidden by the Ivy, and the flowers peep above it.   The best kind for this purpose is the Irish Ivy, but where many edgings are made, it would be very desirable to produce some variety by using other healthy green-leaved kinds; and the variegated ones, too, should be attractive, though no charm of theirs can ever equal the unmatched verdure of the green Ivies in early summer.   It should be observed that an Ivy-band of the width of an ordinary edging is not at all so desirable as when its sheet of green is allowed to spread out to a breadth of more than a foot.   In nearly every courtyard in Paris the Ivy is tastefully used.   Scarlet Pelargoniums are seen to great advantage when grown in boxes placed against a wall densely covered with Ivy, and with it also planted along their front edges so as to hang down and cover the face of the boxes.   One of the floating baths on the Seine has its entrance embowered with Ivy, which looks as much at home as if no river were gurgling beneath.   It is secured by placing deep boxes filled with very rich light soil here and there on the bare space; then planting the Ivy at the ends of each box, devoting the remainder of the space to flowers.   The soil is kept well watered, and the shoots of the Ivy are trained to a light trellis overhead.   In the garden of the Paris Exhibition of 1867, a pretty circular bower was shown perfectly covered with Ivy, the whole springing from a large tub.   Imagine an immense green umbrella, with the handle inserted in a tub of good soil, with boards placed over it, so as to form a circular seat, and the whole arrangement will be understood in a moment.   Such a bower could readily be made on a roof, or on a wide balcony.

An illustration here given of "rocky eaves covered with Ivy," shows a successful attempt to hide with graceful vegetation some caves for storing tools, and also serving as a shelter to passers-by in showers.   These caves are almost completely covered with a mantle of Irish Ivy, which also spreads into the bushes and grass around.   Where the rocky masses forming the grottoes are seen, the effect is good, owing to the rock being well formed.   The

caves are made in a sloping bank backed with trees. It will be
seen from this example that where structures are really required
in gardens it is easy to make them ornaments and not eyesores
in the garden-landscape.

Where there are tall bare walls near a house, they are quickly
covered with a close tapestry of Ivy. If the margin of the grass
around some clump of shrubs or flower-beds looks bare, some

Rocky Caves covered with Ivy.

young plants of Ivy will soon make a wide and graceful edging
which will look well throughout the year with slight attention.
When Ivy is planted thickly and kept neatly to a breadth of
from twelve to twenty inches, it forms a dense carpet of leaves on
the ground. The effect of Ivy-bands outside masses of gay
flowers is excellent, forming, as they do, a graceful setting for
the flower-borders. In some geometrical gardens panels are
edged with stone. These Ivy-edgings associate well with such
stone borderings, while they may be used with advantage in any

style of garden. A garden pleases in direct proportion to the variety and life that are in it; and all bands and circles of stone, all unchangeable geometrical patterns, are as much improved by being fringed here and there with Ivy and the like, as are the rocks on a river's bank.

In the Square St. Jacques there is an example of the way in which the small-leaved Ivy may be used for covering the trunks of trees; the effect being more lace-like than that of the ordinary kinds. It would be well to plant a variety of the green-leaved kinds at the foot of trees. It is not, however, advisable to cover very young trees in this way, as it is apt to interfere with their proper development. With regard to growing Ivy on trees, Mr. George Berry of Longleat makes the following judicious remarks:—

"In almost every park, however small, there are some few trees—old trees that are of no value, and that have matured their growth—that may be given up to Ivy by those who wish to grow it in this manner. It may also be allowed freedom on any inferior under-growing trees that have been overtopped by better ones, of which there are generally too many on nearly every property, particularly where judicious thinning has been neglected until too late to be of any benefit. In natural copses, when not grown for profit, Ivy forms an ornamental feature, especially on the Birch, to whose white bark

Small-leaved Ivy on Tree in Paris Square.

and brown airy twigs the green of the Ivy offers an agreeable
contrast.　Ornamental Fir-clumps, too, with the stems of two or
three of the most inferior trees clad in Ivy, become thereby much
improved in appearance; but the Ivy rarely creeps among the
branches of the Fir; when it has reached the foliage the dense
shade repels its further advance, and then it seems to retrace its
steps and forms pendent festoons.　Lovers of creeper-clad trees
should, however, take care not to allow young growing trees
or any fine healthy ornamental timber to be taken possession
of by Ivy.　It is an indisputable fact that when Ivy is permitted

to cling to and cover growing
young trees, it prevents development of the stem; while
its tightly-laced and interwoven mass of dense plaits
also excludes light, air, and
moisture.　The production
of foliage, too, gradually
diminishes, and when Ivy has
established itself on young
trees, the result is often slow
but premature death."

The Ivy may be readily
grown and tastefully used in
a dwelling-house, especially
in making living screens for
rooms.　This is usually done
by planting it in narrow
boxes and training it up

Ivy on High Window.

wirework trellises.　The boxes being portable, a screen may be
formed in a few minutes in any part of a room.　Sometimes,
however, it is permanently planted, and it is not unfrequently
used to embellish glass partitions between large apartments.　To
make the Ivy-edgings which are so abundantly and well employed
in and around Paris, plants are easily procured in pots at the
markets, on the quays, or of the nurserymen at Fontenay-aux-
Roses, who every year grow it in large quantities.

When used as a screen, Ivy may often be combined with other
creepers so as to produce a variety of pretty effects.　A happy

combination of Wistaria above and Ivy below in the same railing often occurs, and the contrast of colour between the delicate Lilac-blossoms and light green leaves of the Wistaria and the deep glossy green of the Ivy is so charming, that one could wish it were far more extensively employed in such companionship. Ivy also forms an admirable frame for windows, in situations where little else will grow. The window framed in Ivy, as shown in the sketch of "Ivy on high window," was a very high one (four stories) and the effect was very good. A deep box, filled with rich light soil, suits these Ivies best.

In some cases a green screen may be desirable far above the ground-line. It can easily be formed of Irish Ivy, planted in deep boxes of rich light earth or in a trough formed of stone or cement; in such positions the effect of the Ivy is all the more telling from its contrast with the large expanse of stone. The high screen represented in our illustration was formed about twenty feet above the ground, and in a position where it could not be planted in the earth on the ground level. In preparing Ivy for growing against the railings and trellis-work in the various parks and gardens, it is trained carefully during the first one or two years, so that it may cover spaces equably. At the end of the second year the railings are completely covered, and it is then only necessary to keep it properly trimmed.

Ivy over high wall.

The Ivy used by the City of Paris for ornamenting the flower-beds in the squares, the trunks of trees, etc., is grown at the nurseries in the Bois de Boulogne. Towards the end of the summer the propagation of the Ivy by means of cuttings is carried on. Three or four leaves are left on each cutting, and they are planted very thickly in lines in a half-shady position. When they have taken root sufficiently, which generally takes place in the following spring, they are transplanted into pots of four or five inches in diameter. Afterwards stakes are fixed along the rows of pots, and from these are stretched lines of thin galvanized wire; to this slender but firm trellis of from three to five feet high, the plants are trained during the growing-season. At the end of the second or third year they are strong enough to be employed to cover railings, and for many similar purposes. The nurserymen in the suburbs of Paris generally propagate them by layers, which are often rooted in pots. If a wide belt of Ivy is

Screen of Irish Ivy—Boundary to Garden on Banks of Seine at Courbevoie.

desired, the young plants may be arranged in two or three rows, as the French do when making the excellent Ivy-edgings which are here described. In any case, after the plants are inserted the shoots must be neatly pegged down all in one direction.

The reason why Ivy-edgings when seen in England look so poor as compared with those in Paris, is that we allow them to grow uncontrolled, and they get overgrown, wild, and entangled, whereas the French keep them down to the desired size by pinching or

cutting the little shoots well in, two or even three times every
summer, after the edging has once attained size and health.   The
abundant supply of established plants in small pots obtainable in
the markets, enables them to lay down these edgings so as to
look well almost from the first day.

CHAPTER XIV.

THE GARDENS OF VERSAILLES.

THIS being one of the most celebrated gardens in the world, it may profit us to examine it somewhat in detail—were we, however, to treat of it in proportion to its real merits as a garden, a very small amount of space would suffice. Let us pass through the vast stone courtyard and look from the garden-front of the palace. Standing near the palace walls, one first sees a vast expanse of gravel, some marble margins of great water-basins, sundry protuberances from the level of the water, and away in the distance an effect like that afforded by a suburban canal in a highly-practical and unlovely country. A few Lombardy Poplars help the remote vista, but the effect of the whole is from this point of our view lamentable. To the right of the palace is a parterre-garden, with high. Box-edgings, clipped conical Yews and other trees, and numerous statues prominent against dense woods of Horse-chestnut trees. To the left is one of those spreads of gravel and grass, diversified by stone steps, walls, and a few stumpy clipped Yews, forming what are termed geometrical gardens, Horse-chestnut groves starting up beyond it and somewhat relieving the whole. Advancing from the palace, the lower terrace and its surroundings come into view, the faces of the terrace walls are hedged with green ; above the terrace-walls Yew-trees planted and clipped very regularly ; in the centre there is an elaborate fountain, and the dense groves of trees near by again spring up and only just save the scene from bald formality, not to say ugliness. .Versailles is a vast garden, much of its interest hidden behind these kindly groves of trees, but it is about this spot that we obtain the broadest effects of this far-famed place, and may judge how far

o

they are worthy of the praise bestowed on them and of our admiration or imitation.

Versailles is often extolled as the queen of geometrical gardens, and it is certainly a vast illustration of the formal style of gardening. There are in books many dissertations on the several styles of laying-out gardens; indeed some have taken us to China and Japan, others to Mexico for illustration; but when all is read and examined, what is the result to anybody who looks from words to things? That there are really two styles:—one straitlaced, mechanical, with much wall and stone, or it may be gravel; with much also of such geometry as the designer of wall-papers excels in, often poorer than that; with an immoderate supply of spouting water, and with trees in tubs as an accompaniment, and perhaps griffins and endless plaster-work and sculpture of the poorer sort: the other, with right desire, though often awkwardly, accepting nature as a guide, and endeavouring to illustrate in our gardens, so far as convenience and knowledge will permit, her many treasures of the world of trees and flowers.

We read that " we are forced, for the sake of accumulating our power and knowledge, to live in cities: but such advantage as we have in association with each other is in great part counterbalanced by our loss of fellowship with nature. We cannot all have our gardens now, nor our pleasant fields to meditate in at eventide. Then the function of our architecture is, as far as may be, to replace these; to tell us about nature; to possess us with memories of her quietness; to be solemn and full of tenderness like her, and rich in portraitures of her; full of delicate imagery of the flowers we can no more gather, and of the living creatures now far away from us in their own solitude." What, then, are we to think of those who carry the dead lines and changeless triumphs of the building and the studio into the garden, which, above any other artificial creation, should give us the sweetest and most wholesome " fellowship with nature ?" Simply that their doings result from ignorance of what a true garden ought to be. The worst thing that can be done with it is to introduce any feature which, unlike the materials of our world-designer, never changes. Away, then, with the affectation of pretending to enjoy, with the ignorance which believes that there is some occult beauty in, or excuse for, such gardens as this!

GROUPS OF STATUARY IN ROCK GARDEN AT VERSAILLES

It is perfectly true that there are some positions where an intrusion of architecture and embankments into the garden is justifiable, now and then even necessary. The misfortune is that they are often said to be so when such is not the case. The best terrace-gardens in Europe are those built where the nature of the ground calls for them, usually where the ground is steep and rugged; it is in positions like these that they are most wanted in this country. There is no code of taste resting on any solid foundation which proves that garden or park should have any extensive stonework or geometrical arrangement. Many instances could be given to prove that the natural or nearly natural disposition of the most monotonous ground is preferable to the great majority of expensive geometrical gardens. Let us then use as few oil-cloth or carpet patterns and as little stonework as possible in our gardens, and arrange them so that when our sunny season does come they may be full of life and change, and of such beauty as is nowhere to be found in the deadly formalism of Versailles and gardens like it.

In considering this kind of gardening we have a capital example in the case of the Crystal Palace, in the region of the great fountain-basins, where a more dismal impression is received than in any part of Versailles, though the upper terrace at the Palace illustrates some of the best features of the formal system. But at both the Palace and Versailles the vast expense for a poor theatrical effect is not the most regrettable matter; that, perhaps, is the mass of formal, dirty water-basins, with their spouting pipes and crumbling margins; for the purse that creates such delights frequently fails, or at any rate gets tired of the constant expenditure needed, to keep the stone-cutter's work and geometry in good order. There is nothing more melancholy than the walls, fountain-basins, clipped trees, and long canals, of places like these, not only because they utterly fail to satisfy in themselves, but as constantly suggesting wasted effort and riches worse than lost. There are, from Versailles to Caserta, a great many ugly gardens in Europe, but at Sydenham is to be found the greatest modern example of the waste of enormous means in making hideous a fine piece of ground. It has been called a work of genius, but it was only the realisation of a misguided ambition to outdo another sad monument of great means prostituted to a base use—Versailles. But Versailles is a relic of past ages, and was the expression of such knowledge as men possessed of the gardening art at the date of its creation. Backward as we are now, our means for garden-embellishment have increased a hundredfold since Versailles was designed. Therefore this modern illustration of a barbarous style has none of the excuses which might be urged for Versailles. Instead of a desire to express all that we at present know of pure garden-design, and of the wealth of beauty now within our reach, the major idea was to out-Versailles Versailles. There being many mouldering water-basins there, it was thought well to make some vastly bigger. Versailles having numerous tall water-spouts, the best way to glorify ourselves at Sydenham was to make some unmistakably taller! Instead of confining the purely geometrical gardening to the upper terrace, by far the greater portion of the ground was devoted to the more antiquated and baser features of a changeless and stony style of garden-design, and nearly in the centre were placed those vast fountain-basins, with their unclean water and appalling display of pipes. Surely these water-basins are more hideous as garden-sights than the crater of a volcano. The extensive contrivances to enable the water to go downstairs (prettier than the spouting upwards, it must be admitted), the temples impudently prominent, the statues, the dead walls, all help to add to the distracting elements of the central region. The special gardens, too, such as the Rose-garden, so much better if veiled from the great open central scene, are made as prominent as possible.

Redeeming features were here and there charming bits of good gardening and good planting, but the vast geometrical system overshadows the whole, and only towards the outer margin could one feel free from this incubus. Here was one of the finest marginal plantations ever made. Those who knew it, and enjoyed the many fine shrubs and trees it contained, must regret its recent destruction to provide sites for a number of villas which now stare point-blank into the remains of what a few years ago was the most beautiful scene in the grounds. The one thing for which those with feeling for the beautiful in landscape-gardening always felt grateful to Paxton, was the belt of beautiful plantation that so gracefully cut off the grounds from the chimney-pots around. This plantation was formed at a cost of

many thousands of pounds, and contained specimens of nearly all that was beautiful in the trees and shrubs of northern and temperate regions. Wearied with the crater-like dreariness of the great stony region, one could lift the eye to this varied and interesting belt of vegetation, and therein find rest. This plantation has been almost entirely cut down, and long lines of red villas stare into the garden in its place. The consequence is that beauty or repose in the garden-landscape is made impossible. And to what end? For the gain of about £1,200 a year (the ground-rent of these villas) the gardens have sustained a loss which nothing can repair. Unhappily many instances are to be seen of poor design in public gardens, and of precious surfaces of garden-ground frittered away, but of blind destructiveness it would be difficult to find an example to equal this.

In connection with the Crystal Palace one thinks of ruined shareholders; and with Versailles, of the enormous sums wrung from an oppressed people, and put to such a miserable use. And this was the kind of good effected with the money extorted from a starving population! It was merely burying wealth—indeed, it might have been better to have buried it literally, for many would prefer the naked earth to such extravagances in stone, which must be kept in repair at great cost or soon become intolerable even to their builders and designers. When a private individual indulges in expensive fancies, he has little influence to injure any one but himself; but in the case of a public garden which is set up as an example of all. that is admirable, we then have, in addition to the first wasteful expenditure, an object hurtful to the public taste, sowing the seed of its ugliness all over the country.

It may be said that our taste in England is sufficiently assured against this; but it is not so. Many whose lawns were, or might readily be made, the most beautiful of gardens, have ruined them, for the mere sake of having a terraced garden. There is a modern castle in Scotland where the embankments are piled one above another, till the whole looks as if Uncle Toby and a whole army of Corporals had been carrying out his grandest scheme in fortifications. Were such an erection a matter of trifling cost, or one which could be easily removed or even avoided, it would not be worthy our attention; but being so expensive that it may curtail for years the legitimate outlay for a garden, and prevent expenditure in living objects of the highest value, rather than in slow crumbling monotony, too much cannot be urged against it. The style is in doubtful taste in climates and positions more suited to it than those of northern France and England; but he who would adopt it in the present age, and in the presence of the inexhaustible and magnificent collections of trees and plants now within our reach is an enemy to every true interest of the garden.

Versailles is one of the places in which the terraced garden is least appropriate. At Rome, where the immediate environs, unlike those of Naples, Genoa, and many other cities, are not hilly, the fashionable resorts, such as Tivoli and Frascati, were of a character to necessitate the terrace; the rude stone wall of the husbandman supporting a narrow slip of soil for his Olive-trees or Vines became, in the ornamental garden of the wealthy Roman, an architectural feature, varied by vases, statues, etc. It is essential to bear in mind that the beauty of an Italian or geometrical garden of any kind will depend on the predominance of vegetation over the merely artificial. This may be said to be true of all gardens, and so it is, no doubt; but it applies to the terraced style more than to any other, inasmuch as it is in that style that artificial features are most predominant. Terraced gardens, allowing of an endless variety of architectural work, apart from that of the house, have naturally been much in favour with architects and artists who have taken up the profession of landscape-gardener. The landscape-gardener proper, so to say, impressed by "orthodox" custom, and not attempting to think for himself, chimes in with the popular notion that every house, in no matter what position, should be fortified by terraces. Accordingly he busies himself in forming terrace-gardens, usually on level ground, which is unsuitable for them. Hence it comes that vast sums, ostensibly devoted to the garden, are spent on waterworks, fountains, vases, statues, balustrades, walls, and stucco-work. By the extensive use of such materials many a noble lawn is cut up; and, sometimes, as at Witley Court, the architectural gardening is pushed so far into the park as absolutely to curtail and injure the prospect—that is, if the prospect of a noble, well-wooded park or arboretum is better than that of a posing-ground for the objects above enumerated. Many of the

houses before which we see these formidable arrays would themselves seem to require much further embellishment from the hand
of the artist-architect. Indeed, if the cost of the stone and stucco
ornament lavished on the garden, in many cases, were spent on
its legitimate object—the house, it could not fail to be a change
for the better, for architecture as well as gardening. The fact
is, the style is only worthy of serious adoption with us when the
ground favours it, as, to name an English example, at Shrubland.
There it is used, with a very pleasing effect, to lead from the house
down a steep bank to the pleasure-grounds below.

Nothing can be more pernicious for gardens than the too-
popular notion that the right plan is to place a terraced garden
on the best front of the house, no matter what the nature of the

Terra-cotta Mania in Garden, Fortification Style: a Sketch in Suburbs of York.
Example of modern landscape-work. (From the 'Field.')

ground; the fact being that, where the ground is level, a finer
effect results from allowing the turf to sweep up to the walk in
front of the house than from an elaborate terrace, as may be seen
on the north side of Holland House, and at Cambridge House,
and in such gardens as Oak Lodge, where there is a very narrow
terrace. There is, in many cases, need for a formal walk, raised
or otherwise, and, it may be, for a small terrace—points which
will be governed in each case by the position, and sometimes by
the house itself; but, where the ground, as in most English
gardens, is level, there is no occasion for more than a grassy
foreground, which leaves us free to adopt everywhere a purely
artistic and natural style of gardening. In level town-gardens,
where the excuse of formal surroundings is used to justify a

stony style, it is also a mistake. The highest effect is to be obtained, not by carrying architectural features into the usually small town or city garden, but, by securing an absolute contrast between the garden-vegetation and its unavoidable formal surroundings. This contrast should be secured in such cases, not by aiming at the sham picturesque with rocks, cascades, and undulations of the ground, which would be too obviously artificial in such a case, but mainly by the simple majesty of trees and the charm of level turf. Thus it has been affirmed that none but an Italian garden would have suited South Kensington. Well, we had an elaborate garden designed there, and skilfully designed in its way. The plan was carried out with the greatest care; the planting, etc., was done by experienced men, yet the result, as everybody knows, was unsatisfactory in the highest degree. There are many private gardens in European cities, of a more limited extent and with more formal surroundings, which are beautiful in the highest sense, and as devoid of the aspects that offend many in such a garden as that of South Kensington, as if they were in some happy valley far away from the city.

Garden Statuary at Versailles.

One feature of the Versailles gardens deserving special comment is the statuary. Notwithstanding the wealth of art thus bestowed, it is rare, indeed, that a good effect is seen. On the contrary, the result is often spotty and objectionable, as in the Pincio, at Rome, where there is quite a regiment of new busts; and at Caserta, where the clipped masses of shrubs have statues laid against them at regular intervals. In the distance, that is to say, in the landscape, such dotting about of statues and busts is exceedingly offensive, because it prevents the vegetation from expressing itself, so to speak. At a distance of a few hundred yards or feet, the varied forms and hues of a variety of trees and shrubs may be full of beauty, but a line of statues or busts and pedestals ranged along its face, neutralises all good effect. Then, again, in a real garden, there are, or there ought to be, many living objects to invite the attention which a number of statues or other artificial objects may distract. In the very multitude of statues and busts here there is weariness.   One or two fine works, isolated near or in a grove of evergreens, might be introduced happily—the more so if the statue had any associations connecting it with the place; but it would be better to have such works under cover.   No one who witnesses the disfigurement and decay of statues in the open air, here and elsewhere, can doubt, that, for mere safety's sake, all works of any value from an artistic point of view should be under cover.   If the works are of no such merit, it is not wise so to place them that they continually

Statue on Terrace.—Vase from the Basin of Neptune.—Vase Borghese.   (Hachette.)

interfere with the pleasant impressions one receives in a fair garden.   And if these things be true of the green tree, what shall we say of the dry ?   How is it when Venus is leprous with lichen, when Mars is armless, and when the lion has lost his tail ?   In Italy, in the open air, in a drier climate than that of Versailles, statuary is distinguished mainly by mouldiness.   It is not only the moist climates of the north and west that favour the small spreading growths which so disfigure the forms wrought in marble. Everywhere in Italy, from Genoa to Caserta, the statues that have been more than a year or two in the open air are half-covered with a dirty blackish mould-like lichen, which adheres to them as closely as if it were part of the marble itself. The result is grotesque in nearly every garden where statues or busts are seen ; the expression is distorted, or the form defaced, from half its surface being obscured by an offensive blackish lichen. If this would only grow equally over the whole surface, the statues might be mistaken for those of a dusky race, but it persists in growing in great flakes, now throwing black patches over Apollo, and now bestowing on Psyche a discoloured nose. These facts being considered, it will probably be admitted that marble statues are best under cover; and that, in any case, a garden is not the place for them. Another error worth noting is that of placing large groups of sculpture in central positions. In this case, all objections urged against statues hold good ; but here they are more offensive, inasmuch as they occupy the best positions, and frequently destroy the precious quality known as " repose " in landscape-gardening.

Vases of fine design seem as profuse at Versailles as if the gold and marble had been dug up on the spot, but, good in conception and execution as many of them are, they are open to the same objections as the statues ; though, generally, when well designed and properly placed they have a more legitimate use in the garden. But if such vases as these do not, when too numerous and unrelieved, fail to weary us, what chance can the wretched vases, now so profusely scattered over our gardens, have of satisfying ? In the group illustrated the artist has graced the statuary with a few garlands of Ivy, and other shrubs—a liberty which is never permitted in this garden. All who wish to preserve a little quiet grace in their gardens, would do well to be on their guard against the mistaken use of vases now made in country-seats by certain " fashionable " landscape-gardeners. Vases of terra-cotta and artificial stone, often of poor design, are dotted about so thickly in situations unfitted for them as to destroy all repose and good effect. There are many beautiful gardens in which not one vase is seen, and many extensive ones in which half-a-dozen would suffice. Where the nature of the ground necessitates a terrace or a wall, the lines of these are better for being broken by the graceful forms of vases. It is even then

well to be sparing in their use; but, where the nature of the
ground does not furnish opportunities for using them, to scatter
vases about profusely is one of the worst of blunders in landscape-
gardening. The effect reminds one of the Euston Road displays
of statuary-ware; only in making the comparison, it is fair to

*The Colonnade at Versailles. (Hachette.) One of the least offensive of the Stone-work Gardens
though, like the rest, rapidly decaying.*

remember that the owners of these displays have a reason for
showing them which the country-gentleman cannot plead. In
the variety of advice that is offered, it is often difficult to decide
what is best, but one thing proprietors may be assured of, namely,
that an extensive display of terra-cotta and similar rubbish has
nothing to do with either good gardening or good art.

The Orangery here, in a sunk garden to the south of the Palace and the Parterre du Midi, is probably the most extensive known. It is massively built in the face of a terrace, and is more than thirteen hundred feet long by thirty-six wide. It is an immense archway lighted at one side. The collection of Orange-trees here is very large; but as we have already discussed this unhappy phase of horticulture in the Tuileries gardens, little need be said here. The trees are usually placed in the open air about the 15th of May, and are taken under cover not later than the 15th of October, so that they only enjoy the free air and sun for five months out of the twelve. In addition to the Orange-trees, a few other exotics are kept in this structure in winter, and submitted to the same treatment as the Orange-trees at other seasons. These are Justicia Adhatoda, Olea angustifolia, Jasminum azoricum, and Edwardsia grandiflora. They seem to do remarkably well under the treatment usually given to Orange-trees on the Continent, and the Justicia and Jasminum, and perhaps the others, are more worthy of being thus grown than the Orange, since they display their fine flowers in the open air in summer, and are less costly than when grown in stoves or conservatories. The specimens of the Madeira Jasmine are very fine : the rich green shoots drooping gracefully and bearing abundance of flowers. The Justicia and others are said to flower abundantly in their seasons. Considering the success which attends the culture of the Oleander and the sweet-scented Pittosporum under like circumstances, and even when preserved in cellars during the winter, this would seem to point to the desirability of adopting this system, or a modification of it. With us the nearest thing to it is the practice of putting handsome evergreens in tubs for placing in terrace-gardens, etc. But surely it is scarcely worth while doing this with things that we see in every shrubbery! If we do go to the expense of growing plants in boxes in the open air, it is best to select those that will not bear the cold of our winters, but which grow well out of doors in summer.

Few spots at Versailles will please more than the garden or Bosquet du Roi, near the Orangery; and simply because the artificial look, the stonework, and want of repose characterising the greater part of Versailles, are here absent. It is a sweep of grass, surrounded by handsome trees, with a few flower-beds and fine-leaved plants here and there. It is but one of many types of garden-landscape which simple taste and a knowledge of hardy trees and plants may produce. It well shows the unsatisfactory character of the various far more costly gardens in the immediate neighbourhood.

Another interesting spot is the Bosquet des Bains d'Apollon. This is a large picturesque surface of rock, backed by trees and having a pillared grotto or recess about its centre, containing a

Water-spout Gardening at Versailles. Fountains of the Basin of Neptune. (Hachette.)

large group in marble. The rocky banks in front are wildly clothed with trailing shrubs, the Polypody densely mantles the rocks, and the vegetation around is well arranged to suit the scene. It is not for its statuary we are interested in it, but for the rich garlands of vegetation over its rocks. Sculpture has, even in gardens, a very few noble uses, but not many will admire these costly groups—at least, as part of any garden-scheme; though the Ivy and Polypody, trailing shrubs, rock and hardy flowers, that fringe the grottoes, cover many blemishes.

On the fountains and waterworks of Versailles as much or more labour and wealth were lavished by their creators as were perhaps ever before bestowed on such confectionery "art." The Bassin de Neptune is the most important of these creations. As the waters only play on special occasions, and cost about 400*l.* every time they do play, one is justified in considering the basins in their usual dormant aspect. Nothing can look more wretched than any garden exhibiting large fountain-basins. The formality of the surroundings, the mouldering faded margins, the indescribable ugliness of the scenes near the great fountains here, seem only worthy of some lifeless world of geometrical craters and pools.

In landscape-gardening, and even in semi-architectural gardening (if that combination may be called gardening at all), nothing is more difficult and requires more care and artistic judgment than the introduction of fountains, which, far more often than otherwise, serve to spoil the combinations which they are intended to embellish.

The Little Trianon at Versailles.

This is the true garden of Versailles. To enter the gardens of the Little Trianon, leaving the tortured trees and many inanities of the large gardens at Versailles, is like escaping from a desert into a flowery land. The trees are no longer paralysed, mutilated, or starved, but healthy giants; they inspire one with awe and admiration, while those we have just left give rise to pity and annoyance. The Pines of Europe attain here size and dignity, and so do the deciduous trees. In spring, when the tall Cherry-trees are seen here and there, masses of white bloom among evergreen and Ivy-clad trees, the effect is beautiful. The charm, however, of the Little Trianon exists all the year round; though there is no time when it is so delightful as in April or May, when the tender leaflets are swarming out into the warm air, and many trees are tasselled with catkins. The grass is long, green, and pleasant, and, happily, walking on it is not "forbidden," like so many things in France. Housemaid-gardening has not yet deprived it of Cowslips and Ladies'-smocks, which abound in the grass. When shall we cease to mow and mutilate the sweet flowers that love to grow in the grass? It is sad to think of the eternal shaving of lawns and slopes with the mowing-machine; many of these might be bright with lovely flowers in early spring. Many flowers, natives of our own and other countries, would be happy in the turf, which might be cut once or twice a year without injuring their foliage. It is to be hoped we shall some day see a wisely-modified use of the mowing-machine and the scythe. There are

Cottage in the Little Trianon.

many primly-shaven acres in pleasure-grounds from which flowers might be gathered and grasses cut that are now shaved close every fortnight. A carpet is pleasant to the feet, but we do not want carpets everywhere. Pictures, for example, are better still, and these in gardens may be on the grass.

It is a common belief with French people that the climate and soil of Paris are unfavourable to trees. They speak of England as the land of "fine trees." No wonder this is so, considering the mutilation and overcrowding of trees around Paris. Five minutes in the Little Trianon prove that trees grow as well there as in any country. Here, in this "English garden," the trees

were not ruined by being crowded together in close lines or
tortured by clipping. They are too thickly planted in parts, but
this did not prevent them becoming tall and noble trees. Indeed,
of many rare trees finer examples could not be found. Those who
plant with a hope that the trees may survive themselves in

Streamlet in the Little Trianon (Spring).

time, or may excel in beauty or dignity, should plant so that
overcrowding can never injure them. It does injure nine out of
ten of every kind of tree now planted for ornament.

There is one feature in the gardens of the Little Trianon—a

little building overgrown with Ivy and deeply embosomed among
noble trees—which is so picturesque that it matters little
whether it be a reality or a sham, for it is undoubtedly a charming
object; so much so, that few will care to be told that it was originally
built as a *real* dairy.   One cannot wonder that Charles X., when
driven from his throne by the revolution of a single day, lingered
a few hours in the gardens of the Little Trianon, recalling sweet
and bitter memories, before hastening to the frontier and quitting
France for ever.

The young trees planted by Marie Antoinette, and those
previously established during the reign of Louis XV., are now

The Gardener's House in the Little Trianon.

venerable with age, and, during the summer and autumn, throw
the greater part of this pleasure-garden into a soft and pleasing
half-light, which greatly adds to its charm.   Jussieu has left his
landmarks in the garden of the Little Trianon, in the rare and
beautiful trees that still flourish there, most of them (planted in
1764) being now in their prime, and some of them the finest
specimens known of their kind.   The Weymouth Pine, for
instance, and a great variety of American Oaks are very
remarkable, while a Willow-leaved Oak (Quercus salicifolia) has
attained a height of above ninety feet.   There is also a superb
Planera, besides many other fine trees.

Those who have spent any time in the extensive solitudes of geometry at Versailles, and have been happy enough afterwards to cool their eyes among the rare trees and choice variety of plants of what is called the "Fleuriste," will probably preserve an agreeable souvenir of the spot.   It is a little garden cut off from the rest of the Little Trianon grounds, and, like all charming gardens, remarkable by not being "laid out," in the usual sense of the word.   Grass, trees, choice plants, a house and walls

Orangery in the Little Trianon, wreathed with Wistaria in flower.

clad with climbing plants form the elements; the resulting charm is indescribable.   It is only a gardener's garden, but if kings were born to wisdom they would prefer it to the stony solitudes generally spread around their homes by thoughtless "landscape-architects."   For botanists and all lovers of horticulture this garden has much interest, the collection of Rhododendrons and Azaleas being rich, as well as that of other American shrubs. There are also some remarkable trees in this part of the grounds, among them a grand Pyramidal Oak, a Montezuma Pine, and a

P 2

Pinus Lambertiana, which last is so vigorous that it promises
rapidly to attain its native growth of one hundred feet or upwards.
Fine effects are seen in this garden in spring, afforded by a
number of fine old specimens of the early Magnolias in blossom.
They stand up boldly out of low clumps of American and like
shrubs.   The contrast between two such dissimilar types of
vegetation tells well; the flowering-trees are seen to advantage,
and the masses of low evergreens relieved.   In summer there are

French-garden Side of the Little Trianon.

groups of Arundo and Pampas-grass, Tamarix, masses of Cannas,
New Zealand Flax, and many other handsome tender plants
placed out of doors.   These are usually gracefully arranged, and
there is plenty of turf as well as flowers.   At one end there is the
gardener's house, at the other the Wistaria-wreathed Orangery,
both here shown.   The side walls connecting these two are
covered with many beautiful shrubs that benefit by their shelter.
    A series of villanous clipped trees and hedges, mutilated and

suffering from repression and overcrowding, is seen on one side of the palace here. This monstrosity arose from the childish desire to represent various kinds of gardens, a desire which still prevails among us to some extent. Instead of using our knowledge to express all the beauty possible in gardens, and in many ways, some have offered us in the name of landscape-gardening a patch_ work composed of a variety of barbarisms. Having exhausted

View on the English-garden Side of the Little Trianon.

the watery fancies (or misfortunes) of the Dutch, dug up scroll_ gardens of gravel from old books, shaved the branches of trees into dismal uniformity, they have gone even as far as China for models. There is no example of a garden where this patchwork-system has any but a harmful effect. Let us leave such gardening in books. There it always looks better than in fact. Artists are generous in touches that make ugly things graceful. We do not make the garden more varied by such practices. They simply spoil ground that might be used in a beautiful manner. Given the largest and most varied garden in Europe, it would be easy to suggest a hundred beautiful aspects of vegetation not illustrated in it. Therefore it is a mistake in all ways to illustrate in our own day the gardening of the past, even on a small scale.

The aspect of the French-garden side of the Little Trianon Palace may to our advantage be compared with what is called the English-garden side. This side of the Little Trianon well shows the superiority of simplicity and a carpet of grass, as compared with the very different materials often seen before houses. There are some noble trees among those on the little lawn,

Grand Trianon: one of the results of the "Genius of Le Nôtre!" (Hachette.)

notably a very fine spreading Sophora. The open glade of grass allows the forms of the trees to be seen and enjoyed, and the effect is very good. The grass is somewhat rougher and more tossed in appearance than it is in fact, but that must be laid to the charge of the artist—artists not liking shaven surfaces.

There is very little artificial rock in the Little Trianon, and that little is constructed so as to be useless for plants. There are however several small rocky bridges, with shrubs trained over them. Such might be made with advantage in gardens with running water. They could readily be formed so that water-side and Alpine plants and rock-shrubs might be well grown on and near

An Avenue of old Lombardy Poplars at Versailles (near the Little Trianon).

them. The water is the worst feature here. A wide ditch trails through the grounds near the house, and prevents it from being seen to advantage from one side. By the same means the lawn is cut up and destroyed. Needless bridges are of course an accompaniment to needless water. The pond in front of the cottages, etc., would have been enough here, and one brooklet trickling through the grass. The scene however is scarcely wide enough for the successful use of water, except in the form of a streamlet. From any point of view the pond approaches too near the cottage. In many parts the effect of the water is spoiled by rounded margins. This is most noticeable where the water is dragged about in a ditch-like manner near the palace.

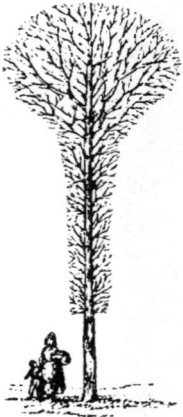

A Shorn Tree ("ideal" form: after years of mutilation the trees are even more hideous).

The gardens of the Grand Trianon near these are part of the series of gardens at Versailles, and very instructive from the point of view of garden-design. They are, perhaps, the most repulsive of all the gardens of the same school yet made. Many other gardens have something to distract attention from the puerile or barbarous nature of their plan, but here the geometry stares at us naked as a prison-wall. They are in a position not demanding a geometrical garden at all, being an adjunct to a pretty little palace, situate on level ground. The illustration on p. 214 gives a feeble idea of one of the dismal prospects which meet the eye of the visitor wandering through the grounds in search of objects of interest or beauty. According to the books, this is a legitimate phase of garden-design—" very well in its place." But the art to which it belongs is that of destroying all beauty, or possibility of beauty, in a spot specially intended by man for his delight.

In speaking of Versailles, it is impossible not to consider the way trees in the streets of that town are mutilated. A huge ladder, reminding one of the shrouds of a ship, is moved along on wheels, and from the top of this a man, armed with a very long-handled bill-hook, slashes away at the trees. It would be difficult to find a more striking example of labour worse than thrown away than that bestowed on clipping trees in France.

Among the Trees, Little Trianon (Spring).

Not only are the trees themselves robbed of all individual beauty
or character, but many places are spoiled by their presence.
Frequently the trees become hideous from disease consequent
upon mutilation ; and what they are in " perfection " may be
seen by the accompanying " model " tree figured (see p. 216) in
one of the best French books on arboriculture.

No necessity for this clipping exists. When trees are planted
in close lines to form a shady avenue, their natural tendency is
to form a beautiful and, though formal, picturesque arch, so that
clipping them to obtain this is a futile barbarism. Do we want
to prevent them spreading forth and filling the streets with their
great wide heads ? If so, we may select trees almost pillar-like
in their habit, as the Lombardy Poplar, the fastigiate Acacia, and
various trees of similar habit. Do we require them flat-headed
and low, so that while shading the hot street they may not
darken all the windows ? If so, we have the Paulownia, of great
shading power, and fine as a street tree on dry soil, without a
disposition to mount much higher than the mutilated Limes so
commonly seen. There are also the excellent Catalpa and the
common and round-headed Acacias, which do not rise higher
naturally than the tortured trees. No lover of trees or gardens
will regret that this miserable practice is now nearly discontinued
with us. We have our walls and pillars, and pyramids of verdure,
but happily the branchlets that form them know not the shears.
We may, indeed, yet see for ourselves, in the few places where
clipping and shearing are still carried on, how wretched is the effect.
In the case of a very old garden, where this system was in fashion
many years ago, it is permissible perhaps to continue the old idea
in our own time, but it is surely absurd to permit a trace of it in
modern gardens. Apart from the question of taste, or rather of
our right to deform beautiful natural objects, there is to be considered the great amount of not unskilled labour necessary to
carry out this absurd practice.

As if to contrast with all these decrepit avenues and monstrous
achievements of the bill-hook, there is a grand avenue of old
and very tall Lombardy Poplars near the gardens of the Little
Trianon, an illustration of which, here given, shows how we may
have, at least, noble walls of verdure without clipping or
mutilating one leaf or shoot. It will also serve to show how

In the Little Trianon (Summer).

desirable it is, in order to concentrate the effect and to obtain
character, that at certain places in the landscape and certain
streets in the town, one particular tree should predominate.
How pleasantly our imagination is stirred by the mention of the
Horse-chestnuts at Bushey Park, the Linden-trees of Berlin, and
the Elms of Windsor ! I am quoting the words of a correspondent
who has paid much attention to trees from an æsthetic point of
view :—" Great beauty is obtained by the disposition of trees in
an avenue, the essential character of which is that it should be
composed of single species. In no way are trees displayed to
better advantage ; they gain character by their fellowship, and
the attention is at once arrested by the uniformity, which, if it
were not confined to certain limited parts of the ground, would
become intolerable. The well-ordered ranks of stately Poplars,
composing the avenue depicted in the woodcut, give a striking
and unique effect to a flat and otherwise featureless piece of
ground. Their grandeur and formality impose upon the imagination in a way which would be quite absent if the road
were bordered by ordinary masses of mixed planting, or by
isolated groups ; but the effect to be produced by an avenue such
as this should be strictly localised. The contrast should be
sharply defined between the formal lines of stately trees and the
open park or gloomy, tangled wood. Another principle not to
be lost sight of is that there should be an object—not necessarily
visible—at either end of the avenue. Let it not be purposeless,
or half the sentiment is lost. In a town, let the avenue lead to
the river, the cathedral, or the central square,—then the object of
the formality will be obvious."

CHAPTER XV.

WINTER GARDENS.

THERE are few things more worthy of the attention of those interested in indoor-gardening in this country than the mode of embellishing conservatories and winter-gardens which is sometimes seen in France, Belgium, and Russia. Winter-gardens in these countries are usually verdant at all times, being filled with handsome exotic evergreens, planted and arranged so as to present the appearance of a small garden of luxuriant vegetation, and not that of the glass shed filled with red pots and prim plants. We build more glass houses than any other nation, but have as yet nearly everything to learn as to the arrangement of the most important of them, or what is usually called the conservatory. This in some form is an adjunct to a large class of country and suburban houses; sometimes it is well placed and an ornament to the house, but more frequently a thing which would seem better placed among the out-offices. As regards the form and style of building little need be said, as the improvement required seems so obvious. When conservatories are built near the house they should always present a somewhat permanent and architectural character. This is desirable for several reasons, chiefly the propriety of having a presentable and lasting structure in such an important position, and the fact that plants in bloom show to greater advantage in a subdued light than in that of the ordinary greenhouse. Those who remember the effect of the flowers under the thick canvas of the great flower-show tent in the Regent's Park, as compared with the aspect of the same plants in a well-lighted conservatory, will at once appreciate the truth of this. It should also be borne in mind that plants worthy of culture for their leaf-beauty alone always associate well with substantial surroundings. But the most important improvement to be effected is in the contents of conservatories. They will never be truly enjoyable until we display in them beauty of form. The aspect of most conservatories throughout the country is paltry in the extreme, except perhaps when the flush of flower in early summer diverts attention from the faults of a structure so little conservative of the elegant forms which make the vegetable world so attractive. As in many instances these structures stare point-blank at the living-rooms of the house, it is clearly desirable to make them presentable. Small subjects, from the Cineraria to the Azalea, may please the enthusiastic amateur, but plants are capable of interesting everybody and not the specialist only. So much however cannot be hoped for the conservatory until a nobler type of vegetation is not only represented but predominates. Flowers of a similar type to the popular ones mentioned abound in our gardens during summer; there is therefore no necessity for giving them prominence indoors : while on the other hand, those tropical and semitropical aspects of vegetation which we can never see in the open air in this country, may be obtained under glass without difficulty. The temperature of conservatories generally is sufficient to develop as rich a type of vegetation as the hottest stove, and without its heat and moisture. The grandest of all the Banana tribe (Musa Ensete) thrives in a cool house, and so do the Palmetto Palm of the Southern States of America, the Fan Palm of Europe, Chamærops excelsa, the graceful Seaforthia elegans, and many other Palms. Nothing even among Palms can surpass the effective grace of many Dracænas, and they all grow well in the cool temperature of the winter-garden. Numerous Ferns, from those great Dicksonias which at the Antipodes rival or surpass the Palms in grace, to the Woodwardias, which spread forth such great fronds, grow under such conditions without trouble compared to that required by commoner and smaller plants. It is not only the Palms, Cycads, Tree-ferns, Dracænas, and fine-leaved plants generally which thrive throughout the year in a cool temperature, that we may enjoy therein ; nearly all similar plants that flourish in stoves would well bear introduction to the cool conservatory or winter-garden after their spring and early summer growth has been matured. Left there during the hottest months, they would be more appreciated than if in a hot stove, and they could be taken back to their winter-quarters in early autumn.

But perhaps the best plea in favour of the fine-leaved plants that can be urged is that they enhance the beauty of the ordinary flowering-subjects in a remarkable degree. By their aid a few flowers will suffice to produce a more beautiful effect than was ever obtained by the abundant use of the blooming plants alone. This is important, and particularly in winter, when flowers are scarce. In winter, too, the aspect of houses arranged on the system advocated is quite as good as in summer, and more grateful from its contrast with the surrounding dreariness. A correspondent of the 'Field' writes as follows to that journal:—
"This subject has long been engaging my attention. Every suburban villa boasts nowadays of its so-called conservatory; but whether such adjuncts are ornaments is most questionable. In nine cases out of ten, I affirm, they are far from ornamental, whether viewed from the inside or the outside, and it is a wonder to me that people consent to have these ill-shapen, ill-adapted greenhouses stuck on to their residences. Anyone visiting the villas built within twelve or fifteen miles of London must have noticed the conservatories, so named, attached to the houses. I ask, are they even sightly?

"But there is a point I wish to insist upon much more than upon the external; it is the arrangement of the plants inside. What do we find as a general rule? Long lines of white stages with sickly, leggy plants in pots all round the house! If people could all hire efficient gardeners, the thing would be different; the conservatory might then be filled with well-grown plants and specimen shrubs. It is needless to say that the gardener could do but little with only one house; what I want to point out is the advantage to be derived from a totally different arrangement of the house. For goodness' sake get rid of all those weakly, insect-infected Cinerarias, Primulas, Geraniums, and others, and plant in borders round the house plants and shrubs alike easy of cultivation and beautiful.

"What I am aiming at is a graceful and novel kind of 'shrubbery' adjoining the house, rather than a house full of pots. Why not make round the house rich borders of the same width usually

WINTER GARDEN ARRANGED IN PICTURESQUE MANNER.

devoted to these unartistic stages, and plant Camellias, Ficus, and other such things?

"The aspect of these houses is equally beautiful in summer and in winter. This is the most thorough praise that can be given to the system. In St. Petersburg, where the climate is intensely rigorous, conservatories are even more appreciated than here at home. When people cannot afford these, you will find their rooms crowded with plants of the Palm tribe and numerous creepers, which thrive well all the winter; and it must be remembered that the windows are not opened from October till April. In the conservatories of the wealthy what do we see? A shrubbery—a maze of luxuriant foliage. It matters not whether there be 50 degrees or 60 degrees of frost: the promenade round the greenhouse—truly a *greenhouse*—is always agreeable, always charming. No words of mine could give you a true idea of the beauty of these places, nor of their utility to those deprived of plants and trees for six months in the year. One requires to see these plant-houses thoroughly to appreciate them.

"Some may object that they are more suited to Russia than to our country. Not so. Is it not a melancholy exhibition to see our conservatories naked, nearly destitute of bloom, during December and January, and equally disheartening to see them full of flowers only when the gardens are becoming gay? Depend upon it, what we want, and what will some day be the cry, is an agreeable promenade attached to the house—not a swarm of little plants in pots, which none but the gardener can name or appreciate. Then, again, look at the simplicity of the cultivation of the plants whose cause I advocate. Plant them fairly in the border, and they will always thrive. Azaleas, Geraniums, etc., are con stantly requiring to be smoked or otherwise attended to. Are you to take them outside, or into another house, each time they require such attention? If not, and the conservatory adjoins the drawing-room, there will not unfrequently be a decidedly unpleasant aroma there. I could go on to show other advantages connected with the system I am endeavouring to put forward; I could attempt a description of the plant-house of the banker, Outchine, at St. Petersburg; but I feel I have already said enough. To my thinking, it is, however, an important topic, and I hope to live to see more interest taken in the beauty of the conservatory,

Q

of its tout ensemble, and less of the rarity of the plants and flowers."

To any person with a knowledge of what the beauty of vegetation really is, there can be no doubt of the correctness of these views. The rule therefore in the conservatory or winter-garden should be to use plants of fine foliage or stately habit. Plant them in beds or borders; grow them in pots or boxes; the means, size, and require- ments of the place must determine on what scale the thing may be carried out. In some degree the effect desired may be produced in the smallest greenhouse. In planting out, select things that continue graceful during the whole course of their lives. Do not plant subjects which, like Acacias, run up to the roof rapidly and only bloom for a week or two in spring, presenting no attraction for the rest of the year. A great many greenhouse plants grow like these, but if we plant out a Palm like one of the hardier Fan-palms, or a plant like the New Zealand Flax or the superb Musa Ensete, they are in perfection at all seasons. Every conservatory should possess, in proportion to its size, a certain number of green and graceful plants, or those distinguished by some peculiar beauty of habit, which are ready at all times for fresh combinations, and look as well in mid-winter as in June. Without these we cannot succeed in the successful arrangement of a conservatory at all seasons without great expense, or even with it. What are flowers unless set in the graceful green among which we find them nestling in a wild state? By the selection of a great number of things which flower profusely— so profusely as to hide the leaves in many instances, the cultivator has often contrived to conceal leaf-beauty. Nature is bountiful in the production of leaves, and in the widest spread of Heath over a mountain, in the densest mass of Bluebells in a wood, or in any natural display of bloom whatever, we find the mass toned down by pointed leaves, and in the case of the spreading Heather by a fringe of Polypody, or even the cushion of mountain-moss. Everywhere Nature sets her flowers in clouds of refreshing verdure, and they err who merely cultivate dense flowering subjects, and do not take care to relieve them with others possessed of grace, and beauty of form. The continental plan of divesting the interior of the conservatory of all formality is well worthy of imitation by us. Usually an attempt to create a picturesque scene in some small spot with formal surroundings has a ridiculous ending; but in consequence of the luxuriant growth of many plants that flourish in the temperate greenhouse, it is possible effectually to hide almost every trace of the building in a few years. With little lawns made of Lycopodium denticulatum, tiny winding streamlets bordered with New Zealand Flax and graceful Grasses, Ferns, and the like; groups of Tree-ferns, Camellias, and Palms, and a plant of the great Musa Ensete, some winter-gardens are made really worthy of the name, and quite as charming as small wild gardens in those sub-tropical climes most favourable to vegetation. Whether the natural system of arrangement be adopted or not, every attempt should be made to soften the lines of the building and to shroud the spot with foliage.

For the following article on the arrangement of a winter-garden in the natural style, I am indebted to M. E. André of Paris, who has had much experience in these matters. "In England, where amateur gardening is so highly developed, and where more attention is concentrated upon the beauty of individual plants than upon general effect, next to nothing has been done towards a picturesque style in conservatories. Even the largest establishments leave much to be desired in this respect. Of course, in a mercantile or a small private establishment where the plants are either frequently removed or where they are awaiting sale, they will be arranged for convenience, like the bottles in a chemist's shop. But it is surprising that in planting the glass palaces of the rich, such as we find at Sion House, or spacious Palm-houses, like that of Kew, so little regard has been paid to general effect. The cause is simply this, that cultivation has alone been considered in England and in most European countries, and that the knowledge of plants has hitherto been limited to experimental culture. Gardeners have ignored the teachings of plant-distribution. Information on this subject can usually only be gained by studying the narratives of travellers, and these, unfortunately, are often incomplete and uninstructive on this point.

To supply in some measure this defect, we shall attempt to show how a winter-garden in the picturesque style should be treated. Before doing so, however, we should mention that there arc some notable exceptions to the monotonous repetitions which we deplore.   In Mr. Llewellyn's garden at Penllergare, in Wales, might have been seen a few years ago an orchid-house aquarium where lovely denizens of the tropics were planted in the admirable disorder which they present in their native forests. True, it was only on a small scale, but the effect produced was most pleasing.   Again, at Paris, in the Garden of Acclimatisation in the Bois de Boulogne, is a large house, which is planted in an attractive manner, representing a tropical scene, with rockwork, a cascadé falling into a pool, and a rivulet meandering through a valley of Selaginellas.   There would be little difficulty in beautifying in like manner the Palm-house at Kew, the large pavilion of the Museum at Paris, the Horticultural Society's fine conservatory at South Kensington, a portion of the Crystal Palace at Sydenham, the large houses at Sion and Chatsworth, etc.

When in Belgium last year I visited the seat of M. Varocqué, at Mariemont, where a new winter-garden, between fifty and sixty feet high, had been erected on the site of an old Orangery, in which a Belgian landscape-architect of some note (M. Fuchs) had essayed to introduce the style I advocate.   Magnificent Palms, Tree-ferns, Cycads, etc., form the principal features in this large building, with an undulating carpet of Selaginellas beneath them. Immediately facing the grand entrance door was an artistic group of rockwork flanked by a miniature basin, and planted with evident care.   But, in our opinion, the result was not commensurate with the pains bestowed.   The walks are too winding, the surface too uneven, the rockery too imposing to appear natural, and the plantations confused, the sides being naked, and the centre excessively dense.   The artist aimed at the picturesque, but he has failed to produce it in consequence of too great profusion, to the detriment of the general effect and the loss of harmony in the details.   We cite this example to show that it is easy to err in carrying out the best of ideas, and that exaggeration in the intended natural style is more to be deprecated than crowding in the unmitigated uniformity of houses with stages and benches.   Even in winter-gardens where the aim has been to produce picturesque effect, there is always something in the structure to remind us of the artificial surroundings.   Thus, walks are indispensable, and they should be of sufficient breadth

to admit of free and agreeable promenading. To try to imitate
the forests of Brazil by compelling the spectator to scramble over
the rotten remains of trunks of fallen trees, rough stones, and
withered Fern-fronds, would be the height of absurdity. And those
interminable tortuous walks are equally opposed to good taste,
with the rectangular paths which remind us of the system and
order of a purely botanic garden. There is a happy medium to
be studied.

An outer circular or slightly devious walk near the well-
clothed side-walls or lights should surround the central area,
where the eye rests upon choice specimens standing out distinctly
upon a carpeting of Selaginella denticulata, trailing Commelynaceæ,
Lippia repens, Tradescantia, and other plants which readily form
a close and compact verdure. The space between the walks and
the walls should be filled with dense masses of foliage effectually
concealing the stems of the plants, and rising gradually from the
walk outwards; and the centre should show isolated trees and
little groups upon an open lawn of creeping-plants. The detached
specimens must not be planted indiscriminately in the central
area, which is surrounded and intersected by the walks. They
should be grouped in combinations or planted singly, according
to size and foliage, and in such a way that the view between their
trunks is uninterrupted; and at the same time their heads should
harmonise together in colouring and outline.

A ground-plan of our ideal winter-garden is given in this
chapter with numbers indicating the positions for the plants
enumerated as suitable.

Instead of undulating the surface in an infinity of insignificant
hillocks, as in M. Varocqué's winter-garden, we recommend
limiting it to two intercepting dells. A longitudinal one from
the rockery, terminated by a bower, under which are placed a
table and seats, and ending, at the side-entrance, in a single
hollow, of which the pool or basin is the lowest point. From this
pool to the flower-bed No. 94, the ground rises slightly, and the
cross walk curves towards the middle in agreement with the
lower ground. The boundary walk is of the same level throughout,
except towards the rockery, where it rises and terminates in four
or five rustic stone steps leading to the alcove. The beds Nos. 94,
123, and 167, should be elevated about two feet above the

walk; and each of the isolated trees should be planted on a very
gently rising mound of earth, with the exception of the groups
on either side of the rockwork, which are on an abrupt slope,
and the large clump on each side of the bed No. 94, which
should be raised about nine inches above the walk and gradually
sloped off.

Let us now proceed to enter into the planting, which is certainly the most important part of winter-gardening. This may
be considered from several points of view, according to the class
of house, whether cold, temperate, or hot, or for orchids or an
aquarium. For the present we will content ourselves with
treating of a warm temperate winter-garden with a mean
temperature of from 65° to 68° Fahr., in which we could place
Palms and similar house-plants that would thrive all the better
for the increased warmth. Previous to planting, due care must
be given to the drainage and the composition and preparation of
the soil. As bottom-heat is the main thing to produce luxuriant
vegetation in plants, it is important that the hot-water pipes
should be properly arranged and covered with flag-stones to
prevent the plants on the walls from being scorched, instead of
being around the outside, and exposed, as usually is the case. If
uncovered pipes are considered absolutely essential along the base
of the walls, a brick or other partition of some sort should be
placed between them and the plants, to prevent too great an
accession of direct heat from the pipes. But a still better method
is to conduct the heat through underground brick channels to
points with open gratings in the walks to allow the heat to rise.
The soil, well drained at the bottom, and crossed here and there
by the pipes we have mentioned, will be warmer and will encourage
the luxuriant growth desired around the walls of the house. A
good drainage of broken bricks and mortar rubbish will suffice for
the subsoil, leaving a depth of about three feet for the mould intended for the plants. Two drains should run below this through
the house, with an outlet to carry off the surplus water. The
composition of the soil may be varied according to the class of
plants it is intended for. But, as a general rule, for strong
growing plants and large Palms it will be found advantageous to
prepare the mass in the following manner:—Upon the layer of
broken bricks and mortar rubbish should be placed a layer of

reversed turves about eighteen inches thick, and upon that a
second formed of—

Stiff loam	-	-	-	-	-	-	3 parts.
Ordinary garden soil	-	-	-	-	-	-	3 „
River, or white sand	-	-	-	-	-	-	2 „
Coarse pieces of earth and brickbats				-	-	1 „
Leaf-mould	-	-	-	-	-	-	1 „

10

Mix this well together and apply it about a foot thick.   Then for
the surface add a layer of about five or six inches thick of peat, loam,
and leaf-mould from hedgerows, or rotten Willow, Oak, or Chestnut
trunks, if attainable, with a tenth part of sand.   The peat should
be but slightly broken up and the roots left in it.   Prepared in
this way, it will be ready to receive the Selaginella, which will
thrive admirably in it and speedily clothe it with verdure.

It will be understood that these three layers, forming a total
thickness of three feet, will not be of uniform thickness all through
the house, because the surface will be undulated.   The measure-
ment of one yard is merely given as a basis or unit, for the total
depth of subsoil in different parts of the house will vary, having,
for instance, a depth of only eighteen inches near the basin in the
centre of the little lawn, and from four to five feet for the clumps
abutting on the flower-bed No. 94.   But the top-dressing will be
equal all over.   The majority of large tropical plants can be
grown in such a compost.   Those which may require special
treatment may be potted in suitable soil and plunged deep enough
to conceal them, and allow the Selaginella to spread over their
surface.   Liquid manure, if used with moderation and judgment,
will accelerate the growth of most plants, including Ferns.   So
much for the preparations for planting.   But the key of the
question, the secret of success, depends above all upon the choosing
and grouping of the plants.   This selection may vary to infinity,
such are the riches of exotic flowers at our command.   It is
difficult to lay down rules on the mode of arranging plants
according to the colour and character of their foliage.   We may,
however, remark that in houses, no matter how splendidly constructed, the effects of uniformity are bad, and that masses of one
species or of one genus of plants should be avoided. The harmony

and grandeur of unity in composition, attained with difficulty even in large parks, is here impossible. The object to be sought, then, is contrast in the foliage and habit of the plants employed. Two species of massive foliage, for example, should not stand side by side, such as a Musa and a Ravenala, or a Coccoloba pubescens and a Theophrasta. But a large tuft of a Strelitzia beneath the shade of a Cocos plumosa is very effective, and a fine contrast is presented to the eye by backing up the grand foliage and yellow spikes of Hedychium Gardnerianum with clumps of Ferns, Bamboos, or feathery Conifers. The rigid foliage of Rhododendrons and Camellias should be excluded, these beautiful plants being reserved for a separate house, where they will better display their charms in a collection.

In dense masses of foliage, like those adjoining the rockery in our plan, the arrangement should be in gradual rising ranks, thick, heavy foliage forming the basis, surmounted by lighter and more graceful forms of Palms and Tree-ferns, whose slender-plumed columns break through the sombre undergrowth. The use of ordinary flowering-plants should be limited to the borders and special beds for them, with the exception of here and there one on the rockwork. We mean such plants as are grown in pots in special houses and taken to the winter-garden for temporary decoration, as—Primulas, Cyclamens, Tulips, Hyacinths, Heaths, Crocuses, etc.

The side-walls, or sashes, should be provided with wire trellis-work or wooden lattice-work against a dead wall, to support climbing-plants all round the house. For covering the surface of the soil nothing is better than Selaginella denticulata; and this should be planted or re-planted in autumn, or in spring, as the dry heat of summer is unfavourable to it. Small fragments, about three inches long, planted four or five inches apart, will soon cover the ground. Above all a good system of shading must be ensured to protect the plants from the direct rays of the sun in summer. The paths may be formed of gravel, and they are best edged with half-plunged portions of rugged stone. The construction of the rockery should be of the simplest kind, composed of a few stones naturally disposed and projecting slightly from the earth so as to be discovered rather than seen. Monumental rock-work should be avoided, and, above all, reject the so-called pretty

stones.   Geological or mineralogical toys may be all very well in
the cabinets of the learned, but they are altogether out of place in
a garden where the object is to show us plants in their native
beauty.   If a small pond be added to the rockwork, it should
neither be absolutely round nor sinuous.

In order to secure a warm, humid atmosphere, so essential to
the well-being of plants, we recommend having the pipe that
feeds the cascade and replenishes the basins made so as to pass
through the boiler, which will sufficiently heat the water in its
transit to cause it to give off a portion by evaporation when dis-
charged.   In this way the atmosphere will be charged with

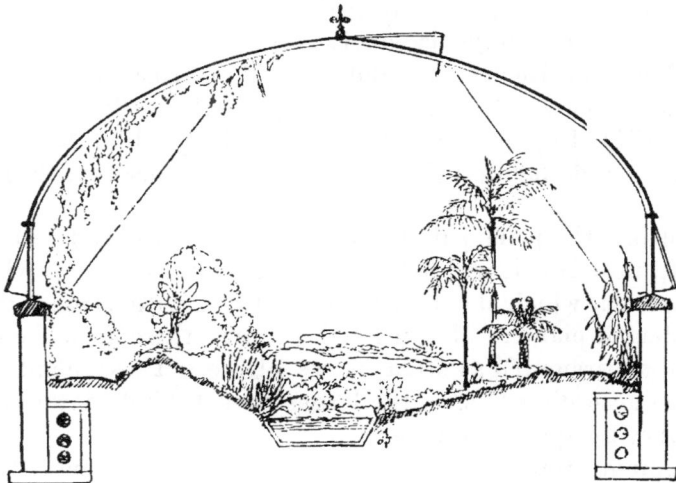

Section of a Conservatory arranged in the Natural Style.

moisture, to the improvement of the health of the plants.   As
regards choice of plants, as has already been observed, it may be
varied indefinitely. These arrangements are, of course, applicable to
a far larger structure than the one under consideration.   In fact
the design is open to modification or expansion almost unlimited.

Distribution of the Plants.

Perennial climbing-plants for placing alongside walls, or for
covering supporting columns, may consist of,—

(1) Aristolochia cordifolia, which is very vigorous, and has

large leaves and enormous flowers; (3) Thunbergia Harrisi, moderately vigorous, flowers numerous; (7) Ipomœa Horsfalliæ; (9) Tecoma stans, which has pinnate leaves and pretty flowers; (12 and 13) Plumbago capensis; (17) Hoya carnosa; (19) Smilax marmorea, leaves marbled with white; (21) S. macrophylla maculata; (23 and 25) S. marmorea; (27) Hoya imperialis, a vigorous kind, bearing corymbs of rich brown flowers; (28) Stephanotis floribunda; (30) Passiflora Decaisneana, a species with large foliage, and large rose and violet flowers; (31) Quisqualis indica; (33) Tacsonia Van Volxemii; (36) Aristolochia leuconeura; (37) Hexacentris mysorensis; (41) Centrostemma multiflorum; (44) Passiflora carmesina; (45) Aristolochia clypeata; (49) Tacsonia mollissima; (53) Quisqualis pubescens; (54) Passiflora trifasciata; (58) Meyenia erecta; (60) Thunbergia laurifolia; (62) Passiflora Buchanani, and (63) P. marmorea, two pretty, vigorous species; (65) Bougainvillea lateritia; (68) Aristolochia gigas; (71) Bignonia incarnata; (72) Tropæolum Lobbianum; (74) Allamanda nobilis; (77) Clerodendron Thomsonæ; (80) Cissus discolor.

Entering the principal doorway of the house and bearing to the left, near No. 1, we shall come to the outer border of which we have spoken, which should mainly be filled with strong-growing fine-foliaged plants. Nothing will prevent these from being increased and renewed as often as we please. These plants being grouped according to size, the larger ones behind may consist of the following species, viz:—

Amomum grana-paradisi, Andropogon squarrosum, Panicum plicatum, Fuchsias, Aspidistra, Dracænas, Begonias, Cyperus, Eugenia, various free-growing tufted Ferns, Ficus elastica, Aralia and Oreopanax, Hedychium coronarium, and H. gardnerianum, Hibiscus rosa-sinensis, Heterocentrum, Hæmatoxylon campechianum, Imantophyllum Aitoni, Laurus Camphora, Plumbago coccinea, Poinsettia pulcherrima, Rogieras, Sparmannia africana, Xylophylla latifolia, Abutilons, Allamanda neriifolia, Pipers and Macropipers, Begonias, Centradenia grandifolia, Franciscas, Gardenias, Hebeclinium ianthinum, Siphocampylus (bicolor and fulgens), Iresine Herbsti, Amorphophallus, Hibiscus liliiflorus, and Marantas, etc.

Above this groundwork of foliage and flowers the following species, with taller stems and stronger habits, may rise:—

2. Musa paradisiaca
4. Oreopanax dactylifolium
6. Alsophila australis
10. Stadmannia australis
15. Anthurium acaule
16. Rhopala organensis
20. Saurauja sarapigensis
22. Dracæna arborea
24. Rhopala Jonghei
26. Theophrasta regalis
32. Musa sapientum
34 Hedychium gardnerianum

35. Cyathea medullaris
37. Chamærops excelsa
39. Artocarpus incisa
40. Musa violacea
42. Hedychium coccineum
43. Carludovica palmata
46. Cibotium regale
47. Castilloa elastica
48. Anthurium cordatum
50. Dracæna fragrans
51. Maranta Lindeni
55. Musa paradisiaca
56. Chamærops stauracantha

59. Ficus Chauvieri
61. Oreopanax platanifolium
64. Sciadophyllum pulchrum
66. Astrapæa Wallichii
67. Anthurium regale
70. Cereus mexicanus
73. Theophrasta imperialis
75. Cyathea dealbata
76. Cocos flexuosa
78. Ficus macrophylla
79. Areca lutescens

The bed No. 94 will be decorated with dwarf, bright-coloured flowers, to be renewed as often as required.

The two groups encircling the portion of green near this bed will be composed as follows:—

Plants with tall stems, but varying in height.

100. Balantium antarcticum
104. Areca sapida
95. Coccoloba pubescens

97. Caryota sobolifera
105. Ficus elastica
109. Laurus Camphora

Of medium size.

101. Pteris argyræa
102. Medinilla magnifica

103. Asplenium macrophyllum

105. Cycas circinalis
108. Dracæna terminalis

Of medium size.

107. Clivia miniata
106. Anthurium leuconeurum

98. Attaccia cristata
96. Crinum amabile
99 Acalypha tricolor

With tall stems.

81. Cyathea beyrichiana
85. Oreodoxa regia
84. Phœnix reclinata

87. Theophrasta macrophylla
90. Rhopala corcovadensis
92. Seaforthia elegans

Of medium size.

83. Amorphophallus nivosus
82. Dracæna australis

89. Croton undulatum
91. Colocasia macrorhiza variegata

88. Asplenium nidus-avis
93. Dracæna cannæfolia
86. Anthurium hybridum

On Lawn.

110. Syagrus botryophora
112. Pandanus ornatus
115. Latania rubra
114. Rhapis flabelliformis
116. Areca sapida

111. Anthurium magnificum
110. Blechnum brasiliense
113. Alpinia nutans
117. Medinilla magnifica

118. Cordyline indivisa
119. Cibotium princeps
120. Pteris argyræa
121. Agave Verschaffelti

Flower-beds Nos. 123 and 167 refilled from time to time with flowering-plants, bulbs, &c.

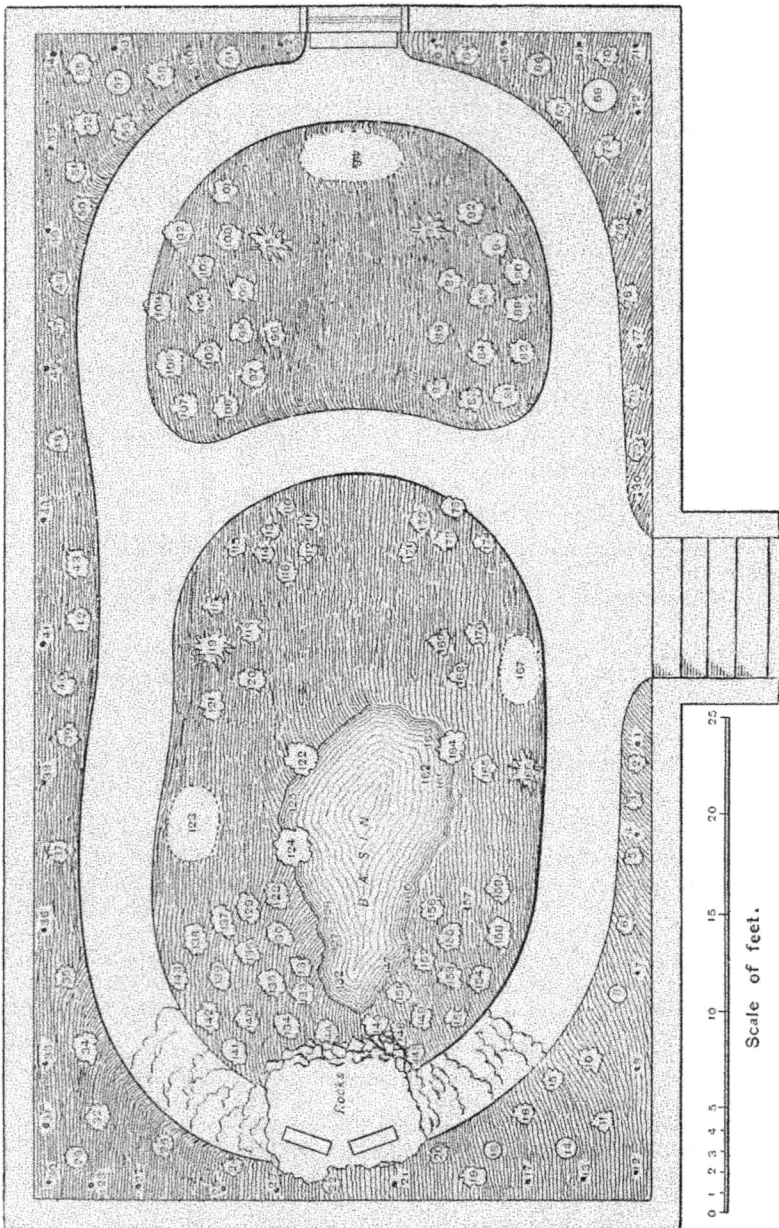

Scale of feet.

0 1 2 3 4 5   10   15   20   25

Ground-plan of Wintergarden: the Figures are referred to in the Text, and serve for both the hot and cool wintergarden.

122. Bambusa Thouarsi
124. Philodendron pinnati-
   fidum
128. Phajus Wallichii
129. Phœnicophorium
   Seychellarum
130. Phormium tenax
   foliis variegatum
121. Pandanus elegantis-
   simus
135. Durio usibethinus
134. Lomaria gibba
133. Carludovica atrovirens
144. Hoya bella
141. Acanthus latifolius
142. Clivia miniata
140. Clusia rosea
136. Ficus Cooperi
139. Musa paradisiaca
143. Pteris cretica albo
   lineata
138. Platyloma falcata

137. Vriesia gigantea
132. Thalia dealbata
147. Philodendron pertu-
   sum
127. Pontederia cordata
126. Nymphæa gigantea
125   „   Ortgiesiana
             rubra
163.   „   cærulea
162. Philodendron Lindeni
161. Vallisneria spiralis
160. Nymphæa dentata
156. Musa Ensete
157. Crescentia regalis
159. Disteganthus basi
   lateralis
158. Cycas revoluta
154. Carludovica plicata
155. Balantium Culcita
153. Lomaria gibba
152. Billbergia zebrina

151. Theophrasta imperi-
   alis
149. Musa sinensis
148. Cocos coronata
146. Pteris argyræa
145. Platycerium grande
166. Verschaffeltia splen-
   dida
165. Bambusa Fortunci
164. Colocasia nymphæfolia
168. Cypripedium barba-
   tum superbum
167. Attalea excelsa
170. Dion edule
171. Cyanophyllum mag-
   nificum
172. Dracæna Guilfoylei
173. Sciadocalyx digi-
   taliflora
174. Cordyline indivisa
175. Croton maximum.

Such are the prominent distinctive features of this mode of grouping the principal furniture in this palace of flowers. As we have already observed, these combinations are capable of endless variations, and numerous small species may be inserted in empty spaces between the larger plants; while baskets of Ferns, Bromeliaceæ, Orchids, etc., may be suspended from the rafters on slender wire. These may either be planted in the baskets, or the pots placed in them, the interspaces being filled with growing moss. The rockery will be adorned with all sorts of plants that will flourish in the interstices between the stones, including a complete collection of Selaginellas creeping amongst innumerable Ferns.

Lastly, dead trunks of trees, fixed in the ground by means of iron stakes to prevent them from falling as decomposition goes on, should be placed at the spots Nos. 8, 14, 18, 29, 52, 57, 69, and covered with tropical creepers and Epiphytes, and a whole collection of Bromeliaceæ, especially Tillandsia usneoides and Orchids. A short time will suffice for these to assume all the picturesque appearance they present in the tropics. Here ends our rough sketch of a warm winter-garden as it might and should be made.

A Cool Winter-garden.

We have given consideration to the laying-out of a winter-garden or conservatory for plants belonging to the warmer regions of the world, and have grouped together such representatives of tropical vegetation as can exist in the same atmosphere. Some greenhouse kinds which acquire larger dimensions under the influence of a more intense heat than they would in a cooler atmosphere, such as certain Palms, Aralias, etc., have been omitted. For instance, the Rice-paper plant, which grows in the open air in the south of France, acquires gigantic dimensions in a hothouse. A specimen of it, thus treated, measured thirteen feet two inches high, and threw out superb leaves, exceeding six feet six inches in length, including their stalks.

In most cases, nevertheless, the plants named for a greenhouse suffer under too high a temperature. Besides, the cool winter-garden is still more valuable than that just described, for, while it is as rich in ornamental specimens, it is more within the reach of moderate means. Very little artificial heat is enough to keep the temperature in winter at a minimum of three degrees above the freezing-point, which is quite sufficient for the period of repose required for many of the plants from Australia, China, Japan, New Zealand, and mountainous tropical regions. One can hardly believe with what numbers of plants, often supposed to belong to tropical climates, a cool conservatory can be furnished. Numbers of our beautiful Palms would flourish under cool treatment; and hundreds of Ferns require no better situation than the shelter of glass. The Dracænas, Agaves, Acacias, Dasylirions, Ficus, Aralias, Banksias, tender Conifers like the Norfolk Island Pine, Yuccas, Grevilleas, Rhopalas, and the Cactuses, would certainly submit to the same treatment, without mentioning the smaller kinds, which only thrive under a low winter-temperature.

The treatment carried out in reference to some tropical species has often no relation to the altitude at which the plants naturally grow. Should a plant arrive from Mexico, it would naturally be placed in a warm conservatory. But as regards the Ferns of that country, they are found between 3,600 and 6,000 feet above the sea-level, that is to say, at the limit where begin the Pines and

Heaths of the sub-alpine region; and it is at this height that the magnificent Alsophilas spring up.

More than thirty kinds of Palm now flourish in our cool houses. A great number grow in the cold regions of tropical mountains, such as the Ceroxylon andicola, which is found at 10,000 feet and upwards. Oreodoxa frigida, and several kinds of Chamædorea, reach as high as the Pine region; Areca humilis reaches to 8,000 feet in Java; Chamærops Martiana to 7,800 feet in Nepal; Phœnix humilis to 6,000 feet; without reckoning Chamærops excelsa of China, Rhapis flabelliformis of Japan, Corypha australis, and others.

Let us now proceed to plant a cool house on the plan already used in the case of a winter-garden. By the aid of the same series of numbers on the plan, we can at once show the different types of vegetation that may be used in each case. We will first give a list of climbing-plants, without which no such structure can be properly adorned :—

1. Rhynchospermum jasminoides
4. Plumbago scandens
7. Passiflora cærulea
9. Mikania scandens
12, 13. Solanum jasminoides
17. Cobæa scandens variegata
21. Thunbergia laurifolia
23. Kennedya violacea
25. Mandevilla suaveolens
27, 28, 30, 31. Senecio mikanioides
33. Tropæolum Spitfire
36. Passiflora edulis
38. Akebia quinata
41. Aristolochia sempervirens
44. Clianthus puniceus
46. Fuchsia coccinea
49. Lapageria rosea
53,54,58. Aristolochia ciliosa
60. Kennedya Maryattæ
62. Tropæolum speciosum
63. Tropæolum pentaphyllum
65. Bignonia Cherere
68, 71, 72. Tacsonia Van Volxemii
74. Lapageria alba
77. Hoya carnosa
80. Clianthus Dampieri

It must here be observed that, for a conservatory of the size named, the number of plants given would be too extensive, and would darken the house too much during winter. We only give the list entire for the use of a conservatory large enough to contain them; for example, from 100 to 150 feet in length, with a proportionate width and height.

The following is a list of plants with noble leaves, and of stately port, that thrive well in a cool house :—

67. Chamærops stauracantha
15. Chamærops excelsa
32. Corypha australis
56. Jubæa spectabilis
102. Sabal palmetto
105. Phœnix reclinata
95. Rhapis flabelliformis
93. Livistona sinensis
84. Seaforthia robusta
90. Oreodoxa frigida
173. Phœnix tenuis
168. Cocos Romanzoffii
159. Areca sapida
166. Glaziova elegantissima
154. Ceroxylon andicola
156. Calyptrogyne elata

149. Seaforthia elegans	137. Chamærops Martiana	95. Phœnix farinifera
134. Brahea dulcis	119. Phœnix sylvestris	105. Chamærops humilis
136. Seaforthia gracilis	105. Cocos australis	102. Brahea nitida.
142. Chamædorea glaucifolia		

Here, then, are twenty-six kinds of Palms, of varied stature, and perfectly suited to form a background of foliage of supreme elegance. We speak of such only as have been proved to succeed ; and if the altitudes at which they grow spontaneously are compared, it will be seen that a conservatory with a minimum of 38° Fahr. is all that they require. It is known that for every six hundred feet of altitude above the sea, the mean temperature decreases one degree. But if we take, as is generally done, the mean temperature of the tropics as 80° at the sea-level, at 6,000 feet it would be only 65°, and at 10,000 feet, 50°, which is equal to the mean temperature of Southern England. It is not, therefore, very extraordinary that the Palms of these high regions, the Chamærops excelsa, for instance, can live out-of-doors in those climates where they have nothing to fear but exceptional winters. If we have not certain data as to this mode of culture, it is because Palm-trees have hitherto been too costly to risk their sacrifice in the open air. The Cycads, although generally less hardy than the Palms above named, are still available for the conservatory, where a low temperature for a short time would not be prejudicial, though they would suffer by prolongation of that temperature. Thus we would advise the following specimens to be planted :—

85. Bowenia spectabilis	169. Encephalartos Alten-	134. Dion edule
96. Cycas revoluta	steini	120. Zamia australis.

Among the Tree-ferns, the following are suitable for the cool winter-garden :—

124. Alsophila australis	116. Alsophila ornata	170. Cyathea dealbata
82. Blechnum brasiliense	140. Balantium antarcti-	151. Todea australis
	cum	

With plenty of space one might add :—

Alsophila excelsa	C. spectabile	Lomaria cycadifolia
Balantium Culcita	Cyathea medullaris	L. gibba
B. Sellowianum	C. Smithii	L. discolor
Blechnum rio-grandense	Dicksonia fibrosa	L. magellanica.
Cibotium regale	D. squarrosa	

COOL CONSERVATORY WITH VEGETATION PLANTED OUT

The following plants, though not so important, deserve a place by the side of these, such as :—

106. Cordyline indivisa
97. Aspidistra elatior
98. Podocarpus Totara
99. Clivia cyrtanthiflora
100. Correa cardinalis
101. Farfugium grande

104. Eucalyptus viminalis
109. Elæagnus undulata
108. Clivia nobilis
107. Camellia japonica, var.
86. Erythrina Marie Bell-
    anger

92. Edwardsia grandiflora
91. Sparmannia africana
87. Ligularia Kæmpferi
83. Brugmansia sanguinea
81. Daphne delphini

To make intervening spaces a little ornamental, any number of less important plants could be added. We next come to plants for decorating the beds of the central portion. For the grass-plot may be taken :—

174. Pancratium mexica-
     num
172. Aspidistra elatior va-
     riegata
171. Agave Verschaffelti
112. Phormium Colensoi
111. Philesia buxifolia
110. Macleayia cordata
113. Linum trigynum
114. Eucalyptus giganteus
115. Aralia Sieboldii
117. Skimmia oblata
117. Rubus rosæflorus
118. Thuiopsis dolabrata

121. Rhododendron Jen-
     kinsii
122. Araucaria excelsa
128. Lomaria gibba
130. Beaucarnea tubercu-
     lata
137. Crowea saligna
143. Aspidium Bellangeri
139. Stadmannia australis
142. Mimosa cultiformis
141. Sparmannia africana
135. Eucalyptus giganteus
134. Thea viridis

144. Platycerium grande
145. Senecio platanifolia
146. Nephrolepis exaltata
148. Dracæna Rumphii
150. Pteris cretica albo-
     lineata
153. Agnostus sinuatus
152. Cyrtomium falcatum
155. Acacia dealbata
158. Pimelea elegans
157. Littæa gracilis
165. Senecio Ghiesbreghtii
164. Musa Ensete

Plants between the borders and the glass may consist of :—

2. Wigandia urens
5. Yucca aloifolia tricolor
5. Woodwardia radicans
6. Viburnum suspensum
8. Xanthorrhœa hastilis or
   Phormium tenax
10. Veronica Andersoni va-
    riegata
11. Acacia lineata
14. Abutilon striatum
16. Hibiscus rosa-sinensis
18. Aralia pubescens
19. Senecio Ghiesbreghtii
20. Nicotiana wigandioides
22. Bambusa Fortuni va-
    riegata

24. Viburnum Arrafuski
29. Magnolia fuscata
34. Aralia dactylifolia
35. Ficus macrophylla
37. Templetonia retusa
39. Siphocampylus Hum-
    boldtianus
40. Solanum Warszewiczii
42. Montagnea heraclifolia
43. Clivia miniata
47. Rogeria gratissima
48. Rhododendron Gibsoni
51. Rhopala australis
52. Rhododendron Nuttalli
57. Pleroma elegans
55. Podocarpus zamiæfolia

59. Phyllocactus Aker-
    manni
61. Fuchsia var.
64. Aralia nerifolia
66. Osmanthus ilicifolius
69. Oreopanax platani-
    folium
70. Bocconia frutescens
73. Helianthus major
75. Aralia papyrifera
76. Hebeclinium macro-
    phyllum
78. Hedychium gardneri-
    anum
79. Desfontainea spinosa

The Palms for a winter-garden ought to be kept in pots up to the period when their leaves divide and show their character, and their stems become at their base as thick as a man's arm. They must not be put in the ground before this, nor until they have been frequently repotted and kept as much as possible in a warm greenhouse where the pots have been plunged in tan. They should be repotted twice a year, in spring and summer, when their growth is rapid, without cutting the roots, and in deep narrow pots. A warm atmosphere, somewhat shady, but without stagnant moisture, is best suited to Palms when young.

A great number of the plants will remain uninjured in the cool winter-garden if frost is kept out; but it is better, as has been already said, to keep up the winter temperature a little over the freezing-point; and even when the sun strikes upon the glass raising the temperature, it will not be necessary to open the house at all during the winter. After February, however, when vegetation is getting active, it will be necessary to give air gradually, and in the evening, to give water. In March we must begin to shade with some light material up to the time that we can uncover the greater part of the conservatory, and perhaps place some of the plants in pots or boxes in the open air. As to the great Palms and Tree-ferns, Dracænas, Aralias, etc., they will be better slightly shaded throughout the year, taking care to give plenty of air. Where it could be done easily, it would be desirable to remove the roof and allow the contents to be refreshed by the summer rains. Plants easily moved, and of fine habit, may be removed to the open garden, where they will be more enjoyable during the hot months than in any house; many of them are all the better for making their principal growth in the open air. Thus managed, with plenty of water and a proper amount of shade, it is very possible to develop beautiful tropical vegetation in such a structure.

As for Orchids, hothouse Ferns, and other stove-plants, which do not bear the temperature of the conservatory without injury, an arrangement might be readily made by which they also could be enjoyed in this structure. A conservatory heated to stove-temperature would be unpleasant to many, while the heat of the temperate house is agreeable to our senses. The best way to secure means for displaying tender Orchids and other plants in the conservatory, is by making a closely-glazed case therein fitted up with rustic shelves. In this might be placed any Orchids, choice Ferns, or not over-large stove-plants that come in flower in winter, spring, and autumn, and by interspersing them with the choicer dwarf fine-leaved plants so common of late in our stoves, a welcome feature would be added to the conservatory. As the plants would only remain in this case during their period of flowering, and fine foliaged plants perhaps a few weeks longer, the position of the case as to light matters little. Against the back or some other wall of the house is of course the best position; and if there be an arched recess, it might be taken advantage of. To heat a little boiler sufficiently to keep any desired temperature in the case would be easy, and to do it with gas would be convenient to many. To make the wall and the shelves in this case of a rustic character is a good and tasteful plan; they should be studded with Moss, which if kept moist will give off the vapour so congenial to stove-plants, and the windows or folding-doors should be fitted with single sheets of glass, kept clear at all times. It would be easy to induce the common Lycopodium, seedling Ferns, and miniature stove Mosses to crowd over the back wall and indeed on every rocky surface in the case, or even to grow on turves placed along the front shelves.

The Plant Decoration of Apartments.

The graceful custom of growing plants in dwelling-rooms is very much more prevalent on the Continent than in England. It is true that we often see a display of flowering-plants in rooms, though rarely subjects distinguished by beauty of form, or adapted for culture indoors. But the day is approaching when the value of graceful plants as house-ornaments will be recognised. That the substitution of life and changeful interest for much that is without these qualities, will prove a gain, few will doubt. Apart altogether from their effect as ornaments, what can more agreeably introduce us to the study of plant life? Rooms are often overcrowded with ornaments, many of them representations of natural objects; but in the case of the plants we may, without inconvenience, enjoy the natural objects themselves.

Those we employ for this purpose now are mostly such as cannot be preserved in health for any length of time in living-rooms. If in addition to the best of these we select handsome-leaved plants of a leathery texture, accustomed to withstand the temperature of hot countries, we shall find that the dry and dusty air of a living-room is not at all injurious to them, and that it is quite easy to keep them in health for months and even for years in the same apartment. The variety of form and grace of outline which many of these plants possess, is very great. Many of them are exotics, rarely seen in England out of stoves, while about Paris they are sold in abundance for the decoration of apartments. The widely-spread taste for plants in rooms explains the prevalence of these graceful plants in Paris gardens and flowershops. The number of Dracænas cultivated in and around Paris is enormous, one Versailles nurseryman annually raising from 5000 to 6000 plants of the bright-leaved Dracæna terminalis alone, by far the greater part being for room-decoration. Among the newer species of Dracænas—not alluding to the coloured-leaved kinds—are some that combine grace with stateliness as few other plants do. They are useful for the centres of massive groups of plants in their larger forms, while the smaller species may be advantageously associated with the Maidenhair Fern and small flowering-plants. They are of the greatest utility in these decorations, and are largely used in all parts. Young Palms are also cultivated to a surprising extent about Paris, and so are all graceful-leaved plants from the Cycads to the common trailing Ivy,—used a good deal to make living screens of.

The following few notes on the principal plants which serve for window and room decoration in Paris are by M. A. Chantin, a cultivator of plants for these purposes on a large scale, and the possessor of a very rich collection of Palms and other exotics. Of these the Palms are without doubt the most important, and are most generally used, because of their hardy character and moderate price. Among the very best are the Fan-palms— Chamærops humilis and excelsa. Corypha australis, although now but little known as a house-plant, is destined in a short time to occupy a foremost place in the decoration of apartments. It is conspicuous for its peculiar beauty, and the number of its leaves, and is, I believe, the most hardy and enduring of all the

Palms for indoor-culture. Cocos coronata and flexuosa are very elegant, and produce a charming effect. Latania borbonica is certainly one of the most valuable plants of this family, as much for the deep yet fresh green of its leaves as for its hardiness and elegant appearance. Phœnix dactylifera, leonensis, and reclinata are very much sought after, and are highly esteemed, as are also Areca alba, lutescens, and rubra.

The following Palms could be used with great advantage in the decoration of apartments; but their high price and great rarity cause them to be not much known, although they accommodate themselves to the atmosphere of rooms as well as any of those previously mentioned. Areca sapida, most of the species of the genus Caryota, Chamædorea amazonica and elatior, Chamærops Palmetto, Elæis guineensis, Euterpe edulis, with its finely-serrated and very graceful foliage; Oreodoxa regia, young plants of which are very frequently used; Phœnix pumila, Phœnix tenuis, Thrinax argentea and elegans, Rhapis flabelliformis, and Leopoldina pulchra.

Next in importance to the Palms we must place the Dracænas. Those which are the most frequently noticed are Dracæna australis, cannæfolia, congesta, indivisa, indivisa lineata, rubra, stricta, terminalis, and umbraculifera. Those most easily managed, and therefore the most popular for window-ornaments, are Dracæna congesta, rubra, and terminalis. Pandanus utilis, amaryllifolius Vandermeerschi, and javanicus variegatus; Cycas revoluta, and varieties of Aspidistra, occupy also a very important place in the decoration of apartments.

The plants composing the following list, although suitable and distinct in appearance, require somewhat more care and attention than the preceding. Several species of Aralia, more especially Aralia Sieboldii; Bambusa japonica variegata and B. fortunei variegata; the different varieties of Begonia; most of the Bromelias, Billbergias, and allied families are very useful, including the variegated Pine-apple, which forms a splendid object for placing in large warm rooms on special occasions. Caladium odorum, for winter decoration, and the species with the beautifully-spotted and mottled leaves, for the summer; Carludovica palmata and plicata; Croton in variety, Curculigo recurvata, and several species of the genus Dieffenbachia. Ficus elastica is a capital plant for

window-ornament, and some years ago was very much employed
for that purpose; but since it has become somewhat common,
Ficus Chauvieri has been substituted for it in many places.
There are many other Ficuses which are suitable for this purpose,
and will be found most useful when they become plentiful enough.
Maranta zebrina is the only species of Maranta suitable for
cultivation in apartments, as all the other species should be grown
and kept in the houses, and only carried indoors when extra
attractions are desired for special occasions. Several species of
Musa are favourites, but principally M. discolor and M. rosea;
Musa Ensete is particularly suitable for room-culture. Monstera
deliciosa was much sought after during recent winters, and has in
most places thriven so well that it has given general satisfaction.
Several varieties of Beaucarnea are suitable for rooms, and
produce a very beautiful and graceful effect when grown in
suspended vases or baskets. Rhopala corcovadense is a plant that
exhales a somewhat disagreeable odour, but it is nevertheless much
in favour on account of its very elegant and graceful appearance during the development of its young leaves. Hecktia
pitcairnifolia is excellent for suspending in baskets. Tradescantia
discolor, Phormium tenax, Rhododendrons, Camellias, Grevillea
robusta, Euonymus, Aucubas, Bonapartea, Agaves, variegated
Yuccas, etc., are also frequent. In addition to the common
Saxifraga sarmentosa, which is frequently seen with its slender
runners pendent from window-baskets in England, sev.ral other
allied species would prove equally useful in the same way—
Saxifraga Fortunei variegata, and S. cuscutæformis, for example.

The family of Ferns, although classed among plants with
delicate tissues, and having a great dislike to dry hot atmo-
spheres, nevertheless furnishes numerous examples which, with
careful management, add very much to the beauty of apartments.
Thus I have very frequently remarked several species of Adiantum,
which wherever they can be preserved in good health, produce a
most pleasing effect. Pteris argyræa, P. cretica albo lineata, and
P. serrulata variegata likewise produce a good effect with their
prettily-marked fronds. Alsophila australis and Dicksonia an-
tarctica are also sometimes employed for decorative purposes in
rooms of large dimensions, where their magnificent appearance
never fails to produce a pleasing impression. Nephrolepis

exaltata is universally useful, and withstands the air of rooms without the slightest injury.

Experience has shown me that Orchids may be introduced into a drawing-room with perfect success, the plants not having suffered in the least by the change of atmosphere. The most suitable are the various species of Cattleya, Vanda, Aerides, and Cypripedium. Doubtless the time is not far distant when we may venture to try many more kinds than we can now afford to do; but even from what we have already done in that way, I entertain no doubt that the Orchid family will eventually furnish the most valuable of all plants for room-decoration. True, they may not live throughout the year in rooms as Ficuses and such plants do, but that is not desirable—their appearance, as a rule, not being prepossessing when out of flower. The quality that they do possess, and that which makes them so valuable, is the thick succulent texture of the flowers generally. This enables them to continue a long time in bloom in a room, and a like kind of texture enables the leaves to stand during the blooming-time without injury.

We ourselves are foremost so far as flowering-plants are concerned, ours being as a rule better grown. One plant, however, cultivated in great abundance around Paris for winter-blooming, is well worthy of increased attention—Epiphyllum truncatum. There are several varieties, and they certainly form most beautiful objects on dull December days. The employment of simple materials is also to be commended. Thus the variegated form of the common Roast-beef plant—Iris fœtidissima—may be seen occasionally used with good effect. We mostly use hot-country plants if we want those that live long in our dwelling-rooms, but this is a true hardy native which well deserves culture indoors. It forms a very pretty plant for room-decoration, requires none but the most ordinary attention, and is easily obtained. In France the plant is rather commonly used as an edging. The Acanthuses too, and particularly A. lusitanicus, used so effectively out-of-doors, are also grown abundantly in rooms, where they do very well.

A sketch here given shows Acanthus latifolius, as grown in a window, but no drawing could represent its superb health and the deep untiring gloss of its fine leaves as they are seen from the street.   The specimen figured was sketched from before the window of a restaurant in the Champs Elysées, where it has not only grown for years but flowered vigorously.   It is quite a hardy plant, but no tropical one is more beautiful in form or colour of foliage.   It is the most valuable of large-leaved room-plants, and far more so than the long popular Ficus elastica, because it is hardy and the easiest of culture in a cool room.   It will be found perfectly at home in cool rooms and halls where no artificial heat is applied.   The plant figured grows in a wooden box in the window.   Everything proved to do well indoors without the protection of a case is a gain to those who wish to grow plants in rooms.

Acanthus latifolius in Window in Paris.

CHAPTER XVI.

A FEW NOTES ON PRIVATE GARDENS.

Wreath of Wistaria above Ivy—(by Roadside, Vincennes to Montreuil).

THE contrast between French and English country life is strongly marked, and nowhere more so than in the garden. The effect of the love of gardens and trees in England is to make the country the most beautiful on earth —parts blighted by smoke and cinders not included. The explanation of the unrivalled charms of rural England is found in the groves that make the landscape lovely with their clouds of verdure and varied forms. The best-cultivated parts of Belgium and France are devoid of such charms from the absence of trees. The streets of many fine continental towns are as arid as a barrack-yard from the same cause. Gardening abroad, as with us, has received a great impetus within the past score of years; in France this is mainly seen in the gardens of the middle-class. In the homes of the old families in France we see no such evidence of love for the art as we have at home; and richly-stored or otherwise remarkable gardens are not so common as with us.   Frequently the chateau-garden is a dismal exhibition of the absurdities of the old school of landscape-gardeners.   Lime and other trees shorn into the form of walls; dreary expanses of gravelled surface; endless straight avenues instead of open spaces where the breezes might play with the grass; crumbling fountain-basins suggestive of mouldering tombs; often an Orangery reminding one of the time when the Orange was our only greenhouse-plant; and statues that one wishes buried with those who carved them.   There are exceptions, and many, but even in the best there is a great deal more of the zoological element that one cares to have in an English garden. The aviary, too, is often disagreeably conspicuous, and the water-fowl plentiful enough to destroy the beauty of the water.   The buildings—hoary with time, and frequently interesting as regards architecture—are seldom surrounded by noble trees.   The absence of these is frequently accounted for by the destruction through wars, especially round Paris, though the stupid practice of lopping has much to answer for.   A revolution in this respect is as much wanted in many gardens in France, as ever it was politically in that country.   The admirable culture that one notices in the market-gardens round Paris and some other cities, is rarely seen in the ordinary chateau-garden, which seldom looks so well cultivated as an average English kitchen-garden.   A few well-trained trees, however, are always to be seen.   The art of training and grafting fruit-trees with ease, seems now to be as deeply engrained into the French as the art of making soup.

It is in the gardens of the middle-class that we may best judge of French gardening.   The merit of these is that they are not wholly sacrificed to the demon of bedding-out, but often contain a variety of plant-form and flowers; they are frequently fresh and pretty in winter, and laid out without the horrid pattern-beds which make the sight of so many gardens far from soothing. In large gardens at home, wise people sometimes get a little freedom from the tormenting beds that have been the worthless stock-in-trade of the landscape-gardener for centuries; small gardens are nearly always ruined by these.   A bed, in the sense of a body of well-prepared soil, is essential in gardens; but it is not necessary that beds should take ugly forms.   The best preparation needed for shrubs or flowers may be hidden beneath the green turf. When men come to see the meaning of real gardening, they will laugh at the endless weary strainings after patterns in beds. They will not admire a garden that is laid out as men used to design wall-paper; now better things are expected of wall-paper designers. Here is an engraving of a little garden on the banks of the Seine near Courbevoie, and in it there are no beds at all in the central parts. With its varied trees and shrubs,

A Paris Garden not spoiled by Beds.

and masses of Rhododendrons against the house, and deep green fence of Irish Ivy, it is quite charming even through the winter. In such a garden one may have as much variety of flowers as may be desired, and one of the ways of best attaining this end is by having groups of beds, simple in outline, a little way from the central scene. All the really fine hardy plants, from Tritomas to Grasses and Yuccas, may be planted to best effect in good ground, but not in formal beds. Where a geometrical series of beds is desired, they certainly will also be best on one side in a quiet nook, and not in the centre of, and dominating, all.

Borders of Ivy, sometimes with great roguish-looking Pansies inside them; well-developed isolated plants, like Yuccas or Acanthus; Ivy bowers; lawns, open and fresh, if small; Pomegranates with coral blossoms; Wistaria wreathed in many ways; lovely straggling of Vines about the walls; Roses often on their own roots, and too often on broom-sticks; noble standard Evergreen Magnolias; groups of tree and herbaceous Peonies on the grass; and graceful tufts of hardy Bamboo, also add to the charms of these little gardens, which are often very quiet and lovely, and which though small have a dignified air, and contain a variety of beautiful life. The walls are nearly all garlanded with creepers, often with a half-wild look through luxuriant

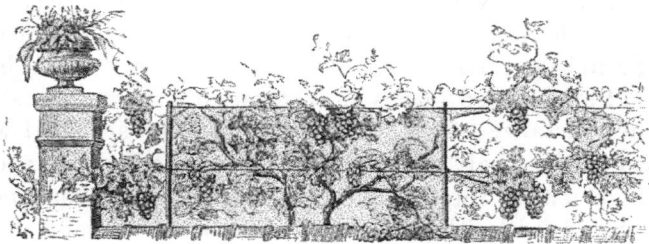

Trellis for Vines on Top of Dead Wall (Vincennes).

growth. So long as we have dead walls, some means of modifying their severity is desirable. In landscape-gardening the dead wall is a serious obstacle to deal with, and so it is in the small garden. In these, however, there is sometimes a necessity for the dead wall as a dividing-line or a screen, whereas in large country-places they are often made where they are needless and objectionable. In small gardens the dead walls, usually bare along the top, may be gracefully wreathed with either climbing-shrubs or fruit-trees, as shown in the accompanying cut. Single stems are easily taken up the wall and trailed along two or three firmly-fixed but slender galvanised wires. In this way much of the harsh aspect of the upper part of the wall is removed. The sketch given was made on the road from Vincennes to Montreuil, a country in which good Grapes are gathered on the trellis; ornamental subjects for such places are numerous enough from Wistaria to Clematis montana.

In Paris there are, besides the suburban gardens, numerous pretty gardens in the city itself, of one of which, thanks to the courtesy of its owner, Madame Haine, an illustration is here given. Enclosed by high walls and buildings, with large trees, a lawn of freshest grass, Acanthuses and Yuccas on the turf, bold Pansies in masses, carpets of the ever welcome Ivy and the Periwinkle beneath the trees, and numerous Wallflowers, it had, on the April day when sketched, many charms not usually associated with crowded cities. In Paris one frequently finds an oasis of trees and flowers and grass hidden by high buildings from the noisy street. In such nooks, finer trees are often found than grow in the public squares. Paris is far richer than London in these pleasant city-gardens. Some town-gardens in London, such as that of Montagu House, may be named as examples of what a town-garden may be made even in London, but they are too rare. The main blemish in the small French gardens is the water, which never ought to be present at all in such places in a so-called ornamental state. It is another instance of the futility of forming artificial water in any form in the small garden, and it is wonderful that people can tolerate cemented tubs of unclean water in spots that might be wholly beautiful with flowers and grass. Cement-margined puddles of this sort, and larger, abound, sometimes associated with very droll rock-work. Sometimes, on the other hand, a little rock-garden is fairly well constructed, but contrasted with the vilest margin of black asphalte to the water-basin.

A disagreeable feature of the Paris garden is the mirror-globe, which is a burnished nuisance in so many otherwise pleasant gardens. I once hoped that this object would never be introduced to English gardens, but lately a very large one was seen in one of our new provincial parks. Lately also a misguided gentleman in the north-western district of London, not content with one or two of these mirror-globes, made himself an avenue of them of various colours. Each huge globe rests on a terra-cotta vase, and the avenue on each side, from the gate to the house, is bordered by vases with mirror-globes. The effect is as good as could be desired for a Shoreditch theatre. Such an object may perhaps amuse children, but surely one is merely expressing the sentiments of all lovers of English gardens, in saying that a globe-mirror is one of the most offensive objects that can be placed in a garden.

The picturesque style of gardening as seen round Paris is mainly distinguished by its tempestuous undulations. Even in the Champs Elysées every patch of turf is waved up and down in the most violent manner, and very often it is so in the little gardens. The adjacent level lines of roadway, footway, or

A Town-garden in Paris.

buildings, contrasting abruptly as they do with all this, show its artificial character at once. When valleys are traced through bits of turf not much larger than a dining-room floor, and surrounded by wide level walks, we get the puerile instead of the picturesque. One might as well attempt to diversify the surface of a dinner-table. In addition, the undulations are stiffly and badly carried out—scarcely an easy, natural gradation is seen.

Sir Richard Wallace's garden at Bagatelle, in the Bois de

Boulogne, offers, in this respect, a pleasing contrast to the many places in which the above-named blemish is conspicuous. Here we have broad easy glades, so gently, though artificially, hollowed, that they rarely suggest the artificial or the incongruous. Here, too, may be seen successful attempts to epen-up charming views, both in the garden, and from it into the surrounding country. Happiest of the features, however, is the way these glades and vistas are planted. Instead of the usual plum-pudding-like mixture everywhere, we have small groves of distinct trees, with turf spreading beneath them, and natural-looking groups of different kinds, and sometimes a cluster of one kind only. There is not a trace of the dot-a-tree-everywhere system, by which so many garden-landscapes are spoiled. Open breezy turf-carpets abound, and afford a foreground from which the various beauties of trees or

The Degradation of Water (in small Garden near Vincennes).

shrubs or landscape may be seen to advantage from the different points of view. Groups of Yuccas are effective here; also groups in threes of various Tree-peonies and other vigorous hardy plants. Many of the older trees, with high stems, are clad with a mantle of Ivy, which, however, is confined to the bole only. Where a number of tall trees thus covered occur, one may sometimes fancy (seeing only Ivy-clad boles) that it is an evergreen-grove, the heads of the deciduous trees being high overhead. Two large groups of artificial rock here are more successful than they generally are in France; both are gracefully embellished with suitable plants, and so well supported with masses of trees and shrubs that they have a picturesque effect in the grounds. Here, however, as in other places, no attempt is made to grow the true Alpine plants in or near these inviting positions; that is work for the future. Where there is so much to praise, one may venture to point out that the artificial water here, as in too many gardens, is rather too much after the duck-pond pattern—too abrupt in its margins, and too near the house. With a graceful bend of the Seine glistening through one of the vistas, it would have been wiser to dispense with artificial water. Such contrasts remind us of the full moon and stars calmly shining down on a Bond-street illumination.

It has long been a fashion with continental lovers of gardening to employ Englishmen to form their gardens; and, among those so formed, there is none more remarkable than Paxton's work at Ferrières, the seat of Baron Rothschild, which is an oasis amid the dreary fields of this part of France. The house, as well as the grounds and almost everything about the place, was the work of Englishmen, and the gardens show an instructive mixture of the best features of the horticulture of both countries. The house is, of course, fortified with a terrace-garden, but this is not too extensive nor overdone with " bedding-out." On its steps, one day, Jules Favre met Bismarck, when he went to plead in vain the cause of prostrate France. The king and Bismarck had their quarters here when the Germans overran the plains around, and gave orders that not a hand was to be laid on anything. Had it been otherwise, the specimen Wellingtonias might have suffered the ignoble fate of thousands of fine garden-trees around Paris during the siege. Probably the finest Orangery in any private garden in France is here, and the Orangery-system of cultivating plants is here seen in its best aspect. Nothing can exceed the health and beauty of the specimens grown in enormous but well-designed tubs, and standing so close together that the dense heads touch, and one seems in an Orange-grove. In addition to the many Orange-trees, there are superb pyramidal Myrtles, nearly twenty feet high, in tubs ; numbers of tubs of the New Zealand Flax and large specimens of the Australasian Araucarias, which do well treated thus. The plan of planting-out Palms and many other fine-foliaged plants in a large house, and with an eye to picturesque effect, is here well carried out, and the effect very good at all seasons. The fresh green Lycopodium denticulatum forms, as usual, the turf of the small landscape in which the flowers look so well. Among trees, good specimens of the weeping Sophora are employed with fine effect near the water at Ferrières. Perhaps

s

its slow growth with us prevents it from being more frequently seen in our gardens.   The remarkable and well-managed fruit-garden here is alluded to in another part of this book.

An unhappy feature is a formal margin of stones around the water, somewhat similar to, but smaller than, that which now disfigures a part of the ornamental water in the Regent's Park.   The individual who causes a neat little barricade of stone to be built around a piece of ornamental water may have genius, but certainly not for landscape-gardening.   The very line of beauty, so to say, where the turf might slope easily down to kiss the water, or the wavelets play amongst a fringe of Forget-me-nots or Arrow-heads, finished off like a manure-tank !   It is too bad.   The line of kerb-stones placed along the margin of the Serpentine, is another " improvement " of the same type.   As a protection to the edge from the action of the water, such things are never of any real use, and, in the case of the Serpentine, the water is frequently below the kerb-stones.   The best margins for artificial water are sand or turf, and, if these are disturbed by the action of the wavelets, they will certainly be more appropriate in their worst condition than cement, bricks, flints, or kerb-stones.

Baroness Rothschild's garden at Boulogne is too extensive and remarkable to be passed over.   From a landscape-gardening point of view the grounds at both sides of the house are more than usually well disposed, there being plenty of open lawns and a variety of good views, particularly on what is called the English side, where there is a considerable space devoted to lawns, water, and shady groves.   On this English side there is a terrace-garden against the house, which, though needless perhaps in its position, has the merit of not being overdone or prolonged into the green garden to its detriment.   On this terrace, strange to say, there are no flower-beds—simply grass and walks—what flowers there are being in jardinières or vases.   From each end of this terrace extends one of those formal shady groves so common in France. The water is well formed and adorned in one part with little rocky islets very naturally constructed, and over which scramble briars and other trailing and wild plants.   A beautiful scene is formed in one part of the gardens by the rich tropical vegetation of the stoves grouped in picturesque masses under trees, the plants comprising Tree-ferns, Giant Cacti, numerous handsome

Dracænas, the large-leaved Musa, New Zealand Flax, and many of the very finest tropical and sub-tropical plants, arranged on high sloping banks.

From among them rise the stems of the native and garden trees which shade and shelter the tenderer plants beneath. These are arranged so that nothing but the beauty of the plants and foliage is observed, the pots, tubs, etc. necessary in the case of such tender subjects being concealed. These plants are placed out-of-doors in early summer, when all danger of frost is over, and are taken in about the end of September. Many of them make free growth in the open air, all are cleansed and refreshed by the summer-rains, and are thus in a better state for passing the winter than if they had made their growth in the hothouses in summer. This system merits considerable attention, inasmuch as plants cannot be so much enjoyed in the hothouses in summer and autumn as in the open air arranged as described. As carried out here, this grouping of the rich collection of plants, and the effect generally obtained, are the most picturesque and satisfactory I have ever seen afforded by tropical plants in a northern country. Here, cut off from the picturesque or English part of the gardens, is a " French garden " well formed, and perhaps the largest and best of its kind. That style of garden means straight walks, straight borders, and rigidity in general plan as well as in details. It is effective but formal, and takes up much space which might be disposed in a simpler and more artistic manner. Notable here were huge plants or masses of New Zealand Flax in large vases. This plant is invaluable for many purposes in ornamental gardening. In the great court before the principal entrance is a little garden in the centre, formed by gigantic Orange-trees in tubs, and other evergreens. This is a good idea, giving as it does a little privacy, and forming a small oasis of verdure in what would otherwise be a very bare and arid space. The most beautiful weeping-tree I have ever seen is here, a large specimen of Gleditschia Bojoti, the leaves divided like a delicate Fern, and the tree giving a shade as light as the Cloud-grass. It does not weep formally and regularly like some other trees, but in an irregular and picturesque manner, while it is free in growth and large in stature. There is a graceful way of training Climbing-roses over old stumps and old trees, which here leads to some very pretty effects.

The great gardens of the Rothschilds and like places, however, must not be taken as representative of the chateau-gardens generally, in which not so much attention is bestowed on the gardens as in England. Circumstances have placed gardening for pleasure and planting in a more advanced condition in our country than in any other. We have got further away from the ideas that led to lopping trees into the forms of coffee-pots than any other people. We have much to do and much to abolish yet. But our privilege of leading the van in this way should incite us to greater exertion still in the cause of progress ; to make the garden more and more a conservatory of beautiful natural objects ; to abolish unmeaning line-gyrations and formality, so that our garden-galleries may be fitted for the reception of the living, changing pictures we may have in them.

A garden horror; the mirror-globe.

CHAPTER XVII.

THE SCHOOL OF HORTICULTURE AT VERSAILLES.

THE once royal and imperial kitchen-garden at Versailles is at last turned into a school of gardening. It is the most suitable spot that could have been obtained about Paris for the purpose. The scheme seems to have been carefully considered, and in all ways deserves success. On visiting some of the suburbs round Paris, places which only a few years ago, immediately after the war, were scenes of what seemed irreparable desolation, we strangers may well be surprised at the great change that has taken place for the better; not only are traces of the destruction wrought by the war unseen, but the gardens and fields look better cultivated than they were before. This result is largely owing to the skill in market-garden-culture and fruit-growing common about Paris and taught in such places as this. It is gratifying to see such minute attention bestowed on the new school of gardening at Versailles, though the burdens of the country prevent its being liberally endowed. This and similar institutions cannot fail to further improve the horticulture and add to the real wealth of the land.

The fruit- and forcing-gardens at Versailles form a large establishment, not so costly nor nearly so fine as those at Frogmore, but containing much that is instructive to the visitor. Generally the crops do not display the high cultivation nor the surface the rapid rotation to be seen in the market-gardens round Paris, but in the culture of hardy fruits there is something to learn. It is a forcing-, culinary, and fruit-garden mainly.

The hardy fruit-growing department is undergoing a gradual and complete alteration, especially as regards the choicer Pears trained as espaliers. So satisfactory is the system adopted, that if English cultivators generally could get an idea of its excellence it would lead to a revolution in our fruit-culture, and a great improvement in the appearance of our gardens.

There is no way whereby we may so highly improve the garden-culture of the Pear as by paying more attention to it as an espalier-tree. It is well known that some Pears suffer in quality by being grown against walls. It is equally certain that a fuller degree of sun and exposure than the shoots and fruit get on a pyramidal tree is very desirable in many parts of this country, especially for particular kinds. Many sorts grow beautifully as pyramids; others, to be had in perfection, must be grown upon walls; but by means of the improved espalier system the majority of the finer kinds may be grown to the highest degree of excellence. The French can certainly give us a lesson we may well profit by, as to the improved appearance, cheapness, and utility of the espalier mode of growing fruit, especially as regards the finer varieties of Pears.

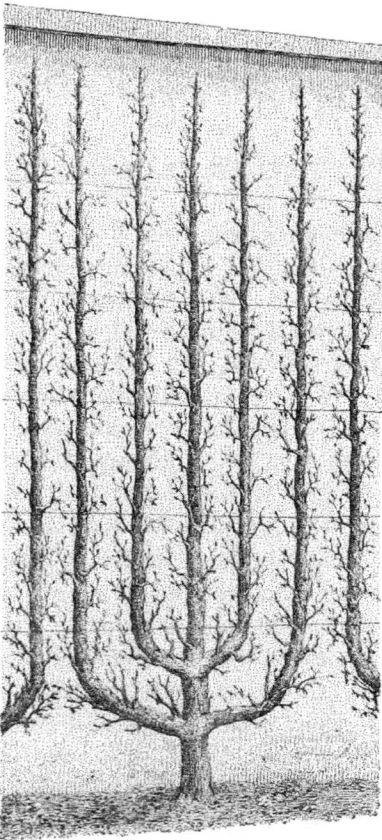

Wall Pear-tree with vertical branches ; ten years planted

Nothing can be uglier or more inefficient than the usual mode of training espaliers in our gardens. It is generally so costly and disagreeable to the eye that in many gardens it has been done away with for these reasons alone. In many instances the espalier-supports are the most unworkmanlike things to be seen, consisting as they do of rough uprights of wood, which soon rot and wabble out of position; thick and costly bolt-like wire, making the whole a cumbrous and expensive construction. The form of tree used, too,

PROFIT AND ORNAMENT ON SURFACES USUALLY BARE.

Outhouse covered with Plum-trees at Versailles. Photographed by Jules Lemercier in April 1877; drawn and engraved exactly after the photograph.

is such that the lower branches become impoverished, and often nearly useless.

To support his espalier fruit-trees M. Hardy, the head of the School of Horticulture, has largely adopted a system which is at

once cheap, neat, and almost everlasting. Instead of employing
ugly and perishable wooden supports he erects uprights of T-iron,
and connects these with slender galvanised wire. These are
tightened with *raidisseurs*, without difficulty. He erects this
trellising nine feet high for less than a shilling a yard run;
but it could not be done so cheaply in small quantities. Then,
instead of adopting the common form of espalier-tree, with

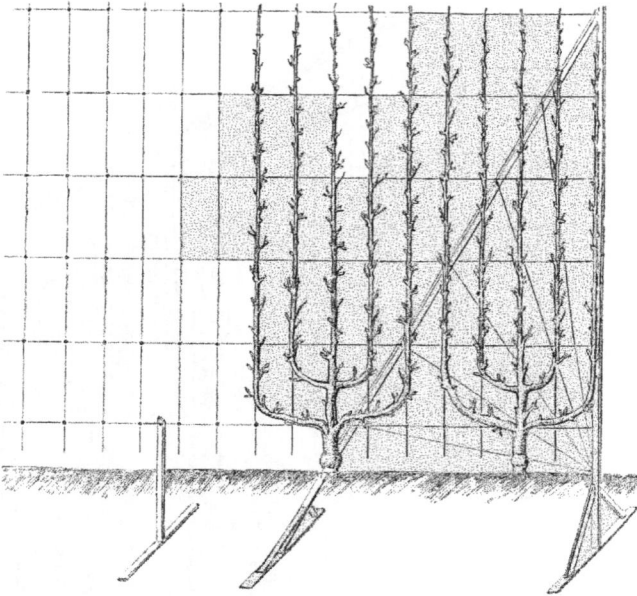

TRELLIS FOR PEAR-TREES : TEN FEET HIGH.

Uprights and stays of T-iron; horizontal lines, slender galvanised wire; ver-
tical lines, pine-wood rods half an inch square and painted green : to these
the ascending branches are trained.

horizontal branches, he more frequently plants trees of which the
branches ascend directly towards the top of the trellis. The
accompanying figures will give a better idea of both trellis and
tree than any description. There is no more important matter
connected with our fruit-culture than this. Those who give their
attention to this system will be led to adopt it, and will much
improve their fruit-culture. The finest stores of Pears to be seen
anywhere are to be found in those French gardens in which a good

length of tree has been trained in this manner. In few places in France is the espalier system so extensively and so well carried out as here. The form here represented is much better than the cordon or single-branched Pear-tree, because a more free and natural development is allowed to the tree: at the same time the

View of portion of square devoted to double espaliers of Pear-trees at Versailles.

trellis is covered quickly, and a considerable variety of fruit may be obtained from a small space. It is very extensively adopted by M. Hardy. upon walls as well as on the neat trellis, of which he has constructed so much. Of course the Palmette Verrier, the fan, or any other form may be trained on these trellises, but decidedly the best of them are such as combine the advantages of

quickness of growth and early productiveness claimed for the
cordon, with the fuller development and natural appearance of the
larger forms.   It should be borne in mind that planting erect
cordons close together, as they must be planted, involves an
amount of expense which is avoided by using trees which have
been allowed to attain a more natural growth.   It takes a good

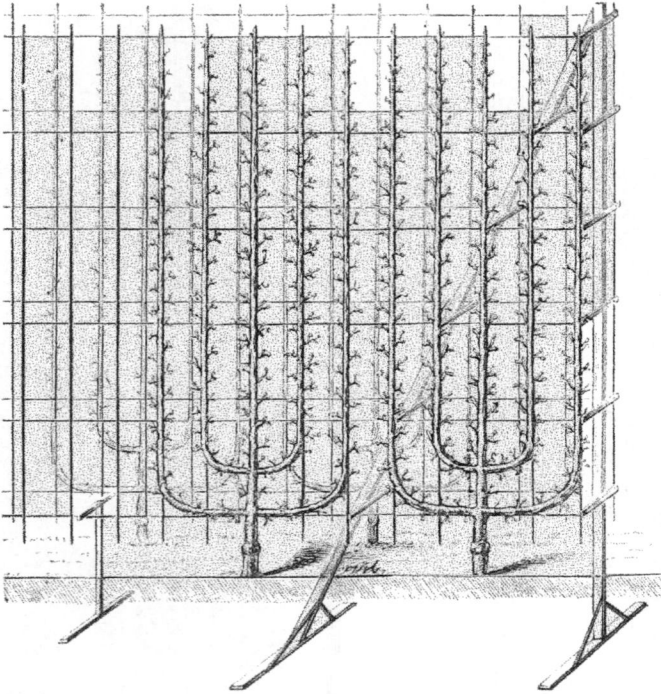

DOUBLE TRELLIS FOR PEAR-TREES : TEN FEET HIGH.

Uprights and stays of T-iron ; horizontal lines, slender galvanised wire ; vertical lines, pine-wood rods, half an inch square and painted green : to these the ascending branches are trained.

many years to form the large style of tree usually adopted; the
general planting of these intermediate forms is therefore to be
preferred.

   Nothing can be neater in the kitchen- and fruit-garden than
lines such as these trained on the trellis alluded to.   There is no
shaking of rough irons or wooden beams, no falling down or

loosening of the wires ; the fruit is firmly attached and safe from

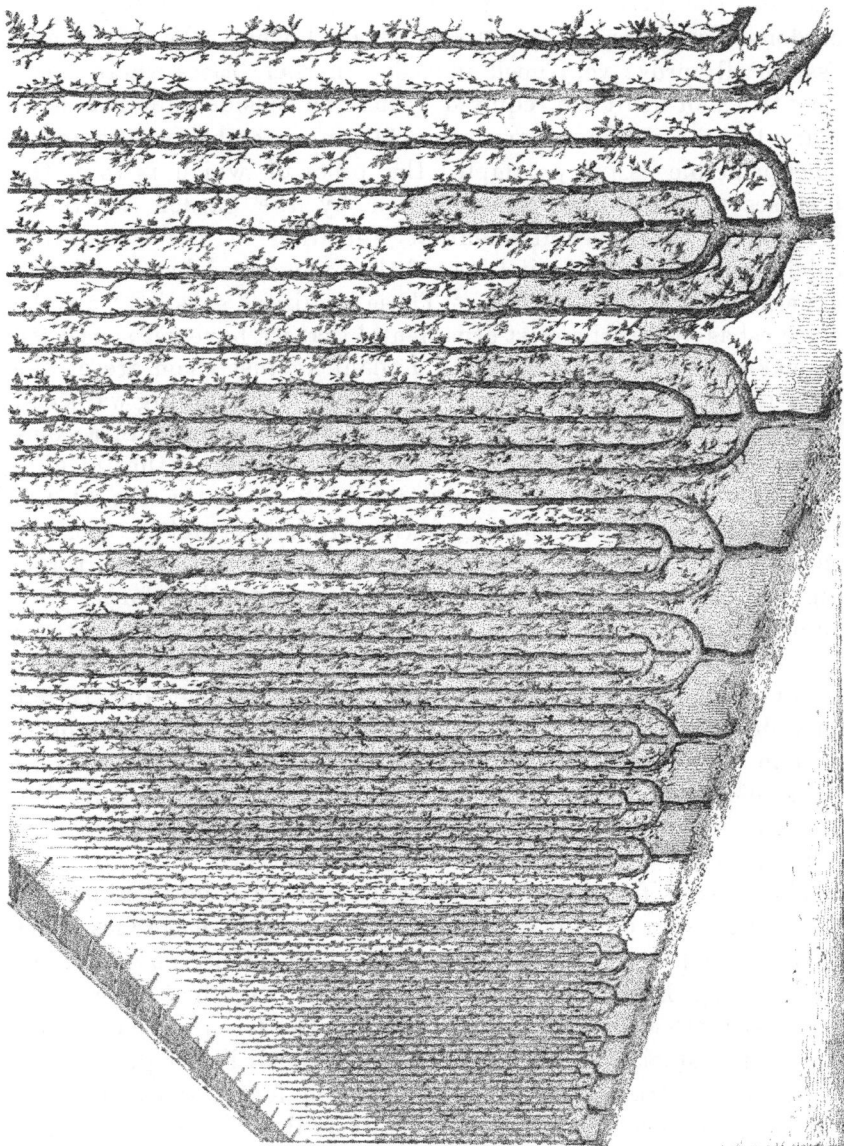

WALL OF EASTER BEURRÉ PEARS IN THE SCHOOL OF HORTICULTURE AT VERSAILLES.

gales, the wood is fully exposed, and the trellis when well covered
forms an elegant dividing line in a garden. The best way to

place them is at from three to six feet from the edge of the walk, and if in the space between the espalier and the walk a line of the cordons elsewhere recommended be established, the effect and result will prove very good indeed. In some cases where large quantities of fruit are required, it may be considered desirable to place them across a square some fifteen or eighteen feet apart. The principle is very simple, the proof of which is that the trellises at Versailles were erected by the garden workmen. M. Hardy, the superintendent at Versailles, is the son of the celebrated writer on fruit-trees of that name, and has had much experience in fruit-growing. "These trellises," says he, "are the cheapest as well as the most ornamental that we have yet succeeded in making, and the trees which I plant against them are of the form that I prefer to all others, for promptly furnishing walls and trellises, and for yielding a great number of varieties in a comparatively restricted space." The mode of employing the uprights of pine-wood painted green and reaching from the top of the trellis to within six inches of the ground is not a common one, though very desirable where the erect method of training the shoots is practised. Of course any other forms may be used with this system of trellising, with slight modifications to suit different kinds or forms of trees. The double trellis shown is simply a modification of the single one, and is not only desirable where space is limited, but also for its economy, for one set of uprights supports the two sets of wires by using cross pieces of iron about eighteen inches long, and at the desired distance apart. However, the engraving shows this at a glance.

The Pear is found to succeed badly here as a low cordon, and to plant it as an oblique cordon at fifteen or eighteen inches apart is considered much too close. A white wall fourteen feet high covered with Easter Beurré Pears shows an excellent example of the best method of growing this Pear. The trees are mostly on the Quince stock and a few on the Pear, but all bear equally well. They are all trained in the five-branched form usually adopted here, and almost cover the tall white wall. The growers here insist on the necessity of having white walls for fruit-trees, and state that dark ones injure both fruit and leaves, while white ones benefit both. White walls, apparently well lime-washed every year, are to be found in every good establishment, whether for Peach, Grape, or other wall-fruit culture. The Easter Beurré may be seen here double-worked on the Curé. The Curé is first grafted on the Quince and allowed to form five vertical branches before it is budded. The Easter Beurré is found to do best when double-grafted, though the trees directly on the Quince and Pear seem to do well. The bare parts of the stems of fruit-trees in this garden are in many cases protected from injury from a strong sun by being neatly co-vered

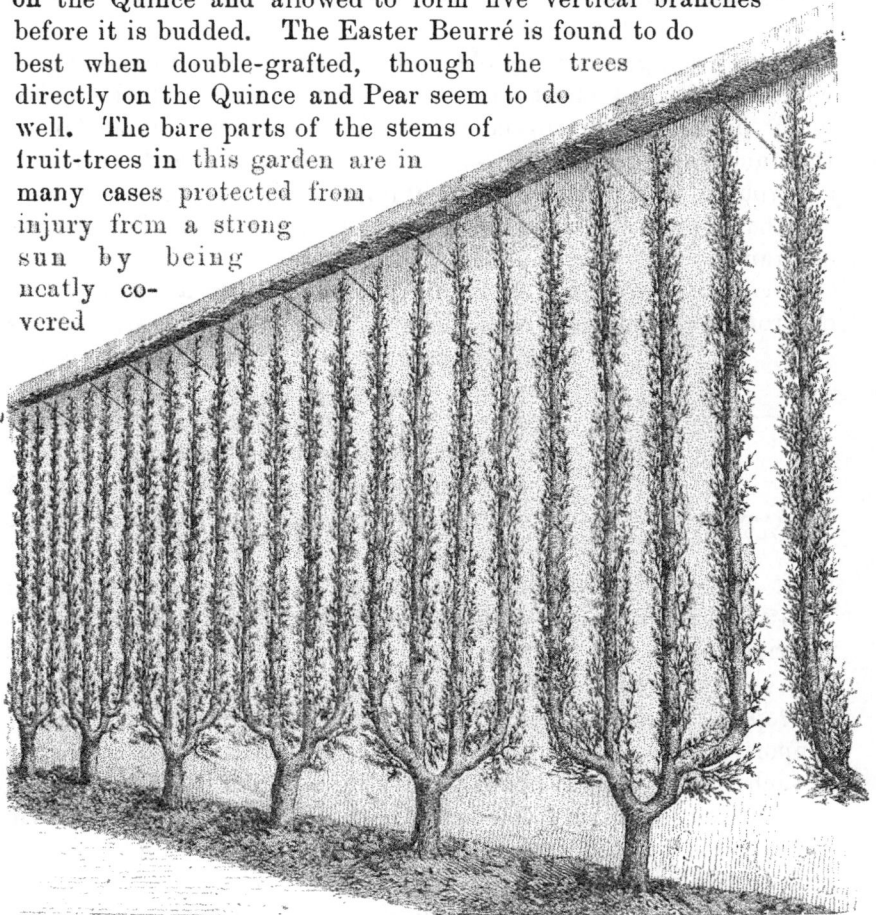

WALL OF PEACH-TREES IN THE POTAGERIE AT VERSAILLES.

Engraved from a photograph taken in April 1877 by Jules Lemercier. Showing the trees when in flower and before the young shoots begin to cover the surface between the erect branches. The trees are protected from frost during the flowering season by straw mats temporarily fixed on the top of the wall. These trees, having vertical shoots, are quickly and easily formed. The wall is perfectly covered with the trees as shown in the engraving, in which no alteration from the photograph whatever has been made.—These Peach-trees are trained in the U-form with vertical branches, and are about seventeen years old. The sorts are the Grosse Mignonne, Madeleine Rouge de Courtoy, Belle Beausse. The wall is about thirteen feet high, and faces the west. The trees took only six years to cover the wall. Each tree produced from 150 to 200 Peaches when in full bearing, but after this figure had been reached the yield was reduced to 150, or even 120, the fruit becoming better in quality as they became less numerous.

with straight straw, tied with willow twigs.   Neatly done, it seems better than the commoner plan of placing slates or boards before them.   Brackets to support straw mats in spring are placed on every wall at a little more than a yard apart.

There are a great many old and worn-out trees in the garden which have a bad effect on its appearance here and there, but many promising improvements are being carried out as far as the funds afforded to the school will allow.   The Pear makes as strong a growth here as in Britain, though some of our growers say that a more fruitful kind of wood is formed in the fine climate of France.

For some years past M. Hardy has carried out a novel system of protecting espalier-trees.   The plan is simply to strain lines of galvanised wire above the top of the espalier, so as to form a low-span roof when covered with rough canvas.   The sides are not covered, but the protection at the top is sufficient to prevent radiation, and to throw off heavy rains when the trees are in bloom.   If there is a wall running at

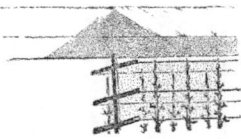

Side view of protection to double line of Espaliers.

right angles with the lines of espaliers, wires are stretched from it so as to form a light support over each espalier ; if not, a post is driven in so as to support and stretch the wire in the firmest way.   The lower of these two lines _____ may be supposed to represent the top of the espalier, the upper a line firmly supported at a few inches above it.   Wires are also stretched at each side of this, at about twenty inches from it, so as to form the outline of a very low-span roof.   It is a matter of little difficulty to stretch canvas over these wires, letting it be an inch or two narrower than the breadth between the outer wires, so that it may be strained tight.   The outer margins must of course be firmly threaded to the outer wires with twine or any convenient tying or rough sewing material.   Here they simply use the stems of the glaucous or hard Rush (Juncus glaucus), which grows wild all over Britain, and find it answer admirably.   A neat ridge is thus arranged over each line of espaliers, which throws off the rain and prevents radiation, thereby saving the bloom from frost and insuring a crop.   The protection is put up before the buds are liable to be injured, and removed when the fruit is set and all danger has passed away. Thus a very cheap and effective protection is secured. The kinds of Pears mostly grown here are Easter Beurré, by which several walls are covered; Duchesse d'Angoulême, of which there is a square of trellising nearly 600 yards long in all, and about nine feet high; Beurré Diel; and Louise Bonne d'Avranches.

The Peach is well grown and trained in some parts of the garden, a form with five main branches being adopted with success. It is analogous to the form used for the Pear in the same garden, and is very readily made. It would be difficult to see walls more beautifully covered with trees than a considerable portion of the peach-walls here. The tree is here almost invariably trained in a vertical manner, and as usual protected in spring with deep copings. I have to thank Mr. Hardy for permission to have some of the Peach and other trees photographed, and for other kindly help.

In addition to the trellises above described,

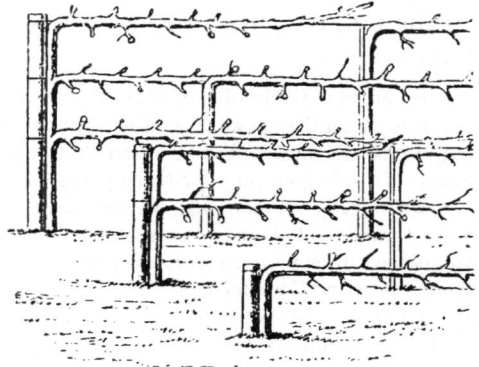

Border of superimposed Cordons at Versailles.

the most remarkable feature of this garden is the presence of a vast number of horizontal cordon Apple-trees, both in single and superimposed lines of two or three stages, all on galvanised wire. The trees are on the Paradise stock, and nearly always confined to a single stem. These trees sometimes bear enormous crops, but the fine Apples are often destroyed by the grub. One border devoted to cordons is about one thousand feet long, and altogether there are over four thousand yards of cordon-trained Apple-trees in the garden. As the greater portion of this length is composed of two and three lines of wires placed at distances of a foot one above the other, there are really more than five miles of horizontal cordon Apple-trees on the true Paradise stock, and it should be observed that though the cordons are often grown in lines one above the other, one plant does not furnish more than one line except at the ends. There, however, it is necessary to take several branches from one plant to furnish the two or three lines of wire starting from the same post. Here, as in many other gardens superintended by experienced fruit-growers, this mode of Apple-growing is preferred to any other, but the enormous number planted best speaks of the estimation in which it is held. The cordons, though generally well managed, are not quite so good as may be seen elsewhere, owing apparently to being too closely confined to the main stem. They are best and most satisfactory when allowed to form a free and regular bush of spurs along the stem. It is a soil as cold, stiff, and disagreeable for fruit-culture as could well be devoted to that purpose.

The programme of this school has been published, and reads as follows :—

The School of Horticulture, established in the Royal Kitchen Garden of Versailles, is placed under the jurisdiction of the Minister of Agriculture and Commerce. Only out-pupils are admitted; the instruction given is entirely gratuitous; and the course of study continues for three years.

Conditions of Admission.—The candidates must not be less than seventeen, or more than twenty-seven, years old at the time of entrance. Applications for admission, drawn up on stamped paper, should be addressed to the Minister of Agriculture and Commerce, so that he may receive them by the 20th of September at the latest. No notice will be taken of any application sent in after that date. Each application must be accompanied by (1) a certificate of the candidate's birth, if a native of France; (2) a certificate of good character, signed by the local authorities; (3) a medical certificate, to the effect that the candidate is sufficiently strong and healthy to undertake the occupation of a gardener. On receipt of these documents, which should be legally drawn up, the Minister, if everything is satisfactory, will authorise the candidate to present himself for an examination, of which he will send him due notice.

Entrance Examination.—Every candidate must undergo an entrance examination in the following elementary subjects : (1) Reading; (2) writing and spelling (from dictation); (3) numeration, and the first four rules of arithmetic. Credit will be given to the candidates for any technical knowledge which they may possess. This examination will be held in the school on the 1st of October, which is the date fixed for the commencement of the academical year and the entrance of pupils. Every candidate who shall pass this examination in a satisfactory manner is at once placed on the list of pupils, and has thenceforth right of entrance into the school.

Course of Instruction.—The main object of the course of instruction pursued in the School of Horticulture at Versailles is to train up skilled and intelligent gardeners, possessing all the theoretical and practical knowledge that is necessary in horticultural operations. It embraces the following subjects : (1) The cultivation of fruit-trees in the open air and under glass ; pomology ; (2) the cultivation of forest and ornamental trees, comprising nursery work in general ; (3) the cultivation of vegetables in the open air, and by forcing ; (4) the cultivation of flowering plants, in the open air and under glass ; (5) elementary and descriptive botany ; (6) the principles of landscape-gardening and garden architecture ; (7) elementary instruction in physics, meteorology, chemistry, geology, and mineralogy, as applied to horticulture ; (8) the elements of zoology and entomology, in their relation to horticulture and arboriculture ; (9) arithmetic and geometry, applied to gardening purposes, such as the measuring of surfaces, finding cubic contents, laying down plans to scale, etc.; (10) line drawing, and sketching plants and implements ; (11) lessons in the French language and book-keeping. The practical instruction is supplied in a systematic course of manual labour, which embraces every operation of gardening. The time is so divided between these two branches of instruction that all the pupils will take part in the work of the garden every day, and thereby acquire the knowledge and manual dexterity which are so indispensable. In addition to the instruction imparted in the school, the pupils will be taken from time to time to visit the principal horticultural establishments, in order to familiarise them with the best examples of practical horticulture and arboriculture.

Examinations at the end of the year and on leaving the School.—At the end of every academical year a general examination will take place for the purpose of classifying the pupils. Those who fail to pass through this examination into a higher division, will cease to be members of the School. Those pupils who pass a satisfactory examination on leaving the school will receive, on the recommendation of the examiners, a certificate of merit from the Minister of Agriculture and Commerce. Moreover, those pupils who distinguish themselves most at the final examination may (if their acquirements and fitness in other respects point them out as deserving of the favour) receive an appointment, for one year's practice, in one of the leading French or foreign horticultural establishments. An allowance of 1200 francs (£48) is attached to each of these appointments, the number of which is not to exceed three every year. It must be understood, however, that these appointments cannot be claimed as a right by those pupils who come out among the first at the final examination. A nomination to one of them will depend on whether the examiners have formed a judgment of the pupil, in the course of the examination, as to whether he is a person likely to make a good use of this complementary means of improvement ; preference being given to those pupils who manifest a desire for further knowledge, and an earnest devotion to their profession.

Bursaries.—Bursaries, six in number, and each of the value of 600 francs (£24), will be annually given to those pupils whose names stand first on the entrance-list, to help to defray their expenses while they remain at Versailles. Holders of these bursaries will receive them in monthly payments of 50 francs (£2). The institution will also receive pupils sent from the departments, towns, and agricultural or horticultural associations, whose expenses are defrayed by the department, town, or association to which they belong. All the pupils, whether holders of bursaries or not, go through the same course of study, practical work, and examinations, and are amenable to the same internal regulations.   In the school, all the pupils stand on the same footing, and are subject to the same rules.

Discipline.—Special rules are framed for regulating the hours of attendance in the school, the employment of time, the course of out-door operations, and the maintenance of order in the establishment.   To each rule is appended the penalty incurred by its infringement.   Every year the course of theoretical instruction is suspended for two months (from August 1 to October 1).   During this time, leave of absence may be granted to those pupils who ask for it; but the director has the power of limiting the periods of absence, or refusing them altogether, in order to enable him to have always a sufficient number of hands to keep the gardens in order, or to carry out any works of importance or urgency.   Any pupil who does not return at the expiration of his leave of absence is looked upon as having left the school; his name is erased from the roll, and cannot be replaced without the sanction of the Minister of Agriculture and Commerce.

The School of Fruit-culture of the City of Paris in the Bois de Vincennes.

Before the war it was determined to found a school of fruit-culture for Paris, and in the spring of 1868 the first trees were planted. In arrangement it is almost identical with the plan given in this chapter and recommended by M. Du Breuil for the north of France. It is situated near the Avenue Daumesnil entrance to the Bois de Vincennes. The first thing remarkable about the new garden is its walls; they are of felt, supported on a rough wooden framework. The felt is first nailed on frames of wood about six feet long by four feet wide, which are dropped into a groove made in the uprights, the stronger framework resting upon a few inches of masonry : the felt is whitened over, and the whole surmounted by a little ridge-like coping. This peculiar form of wall was erected in consequence of the objection of the authorities to have any walls of solid materials in the neighbourhood, which is near the fort : but it has helped to prove that in cold northern countries we may hope to grow good fruit by means of something less expensive than brick walls. These walls are about nine feet high, except at the north end, where they are more than twelve feet.

The garden is in two divisions, one to illustrate the practical

North.

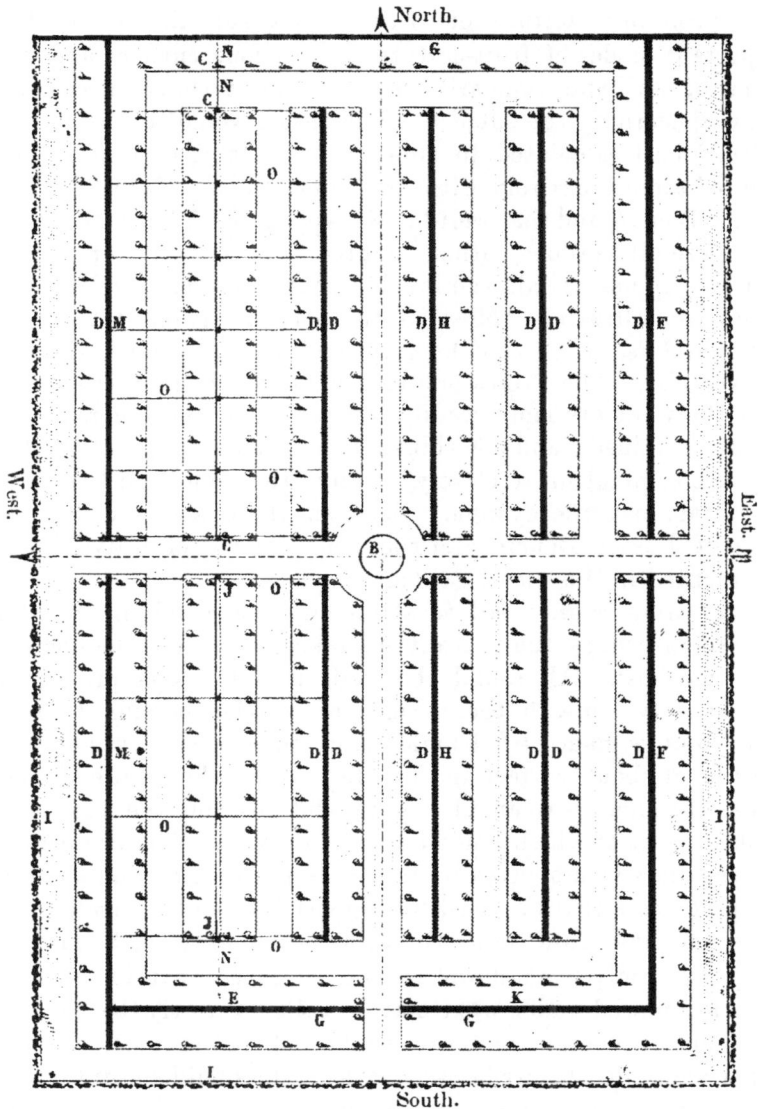

West.

East.

South.

Plan of a Fruit-garden for the north of France (Du Breuil).

B, *cistern. C, double espalier for Apricots. D, west side of walls planted with oblique cordon Pear-trees, 16 inches apart. E, Gooseberries. F, east side of wall, planted with Peach-trees as simple cordons 16 inches apart. G, Cherries as oblique cordons, 16 inches apart. H, Plum-trees, trained in like manner. I, hedge. J, summer Pears, as vertical cordons on espalier. K, Raspberries, cultivated at the foot of the wall. M, wall of Vines. The borders are surrounded by a cordon of Apples, planted 7 feet apart, and 12 inches within the margin of the border. The black lines show the walls, and N and O wires stretched from the walls to support the espalier.*

and profitable culture of fruit for market, the other all the important modes of. fruit-culture, the various curious and useful forms of wall and standard trees, and most things necessary to know concerning the subject. The part devoted to the modes of culture best calculated to afford a quick and certain return is planted almost entirely with the finest of all winter Pears, the Easter Beurré, and that well-known Apple the Calville Blanc. The Pears are all cordons, either planted against walls or espaliers, and the Apples are all the low horizontal cordon. Only the best fruits are cultivated. Most of the cordons against the walls are oblique (thus, / / / /), except on the highest wall, where they are vertical. The Professor's reason for adopting these forms is that the walls are more readily covered by it, and a much quicker return obtained; and he thinks these advantages outweigh the expense of planting so closely, or any other objection that may be urged against the system. Between three and four thousand trees of Easter Beurré, and the same number of Calville Blanc, are planted in this small garden.

One thing cannot fail to strike any visitor taking an interest in fruit-growing—the precautions taken to protect the trees from wet and frost. All round the walls iron brackets project from immediately beneath the permanent wooden coping, to receive wide copings made of felt nailed on a high wooden framework, in lengths of about six feet and two feet wide. These are slipped in under the short permanent coping, and rest on the bracket, the hooked point of which holds them in position. The protection for the espaliers is supported by iron rods projecting from the top of the pine posts that are used to support the double espaliers. On these are fixed thin frames of straw, each at least a yard wide. They are firmly fixed down to the wires, so that in spring the trees are placed under what may be called a neatly thatched shed. No doubt some other material would look better than the straw, but when nailed firmly between laths it does not look untidy ; and, moreover, it is the object of the school to show the cheapest as well as the best way of applying the protections most commonly in use. The use of neat straw mats for protecting walls is very common in France. Posts of pine-wood five or six inches in diameter are employed to support the espaliers, because they are easy to procure; and, to secure their durability, they are thoroughly saturated with blue vitriol before being used.   This is a cumbrous and bad plan, the kind of fruit-trellises employed at Versailles being neater, more durable, and in every way superior.

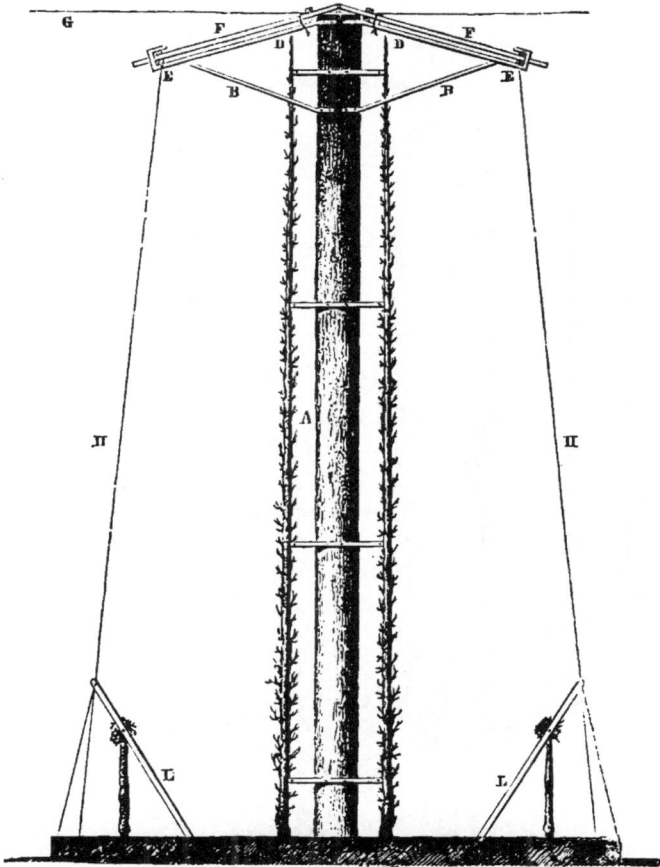

Double Espalier with a row of Cordons on each side, showing mode of protecting the whole in spring (Du Breuil). A, wooden support. B, B, supports for protection. F, F, wide temporary copings of neat straw mats, held by iron brackets. H, H, galvanised wires fixed at E, E, descending at intervals and fixed in the iron posts, L, L, and to stones in the ground. G, one of the lines running across the espaliers from the walls of the garden.

In the garden devoted to teaching purposes only, all the lines which the branches of the wall trees are to occupy when fully formed are indicated by small rattan canes—accurately placed, so

U

that as the tree grows the trainer has merely to attach it to the
rods.   Useless as well as desirable forms of training are shown;
for instance, trees formed like a goblet, with the branches crossed

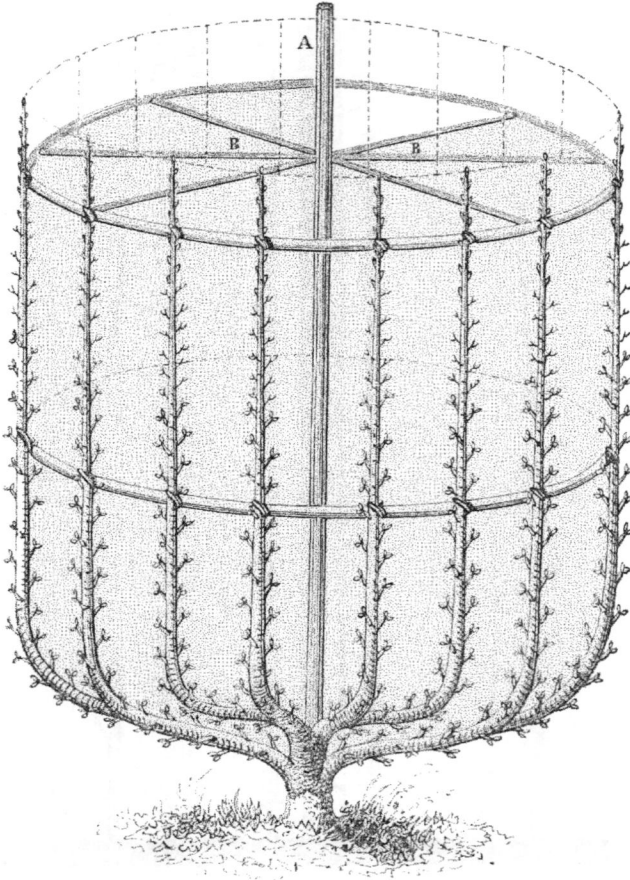

FRUIT-TREE IN THE VASE FORM.

*One of many forms more curious than useful.   A, stake.   B, B, crossed sticks to sustain hoop in
position.   To form a handsome tree of this kind, eighteen or twenty branches are required.*

or ascending vertically.   These are all useless for practical purposes, though they may serve to amuse an amateur; who, however,
would do better to amuse himself with forms more simple and
productive.   The way of making a hedge of Pears is also shown—

a hedge that when once made, and with its branches crossed and intertwined, will support itself — and without doubt neat and productive screens of fruit-trees may thus be made in any garden, and the trees kept quite as neatly as if supported by expensive trellising.   Altogether the place will prove an instructive one, though the School at Versailles will be found by visitors to be more interesting so far as trained trees are concerned.   A model vineyard and a promising young orchard have been planted in the Vincennes School of Horticulture, in which, as in the fruit-gardens a professor gives free lectures to large classes.

Hedge of Pear-trees (half formed)

CHAPTER XVIII.

The Cordon System of Fruit-Growing.

A cordon means a tree confined to a single stem, that stem being furnished with spurs, or sometimes with little fruiting branches nailed in, as in the case of the Peach when trained to one stem. Some have supposed that it means any form of branch closely spurred in ; but this is not the case.   The term is wrongly applied to any form of tree but the small and simple-stemmed ones.   The French have no more need of the word to express a tree trained on the spur system than we have, and they have trained trees on the spur system for ages without ever calling them by this name.

The Apple trained as a Simple Horizontal Cordon, grafted on the French Paradise Stock.

Professor Du Breuil, in reply to a letter requesting him to define the exact use and meaning of the term, replied as follows : " The word *cordon* is derived in French from *corde*.   I employed this expression to designate the forms of fruit-trees composed of one branch, which only bears fruit-buds and branchlets."

He states that, struck with the long period it took to cover a wall by means of the larger forms of trees, he adopted those quick-rising simple-stemmed kinds to cover the walls rapidly and give a quick return.   Hence it is clear that if we call a fan-trained or a horizontal tree a " cordon," we not only misapply the term, but prevent the inventor's simple idea from being understood. However, the figures in this chapter will give a correct idea of what the cordon system is.

A simple galvanised wire is attached to a strong oak post or rod of iron, so firmly fixed that the strain of the wire may not disturb it. The wire is usually supported at a distance of one foot from the ground, and tightened by a raidisseur, a handy little implement described elsewhere in this volume. A raidisseur will tighten several hundred feet of the wire, which need not be thicker than strong twine, and of the same sort as that recommended for walls and espaliers. The galvanised wire known as No. 14 is the most suitable for general use. At intervals a support of wood or iron with an eye in it is placed under the wire on which the tree is trained; thus forming the simplest and best kind of cordon, and the one so extensively employed for making edgings around the squares in fruit-gardens.

By selecting good kinds and training them in this way abundance of the finest fruit may be grown without having any of the large trees or those of any other form in the garden to shade or occupy its surface. The bilateral cordon is useful for the same purposes as the simple one, and especially adapted to the bottoms of walls, bare spaces between the fruit-trees, the fronts of pits, or any low bare wall with a warm exposure. As in many cases the lower parts of walls in gardens are quite bare, this form of cordon offers an opportunity for covering them with what will yield a certain and valuable return. It is by this method that the finest-coloured, largest, and best French apples sold in Covent Garden and in the Paris fruit-shops at such high prices are grown. In Covent Garden

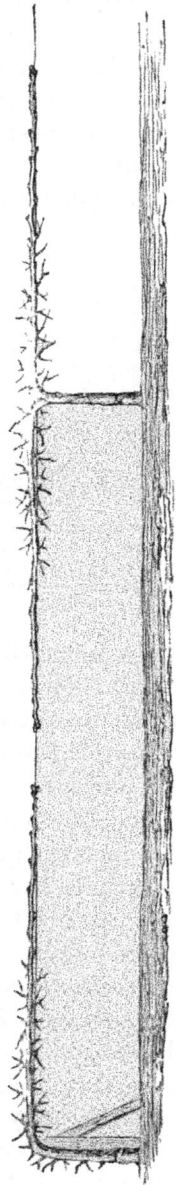

Simple and Double Cordon Trees training as Edgings.

and in Regent Street they are sometimes marked two and three shillings each, and in St. Petersburg they are sold in winter for as much as six shillings each. Considering the great number of walled gardens there are in this country, there can be no doubt whatever that by merely covering, by means of this plan, the lower parts of walls now entirely useless, we could easily supply our markets with the very choice fruit referred to, and be independent of other countries in this respect.

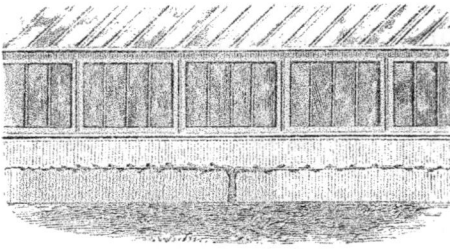

Cordon Tree on low Wall of Plant-house. In this way Calville Blanc, Reinette du Canada, Melon-Apple, American-Mother, and the finer and tenderer Apples may be grown to perfection.

Many will suppose that such very fine fruit must require a warmer country than ours for their production. But by treating them as the French do we may produce quite as good a result, and may, in addition, grow tender but fine apples, like the Calville Blanc, that do little good when grown as standards. The climate in most parts of England will be found to suit them as well as that of France, if not better, because the sun in some districts of France is rather too strong for the perfect development of the flesh and flavour of the apple. There is no part of this country in which the low cordon will not be found a useful addition to the garden —that is, wherever first-rate dessert fruit is wanted. So great is the demand in the markets for fruit of the highest quality that sometimes the little trees more than pay for themselves the first year after being planted. In any northern exposed and cold places where choice apples do not ripen well it would be desirable to give the trees as warm and sunny a position as possible, while the form recommended for walls should be used extensively. In no case should the system be tried except as a garden one—an improved method of orcharding being what is wanted for kitchen fruit, and for the supply of the markets.

When lines of well-grown cordons are completed the whole forms a mass of bold spurs. Some keep them very closely pinched in to the rod, but the best are allowed a rather free development of spurs, care being taken that these are produced regularly and thickly along the stem.

The cordon system as generally applied to the Apple is simply bringing one good branch near the earth, where it receives more heat, where it causes no injurious shade, and where it may be protected with the greatest efficiency and the least amount of trouble.

It is an extension of the best principles of pruning—a wise bending of the young tree to the conditions that best suit it in our northern climate. The fact that by its means we bring all the fruit and leaves to within ten inches or a foot of the ground, thereby exposing them to an increase of heat, which compensates to a great extent for a bad climate, will prove a strong argument in favour of the plan. The form is so definite and simple that anybody may attend to it, and direct the energies of the little trees to a useful end, with much less trouble than is requisite to form a presentable pyramid or bush. It does not, like other forms,

Young Cordon Tree of the Lady Apple trained as an Edging.

shade anything; and beneath the very line of cordons a slight crop may be grown. They are less trouble to support than either pyramid or bush; always under the eye for thinning, stopping, and pruning; easy of protection, if that be desired; and very cheap in the first instance.

A few words are necessary as to the best method of planting and managing the Apple trained and planted around the quarters or borders. In a garden in which much neatness is desirable it would be better to plant them within whatever edging may be used for the walks; but in the rough kitchen- or fruit-garden they may be used as edgings. The reason for supporting the cordon at the height of a foot from the surface is to prevent the fruit getting soiled by earthy splashings. In gardens where it would not be suitable as an edging, the best way would be to plant it ten inches within the Box or whatever kind of edging was employed. In planting, the union of stock and scion must be kept just above the surface of the ground, to prevent the Apple grafted on the Paradise from throwing out its own roots and consequently becoming useless for such a mode of training. The trees should never be fixed down to wire or wall immediately after being planted, but allowed to remain erect during their first winter and until the sap is moving in them, when they may be tied down. Some allow them to grow erect for a whole year before tying them down. They should in all cases be allowed to settle well into the ground before being tied to anything. For general plantings, the best kind of plants to get are those known as "maidens," *i.e.*, erect growing trees about a year from the graft. These can be readily trained down to the wire, or to the wall, in spring. In training the young tree, the point with its growing shoot of the current year should always be allowed to grow, so that the sap will flow equably through the plant, drawn on by the rising shoot at its end. To allow gross shoots to rise at any other parts of the tree is to spoil all prospect of success. If the tree does not break regularly into buds, it must be forced to do so by making incisions before dormant eyes.

A chief point is not to pinch too closely or too soon. The first stopping of the year is the most important one, and the first shoots should not be pinched in too young, but when the wood is a little firm, so that the lower eyes at the bases of the leaves may not break soon after the operation. Stopping should be done at six leaves, as the object is not to have a mere stick for the cordon, but a dense bushy array of fruit-spurs quite a foot or more in diameter when the leaves are on in summer. All the after-pinching of the year may be shorter, and as the object is to regularly furnish the line, the observant trainer will vary his tactics to secure that end—in one place he will have to repress vigour, in another to encourage it. About three general stoppings during the summer will suffice, but at all times when a strong "water shoot" shows itself well above the mass of fruitful ones, it should be pinched in, though not too closely. In some of our nurseries may be seen "cordons" with every shoot allowed to rise up like a willow wand—utterly neglected and on the wrong stock.

As the Paradise keeps its roots quite near the surface of the ground, spreading an inch or two of half decomposed manure over the ground, or in gardening language "mulching," could not fail to be beneficial. This is the more necessary on warm or dry soils, in which the Paradise stock is least vigorous.

The cordons are usually planted too close together in France. When the trees overtake each other it is common to graft them one to another—a very simple operation. If when all are united they should grow too strong in rich ground, the stem of every second plant may be cut off just beneath the wire and the trees will be nourished by the others. When the line is well trained and established the wire may be taken away altogether. If the plantation be made on a slope, all the trees should be planted so as to grow up the incline.

Finally, in winter, the trees will be the better for being looked over with a view to a little pruning here and there; taking care to thin and regulate the spurs when the plantation is thoroughly established, to cut in useless stumps, and to firmly tie the shoots along the

The White Calville Apple.

wire but not too tightly so as to prevent their free expansion.

As the system is chiefly valuable for the production of fine dessert fruit, only the best kinds should be selected; but, as some Apples are of high value both for kitchen and dessert, some of the finer kitchen Apples are included in the following list of such as will be found very suitable: Reinette du Canada, Reinette du Canada Grise, Reinette Grise, Reinette de Caux, Reinette d'Espagne, Reinette très-tardive, Belle Dubois, Pomme d'Api, Mela Carla, Calville St. Sauveur, Coe's Golden Drop, Calville Blanc, Northern Spy, Melon-apple, Cox's Orange Pippin, Duke of Devonshire, Kerry Pippin, Lodgemore Nonpareil, White Nonpareil, American-Mother, Early Harvest, Lord Burleigh, Beauty of Kent, Bedfordshire Foundling, Lord Suffield, Cox's Pomona, Hawthornden, Tower of Glamis, Winter Hawthornden, Betty Geeson, Small's Admirable, and Braddick's Nonpareil. Some of

the best of the above are valuable keeping Apples. The Reinette
Grise may be seen in fine condition in the markets at Rouen in
June, and Beinette très-tardive is good in July. Those who
wish to plant good early Apples might try Borovitsky, and a few
of the best early kinds; but it is better to devote most of the
horizontal cordons to the growth of the finer and later fruits.
Of the above selection the Calville Blanc, the Reinette du Canada,
and Mela Carla must be grown on a warm wall; the Mother,
Melon, and several of the other later and finer Apples will also be
grateful for the same protection.

Of the kinds of French Apples that may be had grafted on the
Paradise abundantly in nurseries all over France the following
are among the best: Calville Blanc, Reinette du Canada, R.
d'Angleterre, R. Grise, R. de Caux, R. très-tardive, R. de

Reinette du Canada trained as a Cordon.

Bretagne, R. d'Espagne, Belle Dubois, Belle Joséphine, Calville
St. Sauveur. As a great number of trees is required for this
mode of planting; as the Apple on the Paradise occupies but a
small space in nurseries compared to other trees; and as it is
very likely that before long there will be a demand for this form
of tree, it is to be hoped that our nurserymen will offer suitable
kinds at a very low rate by the dozen, score, or hundred, as is
the case in France. Till this is done there can be no hope of
the perfect and general success of the system.

As to the culture of the Apple on the Paradise in its earliest
stage in nurseries, M. Jean Durand of Bourg-la-Reine, near Paris,
writes to me as follows:—

" If the Apple-tree is to be grown in the form of the horizontal
cordon, it must be grafted on the variety known to horticulturists
as the Paradise. This variety, which loves a fresh, damp, clayey

soil, cannot be grown from seed, but must be propagated by means of layers or cuttings, which are obtained in the following manner : Having chosen soil of the proper description, it must be well dug and manured.   Trenches, six inches deep and a yard apart, are then opened, and the stocks, which have been prepared previously, planted in them.   They should be pruned down to twelve or fourteen inches in height, and placed in the trenches at a distance of four inches apart, and in such a way that about six inches of the top appears above the ground.   The trenches are then filled in and the ground levelled.

"In the following spring, as soon as there is no longer any danger from frost, the stocks are cut down level with the ground.

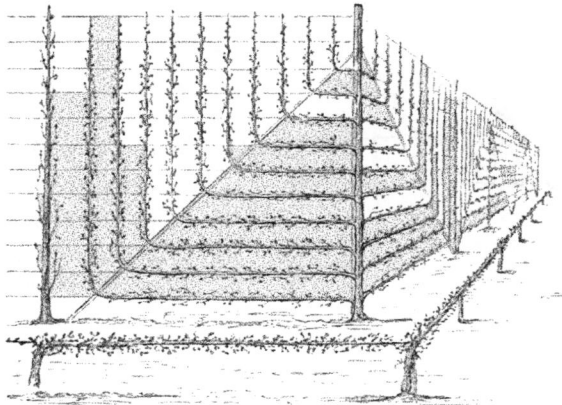

Edging of Simple Cordons three years old in Fruit-garden at Brunoy.

The object of this operation is to develop a number of shoots : these are earthed up about June or July by covering them with a small quantity of earth taken from the trench on each side of the line of plants, so as to cover their bases to the depth of four inches or so.

"In the following November these buds will have taken root; the plants from which they take their origin will give every year a certain number of young plants, and will be alluded to in future as old stools.

"Every year during the month of November the young plants should be stripped from these old stools.   It is necessary above all during the first year to use a strong pair of pruning-shears,

called a *sécateur,* for taking them off in order not to injure the
stools; later on they may be simply broken off. Immediately
after this operation the stools should be covered over with earth.
They will afford young plants for a long time—from five to ten
years, according to the care taken of them—and the suckers thus
obtained will serve for grafting in the nursery.

"The ground which is to receive them should be well dug
and the trees then planted in lines two feet apart, or a little more.
They should be placed sixteen or twenty inches apart and three
or four inches deep. The operation of planting in beds requires
great care. The young plants should be well trimmed both at
top and bottom, so as to give the branches a uniform length of
sixteen inches, and the
ground hoed frequently
until the month of
August, with the double
object of destroying
weeds and keeping the
ground open. At this
period the young plants
are ready for budding,
each subject receiving a
bud at about four inches
above the surface of the
ground. Immediately
afterwards, particularly
in dry seasons, it will

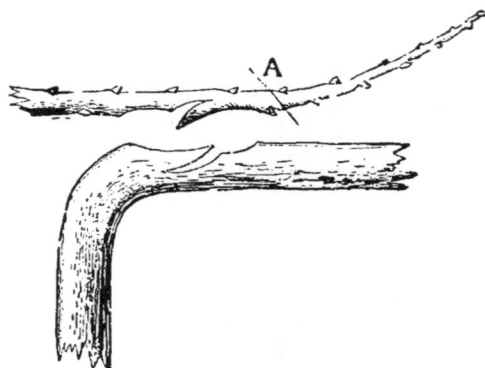

*Grafting by approach, to unite the points of Horizontal
Cordons. The apex of each cordon is cut at A, when
firmly united to its neighbour (Du Breuil).*

be well to give the ground a good hoeing to help to keep it
moist.

"During the winter the plant should be cut down to within
three inches above the bud, and all the remaining shoots should
be stripped off. The following spring a number of small shoots
will make their appearance all over the pruned plant. When
they have reached a length of an inch or an inch and a half, they
should be pinched down to favour the growth of the graft, which
will have grown as large as the other buds. The bud which has
not been pinched will naturally soon exceed in size those which
have been. From this time it will attain sufficient strength to
absorb the sap, and it will be necessary to remove all the other

shoots. This little pruning operation requires considerable caution, and is performed by the aid of the knife. Care should be taken not to confound the graft with the other shoots on the plant. The stem of the stock above the bud being thus deprived of its shoots, serves as a stake to which to tie the young growing scion, which tied loosely is preserved from accident during its growth. At the end of the year this natural stake, having served its purpose, is cut away, and the graft having attained its proper size is ready for transplanting as a maiden plant, and may then be trained into any form the grower may think desirable.

" The Apple thus grafted on the Paradise is, as is well known, a great success throughout all parts of France and the adjoining countries. In proportion to the space it occupies, it furnishes a great quantity of the finest fruit. It is not rare to count seventy or eighty apples upon a little tree whose arms together are not more than seven feet long. This form is due to M. J. L. Jamin, of Bourg-la-Reine. This nurseryman used to sell dwarf fruit-trees of all kinds in pots in the Paris market, and amongst them the now well-known cordon. The form was much appreciated and promptly spread abroad, and after having had some success at a horticultural exhibition held at the Louvre, it was definitely adopted in kitchen- and fruit-gardens under the name of the horizontal cordon.

" To establish the growth of cordons in the nursery a line of galvanised iron wire is stretched horizontally at about fourteen

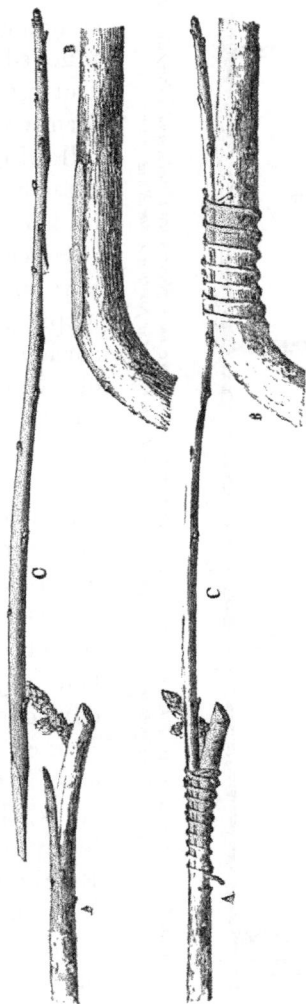

Another Mode of Grafting to unite the Cordons (Du Breuil).

inches above the ground, the ends being firmly fixed. The young trees are then cut down nearly to the level of the wire, and when they start in spring two opposite buds are chosen for the formation of the two arms, and allowed to grow during the summer, the buds on the stem below these being pinched within an inch or so of their base. During the summer the two shoots ought to form a strong cordon fit for transplanting in the following winter. The simple cordon with one branch is formed in the same manner, except that one bud only is allowed to grow."

Since the discussion which took place in the journals concerning the merits of this mode of Apple-growing, I have seen a great number of cordons on the Paradise in many parts of France and in Switzerland, seeking in various districts to ascertain its merits and defects; and am more than ever satisfied of its value. Some have considered that a late frosty season would be fatal to low cordons, and that our climate is too conducive to the production of gross wood, while on the Continent it becomes ripe and stubby, and the trees may be preserved within bounds. If such were the fact, this objectionable tendency should be more developed in the warm parts of north-western France near the sea-coast; but this is not the case. Grafted on the true French Paradise stock, the tree is always good, and keeps perfectly within bounds in parts of France and Belgium as cold and moist as southern England. In a note from Professor Morren, of Liége, he says: "The culture of the Apple as a cordon on the Paradise stock has been extensively tried in this country, and is rapidly extending, particularly near Liége, Verviers, Huy, Namur, and in all the Flemish districts. Hedges of horizontal cordon Apples and Pears are now formed along the sides of the railway between Brussels and Louvain. These plantations were made two

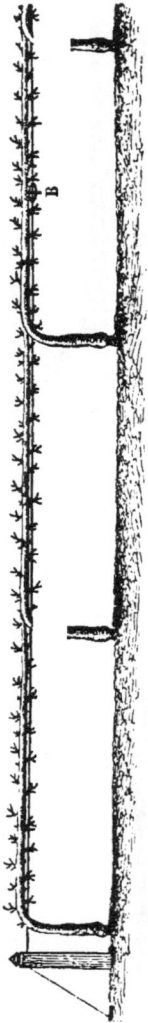

The horizontal Cordon trained as an Edging. Originally the trees represented here were planted too thickly, and after all had been securely grafted together, every second stem was severed. B shows the position of the Raidisseur.

years ago, and have proved very successful. The fruits attain a considerable size, and the experiment promises so well that preparations are being made to greatly extend it." It is improbable that there should be so much difference in the behaviour of trees separated by a few miles of sea! In many continental districts where frosts are quite as severe as here, the cordons escape yearly without serious injury ; and besides, no form of tree is so easily protected in spring, it being so very low.

In conclusion, it may be urged in favour of these cordon Apple-trees : 1. The fruit is larger and finer than that borne on any large form of tree. 2. The tree comes into bearing much earlier —in fact, often bears freely the second summer after being grafted. 3. The growth is dwarfer and much more compact than that of the apple on any other stock, and the tree may, without root-pruning, be kept in a more compact and fruitful form than apples on the Crab may be with that troublesome attention. 4. The fruit being held at an

Simple Mode of protecting Cordon Apple-trees in M. Jamin's Garden at Bourg-la-Reine.

average of one foot from the ground is in consequence benefited by a greater degree of heat ; and from the compactness of the form the leaves and wood enjoy a greater amount of sun than is the case with high trees : it need hardly be said that these are great advantages. 5. The tree being confined to a single stem, and stubby fruit-spurs held near the surface of the ground, there is in consequence no injury to the fruit from wind or the swaying about of branches ; besides, the fruit, if it does fall, is not injured. 6. The trees may be more readily protected than any other form whatever, should protection be considered necessary. 7. They may be more easily attended to in pinching, pruning, and thinning the fruit, and the desired shape attained more readily than any other form of trained tree. 8. Being little taller than a neglected Box edging, they shade no garden-crop. 9. They take up but small space, and the positions best suited to them are those that hitherto have been made no use of. 10. The apple on the French Paradise grows to its highest perfection on stiff loamy and wet and clayey soils, those which are often most

inimical to fruit-culture in these islands. 11. By planting it
against low walls we may grow the fine winter apples now supplied
to the capitals of Europe from northern France.

The testimony of the late Mr. James Barnes, of Bicton, is worth
adducing :—

" I have seen a good many espaliers in my time, but never one that bore a crop
like those little cordons that I saw at Ferrières, Versailles, and amongst the French
fruit-growers. The espalier on the Crab stock, no matter how big and ugly was
the trellis you put it upon, was always with difficulty kept within bounds, always
pushing its vigour to the top branch, whereas the little trees I saw in France
growing on very stiff moist loams were in the stubbiest and neatest condition
that could be desired ; and everywhere I was told that they were scarcely any
trouble, a little pinching now and then, and some attention to see that the spurs
were equally distributed along the line, being all that was required. Why, the
trouble is worth incurring for the sake of having such a pretty garniture to our
walks in spring and autumn. The pinching and training would be pleasant
employment for ladies and young folks, in their few hours' garden rambles,
affording both profitable and amusing exercise. So many tortured forms of trees
have been presented to the public that I do not wonder at those rejecting them
who cannot see the undeniable merits which have been claimed for these cordons ;
but when once they are seen well done, and in working order, everybody interested in a garden will be charmed with them, and the plan will, I venture to
say, be adopted in the largest as well as the smallest gardens in the land. Every
operation connected with the culture of these trees will be agreeable in consequence
of its simplicity ; and it will be a pleasure to have the little trees under the eye,
from the unfolding of the buds in spring to the gathering of the fruit in autumn.
It is to me very surprising that some of our great fruit-growers, pomologists, and
others, who are, I believe, in the habit of travelling in France every year, and
some of them for the past thirty years, did not spy out and introduce this system
long ago, and more surprising still, that it is but recently that we have learned
from Mr. Robinson the real value and nature of the stock (others who have
mentioned it have always recommended the Doucin or English Paradise). No doubt
but for his exposition of the matter we might have gone on for many years in the
future as in the past without knowing anything of value about it, notwithstanding
the proximity of the fruit-gardens of northern France and southern England, and
the abundant intercourse between the two countries. We have brick and tile
edgings in all sorts of fancy forms, pebble, stone, slate, and wooden edgings,
also Grass, Box, Thrift, and many other living edgings ; but when once fairly
understood, the little edging of choice Apple-trees will prove the most popular,
profitable, and useful of them all for the fruit- or kitchen-garden. Apart from
edgings, the plan of planting the cordon on the ends, fronts, and low walls of
plant-pits and glass houses, low walls and fences, small vacancies or spaces
between fruit-trees on walls of any aspect— indeed, on any kind of blank space
on walls—is another distinct improvement ; and, when we have it in full operation,

the specimens of the finer and tenderer fruits grown on this method will be such as we have not yet had in this country."—*Gardener's Chronicle*, February 27, 1869.

On the same subject the late Mr. J. A. Watson of Geneva wrote to the same journal :—

" M. Vaucher, the President of our Horticultural Society, began fruit-growing at Chatellaine, a mile from Geneva, three years ago.   Knowing that he had made large plantations of the horizontal cordons, I paid him a visit early in July with the view of ascertaining their condition.   The plantation is not more than three years old, the garden having been a grass field previously.   In entering the garden the first things that catch the eye are the very neat lines of these little trees running around the borders, and at about one foot from the margin of the gravel walk.   The space between the cordons and gravel is planted with the finer kinds of Strawberries.   The borders margining each square are cut off from the body of the square by alleys, and these are also edged by cordons in the same way.   In most cases two lines of cordons are employed, one above the other, the fruit of the lower line sometimes coming within three or four inches of the ground.   The effect of the whole is neat, and such as would make a tasteful gardener use them for edgings, even if the result they yield be ever so problematical.   But as regards the Apple, with ordinary care there is nothing problematical about it, for the most dense crops already adorn these beautiful little trees.   Here are my notes and measurements of a few of them :—Calville d'Hiver, eighteen inches from the ground, seven feet six inches long, thirty-seven fine promising fruit ; the same kind, seven feet long, seven inches from the ground, twenty-four fine fruit ; Pepin d'Angleterre, six feet long, the fruit fifty-seven in number, hanging at an average of fifteen inches from the ground ; Reinette d'Espagne, three feet six inches long, twenty-four fruit ; the Lady Apple, six feet long, 110 fruit.   These were some of the best examples I saw ; and I need not remind your readers that the fruit, instead of being too thin, is much too thick.   I may safely say that if properly thinned as fine fruit as ever grew will be gathered from these young cordons—so neat in appearance, and at the same time such a source of profit.   I particularly observed that the fruits on the lower line of wire, at an average of about six inches from the ground, were quite as good and fertile as those on the upper wire, at an average height of about eighteen inches—although, perhaps, at some disadvantage from being exactly under the higher line.   I may add, that there are many gardens about Geneva in which these cordons on the Paradise are a perfect success, that they give little trouble to the gardeners, who are always fond of them, be the gardens or the 'help' large or small."

It is not merely in the way it is at present practised in France or elsewhere that the cordon system is interesting and instructive to all taking an interest in the culture of hardy fruits. . It offers a means of training trees so that we may readily give them that protection in spring, the want of which is in nine cases out of ten

the cause of our failures in fruit crops.   Hitherto the best course
to pursue with the borders along our fruit-walls has always been
a disputed point : some contending that they ought not to be
cropped at all ; others that salads and small vegetables might be
grown upon them.

Let us crop the borders with trees trained on the horizontal-
cordon principle as suggested in the accompanying figures, and in
this way dispose of the much-debated question as to what is best
to do with the fruit-borders.   By so doing we should collect such
a valuable stock of fruit-trees immediately in front of each wall
as would render it convenient and desirable to protect efficiently
both walls and borders, and by the same means.   The low cordons
will no more shade the wall than a crop of small salading and
will prevent all need
for disturbing the
border.   Indeed, I can
conceive no greater
improvement in our
fruit-culture than de-
voting to fruit-trees
those excellent sunny
borders that usually
lie at the foot of our
fruit-walls.   By this
plan we should, it is
true, sacrifice some of the more suitable spots for early vegetables
and salads, but we should gain very much more, and the change
would be in every way conducive to the beauty and utility of
our gardens.   When the wall-trees are being attended to the
cordons cannot be forgotten, and the whole will be under the eye
at a glance.

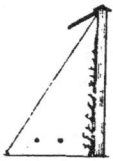

Narrow border in front of fruit-wall, with two lines of horizontal cordons, protected in Spring by wide temporary coping and rough canvas.

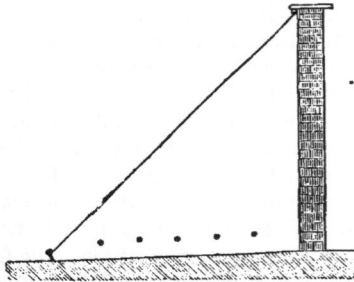

Peach wall and border, with five lines of cordons, the whole protected in Spring.

The Pear may also be grown thus in the highest perfection, and
there can be no doubt that the fruit which may be grown in this
way on the border would, if put to the market test, more than pay
for the expense of protecting cordons and wall-trees at the same
time.   Other fruits will probably be found to submit to this mode
of culture as well as these, and all kinds should be tried by those
with opportunities for making experiments in fruit-culture, those
kinds of a fertile and compact habit being selected for trial.

Should we in time find varieties of our other hardy fruits conform as readily to the cordon system as the Apple on the Paradise, this way of covering borders as well as walls with fruit-trees will prove a gain in the culture of our choice hardy fruits, the importance of which it would be difficult to over-estimate.

Care being taken to protect the borders and walls efficiently from the time of flowering till the fruit is beyond all danger, they may be afterwards exposed to the refreshing summer rains, and then there will be an end to all but mere routine work till the protecting season comes again. Every hundred feet in length of such well-protected wall and border would be equivalent to a well-managed orchard-house.

Simple wooden support for Cordon, the wire attached to a stone in the ground.

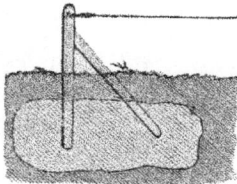

Iron support let into stone.

Iron support, with ratchet wheel at the top.

Although the cordon is so simply supported, it is desirable to know the best means of doing so in a permanent and ready way. The simplest way of all is to drive a tough wooden post in the ground to the required height, and attach the wire to it. The post may be driven in obliquely, or upright; or an iron support with a stay let into a block of rough stone would be as satisfactory as any other, because permanent. A variety of good supports are now offered by houses who erect espalier trellises.

THE PEAR AS A CORDON.—When at Holme Lacy in Herefordshire, a few years ago, I was pleasantly surprised to see a wall covered with Pear-trees, trained as single cordons, and in the finest bearing condition. I learnt from Sir II. Scudamore

x 2

Stanhope, that he had taken some interest in their mode of culture when in France, and made several experiments, this plantation of Winter Pears being one of them. He has kindly furnished me with the photograph from which the sketch was engraved, and the following account of the trees :—

"Allow me to furnish you with an illustration of my cordon Pear-wall, one-half of which, planted in December, 1861, bore fruit in 1864 ; another half, planted in March, 1865, bore fruit in 1868. From the time these trees began fruit-bearing up to the present date, they have been, and are now, perfectly healthy, and have yielded large crops every year, with the exception of two

Wall of Cordon Pear-trees in the gardens at Holme Lacy.

or three trees, perhaps, which may miss bearing each year ; as to the superiority of the fruit, in size, appearance, and flavour, over fruit grown in my garden on pyramids and espaliers, there can be no question. In hot summers it was found necessary to mulch, and even to water them, owing to the Quince stock, on which all are grafted, having more fibres and rooting nearer the surface than the Pear stock. They are trained on a south wall, which, however, is somewhat shaded by large Oaks, and, although this circumstance renders the wall unfavourable for Peaches, I do not consider it has been against these Quince-grafted Pears, as, but for the shade, they would probably have suffered more in hot summers than they have done. I do not, therefore, think a south wall, by any means, a necessity for the successful culture of cordon Pears in the south and west of England.   As to the pruning, my late gardener writes as follows : ' My experience in pinching has never been what I was led to expect; never, but in one solitary instance, have I found the fruit-bud to be the result of that practice, and even that one being so far from home, so to speak,

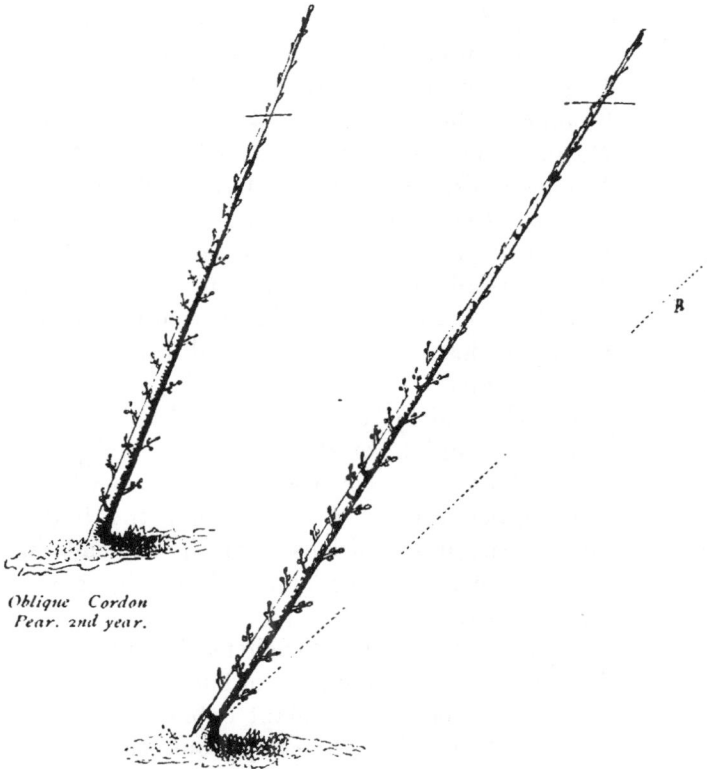

Oblique Cordon Pear. 2nd year.

Oblique Cordon Pear. 3rd year. B is the position which the tree will eventually occupy.

would have to be cut off in order to keep the spur short.   But that was not all, for I have found that what was once a decided fruit-bud would lengthen and grow into wood before the growing season closed.'   I myself certainly think that the pinching cannot be carried out in our climate to the same extent as in France. [Close pinching is a bad English practice—not a French one. In France I never saw fruit-trees pinched in very close.—W. R.] The result with us was to produce too many wood-shoots.   Whether this is the result of a richer soil and a moister climate or not, I cannot say.   The merit of the successful results of the cordon-wall is due to my late gardener, Mr. Wells, now at Osborne Park Nurseries, Potter's Bar.   The following are the weights of some of the cordon-grown Pears, produced by trees which have always been allowed to bear freely, viz. :—Glou Morceau, 13½ oz. ; Beurré Bosc, 12½ oz. ; Beurré Superfin, 14 oz. ; Van Mons, 15 oz. ; Easter Beurré, 16 oz. ; Beurré Diel, 15 oz. ; Zéphirin Grégoire, 11½ oz. ; Triomphe de Jodoigne, 14 oz. ; Joséphine de Malines, 11 oz. ; Doyenné d'Alençon, 13¾ oz. ; Duchesse d'Hiver, 18½ oz. ; Bergamotte d'Esperen, 11½ oz. ; Conseiller de la Cour, 14 oz. ; and fruit from Doyenné Boussoch, Beurré Hardy, Madame Millet, Williams's Bon Chrétien, Figue d'Alençon, and Beurré Sterckmans have weighed equal to these, as have also Duchesse d'Angoulême, and many others."

For the fruiting of seedlings and testing of new kinds, the cordon for Pears is also a good plan, and if the object be to cover a wall in a short time and get a quick return, it is certainly the best way. In this case it enables us to attain our ends in the shortest space of time, and with the least possible waste of space.

Pear-tree trained as a Vertical Cordon. This form is best suited for very high walls, etc.

Some of the leading teachers of fruit-culture in France adopt the oblique cordon as the short way to a quick return, and plant extensively the finest varieties trained in this way; but others ridicule the planting of trees as closely as one would Cole-worts.   For the finest kinds of Winter Pears and for culture on high walls it is well worth adopting, provided the trees can be got at a low price, or grafted on the spot.   None but the very best kinds should be planted, and to begin with, it would be desirable to plant a goodly number of one kind known to succeed well in the neighbourhood rather than a variety of sorts.   The kinds known to do best in this contracted form are *Beurré Superfin, Flemish Beauty, Beurré

Giffard, *Louise Bonne of Jersey, *Marie Louise, Beurré Clairgeau, Duchesse d'Angoulême, *Easter Beurré, and Beurré d'Anjou.

The Pear trained as an Oblique Cordon. This form is best suited for the wall-culture of choice Winter Pears where it is desired to obtain a quick return.

Of these a beginner would do well to take those marked with
an asterisk. As regards the training of the Pear in this
way, it is too simple to require description here. The tree is

merely treated as we train a single branch of a fan-shaped tree, and requires none of the careful pruning necessary to form the more elaborate shapes.   Healthy young plants, a year from the

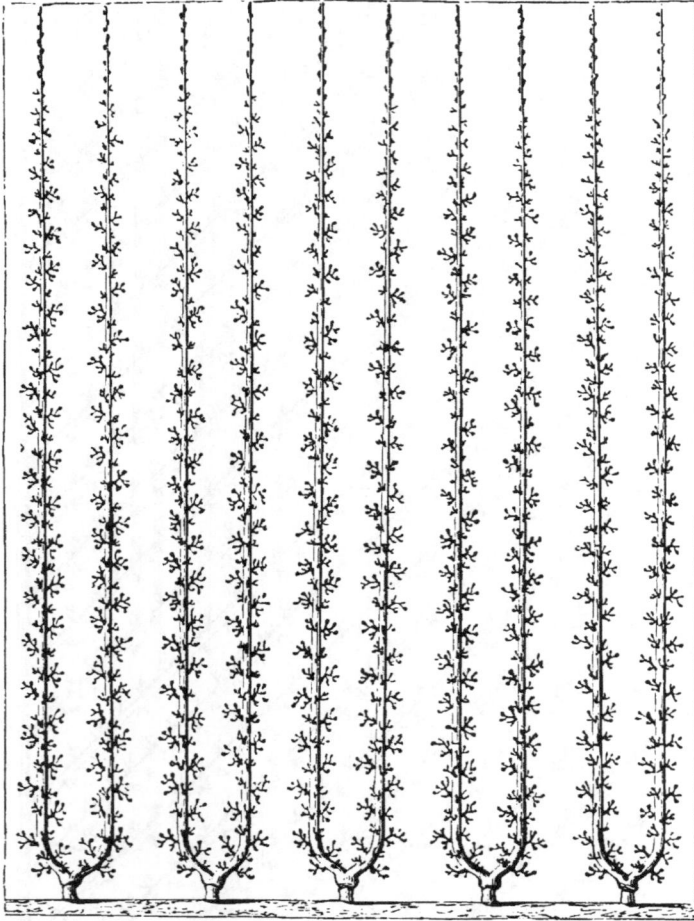

Pear-tree trained in U form for very high walls.

graft, are chosen, planted at from 16 to 18 inches apart, and trained as explained in the accompanying figures.

Sometimes the Pear is trained as a vertical single or double cordon. Of the two forms the single is preferable, and it is chiefly suited for very high walls, the gable ends of outhouses, and the like. It need scarcely be added that the trees in this case should be on the Quince stock.

The Pear may also be trained as a horizontal cordon on low walls, the fronts of glass houses, and as an edging like the Apple. But generally the Pear pushes too vigorously to be trained in this way, while the pendulous habit of the fruit renders it more liable to be splashed. I once saw Uvedale's St. Germain grown in this

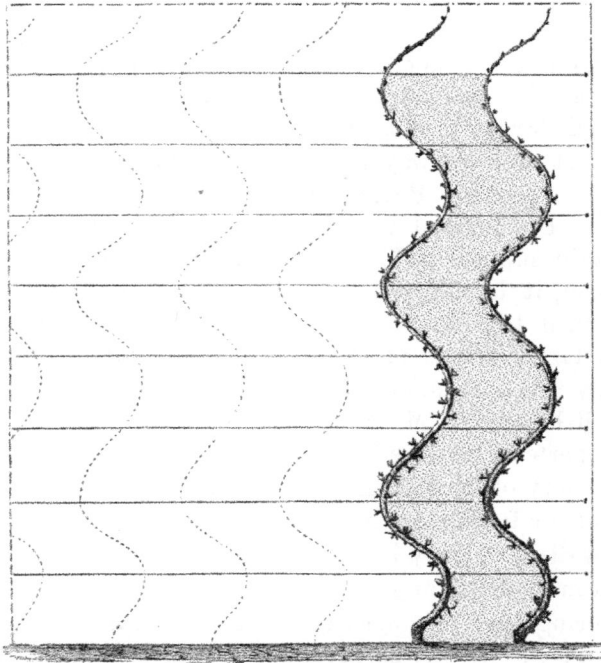

The Spiral Cordon against walls.

way at Chartres, the great fruit sitting on the ground, and quite encrusted with earthy splashings.

The disposition to form a neat compact line of spurs so abundantly manifested by the Apple when well trained on the Paradise is more rarely shown by the Pear. Nevertheless a few varieties, such as Louise Bonne and Beurré Giffard, might be tried; allowing them to attain a greater length of stem than the cordon Apples, and placing them a little higher from the ground.

As regards the Pear as a horizontal cordon, Mr. Watson of Geneva wrote as follows to the *Gardener's Chronicle:*—" I question if there exists elsewhere a more extensive collection of Pears trained on the horizontal-cordon system than may now be seen in M. Vaucher's garden near Geneva. There are hundreds of them, consisting of every good sort that M. Vaucher could buy. Beurré Noirchain, four feet six inches long, had twenty-three fruit upon it; Beurré Giffard, six feet six inches long, twenty-two fruit; those of the last-named kind hanging about four inches from the ground."

The Peach as a Cordon.—With the Peach as an oblique cordon, a good result is attained, the wall being covered very rapidly; and the neat laying-in of a great number of shoots on each side of the simple stem does away with the crowded appearance which a plantation of cordon Pears assumes when old and the stems thickened. But instead of the wood being closely pinched in, as people might suppose in England from reading of the method of one M. Grin, it is nailed in at each side of the branch, more so indeed than if that branch were part and parcel of one of the older and larger forms of tree. I once saw an excellent result afforded by this system against the high back wall of a vinery in the establishment of M. Rose-Charmeux, at Thomery. By its means he perfectly covered his wall in a short time, and gathered a great variety of fruit from a small space. Out of doors it not unfrequently affords equally good results. It is well calculated for high walls, and may be adopted for low ones by training the trees at a more acute angle with the earth.

Considering the time usually required to furnish walls in the ordinary way, there can be little doubt that this mode of training the Peach is a real improvement, where a considerable number of varieties are required from a small space. Apart from that, however, the facility and simplicity with which walls may be covered by this method, and the readiness with which a diseased or otherwise objectionable tree may be replaced, will doubtless prove a sufficient recommendation for cultivators who are not restricted as to space. It should, however, be borne in mind that on very good soils where the Peach grows very vigorously, it will not suit so well as on poor ones where it grows slowly, and that medium-sized forms may be adopted for the Peach as well as for the Pear. The following is a description of the mode of forming it after M. Lepère :—

" There are two modes of growing this form. One, which was recommended by a professor of arboriculture, and frequently put in practice by many amateurs, but which I consider faulty, consists in planting the trees just as they come from the nursery, and training them at once in the oblique form. The inconvenience arising from this method consists in being obliged

Young Peach-tree trained as an Oblique Cordon. 1st year. A shows the first pruning.

Peach-tree trained as an Oblique Cordon. 2nd year's pruning. The leading shoot is cut at A, and the side-shoots at the cross-marks.

to place the tree close to the wall, which crowds the roots too much, preventing them from affording sufficient nourishment to the tree. Besides this, on account of the inclination of the tree, part of the roots are directed towards the surface of the earth or placed in an unnatural position, thereby preventing their full development. By-and-by, the trees that have been planted thus are cut to half the length that they were when they came from the nursery, having a number of weak, useless branches on the lower part, a condition which, as every one knows, is always un-

favourable.   The second method differs from the first, inasmuch
as the plant from the nursery is cut down instead of being planted

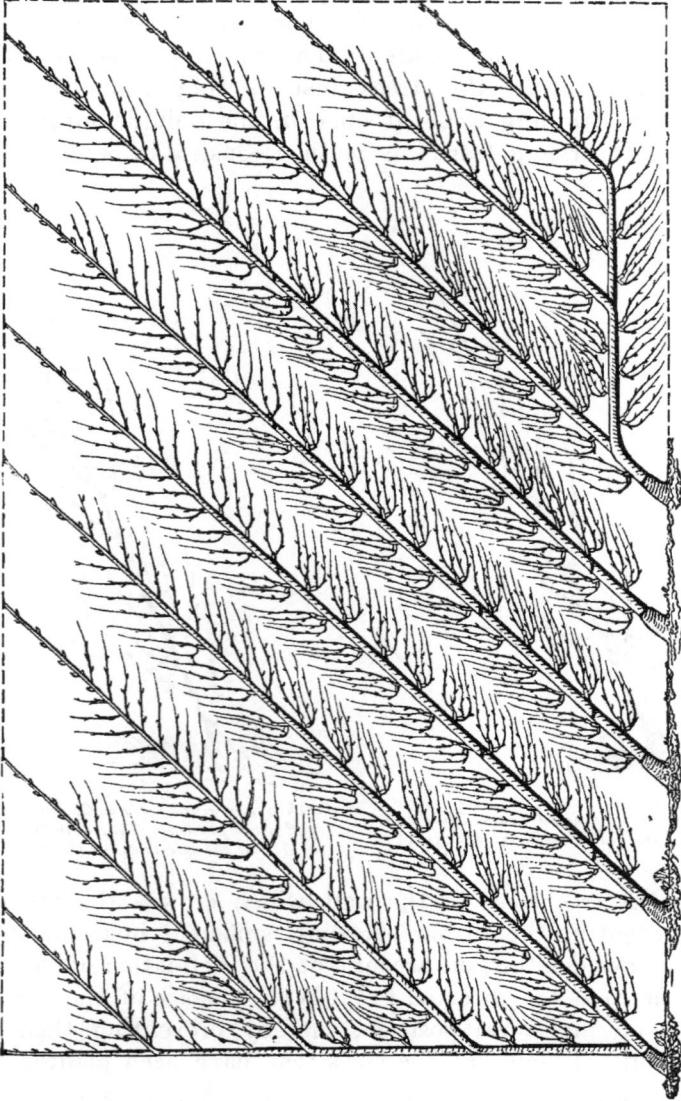

THE PEACH TRAINED AS AN OBLIQUE CORDON.   (*Du Breuil.*)

in an oblique direction.   To obtain the oblique form without
planting the tree in a crooked position, the stem is cut at eight

inches from the graft, and placed in the ground so that the base
of the stem is four inches from the wall, with its extremity just
touching it.   The roots are well spread over the hole and drawn
as much as possible towards the border in which the tree is
planted.   Care is taken to leave a well-placed bud on the side
where the oblique branch is to be formed, and its development
must be encouraged by ruthlessly pinching off all useless shoots.
Under these conditions, the tree grows as long during the first
year as the one planted obliquely and allowed to be of its full
length from the first.   This method is also to be preferred,
because the shoot thus obtained the first year can be left intact
and allowed to attain a development equal to that of the tree planted
according to the first method.   Besides this, the shoot is calculated
to grow faster in consequence of its bark being less
hardened, and each year the terminal point may be
allowed to grow without cutting back.   Sometimes the
terminal bud does not develop, owing to its having
been killed by cold.   In such a case a stronger eye is
chosen lower down to make the desired lengthening.

"As in the case of other forms of training, the
branches of the Peach cordons are allowed to grow in
a more erect position at first than they are finally intended to occupy.   I should advise this cordon form
to be adopted in the case of gardens whose walls are
on the incline, as often occurs, and for soil of inferior
quality where the Peach-tree grows slowly, because

*Young Peach
tree with three
stems, a dif-
ferent variety
being grafted
on each.*

under such circumstances it never attains its full development.
The plan does not answer where the ground is flat and the conditions are such as favour the rapid growth of the tree."

Some fruit-growers think that there is no occasion for resorting
to this simple cordon in the case of the Peach, any more than in
the case of the Pear.   M. F. Jamin, of Bourg-la-Reine, plants in
his fruit-garden a form of tree with three vertical branches, and
if he wants a great variety of fruit from a small space, works a
different variety on each branch.   This figure shows, on a small
scale, the appearance of one of his young specimens, trained on
this principle.   The U and double U forms, described in the
chapter on Montreuil, are also extensively adopted by many
growers in preference to the oblique cordon.

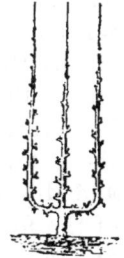

CHAPTER XIX.

THE PARADISE, DOUCIN, AND CRAB STOCKS.

THE stock is as important to the cultivated fruit-tree as the foundation is to the house; if we have not the right stock, all is wrong. The French Paradise stock is the only one that should be used to form cordon trees except on the very poorest and driest of soils. Before the writer had seen the results of using this stock in France and called attention to its merits, it was condemned as useless by our authorities, who described it as "exceedingly dwarf in its habit, and too tender for this climate, unless in very warm and dry soils!" But in fact it is as hardy as the hardiest tree of the forest, not perishing even if thrown with its roots exposed on the surface of the ground, and allowed to remain there through a rigorous winter; and the soils above all for which it is peculiarly unfitted are those that are hot and very dry, while it flourishes on rich, moist loams, and even bad clays—the very soils which often present the greatest amount of difficulty to the British fruit-grower. As will be readily seen, this is simply a matter for experiment, and I appeal to the horticulturists of Britain to settle the question by direct trial, a thing they can so readily do. The "English Paradise" is the Doucin—one that as regards vigour is intermediate between the Crab and the Paradise, well fitted for neat standards, pyramids, and large bushes, but growing too vigorously to furnish anything but disappointment if planted as a low cordon, except on very light calcareous or "burning" soils. To plant the Apple on the common or Crab stock, and expect to form a dwarf fertile tree, is folly. By mutilation and removals we may secure a crop, and keep the Doucin or "English Paradise" within bounds; but what is wanted is a stock that will furnish a dwarf and fertile growth, without any root-pruning or attention beyond that of slight pruning, according to their luxuriance. This we have exactly in the Paradise stock, grown by millions in the nurseries around Paris, and in many other parts of France.

We have next to determine what is this Paradise stock. It need scarcely be said that a plant like this, which exerts so marked an influence on the trees grafted on it, and is so truly valuable for our gardens, deserves to be at least as well known as

FLOWER OF THE FRENCH PARADISE APPLE.
Drawn from nature and engraved by A. Thiebault.

any one kind of fruit, however good. Yet this is so far from being the case that but very little is known about it. To most of the French botanists its origin is involved in obscurity; apparently the clearest account is that of Professor Koch of Berlin, who has paid a great deal of attention to the origin of all our fruit-trees. He says:—" The name Malus paradisiaca appears to have been first used by Ruellius in the year 1537. It is a native of South-Eastern Russia, Caucasus, Tartary, and the Altai Mountains. I have often seen this shrub in the Caucasus, and near the Don and the Volga, where it forms bushes and dwarf trees, frequently accompanied with suckers."

Without attempting to throw any light on the origin of the Paradise, M. Carrière of the Jardin des Plantes has studied its characteristics, compared them with those of the Doucin, and described both in the 'Flore des Serres':—

PARADISE.	DOUCIN.
"Roots much ramified and tidy, short, remaining near the surface, and never tap-rooted. Shrub, bush-like, much branched, the branchlets rather long, and with a lateral tendency, the adults covered with a smooth bark of a reddish colour; lightly pubescent in the case of the young shoots. Leaves lanceolate, elliptical, of a light green above and velvety beneath, finely denticulated, acuminate at the ends, but principally at the base. Petiole broadish and channelled. Calyx, with divisions acuminated and recurved, often contorted, as long as the peduncle. Petals straightly elongated at the base, faintly keeled, borne on a thin base, prolonged into a sort of keel. Ovary on a slender base, pubescent. Fruit higher than broad, lightly ribbed, skin white, flesh sweetish, almost insipid; ripening in July." It flowers more abundantly, and eight days earlier, than the Doucin.	"Roots rather long and strong, tap-rooted. Tree not much ramified, straight in its growth, with branchlets short, large, in adult specimens covered with a deep dull brown bark; very tomentose, and whitened in the case of the young shoots. Leaves broadly oval or nearly oboval, lightly blistered, shining on the upper and pubescent on the lower surface, rather broadly denticulated, scarcely acuminate at the apex, abruptly contracted and round at the base. Petiole broad, scarcely channelled. Calyx with divisions usually horizontal, occasionally recurved, rather large. Petals suboval, nearly blistered, keeled, borne on a base short and rather broad. Ovary on a stout support, covered with a tomentose down, white and thick. Fruit depressed, broader than high, not ribbed, the skin of an intense green, marked here and there with brownish spots: flesh of a high and agreeable flavour; ripening in August."

The Paradise stock has been known in France for between 200 and 300 years. The Doucin would appear to be not quite so ancient, but has been known for at least 160 years. It is used to form low trees, pyramids, wall, espalier, and even standard trees less vigorous and more suitable for gardens than those grafted on the Crab stock and occasionally for cordons on bad and poor dry soils. It is most probably a vigorous and deep-rooting variety of the same species as the Paradise, healthy everywhere, and succeeding well where, in consequence of its habit of surface-rooting, the Paradise would suffer and prove useless. Apples grafted upon the Doucin come into bearing earlier than upon the Crab, and it is admirable for all forms of garden-trees in size intermediate between the very dwarf cordons and bushes and the tall and vigorous orchard-trees.

The Crab stock it is needless to describe. It is the stock on which our Apples have been grafted for ages, and which is the only one employed in the majority of British gardens. It is the natural stock for the Apple, and that on which it grows with greatest vigour ; but it takes a much longer time to come into bearing, and the attempts to keep it of a size suited to gardens by pruning, pinching, and root-pruning which may be seen everywhere, are all efforts thrown away. Thus it will be seen there

THIEBAULT

Fruit of the French Paradise Apple. Drawn from nature and engraved by A. Thiebault.

are three distinct stocks, each suiting distinct purposes, and that those who experiment upon the cordon system of Apple-growing without acting upon or bearing in mind these facts as the most important in connection with the subject, cannot be said to try it fairly.

Of these three stocks, the one which has been most abused and least known, but which will yet prove the most valuable of all as a garden stock for the Apple, is the true French Paradise. When

fairly tried it proves to be of all stocks yet known the hardiest,
most dwarfing in its effects, and most powerful in inducing early
fertility.   This stock, which has been characterised in England as
a thing quite worthless, will, if planted in the coldest and wettest
of soils, instead of sending long roots down into the sour clayey
earth like the Crab and in a lesser degree the Doucin, keep its
wig-like mass of small roots near the surface, and without root-
pruning bear fruit long before the others.   That is the way to
best test its powers of withstanding cold, and the other merits
claimed for it : on all ordinarily rich and cool soils it will be
found to succeed perfectly without root-pruning of any kind.
Growers have only to try it to prove that instead of dying in our
cool climate, and on our moist soils, its general adoption will lead
to marked improvement.   It is necessary to observe that in
trying this stock healthy plants should be secured to begin with.
It has been ascertained that some of our nurserymen who have
tried this stock import the Paradise from France in a very small
state, and then graft it soon after it arrives.   The consequence is
that the little trees have no power to push forth a healthy graft.
If imported in this state they should be allowed one year's growth
before being grafted.

Thinking that experienced growers in the colder parts of North
America might be able to throw some light on the hardiness of
this stock, I wrote to Mr. J. J. Thomas, a pomologist of long
and deserved repute, author of a standard book on fruit-culture,
and pomological editor of the Albany ' Cultivator,' who replied
as follows :—" The French Paradise stock grows well with us on
strong soils, with suitable pruning and cultivation.   Neglected,
and on light soils, it frequently fails after a lapse of several
years.   The oldest trees with which I am acquainted in western
New York are on the grounds of Ellwanger & Barry, at Rochester.
Trees which have been worked on it thirty years old still possess
a fair degree of vigour, having stems six inches to eight inches in
diameter, and the trees are about eight feet high, with about the
same extent of branches.   Twelve-year-old trees are five feet or
six feet high, and four inches or five inches in diameter.   On my
own grounds, which are a strong clay-loam, trees which have
been planted twenty-five years are seven inches in diameter at
the base, and are about ten feet high, with ten feet spread of top.

These have been sparingly pruned. In these remarks I carefully distinguish the true French Paradise, with its peculiar wood and small fruit, with a mixture of sweet and bitter in its flavour."

On the same subject Mr. Such of South Amboy, New Jersey, writes as follows :—

"In my garden I have on this stock many little bush-like Apple-trees that have endured the greatest extremes of heat and of cold. About four winters ago the thermometer fell to 20° below zero, and last summer the heat was intense, reaching 106° to 108° in the shade. In spite of this my little trees are in perfect health. The Doucin stock is also thoroughly hardy. There is near here a small orchard of Apples on this stock, planted more than fifteen years ago, all of which are in full vigour. My trees on the Paradise are like very large currant bushes ; those on the Doucin are from ten to fifteen feet through."

Since the first edition of this book appeared, the Paradise stock has been figured in the 'Florist and Pomologist' (May, 1875), with the following remarks :—

"We have much pleasure in submitting a figure of the true French Paradise Apple, the Pommier de Paradis, which, when used as a stock, is of such inestimable value in inducing dwarfness and prolificacy in other varieties of Apple. Mr. Barron has collected from various sources, British and Continental, a number of Apple stocks, which are growing side by side, so as to admit of easy comparison. Side by side, also, are various Apples worked on the several stocks. There are the Crab stocks (Pommiers francs), with long, spreading, rigid, wiry, tangled branches, of a deep purplish-black colour, and at the time of our visit (April 11) with no vestige either of leaf or flower to be seen. There is the Dutch Paradise, of straggling habit, with olive-coloured shoots, in full leaf, but without a flower. There is Mr. Rivers's Nonsuch English Paradise, destitute of leaf or flower, and Rivers's Miniature Paradise, equally late, and scarcely justifying its name. There is Mr. Scott's Paradise, of very distinct somewhat pyramidal habit, in full leaf, but with scarcely a flower to be seen. There is the Doucin, also of pyramidal habit, and producing flowers early. Then there is the true French Paradise, Pommier de Paradis, obtained from the most reliable sources in France, which must unquestionably bear away the prize for precocity of flowering and abundance of bloom. By precocity we mean not early flowering with regard to season, but with reference to age also; while other stocks of the same age have not reached the fruiting stage, this one has already done so. It is of rather straggling habit, but full of flower. While some stocks at the time of our visit were showing few flowers and others none at all, this one stood out in the row sheeted over with pale pink blossoms. These qualities it very markedly contributes to the grafts. Short compact growth, and early and abundant flowering, characterise the scions grafted on this stock, as they characterise the stock itself. A long row in one of the quarters, consisting of various Apples grafted on this stock, side by side with rows grafted on other stocks, is one of the most striking illustrations of the effects and consequences of grafting it has ever been our fortune to witness. The difference in appearance is so great that it would almost seem as if the one row were cultivated for fruit, the other for timber! By way of illustration we may mention the Rhode Island Greening, a vigorous-growing kind, but which when worked on this stock becomes subdued, assumes a short, bushy habit, and produces an abundance of early bloom. What was formerly grown at Chiswick under the name of French Paradise is quite a different thing, and relatively very inferior. Of course this Paradise stock is not intended for orchard use, where the freer-growing stocks are preferred. The French Paradise stock is of spreading habit, with pale purplish shoots. The inflorescence is abundant, and precocious as to season, and also in relation to the age of the plant. The young leaves are glabrescent, oblong-lanceolate, the apex acute, the base rounded, the margin crenu-lated, the crenulations mucronulate; the petiole is less than half the length of the leaf, setose, and the stipules are linear-subulate, as long as the petiole. The peduncles are about three-quarters of an inch long, setose; the flower-tube glabrous urceolate, reddish, one-eighth of an inch long; the calyx-lobes triangular, gradually acuminate, setose within; the petals concave, oblong-obtuse, tapering at the base into a short stalk, and provided with a few cottony hairs on the inner surface; the styles are crested at the base for a short distance, and there slightly covered with cottony hairs, dividing above into five stigmatic branches. The fruit, which is a really good early eating Apple, is, according to our notes, of medium size, oblate, somewhat angular, yellow, changing on the exposed side to deep golden-yellow, and sometimes having a thin flush of rosy-red. The eye is broad, but closed, sunk in a rather deep cavity. The stalk is short, scarcely projecting from the hollow, which is not so deep as that of the eye. The flesh is pale straw colour, fine grained, solid, juicy, and with a brisk agreeable flavour. It ripens in the middle and end of August, and would form a good useful early dessert Apple, independent of its value as a dwarfing stock for Apple-trees grown in the bush or pyramidal form."

A correspondent of the *Garden* writes, " I find it to be a very difficult matter to procure it (the French Paradise) in this country; and, so far as my experience goes, nurserymen seem to discourage its introduction. Last year I wanted a number of trees on the French stock, and had a quantity sent to me by a nurseryman whom I knew; but the vigorous appearance of the trees made me doubt the stock. Acting upon my advice, the nurseryman wrote to another in the trade, who advertises one of the largest collections of Apples and Pears in England, and stocks of all sorts and sizes, and the result was a letter in reply condemning the French Paradise stock as useless, and recommending another variety of the English Paradise, which the writer of the letter had raised and named after himself, and which it appeared was superior to any other in existence. Not a little annoyed at being put off in this way, my friend took the trouble to procure the plants for me direct from France, and from an undoubted source; and fine well-ripened little trees they were, only about half as vigorous as those I had got before on the English stock. They were planted in March, and some of the trees, though only maidens, bore a few large fine fruit this season, and they are planted in the open quarters of the kitchen-garden. They have also made a good growth, and promise to bear well next year. Besides these, I ordered another lot on the French Paradise, this time from a house north of the Tweed; but was informed they could not be got in England true, and that I must wait until the frost had gone in France, when I should be supplied. I did so, and had them direct from Orleans in April. This is my experience in trying to get the French Paradise stock, which I am desirous of experimenting with."

Trials made in a variety of gardens, apart from that by Mr. Barron in the Royal Horticultural Gardens at Chiswick, have proved all that has been claimed for this stock. Among the most important of the trials were those at Paxhill Park, in Sussex, in the gardens of the late Mr. Northall Laurie ; in Mr. Roger Leigh's garden at Barham Court ; and in Mr. Dancer's fruit-garden at Little Sutton, Chiswick ; where very satisfactory results were obtained. Trials were also made in the Duke of Portland's garden at Welbeck by Mr. Tillery, and as in the cases previously mentioned, with complete success.

Mr. Roger Leigh, of Barham Court, showed at South Kensington such a collection of dessert and culinary Apples grown on this stock as one rarely has an opportunity of seeing. Among the dessert varieties were King of the Pippins, Cox's Orange Pippin, Ribston, and others, not only large but especially handsome, owing to their fine colour ; while the culinary sorts, such as Belle du Bois, White Calville, Reinette du Canada, and others, were remarkable for their great size. These fine Apples are gathered from trees growing in bush or cordon form on the true Paradise stock and in good soil. The fruit thus produced in a Kentish garden is fully equal to the best samples grown on the Continent—a noteworthy fact, and one well worth the attention of cultivators, and especially of those who grow fruit for market.

Preserving Grapes through the Winter without letting them hang on the Vines.

The preservation of Grapes through the winter with the least amount of trouble is one of the most important of all matters to the British Grape-grower. Every cultivator knows to his cost what a serious inconvenience it used to be to keep Grapes hanging all the winter after they were ripe, especially in places where there were a good many houses devoted to Vines. Books on the Vine give directions for regulating the Vineries so as to preserve the Grapes after they are ripe, and every calendar of operations tells us how to manage them in that respect, though the directions are not always intelligible. Here, for instance, is an extract from a recent issue of a gardening-paper :—" Those who wish to keep Grapes hanging as fresh and plump as possible to the longest possible period, must take care not to afford them too much heat, as an excess of this, no matter how dry the structure may be, or how favourably treated otherwise, is sure to cause them to shrivel more or less prematurely. Give only just such warmth to the pipes or flues as will insure sufficient buoyancy to any humidity (!) which may arise in the house as to enable it to make its escape. Independently of the ill effects caused by actual heat, a too-warm atmosphere, even in the driest house, will cause a correspondingly excessive evaporation and consequent condensation." Then of course we must have fire-heat and give air when foggy days occur, "as," says Mr. Thompson of Chiswick—"the mean temperature of this month (November) is on the average little above 40°, and the air is generally saturated with moisture. When this is the case, moisture will be deposited on all substances exposed to the air, if they are not warmer than it is. Grapes that are ripe should therefore be kept warmer than the air, otherwise they will be liable to damp. The application of fire-heat would effect this: but if it were applied suddenly, and without air being given at the same time, the heated air would deposit moisture on the berries; for although these would ultimately acquire the same temperature as that of the air surrounding them, yet for a time they would be colder, and so long as this is the case they would act as condensers of the moisture in the warmer air in contact with them. The more rapidly the air is heated, the greater for a time will be the difference between the temperature of the fruit and that of the air, and of course the slower the heating the less at any time will be the difference. Give therefore, in damp weather, a little fire-heat in the morning, and admit air. If the nights are cold, the temperature of the house should not be allowed to fall lower than 45°." Here then are delicate operations and much trouble to bestow on perhaps half a dozen houses during the winter months. If the vineries are old and badly heated, the task is most difficult; in the best-constructed ones it is a great and needless labour. The trouble of regulating the atmosphere, the expense for fire-heat, and the necessity of keeping the house almost entirely devoted to the Grapes, must render any improvement acceptable.

M. Rose-Charmeux's method of keeping Grapes fresh and plump throughout the winter by inserting the ends of their stalks in bottles of water instead of letting them hang on the Vines for months, was in France accepted as a great boon.   One of the best examples of what can be done in a private place is to be found in the gardens of Ferrières, the country seat of Baron Rothschild. Here is constructed, in addition to very fine and well-filled fruit-rooms, a Grape-room, which is filled with stands thickly hung from top to bottom with all kinds of Grapes   M. Bergman, the manager, by cutting down all his Grapes in harvest fashion, is thus enabled in a few weeks, in fact as soon as the Grapes in the latest houses are ripe, to do as he pleases with the crop of his many and well-managed Vineries.   He can allow the wood to ripen, prune and clean the Vines, or utilise the cleared space of the houses for any purpose that may be convenient, not fearing as we used to do in England, to spill a drop of water or make full use of the house.

The Grapes are cut with a considerable portion of the shoot attached, much as if one were pruning the Vine; the shoot is inserted in a narrow-necked and small bottle containing water, and these little bottles are fixed firmly in a row, so that the bunches hang just clear of each other.   In the first instance two strong uprights are erected, each supported on three legs. Then from one to the other of these uprights, on both sides alternately, are nailed sets of strong laths, two for each line of bottles. These laths are kept an inch and a half or so apart by a piece of wood at each end; in the inner one are made incisions, into which the bottom of each little bottle fits, and then the outer lath has a concave incision in which the side of the bottle rests, so that, caught in the inner and leaning firmly on the outer lath, it holds the stem and stout bunch quite firmly.   Walking space was left between the walls of Grapes; for six or seven rows were arranged one above another on both sides of each support.

Animal charcoal is mixed with water, allowed to stand for some time, and then the water is strained off to fill the bottles.   But there can be no doubt that to put a pinch of animal charcoal in each bottle would prove a better plan of guarding the water from any impurity from the slight deposit of organic matter that might be expected; at least, it does not seem very clear how charcoal removed from the water before the Vine-stem is put in can have much effect in keeping it pure.   However, this is not an important matter, and it is certain that a pinch of animal charcoal, which is very cheap, will keep the water quite sweet. One cultivator who keeps Grapes on a large scale by this method, never uses any charcoal at all, but simply fills his little bottles almost full with water, and then inserts the branches, which nearly close the necks of them. He appeared quite as well satisfied with the plan as those who had taken pains to keep the water sweet. In case evaporation should cause the water in the bottles to fall below the bases of the shoots it is simply necessary to add a little more.

With one-tenth the amount of expense and trouble we may in a Grape-room like this maintain conditions infinitely better calculated to preserve the fruit than is possible in the Vinery. We

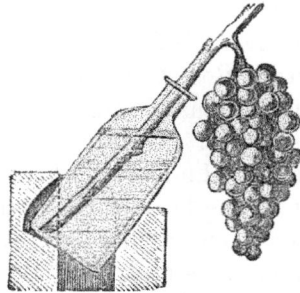

Thomery mode of fixing the bottles.   *Ferrières mode of fixing the bottles.*   *Portion of upright used in Grape-room at Ferrières.*

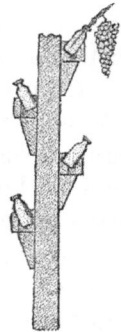

may keep the fruit in the dark, preserve the necessary amount of dryness in the atmosphere, and keep up an equable temperature, all of which conditions are essential to the well-being of fruits. It would be wise, in arranging a room of the sort, to have hollow walls and other contrivances to attain the conditions under which fruit is known to keep best.

As we grow better hothouse Grapes and on a larger scale than any other country, this method has proved of more use to us than to the French. Those who have adopted the system are unanimous in declaring, after several years' experience, that they can keep the fruit as long in this way as upon the Vine, with fewer mouldy berries, and almost without trouble. Having all the stock of Grapes safely housed and away from the attacks of vermin and other interlopers, is another of the many advantages presented by this plan. In places where the stock of Grapes is not sufficient to require a special room for their keeping, part of the fruit-room, or even a dry cellar or store-room, might be adapted to this purpose.

M. Rose-Charmeux, when he originated the plan, began by having a stove and a couple of chimneys to try to regulate the atmosphere of his large Grape-room ; but finding that the Grapes kept very much better without this, he simply devoted to his winter stock of Grapes a large room in his house. It is fitted up in all parts to accommodate handily the little bottles before spoken of, padding the inside of the windows so as to exclude light, and obviate, as far as possible, changes of temperature. The Grapes are cut in October, and preserved in good condition until April, when the earliest of the new crop are ready to cut. He has frequently preserved them till May, and even till August.

A small room in M. Rose-Charmeux's house demonstrates that a similar one in most houses might be made to answer the purposes of keeping Grapes. It has no windows, and scarcely any means of ventilation. The house is heated by hot air ; but while there are openings in the floor of the passages and other rooms to admit this, there are none in this little room in which the Grapes keep perfectly. Thus it is clear that the ordinary dwelling-house will present suitable conditions for the preservation of Grapes throughout the winter. The system was attractive enough when it was considered necessary to construct a room specially to carry it out ; it is much more so now when it has been proved that not only is it unnecessary to take any special means to warm or ventilate the structure, but that the Grapes keep much better without that trouble. The first result of the method was an annual gain to the village of Thomery, which is almost wholly occupied with Grape-culture, of from £4000 to £6000. The system enables the cultivators to keep their Grapes much later than of old, and thus to add considerably to their revenue.

In England the system has been tried and favourably reported on by Mr. Hill of Keele Hall, the famous Grape grower, and by other good growers. Mr. Whittaker of Crewe Hall sent some to a meeting of the Horticultural Society, but he had taken unnecessary trouble by corking and sealing the bottles. The insertion of the shoot into a bottle of water is all that is required, and as the bottles used are little more than wide enough at the neck to admit the shoot, the surface exposed to evaporation is very small.   It has been urged against the method that the Grapes "lose their sugar."   This is not the case unless the fruit is kept a very long time.   The French, in carrying out their experiments, have kept some of their Grapes as long as they could, and have frequently shown them in a nice plump condition long after they ripen their early Grapes.   In these extreme instances a loss of sugar was no doubt perceptible ; but what kind of flavour would

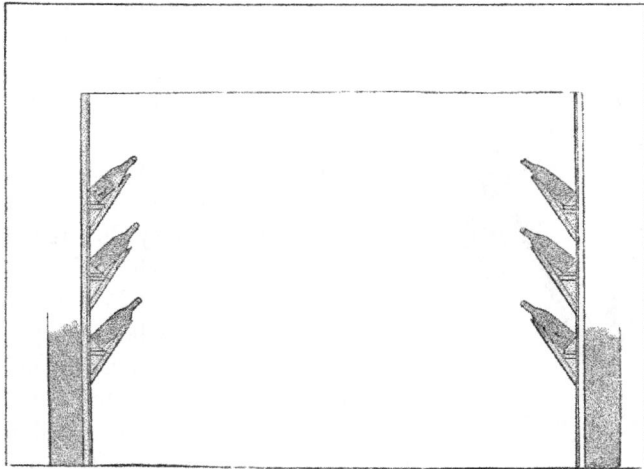

Section of Grape-room at Heckfield. Scale ¼ in. to 1 ft.

Grapes possess if left hanging on the Vine till the summer months when these Grapes were exhibited?   There is no necessity for keeping them till they lose their sugar.   In most of our large gardens Grapes are forced early, and would be ripe before the fruit of the previous year had lost its virtues in the least degree. To be able to clear the Vineries of Grapes two months before the ordinary time, will prove to be a decided gain to all Grape-growers.

Not only has this system been adopted by all our great English grape-growers, but they have modified it by doing away with the necessity for using bottles.   Mr. William Dodds has invented a V tube made of tin or zinc, and suspended by a wire. They are simple in construction, and may be made by any ordinary tinman.

Mr. Kemp has invented what he calls a Grape-rail, which mainly consists in the substitution of a fine trough for the series of bottles.

Mr. Wildsmith's Grape-room at Heckfield is 14 feet long by 10 feet broad and 8 feet high, and is fitted with three tiers of racks running horizontally round the room.   Space is thus provided for a large quantity of fruit.

Messrs. Tillery, Wildsmith, Nisbet, Simpson, Johnston, and a host of others have all adopted the system as a permanent thing.

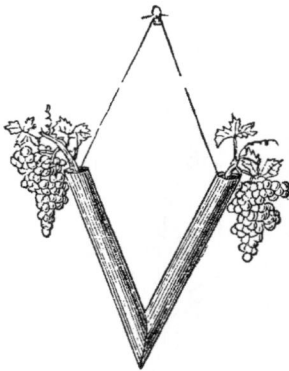

Mr. Dodd's tube for Grapes in Water.

The particular variety of Grape which seems most fitted for keeping in this way is Lady Downe's Seedling; but Black Alicante, Barbarossa, Black Tripoli, Burckhardt's Prince, Royal Vineyard, Gros Colman, Syrian, White Vine, and Trebbiano, succeed well when cut perfectly ripe.   Lady Downe's Seedling may be cut as late as the end of February, and will keep good until the end of June. It may be asked why late Grapes should be kept so long when early forced Grapes can be cut as early as May; but it must be remembered that the difference in cost between keeping late and forcing early Grapes is enormous, whether they are intended for the table or market.   Late Grapes, too, carry better to market than early forced ones.

The advantages of setting both Vines and houses free at so early a period will be appreciated by everybody, more especially by those who are still stricken with the bedding-out mania.   It also gives the Vines greater strength, and allows them to do fuller justice to the pains bestowed upon them.   The conditions of success are simple, and easily complied with.   First, the Grapes must be thoroughly ripe before being placed in the bottles. Secondly, the house must be suitable, *i.e.*, dry and frost-proof, and not liable to unreasonable fluctuations in temperature which induce decay, especially if the Grapes are not fully ripe when bottled.

On these points hangs the whole matter of good or bad preservation. Complete ripeness is easily secured, but a proper house is a more difficult matter. It should be built with hollow walls, to neutralise the effects of both heat and cold; and, though much fire-heat is undesirable, as it causes the fruit to shrivel, provision should be made for its application to expel damp when required—the door

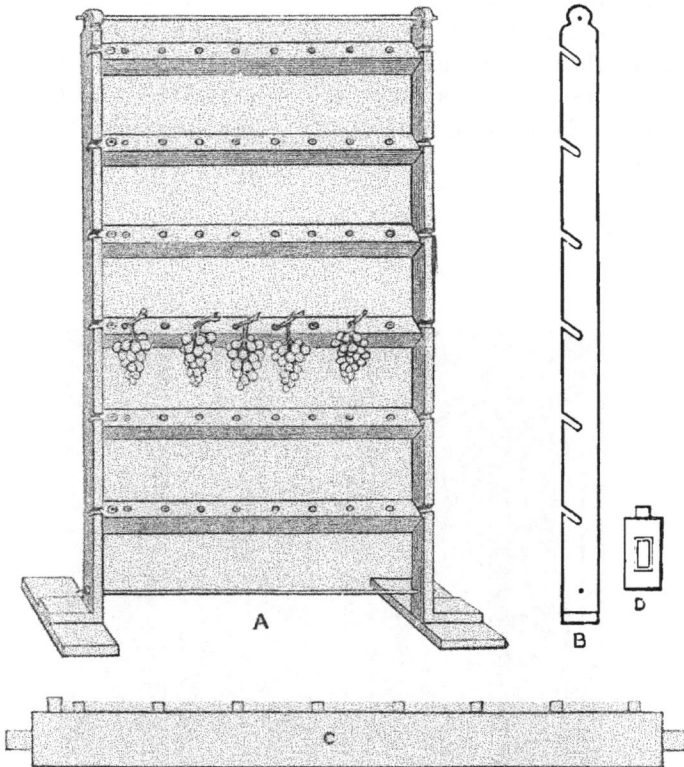

Kemp's Grape-rail.—A, front view; B, side view of support; D, end view of trough; C, side view of trough.

and ventilators being wide open while the heat is being given. The most important point to observe when cutting the Grapes is to see that the whole extent of wood above the bunch be left intact, and not cut off as in the illustration of the Thomery and Ferrières methods of Grape-preserving. The water absorbed by the wood is by this means partially diverted from the fruit into

the branch beyond it, thus preventing deterioration in flavour. If
charcoal is put in the water when the bottles are first filled,
changing the water is never required, and in such a room as that
described evaporation is so trifling that water need only be added
once or twice in the season to keep the bottles full.   Given the
above conditions, and Grape-rooms would soon become as common
as other fruit-rooms, because the Grapes would be certain to keep,
and the Vineries would be set free so much sooner.   Of course,
like most other innovations, it was laughed at when first described
as likely to be a useful system in English gardens. I first noticed
it in use at Thomery in M. Rose-Charmeux's garden there.

Interior of Grape-room at Thomery.

CHAPTER XX.

SOME NOTES ON FRUIT GARDENS.

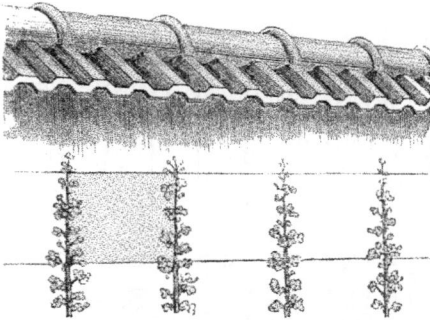

Permanent tiled coping to Peach-wall, Bourg-la-Reine.

MANY French nurserymen have, in addition to the ground devoted to the raising and training of young trees, a private garden or "school" of fruit-culture, in which various trees may be seen in a developed state. The garden established by M. F. Jamin is an excellent example of this class of garden, and being near Paris and easily accessible, should be visited by the stranger interested in fruit-culture. The walls of stone have a coping of overlapping tiles, which project about nine inches. This is, perhaps, as good a coping as any in use, and its effect is neat, much more so than that of other tile copings employed here. The walls are all wired closely and effectively with the galvanised wire tightened by the raidisseur. The walls with the warmest and best aspects are planted with Peaches and Winter Pears, and herein is an instructive lesson.

A most experienced fruit-grower here, one who knows England, gives as his experience that it is absolutely useless to attempt the culture of the finer Winter Pears, the most valuable of all, away from walls, and that it is necessary to place such kinds as the Easter Beurré against well-coped walls with a southern exposure, the soil being of the finest description and the climate that of

Paris.   He could grow some of them in the open, but they would
be uncertain and worthless; and he gives an instance—Beurré
Rance, which is excellent against walls.   The collection of Winter
Pears had only been planted a short time, and yet the crop was
very good, every young tree bearing as much as one could desire
to see upon it.   These Pear-trees were destined finally to assume
the form known as the Palmette Verrier; but the branches were
being trained diagonally, so that they might be furnished and
formed with less trouble and in a shorter time, the sap rising
much more freely and naturally in young branches that ascend
obliquely than when they run in an exactly horizontal direction.
Beurré Diel is also planted against walls here—not that it may

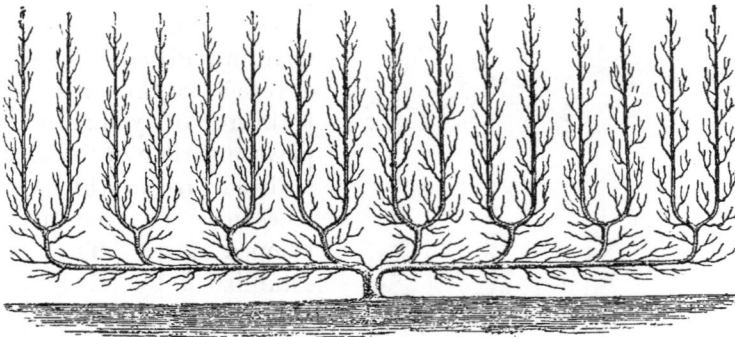

*Peach-tree (Candelabrum) with the vertical branches in the U form, instead of ascending
directly from the mother-branch as in opposite illustration.*

not be grown in the open, but its flowers are very liable to be
injured by frost in spring, and therefore it is placed on a wall to
secure a crop.

   This garden is very instructive, as showing the perfect control
under which the energies of the trees are directed to a useful end
by the skilful cultivator.   Though a nursery-garden where the
more promising young trees are often sold, there are nevertheless
beautiful specimens of trees in it—the Candelabrum Peach-tree
for example.   Illustrations of such trees having usually shown the
tree when bare of leaves and fruit, it seemed desirable that the
public should see some when in full bearing.   The fine example of
a Peach-tree represented opposite has been drawn and engraved
exactly after a photograph taken when the fruit was approaching

ripeness.   It is one of the most interesting examples I have seen
of training applied to a good end, that is to say, where all done
to the tree, is done with a well-directed aim and with a good
result.   A good deal of pruning is often done without either.

In this garden the plan of adopting three upright shoots from

*Peach-tree with 20 vertical branches (Candelabrum form) in full bearing; variety, Chevreuse
tardive; 10 years of age, 33 feet long, 10 feet high; average crop, 400 Peaches of the first quality
and size.   M. Jamin's garden, Bourg-la-Reine.*

one tree, instead of the cordon system, has been carried out.   It
is applied to the Apricot and the Peach, one kind being worked
on each ascending branch, and thus three kinds are borne by each
tree.   There was no indication of a disposition on the part of any
of the trios thus united not to grow agreeably together; indeed,

z

they were as equally balanced and as healthy as could be wished. Where it is desired, by nurserymen or private growers, to have a large number of varieties in a restricted space, this is the best plan of all.

Western and southern walls are found to require more protection and wider copings than those with northern and eastern aspects, the abundant rains being more dreaded than the frost; the

Pyramid Beurré Dumont; 10 years old, 10 feet high, 10 feet wide. M. Jamin's garden, Bourg-la-Reine.

western walls here have therefore a much deeper coping than the eastern. North walls receive very little coping and sometimes no protection at all in the way of a permanent coping, while east walls have one eight inches deep, south walls ten inches, and west walls twelve inches. Surely nothing can be more suggestive to those who have to grow fruit in Britain, the country of rain. This curious difference in the way of protecting the walls according to their exposure, is based on long observation, and it partly explains

to us why the deep temporary copings recommended in this book
are so effective in saving crops.   It may be doubted if they could
have much influence in protecting the trees from intense cold, but
they give complete protection from cold rains, sleet, and snow.

A winged pyramid figured in this chapter from one of the
specimens here, is of a form which commends itself owing to the

*Winged Pyramid, Beurré Hardy; 10 years old, 13 feet high, 6½ feet wide; average crop,
400 Pears. M. Jamin's garden, Bourg-la-Reine.*

avoidance of loss from high winds, the branches being firmly
placed in position.   It is a combination of the espalier and the
pyramid, and is as easy to form as any other to those who have
learnt the rudiments of fruit-culture as taught in France.
The branches are trained in four opposite wings mutually supporting each other by the aid of slender rods of willow, or any
easily-procured stakes.   Such a form must not be classed among

z 2

the mere curiosities of training; in addition to the fruit being
supported firmly, the wood and fruit are more fully exposed to
the sun, and the tree has full room for its complete development.
On deep and strong soils this is of great importance, excessive
repression by the knife producing gross infertile wood. Therefore
free large forms of this kind are as valuable in some soils as the
small forms like the cordon are in others, especially for kinds of
Pear that grow and fare best on the Pear stock.

The handsome palmette form is also well grown here. One

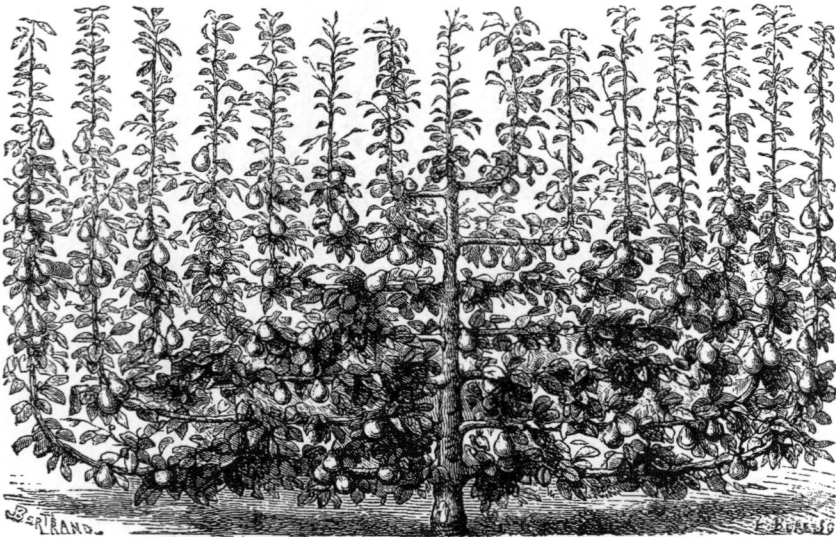

Pear Triomphe de Jodoigne, in Palmette form; 10 years old, 15 feet long, 8¼ feet high.
M. Jamin's garden, Bourg-la-Reine.

specimen in full bearing was photographed, drawn, and engraved
for this work. This is the handsomest of the large forms for trees
in strong soils, and many beautiful examples of it may be seen in
France. Cordon trees are well grown in this garden, and the
horizontal ones forming copings are protected in spring by broom
or other twigs woven into light frames of wood about twenty
inches wide, and supported a few inches above the cordon in
flower.

M. Durand's garden in this town contains also a good example
of a fruit-garden, including a collection of the choicest Grapes

South

North

East

West

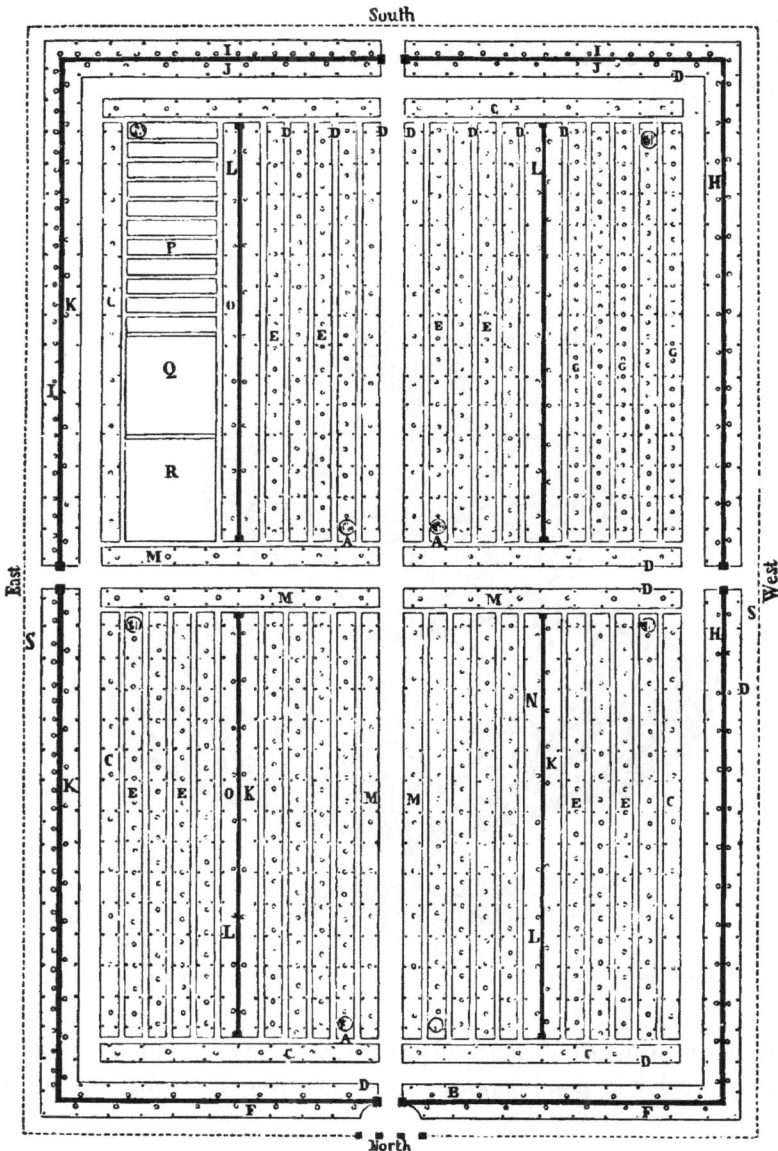

Plan of Fruit garden for the North of France, designed by M. J. Durand, of Bourg-la-Reine, 150 yards long and 80 broad.

References to Plan.—A, Cisterns for water-supply. B, South wall with Peach-trees trained in the fan, palmette, and candelabrum forms. C, Espaliers of Pears in the palmette form, the trees eighteen feet apart. D, Lines of Apples trained as horizontal cordons, planted twelve feet apart and a few inches within the margin of the beds E, Pear-trees in the columnar form, ten feet apart. F, North wall with Cherry-trees, about sixteen feet apart. G, Bush Apples on the Paradise

grown in France. The plan of forming a special garden for fully-trained fruit-trees is well worthy of imitation by growers of fruit-trees for sale.

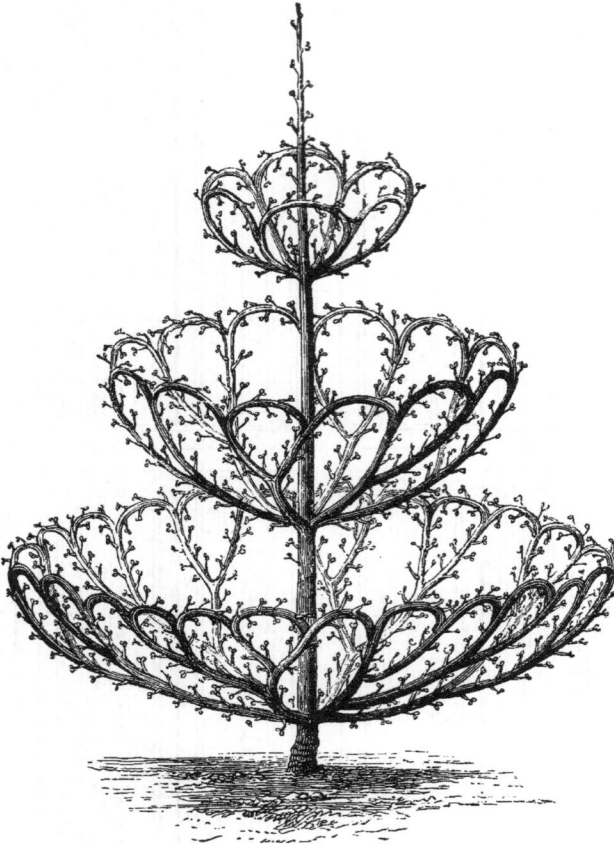

Pear-tree grown by M. Croux, of Sceaux. All the points of the branches have been united by grafting.

On mentioning to M. Durand my wish to have a plan of what he would consider a good example of a fruit-garden in Northern

---

stock, six feet apart. H, East wall with Winter Pears, such as Easter Beurré, Crassane, and St. Germain. I, South wall of Peach-trees with five erect branches, eight feet asunder. J, North wall with Cherries in the palmette form, about sixteen feet apart. K, West wall of Summer and Autumn Pears. LL, Interior walls of the garden. M, Pyramidal Pears, twenty feet apart. N, East wall with Apricots—horizontally-trained trees, planted twenty feet apart. O, West wall with Plums, twenty feet apart. P, Gooseberries. Q, Currants. R, Raspberries. S, Boundary trellis, which may be covered with Vines, or Pears if in a cold climate.

France, he designed one specially for me, which is given in this chapter.

SCEAUX.—In the same neighbourhood are nurseries belonging to M. Croux, and a very good school of fruit-culture apart from the large home-nursery. Many of the trees are trained into very curious forms. The cordons here have grown too strongly, and every second stem is severed. They had of course been previously firmly grafted one to the other. Cydonia sinensis against walls has fruit a foot long in favourable seasons, but is simply a curiosity. Several kinds of Ribes, including the Gooseberry, are grafted on the Red Currant. The remarkable specimen of training figured opposite was shown by M. Croux at the Paris Exposition of 1867, and was

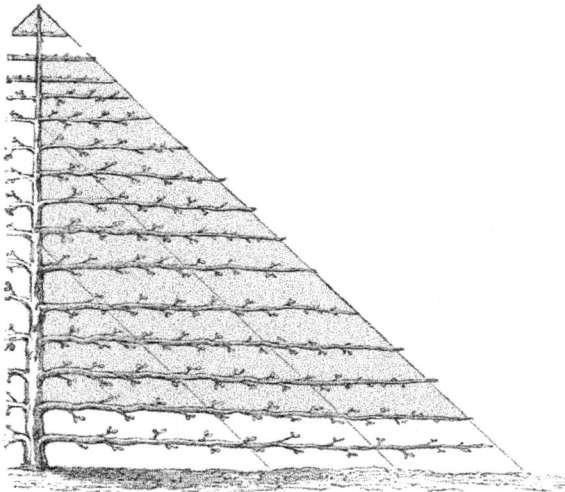

Pear-tree with horizontal branches, supported by slender galvanised wires stretched from a stake at back of the tree to stones in the ground.

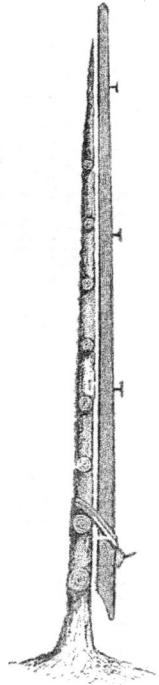

Mode of supporting stake for trees trained as shown in the preceding figure.

much admired. The plant-nurseries of MM. Thibaut and Keteleer near here are well worth visiting.

CHATILLON, FONTENAY AUX ROSES.—Visitors to Bourg-la-Reine or Sceaux may on the same day conveniently visit the garden of M. Chardon in this village. The owner is an amateur, and has a most interesting little garden of fruit-trees. In addition to the common and well-known forms, he has many specimens trained

over walks and bowers, and altogether the garden would well
repay a visit by anybody visiting Paris who wishes to see what
may be done with fruit-trees by an amateur.

SUISNES (Brie-Comte-Robert).--The nursery of M. Cochet here is an interesting one for the fruit-grower. Apples, on the horizontal-cordon system, are planted in large numbers in places formerly only occupied by high box-edgings. They were among the best cordons I have seen in France, some bearing as much fruit as they seemed able properly to develop; yet M. Cochet considered it a very thin crop, and said they frequently have them almost

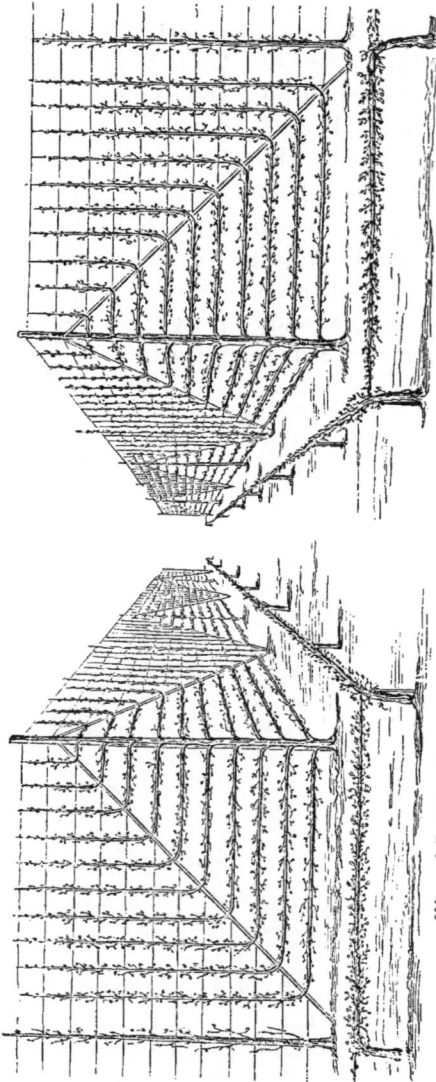

View of Espalier Pear-trees and lines of Apples trained as Cordons in garden at Brunoy.

Plan of Espalier in preceding figure at corner of line.

as thick as they can stand along the line. Several walks
are margined here with two instead of one line of cordons, the
inner line being about three inches higher than the outer one. Of

course many variations may be made thus, but the single line, well conducted and rather freely developed, is the best of all, though there are many positions and circumstances in which two lines, superimposed cordons or other modifications, will prove desirable. M. Cochet has planted almost every good variety of Apple on this principle, and finds they all do well on it. All are grafted on the true French Paradise stock. Some of his fruit from three-year-old plants was remarkably fine, and nothing could look prettier than the handsome Apples along the side of the walks. A much more regular and better effect could be obtained by lines of one kind only, and the training and pruning of them also would be more likely to be performed in the best manner. In nearly all parts of the garden there was abundant evidence that the horizontal cordon for Apples is the best improvement effected in open-air fruit-culture for years.

A line of Pears trained thus may also be seen, but it is a failure, although there was a fine crop hanging on one specimen of the Belle Angevine. When grown in this way the Pear usually manifests a disposition to shoot up " gourmands," or shoots very like those of Willows, from the bend. On walls where the sap has room to spread, this inconvenience is of course not present. The young Pear and other trees here in preparation for wall and espalier culture

Pear-tree in Columnar form

are neatly trained in line by means of tightly-strained galvanised wires. By this means trees fit to place against walls immediately, may be picked out at any time. A good many handsome palmette and other trees are to be seen, but particularly remarkable are those trained in what is called the columnar form. This is simply a tree trained to a single stem, or a vertical cordon, the top being allowed to grow as high as it can, and thus close columns of leaves and fruits are formed as much as fifteen feet high. Nothing could exceed the fine condition

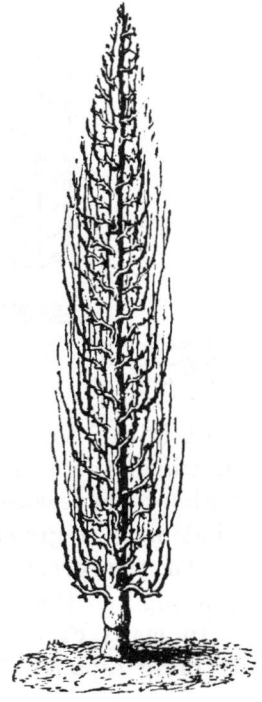

of many of these trees, perfectly laden from top to bottom in many cases, and in many more bending arched to the ground with the weight of their fruit. They were not staked, but when they are grown in a regular fruit-garden it is the custom to connect them securely near the top by a line of wire, so that they cannot bend down with the weight of the fruit. Their advantages are that fruit and leaves enjoy abundance of sun and air. The

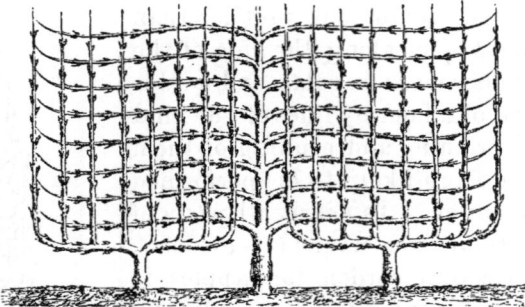

Portion of Self-supporting espalier of Pear-trees, formed of horizontal and vertically trained trees, the points of the horizontally-trained tree grafted by approach to the outer branches only of the vertical ones.

fruit is said to be better flavoured than from the pyramid tree, in which there is usually a good deal of shade, while they are perhaps the easiest of all forms to conduct, and a great many kinds may be grown on a small space. Their drawback appears to be the great height to which they attain, thus rendering pruning and the gathering of the fruit not so easy as desirable.

In many French gardens a peculiarly simple and neat way of training espalier Pear-trees may be seen, and there were good examples both here and in the next place described. It consists of a stout stake for the main trunk of the tree, and of wires running from this to stones or pegs buried in the ground. That the roots of the tree may not be hurt by a large stake, this is sometimes supported by the stem. Besides, the support for the

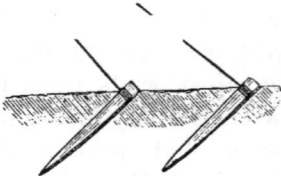

Stake for fixing the wires in the ground.

wires and younger branches is only required towards the top of the tree; hence another reason for not fixing the stake in the ground. It is quite easy to project little stakes from the stouter parts to the young growing branchlets of the tree, and thus keep the points perfectly trained in the desired direction. On the first of November every year, one of the many professors of fruit-culture in Paris, gives and illustrates here a lecture, which is attended by from three to four hundred gardeners from various parts in the neighbourhood.

BRUNOY (SEINE-ET-MARNE).—There is here a very remarkable fruit-garden belonging to an amateur, M. Nallet—a garden which will repay a visit at any time of the year. It is only a few minutes' walk from Brunoy station, passed on the way to Fontainebleau, and within an easy distance of Paris. It is an oblong piece of ground, walled in and with a straight walk through the centre, bordered by two lines of handsome pyramidal trees, cut

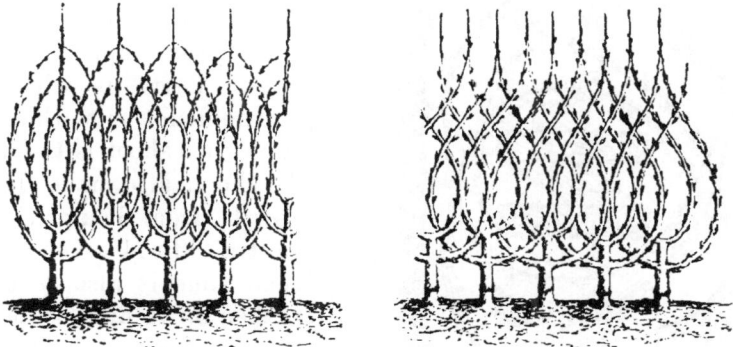

Espaliers of Pear-trees with the branches grafted by approach.

off from the walk by long horizontal cordons. Lines of tall trellis-work run at right angles with the main walk, and accommodate a great variety of trees—many fanciful, and many of the best and most useful forms. The owner considered that, taking bad years with good, an average of ten fruit per yard run of each branch of a cordon tree might be calculated upon. The cordons are never protected, and, here as elsewhere, furnish numerous places which would otherwise not be occupied at all. It is impossible to give the reader an idea of the variety of form to be seen in the fruit-trees, therefore we will confine ourselves to the most remarkable. The garden offers recreation to its amiable owner, and he, while not neglecting the very best forms, also amuses himself occasionally by transforming one or more trees into fantastic monograms and letters. The columnar form is very well developed here, some of the specimens approaching eighteen feet in height. They are regularly staked, and high lines of wire connect them by the tops, so that they are held firmly together.

Numerous palmette trees occur here, and it is noticeable that the lines which the trees are to follow are laid down at first with Willow or other slender flexible rods. This very much simplifies training. The plan is well worth adopting in our gardens even for the simplest vertical forms. There is with this plan no doubt as to the exact course each shoot is to follow. The shoots also make cleaner growth, from being tied to the straight rods when young. Much time is also saved to the men in training by having the lines exactly laid down for the tree at first. Willow-rods do admirably where there are bends of branches. A Plum-tree, trained as a Palmette Verrier, was very ornamental, the lines of fruit darkening the long, neatly-guided branches. Curtains of Pear and other trees, trained on slender trellises of wire, are very well formed.

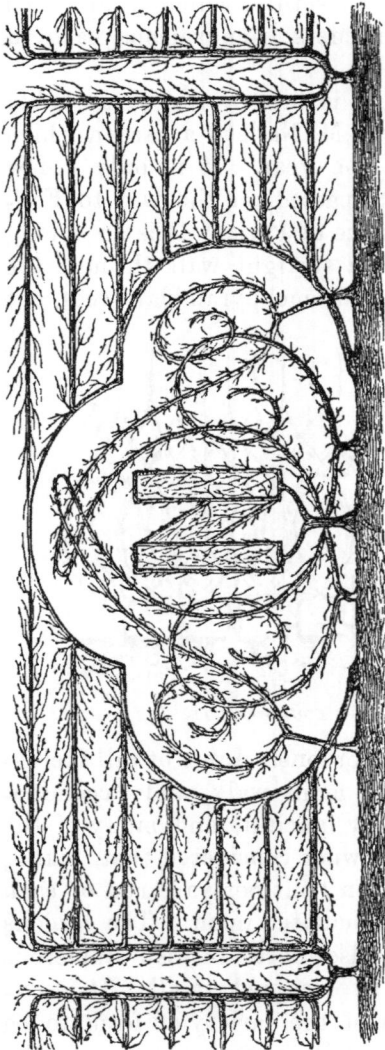

The Peach is grown to some extent against the walls, and successfully, some of the trees looking almost as well as those at Montreuil, though the walls are not so high. A large portion

of the wall-space is devoted to oblique cordons of the Easter
Beurré, and these were in excellent bearing; they had been
planted six years, were about twelve feet long, and bore from ten
to fifteen fruit each.   Planted twenty inches apart, and confined
to one stem, which is never cut back at the point if the wood be
ripe, they soon cover the wall, and as the good fruit of this variety
commands a high price, a quick return is afforded.   In several
small walled gardens made in connection with the chief one of
M. Nallet, the greater portion of the wall-surface is devoted to
Easter Beurré.

The practice of grafting by approach the branches of the Pear-
trees is extensively employed here.   The figures will better
explain the mode of training and the
aspect of the trees in the garden than any
description.   I am much indebted to M.
Nallet for his kindness in sending me
accurate sketches of some of his most
remarkable trees.

A distinct and apparently useful form
of tree I met with here for the first time.
It is called the balloon form, and is made
by taking eight branches from the base
of the tree, and bringing them outside a
circular hoop, allowing one main stem to
ascend erect.   The branches, after growing a little above the hoop, which gives
a desirable uniformity to the base, ascend
at regular intervals to the top, where

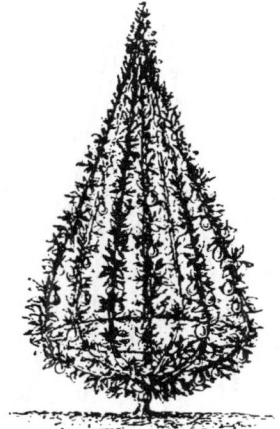

*Pear-tree trained in the Balloon
form, ten feet high.*

they are neatly united to the erect shoot.   The figures will
explain this form, but the stake has been made much too
large by the engraver.   It should be of iron.   This figure is in
other respects a good representation of a handsome specimen
in M. Nallet's garden.   Each branch being kept distinct, and
the tree being well opened up by this system, the result was
very good.   A specimen of the Duchesse d'Angoulême trained
thus was one of the handsomest-looking trees I have ever seen.
The method has more advantages than would appear at first sight
—the long fruiting-branches being thoroughly exposed to the
sun and light from bottom to top, the branches being held

firmly, and the tree being altogether a decided improvement upon
the pyramid for important positions in gardens.

FERRIÈRES.—The fruit-garden here is the finest I have seen in
any private place in France.   There are many beautifully-formed
espalier-trees.   They are more than twice as high as those
usually seen in our gardens, being about ten feet high; but not a
square foot of the whole surface of a
trellis several hundred feet long is without the portion of branch which the
fruit-grower originally intended it to
carry.   The form mostly employed is
the palmette, scores of them being as
regularly formed as if the shoots pushed
and sap flowed at the grower's bidding.
Walks, extending the full length and
breadth of the garden, are bordered with
these high trellises, the effect being very
good.   Other kinds of espalier-trees, of
which the branches do not turn up at
the ends, but run obliquely their whole
length, are abundant here, and are preferred to the Palmette Verrier, which,

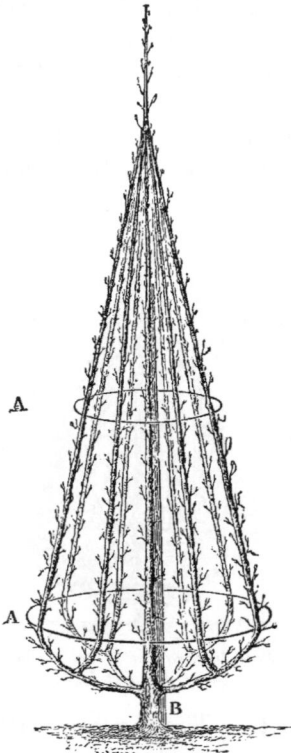

*Pear-tree in Balloon form, seven-
teen feet high and six feet in
diameter.*

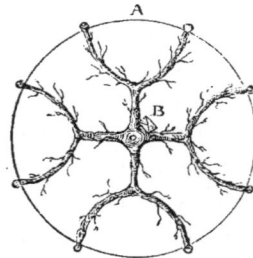

*Plan of Pear-tree in Balloon
form.*

once formed, does not admit of increase in size.   Trellises for
espalier-trees are numerous here.   The reason is that the autumnal
winds are very destructive to large finely grown Pears on pyramidal
trees; on trees fixed to espaliers the fruit will withstand the
strongest September gale.   This is an important consideration for
those who wish to grow the finest kinds of keeping Pears.   This
garden contains hundreds of the finest pyramidal Pear-trees, tall,

firmly and regularly set with branches, each in its turn furnished from top to bottom with fertile wood. There remains the objection that fruit grown in this way and in all respects carefully looked after, is liable to be blown off by an autumnal gale; hence, the grower cannot depend on them as on an espalier. Cordons of the various fruit-trees, mostly simple cordons, are employed, when the aim is to cover the wall quickly and get an early return. Ground-cordons of the Apple form a continuous and frequently inter-grafted line by the side of the walls, and are very useful in the production of fine specimen fruit of the more valuable kinds. There is a deep permanent coping to the walls, and, beneath it, iron stays to support a temporary coping, not less than two feet wide during the spring. A wide coping is placed over the Easter Beurré here, not only when in flower, but throughout the season. It is believed that, in a climate so changeable, and frequently so severe, spotting, cracking, and various other maladies are best guarded against by a deep coping.

LYONS.—Towards the close of the Paris Exhibition of 1867, a noble Peach-tree was shown by M. Morel, trained as a Palmette Verrier, and so well trained as to excite the admiration of all who saw it. M. Morel lives at Vaise, a suburb of Lyons, where I had the pleasure of visiting him afterwards. The wall on which his Peach-trees are grown is on an average thirteen feet high, and it is made of very cheap material—the common earth of the garden. A foundation is made, and the wall raised a little above the surface of the ground with stone, to guard the earth-wall above from injury by frost and wet. Then the earth is laid in and well battered down between boards, and on every layer of earth there is deposited about a inch and a half of mortar. The layers in one wall were about one foot deep; in another—the better wall of the two—they were about two feet deep: and between each layer the thin seam of mortar could be seen. The walls are about eighteen inches thick, and capped with a coping of tiles, under which are inserted iron supports for protection in spring. In this way strong and useful walls are made for fruit-growing and other purposes. The earth-walls cost about a shilling per yard, those of stone about four shillings. The earth-walls, when well made, last for a couple of centuries. A house near at hand, constructed in the same way, has been erected one hundred years.

It is worthy of notice that while the Peach does very well about here as a standard tree, good cultivators find distinct advantages not alone in growing it against a wall, but also in well protecting it when in flower. M. Morel considered that this is of advantage in three ways—firstly, in securing a crop by preserving the flowers from destruction by frost; secondly, by saving the trees from the disease caused by frosts and sleety rains falling on the young leaves and shoots; and thirdly, by the tendency which a wide temporary coping has in making the tree push more vigorously in its lower than in its upper parts. A wide mat at the top of the wall in spring obscures the light to a considerable extent from the upper part of the wall, and this prevents the sap from running rapidly to the top as it generally does. However, a good trainer can always prevent that. These things are mentioned to show that, even in a climate much better than that of Paris, protection to the wall is considered a necessity. The trees away from walls are often attacked by gum and the " maladies caused by the cold of spring," to use M. Morel's words. Does not this suggest the true cause of the miserable aspect of many Peach-trees where careful protection in spring is not resorted to? In numerous large British gardens, with every appliance, the walls are often left exposed or with the most meagre protection—so that there is nothing to prevent the cold rains of spring from falling on the young leaves and flowers; while in many Continental gardens, with but a solitary man to attend to them, careful protection is regularly given. Here, too, each espalier Pear-tree is protected in spring by having a cross-bar fixed over it, by the assistance of which and wires, mats are held over the trees during the season of dangerous frosts.

The portions of the walls here occupied by the old and established trees were perfectly covered with the healthiest specimens; even the bases of the stems and the branches had shoots trained over them. The forms most employed are the Palmette Verrier and the Candelabrum. The pruning is done in winter, when time and weather permit, and not in spring, as is generally the case. There can be little gained by waiting till streams of sap are ascending through the branches, and but slight discernment suffices to distinguish the various kinds of buds in winter as well as in spring. An important point in M. Morel's culture, is that he does not stop the leading shoots, except when one happens to be weak.   In all countries there is probably too much cutting in and shortening back.   As to the state of fruit-growing about here, it is still much in want of improvement, though a considerable advance has been made during the past generation.   Thirty years ago, a dozen Pears of good quality were sold here for eighteen-pence—now worth one-third as much.   This good result has been brought about by popularising really good varieties.

THE REGIONAL SCHOOL OF SAULSAIE.—There are many small departmental schools established with a view to spread a know-ledge of rural pursuits in France—this is one of a few establish-ments with a more extended aim.   It is situated in the department of Ain, a couple of hours' journey from Lyons, and is principally an extensive school of agriculture.   Although Saulsaie is situate much further south than Paris, there can be little doubt that there are many parts of England far more favourable than it to the production of fruit.   The original specimens of the Palmette Verrier are to be seen here, and very fine some of them are.   A marked superiority was observed in the Easter Beurré Pear grown against walls and the same variety grown away from their shelter and protection.   Against walls, where the trees had been efficiently protected in spring, the trees and fruit were in perfect condition. This speaks for itself, and proves that it is to well-managed walls we must mainly look for improvements in the culture of our finer and tenderer fruits.   Here the French actually find that walls are not only a benefit but a necessity for some kinds of Pear.

As the place is very much exposed to storms, peculiar ex-pedients have been resorted to for securing the trees against their influence.   The practice of training trees with the branches crossed and intertwined by way of mutual support, was illustrated here on a large scale, in the case of both Apples and Pears.   Laths and sticks are first used to train the trees into shape, and after the trees have attained their full size, crossing and supporting each other, the supports are removed or allowed to rot away. There were many Apple and Pear trees trained on this principle, and so well and firmly that there could be no doubt whatever that it is perfectly practicable and good, and that the objections which have been urged against it are entirely groundless.   It has been said that the branches would destroy each other by friction : there

2 A

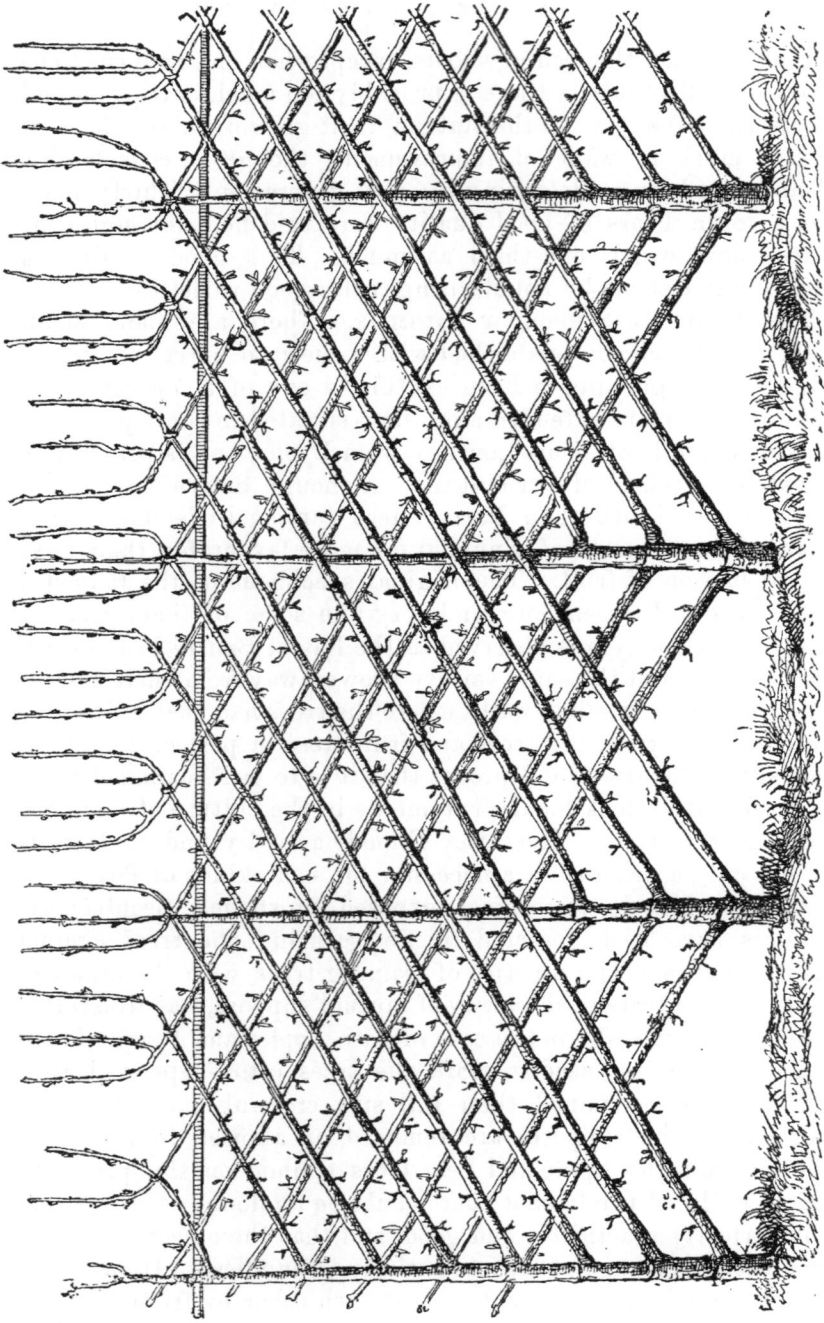

CROSSED AND SELF-SUPPORTING ESPALIER PEAR-TREES AT SAULSAIE.

was ample evidence here that this was not the case, even with the strong winds so frequently blowing. Apple-trees in one fine line of eight feet high, mutually support each other without the slightest injury. There are three stages of branches on each tree, except at the end of the line where they are required to complete it. Having obtained the three tiers of branches, the central stem is retained as a support for the intercrossing branches. It requires eight years to form a series of fine espaliers like those in the Government School at Saulsaie. The shoots at the top are to encourage the sap to flow freely through each branch, and also to prevent very strong growth on the branches. It is thus clear that we may not only much improve the appearance of our espaliers by improved trellising, but make the espalier-trees self-supporting.

In the case of very large pyramids planted here, another expedient to protect them from the wind was adopted. As is frequent in French fruit-gardens, the branches of the pyramids are brought regularly in straight lines from the bole of the tree —that is, the branches form four, five, or six wings, as the case may be; five is the most usual number. In the instance I am describing there are four wings to each pyramid; but the branches, instead of being stopped, as is usually done, are trained in straight lines from one pyramid to the other, so that they cross each other, forming walls of trellis-work, an opening being left at the bottom under which one may pass. In one spot there were regular little squares formed thus between every four trees—in fact, a green wall of from twelve to fourteen feet high enclosed the visitor. I never met with this elsewhere, and it was very well done.

An expedient to give additional support and strength to the espaliers was, when employing the double trellis, to let the two sides meet at top and lean against each other—thus, $\wedge$—instead of placing them vertically, as is the custom. A line of trees trained in the vase-form were united one with the other by a strong arched branch, the branch springing from the top of the vase. The fruit-gardener here, the late M. Verrier, had invented and carried out with much skill, forms to suit a garden open to fierce winds which would render such exposed trees insecure without the strongest support. No garden could afford a better test of the effect of wind on trained trees. Some that were standing singly looked like neat summer-houses. They were pyramids, with the branches brought out from the main stem in six lines, the branches in each line being of course placed exactly one above the other. Trees are trained thus, so that the air and light may fully benefit all parts of them. The character of a pretty bower was imparted to the space between every two wings of the tree by simply carrying an arched branch from wing to wing overhead.

There is here a very well-furnished Peach-wall, made of common earth in the same way as by M. Morel at Vaise-Lyon, except that the base of the wall was made of rough stones instead of solid stone. The coping is of tiles, not sloping down on both sides of the wall, but running clean from front to back, the higher side being reserved for the most important crop. Beneath this coping wooden supports project about twenty inches from the wall, to accommodate a neat straw mat in spring. Espaliers are here occasionally protected with these straw mats by simply projecting from the main support of the espalier two little stays of iron or wood, which carry a rude and cheap span of framework, on which the mats are so placed in spring that the wind cannot blow them off.

There is a School of Dendrology here, with the trees planted in their natural orders, and generally speaking good facilities for teaching young men with a taste for rural pursuits.

DIJON.—The home-nursery of Leconte here is well kept and instructive. It is an oblong piece of ground, about four acres in extent, and walled in on every side, the walls being coped with overlapping tiles. All the space on both sides of the walls was planted with oblique cordon Pear-trees, trained on single galvanised wires, attached to two strong nails in the walls. A wall about fifteen feet high was nearly covered with oblique cordon Pears, and as they had so much room to rise, the position seemed particularly suited to them. Near at hand they were grown to the same height by projecting a trellis above the garden-wall, so as to form a very high screen of cordon Pears above it. This was done by erecting strong uprights of iron to the required height above the wall, and then running galvanised wires from the bottom of the wall to a strong horizontal wire or rod passing from upright to upright at the top. Looking along the walks, cordon Apples could be seen stretching without interruption from one end of the garden to the other, the effect being very pretty. They were planted a few inches inside the box edging, and between it and lines of handsome pyramidal Pears, and, as usual, chiefly to fill up neatly and permanently a space that otherwise could not be usefully occupied.

Angers.—This famous old town is known almost everywhere for its many and large nursery-gardens. It is a fine climate, this of Anjou—so genial as to develop the Tea-plant in perfect health out of doors, and with sun enough to spice the air with the fragrance of that noble evergreen, Magnolia grandiflora, which may be seen used as a promenade-tree in the place immediately outside the main entrance to the nurseries of M. A. Leroy. There are many large specimens and lines of this plant in these very extensive nurseries. The Camellia does perfectly well in the open air, and is grown to an enormous extent, nearly two acres of ground being devoted to the production of young plants, 25,000 being grafted every year. Many other trees and plants are propagated in great quantity—Pears for example. Of one single variety, Easter Beurré, the enormous number of 40,000 plants are grafted annually. Of Duchesse d'Angoulême, 25,000 are yearly required; of Williams's Bon Chrétien, 25,000; that excellent Pear, Louise Bonne d'Avranches, is also required to the extent of 25,000 annually; and Doyenné d'Alençon to 20,000 plants— so that the number of one kind of Pear grown is alone sufficient to form a nursery of itself. Observe the enormous number of Easter Beurré (Doyenné d'Hiver) required. This is the Pear which we import from France in winter. In the region around Paris this kind must be grown against sunny walls. It is folly to attempt its culture in any other fashion in England. Quantities of this fruit are sent from Paris to Russia, where it commands a very high price.

Fifty workmen are sometimes employed in budding here. The fruit-trees are budded as we bud Roses, and those in which the buds fail are grafted in spring. In this way a year is gained. There is a splendid collection of pyramid pears grafted on the Quince stock, many of them of great size and perfect symmetry, the ground being rich and deep, and perfectly suited to the Quince. Every kind of fruit sold or recognised as a variety of any merit is grown here ; Pears to the number of 1,028 varieties; Vines, 550 distinct varieties ; Apples, 800 varieties ; Peaches, 250,

including 45 of the best American kinds; and so on.   The Apple
is planted to a considerable extent as a horizontal cordon, and
many varieties bear abundance of fruit, some of the finer Russian
kinds being gathered early in July.   The following varieties
also bear abundantly as cordons: Joanneting, Astrakan, Winter
Pearmain, Archduchess Sophia, Court Pendu Plat, President
Dufoy, several kinds of Reinette, several kinds of Caville, Transparent, and many others.   It is scarcely necessary to enumerate
kinds, as nearly every first-rate variety does well when trained in
this way and grafted on the true French Paradise stock.

    Rouen.—This district is so near home, and its climate so very
much like our own, that even those who believe the climate of
Northern France to be a delightful one will admit the utility
of noticing the culture of fruit-trees here.   I first visited the
nursery of Mr. J. Wood, an English nurseryman, established here
fifty years.   Speaking of fruit-growing in France and England,
these were his words: " For every single fruit-tree sold in
England there are one thousand sold in France!   Every cottager
with ten square yards of ground buys and plants fruit-trees.   If
it were not so, you would not get so much French fruit in
England."   Generally, he said, the culture of wall-fruit was
carelessly performed in that district, with the exception of the
Pear.   Fine old specimens of Pears against the walls of chateaux
afforded quantities of good fruit.   Alpine Strawberries are grown
here in considerable quantity, and preferred to the common kind.
By covering the ground with a little mulching to prevent evaporation, and giving abundance of water in dry weather, they get
them to bear from early summer to late autumn, gathering
plenty of fruit all through this prolonged season.   When gathered
fresh from the plants, and used with the usual accompaniments,
the best varieties of the Quatre Saisons Strawberry are certainly
excellent.   Mr. Roger Leigh of Barham Court has grown them
extensively of late years, and finds them a great success.   They
occupy ground among the fruit-trees.   On the occasion of a fête,
sixty quarts of this delicate fruit were gathered in his garden on
a single morning.   Various fine kinds are grown ; some not producing runners, which is a great advantage.   Few things are more
worthy of general culture in England than these long-bearing
Strawberries; the climate is even more suitable for them than

that of France. Their merit is not only in their continuous bearing, but in their flavour, which is better than that of many of the larger kinds.

In a letter from M. Fallot, writing from the Château de Maintenon, published in the 'Bulletin de la Société d'Horticulture d'Eure-et-Loire,' the writer strongly urges on Strawberry-growers the advisability of cultivating the Four Seasons Strawberry from seed rather than from runners or cuttings, wherever it may be practicable. There is a wide difference between beds of plants grown on the two systems. The robust habit of the seedlings, their greater productiveness, and the superior beauty and size of the fruit, give them almost the appearance of being different varieties of the same plant. M. Fallot has largely experimented on the three usual methods of propagation by division, by runners, and by seeds, with the result that he estimates their merits as being in the inverse direction of the order in which they are named, that is to say, the roots are inferior to runners, and both inferior to seedlings. The comparative ease, however, with which a large plantation may be made from cuttings or runners has great temptations for the cultivator, whose time is taken up with a thousand other cares. Last year being a damp one, M. Fallot's crop was most successful, the fruits being so large and fine that when brought to table they were thought to be a new variety. The following is his method of culture:—"About the middle of June the best fruit on the finest plants are chosen for seed. They are dried in the sun, and the seeds are washed out, rejecting those which remain floating on the surface. They are sown in the beginning of July in a light soil, raked over and covered with straw; they are shaded until germination has taken place, when more light is admitted gradually day by day. The sowing may be made in pans, which may be exposed to the sun or placed in the shade, as may be thought desirable; they should be watered daily. During the last week in August they are pricked out, leaving about 4 in. between each plant, and in March following they are planted out 12 in. or 15 in. apart, advantage being taken of the first fine days for the operation. All runners are diligently nipped off during the whole year, and also flower-buds until the middle of June. From the end of July the plants are in full bearing until the first frosts set in. The second year's crop is found to be much more abundant than the first, and lasts from the 20th of May until the frosts set in, the plants growing much more rapidly and vigorously than if they had been raised from cuttings or runners. From about the middle of June the plants are well watered every day at the rate of a gallon of water to every ten plants. After the third year's crop the plants are pulled up and destroyed, the order of operations being—first year, sowing; second year, first crop from the end of July only; third year, a full and abundant crop from May 20 until the first frosts set in. The seedling Four Seasons Strawberry being more vigorous in its growth than the others, continues bearing to a later period, but it is not adapted for forcing, the plants produced from division or runners being preferable for this purpose. It is hardly necessary to remind growers that this variety is the only one that can be reproduced from seed; the English and American sorts not only do not yield the variety to which they belong, but produce a mixture of as many kinds as there are plants, and must, therefore, necessarily be propagated by means of runners."

The fruit-garden in the botanic gardens at Rouen contains a good many of what are called model trees, and many cordons; but on the whole, while there is much that is curious, it affords little instruction. Specimens in the U form of trained trees abound. The only noticeable feature was a trifling one—placing Willow-wands in the exact direction in which it is desired to conduct the chief branches. That done, little remains but to tie the young shoots to the Willows as often as necessary. There was one good specimen here of a winged pyramid—*i.e.*, a pyramid having the branches trained in five vertical lines, and with the points united by grafting.

TROYES.—This old town is interesting to the horticulturist from the experienced fruit-growers, MM. Baltet, having extensive nurseries in and near it. Their nursery is extensive and rich in advanced specimens of pyramidal and other Pear-trees. Horizontal cordons, where established, bear wonderfully well. Thus the Lady Apple, well established on the Doucin stock, bore fruit almost as thick as the Apples could sit on a cordon not closely pinched in; but on the Doucin the shoots grow too vigorously, and do not preserve that compact habit which is so desirable in these trees. If the soil were very poor and light and dry, the tendency to over-vigour would be repressed, and the Doucin prove a desirable stock.

How fortunate it is that stocks which possess such admirable qualities are known and easily procured! Suppose the soil to be rich, deep loam, wet, cold, or stiff. By using the French Paradise, we obtain large and beautiful fruit. Plant the same on a very poor, dry, hungry, or calcareous soil, and it is almost useless. Then we have the Doucin, which suits poor soil to perfection, to fall back upon, and thus good results may be produced on soils of very diverse and even very bad qualities. Here, as in every garden, the cultivator considers that cordons " are good, and take up little space." Of course, in a large public nursery like this, little lines of trees under the eye of numerous daily visitors, who may at times buy such of them as they fancy, cannot be exhibited in the perfect state in which they are in private gardens; besides, a number of kinds are planted, and not those known to be best worth growing, and yet sufficient proof of the excellence of the system was here afforded.

Pear-tree with the branches trained in lines exactly above each other, and all the points united by grafting.

There was a good crop of Pear, Beurré Clairgeau, on a hedge formed of that variety. Several similar hedges are formed beside it, and arranged rather closely together, so that plants may be placed between them for the sake of shade. As clipped hedges of Arbor vitæ are frequently employed in France for giving shade to plants in summer, it need scarcely be remarked that the substitution of hedges of good varieties of Pears would be an improvement. The same may be said of many hedges and

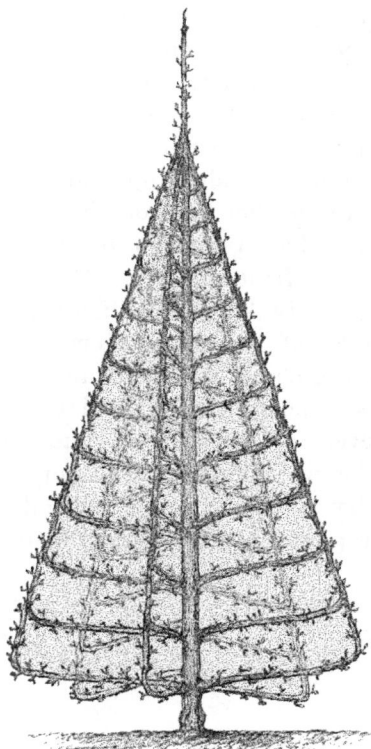

dividing lines in gardens and nurseries everywhere. At first stakes
are used to support the trees, and indeed, some must be employed
till they have attained their perfect development; but afterwards, if properly trained, they will support each other perfectly,
and they may be pruned and kept to look as neatly as if supported
by a costly trellis. Alongside one of the main walks a young
specimen of a very carefully and neatly made curtain of this kind
may be seen. These hedges bear as freely and well as any other
form of Pear-tree whatever. The line of Beurré Clairgeau was
grafted on Quince and Pear stocks alternately. The trees on the
Quince were little better than dead; those on the Pear were fine,
full of fruit, showing that the variety requires the Pear stock.

In another part of the town the Normal School of the department has a garden behind it for the purpose of teaching the
pupils fruit-culture. Here double or superimposed cordons of
the Lady Apple bore fruit in great abundance. The walls were
made of the dried stems of the common Reed, nailed between
rough cheap wooden framework, the mass of stems being about
two inches thick. A flat board nailed along the top at about
seven feet from the ground, afforded about eight inches of coping.
The wall of the school for about four feet from the ground was
very neatly covered with dwarf Peach-trees which bore a fair
crop, and neatly covered a space such as is generally left bare.

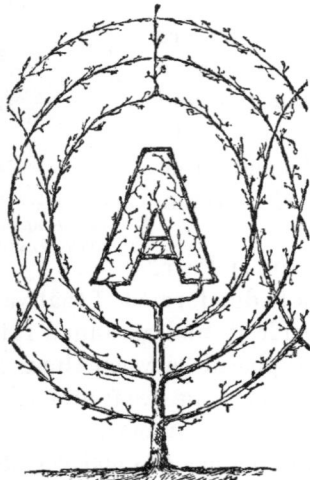

Fantastic training in forming name.

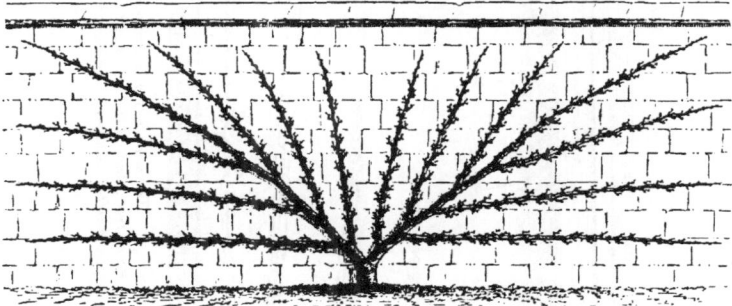

A Spur-pruned Peach-tree.

˙CHAPTER XXI.

THE PEACH GARDENS OF MONTREUIL.

THE finest supplies of Peaches for the Paris market do not come, as perhaps many would suppose, from the sunny south or the balmy west, but from within a few miles of Paris, where they have to be grown on walls furnished with good copings, and receive in every way careful protection and culture. Approaching Montreuil the country is seen covered with good crops of vegetables and fruit to the tops of the surrounding low hills. But getting nearer still to the village, a great number of white walls, about eight or nine feet high, appear, enclosing rather small squares of land, which are almost entirely devoted to the Peach. As the walls are netted over many acres in some parts, the effect from a distance is curious. In the squares are small fruit-trees and all sorts of garden-crops. To the visitor who examines the plantations here it is quite apparent that it is not to the climate that the best growers owe their success. Among the two hundred and fifty cultivators having Peach-gardens here, there are many with very shabby-looking trees on the walls, while those in some of the best gardens are perfect models of health, fertility, and skilful training.

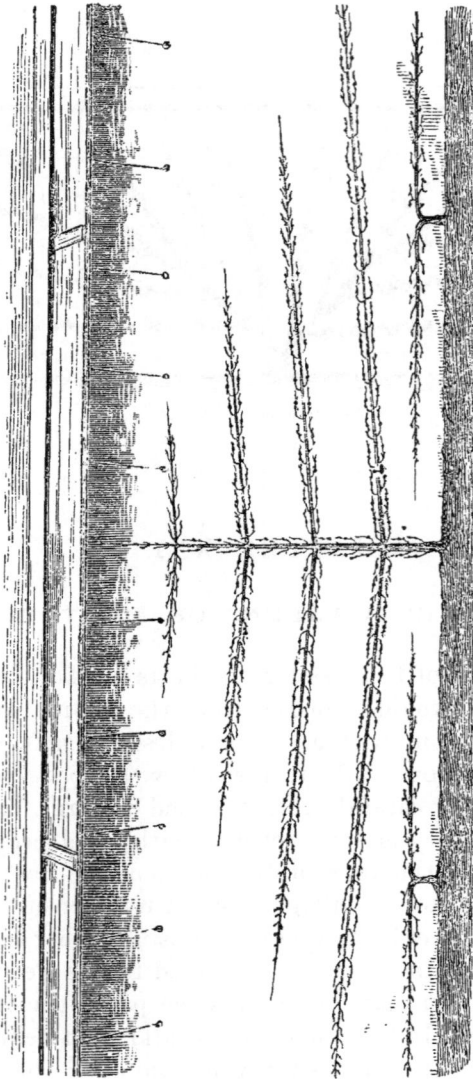

Early Spring Aspect of a portion of Peach-wall in garden at Montreuil, from a photograph. The wall has a permanent coping of plaster, beneath which is a temporary wooden coping twenty inches wide. Beneath the Peach-trees, and in the spaces left bare in consequence of the branches having a slightly-ascending direction, the Calville Blanc Apple, grafted on the French Paradise stock, is trained as a Cordon.

The illustrations to this chapter show their mode of pruning, disbudding, covering bare spaces on the stem, and other processes in the French system, and a glance at any garden-wall with a

Peach-tree will suffice to show the difference between our system and the regular and close-pruning under theirs. A principal aim with them is at securing straight, well-formed, well-furnished, and equi-distant branches, and always to spur in the shoots rather closely in spring.

The garden of M. Chevallier at Montreuil displays examples of cultivation not anywhere surpassed. The first impression is good, for the outer side of the walls is covered with admirable specimens of Peach-trees, the narrow strip forming the border in which they are planted being cut off from the roadside by a fragile fence covered with Vines. This fashion of utilising the outer as well as the inner sides of walls deserves adoption by all interested in wall-fruit culture. There is no aspect whatever of a wall that may not be used to great advantage. Overhead is a permanent coping of plaster, and immediately beneath it, and at intervals of three or four feet, the spokes of old wheels project eighteen inches; on these are placed the temporary copings of boards or mats in spring in this very paradisaical climate. In the

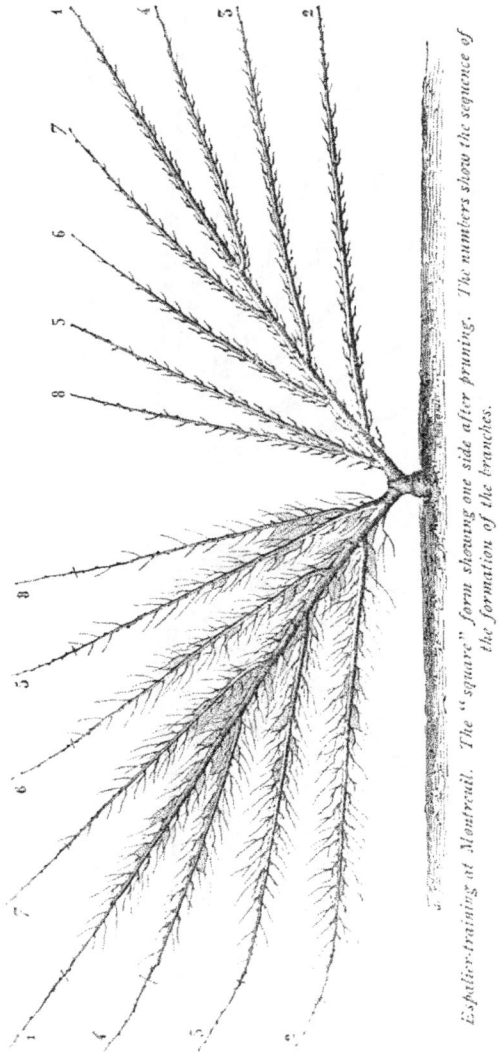

garden admirable culture everywhere prevails. The walls are white—they are whitewashed every year with a view to the extermination of insects,—and the trees are of the brightest and healthiest green. At intervals the knuckle-end of the leg-bone of a sheep projects from the wall a couple of inches only, and at about a foot and a half from the top of the wall. These are placed so as to firmly fix the temporary coping in spring. The boards or neat frames of straw are placed beneath the permanent coping and on the

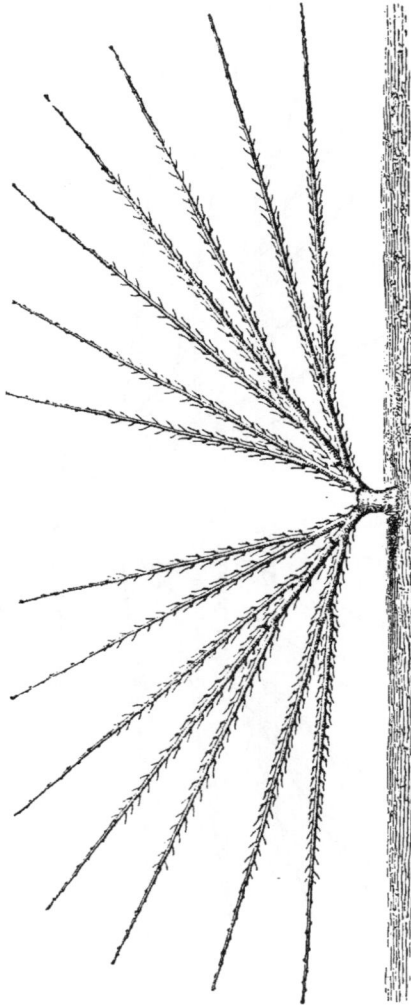

Espalier-training at Montreuil. The Montreuil Fan.

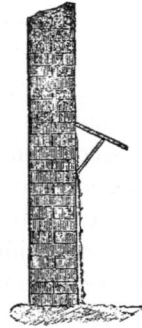

Small Wooden Coping used to protect young Peach-trees in Spring.

supports. The space between coping and brackets being very narrow, there is considerable support afforded to the temporary covering at the back part; by attaching an eye to its under-surface, and firmly tying it with a twig of osier, wire, or strong twine, to the bone projecting firmly below, it is secured from

danger of removal by winds. The cold rains which occur
during the several months while the trees are in bud and flower
and the young shoots and newly-formed fruit tender, run off
the plaster coping on to the temporary one, and from it quite
beyond the trees; while frost is effectually prevented from doing
serious harm by the same means.

To suppose that this protection is merely necessary for the
flowers and to secure fruit, is a
fallacy; a little temporary coping
is improvised here even over quite
young trees without a fruit on
them, simply to guard their
leaves in spring from the maladies
consequent upon the extreme cold
and many vicissitudes of the
French climate at that season.
This extemporised coping is
simply formed by placing little
wooden brackets against the wall
at about four feet from the ground,
and placing thereon a thin rough
board. Such a practice is not
known in England, where there
is of course quite as much
necessity for it. The effect of
the sun on the stem and larger
branches of the tree is also guarded
against, pieces of bark or boards
being placed before the short bole
or base of the tree, the main
branches on the upper parts
being carefully shaded by train-
ing over them the young branches of the current year's wood.

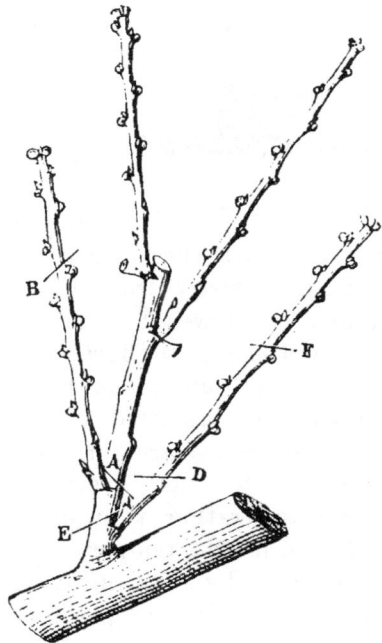

Second Pruning of Fruiting Peach-branch. F is cut at D above two wood-buds to furnish shoots for the following year; B remains to carry the fruit, and the shoot is cut at A. Cut F would only be applied if shoot B did not bear flower buds.

Black marks are traced on the white walls to show the lines
which the main branches of the trees are to follow. In some
cases they are quite simple vertical or horizontal lines, according
as the form to be attained may require; in other places they form
initial letters, flourishes, and other ornamental shapes; for though
the cultivator generally prefers simple and definite forms, he is

also proud of his skill in overcoming difficulties of training, and shows it by these curiously and very successfully trained trees against his walls.   It is only just to state that these elaborately-trained trees bear freely and well; but except for curiosity's sake or for show, they should not be attempted.

Branches of large trees trained nearly in a horizontal position, fifteen feet, were three inches higher at the apex than at the base, a difference which scarcely removed them from the horizontal position, and yet sufficed to give an easy ascent to the sap, and prevent all tendency

Mode of preserving the Lower Part of the Stems from the Sun.

of the branch to shoot vigorously from any point near the base, as is sometimes the case with the branches when placed exactly in a horizontal position.   Apart from this, the growing-point of each main branch is allowed to push freely a little upwards, so as to encourage the sap to flow regularly through the branch, and not halt at any one point to the detriment of all.   Grafting by approach is practised to cover naked branches.   Four to five hundred Peaches are gathered from the best trees, or an average of about ten for every yard in length of fruiting-branch. Cheap and rather thin planks, about twenty inches wide, are preferred for the temporary coping; walls twelve feet high would be benefited by a few inches more.   Cordons of Calville Blanc and other fine Apples are planted plentifully on the spaces between the trees; no matter how well the walls are covered, there is always space for cordon trees between them, in consequence of the branches having an upward inclination.

M. Lepère's garden here is large, and consists of a series of oblong spaces surrounded by Peach-walls, both walls and ground being well covered and cropped.   The Peach is the favourite subject, but neat pyramidal and cordon Pear and Apple trees are also to be seen, and the place is a very interesting one.   Outside the entrance of the Peach-grounds there is a small garden, where against a wall may be seen several capital examples of Peach-trees, the finest being trained after what is called the square form.   This is much admired by the best cultivators, but they

prefer and generally adopt the palm-leaf forms as being the best.
The Candelabrum form is also to be seen in fine condition in this
out-of-the-way nook; it is simply trained by raising vertical
branches from horizontal ones running along near the bottom of
the wall. But as to the form itself, it is not a matter of so much
importance—the two chief points are covering the walls and the

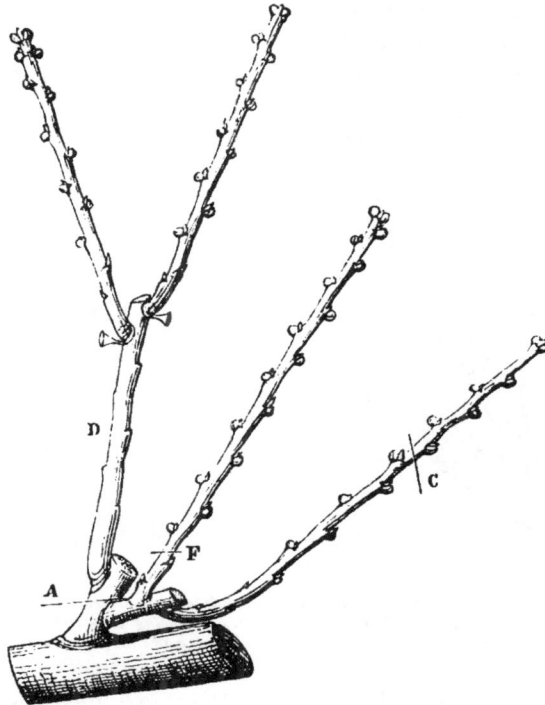

Fruiting Branch of Peach submitted to the third year's pruning. D, which has borne the fruit of the past year, is cut at A; the wood-buds below F will furnish fruiting shoots for the following year; and C will bear the fruit of the coming summer.

treatment of the fruiting branch. Yet it is interesting to notice
the forms adopted by the most successful growers, who, however,
are sure to have several trees most fantastically trained.

An old man, dressed in a blouse, is moving along the walls,
nailing in the shoots here and there, and with him a dozen young
men, his pupils. This is M. Lepère, who has a class twice a
week. The principle of giving a full explanation of their system

2 B

of doing anything well, animates all French cultivators more or less. Did anybody ever hear of an unusually successful English market-gardener or fruit-grower calling a class round him at a low fee, or without fee? The French, though proud of their success in this way, are careful to give it the fullest possible ventilation; and those attending cannot fail to master the culture of the Peach, if so disposed, following the cultivator as, gliding along the wall, he stops and nails in the shoots, cuts out the foremost branches here and there that are not wanted for next year's work; and, in short, does and explains everything before

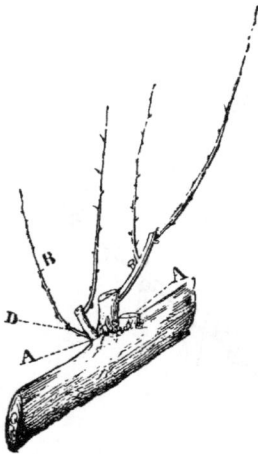

Pruning to replace old fruit-spur: wood-buds are developed at the base, and all the shoots are cut sharp off, as at A

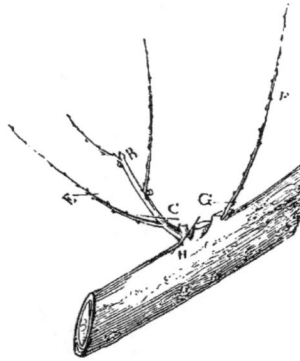

Result of the preceding operation. B is cut at C, producing E, which bears fruit; G, wood-buds; and thus the spur is renewed.

his pupils. M. Lepère has been cultivating Peaches here for a couple of generations, and certainly has reason to be proud of the result.

The well-made walls all run east and west, and are placed within about ten yards of each other. This proximity of the walls is brought about so that many walls may be accommodated on a comparatively small space; so arranged, they are also effective in concentrating the heat and for sheltering. The ground is thus divided into very long narrow strips, the white walls covered with the fresh green of healthy Peach-trees, and the ground planted with fruit-trees, Strawberries, and Asparagus.

The soil is of a calcareous nature, and the long strips enclosed by the walls are generally about fourteen yards across. The syringe is rarely or never used, sulphur being the remedy for spider. The ground is in all cases mulched near the trees, a wide alley being left ; and for preparation of the border they simply trench and manure the ground a couple of feet deep, and about six feet wide. The trees are pruned on the spur system, and are trained to assume a variety of shapes, words and figures. The Candelabrum shape is one of the handsomest and most useful. To form

Spring aspect of Fruit Garden formed in North Germany by M. Lepère fils, on the same plan as the best gardens at Montreuil.

it, two branches are taken along to the right and left near the bottom of the wall. From the uppermost, single shoots are taken at regular intervals to the top of the wall—the lower branch simply running along to the end and rising to the top of the wall, or, in other words, forming a great oblong frame for the interior. Then there is the Montreuil fan shape, but with the divisions somewhat far from the base in most cases, and several modifications of the common horizontal mode of training, which we employ so much for the Pear, but never for the Peach. These seem favourite varieties, and by their means the walls are

2 B 2

perfectly covered—if indeed one can draw any distinction between the walls here, which are all as fresh-looking as a meadow in May.

A form presenting the advantage of the cordon, without its too confined and unnatural development, is very common. It is properly termed the U, bearing a considerable resemblance to that letter much elongated. Frequently this is doubled, and a tree with four ascending branches obtained. These forms are excellent for poor ground, or that in which the Peach grows with but little

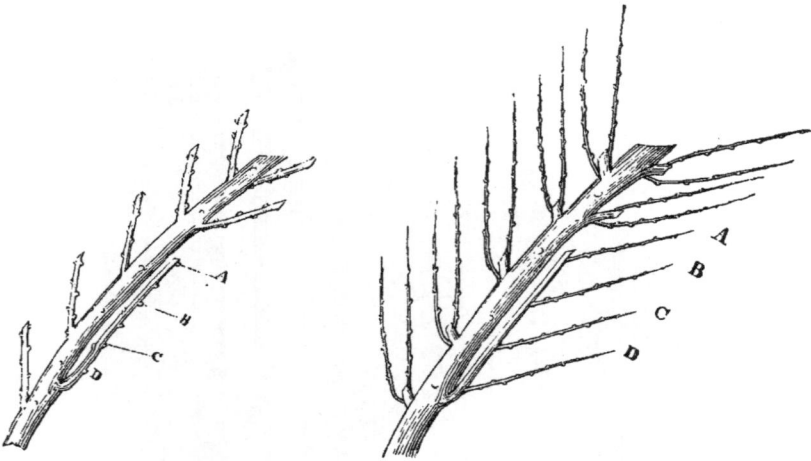

Mode of Pruning to cover bare spaces on the branches of Peach-trees, first year. The shoots arising from the buds A, B, C, and D, are allowed to grow freely, and are nailed in during the summer.

Result of preceding operation, second year. A, B, C, D, are the shoots developed from the buds to which the same letters refer in the preceding figure. This figure shows the appearance of the branches before the pruning.

vigour. The number of fruit borne by the finer examples of trees here range from four to five hundred, and this without in the least injuring the tree. As to the pinching of the summer shoots after they are laid in, it is done according to their strength; but the greater number are pinched at from six to ten inches, and the lateral branches that spring from these are of course pinched also, while weak shortish branches are allowed to grow to their full extension. The pruning is distinct from ours in this: it is done on the spur, and not on the cutting-out principle. We generally leave the shoots of the past year long, and cut away a good deal of the old wood; here the branches are conducted in straight lines and regularly spurred in every year, fruit and wood-buds being left at the base, according to the judgment of the cultivator. The wood of the current year is laid in against the wall with nails and shreds, just in our own way, only thicker, as of course must be the case when a close array of spurs along each shoot has to be obtained. This system is perfectly suited for our wants, provided we take care to protect the young shoots and flowers in spring, as common-sense directs. In any case, the perfect control exercised over the tree, the equable furnishing of fruit-buds in every part,

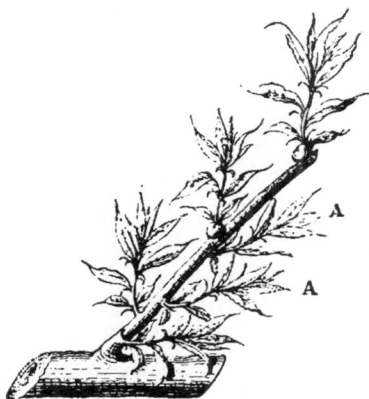

Summer management of the Peach. The shoots above the fruit are retained and stopped, A, A removed, and the two lower shoots furnish the fruiting wood for the following year.

Shoot of Peach without Fruit: the branches A, which would have been retained had the shoot borne a crop, become useless, and the shoot B is cut at C to favour the development of D, D, which will be the fruiting branches of the following year.

and the beautiful symmetry of a tree thus managed, have an interest for all students of fruit culture.

In passing along by the walls, grafting by approach may be seen in operation here and there, with the object of covering naked spots, strengthening shoots, and even adding a young shoot to the base of an old spur that has become too long. An interesting example of its utility was shown by the outer branch of a tree. It is considered very desirable that the lower and outer branch of a Palmette Verrier should be the strongest and highest of all, so as to secure a flow of sap to the lower parts of the trees, instead of allowing it to flow rapidly towards the higher parts, and thus spoil all. In one case, one of the outer branches was feeble and delicate, and did not seem to push much more

Peach-tree trained horizontally: aspect before Pruning. The branches are slightly raised at the points to enable the sap to course through with more regularity.

than to the bend, from whence it ought to have grown strong to the top of the wall. A healthy and vigorous shoot of a neighbouring tree was grafted on it by approach, and in the course of a single season the desired strength was obtained, and the shoot went vigorously to the top of the wall. Not only are the pruner's best precautions taken to secure abundance of vigour and sap in the lower parts of the specimen, but slow-growing and not very vigorous kinds are grafted a little above the middle of the tree, so as to prevent in the completest manner the tendency which the sap has to rush towards the higher points. To show the difference between cultivators, it is sufficient to mention that M. Lepère considers this precaution indispensable; while another distinguished cultivator in the same neighbourhood does not practise it at all, but pinches the upper shoots and deprives them of leaves when too vigorous, and thus preserves the most perfect

Disbudding of the Peach, second year. C and A are removed; B, B, furnish the wood for the following year.

Disbudding of the Peach, second year. If no fruit be borne on E, it is cut at F, leaving G to furnish the fruiting wood for the following year.

health in his trees. This repulsion of the sap to the lower parts of the trees is also effected to some extent by the use of the wide temporary coping, which guards against frost, and keeps the growth down by partly excluding light from the upper part of the wall. When it is removed, and when all danger of frost is past, the sap has flowed so freely into the lower branches that but little trouble is required to keep the tree in a perfectly equable state, all parts of the wall doing a full amount of work. I noticed some walls alongside a road at Montreuil made of blocks of plaster two feet long, one foot high, and five inches thick, forming a strong wall. The blocks are sold at about fifty shillings per hundred.

The walls are about nine feet high, and have a coping of plaster six inches wide. Plaster is very cheap in the neighbourhood, being dug up in quarries quite near to the gardens, and thus it is easy to form a neat and thin projection from the ridge of plaster which forms the top of the wall, by placing boards underneath till the coping sets. This protection is more necessary at the west and south than at the east, the cold rains being more feared than frost, and more difficult to guard against; for while a narrow coping will save the trees from frost, it is not so effective against cold driving rains. It is particularly noticeable that, no matter what form of tree is adopted, all the fruiting branches are

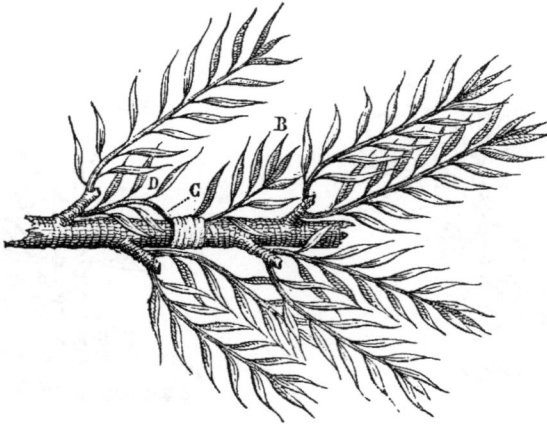

Grafting by approach to furnish bare spaces on the main branches of the Peach-tree. The second spring after grafting, when the Graft has firmly united, the shoot D is cut at C, and B forms a well-placed shoot.

higher at the apex than the base, instead of pursuing the horizontal line, as is the case with us. Perhaps to the passing visitor some of the trees in their full summer dress might appear to have their branches horizontally placed; but even in cases where there is most room for the supposition, the outer ends of the shoots are in fact several inches higher than where they spring from the ascending axis.

Many cordons are to be seen in abundant bearing in the garden, both against the walls and in the open. The Calvilles against the walls were very good, and were not always confined to a single line, but were superimposed. It is a better plan to confine them to a single stem, allowing that to elongate as much as space will permit, that is, if the space to be covered is a mere narrow strip of wall as is the case under these Peach-trees, and the object be to secure a crop of the finest fruit. Some of the Calville and other Apples to be seen here on cordons have nut-brown sears near the apex, showing where the destructive "worm" has been cut out of the fruit ; by taking it in time the fruit is saved, and this attention, which would be ridiculous in the case of ordinary fruit, is repaid in the case of the Calville, for the finest speci- mens of which such very high prices are sometimes received by the owner of this garden. It need hardly be added that such prices are for fruit exceptionally fine, both as to appearance and

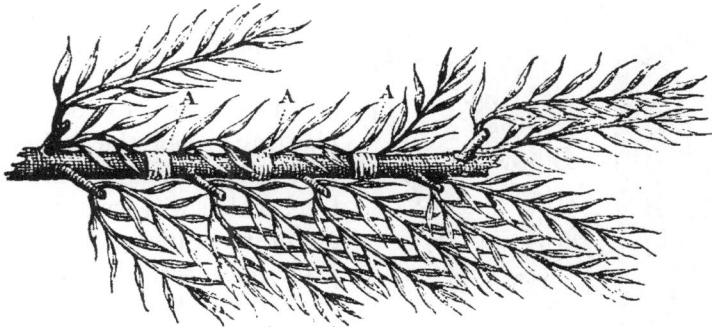

Multiple Grafting by approach, to furnish bare spaces on the stems of Peach-trees. A, A, A, ligatures of Grafts.

size. There are specimens of the Peach trained as cordons bearing plenty of fruit, but they present few advantages in this case that should make them be preferred to forms that are more fully developed. It is not with them, as with the Apple on the Paradise stock, a union that induces a very dwarf development, but, on the contrary, being confined to a single stem they are apt to push too vigorously. M. Lepère had not a word to say in favour of the system.

The U form is so pretty, successful, and generally adopted, that the following remarks on its formation by M. Lepère can hardly fail to be useful :—

"This graceful form is very easy to establish, and I strongly recommend it to those amateurs who have but little wall space to

devote to Peach-growing.   Peach-trees planted in this way afford
the means of growing a number of varieties in a small compass,
and of speedily obtaining a well-trained tree in full bearing.
After having chosen healthy trees, eighteen months old, full of
buds at the base, they are cut down to within eight inches of the
graft at the time of planting.   When the first leaves begin to
appear, two well-placed shoots, situated about six inches above the
graft, are chosen, one on each side of the stem.   These are intended
to form the two main branches that are afterwards to be trained
in the U shape.   The ends of
these two branches are then
turned directly upwards, care
being taken that the extremities
are perfectly free, so that their
development may not be interfered with.

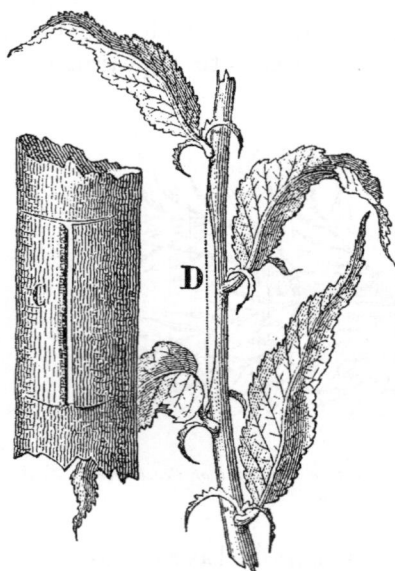

" The space to be given in
planting, when the soil is of the
best kind, is about a yard to each
tree, which will leave an interval
of eighteen inches between each
principal vertical branch, thus
allowing sufficient room for nailing in the summer shoots. When
the soil is not so favourable for
Peach-growing, the trees can be
planted two yards from each other

*Details of the preceding Figures : C, incision of
bare portion of stem ; D, preparation of shoot
intended to furnish it.*

and trained in the form of the
double U.   In this case, as in the
other, the principal branches will
be eighteen inches apart.   Three years ago I planted on a southern
aspect some Peach-trees in the form of the single U.   They
yield on an average one hundred Peaches each every year.   The
wall against which they are trained is ten feet high, and they
were in full bearing the third year.

" I give the preference to this form over the oblique cordon,
because, the principal branches being trained in a perfectly
upright position, the sap is more equally divided amongst the
smaller shoots, and if a tree or two happen to die in a fully

formed plantation, the place they occupy on the wall, which thus becomes empty, is not shaded by the branches of the neighbouring trees. The dead trees can therefore be easily replaced by young subjects from the nursery. This is a great advantage for amateurs who have not always full-grown trees to fill up bare spaces. In the oblique form the inclined position to which each tree is subjected at the time of coming into leaf, causes a disturbance all along the upper edge of the branch, when constant watchfulness of training is not pursued. Besides, if several trees happen to die, and the only trees available to replace them are those from the nursery, the place they will occupy on the wall will be shaded by the branches of the old trees, and the young ones will be injured for want of light and air. As I have already said, the U form is the most easy to train, the most graceful

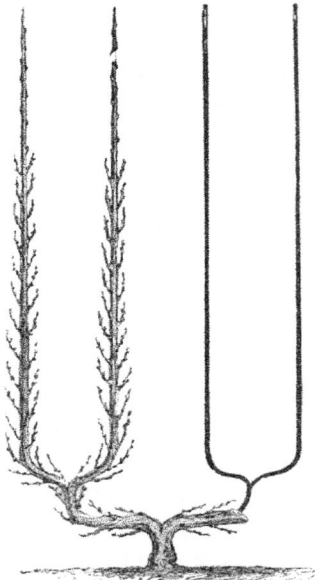

Peach-tree in the double U form. One side is left unfurnished to show the practice of marking on the walls the outline which the tree is to assume.

to the eye, and more prolific than the oblique." In many parts of France may be seen fine results obtained by growing trees on this simple principle. Occasionally the points of trees trained in the U and double U forms are united by grafting by approach. This does not in their case seem to be any advantage.

The reason why the Peach is so successfully cultivated at Montreuil is, that the cultivators pay thorough and constant attention to its wants, with which a life-long experience has made them familiar. The trees are at all times well attended to.

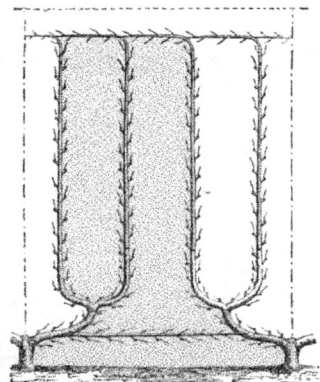

Peach trained in the double U form, with the points of the branches united by grafting.

Quite as good and as certain

results could be attained with the Peach in many of the southern
parts of England and Ireland, particularly if its culture were
made a speciality of, as it is in France.   Indeed, some of our sea-
shore districts would seem to be more favourable for Peach-culture
than the neighbourhood of Paris.   When cultivators devote themselves entirely to a subject, they soon learn all its wants, and, moreover, attend to them at the right moment.   It is, of course, unfair
to expect as much from gardeners concerned with a great variety
of subjects, and often without good appliances for the culture of
any.

It is a matter for regret th:.. public attention has been to some
extent called away from the many uses and advantages of wa⁷⁷⁻
in our climate, and that we have made no progress in protecting
or managing wall-trees corresponding with our advances in other.
respects.   Some persons have gone so far as to say that garden
walls ought to be abolished altogether.   One cannot believe that
such people can ever have seen the excellent results produced by
well-managed garden walls—results as beautiful as profitable.
Why, even if we could erect glass-houses by the economical aid of
a magic wand, the good fruit-grower would still find uses for a
large extent of wall-surface.   As things are at present, all should
aim at greater success in the protection and management of wall-
trees.   Our chief want of success now is due to not preserving
the flowers and tender young leaves from the sleet, cold rains, and
frost, during the cold and changeable spring common to northern
France and the British Isles.

CHAPTER XXII.

FIG CULTURE IN THE NEIGHBOURHOOD OF PARIS.

FIG culture, as practised in the neighbourhood of Paris, is very peculiar and interesting, as well as successful, and is well adapted for the southern counties of England. The Fig bearing well as a healthy standard tree at Arundel and elsewhere in Sussex, without any attention, there cannot be a doubt that the Parisian mode is perfectly applicable in sunny spots in England. It might even be carried out on the railway embankments in our southern counties. The system of culture is founded on the habits of the Fig in the climates of Paris and London. In hot countries the Fig is an evergreen tree, growing and bearing almost perpetually. In cold countries the Fig loses its leaves in winter, and becomes, in fact, a deciduous tree. Then the rudimentary Figs borne at the end of each branch, instead of falling off prematurely, as most other fruits would do, seem to rest stationary; in the spring they recommence their growth, and ripen on into the large, succulent, and well-flavoured Figs supplied to the Paris market in summer. The French call those Figs that require part of two years for their development "figues-fleurs;" those formed in spring and which ripen during warm autumns known as "secondes figues," or "figues d'automne." This rarely in the climate of Paris, and it is to the care of the "figues-fleurs," or Figs formed in the preceding year, that all attention is given. To protect them and the young branches, the trees are trained in long sweeping shoots, pretty near the soil, and in such a form that they may be readily buried in the ground when the winter and its dangers come. The frosts are often of great severity in the neighbourhood of Paris; so great, indeed, that the Fig would have little or no chance if left exposed. So in autumn the cultivators train the branches into four bundles, make a little trench for each, and cover, as shown by the figures, with small sloping banks of soil, protecting the crown of the root by means of a little cone of earth, which merges gradually into the four little ridges that cover the branches. When the plantation is made on deeply inclined ground, a somewhat different system is followed, as is also shown by the illustrations. Most of the details of the culture are taken from Du Breuil's "Culture des Arbres et Arbrisseaux," from the publisher of which, copies of the figures were purchased. I am also indebted to M. Godefroy-Lebeuf, Argenteuil, for making my visits to that town and its Fig-plantations pleasant and instructive. In the climate of Paris the Fig-tree is grown as a low shrub, with free sweeping branches arranged in single lines, or planted all together on a piece of ground devoted to the purpose, and which for want of a better name may be called a "figgery." The branches of these tufty trees are not allowed to grow longer than from six to nine feet, so that the tree may be conveniently buried in the ground during the winter. Those varieties which produce rudimentary Figs in autumn in abundance are the only ones grown, as the Figs of the current year very rarely arrive at maturity. Argenteuil and La Frette are the two most famous localities for the cultivation of the Fig-tree in the neighbourhood of Paris. Before the southern railways were constructed, these two villages used to supply the whole of Paris with all the green Figs that were seen in the markets. The introduction of the Fig-tree into Argenteuil appears to have taken place about two centuries ago. It is cultivated in orchards in deeply dug and richly manured land, the soil of which is of a

Branch of Fig-tree bearing the Figs formed during the preceding year, D ; those formed during the current year, A ; and rudimentary Figs, C.

siliceous, calcareous, and clayey nature, well sheltered from the
north and north-west winds, and open to the south and east.
The cultivation of the Fig extends over a space of one hundred
and thirty acres, the production being somewhere about four
hundred thousand Figs per annum. The variety grown in this
locality is the Blanquette or White Courcourelle, and the method
of growing it is as follows:—

Layers, raised in baskets or in the ordinary way, are planted in
the month of March in holes about four feet six inches in diameter
and one foot eight inches deep, filled with well-manured mould.
The planting is performed in such a way that the roots of the

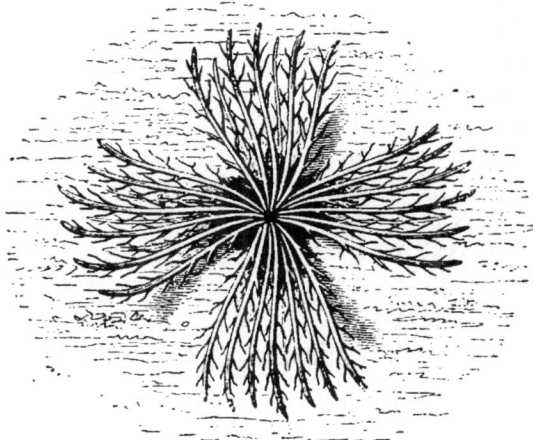

Fig-tree growing on level ground, with the branches grouped in four sets.

layer are buried from ten inches to one foot deep, and that the
stem which springs out of the earth in an oblique direction should
be covered with from three to four inches of earth. To form the
stool more quickly, two layers may be planted in the same hole
instead of only one. In this case the two layers are placed in
lines parallel to those of the plantation at eight inches' distance
from each other, and in such a way that the stems are opposed to
each other in the direction of this line. The surface of the hole
should be at least a foot below that of the surrounding soil. The
rest of the soil is arranged slantwise round the stem of the layer,
so that the rain-water may be easily retained round the roots of
the young trees. The trees are planted five or six yards apart,

the lines being separated by a space of about four yards, so as to form a kind of quincuncial arrangement. These young plants are left to themselves during the whole of the summer, care being taken to keep them from drought by means of frequent watering and careful covering. During the first half of November, when the first cold days set in and the trees are completely bare of leaves, a dry day is chosen when the ground is not too damp, and the young branch is carefully bent downwards until it reaches the bottom of the trench. It is then covered up with a layer of earth a foot deep, to preserve it from the cold. Towards the end of February, as soon as the weather has become mild, the branches are uncovered and the trench is arranged the same as it was before earthing up. The development of the young plant is again allowed to proceed during the summer, to be again earthed up when November sets in.

The third spring after planting, a fine day is chosen towards

Fig-tree with the branches trained in two sets.

the middle of March—the young stem is cut at from six to eight inches from the ground, so as to favour the production of a large crop of shoots, which will afterwards form the principal branches of the tree. These shoots are allowed to grow through the summer, and are earthed up in autumn. This process is performed according to the following directions:—A dry day is chosen when the soil is in a friable condition, so that it will fill the spaces between the branches without leaving any empty places. The soil used should be free from leaves, grass, and straw, which, if they were allowed to come in contact with the buried branches, would cause them to become rotten. It is also necessary to pull off the half-grown autumn Figs, which would rot in the earth, and cause the same mischief as any other decomposing vegetable matter. These precautions having been taken, the branches of the tree are divided into four equal bundles, each being tied together with string. As many trenches as there are bundles of branches are then dug in the ground. Each trench commences at the foot of the tree, and is made of sufficient depth to contain the bundles of branches. They are dug in different directions, according as the ground is inclined or horizontal. In the former case they are dug all in the same upward direction; when, however, the ground is level, they radiate equally from the centre. The earthing up of the branches being accomplished according to these directions,

Showing the Mode of burying the Fig-trees cultivated on level ground, to preserve them from being destroyed by frost in Winter.

tions, each bundle is covered with mould to the depth of eight inches, a small cone being piled up exactly over the root.

Towards the end of February a damp, warm day is chosen for

Fig-tree planted on sloping earth buried for the Winter months.

uncovering the buried Fig-trees. The sooner this operation is accomplished the more forward will be the growth of the tree, and the ripening of the fruit; but the early fruit is often destroyed by the late frosts. For this reason some growers prefer to defer this operation until the end of March, although the trees frequently suffer from being thus suddenly exposed to the heat of

2 c

the sun, and the fruit does not ripen so well.   Others uncover one-half their trees at the end of February, and the other half at the end of March.   By this means a better average crop is insured both in quality and quantity. The branches are sepa-rated from each other by equal distances, so as to avoid confusion, as well as to prevent the leaves from rubbing against the fruit, which would have the effect of blackening them, and render them comparatively worthless. Those branches that are too near the ground are held up by means of forked pieces of wood.   The soil is   carefully   levelled

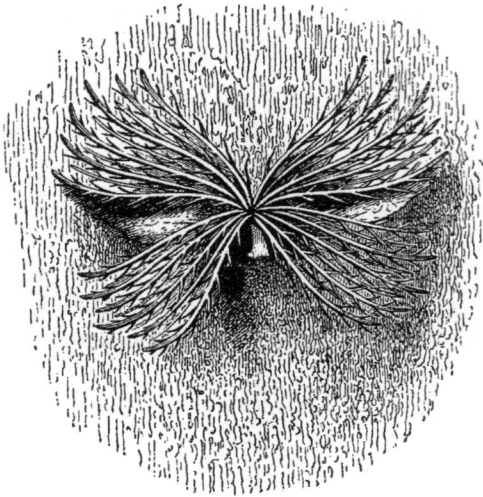

Fig-tree planted on sloping ground, with Earth Basin on lower side to better retain the water.

where the ground is horizontal, a little hollow being made round the root of the tree to hold the rain-water.   Trees that are planted on sloping ground require hollows to be made in the soil, so that the water which flows from the higher ground may be col-lected at the root of each tree.   In this way a proper degree of moisture is insured during the whole of the sum-mer, besides which

Section showing Fig-tree planted on inclined ground, with Earth . Basin to retain the water.

the soil is prevented from being cut up by the rains.   This plan would seem to be peculiarly well suited to plantations on the steep slopes of railway embankments. Henceforward the young shoots growing from the stock are carefully cut off; otherwise they would weaken the larger branches. These precautions are taken during the fifth year.

In the spring of the sixth year the oldest branches are of the form shown in our illustration. The operation of nipping-off the buds at the end of each branch is performed as soon as the un-covered trees begin to show signs of springing into leaf; that is to say, on some fine day the bud on the end of each lateral shoot is pinched off so as to favour the formation of buds on the wood lower down, as well as for the encouragement of any young Figs that already show signs of making their appearance. About one-half of the buds on the side-branches are also pinched off, choosing those that are nearest to the young Figs. Two, however, are always left on near the base of each branch, and one towards the tip, in order to draw up the sap. The end-shoot of each branch is treated in a similar manner, but with this difference, that the bud immediately below the one at the end is allowed to remain on, as well as one or two more for the purpose of producing side-branches, which ought to

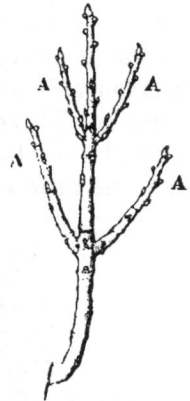

Stem of Fig the sixth year after planting. The points of the shoots A, A, A, A, are pinched off in Spring to favour the development of the Figs, and also of wood-buds at the base of the shoots.

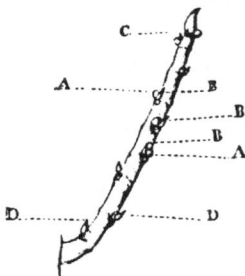

be left about a foot from each other on each stem. As soon as the young shoots are about two inches long, the shoots on all the lateral branches and on the end-branch are nipped off—a fine day being chosen for the purpose. Of the former only a single shoot—the one nearest the base of the branch—is allowed to remain so as to re-place the one which bears the fruit of the year. The shoot at the end of the terminal branch is allowed to remain, and some of the lateral ones intended to bear fruit in the following year. These last are spaced out so that they may receive an equal amount of sunshine without being interwoven or rubbing their leaves against the

Fig-branch with young Figs. The lateral side buds A, B, B, B, are pinched in Spring,—two at the base, D, D, and one at the apex, C, being left.

2 c 2

fruit. As soon as the proper number of branches that each stool ought to bear is reached, all new shoots growing on the parent-stem are nipped off.

Although the Figs which make their appearance during the current year ripen with difficulty, a certain number may be grown in favourable years. Their ripening is hastened in the following manner. Those branches which appear to be most prolific are allowed to retain two shoots at their base instead of only one. The one nearest the base is intended to produce the young Figs for the following year, the other the autumn Figs. In order to force these latter into rapid growth the end of the shoot must be nipped off as soon as it has reached a length of four or five inches. As the process of forcing autumn Figs to ripen makes the trees weaker and less able to produce the buds, or "Fig-flowers," for the next year, only those which are strong and vigorous should be chosen for the purpose.

Should the late frosts destroy the crop of Figs, which may take place before the middle of May, summer-pruning must be resorted to, that is to say, each lateral branch is pruned back to near the stem. This operation causes the sap to flow to the old wood and produce a large crop of shoots. This circumstance is taken advantage of to fill up empty spaces, of course taking care to leave only those shoots growing that are really useful. The shoots are thinned out according to the method already described.

Branch of Fig-tree after the gathering of the crop. Should the year be unusually warm, some of the lower Figs may ripen; if not, they are removed. The shoot that has borne Figs is cut at B.

Towards the end of August a dry day is chosen for cleaning the figgery. The portions of the shoots which have borne fruit are cut off, and useless shoots are taken away just above the lowest eye. If this eye should develop in the succeeding year, it is disbudded in its turn. Withered branches are also removed quite close to the stem, care being taken to cover the wounds with grafting-wax. Some growers leave this operation until the spring of the following year, but prunings made at that time cause a much greater loss of sap, and the wounds made in the tree heal up with great difficulty.

In the spring of the seventh year the lateral branches of each stem are treated like those of the preceding year. The other operations are similar to those already described. The principal branches are allowed to grow longer every year, taking care to allow the fruit-bearing shoots, which are replaced from year to year, like those of the Peach-tree, to remain at regular intervals. When the branches have grown to the length of from six to nine feet, their growth should be checked, otherwise the sap will desert the fruit-bearing branches at the sides, and so cause them to wither away. When sufficiently long the principal are treated in the same way as directed for the side-branches.

The earthing-up to which the branches of the Fig-tree are subjected every year causes them to grow in a horizonal direction a foot or eighteen inches from the ground. This is an element of success, for on the one hand the fruit nearest to the ground receives the greater part of the heat and ripens readily, on the other hand the sab is more evenly distributed amongst the different side-branches. The Argenteuil Fig-trees begin to bear when they are six years old, and are in full perfection at ten years. They live a long time, but it is necessary to renew the long and old stems, which wear out every twelve or fifteen years. For this purpose the requisite number of shoots are allowed to grow on the parent stem to replace those which are cut away in the August following. The soil round the trees should be dug up every year in the spring after having unearthed the branches and

Branch of Fig-tree after the gathering of the crop. C bears the young Figs for the coming year's crop; D is pinched back to help the ripening of some of the Figs of the current year; and the fruit has been gathered from the naked shoot, which is cut at B.

before covering-in the trenches at the foot of the tree. They should also be well watered several times during the summer, and manured every three years. The practice of putting a drop of fine oil into the eye of the fruit just as it colours and shows signs of opening, to hasten its maturity, is employed about Paris, especially during cold summers.

The Culture of the Vine at Thomery.

As it is certain that the culture of the Grape grown against walls in the open air may be attempted with profit over a large part of the southern and midland counties of England, an account is given of the successful and highly-interesting culture of the

The Chasselas de Fontainebleau.

Chasselas Grape near Paris, where it must be grown against walls as well as with us.

Every autumn, quantities of this delicious little Grape may be seen in the Paris markets, packed in small boxes or circular baskets. This variety is not unfrequently grown as an early Grape in this country, under the name of the Royal Muscadine;

but it is not so delicious when forced in our hothouses as when ripened under warm sunshine on the whitewashed walls of Thomery and Fontainebleau. There are several varieties of Chasselas grown in French gardens, all of which are of excellent flavour ; but this is the best of them, and the one most generally grown, as a dessert Grape, for the French markets. The Vine is moderately vigorous in growth, and is easily recognised, even when not in fruit, by its peculiarly blunt-lobed rounded leaves. The bunches are generally small, rarely exceeding a pound in weight even when grown indoors in this country, and grown out-of-doors in French gardens the clusters are smaller still. The berries are

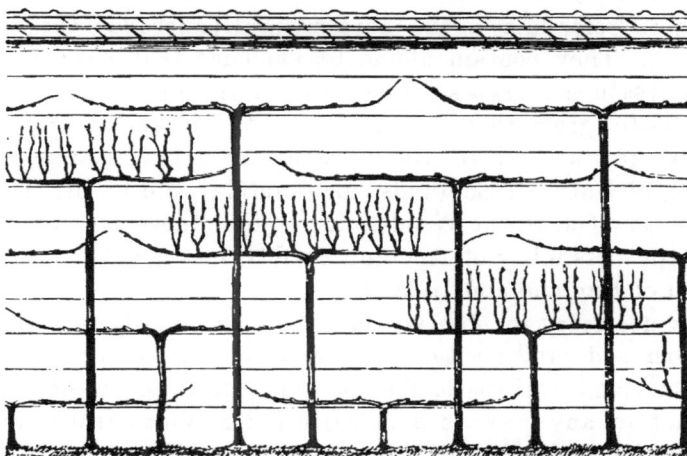

Wall of Chasselas at Thomery, showing the Vines trained as Horizontal Cordons, both in a pruned and unpruned condition.

round and of a clear greenish-yellow colour, acquiring a pink or amber tint, on the sunny side, when fully ripe. Being of a peculiarly sweet juicy flavour, and producing a crackling sensation when eaten, it seems singular that this delicious little Grape does not more frequently find its way to our London markets, as it can be imported quite as cheaply as the Spanish Chasselas and Sweet-waters, and it is greatly superior to them in flavour. It bears packing and carriage well, and the only drawback is that it must be used soon after it is ripe.

When well ripened against walls the French think it the best Grape ever grown, and superior to our hothouse Grapes, fine as

they are.   Here I am simply stating an opinion without en-
dorsing it, merely adding that this estimate is not solely confined
to those who have no opportunity of judging both sides of the
question, but was held by the late Baron Rothschild, who grew all
our finest Grapes, and by some other good judges.   Grape-culture
is often successful against houses with us when it receives mere
chance attention from cottagers and others.   By selecting the
soil and position, and really paying some attention to protecting
and cultivating the Vine, we may grow good Grapes against walls,
even in many places where ground-vineries are now resorted to.
Should any person doubt the possibility of cultivating the Chasselas
and others of our best hardy Grapes in the open air, I have
merely to refer him to the horticultural papers for the autumn
of 1868.   They contain abundant evidence that even with the
rough treatment Grapes now receive in the open air, it is quite
possible to grow them of good quality on walls.   Grapes are
already grown well in the open air in a few places—by Mr.
Darkin, at Bury St. Edmunds, for example; and by Mr. Fenn, in
the Rectory Garden at Woodstock; so that there can be no doubt
about the possibility of ripening good Grapes over a considerable
portion of England and Ireland.

It is necessary to observe that the plan is only recommended
for warm soils and positions, for gardens not having much glass
and yet some wall-space, for covering cottages, out-offices, etc.,
and not in any way as a substitute for Vine-culture indoors.
The Chasselas de Fontainebleau, or Royal Muscadine, is far the
best for culture in the open air in this country.

An account of the Grape-growing at Thomery from the pen ot
M. Rose-Charmeux is likely to convey the most practical information on the subject, and the following is translated from his
'Culture du Chasselas:' from the publishers of which the following illustrations of the subject have been purchased for this
work:—

"At Thomery the soil is of a sandy and clayey nature, and
mixed with pebbles in those parts which are near the river.   The
soil is at all times easy to work.   Near the Seine it lacks depth—
so much so, indeed, that before cultivation it has to be dug and
trenched so as to remove some of the stony subsoil.   Everywhere
else the layer of vegetable mould measures from four feet six

inches to six feet in thickness. This layer is on a reddish clay of about the same thickness, and beneath the clay is a broken-up stratum of building-stone filled with fissures. This building-stone is easily extracted. The Grapes ripen a fortnight earlier in the flinty districts than in those parts in which the soil is deeper and richer.

"The gardens at Thomery, taken altogether, present much the appearance of those of Montreuil-sur-Bois. There is nothing but walls in all directions, distant from each other about forty feet, and ten feet high. This height has

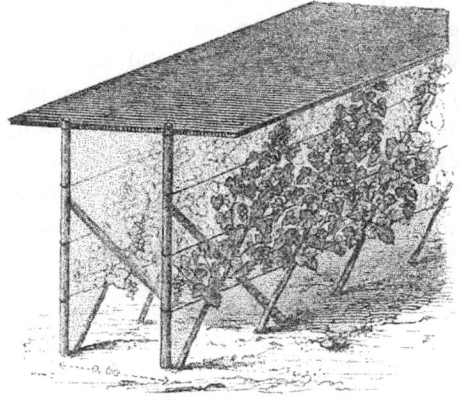

Low Double Espalier, and Mode of Protecting the Vines in Spring.

only obtained during the last fifteen years, before which period they were rarely higher than six or seven feet. The change has been advantageous for two reasons; first, the Grape-growers have been able to increase the space required for their purpose

Section of top of wall at Thomery, showing the projection of the temporary coping.

by taking possession of a larger portion of air instead of having to buy fresh ground; and secondly, the high walls are found to improve the appearance and quality of the Grapes. The walls are built of hard stone quarried in the neighbourhood, the stones being laid with mud only. The face of the wall is then covered with a mortar made of lime and sand, and is finally covered with the same material thinned to a creamy consistence. Every wall is topped with a roof of pantiles, surmounted by a row of gutter-tiles. These roofs project about ten inches, and below them are fixed at every yard iron rods, inclined slightly downwards. These supports project about twenty inches beyond the edge of the tiles, affording altogether a support of at least two feet six inches wide. Upon this is fixed, when occasion requires it a coping of bitumenised felt, or, where economy is necessary, a piece of thin plank. The bitumenised felt is stretched on frames of wood, about ten feet in length by eighteen inches in width, the felt being fastened to them by means of small nails. These frames are chiefly used when the Grapes are perfectly ripe, which is generally about September 15, or when there is danger of the fruit being spoilt by heavy rains. Formerly, before these methods of shelter were employed, large quantities of Grapes were continually lost through

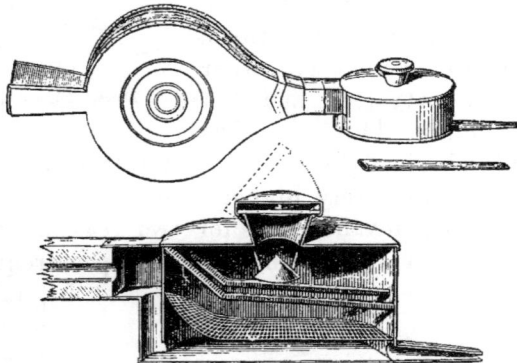

Sulphur Distributor employed at Thomery.

becoming rotten with the wet; since their adoption, however, there is no fear of such a result. The size of the temporary copings to be used is always dependent

Pruning to obtain the two arms of the Cordon.

on the aspect and height of the walls. With walls facing the south and ten feet high, frames containing felt at least thirty inches in width ought to be used. With a western aspect, they ought to be even wider, in order to avoid all danger from the heavy rains. With the old low walls, frames twenty-four inches wide for the south, twenty-eight inches for the west, and sixteen inches for the east, were found to be quite sufficient."

" After selecting a proper position and soil, the most important point is the sulphuring to prevent the Oidium   Sulphur is the effective cure for this pest, and it should be applied directly after the first pinching of the shoots, at a temperature below 96° Fahr. in the open air. If the heat is too great, the young skin of the Grape is liable to become decomposed. In full sunshine at noon the fruit would be burnt up in an hour's time. Sulphuring may be carried on while the dew is falling. There is no fear in this case of soiling the Grapes. The operation should not be deferred until the Oidium has made its ap-pearance. The second sulphuring should be performed when the Grapes are about as large as a pea, or even earlier if the Oidium has appeared at all. It would be pre-

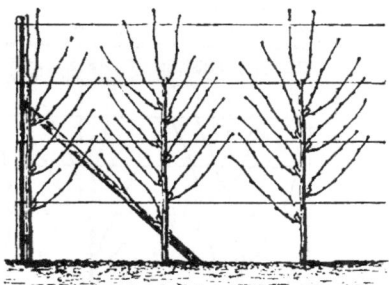

Low Espalier of Vines trained vertically, four feet high.

ferable to sulphur while the Vines are in flower. The operation is performed with sublimated sul-phur, blown upon the Vine with a pair of bellows specially con-

Layer of Vine raised and planted in basket.

trived for the purpose. It may be effectively done without the operator standing an instant in one spot, but passing quickly along the line. In these latitudes heavy rains destroy in part the effect of the sulphur, and it is nearly always necessary to repeat the operation three or four times. If the Grapes themselves are attacked, it is on them that the flowers of sulphur should be applied. It has been remarked that under sunshine the Oidium may be totally destroyed in one hour, a result that may be attributed to the

speedier disengagement of sulphurous acid gas by the heat of the
sun, but it is dangerous to apply it if the sun is too strong."

The pruning of the Vine is so well understood in England that
it is needless to give it here in the full detail with which it is
honoured in M. Rose-Charmeux's book, the 'Culture du Chasselas.' The system as shown
in the illustrations is simply
the well-known spur-prun-
ing practised in nearly
every English vinery. There
are indeed several modifications of training; but this
as everybody knows is of no
real importance. In this

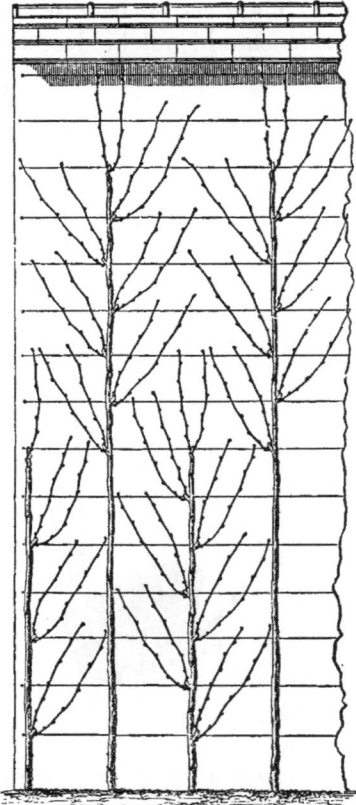

Rose-Charmeux's System of Vertical Training. The Vines are planted at sixteen inches
apart.

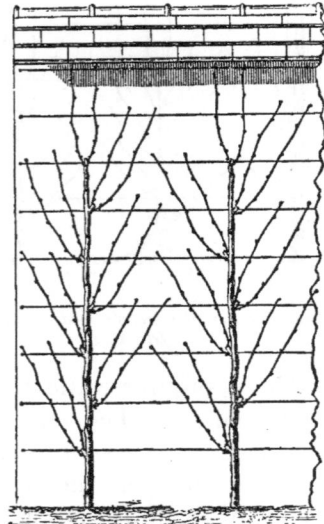

Vines trained Vertically with alternated
spurs, wires nine inches apart on wall;
Vines about twenty-eight inches apart.

case, as with the Vine indoors, the selection of a proper medium for
the roots is of far greater importance than anything else, while the
simplest form and the best system of pruning are without doubt
the same as those seen in our vineries—an erect stem with the
side-shoots annually pruned in.   At Thomery the Vine is fre-

quently trained as a horizontal cordon line over line; but to execute this form well requires time and skill, which only cultivators who devote themselves specially to it can afford, and it may be safely said that letting the Vines run straight up the walls and with their spurs at each side is better than any less-simple mode. The really-important points to bear in mind are—first, the warmer the exposure is, the better for the Grape; second, that the walls are white, or nearly so, as the Vines get more heat on such walls than they do on dark ones, and are maintained in better health; third, that wide and efficient copings are used to permit the fruit to thoroughly ripen in autumn, and prevent its being spoiled by heavy rains; and that the higher walls are found to possess an advantage over the lower ones. The plants are frequently raised in rough baskets for convenience of removal and sale. Several of the appliances here in use are sensible ones,

Movable Scaffold used for thinning the Grapes.

which might be found useful in other ways than that of Vine-culture. For instance, the movable scaffold to facilitate the labours of the women who attend to the walls in summer, the shade to shield them from the sun, and the frame for conveying a number of small baskets laden with Grapes from the walls to the Grape-room.

Grafting is frequently performed, and chiefly to replace a bad by a good variety, or to hasten the fructification of a new one. The plant is cut down to within nine or ten inches of the soil, and with the gouge an incision is made on the smoothest side, a corresponding cut being made in a scion or in the stem of a young plant, both of which methods are here shown. The grafting is performed as soon as the sap begins to move in spring, and the grafts are tied and covered with grafting-wax (see illustration).

A particularly noticeable feature in the cultivation is that the young Vines are as a rule planted at a considerable distance from the wall—say a little more than three feet, and the stem laid into the ground to near the base of the wall. Sometimes the stem is allowed to rise some distance from the wall, and in the following year when it has grown a little it is again lowered and

Shade to protect the Grape-thinners from strong sun.

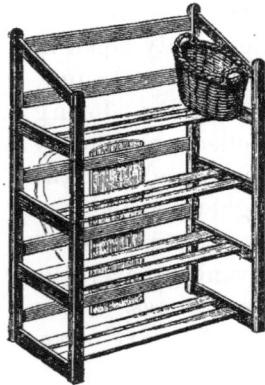

Frame for carrying small baskets filled with Grapes from the walls to the store-rooms: four feet high at back, thirty-one inches wide, and ten and a half inches deep.

taken to the wall. This method is obviously pursued to secure a number of vigorous roots spread over a large surface. Where the ground is stony and poor it is probably a good plan.

As regards the forcing of Grapes at Thomery, there is little to note of any importance to the British Grape-grower, who is certainly in advance of all others as regards the indoor-culture of this old and ever-popular fruit. Nevertheless, M. Rose-Charmeux's garden exhibits such an advance on the ordinary style of forcing Grapes around Paris that it deserves a few words. "The walls of the pits are of brick; the highest, towards the north, measures about five feet in height; the front wall being only about two feet high.   The width of the hothouse at its base between the walls is about four feet six inches, and the length indefinite.   The higher wall is covered on the top with a deal board a foot wide and projecting towards the south; the lower wall is covered in the same way with a board five inches wide. The walls ought to be rough cast, and kept perfectly white like those of the gardens.   Bars of iron serve as supports to the frames, and to keep the walls in their places when the frames

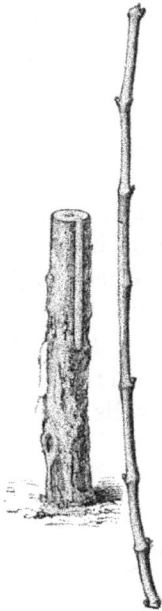

Mode of Grafting the Vine at Thomery.   *Mode of Grafting the Vine, by approach, practised at Thomery.*   *Gouge used in Grafting the Vine : ten inches long.*

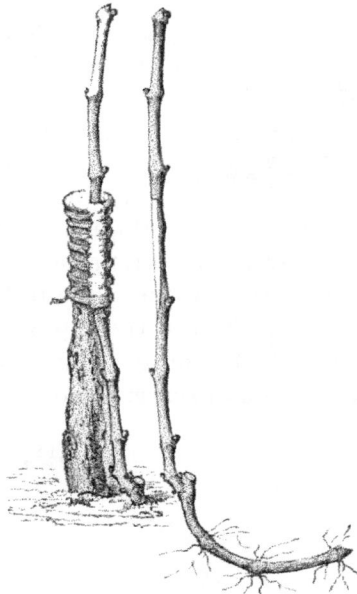

are taken away, and rods provided with holes are placed in the middle of each frame so that they may be opened to different heights according to circumstances.   A copper hot-water pipe, four inches in diameter, serves to warm the structure, and an entrance-door is constructed at each end.   Grape-forcing begins from the 15th to the 25th of December, in order to have ripe fruit by the end of April.   During the first fortnight the heat is not allowed to rise above 58° F. to 65° F.   In a fortnight

it is allowed to rise to 78° F. or 80° F., from which time until
the Grapes are ripe the heat is maintained at from 80° F. to
88° F. The time of flowering requires a great deal of attention,
for on it depends entirely the success of the result. In order
that fecundation should take place under the most favourable
circumstances, and that the Grapes
should be well formed, it is absolutely necessary that the temperature should be maintained
between 78° F. and 88° F. ; also
that the Vine should have plenty
of light and dry air.

"The low span-roofed house is
constructed in the following manner :—On the east and west are
built two small brick walls twenty-
eight inches high, and in the centre

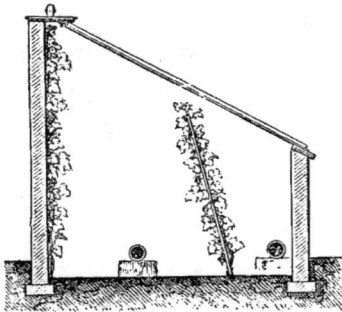

Small Pit used for Forcing the Vine.

of the enclosed space are placed strong posts about five feet high,
and distant from each other about three feet. A plank fourteen
inches wide, nailed on the top of these posts, ties them together
solidly and forms a sort of coping. This plank is covered with
sheet-zinc, and bars of iron are carried from it to the walls serving
as supports to the
lights. At each
end a door is con-
structed for the
attendants to go
in and out, and on
each side is a
thermometer for
regulating the
temperature. The
interior of the
hothouse is about
ten feet wide at

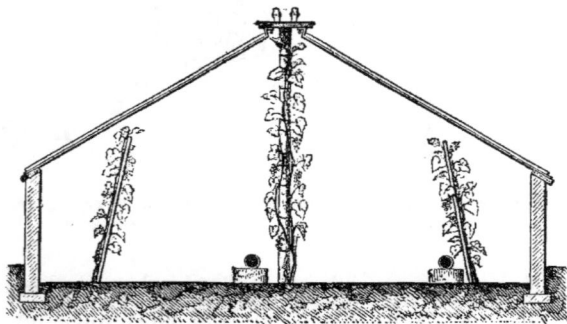

Small span-roofed Pit for Forcing the Vine : ten feet five inches wide,
and five feet five inches high.

the base, so that the rows of Vines are distant from the side-
walls about eighteen or twenty inches, and one side gets the
effect of the sun in the morning, the other in the afternoon. Two
rows of pulleys are attached to the wooden coping for working

the straw mats, which ought to be taken off every morning and replaced in the evening."

Thus M. Rose-Charmeux speaks of his forced culture of the Vine. In addition to the houses here figured and alluded to, he employs a well-constructed portable lean-to house—portable because the French yet believe in the virtue of the plan of alternately forcing and resting their trees, a system which we have long ago proved to be worthless.

The following is a French mode of training Vines on walls, and a very good one; the walls are trellised with split pieces of Oak which last nearly as long as the walls themselves. The Vines are planted against them about six feet apart, as there are three tiers of Vines, or cordons as they may be termed. The distance for each Vine to run horizontally is something like nine feet or so; the horizontal shoots are tied to the first bar or lath, and the rest of the space is left for the summer-shoots and fruits, only one bunch of Grapes being left on each pair of shoots. The shoot that fruits this year does not bear fruit next, and so on throughout. It is a simple and quick way of covering a wall, and one which in the southern part of England might be advantageously practised.

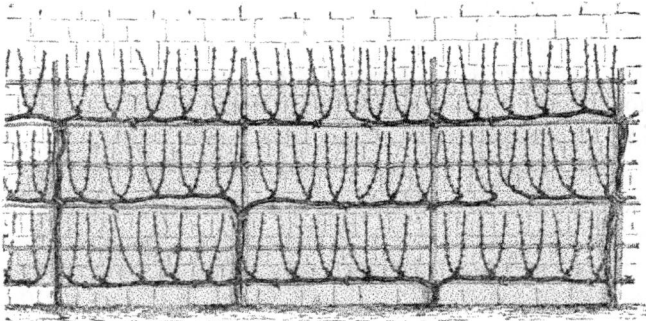

French mode of training Vines on open Wall.

CHAPTER XXIII.

Training.

In France the commonest garden-labourers frequently possess a knowledge of pruning and training trees which we might look for in vain anywhere in this country; and by way of illustrating their skill in this way, we cannot do better than describe their mode of forming two of the most popular forms of fruit-trees— the Palmette Verrier and the Pyramidal Pear-trees, chiefly after Du Breuil. The Pear will serve to illustrate training and pruning as well as any other tree, and the principles laid down will apply to other fruit-trees.

The Palmette.—Wherever large wall-trees are grown, the simple and beautiful form known to the French as the Palmette Verrier is sure to obtain a place among them. It is the finest of large forms, and is preferred by many of the best French cultivators to any other, though for quick returns the vertical forms now begin to supplant it in some gardens. The reader may think it impossible to attain such perfect shape as is shown in the illustrations, but there are many trees even more beautiful than those represented. This figure also shows the advantages of the kind of support used in France for espalier-trees as compared with our method of using rough wooden or iron posts and strong bolt-like wire. It will be seen that the tree differs from the form of Pear-tree that we are in the habit of placing against walls; it is easy to point out its advantages in securing an equal flow of sap to all the branches. In the common horizontal form strength and fertility are apt to desert the lower branches, in consequence of their not possessing a growing-point to draw the sap through, and particularly when constant care is not taken to repress the upper portions of the tree by summer-pinching. The form here figured, in common with all very large wall and espalier

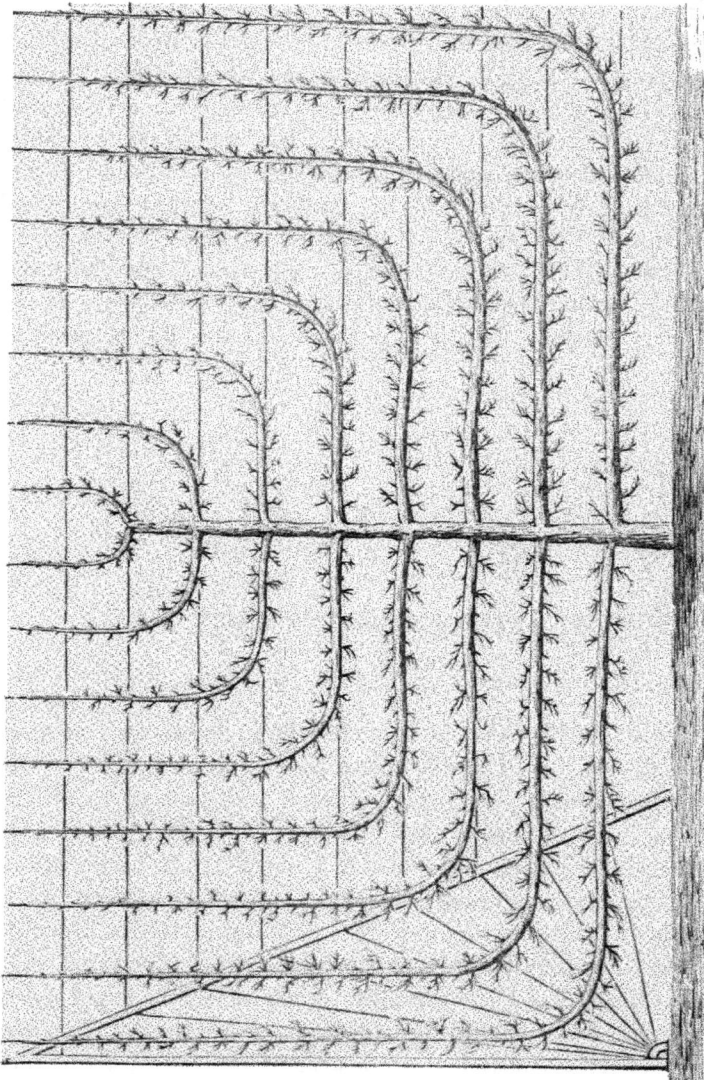

PEAR-TREE TRAINED AS A "PALMETTE VERRIER,"

On trellis ten feet high, supports of T iron, horizontal lines slender galvanised wire (No. 12), wires united in strong ring at base to secure rigidity in end supports.

trees, takes a long time to complete. Given a wall 10 ft. or 12 ft. high, and 20 ft. or 24 ft. long, to be covered with a tree

2 D 2

of this shape, it would require fifteen or sixteen years to form it. By adopting a more contracted form based upon the same plan, we may cover the wall or trellis more quickly.

The Palmette Verrier is named after the fruit-gardener at the Ecole Régionale de la Saulsaie, with whom it was first observed. To form the tree, we have in the first instance to plant a young tree which, as so much care is about to be exercised upon it, should be of the primest quality. In forming this, as all other fruit-trees, the usual and most economical custom is to choose plants about a year old from the time of grafting, or what are called "maiden plants." Trees more advanced might be bought to make the same form more quickly, but they will be more expensive the further they are advanced beyond what is called the "maiden" stage. The young trees should be allowed to

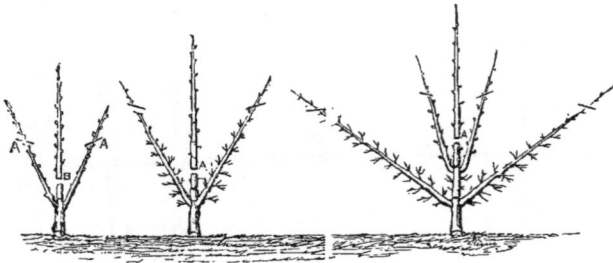

The Palmette Verrier.

Second pruning.   Third pruning.   Fourth pruning.

remain a year or so in their positions before being cut, so that they may root well. At the first pruning the young tree is cut down to within a foot or so of the ground, and just above three suitable eyes, one at each side to form the two lowermost branches, the third a little above them and in front to continue the upright axis. Of course all the eyes, except those that are to send forth the first three shoots, must be suppressed in spring. Although the tree in the illustration looks so very exact and regular in its lines that the branches appear as if they had been "bent in the way they should go" at a very early stage, it is not so; they are at first allowed to grow almost erect, and are after-wards gradually lowered to the horizontal position. During the first year of the young tree possessing three shoots, care must be taken (as at all times) to secure a perfect equilibrium between them. If one grows stronger than the others, it must be loosened from its position on the wall and lowered. This will divert the sap so as to strengthen the rest. Nothing is more easily conducted than the sap, if a little attention be paid to it; if neglected, it soon rushes towards the higher points, and spoils the symmetry of the tree.

At the second pruning they must be cut at B, and about a third of the length of the side-shoots must also be cut at A A, in preceding figure. If one side-branch happens to be stronger than the other, the stronger one must be cut somewhat shorter. In cutting and pruning wall-trees the cut should be made above a front bud, so that the wound made by the knife may be turned towards the wall,

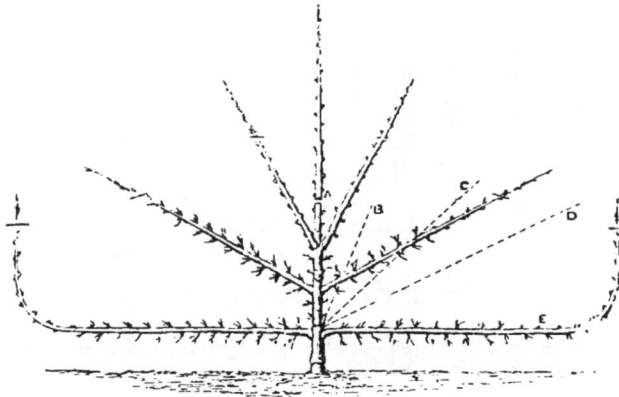

The Palmette Verrier. Fifth pruning.

and away from the eye, from which, of course, it will soon be effectually hidden by this front bud developing into a shoot, and thickening at its base. During the second year no more branches must be permitted to grow, because the trainer desires to throw all the strength he can into the lower branches, which are to be the longest. Sometimes, however, the strength of the lower branches will permit the second stage of branches to be made during the second year of training. At the third pruning the central stem is cut at six inches or so above the previous incision, which is indicated by a slight ring, and a third part of the new growth of the side-branches cut off, as shown in the illustration. Here, again, we cut above and inside three promising eyes to obtain a new set of branches, and each succeeding year add another series until the tree is formed.

At the end of the following growing-season the specimen will have
advanced sufficiently to allow the lower branches to be bent up
towards the top of the wall, and will begin to look shapely. The
fifth stage of pruning is well shown in the illustration, which is
an exact representation of what the tree ought to be—A, and the
cross marks indicating where the incisions are to be made. Above
all things it is necessary to keep the growth and flow of sap
equal, not only for the sake of symmetry, but also to insure
perfect health and fertility; for if one part be allowed to grow
grossly at the expense of another, an awkward state of things will
soon take place. Sometimes, when the vegetation is very vigorous,
time is gained in the making of this form by pinching the central

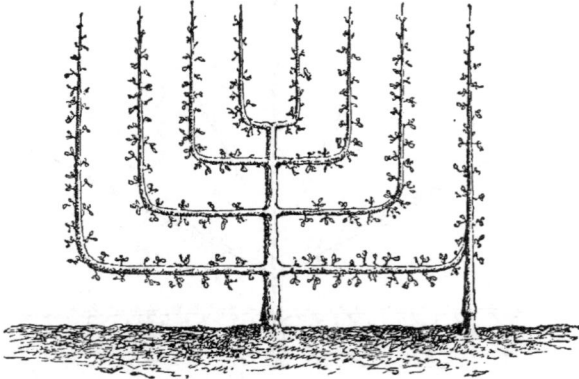

Palmette Verrier, with weakly outer Branch completed by Grafting.

growth at eight inches or so above the highest pair of opposite
branches. It then breaks again, and care is taken to secure two
side-shoots and an erect one. Thus, with attention, and in good
soil, two stages of branches may be secured in the same year, but
this must not be attempted till the proper formation of the two
lower branches is secured. The dotted lines in the figure showing
the fifth pruning indicate the positions that have been successively
occupied by the branch E, while in course of formation, and show
that it is by no means necessary to train a young branch from the
beginning in the exact position it is required to take. In fact,
this form is only to be well and easily finished by allowing the
young shoots to first grow and gather strength in an erect or
oblique position. The branch E was adjacent to the central

branch when young, and was at B; then it was lowered to C, next year to D, and finally to its horizontal position. Some care is required to make the bend of the shoots equal and gently rounded. If the tree is trained on a wire trellis, it is best before it becomes necessary to bend the shoots, to place two bent rods in the exact position desired. They must be fixed at exactly equal distances from the main stem, and be equal in curvature. It is then an easy matter to attach to them the growing shoot, which will soon harden to the desired bend. Against a wall it may be readily directed with shreds and nails; if the wall be wired, bent twigs may be applied, as on the trellis. Like care should be bestowed upon the other bends, as they require to be made; but of course the outer and lower one is of the greatest importance. As this form is not at all presentable if the outer branches be incomplete, grafting by approach is sometimes employed to repair any such defect.

This mode of training is too little practised in our country, and being applicable to many forms of training, I can strongly recommend it, having

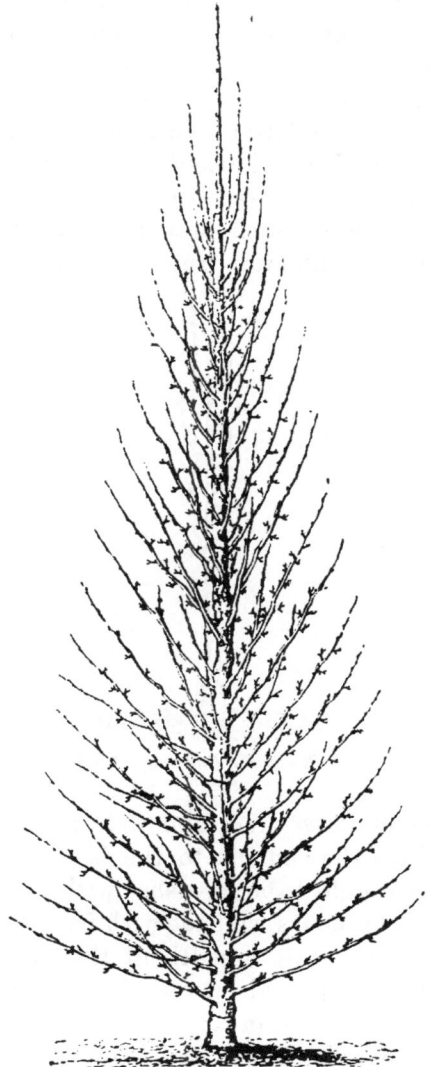

Pyramidal Pear-tree.

frequently witnessed the good effects produced by carrying it out carefully.

Pyramidal Training of the Pear-tree.—This culture is, considered from the stand-point of beauty alone, as desirable as any with which amateurs interest themselves. I have seen in very small gardens in France, pyramidal Pear-trees, which if they never afforded a fruit, would be beautiful objects; and there are few " avenues" prettier than those of Pear-trees in little town-gardens in Paris. In the fully-formed pyramid, in addition to its symmetry will be observed the straight clean growth of each branch, springing at regular intervals from the main stem,

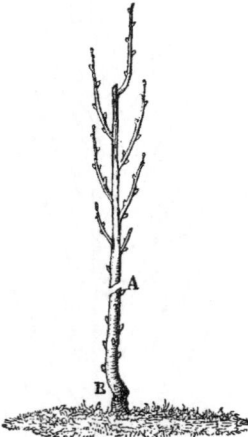

Pyramidal Pear-tree. First pruning.

Top of Young Pear-tree. B, the leading shoot. A A, shoots requiring to be pinched.

which is so erect and well furnished. From the summit to the base such a tree ought to be garnished with nothing but branches well set with fruit-spurs. The greatest breadth of the pyramid should equal about one-third of its height. Pyramidal trees may be purchased in all stages; but trees ready-formed are costly, and as many would prefer training their own, and as those who plant on a large scale will find it economical to begin with trees a year from the graft, we will commence with a " maiden tree," letting it grow one year in the ground before pruning it. The small cut represents the first pruning of this young tree, and its appearance one year after being permanently planted, or two years from the graft. B shows the union of stock and scion; and the terminal bud, A, just below where the shoot is cut should be placed on the side opposite to that on which the scion was inserted, as shown in the figure, so that the stem of the tree may rest perpendicularly on its base. It is by attending to such little points as this that the French get that perfectly equal distribution of sap which is so essential to the satisfactory management and prolonged fertility of trained fruit-trees. The summer following the first pruning, the young trees push with great vigour, and their shoots should be thinned when a few inches long, removing every shoot from the base of the stem to a height of about one foot, and thinning out those above this point to six, seven, or eight shoots; reserving of course the best-placed shoots, and taking care to have them arranged as far as possible at regular intervals. Should they in the course of the year assume an irregular development, pinching with the finger and thumb must be resorted to. For instance, in the cut opposite,

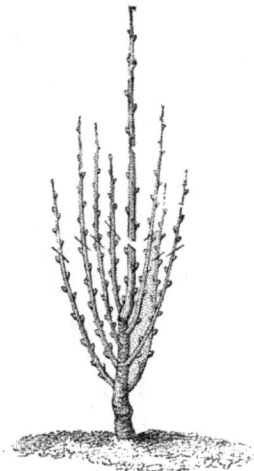

Pyramidal Pear-tree. Second pruning.

Leading shoot of Pear-tree, showing incisions A, A, A, made above the buds required to break strongly.

the shoots, A A, have pushed too much; and one of them rivals the leading shoot, B; they therefore are pinched, merely taking off an inch or so. The second pruning has for its object the production of a new set of lateral branches, and the further development of those already obtained. It is evident that to secure a beautiful tree, the branches must spring forth regularly from the main stem, which they are not likely to do if the tree is left to itself. The illustration of "leading shoot of Pear-tree" shows the way in which the careful cultivator furnishes his stem, as regularly as could be desired. The eyes which he desires to break strongly have an incision made above them, as shown in the figure. This is particularly desirable as regards the lower part of each successive growth of the erect stem; the vigour of the rising current of sap often pushing

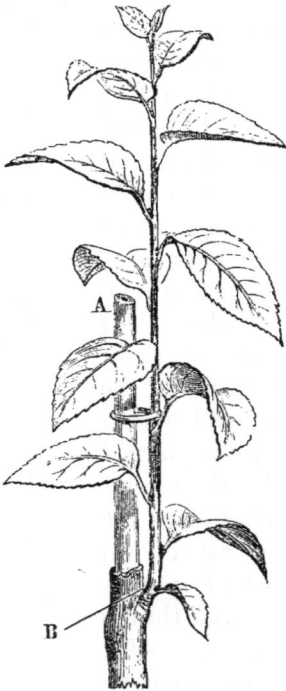

A, part of old leading shoot barked and left to tie the young shoot to. It is cut at B when the shoot has arrived at maturity.

A, the best position at which to prune for the terminal bud.

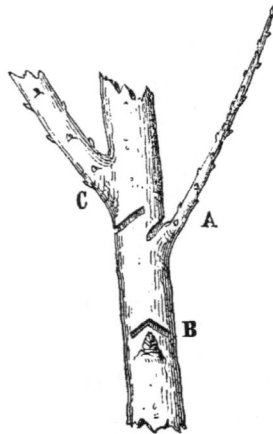

A, B, C, incisions made above and below branches and buds to check irregularity of growth.

towards the higher buds, and causing the lower part to be poorly furnished. These incisions, A, A, A, must be carefully performed on the young branch—deep enough to penetrate the sap-wood, and yet not so deep as to hurt the slender rising point. The top of this shoot, instead of being cut off, has been barked for some portion of its length above the bud that has been selected to continue the growth of the coming summer. To this barked portion the young shoot is trained, and a perfectly vertical growth for what we may term the pillar of the tree is thereby secured. The bark is neatly cut round above the upper eye; the branch is cut off at about four or five inches above that point, and then the bark is taken clean off. When the young leading shoot is long enough, it is fastened to the bare portion of the stem.

In pruning the tree considerable judgment is required, so as to get the base of the specimen well furnished, and secure fertility in the fruiting-branches. Several of the figures here given will explain the practice; which is, to cut them of the greatest length at the base of the tree, and gradually shorten them as the top is reached. The nearer they spring to the soil, the longer they must be left, or, to be more precise, only a third must be cut from the points of the lowest branches; half the length may be taken from those situated between summit and base; and lastly, three-quarters may be cut from the most elevated. In cutting-in the

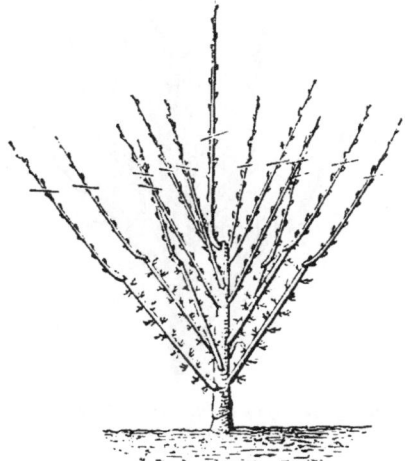

Pyramidal Pear-tree. Third pruning.

lateral branches, the perfectly oblique direction which it is desirable they should take must be borne in mind in the pruning, and the terminal bud of each left as far as possible, as in the figure showing this. In case of a very irregular development among the laterals, incisions are made above a weak branchlet to encourage it, and below a strong one to retard it until the equilibrium of the branches is established. Incisions are also made before a dormant bud that has failed to become developed into a lateral. The weak shoot is not cut, or but very little; the strong one is cut to below the level of the one it is desired to encourage. These incisions should be performed with a little saw, so that the cuts may not soon heal over. The incisions should penetrate sufficiently into the layer of young wood to well intercept the sap-vessels.   If with all these precautions there are objectionably-bare spaces on the stem, they may be remedied by grafting by approach, that is to say, turning back a vigorous branch to the main stem, and grafting it on to the bare space; or if this cannot be done, inserting a short ordinary graft in the stem.   This, however, with good management, will rarely be necessary.

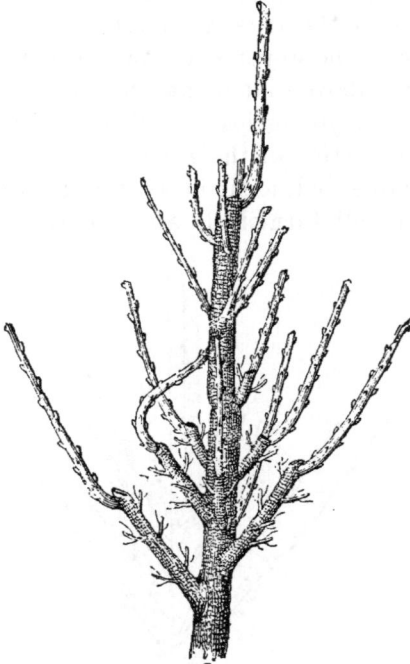

Grafting by approach, to cover bare spaces on Pyramidal Trees.

Having trained the branches straight, the next point is to see that they follow the desired oblique line; and it will be seen by the illustrations that the disposition given them is better than the one they assume under a less careful system.   The light enters freely to all parts of the tree; the more important part of it is under the command of the eye and hand, and the top is prevented from running away. This, however, is more owing to the fine formation of the lower branches than to the position they assume, though certainly such free and straight outlets for the rising sap are very effective in preventing a gross development above, and consequently in keeping the tree in the condition desired.   During the summer following the second pruning, the operations for maintaining the lead with the vertical branch, and equality

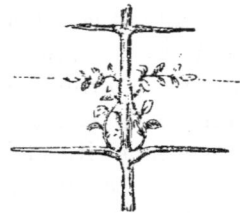

Grafting by approach as applied to Wall and Espalier Trees.

among the lateral shoots of the new growth, must be carried out as before described.   In the third pruning the young lateral branches of the preceding summer are cut in much shorter than the lower ones to favour the development of these.

At the fourth pruning the lower branches are not cut nearly so long as in the previous pruning, because they have now attained to almost the desired length and vigour. The new branches of the second series are left somewhat longer, and the pruner looks more to the top-structure, so to speak. The wisdom of forming the base well at first will be apparent. During the summer

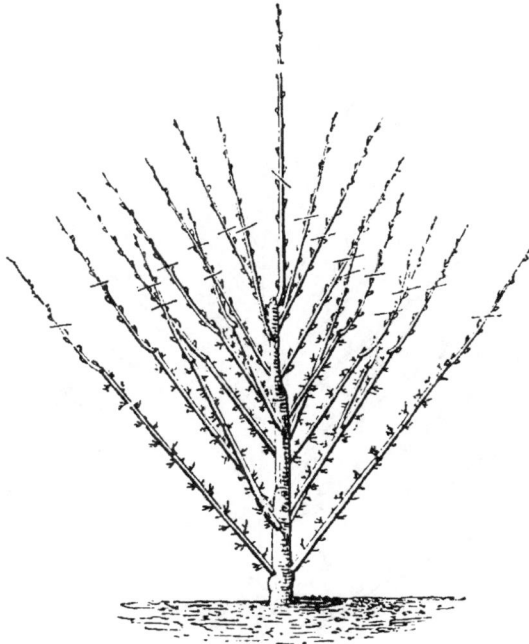

Pyramidal Pear-tree.   Fourth pruning.

following the fourth pruning before described, attention should be given to the young branches at the top of the pyramid, as well as the side ones. As the lower branches will have nearly reached their full length, a too vigorous growth of the terminal shoot of each must be prevented by pinching.

The next figure shows the aspect of the tree at the fifth pruning, and how the pruning is performed. As is well seen by glancing from B to A in this figure, the new growth of the lower branches is cut very short, while the higher the remaining superior branches are, the longer are the portions cut off. The succeeding prunings differ nothing in principle from the others, future development taking place principally in the middle and higher parts of the tree. Care should be taken to guide in the desired direction by means of twine, and sometimes slender stakes, any branches that may have deviated from it. Thus the pruning is carried on till

Pyramidal Pear-tree. Fifth pruning.

the tree becomes a large and perfect pyramid, the laterals being well pinched in, and in every case a free terminal shoot being allowed to proceed from each, so that the tree may be kept equally balanced and the sap freely conducted through each branch. They may of course be cut back well every year; always, however, at a bud likely to furnish a good shoot for the following season.

It is very questionable if the mathematically-designed pyramid

here alluded to be so desirable for gardens generally as a flatter
and less pointed form. For example, the pyramid as represented

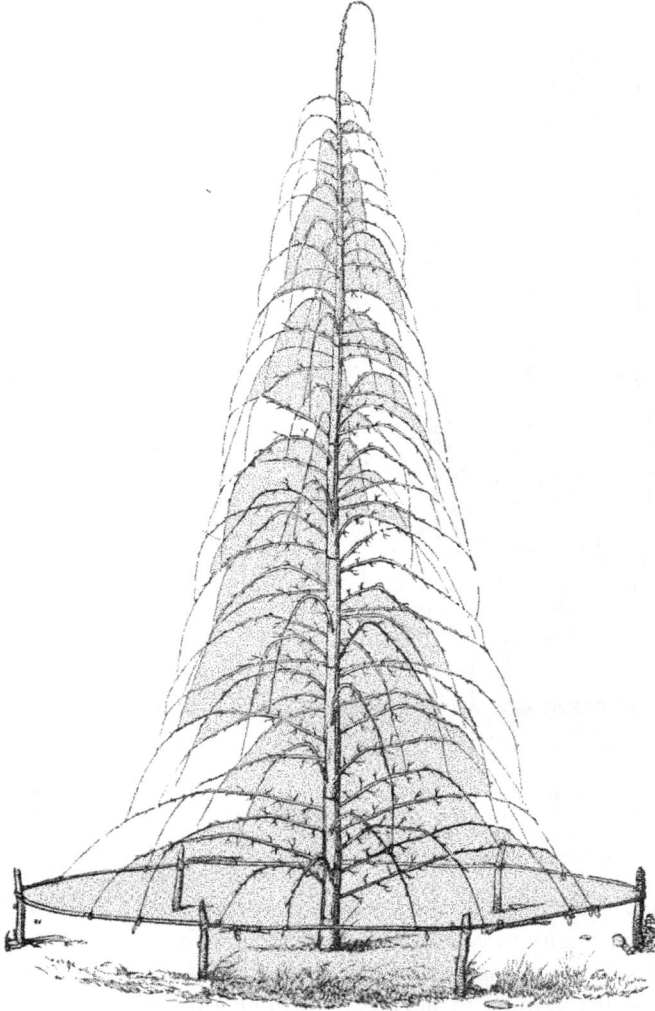

Pyramidal Pear-tree with drooping Branches.

at the time of its fourth or fifth pruning is in outline preferable
to the tall cone-like pyramidal trees.

Occasionally the pyramidal Pear has its branches bent downwards, some thinking that this induces a more fruitful habit;

there is no evidence, however, proving this form to be better than the simple pyramid.

The excellent practice of cutting in pyramidal and other trees that happen to be worthless varieties, and re-grafting them with superior kinds, is much practised by the French growers and amateurs. This system is quite as applicable to wall-trees as to pyramids or standards. In numbers of our gardens great good might be effected by re-grafting with good varieties, and doing away with the worthless ones so very commonly seen. The columnar mode of training to be seen here and there in France, is considered better than the pyramidal form, where saving of space is an object, and where too much shading of the crops by the trees is undesirable. The woodcut on page 333 shows a tree before the winter-pruning takes place, and, as will be seen, it is an erect stem densely furnished with short fruiting-branches.

Wall Pear-tree re-grafted. On each of the branches A, B, C, D, a graft has been placed. The graft at C failed, and consequently a shoot, e, is allowed to ascend; so that it may be budded the autumn following the grafting.

Except on the Quince in suitable soils, it is not likely to present many advantages; for if on the Pear and confined thus closely to a fastigiate bundle of shoots, it would in all probability run too high to permit of proper annual pruning or of the crop being gathered with convenience. Judging by the strength and thickness displayed by our old horizontal wall-trees grafted on the Pear-stock, we should, if we adopted a contracted form like this with trees worked on the Pear, in a few years have objects more like rustic gate-posts than trees.

It is not uncommon in English gardens to train the branches of
the pyramidal Pear in a pendulous fashion; and it is a system

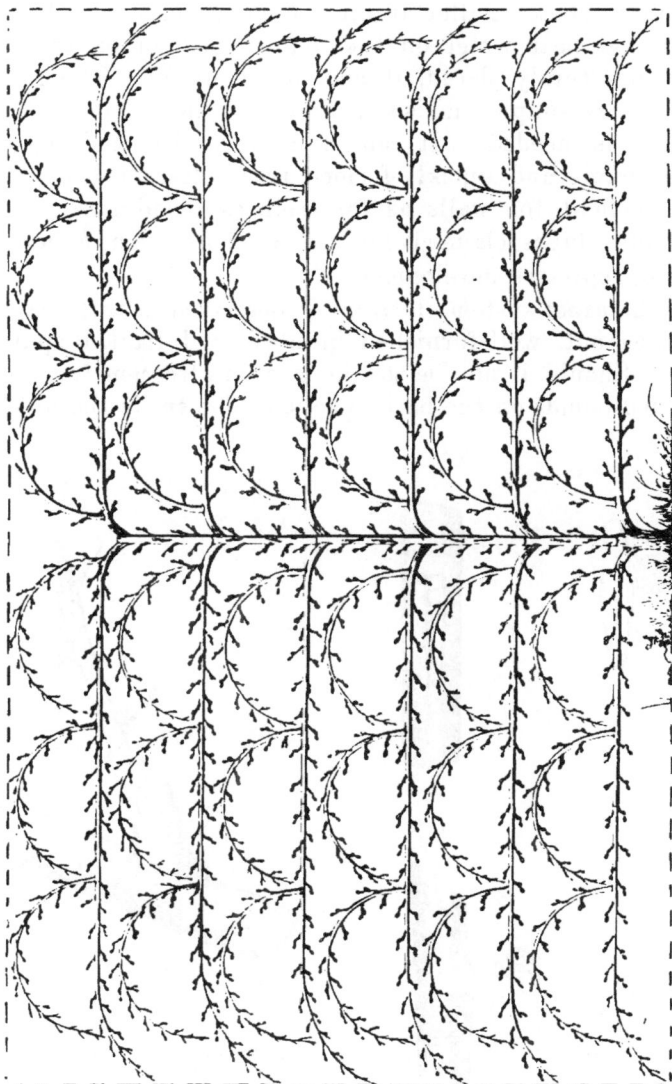

Pendulous Training of Wall Pear-tree.

admired by some, though somewhat more troublesome to form
than the simple pyramid. The figure represents a manner of
applying a modification of the same principle to the ordinary

horizontally-trained Pear-tree.   I do not say that it is as good as
it is graceful in appearance, believing in simple, easily-conducted
forms, but as these smaller arching branches may be established
on kinds that bear better on the young wood, or on trees with
the branches thinly placed, it may prove useful.   The mode of
formation is so simple and so easily established that no further
description is needed.   It cannot however be said too often
that the simple and quickly-formed trees, described elsewhere,
are as excellent for walls as for trellises, combining as they
do the advantages claimed for the cordons with a not too-
contracted, repressed development.

When the exact system of training described in this chapter is
well carried out, well-furnished branches and fruitful spurs are
the rule.   Should it not be so, the growers frequently resort to
grafting fruit-buds on the bare spaces, as shown by the following
figures :—

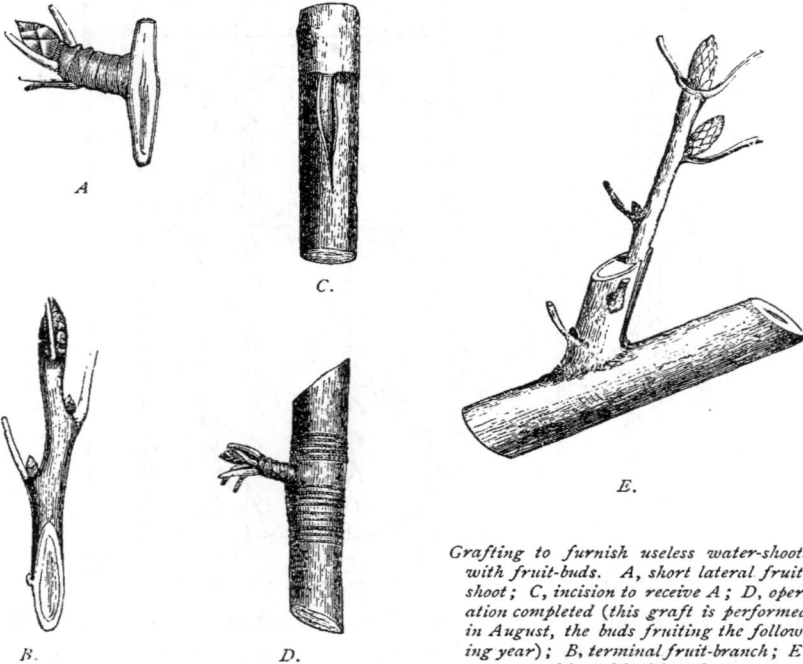

*Grafting to furnish useless water-shoots
with fruit-buds. A, short lateral fruit-
shoot; C, incision to receive A; D, operation completed (this graft is performed
in August, the buds fruiting the following year); B, terminal fruit-branch; E,
crown-grafting of fruiting-shoots on gross
unfruitful ones.*

The greatest attention is paid to the proper and neat pinching and pruning of the shoots, as shown by the following figures :—

Proper mode of cutting shoot.   *Shoot cut too long.*   *Shoot cut too low.*

Young shoot of Pear pro-   *Shoot of Pear pinched too*   *Result of over-pinching.*
perly pinched at about   *short.*
four inches from the base.

Another result of over-   *Pinching of the second growth*   *The stipulary shoots forced into*
pinching.   *of the Pear.*   *growth by the removal of the prin-*
                                         cipal shoot, A.

CHAPTER XXIV.

Fruit Culture: How are we to improve?

The discussion on French and English fruit-growing which took place in the 'Times' a few years ago, and afterwards spread through various other journals, was, like most discussions, not calculated to leave much impression on the public mind as to the best course to pursue. For this reason, therefore, in this chapter I propose to enter at some length into the matter. The fruit-question is not one that merely concerns those who can devote time and money to the pleasures that gardening affords; it is a question for the general public of especial importance when considered in relation to the market-supplies of our cities and towns.

Considering the hardiness of the Pear, its keeping-qualities, and its great variety, it is the most valuable dessert-fruit that can be grown in northern latitudes. A perfect Peach may be preferred to a first-rate Pear, but by properly selecting varieties of Pears we may have them in perfection during eight or nine months of the year, and the variety in flavour is perhaps greater than in the case of any other fruit. We are quite behind the French growers in its production. Our stocks of Apples are usually good and abundant; our stocks of Pears are frequently scarce and very poor in quality. In many gardens a really good Pear is almost as rare as a Mangosteen. We can increase the quantity and improve the quality of our Pears in a tenfold degree over the greater part of England and Ireland, and even in time to come make an article of export the fruit that we are now obliged to import so largely.

No doubt the brighter sun of France is more favourable to the culture of the Pear than our own climate; but it is equally true that by the aid of walls for some sorts, by judicious selection of ground, locality, and kinds, we may grow it to perfection. The quantity of Pears the French send to our markets is surprising. Messrs. Draper, the salesmen of Covent Garden, showed me by their books that from one importer alone they sold from 60*l.* to 100*l.* worth of French garden-produce (chiefly Pears) each market-day ; and a fruit-merchant has told me of one dealer in Pears who annually collects in France and sells in our markets 10,000*l.* worth of that fruit.

It is a mistake to suppose that the climate does all this for the French—the winter and spring in many parts of Northern and North-central France being quite as difficult for the fruit-grower as they are in England. The Pear loves a moist, genial climate, and in many parts of England and Ireland our advantage in this respect will be found to compensate in some degree for the difference in sunlight. Some Pears are grown better in England than in France, and it is a curious fact that some which ripen and go off quickly in the neighbourhood of London remain in an eatable condition much longer and acquire a more delicious flavour in the cooler climate of Yorkshire. Let it be borne in mind that we are talking of the culture of a fruit which grows in a wild state as far north as Southern Sweden, and then we can estimate at their true worth the objections of those who say that our climate prevents any improvement, and who, perhaps, immediately afterwards assert the superior quality of British-grown fruit. Nature is our willing handmaid in this matter, and we have it in our power to place this fine fruit within the reach of all, and render ourselves quite independent of foreign growers. I do not say we could grow such big Belle Angevine Pears as are sold for a guinea apiece ; but that is of no consequence, as these are valueless in point of flavour.

There are various ways in which we may improve the culture of the Pear, and the first and best is by paying more attention to it as a naturally-developed standard tree—in a word, by an improved system of orcharding. Upon orchards we must chiefly depend for the supply of our large cities and towns. This subject, in its commercial aspect, may be left to the growers of fruit for the market, but the country-gentleman and large farmer—in fact, everybody possessing a hedgerow, field, or shrubbery—cannot be too strongly urged to use the great opportunities they have for growing Pears. They grow useless shrubs and weedy trees in many places where the finest fruit might be grown with little trouble beyond that of gathering it; there are numbers of farmers, who hardly ever see a good fruit of this kind, in possession of lines of hedgerow where the trees would grow as healthfully from among the lower brushwood as any subject that now embellishes them; and there are many owners of gardens, who now go to market for their fruit, who might gather it from places in their little shrubberies at present entirely devoted to miserable bushes of Privet. I know well the kind of objection that is made to some of these suggestions—the boys would gather the fruit, etc. Little blame to the boys for making an occasional raid on the little fruit that comes in their way, but if the fruit were as plentiful as it might be they would not be so troublesome.

There is another aspect of the question which may also well commend the growth of Pears and other hardy fruits in ground now profitless. It is often thought that Nature is usually sparing of leaf-beauty where the flower is highly ornamental, and stingy with flowers where leaves assume large proportions and elegant outlines; and, to a smaller extent, that she is apt to bestow her favours in a like way as regards fruit. Nothing can be further from the fact than this supposition. When we consider the flowering charms of the greater portion of our fruit-trees, we ask Why are they not more planted for the sake of their beauty alone? Take the Apple in its countless varieties, and consider that, if it did not give such crops of fruit, beautiful to look upon, and more delicious in flavour than half the boasted fruits of the tropics, it would be sought after for the sake of its blushing flowers, which turn the orchard into fairyland. But it happens to bear fruit of various colours, sizes, and flavours, and, of course, that is a reason why we have hitherto not employed such a beautiful hardy tree in the pleasure-garden. Then we have the Pear, which comes in earlier, and furnishes snowy masses of bloom; and with a more picturesque and handsome habit than the apple. From nearly every hardy fruit we may reap a like harvest of floral beauty—Almonds, Apricots, Cherries, Crabs, Medlars, Peaches, Plums, and Quinces, being all more or less ornamental. And as perhaps some curious persons here and there may not object to plant beautiful flowering fruit-trees because they also bear precious and handsome fruit, they have only to place these objects in any open spots, in pleasure-grounds, by wood-walks, in the fences at intervals, instead of the worthless bushes that now too often occupy them—and, in a word, in the numberless positions where trees good for neither timber nor flowers now take up valuable ground.

Then there is the ornamental orchard. Usually the orchard is, of all spots, the most formal; but there is no need that it should be so, as anyone with extensive pleasure-grounds can quickly prove. At Meudon, where an ornamental orchard was formed, the position was a valley-like hollow, but in an elevated position—just the spot to make a compact Pinetum. Instead of planting it with trees and shrubs of the ordinary type, it was resolved to embellish it with well-arranged groups of fruit-trees. On one side a large clump was devoted to handsome pyramidal Pear-trees, on another to Apples, another to Plums, and so on. The grass was not broken up, nor any of the ornamental features of the spot interfered with in the least. It need hardly be pointed out how varied, as well as useful, such an arrangement might be made. There might be mixed groups of new and untried kinds, as well as masses of tried ones; there might be isolated specimens of various kinds on the grass, from an Apple on the dwarf Paradise-stock to a fully-grown and handsome Pear. Fruits little known or of doubtful utility, like the Eugenia or the Cherry-plum, might be associated with the others with greater propriety than in the fruit-garden proper. Such things as the American Blackberries—and very fine some of these are— would find a congenial home; so would the Dewberry and the various Cranberries. The relatives of our common fruit-trees might of course be planted in the near neighbourhood for comparison's sake; standard Peaches, Figs and Apricots might be tried with safety if the garden were in the south; and the whole would prove one of the most interesting features in a country-place.

It should be remembered that some of our hardy fruits are capable of affording quantities of wholesome food; but before they do so efficiently we must take them out of the class of things that are carefully walled-in in gardens, overdone with kindness, or injured by unnatural pruning, and recognise the fact that many excellent kinds are as hardy and easily grown as the Blackberries and Sloes of the hedges. For the purposes herein suggested thoroughly hardy and free-growing sorts should alone be selected; but it must not be supposed that first-class fruit, even of the continental varieties, cannot be produced in this way. In the gardens at Oak Lodge, Kensington, is a very large and handsome Pear-tree growing among Rhododendrons and other choice shrubs which adorn the margin of a piece of rock-bound water. It is a fine old tree of the Beurré Diel, which, without pruning or attention of any kind, produces abundantly such good fruit, that, of twelve samples of the same variety laid before the Fruit Committee of the Royal Horticultural Society, the fruit of this tree was pronounced the best. This is not mentioned as a remarkable instance, but merely to prove that the finest Pears may be grown by the simplest means, and that the tree is worth cultivating for its beauty alone. The garden of Oak Lodge is the best-designed town-garden in London, and Mr. Marnock, who arranged it, left several of these old Pears in conspicuous positions when laying out the place solely for their beauty as trees, apart from their fruiting qualities. Therefore it is clear that we may effect considerable improvement by planting this tree in shrubberies, pleasure-grounds, and like positions, and in many wild and semi-wild places, both in enclosed private grounds and in the open country. There can be no doubt that enormous quantities of good fruit could be grown upon railway-banks now useless, and from which fruit could be so readily conveyed to market; on this point, however, we shall have more to say by-and-by.

The accompanying illustration shows a type of fruit-garden common enough in and near Paris, and which deserves the attention of all interested in the improvement of small properties. A mere spot of ground is planted with carefully-selected and choice fruit-trees well trained, and the result is, even from an ornamental point of view, better than it often is where subjects are planted that have only beauty to recommend them. The view is from a sketch taken in winter by M. François Courtin, of a small garden facing the street leading from Vincennes to Montreuil. Beneath the trees Pansies, Pinks, and other hardy flowers grow: the presence of the trees does not prevent the little garden being made gay with flowers. In winter, the graceful pyramidal Pear-

trees and well and simply-formed Peach and Plum-trees against
the walls certainly often look better than little gardens arranged
with another aim. In spring there is the beauty of fruit-tree
blossoms, and in autumn the crown of trees—good fruit. The
art of the engraver, even in its best form, can give but a suggestion
of such a garden, but probably this will show how desirable it is
to make, more than ever, full use of our opportunities of planting
fruit-trees in small gardens.

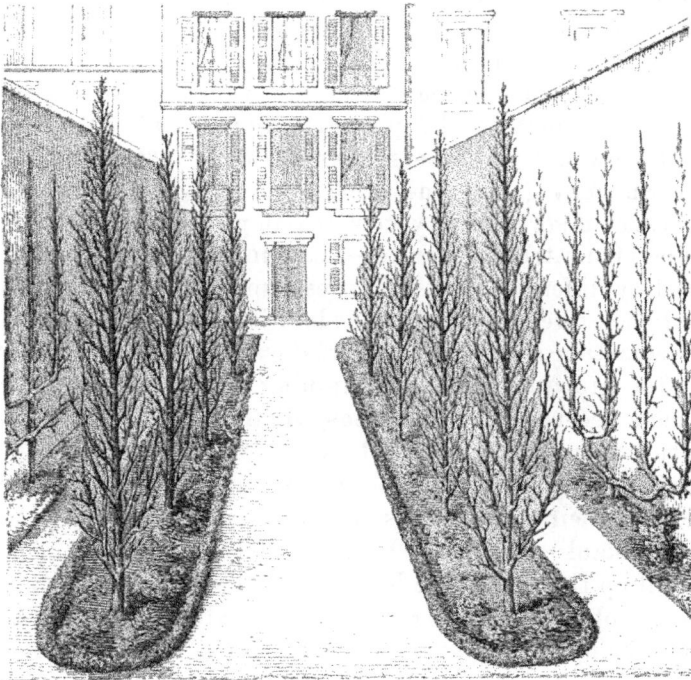

Fruit-trees in a Front Garden (Vincennes).

The second way in which we may improve the cultivation of the
Pear is by planting it to a greater extent as a pyramidal tree,
grafting on the Quince where the soil is rich, moist, or deep. On
many dry and sandy lands the Pear must be grown on its own
stock, and for orcharding purposes generally that may safely be
pronounced the best. We shall never have a good supply for
market till we pay more attention to the Pear as a freely-developed
standard tree; we shall never have a first-rate supply of Winter

Pears till we pay more attention to Pears on walls than we do at present. The French, from whom we have adopted the pyramidal form, employ it to an enormous extent, but do not stop there. It is in planting the pyramid that most of our improvement in this direction has taken place for a good many years back. Almost every nurseryman has now a stock of the tree in this form, and we cannot employ it too much, provided sorts that ripen well in ordinary seasons are selected ; but there are other ways of equal importance. The pyramid is so pleasing in outline, and indeed in all other respects, that, although so highly suited for the kitchen or fruit-garden, it should by no means be confined to either. Handsome specimens and groups may well be introduced in favourable spots in the pleasure-ground and shrubberies, and thus the owners of those numerous small ornamental gardens near towns may gather fine fruit.

Another important way towards improvement is re-grafting worthless fruit-trees. Fruits—Pears in particular—are strangely affected by different soils, localities, aspects, etc. A fruit may be found to be extremely good in one locality, and worthless in others. Thus, sometimes after taking great care in planting fruit-trees, and after growing them and training them for many years until they have become good specimens, so far as fruit is concerned they have turned out to be but cumberers of the ground. Many, doubtless, have proved the truth of this assertion, and yet have hesitated to destroy their trees because of the beauty of their appearance and the blank occasioned by so doing, years being required to again fill up the space thus left bare. The plan now recommended, however, obviates all disappointment; all that is necessary to be done being to re-graft as the illustration indicates. It is easily accomplished, and it is astonishing how soon a tree is thus re-furnished and in full bearing condition after being re-grafted.

The advantages of the process may be summed up thus :—

1. It enables us within two years or little more, to obtain a full-sized fruitful tree of a new variety, which otherwise could only have been done at the expense of planting and training a young one for ten or twelve years. 2. Double-grafting on a well-seasoned stock assists the fruiting properties of many shy bearers. Many Pears very commonly found in this country ought to be re-grafted, and much good may be effected by the process.

Let us now turn to the third way of improving the culture of the Pear, and one that has been comparatively neglected for some years

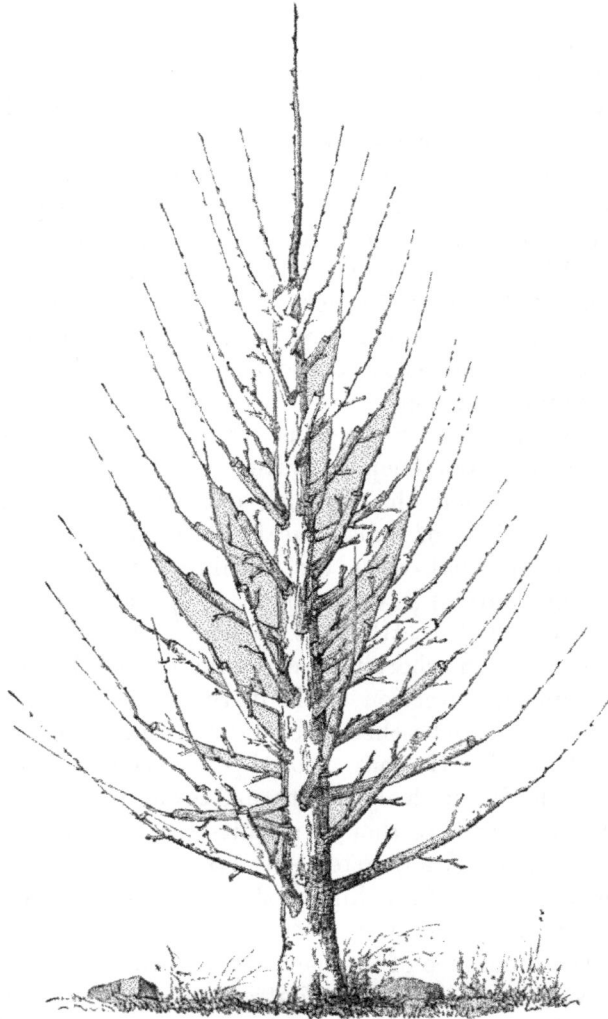

Pyramidal Pear-tree Re-grafted.

past—that is, the Pear on walls.   Here we are certainly behind-hand, and do not appear to have made much progress for a very long time.   Perhaps it may be thought that the French might dispense

with walls; but no such thing.   They find them indispensable for
the perfect culture of the finer Winter Pears ; and were they not
to use them, they could never obtain such a stock of these as they
have.   Yet we have for a long time past been paying attention to
almost every kind of garden-improvement except this important
one.   It is true that walls are expensive, but once reared it is a
great pity to neglect them; and, apart even from garden-walls,
there are numerous places with as much wall-surface naked and
useless as, properly covered, would yield a good supply of fruit.
Few things combine beauty and utility more than a well-covered
wall of Pear-trees; and the creation of such is not a matter of
difficulty.   With walls it may safely be said that our climate is as
good as that of Northern France.   Most large gardens would be
benefited by having a much greater proportion of wall-surface
than they have at present; to many small ones they would also
prove a desirable addition.

Of whatever material the wall be made, it will be desirable to
whiten its surface and keep it white.   Black and dark-coloured
surfaces absorb heat in the daytime, and give it out again during
the night in the form of radiant heat; from which facts we might
perhaps conclude that walls for training fruit-trees should be
black, or at any rate of a dark colour.   Direct experiment was,
however, necessary to settle this question, and M. Vuitry, who
employs his leisure in arboriculture, communicated the results of his
experiments in this direction to M. du Breuil, leaving no doubt as
to the proper colour to be chosen for walls against which fruit-trees
are to be trained.   He has proved—1st. That a thermometer
hung during the day with its face turned towards a white wall, at a
distance from it equal to that of a fruit-tree trained against it—
i.e., about an inch and a quarter—always showed a mean temperature of nearly 6 deg. Fahr. higher than one hung against a black
wall under precisely similar circumstances.   2nd. That during
the night the difference of temperature shown by these two thermometers was inappreciable.   Contrary therefore to the opinions
entertained by many persons, it seems evident that the walls
must be whitened when we wish to give the trees trained against
them the maximum amount of heat to be obtained in the particular climate and aspect.   Indeed, it is precisely the plan that has
already been pursued by the fruit-growers at Montreuil for Peach-

trees, and at Thomery for their Vines, it having been frequently remarked that trees trained against white walls were healthier than those nailed to more or less dark-coloured ones. This result is easily explained, for not only does the lighter colour reflect more heat back to the trees, but by this means they receive a greater quantity of light; and it is well known how greatly vegetation is stimulated by these agencies. Walls of a light tint are advantageous in another way, for they not only reflect light and heat on the particular trees trained against.them, but also on the others in their immediate neighbourhood. By abundantly planting the finer Winter Pears against walls with a warm exposure and whitewashed surface, we may within half-a-dozen years gather such crops of the really valuable Winter Pears as have never before been grown in this country.

Another improvement must of necessity accompany this, and that is, the French method of wiring garden-walls. We cannot use nails with concrete and earth walls, and even if we could the deliverance from nails would be a great point gained; the French mode of employing a little raidisseur or tightener on each wire, and using very slender galvanised wire, is perfect in its way. It will be found to save much time and greatly improve the appearance of garden-walls. We must also adopt the improved kind of espalier elsewhere described.

The upright mode of training wall and espalier trees, of which some of the best examples in France have been photographed and engraved for this book, must also commend itself to anyone interested in fruit-culture.

The U form, or double cordon, is best suited for a very high wall or fence, and if the trees are planted three feet apart, and the side laterals regularly pinched in, the wall becomes quickly furnished, which is the great merit of the system; another also being the large variety of fruit that can be had from a given space, and the ease with which a failing plant or bad variety can be replaced. The first cost for so many plants is necessarily great if the grower does not graft his own trees; but quicker returns soon make up the deficiency in this respect. The same kind of tree may also be trained obliquely, many preferring this to the vertical mode, on the supposition that the flow of sap is less rapid, and that, consequently, the trees are more disposed to form fruit-

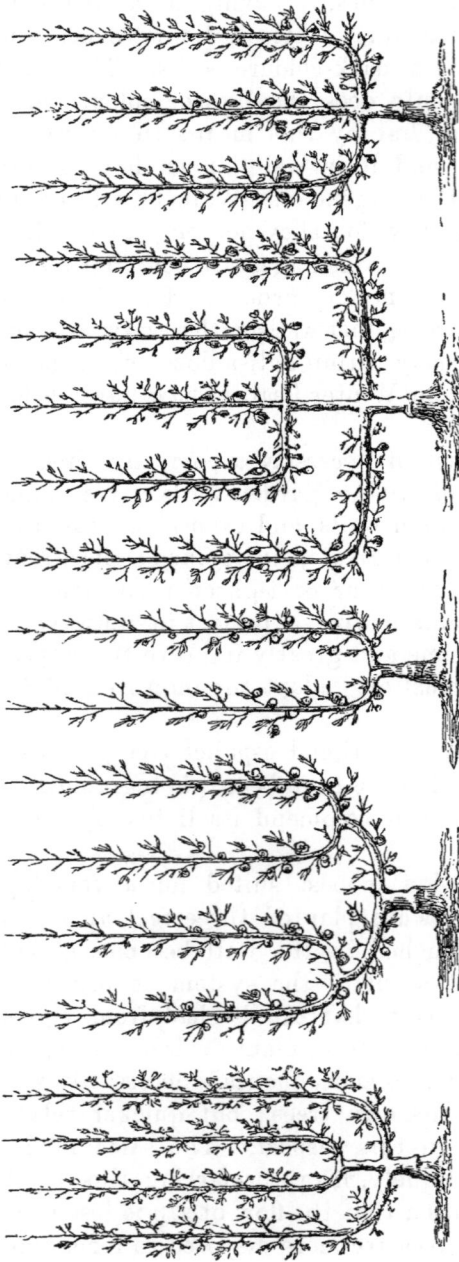

Varieties of Vertical Training.

buds than they otherwise would be. The tree with three erect branches is suitable for the same purpose as that with two, but can be planted on proportionately lower walls or trellises, and, if deemed advisable, the middle branch may be formed by another variety being grafted on the stock. The four-branched tree is well adapted for strained-wire fences, round vegetable quarters, sides of walks, and other boundary lines, and being as easily formed as the old-fashioned espalier, should be adopted in lieu of that mode of training for choice kinds of Apples and the hardier Pears. Strong "maiden" trees, planted five feet apart, and cut back to form the two outer and central branches, will in two years present the appearance represented by the woodcuts—that is if summer-pinching and tying have been attended to. The double U form is one of the handsomest modes of training yet adopted, and being very simple, and therefore readily put into practice, should be carried out largely, even in the most conspicuous positions. The woodcut fully explains all that is wanted as to the best mode of forming the tree, care being required to have all the branches equi-distant. All the above modes of training are calculated to supersede the ordinary espalier, which is often an eye-sore in many otherwise good gardens. The vertical and horizontal style combined, the Palmette of the French, is well suited for the formation of large trees.

The accompanying wood-cut represents one of the simplest and best forms of tree for rapidly covering walls with choice Pears. Before this and like forms the old horizontal pattern, which took so many years to form, must give way. Among the many advantages that belong to the upright form may be mentioned that of simple training. To establish such trees, all that need be done is to take a young tree of from three to seven branches, and place the branches as nearly as may be in the desired position. It is not even necessary to have the branches exactly opposite, as without that the wall may be perfectly covered. With trees of this kind a very few years' growth will suffice to cover a wall that would not be covered in sixteen years by the old method. Trees on this plan may be five-branched or seven-branched. There is no trouble in training. Young trees may be taken from the nursery, and their branches placed in the desired direction against the wall. The above specimen was sketched in M. Godefroy-

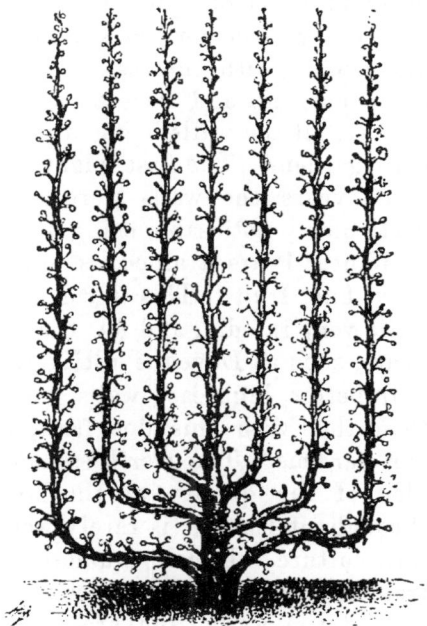

Upright Pear-tree for Wall (Argenteuil).

Lebeuf's garden at Argenteuil, where there is a wall beautifully covered with fertile trees in this form.

As regards trials made with a fruit-garden after the French method in England, thanks to the spirited and judicious plantings made by Mr. Leigh, of Barham Court, we have now in Kent a fruit-garden made after French models, and of the highest interest to growers of hardy fruit everywhere. Not content with trying modes of training more in fashion abroad than with us, or plantations of approved kinds of fruit on the cordon system, Mr. Leigh has formed several new fruit-gardens; and these are replete with interest. There is a very large number of trees planted, and several acres of ground devoted to fruit-culture, all the walls being white as in a neatly-ordered French fruit-garden. The first plantations were made in 1872, and in three years the walls were covered with bearing fruit-trees; particularly noticeable being a wall covered with the finer kinds of Winter Pears, trained as single oblique cordons, and bearing very fine fruit. This form is well suited for covering high walls very rapidly, and for the production of the finest Winter Pears, such as Doyenné d'Hiver. Those having high south, or, still better, high east walls, could hardly do better than plant them thus with this fine fruit, so seldom seen in perfection in our gardens. The worthless specimens usually grown give no idea of the quality of this unsurpassed Winter Pear, which, throughout Europe, is rarely worth eating except under careful wall-culture. Equally numerous at Barham Court are the erect-trained five or seven-branched trees, which quickly run to the top of the walls, and are very easily managed. They are a marked improvement on the old horizontally-trained Pear-tree, which took so long to form; Plums, Pears, Peaches and Apricots are thus trained here, and, so far, they promise a very good result. There are several walled gardens facing pleasantly to the sun, on a gentle slope, and there is plenty of wall-space, some of which is of whitened felt, as in the Paris Municipal Garden, in the Bois de Vincennes. This, however, is not a desirable material to use, brick or concrete walls being far preferable. Most of the walls here are neatly wired. Throughout each garden run lines of light but strong trellis-work for Pears—a great improvement on the

" fixings " for the old espalier. The espaliers here are, in many cases, ten feet high. Trees with erect branches soon cover these to the top, and the effect is better than that of the old-fashioned espalier, while the great height prevents the need of repressing the trees over much. The amount of galvanised wire used in the garden is very great, but the expense will be justified by the security afforded to heavy fruit during autumnal gales. Much destruction to the finest fruit arises in that way. Probably in no garden in England have so many of the little horizontal cordons been tried as here. They do admirably, and, though many of them were only recently planted, the lines are now dotted with large fruit, some of which is the finest of its kind to be seen. Here are also Ribstone Pippins trained in this manner, and the fruit is much larger than that grown in the ordinary way. The Ribston is one of the fruits which would well repay culture in this way. Popular and excellent in quality, as it is, everybody would admire extra fine samples of it, and in our markets they would fetch a very high price. It is, of course, needless to grow kinds of fruit in this way that may be had as good as we require them by more simple modes of culture. The little cordons are nearly all grafted on the true Paradise stock. Rivers' Nonesuch is also found to be good on a dry bottom, but grows stronger than the true Paradise. Where any other stock is used the growth is too rampant for this mode of training. The Lady Apple bears well here, and ripens satisfactorily on cordon trees; so does the White Calville. A mode of training these and other tender Apples on very low wooden walls formed of one or two boards is recommended by Mr. Leigh to his cottagers as a substitute for brick walls. The quantity of fruit already borne by the young trees is surprising. Horticulture is much indebted to Mr. Leigh for thus testing, in a thoroughly practical, intelligent way, questions of much importance.

Of all our wants in connection with the Pear, that of the spread of good varieties is perhaps the greatest. Naturally, or rather I should say in a wild state, the Pear is a poor fruit about an inch and a half long ; and from this has been gradually developed the splendid race we now possess. Scattered through our gardens and orchards in all parts of this kingdom, there are scores of kinds which are practically of little more use than the wild

2 F

fruit-trees of the woods and hedgerows. But apart from all these worthless varieties, named and unnamed, that occupy valuable ground, there are numbers which are regularly sold in our nurseries, possessing fine names, and which yet are practically useless to the cultivator. Let us suppose the case of a person wishing to commence Pear-culture—he has some slight knowledge of other branches of horticulture, and expects that the long list of the varieties of Pears which he finds in his nurseryman's catalogue will resemble each other pretty much as his Verbenas or Pansies do. Taken by the different names and descriptions, he seeks variety, only however to find disappointment. A wide selection of varieties is an evil in every way. It requires much skill on the part of men who have studied gardening all their lives to know what to avoid in these lists; how very dangerous, then, for the amateur, or for those who have only slight knowledge of the matter, to make a selection! Let us glance for a moment into some of the fruit-catalogues. It is needless to state how very much the Pear varies. Here is a catalogue naming, describing, and numbering nearly 400 kinds. People suppose that giving long lists of this kind is for the sake of selling a great number of varieties; but that course would be so clearly a mistaken one, that one cannot suppose an intelligent person persisting in it. The presence of bad and unsuitable Pears everywhere throughout the country simply tends to retard the culture of this noble fruit; whereas the distribution of the really good kinds in abundance would create such a demand for them as would cause the trade in young trees to increase tenfold.

The compilers of the catalogues alluded to do not follow the example of the famous M. de la Quintinye, chief gardener to Louis XIV. at Versailles, whose list was lengthy, although published so very long ago, but who conscientiously divided it into several sections—viz., "good Pears," "indifferent Pears," and "bad Pears!" This was honest in M. de la Quintinye, and would be admirable in a nurseryman. The spirit of expurgation was strong in this old gardener, and he follows the bad list with another—a long one—heading it—"Besides the Pears which I know not, here is a particular list of those which I know to be so bad that I counsel nobody to plant any of them." This, observe, was in France, where a greater number of kinds arrive at perfection than is the case with us, and where a greater number of varieties are grown. Although our nurseryman-friend, with his long list, is somewhat of an exception, the lists of others of our fruit-tree raisers are much too long to be any real guidance to the amateur. There is less general craving for novelty in fruits in France than in England. At Angers, in one of the largest fruit-tree nurseries in France, the following seven sorts only are raised in large quantities:—Williams's Bon Chrétien, Duchesse d'Angoulême, Easter Beurré, Louise Bonne, Beurré d'Amanlis, Beurré Diel, and Beurré d'Aremburg. On an average, from 30,000 to 40,000 trees of each of the first two are sold every year, and about 20,000 of the other five put together. Even the best of the new varieties find scarcely any sale.

The following may be taken as the best Pears for culture in the British Isles of the many hundred kinds known :—Doyenné d'Eté, Jargonelle, Williams's Bon Chrétien, Louise Bonne of Jersey, Jersey Gratioli, Urbaniste, Fondante d'Automne, Beurré d'Amanlis, Suffolk Thorn, Seckel, Comte de Lamy, Flemish Beauty, Désiré Cornelis, Marie Louise, Baronne de Mello, Thompson's, Beurré Bosc, Duchesse d'Angoulême, Beurré Diel, Beurré Hardy, Maréchal de la Cour, B. Superfin, Doyenné du Comice, Glou Morceau, Winter Nelis, Beurré Rance, B. Sterckmans, Joséphine de Malines, Bergamotte Esperen, Easter Beurré.

Of these, Beurré Bosc, Duchesse d'Angoulême, Beurré Diel, Doyenné du Comice, Glou Morceau, Beurré Rance, Joséphine de Malines, Bergamotte Esperen, Easter Beurré, Beurré Sterckmans, Désiré Cornelis, and Winter Nelis, should be grown against walls. In some cases they may afford a satisfactory result away from them, but if grown against white walls they will in all cases be highly improved, and some of the very best of them are only to be had in perfection when thus grown. As wall-space is often limited, and as it is necessary to have the warmest walls to perfect the finest Winter Pears, it is desirable to be very particular indeed when selecting Pears for wall-culture ; and Easter Beurré, Doyenné du Comice, Glou Morceau, Beurré Rance, Joséphine de Malines, and Bergamotte Esperen, should be abundantly planted against walls wherever a supply of first-rate Winter Pears is a want.

Some of our authorities on fruit-growing give the Easter Beurré

2 F 2

as one which should be planted as a bush or pyramid, and say it
is " mealy and insipid from walls." But the fine Easter Beurrés
which adorn our tables in winter and spring are grown on walls
in France. All of the same variety are grown in like manner in
the school of horticulture at Versailles; and as soon as a wall is
cleared of other varieties of Pear-trees there, it is immediately
planted with the Easter Beurré—so much is this fine variety
esteemed. The quantity of its fruits sold in the markets of
Europe during the winter-season is something incredible. It is
perhaps the most valuable of all Winter Pears; and the chief, or
almost the whole supply comes from France. The climate does
it, some will say, but such is not the case; for if left to the
climate unaided, we should have few fine Easter Beurré Pears in
Covent Garden in winter. And the same remark applies to other
varieties of Winter Pears. The flavour is said to be inferior when
grown against walls. Let us try them against white walls as the
French do, and see if we cannot nearly or quite equal their Pears
in size, and quite equal them in flavour. We have been for years
planting them as bushes and pyramids, and paying little or no
attention to their culture against walls; hence our deficiency of
good Winter Pears—those which are by far the most valuable
of all.

Having taken sufficient care to select the very best varieties,
and to place them in positions where they are likely to succeed,
there is more to be done in getting rid of the bad ones. They
abound in every part of the country, and take up space in which
the best kinds might and should be growing. This prevalence
of bad kinds not only results from the greater scarcity of the
good varieties in bygone days, but also from the large number
of inferior kinds that are still offered for sale. In very many
cases the tree is worthless, because it has not been planted in a
position to ensure success. It frequently happens, for example,
that the finer kinds of Winter Pears, and those which the French
grow against walls around Paris, are in Britain sent out as suitable for pyramids. All worthless Pear-trees should be destroyed,
and good kinds planted or (happily there is an alternative) the
others re-grafted with good sorts. Another point would be gained
if the custom of growing inferior kinds from pips—which is
common among farmers in some fruit-growing districts with

Pears as well as other hardy fruits—were abandoned, and only first-rate and hardy kinds planted or grafted.

As to Apples, it is well to bear in mind that a good hardy kind on a well-managed standard or naturally-developed tree is the best for the supply of the markets with all but the very best fruits, and for all ordinary purposes; and that the system of orcharding in the London market-gardens is on the whole a good and safe one. Generally speaking our Apple-culture is not to be complained of, though it may certainly be improved. There is in this country a large demand for fruit of the finest quality that can be obtained, both in the case of those who buy all they use and those who grow their own. In these islands it is also generally admitted that to keep the sun from the general contents of our gardens by shading them with Apple-trees is anything but desirable, and therefore the cordon trained as an edging is recommended. It has been proved that where well managed these will, if placed alongside the walks in the kitchen and fruit gardens, furnish abundance of fruit of the finest quality. In many places the positions in which the cordon-plantation may be made are unoccupied. The system will have to encounter prejudice and bad management—but as soon as well-managed specimens are seen in our gardens it will spread rapidly, and prove a boon wherever perfect fruit is desired. In Northern England and in Scotland, where every ray of sun is required, many gardens are shaded and half destroyed by old standard Apple-trees.

The Peach attains the finest possible condition when well grown against walls in England. In other countries it may be grown freely as a standard tree; in none can they produce finer or better fruit than may be gathered from walls in England and Ireland. France has very diverse climates—some in which the Peach grows well as a standard—but the best Peaches grown in France are gathered from walls in those parts where the climate is most like our own. Good specimens of Crawford's Early Peach have been gathered from pyramid trees standing in the open quarters of the Rev. Mr. Benyon's garden in Suffolk; therefore it is certain that in the midland and southern parts of the British Isles the Peach may be grown against walls to the highest degree of perfection; and in favourable parts of the south, early Peaches may be grown with success as a standard or bush tree, away from

all protection. There can be no doubt whatever that if we pay
as much attention to the Peach as the cultivators of Montreuil
do, we can attain quite as good a result. Our good fruit-
growers understand its culture well enough ; but of late years
public attention has, by various means which need not be detailed
here, been called away from the fact that, with walls, we can
produce the finest fruit in the world, and without them do little
or nothing with the choicer fruits. The " power of the climate "
in Paris may be very wonderful, but there is one thing it cannot
do better than our own—it cannot produce a better Peach than
is often gathered from walls both in England and Ireland. It
would be thought, perhaps, that with their climate, the French
would be able to dispense with protection to the trees in spring,
and altogether leave their trees more to nature than the British
gardener ; but exactly the reverse is the case. The French Peach-
grower takes care to have a good protecting coping to his wall.
With us it is not uncommon to see the culture of the Peach and
Nectarine attempted without any coping at all. Of course we
want this protection as much as the French, or more so. Over
the greater part of the country, without question, the Peach may
be grown to the highest degree of perfection, and yet, though few
Englishmen could manage, as Dr. Johnson did, " seven or eight
large Peaches of a morning before breakfast began," they may well
say with him that getting " enough " of them is indeed a rarity.
To succeed with the Peach in the open air, we must remove it
altogether from the chance culture now bestowed upon it ; give
it full attention in spring and early summer; select suitable soil
in the first instance, and thus avoid expense for what is called
made ground. We must take care to protect the trees in spring,
as the careful French cultivators do; and take advantage of the
new and cheap ways of erecting walls. No chance culture on any
walls that may happen to surround the place will alter matters
much.

    We may do a good deal more than at present with our unoc-
cupied walls. Probably many readers who live near Oxford can
testify to the beauty and profit that result from the villagers
covering their walls with Apricot-trees. The same may be done
in many parts of England where such a thing is not now to be
seen ; but in the case of cottagers and others the only thing likely

to do good is example. If they see a specimen of successful fruit-culture in small gardens like their own, they need no other encouragement. And perhaps a present of a few good kinds of trees and a few minutes' advice from the gardener, would be more productive of benefit to cottagers than many other things now given them in a charitable way.

As to our various other hardy fruits, including the Apple and Pear, there can be little doubt that it is to good orchard-culture we must look for the increase of our supplies. The word orchard is familiar enough in our ears, but a really good orchard is as rare round country seats as if it were not a British institution. There are farmers and market-gardeners and fruit-growers who have the finest orchards; but at the country seat, with generally every opportunity to select a good site, it is surprising how rarely even a presentable thing of the kind is attempted. Indeed, in some parts of the country it is never thought of—the ordinary type of kitchen-garden being considered sufficient for all attempts at fruit-growing. The surface cannot of course be devoted to standard trees, as they hide the light from the necessary crops, and the walls and dwarf trees, if such there be, are those upon which we depend. Now good culture of trees on walls is far from being as common as might be desired. But supposing that the wall-culture is good, and that the most is made of the space, it is hardly sufficient to yield a crop of fruit for all purposes. If the walls supply a good dessert for a reasonable length of time, it is as much as is expected of them, and more than they generally do. They who secure a good crop of Winter Pears, who can command really eatable specimens of this fruit during the winter and spring months, are few in number. The walls can only supply a portion of the choicest fruit—chiefly of those kinds which require the additional heat of a wall for their perfect development and flavour. Standards we see are not much grown; they shade the ground too much, and the ground-crops are better when fully exposed to sun and air. In some places the culture of bush and dwarf pyramidal trees is carried on successfully, but in general it is so backward that nothing like a good crop is gathered. Besides, all dwarf closely-pruned and accurately-trained trees involve considerable expense and time, which it would be unwise to bestow on kinds producing as good a result when grown as standard

trees, requiring hardly any attention, and actually permitting of
as good a crop of vegetables being gathered from under them as
if the trees did not exist.   Perhaps there may be a few espaliers
in the garden; but they are usually so very few and so badly
managed that little fruit is got from them.   It follows, then, that
in private grounds there is as a rule no source from which an abundant stock of the better kinds of hardy fruit may be gathered.
The wisest way to increase the supply of good fruit in any given
locality is to plant an orchard, carefully choosing the site, and,
above all things, selecting the very best kinds, all perfectly hardy,
and such as ripen their fruit every year, be the season what it
may.   Such an orchard would be very convenient near the garden,
in fact might form part and parcel of it; as however the care
required is nearly none, except the pleasant one of gathering the
fruit, it would not matter much about its position.   The first
consideration should be the selection of the most suitable soil
available.   Not an inch of space of the whole need be lost.   All
the trees should be allowed to grow as standards, and the crops
gathered from them would soon put to shame the crop on the wall
or dwarf tree.   All the wall, dwarf, and espalier trees might then
be exclusively kinds that require some additional heat or attention, or to which the shelter and support of the espalier and the
cordon systems are an advantage.   As protection of some kind
might be provided for most of these carefully-trained trees, it
would of course be wise to include among them all the sorts
most liable to injury by spring frosts; and such kinds are so
abundant that all the walls and espaliers might well be devoted
to them.

Great improvement in fruit-culture may be effected by the
judicious thinning of the branchlets of standard orchard and
garden trees.   The natural tendency of trees of the Apple order,
to which most of our fruits belong, from the Hawthorn of our
hedges to the showy-flowered Chinese Pear, is to produce a dense
profusion of bloom, and consequently of fruit.   Sheets of white
or pink blossoms in spring, and showers of pretty fruit in
autumn, usually adorn them.   And the tendency is as apparent
in the newest and largest Apple and Pear as in one of those
American Thorns laden with crowds of bright scarlet haws.   For
ages and ages man has raised our hardy fruits, until they so vary

in flavour, size, and beauty of colour that they puzzle system, and until some of the varieties have no more likeness to the aboriginal native than a Life Guardsman has to a chimpanzee. Yet in one point they still inherit their marked native trait— profuseness in bud and fruit. It is true that by selection the fruits have become so large that the improvement to be had by judicious thinning is not likely to present itself to many cultivators ; but one trial of the system will convert the most sceptical.   Nature's tendency is to the production of myriads of individuals, whereas in the case of our fruits we require size and perfection of the individual rather than mere quantity.   Let it be duly considered that the total weight of finely-developed fruits may equal, or nearly equal, an unthinned and half-starved crop, and perhaps be worth three or four times more in money value.

Generally the practice is to leave the crop as much to nature as regards thinning of the branchlets as we do that of the Ash or Blackberry.   One year the tree bears a great crop of fruit, and the whole of its vigour is so drawn up by the many hungry feeders that little remains to form fruit-spurs for the following year, and such as are formed may lack vigour to set.   Then comes a year of effort in the production of wood and spurs, and perhaps by the end of autumn there will be a score, or even two score, fruit-buds on one fruit-spur, where one, two, or at most three, would be sufficient.   Now, if all be allowed to set, the result will be a dense crop of poor fruit, which, if submitted in the market-test, will prove of little value.   But if these spurs be thinned so as to concentrate the energies of the tree in fine and succulent fruit, there will also rest sufficient strength in it to form at the same time a medium crop of fruit-buds likely to afford a crop the following year, and to induce a more regularly-fertile habit in the tree.   By following this thinning-system we may, in fact, get good and valuable crops every year ; and by the other the alternate and useless profusion before alluded to.   The Pear requires this attention as much as the Apple when grown as a standard or freely-developed tree ; but, in consequence of being much more grown in a dwarf and contracted form, on espaliers, walls, etc., and much pruned, the want of thinning is not so often seen as in the case of the Apple.

No method of growing these trees in the open air is better than the freely-developed standard tree, if the thinning-process be well carried out. The tree should be opened up in the usual way as regards its main branches, but equal attention should be given to the regular and bold thinning of the fruit-bearing branchlets; and even to the thinning of the spurs, where there is plenty of time to do so. In one large orchard-plantation of Pears to the west of London the fruit has brought more than double the amount of money during the last few years, since the careful pruning and thinning of the trees, than it did when left to nature. The thinning of the branchlets should not be performed till they have begun to bear fruit-buds in too great abundance.

The following are the names of the kinds of hardy fruit that do best as standard orchard-trees :—

Pears.

Jersey Gratioli	Louise Bonne of Jersey	Doyenné d'Eté
Doyenné du Comice	Suffolk Thorn	Comte de Lamy
Citron des Carmes	Thompson's Pear	Knight's Monarch
Jargonelle	Beurré d'Amanlis	Althorpe Crassane
Williams's Bon Chrétien	Swan's Egg	Marie Louise
Aston Town	Croft Castle	Beurré Superfin.
Beurré de Capiaumont		

Apples.

Borovitsky	Cox's Orange Pippin	Court Pendu Plat
Early Harvest	Early Nonpareil	Golden Harvey
Irish Peach	Golden Pippin	Sam Young
Joanneting	Ribston Pippin	Sturmer Pippin
Summer Golden Pippin	Sykehouse Russet	Beauty of Kent
Lord Suffield	Bedfordshire Foundling	Dumelow's Seedling
Keswick Codlin	Hawthornden	Royal Pearmain
Adams's Pearmain	Yorkshire Greening	Tower of Glammis
Blenheim Pippin	Golden Noble	Pitmaston Nonpareil.

Plums.

Pond's Seedling	Gisborne's	Prince Engelbert
Early Rivers	Victoria	Damson.
Orleans		

Cherries.

May Duke	Late Duke	Rival
Early Prolific	Knight's Early Black	Mammoth.
Bigarreau	Belle Agathe	

Apricots.

For Standard Trees in the Southern Counties.

Breda	Brussels	Turkey	Moorpark.

Figs.

For the Southern Counties.

Black Ischia　　　　Brown Ischia　　　　Brown Turkey　　　　Courcourcelle Blanche.

Medlars.

The Nottingham is the best kind.

Nuts.

Lambert's Filbert (Kentish cob) is the best.

Purple Filbert　　　　Pearson's Prolific　　　　Cosford (also good).

Of the Quinces the Portugal is the best.

Of the various waste spaces where good fruit might be grown the most conspicuous are the railway-embankments. Here we have a space quite unused, and on which for hundreds of miles fruit-trees may be planted, that will after a few years yield profit, and continue to do so for a long time with but little attention. I am not aware that any attempt has been made to cultivate fruit-trees on these places in England; but learning that one had been instituted in France, I went to see the experiment which has been made for a distance of eight leagues or so along the line from Gretz to Colommiers—Chemin de fer de l'Est. The French see the great advantage of utilising, in this way, spots at present worthless, and they are beginning to work at it.

A cheap fence of galvanised wire runs on each side of the line, and on this Pear-trees are trained so that their branches cross each other; and, though only in their fourth year, they are at the top of the fence. In some parts they are trained in like manner on the slender but very cheap and slight kind of wooden fence, so common in France. By training them in a way to cross and support each other, before the time the fence decays the trees are perfectly self-supporting, and form a very neat fence themselves. This is a plan well worth adopting in many gardens where neat dividing-lines are desired.

Those who have travelled by day from Brussels to Louvain, or from Leopoldsdorf to Soleman, on the Belgrad, Gratz, and Vienna line, cannot fail to have remarked that the railway is flanked at intervals on both sides by Apple and Pear trees, either growing naturally or trained as espaliers.

According to Dr. Morren's report in the 'Belgique Horticole' of February 1869, the trees planted three years previously between the first-named towns had so far thriven exceedingly well, their branches already reaching up so as to form a third and fourth stage, and in the spring of 1868 the majority of them blossomed. They are placed seven feet apart, and trained on a fence of posts, thin horizontal iron bars, and cross rails, the posts being five feet in height by three inches or four inches in diameter, and the wooden rails one inch broad by two-fifths of an inch in thickness. The fence costs about threepence the running foot, and the wear and tear is estimated at one penny. When iron wire is used—and old telegraph wires come in most usefully for the purpose—it may be attached every ten feet to a four feet high oaken post, the lowest wire being one foot and a half, the second two feet and three quarters, and the third nearly four feet above the ground. One tree may be planted close to a post, and one midway between post and post—the trees will in that case be five feet apart; and if the plan of alternating a horizontal espalier with the columnar pyramidal form be adopted, the fence will in a few years assume the appearance indicated by the accompanying sketch.

If preferred, smaller intermediate posts may be used as supports for the

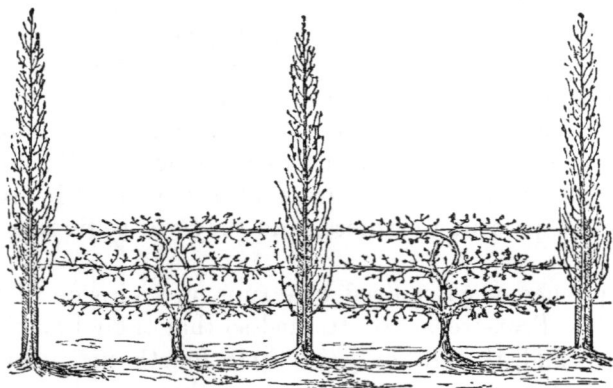

Fruit-trees along Railway.

espalier trees, and to facilitate training of the branches, the wires extending from them to the large posts may be made to slope upwards. As regards the method of training and managing a horizontal espalier fence, the following details may be of service:—A strong, well-rooted Pear or Apple tree, one year from the graft, is planted without being cut, at the place intended for it in the row, and about the middle of the ensuing May, when the sap is in full movement, is bent down and fastened in a horizontal position to the lowest wire. To encourage the putting forth of fruitful side-shoots along its whole length, incisions are made before all the dormant eyes, while too-vigorous shoots are pinched in. A good even growth of fruit-wood will shortly be the result. Owing to the accumulation of sap at the point where the young tree is tied down, the shoot there thrown out will be stronger than any of the others; it must be allowed to grow freely, and be attached in an almost upright direction. In the following year it will require to be bent down and fastened in the opposite direction to the stem from which it sprang, and it then forms the second arm of the tree. To form the second stage of branches, which is the next operation, a shoot must be taken from arm No. 2, and, after being carried up as far as the second wire, be bent down and fixed horizontally. From this third branch, by repeating the operations of the stage below, a fourth leading branch is formed, and the second stage is then complete. As regards the upper or third stage, it may either be formed in the same or in a slightly-different manner from the first and second, and in the sixth year the extremities of the two lower branches will require to be drawn up, and either grafted by approach or otherwise attached to the two uppermost. If the tree push forth very vigorously at first, its two leading shoots may be allowed to grow in an upright direction in the same year, and afterwards be attached horizontally to the wire.

Respecting the cultivation of columnar-pyramidal trees—a form to be preferred where, on account of the corn-crops, much shade is undesirable—a good plan is to put in strong, healthy plants two years from the graft, and the first operation will consist in pruning away all side-branches above the union of scion and stock. Incisions are afterwards made above the eyes, with a view to cause them to break out strongly, and in the following spring, the lateral shoots thus developed must

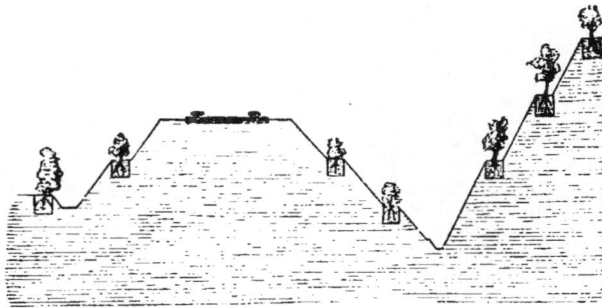

Section of Railway-embankment and Terraces for Fruit-trees.

be cut short back. During the second year, the same mode of proceeding as regards incisions and cutting back of side-shoots (to about one inch in length) should be continued, and the point of the main stem will require to be somewhat shortened. Later on, as the tree shoots upwards—and it will, if permitted, attain a height of fifteen, twenty, and even twenty-five feet—the topmost lateral branches must be pinched, whilst the lower ones are regularly cut back and not allowed to extend beyond one foot from the main stem. If incisions have been made in the latter as above directed, and successive prunings properly attended to, the tree will be clothed from summit to base with short fruiting-branches, and in five to seven years from the time of planting will begin to yield.

When it is proposed to utilise the slopes and embankments of railways for fruit-growing, the system of planting the trees, whether espalier or free-growing, on terraces some two or three feet in width, will be found in many cases a very advantageous one; and not only Apples and Pears, but Cherries, Plums, Gooseberries, Currants, Strawberries, Filberts, Walnuts, and other kinds of fruit and wood suitable to the locality, may also be successfully cultivated.

On some of the State railways of Sweden the plan is found to work well of engaging a competent man to superintend the cultivation of a certain number of station orchards and gardens, and perhaps it might answer to make some similar arrangement in connection with the planting, pruning, training, etc., of fruit-trees grown on the sides of the line. Railway employés in those localities where the traffic is small, would thus be enabled to make a profitable use of their spare time, and, under the direction of an efficient staff of pomologists, be the means of turning to good account thousands of acres of what is now waste, unproductive land.—*S., in ' Field.'*

In France and Belgium it is often the case that, instead of the trees being in the form of standards, they are trained as is represented in the accompanying engravings, so as to form a hedge. Established trees crossed in this way should not be allowed to get into a rough hedge-like condition, but, on the contrary, should be trained as neatly and perfectly as trees on a

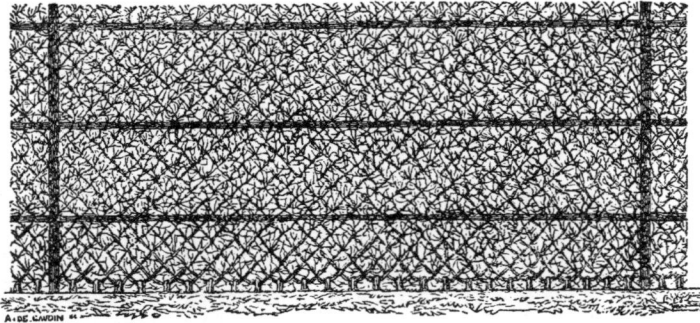

Fruit-hedge fully furnished.

trellis or wall. No fraying of the branches, resulting from their being interlaced, need take place. A shoot should be taken along the top so as to act as a finish and tend to hold all tightly together, and, thus constructed, the whole will look much firmer and neater than the ill-trained espaliers that one too often sees. These fruit-hedges might well replace useless hedges and other fences in many gardens and country-places.

A correspondent well conversant with fruit and fruit-culture in England, sent me the following note with sketches:—

"During a recent journey through a part of Belgium I was struck with what appeared to me to be a very excellent method of turning railway-fences to good account. For miles along the road between Aix-la-Chapelle and Brussels the fences on either side of the railroad consist of wooden posts 4 inches square and

4½ feet out of the ground, with four pieces of straight wire nailed to the outer side ; between the posts four long, thin sticks are tied diagonally ; the fencing is then covered with cordon Apples and Pears of the most suitable kinds for market and other purposes, the Apples being worked upon the Paradise stock. They are planted in front of and between each post, and trained

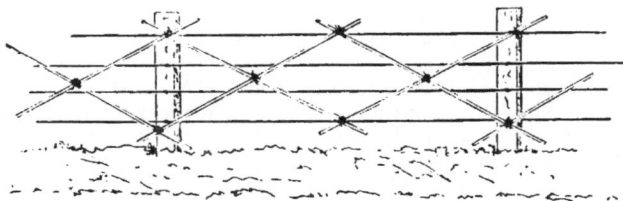

Form of Fruit-tree Fence.

obliquely to the sticks fastened to the wires. The trees appeared healthy, short-jointed, well-trained, and likely to be very productive. I could not help thinking of the thousands of once fruitful acres which the railways in this country have thrown out of cultivation and the desirability of devising some plan for reclaiming and turning to profitable account some part of this lost inheritance. I know there are great difficulties in the way ; these may be thought too .formidable to be surmounted, but where the iron road passes through a flat country, and one

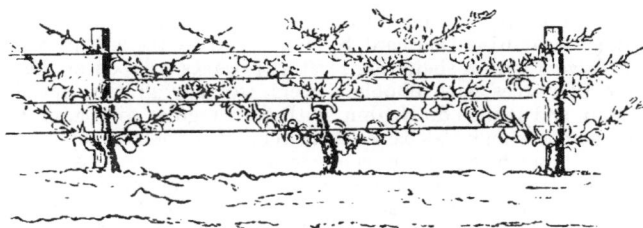

Railway Fence furnished with Fruit-trees.

suitable for fruit-cultivation, there are always portions of land on each side, and often corners and triangular pieces hitherto left waste, and I cannot help thinking they might be made useful in helping to furnish some of the food required for the support of our people.—W. N."

ORNAMENTAL PEAR-TREES.—As this book was going through the

press, the following notes, by M. C. Baltet, of Troyes, were published in the ' Revue Horticole ': as they are so interesting, and so likely to be useful to all who care for fruit-trees for their beauty, they are given here—

"A group of prolific, large-fruited varieties, such as Beurré de l'Assomption, Williams' Bon Chrétien, Van Marum, and others, will always be a source of delight to the lover of fruit, but the artist will look for effect from the natural appearance of the trees. If he wishes for luxuriant growth, he will find it in the branches of the Pear known as the Curé, Louise Bonne d'Avranches, Conseiller de la Cour, and others. The Beurré Hardy, Vauquelin, and Duc de Nemours have long upright branches, while those of the Beurré d'Amanlis, Bon Chrétien, and Triomphe de Jodoigne spread out more or less horizontally, or even curve downwards. The latter tree is the type of hardiness and vigour. Arbre courbé, Nouvelle Fulvie, and Marie Louise would not be out of place as drooping trees ; while to rival the pyramidal varieties of the Robinia, the Oak, the Birch, and the Elm, we may admit a group of Pear-trees which grow naturally in this shape, such as Fondante du Panisel, Beurré de Nantes, Fondante de Noël, Beurré d'Angleterre, and a number of others, including Charles Ernest, a new and excellent variety. The 'curious,' as they were called in the days of La Quintinie have already borrowed from the domains of pomology such subjects as the Weeping Pear, the Mount Sinai Pear, the Sage, Willow, and Almond-leaved Pears, etc. ; but their fruit is insignificant. The beautiful foliage of the Sucrée de Montluçon, Delpierre, Triomphe de Jodoigne, etc., is rivalled by that of the Mikado and Daimyo varieties, which are of Japanese origin, with large, thick, and somewhat cottony leaves. China furnishes us with two sorts, the thick, shining, and ciliated leaves of which change to amaranth red in the autumn, like certain Maples and Sumachs. Amongst our own sorts, we have the German Kopertscher, the Belgian Délices de Jodoigne, the American Philadelphia, and Gile-ô-Gile, which present the same character. The observer who takes notice of the particular characters of each variety will know that Marie Guisse, Monseigneur des Hons, and Royale d'Hiver are the first to show their buds in the spring, while Martin sec, Madame Loriol de Barny, and Herbin seem loth to shed their leafy clothing in the autumn. Bonne d'Ézée and Doyenné d'Alençon are the earliest to flower, and Alexandrine Douillard, Sylvange, and Nouvelle Fulvie protect their clusters of flowers with a sheltering rosette of leaves as soon as they open. If we wish for Pear-trees with double flowers, we may gratify our desire with Comte Lelieur and Beurré de Naghin, with their regular corolla, or the double-flowered Bergamotte and Calebasse Oberdieck, with their drooping petals, will satisfy us. Without being able to compete with the coloured barks of the Birch, the Golden Ash, the scarlet Dogberry, or the veined Maple, we may content ourselves for the present with the Ash-coloured bark of the Bési Dubost, the ochrey Passe Colmar, the violet Beurré Giffard, the purple Doyenné Flon aîné, the dark brown Bon Chrétien de Bruxelles, the bright-barked Fondante Thirriot, the sombre Rousselet, and the yellow-green and sepia-veined and variegated varieties Beurré d'Hardenpont and d'Amanlis, Verte longue, Saint-Germain, &c. Amongst our ornamental shrubs we have examples which have their bark curiously split, crannied, and gabled, but we can match them with Van Mons, Deux-Sœurs, Angélique Leclerc, Beurré Lebrun, and others, the latter having a vigorous stem, which looks as if it had been sprinkled with carmine. Wildings will furnish us with prickly varieties, and the study of local fruit has provided us with the Poirier de Fosse, which, in the department of the Aube, is as large and tall as an Oak."

CHAPTER XXV.

CONCERNING CERTAIN IMPLEMENTS AND APPLIANCES USED IN FRENCH GARDENS.

THE CLOCHE.—This is simply a large and cheap bell-glass, which is used in every French garden. It is the cloche which enables the French market-gardeners to excel all others in the production of winter and spring salads. Acres may be seen covered with them round Paris, and private places have them in proportion to their extent—from the small garden of the amateur with a few dozen or score, to the large one where several hundreds are required. They are about sixteen inches high, and the same in diameter at the base, and cost in France about a franc a-piece, or a little less if bought in quantity. The advantages of the cloches are—they never require any repairs; they are easy of carriage when carefully packed; with ordinary care they are seldom broken; they are

The Cloche as used in Winter-Lettuce culture.

easily cleaned; are useful for many purposes besides salad-growing; for example, in advancing various crops in spring, raising seedlings, and striking cuttings. Every garden should be furnished with them according to its size; and when we get used to them and learn how very useful they are for many things, from the developing of a Christmas Rose to the forwarding of early crops in spring, they will be much in demand. It is not only in winter that they are useful, but at all seasons, both for indoor and outdoor propagation and seed-sowing. In France,

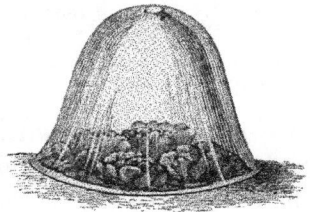

2 G

seedlings of garden-crops likely to be destroyed by birds or insects are frequently raised under the cloche.

In a recent number of the ' Comptes Rendus,' M. Th. Schlosing points out that the power of absorbing mineral ingredients in solution from the soil is diminished by cultivating plants under glass, and thus lessening the amount of evaporation from their surface. A Tobacco-plant so grown absorbed 17 per cent. of mineral matter, instead of 20 per cent., as it would do under ordinary circumstances. The production of vegetable acids was diminished by one-half—that of resin and cellulose to a less extent; while the nitrogenous ingredients were not materially decreased. Starch was present to the extent of 20 per cent., instead of to 100th per cent. only. Thus when evaporation is reduced in amount, a portion of the starch remains unused, and consequently accumulates in the plant. Assuming the correctness of M. Schlosing's conclusions, the immense importance to cultivators is obvious; as the two staple food-ingredients, the nitrogenous matters and the starchy ones, can be augmented by limiting evaporation.

Usually the cloche is made without a knob, as that appendage renders their package a much greater difficulty and increases the cost, so that practical men use only the one without the knob. When not in use the cultivator puts his cloches in some by-place, in little piles of half a dozen each, small pieces of wood being placed on the top of each to prevent them from settling down firmly on each other. Workmen used to them carry two or three in each hand in conveying them from place to place, by putting a finger between each. In commencing to use them in our gardens it would be well to see that they are placed in some spot where they will not be in danger of breakage. The cloche must not be confounded with the dark and very large bell-glass that was in common use many years ago in our market-gardens, and which may yet be seen here and there. These were even dearer than the hand-glasses which superseded them. The French cloche does not cost one-fourth so much as a hand-light—and, moreover,

The Cloche as used in the raising of Seedling Plants.

does not require painter, plumber and glazier for keeping it in repair.

How to procure these cloches has hitherto been a difficulty. Many have been deterred from employing them by the trouble, expense, and loss consequent on ordering them from France. Messrs E. Breffit and Co., proprietors of the Aire and Calder Glass-bottle Company's Works in Yorkshire, well known for its productions, now produce them on an extensive scale. It is well that the manufacture of the cloche has been taken up by a firm with every means of carrying it on in the best manner, and with stores in the North and in Liverpool, as well as in London. Messrs. Breffit and Co.'s offices are at 83, Upper Thames Street, E.C. ; their stores at Free Trade Wharf, Broad Street, Ratcliff, E., and at

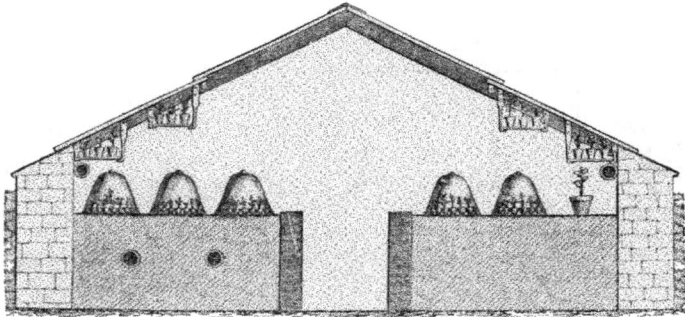

The Cloche as used in the Propagating-house.

120, Duke Street, Liverpool—and their manufactory at Castleford, near Normanton, Yorkshire, at any of which addresses orders will be taken and executed as soon as possible. They can also, of course, be obtained through various retail glass-houses.

CARRIAGE FOR TRANSPORTING ORANGE-TREES.—The fashion of growing large Orange-trees in tubs is so general in France that some efficient means of moving them from place to place is necessary. Many contrivances have been tried, and several are in use, but the best and handiest is that employed for the carriage of the large specimens in the gardens of the Tuileries. For the following notice of it I am indebted to the late Mr. John Gibson : " The machine used in the gardens of the Tuileries for removing large Orange-trees in tubs, of which a longitudinal representation is here given, is the most useful contrivance I have

2 G 2

séen in use for this purpose. Its simplicity and the facility with which the tubs are lifted for transit are its chief recommendations; no taking to pieces or removal of the side-beams, prior to loading, is necessary, beyond the removal of the hind axle, which consists of a strong wrought-iron bar with a hook at each end, the hooks fitting into eyes fixed on the inside of the stock of the hind wheels. They are made fast with a pin through each hook; when this bar is removed the machine is backed to the tub, one of the hind wheels passing it on each side until the tub is midway between the fore and hind wheels where the lifting apparatus is fixed. This being done the axle-bar is fixed and the machine is ready for loading.

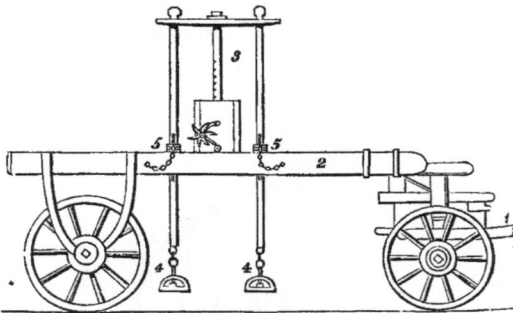

. *Carriage for transporting Orange-trees.*
1. *Fore carriage.*   2. *Side-beams.*   3. *Lifting-screw.*
4. *Stirrups for carrying Tub.*   5. *Pins.*

"The stirrups attached to the lower end of the upright lifting-rods are now lowered to the bottom of the tub by means of the rack and pinion machinery until the two iron bars, which are previously pushed under the tub, can be placed in the four stirrups; this being done, all is ready for lifting the tub in an upright position by the rack and pinions, which are worked by a man on each side. When the tub is high enough for travelling it is secured by means of a pin through the four

Truck for moving Plants in Tubs and large Pots.

upright lifting-rods inserted at 5 in the illustration; the tub being lowered on to the pins for travelling. The whole operation does not occupy the three men required to work it more than two or three minutes. The machine is drawn by one horse, and it will be seen how easily and quickly the superb Orange-trees alluded to are brought from their hibernatory in the spring to their summer-quarters, and as easily taken back in the autumn. The fore part of the machine is made to 'lock' so that it turns in little more than its own length. It is in every respect a most complete apparatus for this and for like purposes."

TRUCK FOR TUBS OR VERY LARGE POTS.—This very handy little truck is what the French use for moving large plants in tubs and large pots. It would be difficult to find anything more useful in its way. Large specimen plants are quickly and easily moved by this means. The pot or tub is caught by the little iron feet, then thrown on its side and tied firmly if a long distance has to be traversed.

GRAFTING MASTIC.—The thorough knowledge of grafting possessed by the French led them long ago to invent various kinds of grafting-wax or mastic, which greatly facilitate grafting. These, while distinct improvements for propagators and practical gardeners having much grafting to do, render grafting on a small scale by amateurs a pleasant operation. The mixture commonly employed for grafting in this country is not such as many amateurs care to make, and now that grafting-mastic is readily procurable it is scarcely worth while making our old-fashioned unpleasant preparation for the sake of a graft or two. The best of the French compositions for grafting is that called *Mastic l'Homme Lefort*— an awkward name for an excellent article now procurable through seedsmen.

IMPROVED FRUIT-SHELVES.—In the Pear-room at Baron Roth-schild's at Ferrières there is an excellent plan for arranging the fruit—the successive shelves of fine Pears being so formed that every individual pear can be examined without touching it. In the case of a fruit requiring so much care as the Pear does, from those who desire to have each variety, or even each perfect specimen, used at the right moment, this is an important improvement. In the Pear-room at the Versailles School of Horticulture the old flat form of bench is in use, and all the shelves are closed in by wooden doors, so as to exclude the light from the fruit.

PLOUGH-HOE.—This is used for cleaning the numerous long straight avenues in national and other large parks. A few men, each guiding one of these, clean the weeds from an avenue almost as quickly as they can walk along it, but the texture of many walks would not permit of its use at all. At St. Cloud and other places where it is used, the surface is quite sandy, and wherever

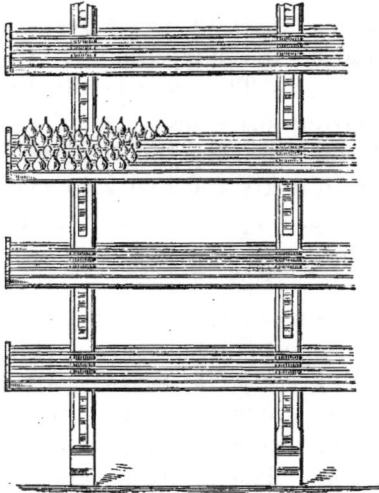

Portion of Pear-stand at Ferrières.

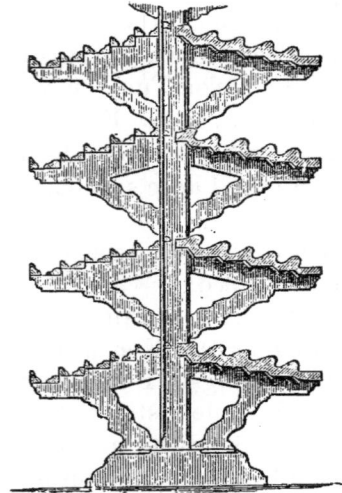

End View of Pear-stand.

this is the case it may be used with advantage, particularly in places where many wood-walks and drives have to be kept in order. They could not be used on such firm walks as we have about London.

FRAMES FOR FORCING.—The French market-gardeners use a great number of frames, and it is by their aid they procure most of the tender and excellent forced vegetables sent to the markets in early spring. These frames are made of very rough wood; are narrow— not exceeding four feet in width; and arranged in close lines completely immersed in the heating-material. They are usually about twenty inches high at the back and fourteen in front. Undoubtedly the principle is better and cheaper than our own. We employ large and well-made frames in private gardens, and for the most part place them so that all but the base is exposed to the influence of the weather

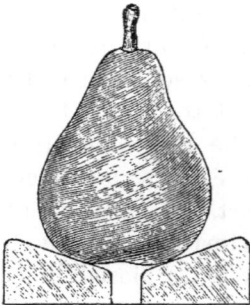

Section of Pear-rail in the Fruit-room at Ferrières.

and the plants therein are more liable to changes of temperature and cold. By having the frames narrow, all the sidework rough and cheap, and the frames placed in close lines, the greatest amount of heat is obtained at the smallest cost. By having nothing but the surface of the glass exposed, little heat is lost, and when the frames are covered by the neat, warm, and flexible straw mats, they are as snug as could be desired. When

it is only desired to pre-serve half-hardy plants through the winter, the spaces between the rough-sided frames are merely filled up with leaves and

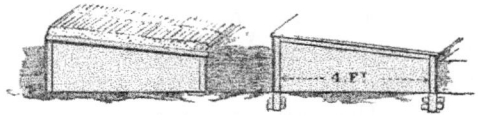

Narrow Frames used for Forcing.

slightly-heating materials.   A space of about two feet is left between each frame, or just enough for the convenience of the workmen.   Generally the frames are made by the workmen of the market-gardens : two stout posts being driven firmly in at one end, and an end-board nailed to them.   Then at every four feet or so minor posts are driven down, and the rough front and back boards nailed to them. Numbers of them are also made on a plan by which they can be readily taken to pieces and stored in a small space while not in use. By this means the ground covered by forcing-frames in winter is rapidly cleared for ordinary open-air crops in summer.

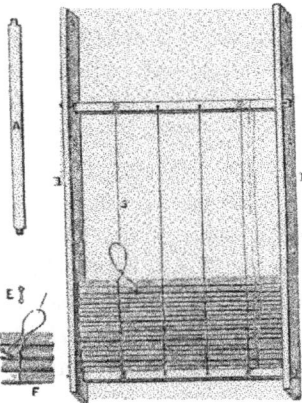

Frame for making Straw Mats.

MATS FOR COVERING PITS AND FRAMES.—In our cold and variable climate, the winter-covering for many minor glass structures is of the greatest importance.   It is a thing generally managed in a very expensive and by no means satisfactory way. The French mode of doing it is much cheaper, neater, and more effective ; and in passing through their market-gardens and forcing-grounds in winter, it is one of the first things that seems worthy of imitation by the English horticulturist. The covering used consists of straw mats about an inch thick, the sides as neat as if cut in a machine, the mat knit together by twine, and its texture such that it may be rolled up closely.   These mats are not only much better as a protection than a bast mat, but cost much less than that, while, in point of appearance and amount of protection given, the advantage is all in their favour.   The preceding figure represents a simple frame used for making these mats in the nurseries of M. Jamin, the celebrated cultivator of Orange-trees, who thus describes it :—" Get two pieces of timber (1) about three inches thick, four inches wide, and as long as required.   Pierce these timbers, as shown in the figure, and introduce the bar A in the holes to maintain the same width between the sides, and support the nails or screw.   These nails are to keep the string tight (5).   The bar may be shifted from hole to hole so as to make mats of any desired length.   The length of the string must be about three times that of the straw mat, and rolled round a little reel, shown at E.   The straw must be placed on the machine so as to have

Straw Mat (Paillasson) used for covering Frames.

all its cut or lower ends close · against each side, the tops meeting in the middle, and so as not to have the mat thicker than three-quarters of an inch when finished.   The stitches must not be wider than three-quarters of an inch, and are worked as follows (see F in the figure).   Take a little of the straw with the left hand, and work the reel with the right, first over the straw, then over the looped string, coming back underneath, and swiftly passing it between the two strings, pulling tightly and pressing the straw, so as to have a flat stitch, and not thicker than three-quarters of an inch at the most.   The same operation is repeated until the mat is finished.   The machine described has been at work for the last twenty years in our nursery at Paris, and is still as good as new.   An ordinary workman may make daily from thirty to forty yards' run of these straw mats with it."   There are several frames for this purpose, and also a machine for making the mats so indispensable in the French garden; but the one just described is the simplest for private use. Most innovations of this sort are adopted slowly; but that people would immediately use this, if they had an opportunity of seeing it in working order, there can be little doubt. In France they are found so useful that they are employed for many purposes besides that of covering frames, and they form an efficient temporary coping for walls in some cases. In all gardens where men are regularly employed they may be made during bad weather in winter; and as there is often difficulty in procuring enough useful indoor work for men at such times, the making of the mats will be a gain from that point of view alone. In country-places, where straw is abundant, their cost would be trifling.

Sécateur.—This is an instrument that all who prune should possess. It is seen in the hands of every French fruit-grower, and by its means he cuts as clean as with the best knife and much quicker. Men cut stakes with them almost as fast as one could count them; they have recently made some large ones for cutting stronger plants—such as the strong awkward roots of the Briars collected by the Rose-growers. Of these sécateurs there are many forms. First we have the Sécateur Vauthier, a strong and handy instrument. Its sloping semi-cylindrical handles have their outer side rough, which gives a firm hold; the springs, though strong, resist the action of the hand gently; the curvature of the blade and the adjustment are perfect; and lastly, the principal thing, the action is so easy as never to hurt the hand. " During the many years of my experience," observes M. Lachaume, a fruit-grower who describes this implement in the ' Revue Horticole,' " I have used tools of all kinds, and the tools have also used me a little; but I have never met with anything which gave me so much satisfaction as the Sécateur Vauthier. Every desirable quality is combined in it, and I recommend it with perfect confidence. The strongest branch will not resist its cutting, nor a single branch, however hard to get at, be inaccessible to it. Another great advantage this sécateur possesses is a double notch on the back of the blade and hook, which enables the operator, when employed at his trellises, to cut every wire without using the pincers." The Sécateur Lecointe is another variety much recommended. It is said that this form of spring secures an easy and gentle action of the instrument, and has the advantage of lasting longer than others, from not being so liable to break, while it secures a firmness and evenness in working which is not otherwise attained. A further improvement is pointed out in the fastening, which consists of a stop that catches when the two handles meet, a projecting portion on the outside acting as a spring which is to be pressed when the instrument is required to be opened. Then there is the sécateur of older date than the preceding, the one more generally used. It is much employed at Montreuil. There can be no doubt that where much pruning of any kind is done, and particularly pruning of a rather rough

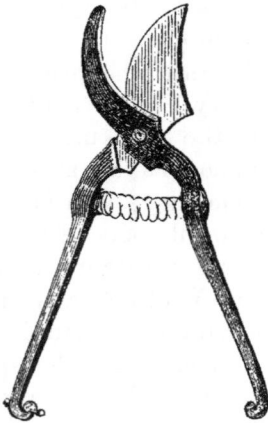

The Sécateur Lecointe.

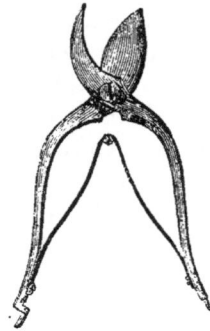

The Common Sécateur.

nature, the sécateur is a valuable implement. For pruning in which great nicety of cutting is required a good and properly-shaped knife is best. The sécateur was invented by M. Bertrand of Molleville.

THE RAIDISSEUR.—This is the name for the little wire-straining

The Raidisseur.

implement which plays such a very important part in wiring garden - walls, or erecting trellises for fruit-growing in France. It is an implement which, though insignificant in itself, is calculated to make a vast improvement in our gardens and on our walls. It will save much labour, and make walls or permanent trellises for fruit-growing far more agreeable to the eye and useful to the cultivator than ever they were before. There are various

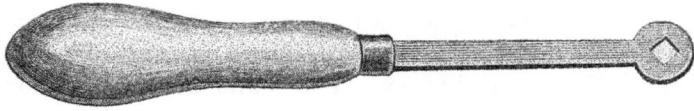

Key of Raidisseur.

forms which need hardly be described, as they are so well shown in the accompanying cuts. The first is a reduced figure of one about three inches long. The engraver has placed it in the best position to show its structure. The wire that passes in through one end is slipped through a hole in the axle; the other end is

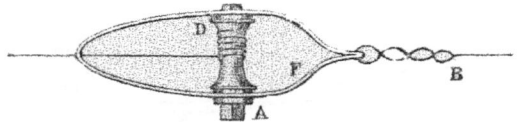

Collignon's Raidisseur.

attached to the tongue, as shown in the engraving, and then by the aid of a key, placed on the square end of the axle, the whole is wound much as a violin-string is wound round its peg. The

Side View of Collignon's Raidisseur.

first form figured is very much used in the best gardens, and seems to do its work effectively. The next Raidisseur here figured is that invented by M. Collignon and recommended by M. Du Breuil. It does not differ much from the preceding. D shows the point of insertion of the wire that has to be tightened; B the fastening of the other end of the wire; and A the head on which the key is placed. The foregoing kinds are, like the wire, galvanised. The best of these tighteners cost but a few pence; but even if they

Thomery Raidisseur.

were not cheap, it would still be profitable to employ them, in view of the great saving they effect, by allowing the use of a very thin wire, which besides being quite as efficient is infinitely neater than the bolt-like wire employed here. They have a still better and simpler raidisseur in use at Thomery. It is simply a small piece of cast-iron costing little more than a garden-nail—so small that its presence on wall or trellis does not look awkward as some of the larger kinds do, but for all that, it is a very effective tightener. The walls at Thomery are very neatly wired by its help, and it is equally useful for espaliers. I have indeed never visited a garden in which the walls and trellises were so neatly done, and all by means of this simple strainer and the galvanised wire.

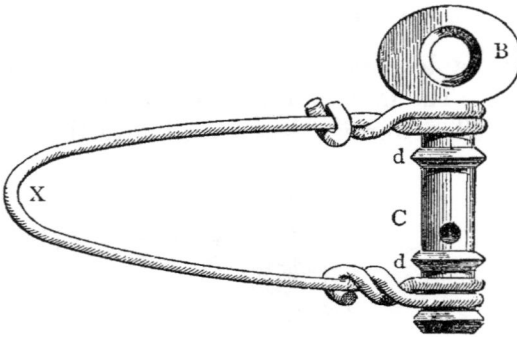

Borel's Raidisseur.

Mr. Palmer of Versailles writing in the ' Garden ' on this subject says : " Among the numerous ' raidisseurs ' manufactured in France there is none, perhaps, more effective and simple, and certainly none cheaper than the tightener made by Borel, of 10, Quai du Louvre. It consists of a small iron bolt with a flat head, of the exact size here given. The hole in the flat head B is used for winding up the bolt by means of a nail or round piece of iron. The hole at C is for introducing the end of the wire to be wound up, which coils away between the flanges (d d). The bolt revolves between the coils of the stirrup-shaped wire loop X, which is itself fastened by a wire to the end-post or hook of the espaliers. The whole affair, with the wire loop ready mounted, is sold for three-halfpence. Before this last raidisseur was invented, I had successfully used for many years the following plan of tightening wires. I made a loop somewhere about the middle of my wire by twisting it round a cylindrical piece of iron or bolt, which I left in it to prevent its closing, while I stretched the wire by hand and fastened the two ends. This done, I gave the bolt as many turns as were necessary to obtain the required degree of tension, and then withdrew it. I could at any future time give an additional turn or two when required.   If the wire be very long, several loops may be made at equal distances apart.   This method of tightening has this advantage over almost all others, that if the power applied be too great for the strength of the wire it will always give way at A, never at or beyond B ; thus the loop alone comes off, without at all affecting the tightened wire."   M. Jean Sisley, of Lyons writes : " A fruit-grower of our city—M. Ravet

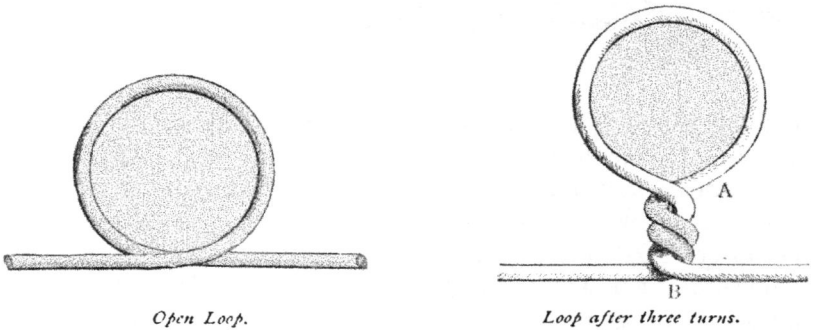

Open Loop.

Loop after three turns.

— uses the following simple and effective mode of tightening wires.   On the wire to be tightened he makes a loop A (as in the figure), through which he passes a piece of wire (B), which he turns round the pole C, to which the wire is to be fixed, and with pincers he twists the two ends (D) till the wire is tightened. Many persons who use the raidisseurs hitherto employed, have

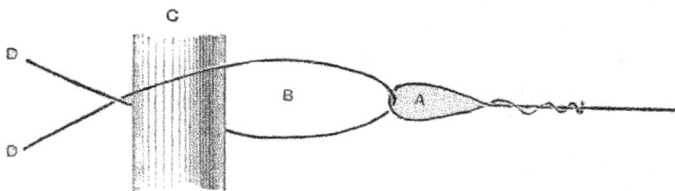

complained that it is sometimes difficult to tighten the wire properly with them.   The raidisseur has been turned up to a certain point, and the wire is still rather loose, but another turn of the raidisseur will break it, and to avoid this the wire is allowed to remain slack, which is very unfavourable to effective training, and moreover has a very slovenly appearance.   The screw and bolt tightener obviates this difficulty.   A glance at the next cut will show how it is used.   One end of the wire having been made fast to the upright (as at A), and the other end secured to the head of the raidisseur (as shown at C), the nut B is then screwed off, and the screw end having been passed through the upright (as at D), the nut is again screwed on and tightened with a pair of pincers or a bolt-wrench, until the wire is brought to a proper degree of tension. It will be seen at once that the screw allows of great nicety of adjustment, without involving too much straining or any slackening of the wire." These contrivances, and numerous improvements and modifications of them, are now sold by various English houses who make a speciality of galvanised wire-work.

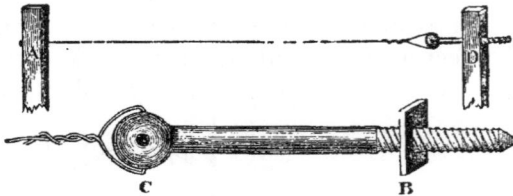

MATERIAL FOR TYING PLANTS.—The tying of plants, fruit-trees, and many things in gardens, occupies a great deal of time, even in small places. The material usually employed is bast matting, and in most large gardens a number of bast mats are annually cut up and used for this purpose. Of late years they have trebled in price. This expense may be done away with, and a much better material secured, by simply planting a few tufts of the common glaucous Rush (Juncus glaucus) in some moist spot; where much tying is to be done, a few dozen tufts may be planted. The stems of this plant are smooth and ready for use at any moment, and are suited for tying everything except the strong or " mother branches " of fruit-trees (for which twigs of the Yellow Osier are best fitted) and the finest and youngest shoots of hothouse-plants. The Rush may be cut green and used at once, or it may be cut soon after flowering and stored for winter-use in a dried state. When wanted in winter it is desirable to steep it in water a couple of hours before it is used, to insure the requisite flexibility. It forms a neat and lasting tie, and is not knotted like the matting, but simply twisted, then pinched off with the nail or cut with the knife, and one of the ends turned back a little. For tying the young shoots of fruit-trees to an espalier it is admirable, as it is for most other purposes of training. When men are accustomed to it, they work with greater facility with it than with any other tying-material. The dried grass of Lygeum Spartum is also used in France to a great extent for garden-tying. It is a Spanish grass, and will grow on any warm soil. It is suitable for very strong and durable tying. Thus the two best materials for this purpose may be grown in any garden without cost. Even if the bast matting were as cheaply got as these, the fact that the Rush and Grass are ready found in twine-like fashion, should make us prefer them. In tying carefully it is necessary to twist the matting, and thus a good deal of time is lost. In addition to the above hardy plants, the

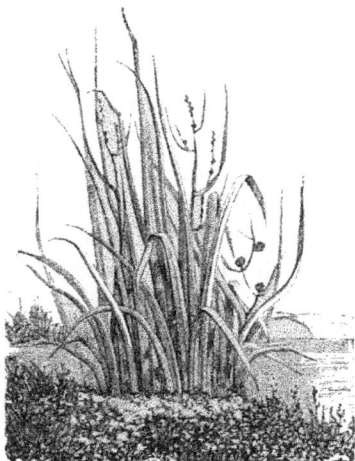

Bur-reed (Sparganium ramosum).

Reed-mace (Typha latifolia).

" Grass " of which may be directly used for tying, the leaves of the New Zealand Flax (Phormium tenax) are very largely employed for that purpose about Paris. This plant is grown everywhere for room-decoration. The long leaves being produced in great abundance, the old leaves that are cut away should be preserved, thus securing a strong and excellent material for tying.

MATERIAL FOR TYING GRAFTS AND BUDS.—The dried stems of Sparganium ramosum, the Bur-reed, have replaced woollen thread for budding-purposes in France. In texture they are peculiarly suited to this purpose, being soft, dense, elastic, and tough, so as to enable the operator to secure an effective tie. The plant is a common Water-weed about three feet high, growing everywhere in Britain along the margins of ponds, streams, and ditches. It is therefore a very cheap material, and may be cut and stored in any quantity for budding and grafting purposes. It is in extensive use in some of the largest and best nurseries in France. The stems of the common Reed-mace (Typha latifolia) are used for like purposes, but not so extensively. By means of these, many French grafters have been enabled to do away with all expense for woollen and cotton thread. The Sparganium is gathered in summer when fully grown; the leaves, which are united at the base, are separated, and then hung up in bundles to dry in a shed or barn. When required for use they are cut to the necessary length, from fourteen to twenty inches, steeped in water for a few hours, and then slightly dried by pressure or wringing. In large field-nurseries, where there is no water, bundles of the Bur-reed are kept moist and flexible by being buried in the earth, and they may also be kept so by placing them in a cellar. It must not be used very wet, and if too dry it is more liable to crack. It is found to bend best when applied edgeways to the body which it is to envelope, and slightly twisted. For all kinds of budding and grafting, except large cleft-grafting and the like, it is as good a material as can be found.

PROTECTION FOR WALL AND ESPALIER TREES.—Having several times spoken of the deep temporary copings the careful French cultivator uses for his fruit-wall, I here give a rough figure showing a section of the tile-coped wall, and projecting from beneath it the supports for the temporary protection. The French take a good deal of trouble with temporary copings, and find them of the greatest value in getting regular crops; for the frosts are severe in the northern parts and all around Paris, and, in fact, over nearly all the region north of the river Loire—the most important fruit-growing districts of France. The best appliance of this kind consists of narrow lengths of bituminised felt nailed on light frames from six feet to eight feet long, and about eighteen inches wide. The use of these on walls devoted to the culture of choice Pears, Peaches, etc., results in a marked improvement. The temporary coping has a great advantage in being removable, so that the trees may get the full benefit of the summer-rains when all danger is past, and not suffer from want of light near the top of the wall, as they would if such a wide protection were permanent. I believe that similar copings would be much more effective than any of the netting and canvas protections now in use in English gardens. The commonest temporary coping seen in France is made of straw nailed between laths; it seems to answer its purpose very well, but it is not so neat as that made of bitumenised felt. Whatever kind of protection may be employed, care is taken that it shall throw the wet well off the wall; the slightest experience of the effects of frost on vegetation will show the wisdom of this course. Of what does it avail to place a net or a few branchlets

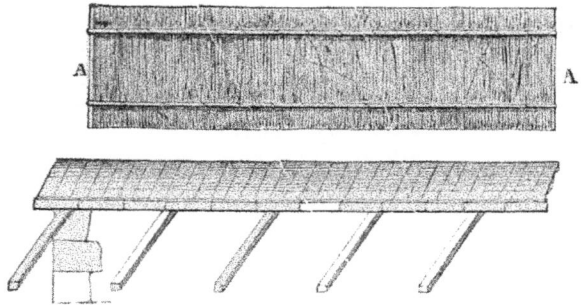

Mode of Protecting Walls. A, Straw Mat, two feet wide, held between laths, for placing beneath the permanent copings while there is danger of Frost.

of trees before a fruit-wall, if we allow the cold rains and sleet to fall on every tender brush of stamens?

WIRING GARDEN-WALLS.—The one practice among French horticulturists most worthy of adoption by the English fruit-grower is their improved way of placing galvanised wires on walls, or in any position in which it may be desired to train fruit-trees neatly. Several strong iron spikes are driven into the brickwork at the ends—in the right angle formed by two walls—nails with eyes in them being driven in in straight lines, exactly in the line of direction in which the wire is wanted to pass. The wires are placed at about ten inches apart on the walls, and the little hooks for their support, also galvanised, are fixed at about ten feet apart along each wire. The exact distance between the wires must, however, be determined by the kind of tree and the form to be given to it. If horizontal training of the branches be adopted, the wires had better be placed to form the lines which we wish the branches to follow; if the branches are vertical, we need not be so exact. The wire—about as thick as

2 H

strong twine—is passed through the little hooks, fastened at both
ends of the wall into the strong iron nails, and then made tight
with the raidisseur. The wires remain at about the distance of
half an inch or three quarters from the wall. If we consider the
expense of the shreds and nails; the destroying of the surface of
the walls by the nails, and the leaving of numerous holes for
vermin to take refuge in; the great annual labour of nailing, and
the miserable work it is in our cold winters, it will be admitted
that a change is wanted badly. This system of wiring a wall
above described is simple, cheap, almost everlasting, and excellent

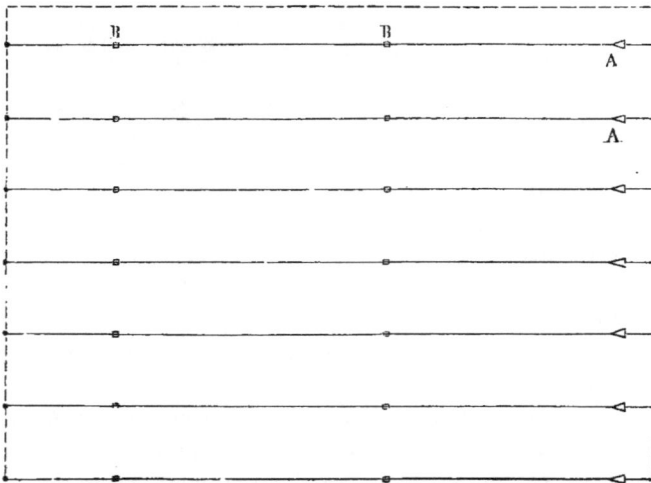

*Mode of arranging Wires on Walls for training Fruit-trees with Vertical or Horizontal Branches.
A, Position of Raidisseur; B, Nails with eyes, through which the Wire is passed.*

in every particular; and before many years elapse these advantages must force it into universal adoption in our fruit-gardens.
A man may do as much work in one day along a wall wired
thus as he could do in six days with the nail and shred. Since
the publication of the first edition of this book various houses
took up the idea and have wired many garden-walls in the
way above described, in many cases effecting improvements in
details. Given a concrete wall (as described elsewhere in this
book), smoothly plastered, and wired thus, fruit-trees could
not, in a northern country, be in a more excellent position. The
temporary coping taken off after all danger from frost had past,
every leaf would be under the refreshing influence of the summer-

rains, all the advantages of walls as regards heat would be obtained, and the syringing-engine would not be defeated by countless little dens offering comfortable breeding-places to the enemies of the fruit-tree, while the appearance of the wall would be all that could be desired.

The wire and the raidisseur are also efficiently used in doing away with any necessity for nailing in training the Peach and other trees, when trained as cordons, as shown

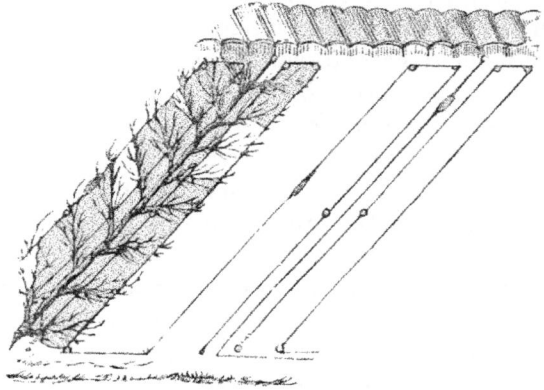

Wall Wired for Oblique Cordon Training.

in the accompanying figure. When the lines which the wires are to follow are fixed upon, bolts and eyes are driven in the wall, the wire being fixed to and passed through them, and then made firm.

The French apply the term " espalier " to their wall-trees, and in adopting the word from them we have transferred it to trees standing in the open, but trained in a similar manner. They term our espalier "centre-espalier," but the terms wall-tree and espalier are distinctly and generally understood among us, and therefore it is better to employ them in their usual sense. The simplicity and excellence of their mode of making supports for espaliers will be better shown by the figures in the account of the Versailles School of Horticulture than by verbal description. The mode of making trellises for espalier-trees now extensively

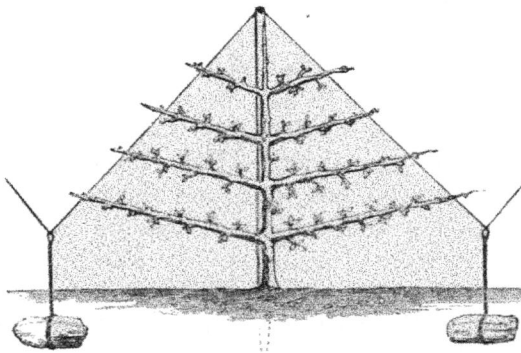

Trellis for Young Trees in Nurseries. Page 456.

2 H 2

adopted in France is far superior to our own mode, and owes its excellence to the abundant use of slender galvanised wire and the little tightening implements, or raidisseurs. The wire is sold in twenty-three different sizes. Of this an intermediate size, 12, 13, or 14, is that best suited and usually selected for strong and permanent garden-work, albeit a mere thread to the costly thick iron wire we use. The sizes appropriate for cordons, trellises, etc., are sold at from 30s. to 44s. per mile, so that the material is cheap enough. It is sold by weight, No. 12 size being 31s. per cwt of 1241 yards, and a smaller size 34s. per cwt. of 2031 yards. Of course smaller quantities are readily obtainable.

In some of the nurseries a simple kind of trellising is used for training young wall and espalier trees. It is useful in enabling the French to keep in stock trees for these purposes to a greater age than is the case in our nurseries, and for various purposes should prove useful to the grower of young fruit-trees. A larger and modified application of the same plan would do well for large espalier-trees; indeed it is applied with good effect and perfectly suits a method, not uncommon in France, of keeping the upper branches of trees, trained horizontally, shorter than the lower ones so as to secure greater vigour in the lower branches. This trellis may be established at a trifling cost by using light posts of rough wood, or, if permanence and greater strength be desired, of T-iron. In either case the posts must be firmly fixed. The wire should be passed through a hole or strong eye in the top of the pole, and fixed with stones or irons in the ground. In order to train the shoots straight, their rods may be extended from the post to the wires with but little trouble. Other illustrations of the neatest and best trellises in use in French gardens occur in several parts of this book.

EDGINGS FOR PARKS, PUBLIC GARDENS, SQUARES, DRIVES, ETC.— The edgings in gardens have a very important bearing on their general aspect, and often on their cleanliness. An edging much in use in the public gardens of Paris is made of rustic rods of cast-iron, in imitation of the little edgings of bent branchlets that many are familiar with. They are evidently cast from the model of a bent branchlet, generally about as thick as the thumb, but they are of various sizes. These irons are placed in the ground firmly, and are very easily fixed. The fact that they are not stiff, ugly, and tile-like prevents their offending the eye if one or two should fall a little out of the line here and there; this is nearly impossible, as they are tied by a scrap of common wire at the place where every two sticks cross each other. They are so plunged in the walk, or by the side of the walk, that about six inches of the little fence appears above ground. This, however, may be varied with the size of the subjects which they are used to margin; six or seven inches is the usual height for edges for ordinary purposes. In parks and pleasure-grounds, however, we usually have edgings of grass, so it may be thought that iron edgings are useless therein; but the little fences of bent wood which furnished the idea for these iron edgings were generally used to prevent grass near drives and walks from being trodden upon, for which purpose those now recommended will answer better. In much-frequented places along drives, and in public gardens, parks, and squares, their chief merit will be found.

THE SÉCATEUR.—As this edition was going through the press, the following note as to the utility of the sécateur (already described) came to hand :

"I have used this useful French pruner for several years. Last season I had occasion to lower two old thorn hedges, which had been shorn for more than forty years. I fixed up a number of stakes, stretched a line the required height, and employed a good workman to cut off the top in an even manner with the sécateur, lowering it 18 inches in order to bring a beautiful landscape into view. The work was done in a very even way, and in less than half the time the shears and saw would have taken, the stem being the size of a man's thumb. When such are bent by the hand the cut is then made much more easily, by one edge chiefly. I find the sécateur most useful for all kinds of shrub pruning. I have three in use, two of the largest 9 inches long, which I find the most useful, and which cost 6s. 6d. I have never found the spring of the large size get out of order. The rivet should be kept oiled, and then the shears readily spring open."— J. GARLAND.

CHAPTER XXVI.

The Market Gardens of Paris.

It has frequently been said that the minute division of property
in land retards the improvement of agriculture in France.   It
may be so with farming, but it certainly does not hold good with
markét-gardens.   These in and around Paris are very small, but
they are the best and most thoroughly-cultivated patches of
ground in Europe.   Every foot of earth is at work; and cleanliness, rapid rotation, deep culture, abundant food and water to the
crops—in a word, every virtue of good cultivation—are there
to be seen.   It is doubtful if such good results could be obtained
from large market-gardens, and certainly in no part of Britain is
the ground, whether garden or farm, so thoroughly cultivated as
in these little family gardens, as they may be called, for they are
usually no larger than admits of the owner seeing every crop in
the garden at one glance.   The Paris market-gardeners as a class
keep to themselves, and each seems content with about as much
ground as gives occupation to his family.   They are as a rule a
prosperous class.   The gardens vary in size from one to two, and
occasionally three acres, are usually walled-in, and contain a
cottage, a few sheds, and a well.

In the neighbourhood of our English cities the price of ground
is high—according to our scale that around Paris is very high
indeed, the rent varying from £24 to £33 per acre.   On entering
upon a market-garden the tenant has to pay in addition to his
rent from £200 to £600 for stock, fixtures, etc.   Manure forms
a very considerable item in the expenses of these gardens.   One
market-gardener paid £20 a month for manure.   His garden was
about three English acres in extent, which is much larger than

usual. Manure would appear to be dearer than in London, and
it is used very profusely, some of the crops being grown in almost
nothing else.   From the beginning of May to the end of November
the market-gardeners have no use for hotbeds, still every day
arrive loads of stable-manure, which piled meanwhile into rick-
like heaps, will be used chiefly in winter and spring.   In November they commence to make the hotbeds, and as stable-manure
continues to arrive every day it is mixed with that which has
been gathered during the summer—this making beds giving a
moderate degree of heat.

But a more important and expensive item is the watering.
The Parisian market-gardener, if not a " scientific " man, would
appear to be fully aware of the fact that by far the most important
constituent of vegetables is water.   It is mainly owing to the
abundant watering of these gardens, that the Paris markets are
throughout the hot season better supplied with crisp, tender, fresh
vegetables than any other capital in Europe.   Almost every
market-garden has its pump worked by the horse of the establishment—the Naudin system being generally preferred.   The water
is thence conducted into barrels plunged nearly to their rims
in the ground at regular intervals over the garden, and from
these distributed by copper watering-pots made to discharge the
water very quickly.   This constant watering involves a considerable expenditure for labour, one or two men being nearly always
employed at it in each little garden during the sunny months.
The system of watering with the hose, generally adopted in the
city of Paris, could not fail to attract the attention of the market-
gardeners : it is already used by several of them   In these cases
the pump is employed to elevate the water to a cistern placed a
few yards above the highest point of the garden.   I examined
a garden thus arranged, and found the system very satisfactory.
Twenty-seven outlets for the water were established over the
surface of a garden about two acres in extent.   To these a hose
of india-rubber is attached, with a few feet of copper tubing and
a large much-perforated copper rose or distributor at its other
end.   From this, when the water is on, it flows in a gentle but
copious shower ; and the apparatus may be managed by a boy.

Nobody could pass suddenly from our own markets and market-
gardens to those of Paris in the middle of a dry summer without

being forcibly taught how advantageous would be a good supply
of water in our gardens.   It is the custom to grumble about our
climate—the " dull," " cloudy," " changeable " climate of Britain ;
to speak of that of other countries as paradisaical, and to attribute
all our failures to " want of sun," but if we have a warm and
sunny season our market-supplies immediately run short, owing
to the absence of any preparation for watering garden-crops.   In
some dry seasons market-gardeners who are accustomed to realise
hundreds of pounds for a crop, gather barely as much of it as
would make it worth while sending to the market ; while the
private growers are quite as badly off.   Often in hot summer
when Cauliflowers in British gardens have almost disappeared
owing to the drought, they may be measured in the market-
gardens of Paris a foot in diameter and of the finest quality.   We
have vegetables, salads and the like when the weather is dewy
and favourable, and where the climate is moist ; but a few weeks
of drought puts an end to their goodness, and should it continue,
everything becomes worthless.   Are we in a position to boast of
our horticulture while this is the case ?   Does the routine work,
which merely waits upon the seasons thus, deserve the name of
skill ?   It is instructive to note that the very things which our
watery and cloudy clime is supposed to be most favourable to, are
to be found in greatest perfection with the French, in the drier
and, for vegetables, less favourable climate of Paris !   The secret
of it all is that the French market-gardener, in addition to tilling
and enriching his ground in the best manner, waters thoroughly
and repeatedly every crop requiring water for its perfect development.   Few need be reminded of the many things of which water
is almost the life.   Extract the water from a juicy Lettuce, or
any other garden vegetable, and what remains ?   Our soils are
of course saturated with water in winter, while in summer the
need of it leaves the vegetables mere accumulations of tough fibre.
I am not sanguine enough to hope that any words of mine can
induce cultivators to adopt plans for watering gardens effectively ;
but there can be no doubt whatever that it would be a decided
advantage to mark off in every large kitchen-garden a portion of
ground near the best supply of water, to make it rich and light,
and keep it thoroughly moist during the dry warm months ; so that
a few crisp delicate salads and vegetables may not during a dry

season be as impossible with us as in the Sahara. This small division might be established in most places at a trifling cost; while the result would be so satisfactory that it would probably soon lead the grower to adopt the same plan on a larger scale. It need hardly be added that it would not be necessary to take such precautions in very moist districts in the British Isles; but there are many districts where a modification of the Parisian plan would prove a decided advantage.

Noticeable in these market-gardens is their rich verdure at nearly all seasons. In the ordinary kitchen-garden there is often as much space wasted in needless walks and alleys as goes to form one of these little gardens which occupy and support a family. Custom, time, and authority are all arrayed in favour of a series of walks in the kitchen-garden, and yet they are as wrong as they can be. For the following reasons there should not be any walks in a perfect kitchen-garden :—

First. Convenience of Watering and Irrigation.—Even in our moist country good vegetable culture is not everywhere possible without watering or irrigation. As gardens are at present arranged, watering is difficult, and irrigation impossible, without spoiling all the walks, gravel, and edgings. In many parts of the country, especially in Scotland and the moist parts of Ireland, the need of thorough watering or irrigation is not known; but in England it is seriously felt. Three warm days in July show their effect in Covent Garden, inconvenience the housekeeper, and injure and reduce the supplies of vegetable food at a time when these are more than ever important for health. It cannot be said that either our kitchen- or market-gardening is what it should be so long as we are unable to reap benefit instead of loss from the sunny weather. In a garden properly irrigated, a few weeks of warmth would give us a better result than we should obtain during a similar number of cold or cloudy days. Therefore we shall never have a good system of kitchen-gardening till all crops liable to suffer from drought are as promptly and effectually watered as a small plant growing in a pot.

Second. To Secure Good Culture.—To get the best result from a piece of ground devoted to vegetable-culture, it is necessary that the whole of it be thoroughly turned up, and enriched from time to time. Walks and hard alleys, gravel, etc., prevent this from being done with ease and thoroughness. The whole surface of a perfect kitchen-garden should be as freely open to the labours of man, or horse, or spade, as a heap of loam lying in a compost-yard. In the orthodox kitchen-garden, the men may frequently be seen carefully scraping their boots, just as if they were going into a drawing-room or a Turkish bath. Half the ground thoroughly cultivated would be better than the large areas we frequently see bare or badly cultivated. As regards the convenience of moving composts and the like, that is more easily secured in a garden free from all obstructions in the way of well-gravelled walks and neatly-kept edgings. In a very large garden, a firm cart-way might in some cases be desirable, but the fact is that the space really necessary for the kitchen-garden proper, under a good system of culture, is of a size that a walk or cart-way leading to it is all that is required. The best system for the kitchen-garden is a thorough trenching and annual enriching; afterwards, and throughout the seasons of greatest growth, such cropping of the surface as never allows the ground to be idle; this system is most easily pursued where there is nothing needlessly in the cultivator's way.

Third. Because Walks are Needless as a Convenience among Kitchen-garden Crops.—Permanent walks may be a convenience among choice dwarf fruit-trees, small fruits, plantations of herbs, etc., but nobody who considers the matter fully will say that they are needed among succulent crops, such as Cauliflowers, Kidney-beans, and the like. A walk in itself is ugly, and a few lines of a useful well-grown crop are far preferable in appearance; as to inconvenience from mud, &c., there is none, because in any case the cultivator or gatherer has to get on the ground, and in the usual style of elaborately laid-out gardens he has always the needless trouble of taking care not to soil the walks. In a well-drained garden there is little fear of mud. In case one of the main lines of walk passes through or near a kitchen-garden, we need not consider it, because that is a question concerning the general convenience of the place. It has nothing to do with the present question—the need of walks in the kitchen-garden itself.

Fourth. Cleanliness and Neatness.—It is much easier to keep clean a garden, the whole surface of which is devoted to crops, than one where a large area is bare, and continually offering in edgings and in gravelled surfaces sunny welcome to the seeds of weeds. Under a better system, all the trouble of cleaning the walks, and keeping edgings, etc., in order, would be saved. As to appearance, there is nothing nearly so beautiful in the ordinary kitchen-garden as may be seen in a garden where the whole surface throughout the growing season is covered with healthy green vegetation.

Fifth. Because of Modern Wants.—The kitchen-garden is now planned as it used to be when most of the flowers, fruits, etc., were grown within its walls. In those days there was absolute need of walks in the kitchen-garden, from the season of the Golden Crocus to that of the Christmas Rose. But we have changed all that. There has long been a desire to separate fruit-gardening from kitchen-gardening: the wisdom of this view need not be discussed here, but there can be no doubt that in most gardens flowers—hardy as well as tender—have left the kitchen-garden for good.

Sixth. Economy.—In many kitchen-gardens there is quite a mile of broad, gravelled walks, mainly for the " convenience " of those who have to perform the pretty frequent labour of cleaning them and the edgings, etc. Space may not be very precious in the places spoken of, but it is none the less true that the ground often wasted in walks would be sufficient to grow vegetables for a large family. It is obvious that a market-gardener who tried to do his work in a paradise of walks would soon be heard of in the Bank-ruptcy Court. None of them however are simple enough to go to work in this manner. But it must not be thought that their gardens are always untidy because of the absence of walks. In most countries, the better class of market-gardens are models which the private gardeners might well study, even from the point of view of neatness and appearance. Is it needful to speak of the absurd waste of means in the making and keeping of walks, edgings, etc., not merely useless, but the source of perpetual loss of time and means ?

Various other reasons against the common practice could be given, but they are not needed. The present system is so firmly rooted that few will be able to change to a better plan soon, but, nevertheless, the opening of the question will probably do good. In the present state of horticulture, where so much remains to be done, we can ill afford to spend means and energy in the wrong places. Frequently it will be expedient to leave things as they are in the case of fairly well-formed gardens ; but in the case of laying-out a new garden, it would certainly be better to separate the fruits—large and small—wholly from the kitchen-garden ; also, all such plants as herbs which do not require deep or frequent culture, all store or nursery beds which are often visited, frame-ground, and plunging-beds, should be removed from it altogether. Such walks as convenience demands might be made in the fruit and other departments. The kitchen-garden itself might be formed or sheltered in whatever way the needs of the place might suggest. No walks should be seen in it ; it would, in fact, be treated as one plot of ground in the highest state of culture to which drainage, trenching, manure and water could bring it.

A great deal of the success of the Parisian market-gardeners is due to a close system of rotation, eight crops per year being frequently gathered from the ground. Were it not so the culti-vators could not succeed, so very limited is the ground each pos-sesses. A considerable portion of the surface in one garden I visited was devoted to Cos Lettuce, and very fine specimens they were ; but beneath them there was a dark green carpet of leaves very close to the ground—the leaves of the Scarolle, which forms such an excellent salad. The young plants have room to grow now amongst the closely-tied-up Cos Lettuce ; but the moment the Cos is cut for market, the Scarolle has fuller liberty, and with abundance of water soon itself covers the ground. Then perhaps some young plants of another vegetable are put in at regular intervals in the angles between four plants of Scarolle, the new crop being vigorous and halfway towards perfection when the great smooth Endive is ready for the market. As an illustration of the cropping, the cultivator described to me that of a portion of his ground for the past year. In the earliest spring the ground was occupied by Cos Lettuce, and from between them a crop of Radishes was gathered. Cauliflowers were planted early among the Cos, and as they approached maturity the ground was of course wholly occupied by them, as one could not well put anything beneath a crop of well-grown Cauliflowers. When they were cut in May and June, an opportunity occurred of giving the ground that thorough culture and preparation which such a course of heavy cropping demands.   Then a crop of Spinach was sown, and in the Spinach Cos Lettuce.   As soon as the Spinach was cleared off, a crop of Endive was placed alternately with the Cos.   Then small Cauliflower-plants were put in, yielding a fine crop in the autumn, and after them a small quick crop like Corn Salad, and afterwards the ground was covered with frames.

Like everything else in Paris, and in France generally, the condition of these market-gardeners has much improved during the past generation.   Some of the crops, and particularly the forced crops, are now brought to invariable perfection in low narrow wooden frames. Eighty or ninety years ago, however, the market-gardening of Paris was much less perfect ; fewer crops were gathered during the year, the art of forcing early vegetables and salads was in its infancy, and the most advanced market-gardeners had not got beyond the use of the cloche to force their vegetables.   The workmen employed in these market-gardens work, like their masters, hard, but are better paid than men of similar occupation in England.   From inquiries made of different cultivators, it seems wages are from £2 to £3 per month with board and lodging. They have no fixed hours for work as with us, but in summer begin with the dawn and in winter hours before it.   The men board at their master's table.   M. Courtois Gérard said that to cultivate a garden of two and a half acres devoted to forcing in frames, and open-air culture, it is necessary to have five or six persons—that is to say, the master and mistress, two men, a girl and a boy.   As to the masters, I was informed that many of them could not read or write ; but I noticed notwithstanding a good barometer in each house.   They well know the value of this instrument, and consider it of the greatest use in cultivation, by helping them to take precautionary measures and to adapt work to weather.

These men have their vicissitudes notwithstanding the vigorous industry and excellent system of culture which is general with them.   Some that I visited devote a considerable portion of space to a difficult crop—Cauliflower-seed.   This takes a long time— more than a year—to bring to perfection ; one market-gardener in the habit of growing large quantities of it for Messrs. Vilmorin, Andrieux and Co., had scarcely gathered two pounds of it one year in consequence of the great heat of the season.   There is a

Mutual Aid Society among these market-gardeners. To give an example of the way they work, I have merely to state that when a body of provincial cultivators were almost ruined by inundations, the Paris society sent them more than 1200 lbs. weight of seeds to begin again with. Generally they seem independent, and are said to accumulate money, and often to retire comparatively early in life from active work. Few will doubt that it is better to have a large class of small proprietors in a thrifty and independent, though humble condition, than one individual with many acres, and every soul employed by him without anything to call his own.

The opinion prevails widely in England that the smaller the holding the worse the culture. It may be so in some cases; very small holdings and very high culture are the rule around Paris. The owners are certainly as hard-working and, apparently, as poor as any independent workers can well be, but they appear to gain, at least, as good a livelihood as the farmers who try to cultivate a hundred or more acres in the best parts of Canada. This Paris market-gardening is, however, so essentially peculiar and special that it would be unsafe to deduce any broad conclusions from it alone. The culture in the open fields round Paris is far inferior, and very imperfect. Hence, the vegetables raised in that way are inferior to those seen in the London market. In and near Paris one rarely sees much variety in one garden; the tendency is to special culture. Thus, one whole town and its environs is devoted to Asparagus, another district to Garden-turnip culture. Mushrooms form a speciality, and even the forcing of Asparagus is sometimes made the main effort of a life. One may look in vain in any of these gardens for either Rhubarb or Seakale. It is odd to reflect how slowly and curiously ideas sometimes travel. In the deserts of Utah, in the garden of a Mormon elder; or, farther still, away on the coast range of the Pacific in a Californian garden, Pie-plant (Rhubarb) and Seakale are as well known as the Potato. Cross the English Channel, and we find a land where they are seen no more, except, perhaps, in very rare cases as curiosities.

According to some figures quoted by M. Joly before the Central Horticultural Society of France, and taken from the records of their Custom House, the total quantity of fruits exported to England,

Belgium and Germany amounted in 1874 to nearly 80,000 tons, or more than double that in 1873. Of dried vegetables over 23,000 tons were exported in 1874, Chestnuts 6000 tons, and of Potatoes the enormous quantity of nearly 175,000 tons. The amount of money we now pay to the French for garden-produce is considerable. The weights are surprising enough in themselves, but when it is considered that a great deal of the produce is of the very choicest description, fetching high prices (as in the case of Early Asparagus, choice fruit, Winter Lettuce, etc.), then the meaning of these figures may be better understood. Our growers, and, perhaps, our politicians too, would do well to bear such facts in mind, for there must be some points worth studying in the conditions which give rise to such a state of things.

Gourd of the Paris Market.

CHAPTER XXVII.

ASPARAGUS CULTURE.

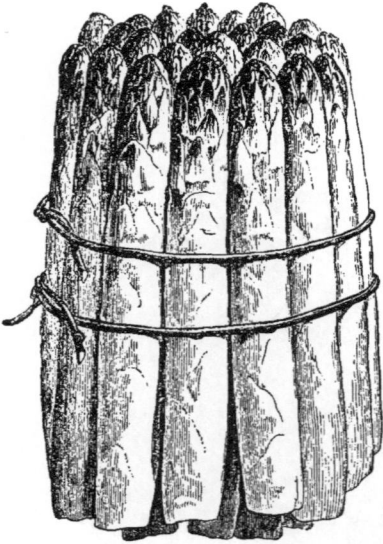

ASPARAGUS is grown much more abundantly and to a much larger size in France than it is in England. The country is half covered with it in some places near Paris; farmers grow it abundantly, cottagers grow it—everybody grows it, and everybody eats it. Near Paris it is chiefly grown for market in the valley of Montmorency and at Argenteuil, and it is cultivated extensively for market in many other places. About Argenteuil 3000 persons are employed in the culture of Asparagus. It is grown to a large extent among the Vines as well as alone. The Vine under field-culture is cut down to near the old stool every year, and allowed to make a few growths, which are tied erect to a stake: they do not overtop the Asparagus, but on the other hand, it, when strong, shows well above the Vines. It is not in distinct lines among the Vines, but in tufts widely and irregularly separated. One plant is put in each open spot, and given every chance of forming a large specimen, and this it generally does. When the stems get large and a little top-heavy in early summer, a string is put round all, so as to hold them slightly together (the careful cultivator uses a stake), and the mutual support thus given prevents the plant from being injured by winds. It is liable to be twisted off at the " collar " by strong winds, especially in wet weather, when the drops on every tiny leaf make the foliage heavy. The growing of Asparagus among the Vines is a very usual mode, and a vast space is thus covered with it about here. It is grown in other and more special ways, though not one like our way of growing it, which is decidedly much inferior to the French methods.

Perhaps the simplest and most worthy of adoption is to grow it in shallow trenches. Extensive plantings look much as a Celery ground does soon after being planted, the young Asparagus plants being in a shallow trench, and a little ridge of soil being thrown up between the lines of Asparagus. These trenches are generally about four feet apart. The soil generally is a rather stiff sandy loam with calcareous matter in some parts, but the soil has not all to do with the peculiar excellence of the vegetable. Soils on which it would flourish equally well are common in England. It is the careful attention to the wants of the plant that produces such a good result. Here, for instance, is a young plantation planted in March, and from the little ridges of soil between the shallow trenches have just been dug a crop of small early Potatoes. In England, the Asparagus would be left to the free action of the breeze, but the French cultivators never leave a young plant of Asparagus to the wind's mercy whilst they can find a stake of oak about a yard long. When staking these young plants they do not insert the support close at the bottom, as we are too apt to do in other instances, but at a little distance off, so as to avoid the possibility of injuring a root ; each stake leans over its plant at an angle of 45°, and when the shoots are big enough to touch it or be caught by the wind, they are tied to the stake. The ground in which this system is pursued being entirely devoted to Asparagus, the stools are placed very much closer together than they are when grown among the Vines, say at a distance of about a yard apart. The little trenches are about a foot wide and eight inches below the level of the ground.

The young plants are placed in these trenches very carefully. A little mound is made with the hand in each spot where a plant is to be placed, so as to elevate the crown a little and permit of the spreading-out of the roots in a perfectly safe manner. The planting-season at Argenteuil lasts from the first week in March to about the 20th of April. The best Asparagus in France is grown here, and by one system mainly. The plants, one-year seedlings (never older), are planted in shallow trenches 7 in. or 8 in. deep, the plants a little more than one yard apart, and the lines 4 ft. apart; no manure is given at planting; no trenching, or any preparation of the ground (beyond digging the shallow trench) takes place   In subsequent years a little manure is given over the roots in autumn ; the soil, thrown out of the trenches and forming a ridge between them, is planted with a light crop in spring. In all subsequent years the earth is placed over the crowns

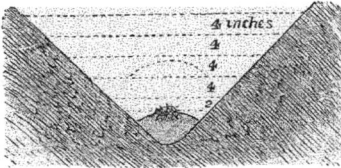

This Figure shows the depth of the successive annual earthings given to the Asparagus. After four or five years' growth the ridges disappear, and the highest points of the ground are those over the crowns of the roots.

in spring and removed in autumn. The culture is for the most part conducted by peasants on their own ground. Under this system good results are obtained in various soils, the only difference being that on cold clay soils the planting is not quite so deep. Every winter the growers notice the state of the young roots, and any spot in which one has perished they mark with a stick, to replace the plant the following March. Early every spring they pile up a little heap of fine earth over each crown. When the plantation arrives at its third year they increase the size of the little mound, or, in other words, a heap of finely-pul-

Planting Asparagus ; Trenches at Planting-time and after a Season's growth.

verized earth is placed over the stool, from which some, but not much, Asparagus is cut the same year, taking care to leave the weak plants, and those which have replaced others, untouched for another year.

The process of gathering is interesting to the stranger. Asparagus-knives of various forms are described in both French

and English books, but one is confidentially told by the growers
that they are only fitted for amateurs who do not care to soil their
fingers. The cultivators here never use a knife. Each crown or
root is covered with a little mound of loose earth; through the
top of this the tips of the strong, thick shoots are seen appearing.
In the light the young shoot first assumes a delicate rose-purple
hue. For gathering it is not enough for the shoot to be visible
on the surface; it must be one inch above it, so as to show the
slightly-rosy tip. Gatherings are made every second day about
the end of April, but in May, when the growth is more active,
the stools are gathered from every day. Given a shoot emerging
from the earth ready to gather: the slightly-hardened crust
around the emerging bud and on top of the little mound is pushed
aside, the fore and middle finger separated are then thrust deeply
into the soft mould, pushing the earth outwards. If a rising
shoot be met with on the way down, it is carefully avoided. A
second plunge of the two fingers and pushing out of the earth
usually brings them to the hardened ground about the crest of the
root; the forefinger is then slipped behind the base of the shoot
fit to gather, and pushed gently outwards, when the shoot at once
snaps clean off at its base. This plan has the advantages of
leaving no mutilated shoots or decaying matter in the ground.

Once gathered, care is taken that the shoot is not exposed to
the light, but placed at once in a covered basket. As soon as the
stalk is gathered, the earth is loosely and gently raked up with
the hand so as to leave the surface of the mound as it was before,
not pressing the earth in any way, but keeping it quite free.
The shoots are not rubbed or cleaned in any way—it would disfigure them, and they do not require it. Asparagus in a green
state is only cut here for soup, etc., and for that only inferior
shoots. We sometimes see observations as to the great superiority
of the green-cut Asparagus over that blanched in the above
manner; but they are invariably written by persons who know
the ordinary green form only, or the withered blanched stalks
eaten long after being gathered. But those who know what good
Asparagus really is—and we speak now of good judges in Covent
Garden as well as in France—know well that in flavour green
and properly-blanched Asparagus are very different things, and
that the blanched is the better and more delicate. Let us on the

question of gathering hear the French side :—" In certain localities they do not yet value the distinction between blanched and green Asparagus, and occasionally prefer the last. That is an error very prejudicial to the consumer's interests. Properly-blanched Asparagus is infinitely more tender and delicate. All Asparagus cut when it is green is not fit to be eaten in the ordinary way, but may be used cut up small as an accompaniment to other dishes. To serve up green Asparagus is to dishonour the table! In the markets of Paris the green Asparagus is worth one franc a bunch, when the blanched is worth three francs; they do not eat it (the green Asparagus)—it serves for the manufacture of syrup of Asparagus.—V. F. Lebeuf " of Argenteuil.

There was originally but one single variety of edible Asparagus (Asparagus officinalis), from which have come the commonly-grown sort and larger variety (A. major) ; the former of which has given birth to the early kinds known as Hâtive rose d'Ulm, de Hollande, et d'Argenteuil, and the latter to the late kinds of the same names. Culture and selection has so great an influence upon vegetation, that it improves the constitution, habit, and even the flavour. It is by dint of observation, care, and patience, that the growers at Argenteuil have been able to improve Asparagus, have created the two varieties " early " and " late," and have settled or established them in a manner to render them superior to the original type in size and quality. The favourite is the Argenteuil Early Asparagus (Hâtive d'Argenteuil), because it gives heavier crops and is ready ten days earlier than the earliest other sorts known. Under good culture the late Argenteuil Asparagus measures from 3 to 6 in. in circumference at 8 in. below the tips; and is better than the early sort where there is not much depth of soil. Although the crops are lighter for the first few years than the early variety, it remains productive much longer, the stems, in some Asparagus-grounds 27 years old, being found to measure from 2½ to 3 in. round. The early Argenteuil Asparagus gives stems of 2¾ to 6 in. round at 8 in. from the tips. It grows higher than the late sort, sometimes attaining a length of 10 ft. It is very vigorous and cares little for richness of soil, which should, however, be at least 10 in. or a foot deep, as the roots rise nearly half an inch every year. It begins to yield in the third year, and gives large crops from its sixth to its fourteenth or fifteenth year, after which the stems, though plentiful, are rather smaller. In good cultivation it lasts from 18 to 20 years. The Dutch Asparagus has stems from 1 to 3½ in. round at 8 in. from the tops, and attains a height of about 4 ft. It is not so fine in any respect as the Argenteuil kinds, and requires a richer and deeper soil, so its culture is generally abandoned. Among its other defects, it grows hard very quickly, opens out at its points, and becomes green in 24 hours. At the Halles at Paris it fetches 10d. per box, while the Argenteuil Asparagus realises 2s. 6d. or 3s. This statement as to the varieties is on the authority of M. Godefroy-Lebeuf, of Argenteuil. It is commonly believed in England that there is no real distinction between the different varieties of Asparagus. In conversation, however, with trust-worthy growers at Argenteuil, and from what I saw there, I think there can be no doubt that there are at least two distinct kinds, an early and a late.

The French mode of cultivating Asparagus differs from our own in giving each plant abundant room to develop into a large healthy specimen ; in paying thoughtful attention to the plants at all times ; and in planting in a trench instead of a raised bed. They do not, as we do, go to great expense in forming a mass of the richest soil far beneath the roots, but rather give it at the surface, and only when the roots have begun to grow strongly.

The following from a French gentleman well acquainted with the culture may be useful here :—

" In February, should the weather be favourable, form the ground into ridges 4 ft. wide and 1 ft. high, and in March or April, according to the weather, make a trench between each ridge a few inches deep, and plant on little hills or elevations 3 ft. apart, cautiously spreading out the roots, and covering them with 1 in. of good compost; then add an inch of fine soil. A stick should be inserted obliquely to protect the roots and to which the small stems can be fastened when they require support. Keep the ground clear of weeds and destroy all slugs, snails, and Asparagus beetles ; the latter lays its eggs on the stems, and when the larvæ are hatched, they destroy the young plants. Water two or three times during the summer with liquid manure if needed. In the autumn, when the stems have withered, cut them down to I in. or 2 in. in height, and remove the soil from the roots, leaving only about 1 in. or so of covering, and put a light layer of old manure or compost from 2 in. to 3 in. in depth over the roots. Thus covered, the roots will never get injured by frost and the ground will be enriched.

" Second Year.—In February or March fork up the bed, making small hillocks 5 in. or 6 in. high over each plant. Make good any plants that may have failed, and cover the whole bed with a layer of rotten manure ; this will keep the soil in good heart and in an equable state as to moisture, therefore no more watering will be required ; destroy weeds and insects, and tie the stems to their sticks in order to prevent the wind shaking the roots.   In autumn cut down the dry stems to a few inches above the ground ; again make up the ridges between the lines, leaving the roots 1 in. or 1½in. deep.

"Third Year.—In February level the ground as in the preceding spring, and remove what was left of the stems ; over each plant put a little hill of soil.   A few heads may this year be cut for use from each plant, but cutting must not be continued later than the 15th of June.   Every year in autumn and in spring the same operations must be gone through as in the preceding season.

"Fourth Year.—The heads may now be cut for use, but be careful to discontinue cutting by June 25 ; after that allow all the stems which appear, to run up.   The roots having now attained full development, must be kept during spring under a hill of soil 10 inches deep.   The cutting-time being over, the bed may be levelled if preferred ; every autumn apply plenty of manure, and every spring mulch between the hills with fresh manure to prevent the soil becoming hard. Salt dissolved in water and applied in spring will be found advantageous.   All seeds should be picked off as early as can be done ; do not let them fall on the ground in autumn, otherwise a quantity of useless young plants will appear to the detriment of the bed.

"The distances at which the plants stand apart may appear too great, but wide planting is the great secret as regards getting fine Asparagus ; besides, the number of heads produced is double, and their size three or four times larger, than they would be in crowded masses, thus showing a large balance in favour of plenty of room.   The celebrated Argenteuil Asparagus, so largely imported to Covent Garden, is grown in a way similar to this.   It is a practice in some provinces in France to plant Asparagus in vineyards between the lines of Vines.   In this case the roots stand at 3 ft., 6 ft., and even 9 ft. apart, and though the ground may not receive any manure for twenty years, the produce is large and the quality excellent.   Planting among Vines is much practised in Burgundy.   Immense quantities of Asparagus have been planted in several parts of France and Germany for market-purposes ; they are for the most part cultivated with the plough, and supplied with chemical manure ; the result is generally good.   In order to insure success, take up the plants from their seed-bed with every possible care ; throw away every one cut or broken, and use only such roots as have a healthy appearance, and strong, well-developed buds ; do not expose them to the air ; on the contrary, put them into a basket in wet Moss immediately they are taken up, and keep them there until they are planted.   " D. Guihéneuf."

The forcing alone of Asparagus throughout the autumn, winter, and early spring, is an industry of considerable extent.   In one of the most recently-organised and active of these gardens about half an acre of glass is devoted solely to the forcing of Asparagus, and a supply is obtained from early in September to the end of

April.   It is forced in three ways— in houses heated with hot
water; in frames sunk in the ground and heated in the same
way ; and lastly, in frames plunged in warm stable-manure.   It
appeared to be forced with equal success in each case, though the
stable-manure seemed to offer the simplest means.   As usual here
the frames are small—about 4 ft. wide ; the roots are placed
directly on the manure, not flat as they would be in the open

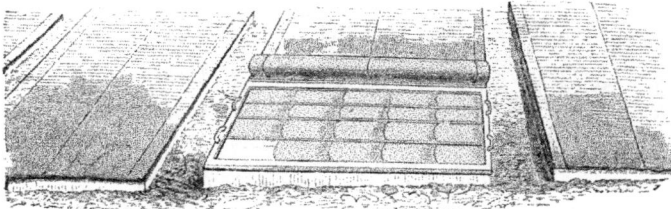

Frames used for Forcing Asparagus.

ground, but packed as closely as possible, from 500 to 2000 roots
—according to size—going under one light ; a mere sprinkling
of soil is placed over them.   As a result, the shoots come up very
thickly.   The roots employed are strong fine ones three years from
the seed ; as many as five crops of roots follow each other throughout the autumn, winter, and spring in the same frame.   The
universal straw mat is used to cover the frames at night.   A

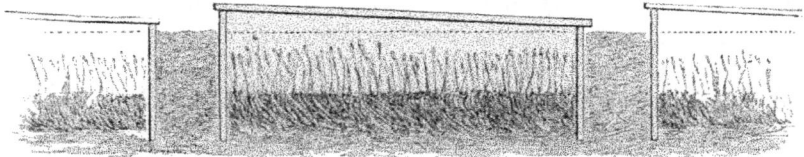

Section of Frames for Forcing Asparagus

dozen persons were employed solely in gathering and " bundling "
the Asparagus for market, so that the quantities gathered for
use are very considerable.   All is done in the simplest and
rudest manner, the securing of good crops being the only thing
considered.

The old mode of forcing Asparagus, still practised to some
extent, chiefly consists in digging deep trenches between beds
planted for the purpose, covering the beds with the soil and with

frames, filling in the trenches between the beds with stable-manure, and protecting the frames with straw mats and litter to keep in the heat.   In the beginning of November the pathways between the beds of Asparagus are dug up about two feet in depth and width.   The soil coming from the pathway is divided very carefully, and put about eight inches thick on the surface of the bed.   The trench is filled up with new stable-manure, not litter, and frames placed on the bed.   The manure should rise as high as the top of the frames, and the lights be entirely covered with mats and litter to prevent the heat accumulated in the frame from escaping.   In about a fortnight or three

Preparation for Forcing Asparagus.   The trenches are dug out and filled with stable-manure, the earth being heaped on the beds.   These are covered with rough frames, up to the edge of which the heating-material is piled.

weeks, the Asparagus begins to show itself on the surface of the bed.   Many market-gardeners cover the whole of the bed inside the frame to a thickness of three or four inches with manure to force the vegetation more quickly, but in this case the manure must be removed when the Asparagus begins to shoot.   When the shoots are about three inches out of the ground they may be cut.   The mats must be taken off in the daytime, but the heat must be well kept up or the roots and buds will fail to push.   The beds are forced every second year only.   The gathering of the Asparagus may continue for about two months, but no longer, or the plantation would be injured.   When the gathering is over, the frames and linings are taken away, and the soil which has been dug up from the alleys is put back again.

The preceding note applies to the forcing of the better qualities of Asparagus chiefly.   There is a garden at Clichy in which quite a speciality is made of forcing the smaller-sized Asparagus for soups, stews, etc.   It contains a number of iron houses, on the same plan as those in the Jardin Fleuriste, already described. There are frames within each house, just as in propagating-houses, and beneath them the Asparagus is forced for the markets, in large quantities.   The houses are heated with hot water, and the culture in other respects resembles that practised in forcing-gardens in England—that is, when the plants are taken up to be forced indoors or in pits. The very large table Asparagus is never forced.

Where so much Asparagus is grown both for home consumption and exportation, the need for effective bunching-implements has led to various improvements in these, some of which are figured here—after the ' Revue Horticole.'

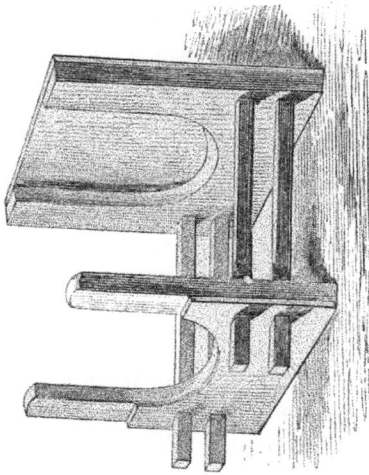

Asparagus Buncher most commonly used in France. The front piece slides backwards or forwards to suit the length required.

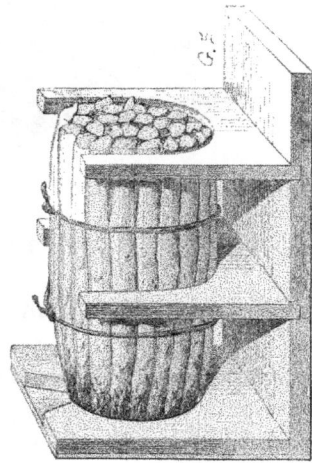

Sartrouville Buncher (filled). None of the parts are moveable. The tips of the Asparagus are kept close together by being dropped through the wedge-shaped opening at the back.

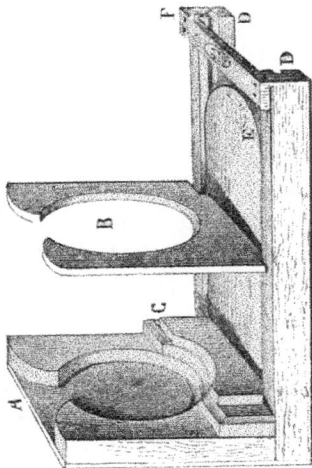

Argenteuil Asparagus Buncher (closed).

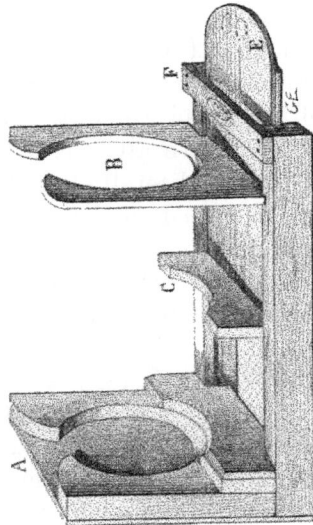

Argenteuil Buncher (open). DD are grooves in which slides the board E on which are fixed R and C; the cross-piece F is added to increase durability. The circles marked near E indicate that there are two cavities underneath to facilitate the sliding of E.

CHAPTER XXVIII.

SALADS IN PARIS.

THE market-gardens immediately round Paris are, in spring, for the most part covered with glass—large clear bell-glasses, about 18 inches high, and small shallow frames. In each large glass a huge Cos Lettuce rises nearly to the top, while at its feet—pigmies round a giant—there is a ring of those dwarf tender Lettuces so much sought after in winter and early spring. The icy breath of the north is probably blowing over the garden; but the plants are well screened from it, sitting in the sun within their glass homes. We have all laughed at Sydney Smith's " bottled sun-beams ;" but we literally have them here. Sometimes these glasses are thickly placed on shallow hot-beds, when used for winter and early-spring crops ; sometimes on slightly-sloping beds of rich light soil. The bell-glasses are used, for the most part, for the production of Cos Lettuces; the shallow frames for the Noire Lettuce, so much in demand in winter. The culture of Salads in the suburbs of Paris for the supply of its markets and the markets of many other cities, is one of the most interesting examples of successful cultivation it would be possible to name. The sugges-tion that climate is the cause of the superiority of the French in this respect, will no doubt occur to some. It is not so, however. By the adoption of the methods to be presently described, as good salad as ever went to the Paris markets may be grown in England and Ireland during the coldest months of winter and spring. The winters in Northern France are severer than our own, and there are many spots in England and Ireland which are preferable to the neighbourhood of Paris for this culture. Near that city may often be seen Cos and Cabbage Lettuces looking as fresh under their coverings in the middle of winter, when the earth is frostbound, as Lilac-buds in May: had they been treated as ours usually are, they would have presented a very different appearance. As ordinary cultivation suffices to grow them with us in summer, and as

Cloches over Lettuce in Spring.

in winter and early spring our tables are supplied from France, it is only as regards these supplies that we want improvement.

The first and chief thing towards it is to procure some of the large bell-glasses or cloches used for this purpose. They are cheap, require no repairs, and are easily cleaned and stored when not required. The troublesome task of giving air is done away with in their case. Without air on "every possible occasion" the British gardener attempts nothing under glass. By adopting this simple protector, he may forego that ceaseless trouble in Lettuce-growing throughout the winter and early spring. In the hotter weeks of autumn, these glasses are tilted up on one side for an inch or so, with a bit of stone placed underneath; but when once winter comes they are placed down quite close, and are all through the winter in the same condition as Wardian cases. By the way, the French recognised this principle of the Wardian case long before we did, and what is more, have made a far more practical use of it. For all sorts of winter Salad-growing this huge bell-glass is infinitely superior to anything that we use for like purposes. The plants get full light at all times, and are not in the least "drawn" or injured by the confinement, the light

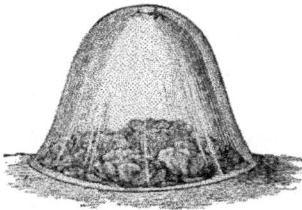

Plants of the Lettuce Petite Noire under the Cloche in October.

coming in so freely at all points.   The glasses are nearly sixteen
inches in diameter, and about as much in height.   For the winter-
work they are sometimes placed on sloping beds with a sunny
aspect ; the beds being wide enough to accommodate three or
four lines of glasses.   In early autumn these beds are made and
the plants placed upon them, so that they can be readily covered
by the bell-glasses when the time comes at which growth is
checked in the open air.   It should be added that the ground
chosen is very rich and light, and the Lettuces are sown at
intervals of a fortnight or so, to secure a succession.   The plants
put out in September for the early and mid-autumn supply may
not require to be covered if the weather be fine ; and if they
should happen to require it, the glasses are tilted up a little as
before described.   But when the sun begins to fail and the cold
rains to check growth, about the end of October, then the crop to
be cut in the following month must be covered ; and when towards
Christmas the frost begins to enter the ground, the glasses must
be firmly pressed down, and a deposit of leaves and litter placed
around and between them.

Thus, while everything else is at rest in the grip of ice, the
plants will be kept perfectly free from frost, receiving abundant
light from above, and growing as fresh as early summer leaves.
A deeper layer of the surrounding litter will be necessary in case
of severe frost.   Covering the glasses a little more than half-way
up with a rather compact body of leaves and litter, effectually
secures the contents from sharp frosts.   When very severe winters
occur, mats made of straw are spread over the tops of the glasses ;
and should heavy falls of snow occur while these mats are on,
they will enable the cultivator to carry it away bodily ; it should
on no account be allowed to melt on the beds or in the alleys
between.   In late spring the cloche is not required, nor is it used
for any except those crops that require artificial assistance.   Thus
the March and April supply is planted in October on a bed of
light soil, with a surfacing of an inch or so of thoroughly-rotten
manure or leaf-mould.   These little plants are allowed to remain
all through the winter unprotected ; and when in spring the most
forward Cloche Lettuces are cut, the glasses are immediately
placed over the most advanced of the little ones that have remained
exposed.   By that time they have begun to start up, encouraged

by the early spring sun, and from the moment they receive the additional warmth and steady temperature of the cloche they commence to unfold their fresh and juicy leaves, and finish by becoming great-hearted and tender products. In the first instance three or five little plants may be put under each glass, and these thinned out and used as they grow, so that eventually only one is left, which often grows almost too big for the glass. No water is required, as the ground possesses sufficient moisture in winter and spring, and evaporation is prevented by the glasses and the protecting litter that covers the little spaces between them. Thus a suitable moisture is kept up at all times, and the conditions that best suit Lettuces are preserved by the simplest means.

With the same glasses the various small saladings may be grown to perfection. Thus, for instance, if Corn Salad be desired perfectly clean and fresh in mid-winter, it may be obtained by sowing it between the smaller Lettuces grown under these glasses; and so with any other small salad or seedlings that may be gathered before the more important crop requires all the room. These bell-glasses will be found of quite as much advantage in the British garden as they are in France; they will render possible the production of as fine winter salads in our gardens as ever the French grew; they will enable us to supply our own markets with a commodity for which a good deal of money now leaves the country; hence their adoption is important for all who care for delicate winter salads. At present the home-grown produce is so inferior at that season, that it is generally avoided, and rightly so; for Lettuces when hard and wiry from alternations of frost, sleet, and rains—slug-eaten and half-covered with the splashings of the ground, above which they hardly rise—are not worth gathering. And though they may be grown well in frames and pits, the method herein described is, when properly carried out, better and simpler than that. To understand the cloche and its use will not suffice; it is well to observe the culture of the varieties suited for each season.

Culture of the Lettuce Petite Noire.—This kind is grown to an enormous extent; these are the Lettuces sent from Paris to Covent Garden throughout the autumn and winter. Few, however, sow it before the first days of September. It is sown on light, rich ground, well and deeply stirred, and covered with an inch, or a little more, of thoroughly-decomposed fine stable-manure. The surface is made level and somewhat firm, and the impressions of the number of cloches it is intended to use made upon it. One cloche will prove sufficient for a private garden at one sowing; a few suffice for the wants of a market-garden. The Lettuce-seed is then regularly sown within the ring formed by the impression of the large bell-glass, and covered with a very slight coat of fine rich soil. Then the cloche is put on, the rim being gently pressed into the light rotten mould. Shade is given when the sun shines strongly in early autumn, but air is never given. A peculiarity of this excellent Lettuce is that it grows best without air.

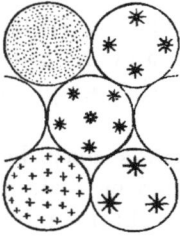

As soon as the seedlings are strong enough to transplant, they are pricked out, about thirty under each cloche. This transplantation is done at a much earlier stage than is the case with us. The plants are not allowed to get crowded, but are taken up gently and without disturbing the roots; soon after the cotyledons are developed and when the first leaves are beginning to appear. In transplanting, a surfacing of very fine and thoroughly-rotten manure is placed over the earth to the depth of an inch, and the earth is often thrown into beds sloping to the south, so that the cloches may enjoy the full sun. Whether the beds are flat or sloping, they are wide enough for three ranges of cloches placed in an alternate manner, so that very little space is lost between them. Before transplanting, the ground is marked by the impression of a cloche, and the little seedlings are inserted by the finger in the soft mould. Instead of getting drawn, as would be the case if they were left together for a longer period, the plants spread out into neat firm little rosettes, their leaves lying close to the ground, for the light comes freely through the clear cloche, and there is not a sign of ill-health or speck of dust to be seen on the leaves. The strongest batch of those that in September were in the rosette stage, under the cloches, are transplanted into their

Diagram showing the several stages of Lettuce-culture under the Cloche. The minute dots represent the seedlings, which are pricked off when very small, as shown in the circle with twenty-four asterisks. The central ring is the plan of a Cloche with one Paris Cos Lettuce in the middle, and five Cabbage Lettuces around it; above it, one with four plants of a Winter Cabbage Lettuce; and beneath it, one with three plants of the Cos.

final places before the 15th of October, planting four under each cloche. They supply a great want, coming in in perfect condition towards the middle of winter.

Sometimes the crop is planted out in the narrow frames common to Paris market-gardens, turning over the old beds before planting. The frames being shallow the plants are near the glass, and as soon as planted the lights are put on, but, instead of giving air by the aid of these lights, the greatest care is taken to keep it out. No matter whether under cloche or frame, the Petite Noire must never get any air. Should severe frost occur, the glasses may be protected with straw mats. It must be observed that when the plants are transferred into the places where they are to attain their fullest size they are removed with good balls, and with some care to check their growth as little as possible. The plants pricked out in October are ready to cut at the end of November or beginning of December, when this Lettuce begins to come into general use. In addition to the crop put out during the first half of November, another is sown at that season, in the way before described. Should very severe weather render the Lettuces liable to suffer, dry litter is placed between the cloches, and higher up at their north side, so as to prevent the frost from entering the ground, and the contents of the cloches are daily exposed to the light and sun, except when they are frozen, when the covering is kept on or increased. The forced culture in the small narrow frames usually begins about the end of November. At that period a hotbed is prepared, sixteen inches thick, and about 55° F. in temperature, spreading on it some of the never-failing, thoroughly-rotten manure, and on it are planted seven lines of Petite Noire. This plantation requires greater care than those placed under the cloche, in consequence of the warmth and humidity; decaying or spotted leaves have to be picked off when they occur, and the plants must be protected with the mats more than those not excited by heat. The frames are surrounded by fermenting manure, which also fills up the alleys between the little frames to the upper edge of each.

At the end of January or beginning of February the last forced crop of Petite Noire is planted, under cloches placed on a gentle hotbed a foot deep, and covered with about four inches of the same mould-like manure, the bell-glasses as usual being placed

in three ranks.   The bed for them may be made wide enough for
six (three lines on each side of a narrow alley), or for three only.
In this January or February planting, four plants of Petite Noire
are planted under each cloche, and one Cos in the middle.   The
tender Petites Noires are gathered in February and March; the
Cos remains a little later, nearly filling up the glass and forming
one of those superb Lettuces to be seen in all our great towns
in early spring, and which are usually supposed to come from
some paradisaical climate, instead of the ungenial winter-climate
of Paris.   Certainly the climate that would produce them without
protection at the period spoken of should be mild indeed.

LETTUCE VERTE MARAÎCHÈRE.—This Lettuce is sown about the
first fortnight in October in the open air, or on a sloping bed under
a cloche.   It is pricked out, and twenty or thirty are generally
placed under one glass, which is taken off every time the weather
permits.   As it often happens that, in spite of the care taken
with it, this Lettuce will grow too tall, it is generally taken up,
and transplanted some time in November.   For this purpose a
new sloping bed is prepared and the plants are pricked into it
immediately, only eighteen or twenty being put under each glass.
From this moment they receive the same care as the other
Lettuces sown at the same time.   Towards the end of December
or the beginning of January planting in frames and under cloches
is begun.   In each frame eight rows are placed, each consisting
of twenty-five plants, so arranged that there is a Petite Noire
and a Cos Lettuce alternately.   Under the cloches they are
arranged so that there are four of the former to one of the latter.
The Cos Lettuces thus grown may be gathered at the beginning
of February, after which the beds are planted a second time,
towards the end of February or the beginning of March ; that is
to say, when the severe cold is no longer to be dreaded, a single
plant is pricked out in the little spaces between the cloches.   As
soon as the Cos and the Petite Noire Lettuces planted beneath the
bell-glass are gathered, the glass is used for the second crop.   By
this method the crop may be gathered about three weeks after.
At the same time warm borders on the south side of walls are
also planted with Cos Lettuces.   Ten or twelve rows are drawn,
according to the size of the border, and planted with Cos Lettuces
about twelve or fourteen inches apart.   After this crop has been

Lettuce—Grosse Brune Paresseuse (Summer).

Lettuce—Crêpe (Spring).

Palatine (Autumn).

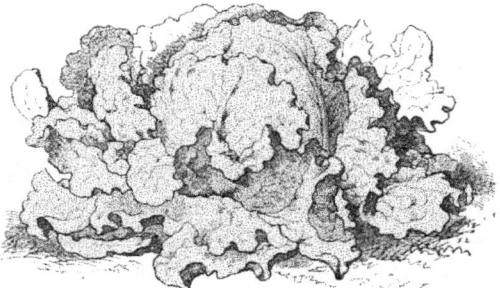

Lettuce—Batavia blonde (Summer).

Lettuce—Romaine verte d'hiver.

Lettuce—Romaine blonde maraîchère.

Some Lettuces of the Paris Market (Vilmorin).

2 K

planted out, a few Radishes, Leeks, or Carrots are sown between
the Lettuces.   Generally speaking, these Cos Lettuces are fit to
gather towards the end of April or the beginning of May.   Some
market-gardeners also sow Cos during the month of August,
which, planted out in hotbeds under bell-glasses, are generally fit
for gathering in December and January.

GOTTE LETTUCE.—This Lettuce cannot be raised in the same
way as the Petite Noire, because it will not come to perfection
without plenty of air.   It is not so early as the Petite Noire, but
is much esteemed, growing larger and more perfect than that
variety.   The Gotte Lettuce is sown from the 20th to the 25th
of October on a sloping bed, and the
same method of after-treatment is adopted
as in forcing the Petite Noire, although
it is less damaged by frost.   Being a later
kind, it may be left in the bed until the
Petite Noire is all gathered, when it may
be used to fill the vacant places in the hotbeds.   The manure of
the hotbeds should be left undisturbed, but the soil in the frames
should be well forked and made even.   Towards the end of
January or beginning of February the Gotte should be planted in
the frames.   It should have plenty of air, whenever the weather
will allow it, by propping up the back of the light.   If the
Lettuce does not heart early when protected, the light should be
removed as soon as the fine weather makes its appearance, so as to
allow it to come to perfection in the open air.   Instead of planting
the Gotte Lettuce in a frame, it may be planted on a hotbed under
cloches arranged in three rows, three plants being placed under
each, taking care to preserve them from frost in the usual way,
and to give them air whenever the weather will permit.   It may
also be planted in the open ground under a cloche.   The earth is
well dug and raked, and an inch and a half of well-decomposed
stable-manure thrown over it, smoothed and flattened.   The
cloches are then placed in alternate lines, with three plants under
each.   When the plants have struck, air should be given them
whenever possible.   This variety when planted in frames at the
end of January, arrives at perfection by the end of March ; when
planted under cloches in February, at the beginning of April ;

Lettuce Gotte.

and when planted under cloches or in frames at the end of February, towards the middle of April.

The Passion Lettuce—Laitue de la Passion, as it is called—is the only Winter Lettuce grown in the neighbourhood of Paris in the open air. It is sown from the 15th of August to the 15th of September, according to the soil which is to receive it, and is pricked out rather thinly in October. It is generally left unprotected through the winter; however, it is prudent to defend it against severe frosts by covering it with long litter, which is taken off and put on again as often as necessary. This Lettuce is generally fit for gathering towards Passion Week, from which circumstance it derives its name. As regards the best varieties of Lettuce of the Paris gardens for the different seasons, I am indebted for the following note to M. Henri Vilmorin of Paris. "Forcing kinds: Crêpe à Graine Noire (Petite Noire) and Gotte; for spring use, Gotte à Bord Rouge and Blonde d'Été; for summer use, Blonde de Versailles and Batavia Blonde; for autumn, Palatine; for winter and early spring, Passion and Morine; and for all the year round, White Paris Cos.

The Barbe de Capucin is the most common of all salads in Paris

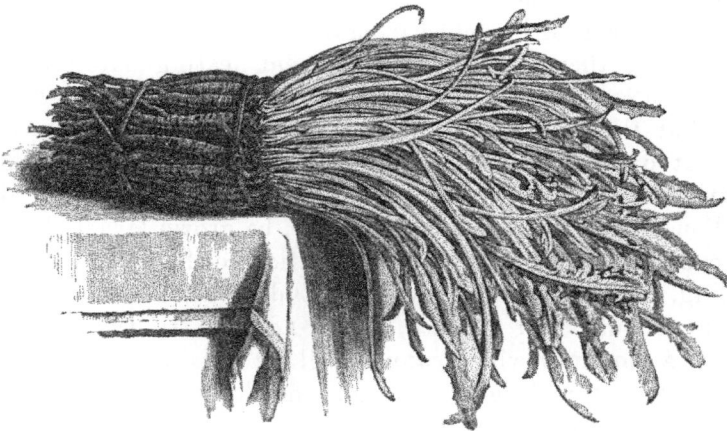

Barbe de Capucin.

in the winter and early spring. It is perhaps too bitter for some tastes, but is well worthy of culture in small gardens, being so very easily forced when other salads are scarce.. This salad may be had with the least amount of trouble in a cellar, or any dark place where a little heat might be used to start the blanched leaves in winter.   Should the taste be too bitter to those unaccustomed to it, or who do not like bitter salads, the addition of Corn Salad, Celery, or Beetroot, improves and modifies the flavour, and makes it a very distinct and agreeable salad.   The gardeners of the commune of Montreuil sow every year in spring a large quantity of common Chicory for the purpose of forcing the Barbe de Capucin.   In autumn the roots are taken up with the fork, care being taken not to break them.   They are then laid by the heels so as to have them always ready for use; and in October, the season when such work is usually commenced, a hot-bed about sixteen inches deep is prepared, the heat of which is from 65° to 80° Fahr.   The most favourable position for such a hotbed is in a cave or in a deep cellar without light or air.   When the heat of the bed has somewhat abated, the plants are tied up in bundles after carefully removing all the dead leaves and other portions liable to produce mouldiness, after which they are placed upright on the bed and watered.   From the time the Barbe begins to grow, these waterings must be given with judgment, so as to prevent the interior of the bundles from rotting.   At the end of fifteen or eighteen days, the salad is long enough to be gathered. The Chicory can be blanched from autumn up to March and April; after every gathering, however, the spent heating-material should be removed, and replaced by a fresh supply, so as always to keep the bed at the same degree of warmth.   Chicory possesses many excellent qualities, which should recommend it to more general attention than it now enjoys.   It is of easy culture, is not at all fastidious as to soil, and may, therefore, be grown largely by those who cannot devote much time or attention to the culture of choice salading.   Even where Lettuces and Endive are extensively grown, Chicory should find a place, as its addition to the salad-bowl imparts a piquancy which cannot well be obtained by any other ingredient.   It is largely used and much esteemed as a winter salad in many parts of France, and, in common with the Dandelion, it there enjoys the reputation of possessing peculiar blood-purifying principles.

SCAROLE (Broad-leaved Batavian Endive).—This fine salad occupies a considerable space in the culture of the Paris market-gardens.   It ought to be more generally grown in England, being easy of cultivation, very large, and forming an excellent salad; indeed, it is on the whole perhaps the best we have. The mode of blanching is very simple : the leaves of the plant are gathered up, and a single straw tied around them. This is only done five days before the Scarole is ready for market. A crop of this nearly ready to blanch in September, was the second crop of the same plant that had been on the ground—the first and best having been gathered a few weeks before. Some of the finer specimens of this second unblanched crop measured twenty and twenty-one inches in diameter on the 7th of September.

CORN SALAD OR MÀCHE.—This plant is very much used in Paris, and is excellent as a salad. It is peculiarly agreeable when mixed with a sprinkling of Celery. The culture is of the simplest kind, the seeds being often sown amongst other crops. The Ronde variety is sown about the 15th of August, and at intervals till the end of October. That sown in August comes in for the autumn consumption; that sown in September for winter use; and that sown in October is used in spring. During hard frost the crops to be gathered during winter are covered with long litter. Màche Régence is sown in October, and is sown more thinly than the preceding; it is considered the best variety. It may also be raised in the spare places between the plants, under cloches, in any open surface between plants in frames, or any cool light garden-structure.

CHAPTER XXIX.

Some Vegetables of the Paris Market.

A visit to the markets of Paris is sufficient to interest many in the vegetable culture of that capital. There is so much difference in the supplies to that market and the London one that there is much to be learnt on both sides. That so great a difference should exist in the market-produce of cities so near each other is remarkable. The Parisians make as much use of the Seakale or Rhubarb as we in England do of the Breadfruit-tree; and one who leaves London in a hot and dry July, having failed to get a salad at dinner, arrives in Paris next morning, and finds the markets full of every variety of salading as tender as if the climate were a perpetual May. Although abundant intercourse has long existed between the two countries, yet from the fact that the visitors are rarely men capable of appreciating differences and their value and causes, and the difficulty of getting information about the subjects, noticeable improvements have not been exchanged from side to side.

The Carrots of the Paris Market.—Every visitor to the Halles of Paris or the streets near them during the earlier hours of the day, must have noticed vast quantities of dwarf, tender little Carrots. These indeed, sent from Paris, are seen in many other cities. They are always fresh, always to be had, and contain none of the tissue which makes the coarser Carrots so much less valuable. Even when we do grow the best varieties of dwarf Carrots in this country, they never present the cleanly appearance of those of the Paris market-gardens, nor are they so tender and good. The French, who are difficult to please in respect to this vegetable, never make use of field varieties for cooking, except in cases of necessity. In France, also, where its cultivation is most extensive and the best carried out, all the known varieties are more or less made use of according to their value; but the choice small kinds are grown everywhere, even by the poorest people. The varieties grown in this country are not so numerous, are inferior in quality, and badly grown, compared with French kinds. In gardens this is most observable, and the consequence is the London markets are stocked chiefly with the Surrey Carrot, a tough variety, without flavour, and with a heart like a walking-stick. It is, moreover, difficult to cultivate, on account of the deep soil it requires; while, on the other hand, the finer cooking varieties accommodate themselves thoroughly to soils of medium depth.

French Forcing Carrot (Carotte très-courte à châssis).—This variety is the smallest and earliest Carrot, chiefly used for

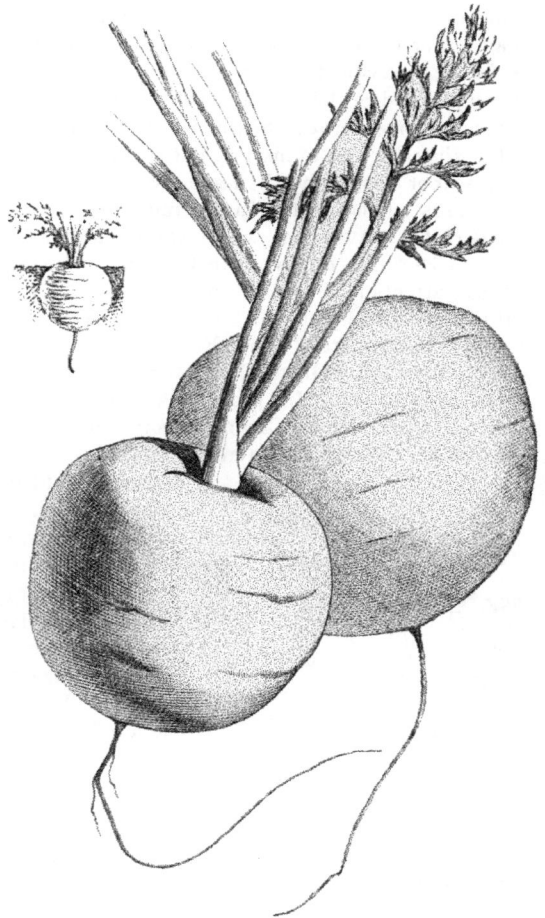

Early French Forcing Carrot of the Paris Market.

forcing. It is a great favourite among the Parisian market-gardeners on account of its extreme earliness. The root is from $1\frac{1}{2}$ to 2 inches in size, nearly round, and terminates in a very fine tape-like fibre. It is pale straw-coloured when grown under glass during the winter, but scarlet when raised in open ground. The flesh is very tender and finely flavoured; and it has scarcely any fibry " heart " in the centre.

The top is greenish and hollow-crowned; the leaves few and small. This affords a fair supply of fresh Carrots all the year round. Recently, bunches of this variety have made their appearance in Covent Garden Market, but the freshness of such tender roots is spoiled by their journey from Paris to London. The preceding cut shows the true shape and natural size; but inferior stocks, producing conical roots neither so succulent nor so early, are often met with. This valuable Carrot ought to be used only for forcing. Sowings should be made on hotbeds having a medium temperature, from November to February, for use from February until May. For early crops sown in warm borders, the Scarlet Horn will be found to be far better adapted. Market-gardeners sow the Early French Forcing Carrot in August and September, and after protecting it in winter, sell it in the spring for newly-forced Carrots, to which they bear some similarity after a sharp brushing before they are sent to market, but the difference may be easily detected by their deep scarlet colour, and the leaves being cut off the roots. In addition to this, the skin is rough and the flavour much inferior, whilst newly-forced Carrots are smaller, of a straw colour, with a shining skin, and are always tied up in bunches by their long thin leaves; both kinds may sometimes be seen at Covent Garden. Special attention should be paid to this variety, which really deserves general cultivation. The following are its synonyms—French Forcing Carrot, French Forcing Horn Carrot, Very Early Forcing Carrot, Very Early Scarlet Horn Carrot, Very Early Short Horn Carrot, Early Forcing Horn Carrot, Very Early French Carrot, etc. In France its synonyms are Carotte grelot, Carotte très-courte à forcer, Carotte Carline, Carotte toupie, Carotte à châssis.

SCARLET HORN (Carotte rouge courte).—A popular early variety, the most generally cultivated for the first crop in the open ground. The root is deep scarlet, 2½ to 3 inches long, and 1 to 1½ inches thick. It is nearly cylindrical, slightly tapering, and terminates abruptly. The flesh is very tender, and highly flavoured. The top is greenish, and hollow-crowned; and the leaves of a medium size. It can be used for forcing exactly like the preceding kind, but being of a larger size it is not quite so early, therefore the best time for sowing is in February, on a warm exposed border; and, if well protected, in case of severe weather, a fair crop of new Carrots may be expected by the beginning of May. Sowings made subsequently from March to May will afford a fair supply during the whole summer where large roots are objected to. On account of its small size it is not suitable for winter storing. This kind is often mistaken or sold for the French Forcing Carrot, although the two plants differ much, both in size and earliness. The following are its synonyms:—Early Horn Carrot, Early Scarlet Horn Carrot, English Horn Carrot, Dutch Horn Carrot, Carotte rouge courte hâtive, Carotte rouge courte d'Hollande, etc.

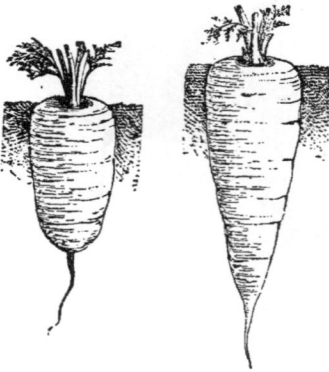

INTERMEDIATE SCARLET (Carotte rouge demi-longue pointue).—This is the

Scarlet Horn.   *Intermediate Scarlet.*

best variety for general use; it has beautiful scarlet roots, 5 inches long and from 2 to 2½ inches thick, tapering and sharp-pointed. The flesh is highly flavoured and of the best quality. The top is greenish, hollow-crowned, with a few vigorous medium-sized leaves. This excellent kind ought to be grown for the main crop in every garden, as it is very hardy and gives large crops. It is the best and the most useful kind for winter storing; it grows in almost every kind of soil, and, provided the plants are kept sufficient distance apart, it will resist drought better than any other garden kind, besides losing little or nothing of its valuable properties. Sown from March until June, in rows from 9 to 12 inches distant, the plants are thinned as soon as possible, and kept from 4 to 5 inches apart, according to the quality of the soil, as soon as they attain the size of a pencil. Hoeing and watering, in case of extreme dryness, will aid development and ensure a good crop of excellent Carrots. It is known under a great many names, according to the country in which it is grown; and, on account of its productive qualities, it has been cultivated sometimes in the field, yielding as much as 14 to 15 tons to the acre.

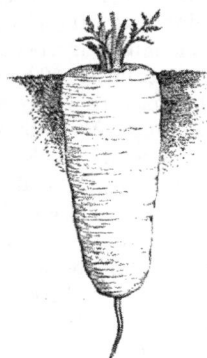

INTERMEDIATE SCARLET STUMP-ROOTED (Carotte rouge demi-longue obtuse).—This is a French variety, similar to the last described in its quality and uses. The root is deep scarlet, from 4 to 4½ inches long, from 1½ to 2 inches thick, and almost cylindrical in shape. The root is stumpy, the top greenish in colour and hollow-crowned. It is an improvement on the preceding kind, which it has supplanted in many gardens, though less hardy and occasionally more affected by drought. It is a valuable variety for autumn and winter storing.

Intermediate Scarlet Stump-rooted.

It has enjoyed a popularity in France extending over thirty years, and is now much used in America, Germany, and Belgium; but its introduction into English gardens has been very gradual and partial. It requires the same culture as the Intermediate Scarlet Carrot, and is an exceedingly valuable kind that should, if possible, be always found in the list of winter-vegetables.

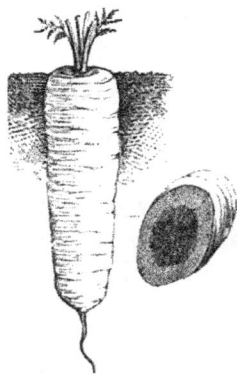

INTERMEDIATE NANTES SCARLET (Carotte rouge demi-longue Nantaise).—This is of recent French introduction, having a close analogy to the two preceding varieties. The root is a deep red in colour, 4½ inches long, from 1½ to 2 inches thick, and bluntly-cylindrical in form; the top is greenish in colour, with a hollow crown. The leaves are of medium size; the flesh is very superior in flavour and quality, the heart being less developed and more tender than in other varieties, and both for sauces and stews it is a most desirable kind. It is a valuable

Intermediate Nantes Scarlet.

acquisition to the kitchen-garden. Although it is an earlier variety than the two preceding ones, it is not sufficiently so for forcing. Sown from March to June, it will produce an excellent crop in the autumn and throughout the winter. On account of the delicacy of this Carrot, considerable attention and care must be devoted to it during growth, which however will be amply repaid by the results. It is sometimes called " Carotte sans cœur."

Forcing Carrots.—The French Forcing and the Scarlet Horn Carrots are the best for this purpose, but the first is to be preferred. The forcing is thus conducted:—Prepare mild hotbeds 2½ feet thick in November or December, and 1½ or 2 feet in January or February; put on the frames, cover the bed with 5 or 6 inches of rich soil or mould, and as soon as the whole is sufficiently heated, sow the seed broadcast, cover with half-an-inch of mould, smooth the surface, and place mats over the glass until the seed comes up. Should the interior get dry, give a slight watering, but damp must be guarded against. The plants must be thinned to half-an-inch apart as soon as they have four or five leaves. Air must be admitted as often as the temperature will allow of it; this will give strength to the seedlings. The heat must not exceed 60° during the day and 50° at night; this may be easily regulated by tilting the glass. In the case of sharp frost, covering with mats is preferable to artificial heat. Shading, if needed, must not be omitted. A November sowing, if well managed, will produce fine young Carrots at the end of February, and through March and April. Subsequent sowings—in December for March to April, in January for April to May, and, lastly, in February for April to June—are required by market-gardeners; but, in private gardens, the first bed should be made in November and the second in January; these will afford an ample supply until new open-ground Carrots are fit for use. Where frames are not available, prepare at the beginning of February, in some warm corner, a bed of hot material mixed with leaves, covered with 4 or 5 inches of mould; sow the seed and protect with mats supported with sticks or other apparatus. As soon as the seed comes up remove the covering every day as frequently as the weather will permit, and the crop will be ready by the end of April and through May. Parisian market-gardeners mix seeds of Radish and Lettuce with those of Carrots, they being ready for use before the Carrots, which are then left to produce a second crop; a practice not advisable, nor is that of planting Cauliflowers among forced Carrots.

D. Guihéneuf.

Culture in the Open-air.—The first sowings are made in the open-air in the month of September. During frost care is taken to cover the young crop with straw, which is removed whenever the weather is fine enough. When this sowing is successful the crop may be gathered towards the month of May. Other sowings are made in February and March, from which time they may be continued regularly until July. But at whatever time the sowing takes place, the ground ought to be well prepared, and the seed sown broadcast. After the seed is sown the ground is slightly covered, then trodden down with the feet, and a layer of fine and thoroughly-rotted manure spread over the whole; the

ground is then raked lightly, and watered whenever it is necessary. As soon as the young plants make their appearance, the
crop is carefully thinned out. Three months after the sowing,
the more forward Carrots may be gathered, the results of the
later sowings being left until November.

Mr. Cornhill writes to the 'Garden': "I should like to see the
French Early Horn Carrot more extensively grown than it appears
to be. I would especially recommend a trial of it to the owners
of small gardens. I venture to assert that those who have
habituated themselves to a supply of this root during the spring
and summer months will not easily make up their minds to forego
the luxury. In all French kitchens this little Carrot is almost
indispensable, and this is not to be wondered at, for both its
appearance and flavour are good. The first crop, where it is
possible, should be sown on a moderate hotbed in January, taking
care that the soil employed is tolerably rich and well sweetened—
the best material I have found for this purpose is the clearings of
old hotbeds which have been turned over and over for several
years, and have become reduced to the consistency of mould.
Where a supply of this does not exist, any kind of free well-worked
soil may be taken. When the seed is up, thin out to about four
inches, and care must afterwards be taken to admit plenty of air
on all favourable occasions, so as to prevent drawing and to cover
up in cold weather. The first sowing in the open ground should
be made about the middle of February, choosing a well-sheltered
and rather dry spot. Thoroughly break and pulverise the soil,
which should be fairly rich; it is well to fork-in a good dressing
of soot and lime, which give substance to the tops and will free
them in a great measure from the ravages of grubs. The seed
may either be sown in a four-feet bed or in drills; if the latter
be preferred they should be drawn with a good broad hoe, making
them as wide as possible. It is advisable to sow the seed moderately thick to ensure a plant, thinning very early. By leaving
them thus they may be drawn as soon as the flavour is well
defined. By thinning out methodically and regularly over the
whole bed in this manner, a small piece of ground will yield a
continuous supply; in fact, it is surprising what a quantity can
be grown on the space; by leaving them rather thick they can be
pulled early, which forwards the season, and as the crop advances

in size, so, from the constant thinning, they acquire the room necessary to their development. It is, however, preferable not to depend upon one crop, and successional sowings should be made in the beginning and latter end of March, and again in April."

Turnip-rooted Celery.

The root, which is the only valuable portion of this Celery, is a stout tuber, irregularly rounded, frequently exceeding the size of one's fist. This Celery is sown in the neighbourhood of Paris in February, on a hotbed; but in the open-air, during the second fortnight in April, or even later. The plants are pricked out in nursery rows, and are transferred to their permanent quarters during the second fortnight in June. The roots are fit for use in September, October, and November, according to the progress they have made. Cultivators are in the habit of cutting off several of the large leaves of the plant, besides off-shoots, and then of earthing-up the plant—a practice which tends to increase the size of the tuber. Though generally eaten cooked, it is sometimes used, cut in slices, in a raw state in salads. There are two or three varieties of this Celery, the largest being the common Parisian variety; the Erfurt has a smaller root, but is at the same time earlier and more delicate. Well grown and properly cooked, this is an excellent vegetable—quite distinct from our ordinary Celery, which is never so well grown in France as in England or America.

Turnip-rooted Celery.

The Cardoon.

The Cardoon is much more grown and eaten in France than in England, and its culture is well understood. There are several varieties, some of which are spiny, whilst others are destitute of prickles, or nearly so. The principal varieties are, the Cardoon of Tours, a spiny variety which Parisian gardeners prefer to all others; the Spanish Cardoon, which is more cultivated in the south than in the north of France; the Cardoon Plein Inerme, which is almost as fine as the Cardoon of Tours, and which has the advantage of being free from prickles; and finally, the Cardoon Puvis, much sought after in La Bresse and in the neighbourhood of Lyons. The Cardoon Puvis is an almost spineless variety, readily distinguished from those already named; the leaves are larger and shorter than those of other Cardoons, which has given rise to the name it bears in some localities—the Artichoke-leaved Cardoon. The way the fine Cardoons of the Paris market are raised is as follows. The ground requires well pulverising and a rest from heavy cropping; it matters little how poor or stiff the soil, so that the bottom be dry. The exposure must be an open one, as they require a free circulation of air and all the sun possible. Having marked off the spaces for the trenches and ridges, allowing six feet for each, those marked out for the ridges are manured well and dug, for the improving of the ground for other crops, as well as providing for the Cardoon, must be kept in mind. The trenches are next dug out one foot deep, laying the soil right and left on the ridges, and breaking the lumps well as the work proceeds. The sides of the ridges should be well sloped off, and beaten smooth with the back of the spade. A compost, previously prepared, must now be wheeled into the trenches to a depth of four to six inches, consisting of about equal parts of chopped turfy soil, good, solid, half-rotted manure, and road-drift or fine ashes, and if at hand some burnt clay. This is forked into the trench in such a manner as to keep the compost merely covered, while the ground below is loosened to the depth of a foot at least. The trench ought to lie uncropped until the season for planting out the Cardoons has arrived, by which time the ground will be in fine order to receive them. Two rows of Dwarf Peas are generally sown upon the ridges, and a row of Spinach between; these will be off before the Cardoons require earthing-up. In the first week in May sow the seeds in thumb-pots, placing two sound seeds at opposite sides of the pots, and plunge the pots in a cold frame, which must be kept close until the plants appear, when plenty of air is admitted, to prevent them drawing up weakly. In a fortnight after the plants are up, they will be strong enough to plant out in this order—one row up the centre of each trench, 18 inches apart, and a row two feet from it in quincunx fashion on each side. Planting two plants together is to guard against losses by insects, and when all danger from this is over, the weakest can be destroyed. Raising them in pots, instead of sowing them in the ground, is to prevent gaps in the rows, and to give the opportunity of having all the plants in the ridge of equal size, so that when earthed-up, the plants being alike in strength, the same quantity of soil will be required for all. The weakest plants may be kept in the cold frame ten days longer, which, with a second sowing, will give a succession. Water the newly turned-out plants, and loosen-up the soil between them. If dry weather succeeds this operation, the plants will require watering once or twice, until they get established, after which they will only require to be kept clear of weeds till October. This will be most advantageously done by forking among them occasionally, and thus keep the weeds in check, and promote the growth of the plants better than by using the hoe. In the beginning of October, the most forward trench of plants will have attained their full growth, and a sufficient number of well-twisted hay-bands must be provided for winding round them. Taking advantage of a fine dry day, commence by carefully bringing all the leaves into an upright position, in which they should be held by one person while another fastens the hay-band round the bottom of the plant, and winds away tightly until the whole of the stalk is bound round, and the end of the rope secured. When each row is completed, earth-up till the bands are covered with the soil, which should be pressed very tightly round the plant at the top, to exclude air and moisture as effectually as possible. Hay-bands are said to rot the plants; but, by deferring the earthing-up till October, and by twisting the bands well, and fastening them tightly round the plants, very few failures occur. Some have tried blanching by fastening the leaves closely together with string and matting, and putting an earthen drain-pipe over the plants, and filling up with sand. This plan answers admirably; the whole of the leaf-stalks becoming perfectly blanched, quite crisp, and fit for use. The adoption of this plan prevents the loss of room occupied by the ridges, as no soil would be wanted for earthing; but it takes a pipe seven or eight inches in diameter for a well-grown plant, and these, if many are required, are expensive.

The finest Cardoons can only be obtained by frequent and copious watering, the quantity being increased as they grow larger. If the weather is warm and dry, at least a potful of water should be given to each plant every other day. The Cardoon is so fiercely armed that it requires a little care to get at the great plants to tie them up, etc., without being severely pricked. To obviate this, three sticks are used—one of them short, and connected with the other two by strong twine. The illustration will show this simple contrivance and the mode of using it. The workman standing at a safe distance pushes the two handles under the plant, and then going

Mode of Tying-up the Cardoon for Blanching.

to the other side and seizing them, soon gathers up the prickly leaves. Another workman then ties it up in three places, and then straw is placed round and tied so as quite to exclude the light. In three weeks the vegetable is as well blanched and as tender as could be desired. To blanch the Cardoon properly and render the leaves perfectly tender, it should be deprived of light and air for at

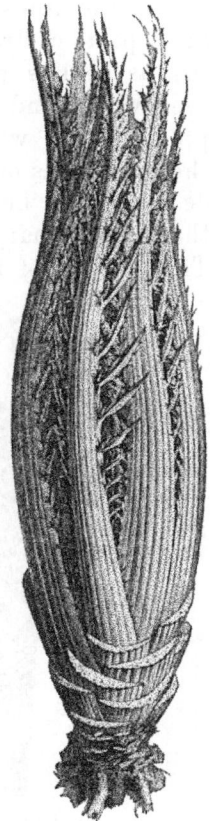

Blanched Cardoon.

least three weeks. It is then cut just below the surface of the earth, and divested of its straw covering; the withered leaves are sliced off and the root trimmed up neatly. If it is desirable to preserve the Cardoon for winter use it should be simply tied up, as before directed, in the month of November, and uprooted carefully with a ball of earth attached to it, and plunged in fine rotten manure or leaf-mould in a dark cellar. The decayed leaves should be removed every week or so. Under this treatment they become sufficiently blanched in a fortnight, and may be preserved in a good condition for at least two months.

GLOBE ARTICHOKES.—Artichoke-culture is of more importance in France than with us, and there is considerable difference among the kinds grown. The Artichoke is extensively cultivated in all parts of France—in the north as well as in the south, in the east as well as in the west; but it does not prosper equally well everywhere, and each province has its variety, to which it gives preference or which thrives better than other kinds. Amongst these varieties ought to be mentioned the large green Artichaut de Laon, the heads of which have scales more fleshy at the base than the ordinary kind, and not placed very close one to the other. This is one of the best varieties known, and one that is most commonly cultivated in the neighbourhood of Paris, especially at Aubervilliers. Varieties are apt not to come true from seed, and they require, besides, more time than offsets before they are fit for consumption; the latter mode of propagation is, therefore, that most generally adopted. Near Paris the offsets are taken off in spring; in other districts the operation is deferred till autumn, as this is thought to produce better and earlier returns. The process is as follows:—After stripping off the soil from the base of the plants,

De Laon Artichoke.

without pulling them up, the suckers, which grow at the collar, are removed with a heel, or portion of the stem, attached to them; and from amongst these offsets the strongest should be chosen for planting. The soil which is destined to receive them having been well prepared, the offsets should at once be planted in lines, at a distance apart of about two feet six inches each way, taking care to heap up the earth round the

Navet gris de Morigny.

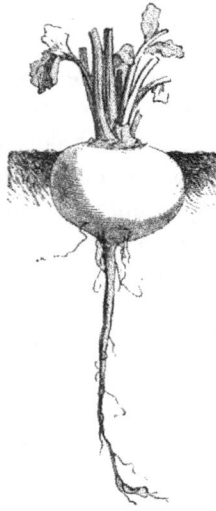

N. des Vertus rond.

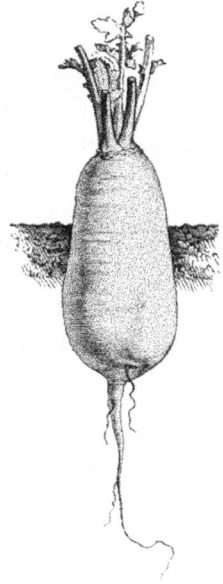

N. des Vertus Marteau.

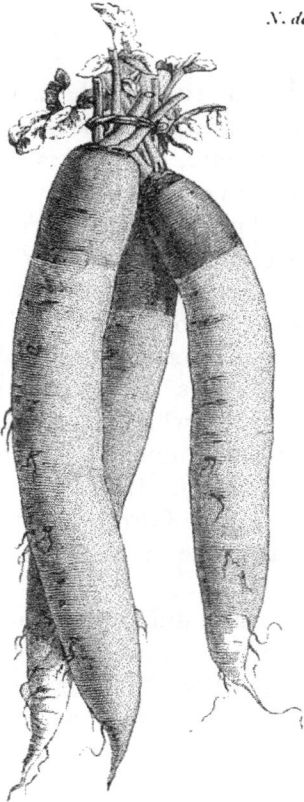

N. de Meaux.

Navet Jaune de Montmagny.

Some Navets of the Paris Market (Vilmorin).

2 L

stalks and to water if the weather be dry. Some prefer planting
in pots until the offsets have fairly rooted, after which they may
be planted out with a ball. Artichokes thus treated are fit for
use sooner than under the ordinary method. In all cases, if the
planting has been properly conducted, a large number put in in
April will be fit for use in the autumn of the same year. Frequent
planting of this kind encourages a succession of good heads,
whereas leaving the plantations long in one place causes all the
heads to come in at nearly the same time. The De Laon variety
is considered the best; Camus de Bretagne is the kind that is
used raw.

NAVETS.—The long white Turnip, of which such large quantities
are now being brought from Paris to the London market, is
the Long Early White Navet des Vertus. The only district
about Paris that will grow this very early Turnip is the valley
on the banks of the Seine, opposite le Pecq de St. Germain and
Marly, between Le Vésinet Chatou and the river. The principal
villages where the cultivation of this Turnip is carried on are
Croissy and Montesson, especially the former, hence this Turnip
is known in the Paris market as the Navet de Croissy. It is
almost impossible to grow good early Turnips in the spring and
summer on a large scale in the open ground; either they do not
form well or else they flower without forming at all—that is to
say, when they escape the ravages of the grub or beetle. In the
Croissy district the soil is sandy, the climate somewhat cold, and
the air saturated with moisture, conditions all of which are
favourable to the cultivation of this Turnip, which elsewhere can
only be grown from seed sown in July and August. The Croissy
cultivators also produce large quantities of the early round
Parsnip and half-long early round scarlet Carrot, of both of
which varieties enormous quantities are seen in the Halles and
other Paris markets.

THE MELONS grown about Paris are quite different in race and
flavour to ours, being nearly always of the Cantaloup race. All
the Cantaloup Melons resemble each other, but vary greatly
under different kinds of treatment. In France, as is often
the case in England, almost every gardener has a so-called
variety of Melon. Their flavour depends entirely on the
time when the fruits are removed from the plant—not too

soon before and not too late after they are ripe. French gardeners never leave a Melon to ripen on the plant. There is no doubt that in this country Melons are left too long on the vines after being ripe, and hence their occasional bad flavour. In fruit-shops, too, they are exposed in windows, and their flavour is destroyed in a short time. The Cantaloup Prescott is a fine Melon when well grown and gathered at the proper time. It is re-

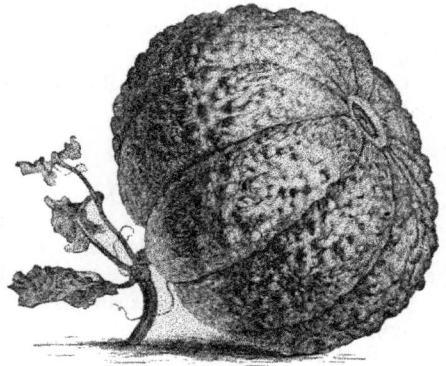

Cantaloup Melon of the Paris Markets.

markably refreshing without being too sweet and sickly, as some of the varieties in this country are.

SOME VEGETABLES GROWN OR USED IN FRANCE.
(D. GUIHÉNEUF.)

ARTICHOKE, green, purple and large Laon (raw or boiled); the young white leaves for salad.

BASELLA, alba, and rubra.

BEANS (*Broad*), Seville long pod, purple seeded, purple flowered; des Marais.

——— (*Runners*), large Soissons, Rice, Asparagus; black algerian, purple podded (both these latter are edible podded); mont d'or butter.

——— (*Dwarf or French*), choco-late; white flageolet; green flageolet; early wrinkled-leaf flageolet; dwarf Soissons; black algerian, white butter, spotted white-podded (all three edible podded), and many others; *Dolichos*, several varieties.

BEET-ROOT, rough bark, or crapau-dine; early flat Bassano.

BENINCASA CERIFERA.

BORECOLE, or KALE, Palm-kale.

BRAKE (young shoots).

BURNET, in salad.

CABBAGE, Baccalan, early and late; St. Denis; Vaugirard, for winter; Savoy, long-headed; Norwegian (very hardy); Tronchouda, curled; Russian; Chinese.

CARDOON, several sorts.

CARROT, earliest French forcing, or grelot; Nantes; pale red Flanders; white transparent; purple.

CAULIFLOWER, dwarf Lenormand.

CELERIAC, common, Erfurt, curled.

CHERVIL, sweet-scented; tuberous-rooted.

CHICK PEA.

CHICORY, large rooted; Witloef; common (Barbe de Capucin); spotted.

CHENOPODIUM, Good King Henry; quinoa (as Spinach).

CLAYTONIA CUBENSIS, salad.

CORCHORUS OLITORIUS, salad.

CORN SALAD, large seeded; Italian; variegated.

CUCUMBER, large white, green, yellow; Russian; Grecian or Athenian; snake; Arada.

DANDELION, improved.

EGG-PLANT, long and round purple, long white, striped, black.

ENDIVE, Italian, Ruffec, Rouen; Batavian en cornet, for winter.

EVENING PRIMROSE, salad.

FEDIA CORNUCOPIÆ, salad.

FENNEL, sweet (in the south).

GOURD, potiron jaune.

HOLY THISTLE (young leaves for salad).

HOPS (young shoots like Asparagus).

ICE-PLANT, salad.

KOHL RABI, Artichoke-leaved.

LEEK, yellow Poitou.

LENTIL.

LETTUCE, early Paris market (for forcing only); yellow Berlin; brown Genoa; blonde Versailles; Bossin; Perpignan; spotted; winter, large white cabbage.

—— (*Cos*), spotted; blood-red for winter; Artichoke-leaved.

—— (*for cutting young*), Oak-leaved; yellow Dutch; curled; Lactuca perennis; Lactuca augustana.

LOTUS tetragonolobus.

MARTYNIA PROBOSCIDEA, pickling.

MELON (*Open ground*), cavaillon, maraîcher, and de Tours.

—— (*Cantaloup*), noir des Carmes, prescott à châssis, fond blanc (these three chiefly for Paris market).

NETTLE (young and tender leaves for salad).

NIGELLA AROMATICA (seasoning).

OKRA, long and short (for pickling and sauce).

ONIONS, pale red Niort; Pear-shaped; Trébons; Catawissa.

OXALIS, yellow, white, and red (roots and leaves).

PATIENCE DOCK (like Sorrel and Spinach).

PEAS, clamart, early and late; purple podded, Sabel, Leopold II.

—— (*Sugar*), tall; giant grey-seeded; grey seeded; white podded; yellow podded; very dwarf; dwarf white wrinkled.

PEPPER or Capsicum, all the varieties, chiefly in the south for pickling, also roasted with oil and vinegar.

PHYSALIS pubescens (yellow Alkekengi).

PICRIDIUM VULGARE, salad.

PLANTAGO CORONOPUS, salad.

POTATO, Marjolin (the earliest); Saucisse; Reine blanche; Vitelotte (salad).

PURSLANE, yellow, for salad; green, for boiling.

RADISH, early rose turnip; extra early white turnip; purple turnip; black turnip; large Gournay; long white green top; long purple; long Rave tortillée du Mans.

RAMPION, salad.

RAPHANUS CAUDATUS.

ROCKET (Brassica eruca), salad.

RUSH NUT (roots).

SALSIFY (leaves blanched for salad).

SCOLYMUS HISPANICUS (like Salsify).

SHALLOT (the true kind, not that now used in London).

SKIRRET, for the roots.

SORREL (daily in Paris).

SPINACH, Lettuce-leaved; large Viroflay.

SWEET POTATO (in sorts).

SWISS CHARD, curled.

TURNIP, des vertus marteau; de Meaux; de Teltau; long black; early white strap leaf; de Bortsfeld.

WATER CHESTNUT, boiled.

YAMS (in varieties).

Mouth of Mushroom-cave at Montrouge.

CHAPTER XXX.

MUSHROOM-CULTURE IN CAVES UNDER PARIS.

MUSHROOM-GROWING as carried on beneath Paris and its environs is the most interesting example of cultivation under difficulties of which we have any knowledge! To get a fair idea of it it is necessary to visit one of the "Mushroom-caves" at Montrouge, just outside the fortifications, on the southern side of Paris. The surface of the ground is mostly cropped with Wheat; but here and there lie blocks of white stone, which have recently been brought to the surface through well-like openings, the stone being mined like coal. We find a Mushroom-grower after some trouble, and he accompanies us across some fields to the entrance of his subterranean garden. Through the circular opening or mouth of the pit protrudes the head of a thick pole with sticks thrust through it. This pole, the base of which rests in darkness sixty feet below, is the only road into the cavern. Down the shaky pole we creep, and soon reach the bottom, from which narrow passages radiate. A few small lamps fixed on pointed sticks are placed below, and, arming ourselves with one each, we commence slowly exploring tortuous passages dark as night and perfectly still. The passages are so low that frequently we have to stoop to avoid the pointed stones in the roof. On each hand there are little narrow beds of half-decomposed stable-manure running along the wall. These have been formed quite recently, and have not yet been spawned. Presently we arrive at others in which the spawn has been placed and is " taking " freely. The grower pointed with pride to the way in which the flakes of spawn had begun to spread through the beds, and passed on to where the beds were in a more advanced state. Here we saw small, smooth ridges running along the sides of the passages, and wherever the rocky subway was more than a few feet wide two or three little beds were placed parallel to each other. These were nearly new, dotted all over with Mushrooms no bigger than Sweet-pea seeds, and affording an excellent prospect of a crop. They contain a much smaller body of material than we employ for Mushroom-beds. They are not more than twenty inches high, and about the same width at the base; while the beds against the sides of the passages are not so large as those placed in the open spaces. The soil with which they are covered to the depth of about an inch is nearly white; it is simply sifted from the rubbish of the stone-cutters above-ground, and gives the recently-made bed, when moistened, the appearance of being covered with putty.

Passages in Mushroom-cave.

Although we are from sixty to eighty feet below the surface of the ground, everything looks trim and scrupulously clean. A certain length of Mushroom-bed is made every day in the year, and as the men finish one gallery or series of galleries at a time, the beds in each are equally forward. As we proceed to those in full bearing, creeping up and down narrow passages, winding always between the two little narrow beds against the wall on each side, and passing now and then through wider nooks filled

View in Mushroom-cave at Montrouge.

with two or three lines of beds, daylight is again seen, this time coming through another well-like shaft, formerly used for getting up the stone, but now for throwing down the materials for the Mushroom-beds. At the bottom lies a large heap of the white earth before alluded to, and a barrel of water—for gentle waterings are required in the cool, black stillness of these caves.

We find but little unpleasant smell, for the galleries are all thoroughly ventilated, not only for the sake of the labourers, but of the Mushrooms, which would not thrive in confined air. If the air were not frequently changed, the workmen, the lamps, and the gases given off by the slow fermentation of the material would soon render the quarries unfit for the culture. The ventilation is accomplished by means of small shafts here and there, surmounted by wooden chimneys, with the upper end cut at an angle. The top of the chimneys is above the level of the mouth of the principal shaft, and the bevelled edge turned towards the north. The number of ventilating-shafts and their distances apart must be regulated by the special wants of each mine. Frequently the Mushroom-growers content themselves with using the ventilating-shafts constructed by the former owners of the pit, seeing that the construction of each shaft costs from £8 to £40, according to its depth. It sometimes happens that two quarries communicate, in which case the ventilation is an easy matter; it is, however, necessary to guard against strong draughts and sudden changes of temperature, which would interfere with the well-being of both the men and the Mushrooms. For this purpose the usual means employed for the ventilation of coal-mines, such as fires and trapdoors, is adopted. When the entrance to the quarry is by a horizontal gallery, as at Méry, level with the road, the ventilation is comparatively simple, and the work of cultivation much easier. The caves are let at from £6 to £16 per month, according to the extent and height of their galleries, and the facilities for ventilating them. Atmospheric variations, both inside and out, must be narrowly watched, so that the temperature of the quarry may not rise or fall too far above or below the average, and that the ventilating-currents may always be kept in the same direction and of the same strength. If the beds are in a cavern, the draughts should be in the direction from north to south, and the ventilating-shafts and their dampers should be so constructed that the quantity of air necessary for the proper growth of the Mushrooms may be obtained at will. Proper watering plays a great part in Mushroom-culture; means must, therefore, be taken for obtaining a sufficient supply of water in the quarry itself. It often happens, however, that the opening of the quarry and the locality of the beds are far away from any dwelling or well, in which case the water is conveyed to the mouth of the shaft in large barrels holding about 130 gallons. By means of a sail-cloth hose, which is attached to the tap of the barrel, the water is lowered to the bottom of the shaft, where it is stored in large tubs or tanks. In some quarries sufficient water filters through the rock for the supply of the beds.

Once more we enter a narrow passage, and find ourselves between two lines of beds in full bearing, the white " button " Mushrooms appearing everywhere in profusion along the sides of the diminutive beds. As the proprietor goes along he removes sundry bunches that are in perfection, and leaves them on the spot, so that they may be collected with the rest for the morrow's market. He gathers largely every day, occasionally sending away more than 400 lbs. weight, the daily average being about 300 lbs. We are now in an open space, a sort of chamber, say 20 feet by 15, and here the little beds are arranged in parallel lines, an alley of not more than four inches separating them, the sides of the beds being literally blistered all over with Mushrooms. Frequently the Mushrooms grow in bunches or " rocks," as they are called, and in such cases those that compose the little mass are lifted all together.

The sides of one bed here had been almost stripped by the taking away of such bunches, and it is worthy of note that they are not only taken out, root and all, when being gathered, but the spot in which they grew is scraped out, so as to get rid of every trace of the old bunch, the space being covered with a little earth from the bottom of the heap. It is the practice to do this in every case, and when the gatherer leaves a small hole from which he has pulled even a solitary Mushroom, he fills it with some of the white earth from the base. The Mushrooms look very white, and are of prime quality. The daily gatherings, and the absence of all littery coverings and dust, secure them in spotless condition.

These caves not only supply the wants of Paris, but greatly those of England and other countries, large quantities of preserved Mushrooms being exported, one house alone sending to our own country no less than 14,000 boxes annually. To traverse the passages any further is needless—there is nothing to be seen but

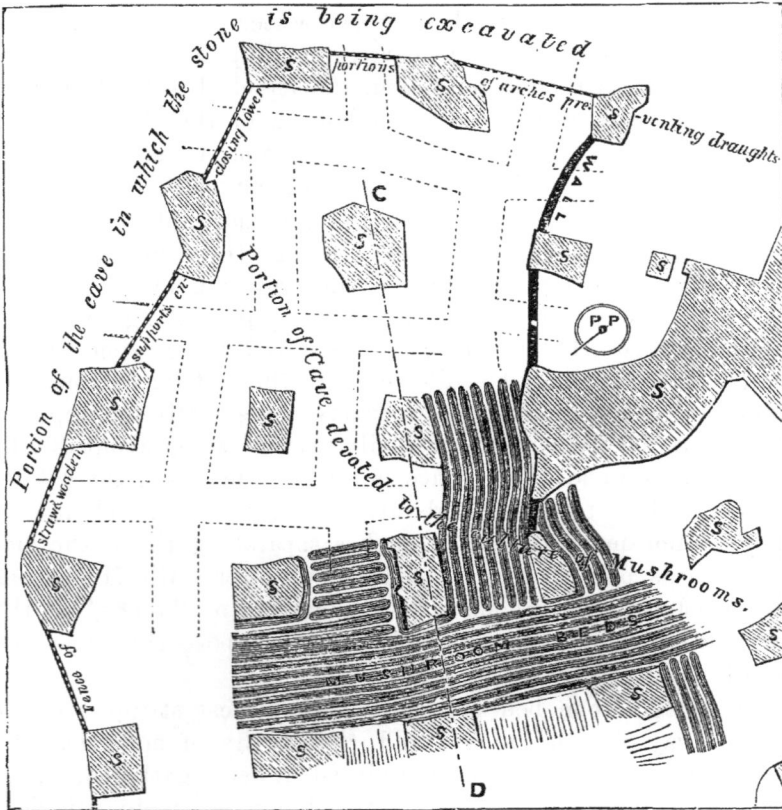

Plan of large Subterranean Quarry at Fortes Terres, Frépillon. S, S, S, represent the plan of the bases of the huge supporting pillars, and the dotted lines their union with the roof. D, C, shows the line of the section shown in the following cut, and P, place for preparing the plaster.

a repetition of the culture above described, every available inch of the cave being occupied. We find our way to the bottom of the shaft, carefully mount the rather shaky pole one by one, and are glad to find ourselves in the hot sun in the midst of the ripe Wheat. In traversing the fields, two things relating to

Mushroom-culture are to be observed—heaps of white gritty earth, sifted from the débris of the white stone, and large heaps of stable-manure undergoing preparation for Mushroom-beds. That preparation is different from what it receives in England. It is ordinary stable-manure thrown into heaps four or five feet high, and perhaps thirty feet wide. The men were employed turning this over, the mass being afterwards stamped down with their feet, a water-cart and pots being used to thoroughly water the manure where dry and white. This cave is but a sample of a number in the immediate neighbourhood of Paris. In the Department of the Seine alone there are 3000 stone quarries; those which have been abandoned as such and which are situated close to Paris, at Montrouge, Bagneux, Vaugirard, Méry, Châtillon,

Section following the line C, D, in preceding figure.

Vitry, Houilles, and St. Denis, are used by the 250 Mushroom-growers of the Department.

We will next visit a Mushroom-cave of quite another type at some little distance from Paris. It is situated near Frépillon, Méry-sur-Oise—a place which may be reached in an hour or so by the Chemin de fer du Nord, passing by Enghien, the valley of Montmorency and Pontoise, and alighting at Auvers. There are vast quarries in the neighbourhood, both for the building-stone and plaster so largely used in Paris. As many as 3000 lbs. weight of Mushrooms were at the time of my visit sent daily from Méry to the Paris market. The Mushroom has rather mysterious habits, for after a time the great quarries seem to become tired of their occupants, or the Mushrooms become tired of the air; the

quarries are then well cleaned out, the very soil where the beds
rested being scraped away, and the place left to "rest" for
a year or two.

The distant view of the entrance to these quarries has much the
appearance of an English chalk-pit. But there is a great rude
arch cut into the rock, and through this we enter, meeting presently a waggon coming forth with a load of stones, the waggoner
with lamp in hand. To one who has seen the low-roofed Mushroom-caves near Paris, the surprise is great on getting a little way
into this one. At least it is so as soon as one can see; the darkness is so profound that a few candles or lamps merely make
darkness visible. The tunnel we traverse is nearly regularly
arched, masonry being used here and there, so as to render the
support secure and symmetrical, the arches being flat at the top
for six feet or so across, and about twenty-five to thirty feet
high.

Presently we turn to the right, and a scene like a vast subterranean rock-temple presents itself. At one end are several of us
with lamps, admiring the young Mushrooms budding all over the
lines of beds which, serpent-like, long and slim, stretch away to
some 150 feet distance where a group of men is at work at the
beds. From both sides of this gloomy temple start the dark
openings of avenues at short intervals, and the floor of all is
covered with Mushroom-beds. These beds are about twenty-two
inches high and as much wide, and are covered with silver sand
and whitish clay in about equal proportions. In some parts of
the cave the work of ripping out the stone by powder and
simple machinery continually goes on. The arches follow the
veining of the stone, so to speak; their lower parts are of hard
stone, the upper ones of soft, except the very top, which is again
hard. There is but a slight crust of stone above the apex of each
arch, and above that the earth and trees. Running in parallel
lines, and disappearing from view in the darkness, one knows not
what to compare the beds to, unless it be to barked Pine-trees
in the hold of a ship.

As the beds are regularly gathered from every day, no very
large Mushrooms are seen. They are preferred at about the size
of a Chestnut. If the old superstition that a Mushroom never
grows after being seen by human eyes were true, the trade of

a Mushroom-grower would never answer here, as the little budding " buttons " are watched every day. The average daily gathering from this cave is about 880 lbs. weight, and sometimes that is nearly doubled. Even when the crops reach their lowest ebb, about 400 lbs. per day are sent to market. The proprietors of the larger quarries are coming to the conclusion that culture on a more limited scale gives the best return in proportion to expense, the care and supervision required by so many miles of beds being too great.

All the manure employed is brought from Paris by rail, as the place is twenty-five miles from that city by road. In the first place, so much per horse per month is paid in Paris for the manure; then it has to be carted to the railway station and loaded in the waggons; next it is brought to the station of Auvers, and afterwards carted a couple of miles to the quarries, paying a toll for a bridge over the Oise on the way. One grower at Méry-sur-Oise uses as much as 300 tons per month. It is placed in large flat heaps a yard deep by about thirty long and ten wide, not far removed from the mouth of the cave, and here it is prepared, turned over and well mixed three times, and as a rule watered twice. About five or six weeks are occupied in the preparation, long manure requiring more time than short. The watering is usually limited to parts where it is dry and overheated. Every day stable-manure is brought from Paris; every day new beds are made and old ones cleared out—the spent manure, useless in Mushroom-culture, is much in demand by farmers and gardeners, it being very useful for garden-purposes, particularly in surfacing or mulching. The advantage the cultivator has in these caves as compared with the mine-caverns near Paris, is the taking his materials in or out in carts, as easily as if the beds were made in the open air. Many men are employed in the culture here, the daily examination of so large an extent of beds being a considerable item in itself. Here and there a barrier in the form of straw nailed between laths may be seen blocking up the great archways to a height of six feet or so. This is to prevent currents of cold air wandering through the vast passages.

The mode of preparing the spawn here is entirely different to ours. The French growers prefer virgin spawn—that is to say, spawn found naturally in a heap of manure. But as this material cannot be obtained in sufficient quantity to meet the wants of such extensive cultivation, they frequently put a small portion of it into a freshly-made Mushroom bed to spread, and instead of allowing this bed to produce Mushrooms it is all used as spawn. In this case the small bed devoted to the propagation of spawn is placed in the open air, and covered with straw, and as soon as it is permeated with the spawn it is carried into the caves and used. As the making and spawning of beds is a process continually going on, spawning-beds of this sort must be ready at all times. It is never made into bricks as with us, but spreads through short, partly-decomposed manure.

A bed in the open air, which is exposed to all the accidents of the weather, may be spawned with dry old spawn, such as may be taken from the stock kept for sale. Experience, however, has shown that, for Mushroom-beds in cellars or quarries, it is better to allow the spawn to become damp, and undergo a kind of stratification before being used. For this purpose, the cakes are placed in rows on the floor of the cellar or cavern, and allowed to remain for about eight or ten days, until the dampness of the atmosphere has caused the filaments of spawn to swell up and resume their normal roundish form, whitish colour, and felted appearance. It is of importance only to expose a sufficient quantity of spawn to the damp for immediate use, for it will not bear being dried and damped again. It must also be remembered that the spawn must be exposed at such a time that it will be ready for use when the Mushroom-bed is at the proper temperature. If the spawn remains too long in this preliminary damping its sporules become swollen with the damp, and, not finding a suitable temperature for their development, they wither away. The stratification of the spawn advances the gathering of the first crop of Mushrooms by eight or ten days. It is for this reason, amongst others, that the Mushroom-growers in the Paris quarries often take their fresh spawn from beds already in work, except when they desire to obtain an entirely new "strain." When the bed has reached the proper temperature, the Mushroom-grower chooses from among the beds already in bearing the one which appears in the healthiest condition, that, in fact, in which the spawn-filaments are most numerous, thickest, and cling most closely to the particles of the manure. The best time for taking

Sectional View: Operations as carried on in the Mushroom-caves at Montrouge.

the spawn from a young bearing-bed is just when the young
Mushrooms are first appearing. The bed thus selected is
broken up, and the cakes of spawn removed, and broken into
lumps of about the size already described. This kind of spawn
is in the best condition for yielding an early and abundant crop
of Mushrooms, which may be gathered at least twenty days
sooner than if dry spawn had been used.

To soil a mushroom-bed, the Paris growers use the chips and
powder of the stone which has been taken out of the quarry, and
which may be procured in large quantities either on the floor of the
quarry or on the surface of the ground around the shaft. This
rubbish is passed through a sieve, and the finer portions mixed
with light, dry earth, in the proportions of three of the former
to one of the latter. The mixture is then watered so as to form
a dry putty-like paste, in which the fingers will leave an impression. The addition of the earth to the powdered stone favours
the development of the Mushroom. Great care must be taken in
selecting the cakes of spawn, only those flakes being chosen which
show an abundance of bluish-white filaments well knitted together and having a characteristic odour of Mushrooms.

Among the spawn may sometimes be found a spurious kind,
which must be avoided. Such patches are a kind of fungoid
growth which spreads very fast, an almost imperceptible spot being
sufficient to infect and kill a large quantity of healthy Mushrooms.
This disease the French growers call *la molle,* or *la mole.* As
will be seen by the illustration, the Mushroom when attacked by
this disease loses its shape, and forms a spongy mass full of
granules. The skin which covers this shapeless cottony mass is
pure white at first, but speedily changes to a yellowish-brown as
it rots away. It emits a disgusting odour, and the inside becomes
filled with brown threads, which are sure signs of decomposition.
Sometimes the edges of the cap turn upwards instead of downwards, and the gills become united into a spongy mass which
sticks to the edges of the cap. As soon as the diseased Mushroom
comes into contact with the air it turns brown, and exhales an
odour like that of putrifying meat. When the disease shows
itself in only a few isolated cases, the Mushrooms attacked are
promptly removed from the beds and quarry; but if it has
been allowed to spread, the whole of the bad and diseased spawn

2 M

must be removed and carried away to a distance. The cause of
this disease is at present uncertain, the opinions of practical
Mushroom-growers being divided on the matter.   Some attribute it to lack of cleanliness when the beds are being
broken up. Others say that the remains of old manure mixed
with the soil of the quarry generate dampness underneath the
beds, and as this moisture cannot be absorbed by the stone surface
beneath, it gives rise to the "molle."   According to this
hypothesis, the remedy would be to thoroughly scrape the surface
of the ground on which the bed rests.   Others say that the

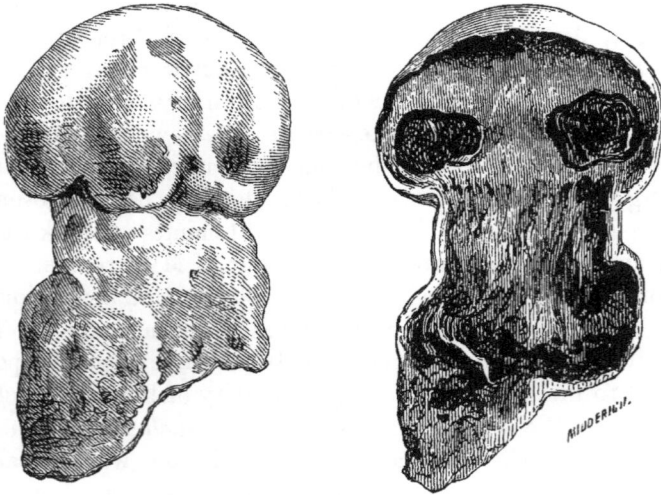

Mushrooms attacked by the "molle."—(Lachaume.)

"molle" is the consequence of the beds being too much crowded
together in a confined space. According to them, the vapours
produced by the fermentation of the manure become condensed
on the walls, and, mixing with the natural infiltrations, fall upon
the beds, and bring about the decomposition of the manure.
They base their opinions upon the fact that it is in the summer,
when the heat is great, that the "molle" makes its appearance in
quarries with low roofs, and that it is much more rare in quarries
which have high roofs and strong currents of air circulating
through them.   But in any case, no matter what may be the

cause, the remedy is the same, that is to say, to thoroughly break up and remove the surface upon which the beds are built. Another disease which sometimes attacks the spawn is known to the Paris growers under the name of verdigris. It makes its appearance in the form of very small greenish granules of the colour of verdigris, and having a peculiar smell resembling chloride of lime. The same remedy is used as in the case of the "molle." It is supposed to be the result of the decomposition of foreign substances which have become accidentally mixed with the spawn. Mushrooms grown from spawn attacked by verdigris are poor and sickly, and probably possess poisonous properties. The smallest particle of iron in the beds of manure is avoided by the spawn, a circle around remaining inert.

The gatherings are made in the quarries at a very early hour. At one o'clock in the morning the Mushrooms are gathered which at a later hour are sold in the open market. The Mushroom-gatherers are each provided with two large baskets, which they carry on their backs knapsack fashion—one to receive the Mushrooms, the other containing the soil with which to fill up the gaps left in the beds after the gathering. The proper way of gathering a Mushroom is to seize it in one hand by the cap, at the same time giving it a slight twist and pulling it gently upwards, so as to detach it from its roots without disturbing the little Mushrooms that are growing round its base. The gathered Mushroom is dropped into the empty basket, and the hole which it has left behind it is filled up with a pinch or two of soil from the other. In some quarries the gatherers pick the Mushrooms and leave them in little piles on the pathways, or on the beds themselves. They are followed by women, who pack them into baskets, and by men who fill up the gaps left in the beds. The beds are then smoothed down with the hand, and if they appear to be too dry they are watered. The baskets should be covered over with a cloth, to avoid all contact with the air, which is apt to turn the Mushrooms brown. The contents of the smaller baskets are then packed into larger ones holding from 23 lbs. to 35 lbs. and sent to market. Mushrooms of good quality are sold wholesale at 8d. to 10d. per pound according to the season. The gatherings are continued daily, but do not yield the same quantities regularly. The time that beds will continue to bear depends on the materials employed, and the manipulation to which they have been subjected. The inside and outside temperature have also a great influence. In quarries with a low roof the temperature is always high, and vegetation is consequently more rapid. The duration of the crop is from forty to sixty days, and the yield rapidly diminishes towards the end of that time. In quarries with high roofs, or which open on to the road, the temperature is lower, the vegetation is less active, and the bed lasts longer. In some high-roofed quarries the beds will bear for three or four months.

A useful contrivance for facilitating the watering of the beds has lately been invented; it consists of a portable water-cistern

View in old Subterranean Quarries devoted to Mushroom-culture, and in the occupation of M. Renaudot.

to be strapped to the back and fitted with a rose and tubing, so that a workman may carry a larger quantity of water, and apply it more regularly and gently than with the old-fashioned watering-pots—while one hand is left free to carry the lamp. An iron frame was also invented, in which the bed was first compressed and shaped, the frame being then reversed and the bed placed in position. This method of forming the beds was afterwards abandoned, owing to its being impossible to avoid fissures between the lengths. On an average 2500 yards of beds are made here every month. Simple mechanical contrivances to facilitate the operation would, therefore, prove of the greatest advantage to the cultivator.

In addition to the caves in the localities above alluded to, there are other places near Paris where the culture is carried on— notably at Moulin de la Roche, Sous Bicêtre, near St. Germain, and also at Bagneux. The equability of temperature in the caves renders the culture of the Mushroom possible at all seasons; but the best crops are gathered in winter, and consequently that is the best time to see them. I, however, saw abundant crops in the hottest part of a very hot season. These Mushroom-caves are under government supervision, and are regularly inspected like any other mines in which work is going on. As regards the depth at which the culture is carried on, it varies from twenty to one hundred feet, sometimes reaching 150 and 160 feet from the surface of the earth. The caves are so large that sometimes people are lost in them. In one instance the proprietor of a large one lost himself, and it was three days before he was discovered, although soldiers and volunteers in numbers were sent down.

The Mushroom reared in the Paris quarries is always much smaller than that which grows naturally in meadows. The earth for "soiling" is very poor, and contains but little humus; but this comparatively slow growth is advantageous from a commercial point of view, medium-sized Mushrooms selling better than very large ones in the Paris market. The French growers, according to M. Lachaume, divide the edible Cave-mushroom into the following varieties:—

1. The Small White Mushroom, whose cap is from $\frac{3}{4}$ in. to $1\frac{1}{8}$ in. in diameter; the stem is 2 in. in length, and its flesh is more spongy than that of the cap. This Mushroom is greatly esteemed, and it is always eaten whole.

2. The Large White Mushroom. The cap sometimes measures as much as $3\frac{1}{4}$ in. in diameter without the edges of the cap ceasing to turn inwards, the stem is relatively short, measuring about an inch in diameter, and is milk-white; the skin of the cap, which is firm and fleshy, is slightly torn, and the gills are light pink.

3. The Cream-coloured Mushroom. The stem is 2 in. in length, and $\frac{1}{4}$ in. in diameter, and milky white. The cap is from $2\frac{1}{8}$ in. to $2\frac{1}{3}$ in. in diameter. The skin is torn and clouded with cream-coloured spots on a white ground, and the gills are of a beautiful light pink.

4. The Grey Mushroom.   This variety attains the largest proportions of any.   Its cap sometimes measures $13\frac{1}{8}$ in. in diameter, the open portion near the stem being as much as $4\frac{1}{8}$ in. across.   The skin of the cap is greyish buff, and is generally torn into silky filaments.   The stem is about 2 in. high, and $1\frac{1}{8}$ in. in diameter; the ring is highly developed, and conceals the gills when the edges of the cap are open.   The flesh is very firm, remarkably white, and emits a rich odour.   In spite of these good qualities, this kind is less sought after than the others.

These varieties are pretty constant when grown under the same conditions, but I have seen spawn of the cream-coloured variety, when sown in a quarry, yield Mushrooms of the pure white variety, which would seem to indicate that the conditions under which they grow have a great influence.   To be certain of the variety we are cultivating, we must grow successively two crops from virgin spawn, so as to leave the soil and the nature of the manure sufficient time to exercise their influence.   For instance, virgin spawn grown on pigeons' guano may, when a bed is first sown with this spawn, give a white or cream-coloured Mushroom, but the virgin spawn, grown on the same bed, having been influenced by the horse-manure, may produce a variety at the second crop.

In his little work on the 'Culture of the Mushroom,' M. Lachaume gives a description of a method of growing Mushrooms without manure, which he has adopted with great success.   He takes a cubic yard of old lime-rubbish, and reduces it to fragments the size of a Hazel-nut.   The mass is then moistened and transferred to a dark cellar.   This mass, from containing large quantities of nitrous salts, greatly favours the development of the Mushroom.   Against the wall a sloping bed is made with the lime-rubbish about two feet, three inches wide, and two feet high, the lower edge being kept in its proper place by means of thin boards. The surface is then smoothed with the hand, and pieces of spawn are inserted all over the bed, at eight inches apart.   The sowing being completed, the whole is covered with river-sand or fine stone-dust to the depth of an inch and a half.   The sand should be fresh, and not too damp, but as soon as the surface of the bed becomes dry it should be lightly watered with a solution of salt-petre, two ounces to the gallon.   The beds must be watered with great moderation, for any excess of moisture would rot the spawn. At the end of about six weeks the Mushrooms ought to begin to make their appearance. By following this inexpensive process, and by renewing the bed from time to time in a different part of the cellar, we may, according to this writer, obtain a plentiful supply of Mushrooms all the year round.

Mushrooms are subject to the attacks of mice, rats, snails, woodlice, beetles, flies, and mites. The remedies used for these are as follows:—For rats and mice, ordinary traps; for the grey snail, placing here and there little heaps of damp bran or bits of Cabbage-leaf, and examining these at night; for woodlice, placing hollowed halves of Potato, and in the morning plunging these into boiling water; for beetles, perseveringly hunting them out, taking care, however, not to damage the spawned portions of the bed; for flies, by placing a number of pans of water with a few drops of oil of turpentine or soapy water added, or by a floating light; for mites (a parasite of the beetles, found in crowds upon the scraps of straw litter), by watering the spot with water in which fresh lime is held in suspension.

In old times the market-gardeners of Paris used to grow the Mushroom in the open air to a large extent, but not so much so since it has been grown in the caves. Nevertheless there may still be seen a good deal of space in the open air covered with beds, especially in winter. They begin with the preparation of the manure, and collect that of the horse for a month or six weeks before they make the beds; this they prepare in some firm spot of the market-garden, and take from it all rubbish, particles of wood, and miscellaneous matters. After sorting it, they place it in beds two feet thick, or a little more, pressing it with the fork. When this is done the mass or bed is well stamped, then thoroughly watered, and finally again pressed down by stamping. It is left in this state for eight or ten days, by which time it has begun to ferment, after which the bed ought to be well turned over and re-made on the same place, care being taken to place the manure that was near the sides of the first-made bed towards the centre in the turning and re-making. The mass is now left for another ten days or so, at the end of which time the manure is about in proper condition for making the beds. Ridge-shaped beds—about twenty-six inches wide and the

same in height—are then formed in parallel lines at a distance of
twenty inches one from the other.   The beds once made of a firm,
close-fitting texture, the manure soon begins to warm again, but
does not become dangerously hot for the spread of the spawn.
When the beds have been made some days, the cultivator spawns
them, having of course ascertained beforehand that the heat is
suitable.   Generally the spawn is inserted within a few inches of
the base, and at about thirteen inches apart in the line.   Some cultivators insert two lines, the second about seven inches above the
first.   In doing so it would of course be well to make the holes for
the spawn in an alternate manner.   The spawn is inserted in flakes
about the size of three fingers, and then the manure is closed in
over and press-
ed firmly a-
round it.   This
done, the beds
are covered
with about six
inches of clean
litter.   Ten or
twelve days
afterwards the
growers visit
the beds, to see
if the spawn
has taken well.

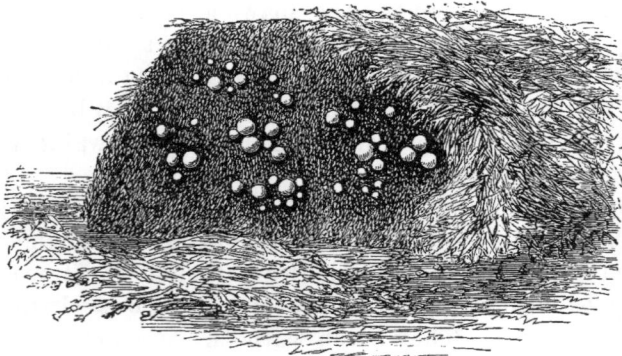

Mushroom-bed in Open air (January).

When they see the white filaments spreading in the bed they
know that the spawn has taken; if not, they take away the
spawn they suppose to be bad and replace it with fresh.   But
using good spawn, and being practised hands at the work, they
rarely fail in this particular; and when the spawn is seen
spreading well through the bed, then, and not before, they cover
the beds with fresh sweet soil to the depth of about an inch or so.
For cover, the little pathway between the beds is simply loosened
up, and the rich soil of the market-garden applied equally, firmly,
and smoothly with a shovel.   With these open-air beds they
succeed in getting fine Mushrooms in winter.   A covering of
abundance of litter is put on immediately after the beds are
earthed, and kept there as a protection.

The daily production of Mushrooms in and around Paris is estimated at about twenty-five tons, worth about £1000, or close upon £400,000 per annum. This goes either to the market, to the preserved-provision manufacturer, or to the provinces. One preserved-vegetable factory takes no less than two hundred tons of Mushrooms a year. Growers make special arrangements with large consumers at an all-round price of about £2 10s. per hundredweight. One of the largest growers is M. Gérard of Houilles and the quarries near St. Denis. He employs nineteen horses and fifty men, and his daily expenses amount to £20. He has over four miles' length of beds in his different quarries. M. Renaudet, of Méry-sur-Oise, sends eighteen tons of Mushrooms to market every month. There are in Paris about fifty agents who have the monopoly of the trade, and who supply the shops and restaurants, the stalls in the markets, the manufacturers of preserved vegetables, and, to a certain extent, the provinces. In addition to those eaten fresh, Mushrooms are preserved in large quantities in a variety of ways, by drying, by desiccation, by grating to powder, by bottling in butter or oil, and also in tins.

Cave-mushrooms as gathered.

CHAPTER XXXI.

Lilacs of the Paris Gardens.

Lilacs, like Ivy, are of more importance in France than with us. After the sweet Violet—sold by millions of bunches—perhaps the most welcome plant in the flower-shops of Paris in winter and spring is the white Lilac. It has for a good many years been popular in Paris and other continental cities, and more recently has been frequently seen in Covent Garden, invariably imported from Paris. The production of this white Lilac has long been a source of interest to cultivators. On seeing snowy fragrant masses of it in the shops so early as October, many persons have supposed it to be a white variety of Lilac, but this is not so; it is the common kind forced into bloom in the dark, and, though the blossoms are of as pure a white as most white flowers, they are simply blanched, just as the shoots of Seakale are. At first, the white variety of the common Lilac would seem to be the most suitable for forcing in this manner, but those who have tried it found it much less so. In the dark it does not make such a vigorous growth as the common Lilac, and, oddly enough, the flowers do not come of so pure a white. The French force the common Lilac in great quantities for yielding these white blossoms, both in pots, and planted out in beds under glass. The plants intended to be forced are cut round with a spade in early autumn to induce them to form flower-buds more abundantly, and this also facilitates their removal in a compactly-rooted manner at a later period of the same year. On being taken up and placed in the house in which they are to be forced, they are at first kept somewhat cool, but soon the heat is increased till it reaches from 80° to nearly 90°, and abundance of moisture is supplied at the same time, both at the roots and over the tops; in the latter case by syringing with tepid water. The chief point, however, is, that from the day the plants are placed under glass they are not allowed to receive any light, the glass being completely covered with straw mats. Thus they gather white Lilac blooms before the leaves show themselves much. The heat and moisture and complete darkness effect all that is desired. The Paris growers commence to cut the white Lilac at the end of October, and continue to do so till it comes into flower in the open ground. For many years, the forcing of Lilacs in France was confined to one or two Parisian nurserymen, who kept the process a secret, and to whom it proved a source of income, as the flowers, which were pure white, were eagerly sought after, and as the growers of them had no rivals in the trade, they were enabled to ask almost any price they pleased for them. The white Lilac blossoms have rarely been seen in England except when imported; but since the appearance of the first edition of this book the production of white Lilac from the common kind has been tried with success. Mr. Howard of Bedford Hill, Balham, has produced it abundantly, and in a simple manner. In autumn and at various periods throughout the winter, he dug up some bushes of the common Lilac and placed them in a darkened shed used for forcing Seakale, etc. This structure is heated by a hot-water pipe which passes through it, but not to so high a temperature as that used by the Paris growers. From this shed, in which the bushes flowered abundantly through the winter, Mr. Howard has gathered quantities of pure white Lilac, with its fragrance perfect. Thus it is proved that the production of this addition to our winter forced flowers may be effected with little trouble.

Recently some careful observers in France have ascertained that darkness is not essential to the production of white flowers from red varieties. The harsh treatment Lilacs often receive out-of-doors, should turn the attention of indoor gardeners to their culture in pots now that it has been proved that they may be flowered easily in a room without the aid of a forcing-house. In this way the season of these sweet flowers may be greatly prolonged, and the flowers are often better indoors in March than in the garden in a harsh May. The French sometimes graft them on a dwarfing-stock, one of the Privets. Enterprising nurserymen could scarcely confer a greater benefit on all who care for flowers in the house, than preparing Lilac-bushes for flowering in windows in town and country. It would prolong so delightfully the season of this too short-lived flower. I look forward to seeing them plentiful in London houses, where the absence of strong light would tend to subdue the reddish pigment and give us the pale but sweet flowers. The subject is a very interesting one, so both sides of the question are here given; but I am glad to find that experiments by M. Lavallée and others in France place the matter beyond all doubt as to the facility of their production in the light.

I extract the following particulars respecting the production of the white variety of the coloured Lilac from an interesting article by M. A. Lavallée, Secretary-General of the Société Centrale d'Horticulture de France, published in a recent number of the Society's journal:—In December, 1876, M. Lavallée laid before the Society several branches of the Red Marly Lilac with perfectly white flowers, and at several subsequent meetings he exhibited similar specimens, all of them produced upon a system differing from that generally adopted. The most usual method of obtaining the artificial white Lilac is to grow the plants in a greenhouse from which every ray of light has been carefully excluded, but M. Lavallée has proved, by repeated experiments, that absolute darkness is not essential for producing the white flowers. The effect of darkness, perfect or partial, on the plants is due to the well-known principle of vegetable physiology, according to which the colouring-matter of leaves known to chemists as chlorophyl—itself, by the way, being a mixture of variously-coloured constituents—can only be perfectly developed under the influence of light. This principle has long received valuable applications in the blanching of Seakale, Celery, Endive, Asparagus, etc., but it is only lately that it has been applied to the bleaching of flowers, and, as far as I know, in the case of the Lilac only. M. Lavallée goes on to point out the needlessness of growing the plants in perfect darkness, and observes that the mistake which horticulturists have made has arisen from the fact of their having confounded two distinct notions, the one being that leaves grown in darkness are pale or colourless—the other, the absence of colour in flowers in which the colourless principle has never been developed, and which therefore remain white.   According to M. Lavallée, specimens of the artificial white Lilac were first exhibited to the Society by M. Laurent in 1860.   These specimens excited a great deal of interest and surprise amongst the members of the Society at the time, and a commission was appointed to investigate the means by which M. Laurent succeeded in obtaining such beautiful results.   M. Laurent's mode of procedure was found to be very simple.   It consisted in forcing the plants in a hothouse heated to 80° Fahr., and kept in a perfect state of darkness.   M. Laurent, however, allowed that it was not impossible now and then to obtain white flowers on plants grown in broad daylight.

At the same time the commission reported on the results obtained by another Paris grower, M. Berthelot, who, also engaged in forcing Lilacs, produced the same effect in the full light of day, using for the purpose a well-lighted house, heated to a high temperature.   From this fact M. Duchartre, who acted as reporter to the commission, concluded that heat as well as absence of light was capable of preventing the formation of the colouring-matter in the petals of the Lilac.   M. Lavallée has thoroughly tested both these totally-different methods of arriving at the same result, and has succeeded in obtaining perfectly-white flowers in both cases.   He is decidedly of opinion, however, that white Lilacs, grown in an ordinary well-lighted house, give thicker and larger bunches of flowers, and which last a longer time than when M. Laurent's method is employed, and finally, that the open-daylight mode of culture requires much less care and attention. Some 9 ft. or 10 ft. of a frame in a Dutch greenhouse were devoted by M. Lavallée to this experiment, the Lilac-plants being planted so that their buds were within from 8 in. to 1 ft. of the glass.   They were then left to themselves for nearly three weeks, the house being kept at a temperature of from 68° to 72°.   At the end of this time the Marly Lilac was in full bloom, while the Charles X. variety did not blossom until four or five days after. It has been stated that the last-named beautiful variety could not be forced, but M. Lavallée has proved this to be a mistake.   It seems, however, that in the early part of the season it does not always come to perfection, the plants placed in the forcing-house by M. Lavallée in November having failed to flower; but after the beginning of December it is the best variety for forcing.   Two specimens of the Charles X. variety were shown by M. Lavallée, both of which were grown in the light, but under different conditions of temperature. The first one, which had pale lilac flowers, was placed in a house heated to a temperature of 68° Fahr. on December 23, 1876, to force its growth. At the end of four or five days the flower-buds began to make their appearance, and it was transferred to a cool house, the mean temperature of which was 40° Fahr. The flowers began to open about January 10, and were of a pale lilac. The shade of colour having been carefully noted, M. Lavallée replaced the plant in the forcing-house, which was now at a temperature of 70° Fahr., in order to see if the heat would have the effect of destroying the small amount of colouring-matter already formed; but not the slightest change took place, the flowers preserving exactly the same tint. The second specimen had perfectly-white flowers, and was put in a well-lighted forcing-house on December 30, where it remained until it was exhibited to the Society. Two specimens of the Marly Lilac, with equally white flowers, were also shown. They were grown in a well-lighted forcing-house at a temperature of 72° Fahr. To vary the experiment, several plants which had produced pale lilac blossoms in a cool house were transferred to a perfectly-dark forcing house, but without the slightest change taking place in their colour.

From these experiments we may draw the conclusions—that a prolonged heat of from 68° to 72° Fahr. prevents the formation of the colouring-matter in the petals of the Lilac, but that when once it has been formed, this temperature is incapable of destroying it, and that a temperature of 40° Fahr. has no influence on the colouring-matter of the flowers of these plants. M. Lavallée therefore supposes that it is on account of the rapidity of their growth in the forcing-houses that these Lilacs produce colourless flowers, and that darkness has nothing whatever to do with the phenomenon; also that when the Lilac is forced into blossom in fourteen, fifteen, or even twenty days, the colouring-principle has not sufficient time to develop itself. Whenever, therefore, we wish to obtain Lilac with white flowers, all we have to do is to place the plants in a forcing-house, the temperature of which is kept at 68° Fahr., without seeking the aid of darkness. This method of producing artificial white Lilac is extensively practised by the country people in the neighbourhood of Antwerp. They simply plant the common Lilac in tubs at the proper season, and place them in their living-rooms, close by their stoves, which are never allowed to go out. The plants flower well, the flowers being always perfectly white. The same result is obtained by cutting off the flowering-branches at an early stage, placing their extremities in a bottle of water, and keeping them in a forcing-house or in a well-warmed room.

It has been said that when the Persian Lilac is grown in a forcing-house it will not yield colourless flowers like its congeners, but M. Lavallée has obtained identical results with this species. He attributes the want of success hitherto to the fact that this Lilac is of very rapid growth, and that a lower temperature, say from 60° to 64° Fahr., is sufficient to make it produce colourless flowers, which would not resist a greater degree of heat. These experiments have been repeated by several members of the Society, who have endorsed the correctness of M. Lavallée's conclusions.

LILACS IN THE OPEN AIR.—About the first day of May the Lilacs are in full beauty in many of the public gardens of Paris, and form at that season the principal attraction. The bushes are pruned closely for two reasons—to insure a strong bloom, and to keep them about the same size every year. They are in lines, as a rule, like soldiers, only more regular. With us this lovely shrub is often left to perish and starve from overcrowding. It is something even to train a common shrub; for so much we have to be grateful in Paris, where the State gardens are virtually in the hands of architects, engineers, and other persons who know little about gardening, and have no sympathy with right efforts therein. The true way to grow Lilacs is not that used in Paris. One ought, perhaps, to apologise for wasting words about a subject that apparently never has excited the least attention. The right method would be to group Lilacs naturally on the Grass, or on mounds or slopes, allowing each bush room enough for its full development. It should not be starved above or below ground; it should not be tortured into anything like a broomstick and balloon-head as in Paris, or contorted by neglect as with us. It should be allowed to assume a natural form, and be pruned so that form is never interfered with; moderate thinning of the branches to secure a vigorous bloom would be desirable. There are now so many fine varieties of Lilac that varied and most beautiful small groups or groves could be formed of them alone. To have a Lilac group, or several, or a small grove, or even a few thoroughly well-grown specimens, would be infinitely better than the common plan of scattering a number of plants through the shrubberies to dwindle or to perish.

As regards Lilacs in the open garden we appear to be satisfied with the common variety. It is to be regretted that such excellent kinds as Dr. Lindley and Charles X. are not planted in preference to, or at least to an equal extent with, the commoner kinds. These are limited to three : Syringa vulgaris, S. dubia (or rothomagensis), and S. persica, with a few of their varieties ; and it is one or other of these kinds we are sure to see in our gardens or pleasure-grounds. In France, however, there is no such poverty of selection. There Lilacs are grown more frequently as specimens both in public and private gardens, and are often carefully pruned with a view of securing finer trusses of blossom. Many accustomed to the one kind so often half-starved in London shrubberies, and like so many other fine hardy shrubs treated as if unworthy of culture or attention, might be surprised to see such a list as the following from a French catalogue of handsome kinds more or less distinct.

Alba	Docteur Nobbe	Moritz Eichler
Laciniata	Ekenholm	*Philémon
Rubra	Flore pleno	Président Massart
*Aline Mocqueris	Géant des Batailles	Prince Impérial
Ambroise Verschaffelt	Général Schmidt	Princesse Camille de Rohan
Amœna	Gloire de la Rochelle	Princesse Marie
Béranger	*Gloire de Moulins	Professor Stœckhard
*Blanc Virginal	Goliath	Purpurea
*Carne à Grande Fleur	James Booth	Rubra insignis
Charlemagne	Justii	Charles X.
Croix de Brahy	Karlsruhensis	*Saugé
*De Croncels	König Johann	Spectabilis
*De Laval	Langius	Triomphe d'Orléans
*De Trianon	Lovaniensis	Vallettiana
Delépine	*Madame Kreuter	*Ville de Troyes.
Doctor Lindley		

As regards the best kinds of Lilac, M. C. Baltet, who has had excellent opportunities of judging, recommends those in the above list with an asterisk affixed as the kinds most worthy of culture among the varieties raised in recent years. He has observed more than fifty kinds growing in his garden, and among them he considers there are twenty good ones.

Pansy Basket of the Paris Market.

CHAPTER XXXII.

" Went out at early morning, when the air
Is delicate with some last starry touch,
To wander through the Market-place of Flowers
(The prettiest haunt in Paris), and make sure
At worst that there were roses in the world."
E. B. BROWNING.

FLOWER, FRUIT, AND VEGETABLE MARKETS.

No garden in existence possesses half the variety of the flower, fruit, and vegetable departments of the Halles Centrales, and it is a variety that is perpetual, for every day brings fresh materials, every week changes of supply. About twelve o'clock at night, before Paris has gone to bed, the growers have already arrived on the spot and begin to expose their freshly-gathered produce in the market or on the wide footways of the streets around, and for eighteen hours after that time the whole scene is one of animation. With its merry clatter of ten thousand tongues, the Central Market of Paris offers, particularly in the early morning, a never-failing source of interest, even to those who confine themselves to the study of the human species. But we who love Violets and those little fresh Rose-buds that look as if born in May and gathered before they were kissed by the sun, and on whom, perhaps, the brightness of some of the faces set in the white

2 N

caps is not, in consequence, wholly .lost, may find much to interest us here. Many who see this market in perfection in summer and autumn do not know it in early spring. The bitter cold of the early spring morning has no noticeable effect in reducing the numbers who usually throng the market, though it certainly must mar their comfort. The large extent of the Great Hall, however, saves them from such drenchings as the people suffer in Covent Garden on a wet morning. The piles of Mushrooms are among the most interesting of the things to be seen., These are thrown out on wide benches, and heaped up as any common roots might be. As to quality, these Mushrooms are excellent indeed ; nearly round, on an average about the size of a Horse Chestnut, perfectly white, fresh and delicate in texture and flavour, they look as if each was selected by an epicure from the myriads often seen on a hill-pasture on an autumn morning. These Mushrooms all come from the depths of the old stone-mines beneath Paris and its environs. Almost equally round, and chubby, and tender, are the little Carrots. Piles of large Pumpkins strew the ground ; these have been kept through the winter, and form, when green vegetables are scarce, an important article of food.

In the United States, long-keeping Gourds are quite as important a crop as the Turnip is with us, if not more so. It would, therefore, seem desirable that their value should be better known in England, where they are as easily grown as the Vegetable Marrow, the only Gourd now popular with us. · As compared with the large Gourd of the Paris market and the best Squashes of the Americans, the Vegetable Marrow is of little importance as a food-supply. The common garden Turnips are seen here, but are not so abundant as the Navet, which many think better, and which is pretty regularly supplied to Covent Garden from the Paris gardens. But there is another curious Turnip here—the Navet de Meaux. This is a singlar-looking kind, usually more than a foot long, frequently curled in form, and only as thick as a Cucumber. These are sent to market in a peculiar manner. The top is cut clean off, a hole pierced an inch below the cut, through which a few straws are passed, which permit of a dozen roots or so being strung in a bundle together. These Turnips remind one of the huge white Radishes that are seen ·in the Chinese quarter of

San Francisco, but are not so large as the snowy ones of the careful Chinese gardeners. Passing by many vegetables common to London and Paris markets, we observe that the Shallot offered everywhere here is the true kind, a distinct species with a slender bulb and a grey coat, whereas the Shallot now commonly sold in London, and evidently a small variety of the common Onion, is a roundish bulb, with a shining dark brown coat. Some not very important vegetables, almost out of date with us, are here yet seen in abundance, such, for example, as the Rampion, with its long and slender creamy-white roots, which are grown to perfection in the light rich soil of the market-gardens. Quantities of Green Peas, from the south, and piles of Globe Artichokes, do not interest us much in early spring, because they are obviously products of a fairer clime; but the great feature of the market is the quantity of excellent saladings of every kind, from the long tufts of Chicory (blanched in caves), to the fresh green rosettes of the tender Lettuce, which Paris is never without. Those sent from Paris to the London market, however good in quality, are never seen there to such advantage; their freshness is tarnished by packing and the journey. Though the whole process of growing these saladings is carried on within the very walls of Paris, there are many who suppose them to be (like the Green Peas and the Artichokes from Africa) the produce of a much warmer climate. There is no market where business is more expeditiously done than here; but what interest us most are the provisions made for the retail trade—for the purchases of the general public. In Paris far more than in London it is the custom to send to the market daily from every class of home. The buyer goes where numbers of competitors are side by side, and where the majority of vegetables exposed are fresh from the gardens.

In London as regards the quality of the products when delivered by the grower, there is rarely anything to complain of, for the market-gardener is usually an excellent cultivator; but the bruising and filth and delay they encounter, owing to imperfect market-arrangements, before reaching the customer in London, often render them barely edible, while the very poor, in buying the cheapest, often get that which is absolutely unfit for human food.

There is no country in the world where vegetables can be

2 N 2

grown more abundantly and cheaply than in the country round London, which can pour its produce into the great centre in an hour or two by rail, and yet for the want of spacious markets, and proper regulations, the London public is to a great extent deprived of advantages enjoyed by most cities and towns in Europe. As for our chief fruit and vegetable market, it is a disgrace to civilisation.   So long as the largest and richest city in the world depends upon Covent Garden as at present arranged, for its fruits and vegetables, so long must it find them very deficient.   The want of room alone is sufficient to frequently make important differences in the prices, not to speak of the treatment the produce gets at all times, especially in wet weather.   What a contrast to the central market in Paris !

Can we not secure a good wide market accessible to river, rail, and streets somewhere on the Thames Embankment, and leave Covent Garden to one or two branches of the trade ?   Can nothing be done to remedy a state of things which is not only a strong evidence of the want of orderly rule in the management of London, but which must have a bad effect on the supplies of almost every family. The cattle-market at Islington and the meat and poultry market in the City are excellent; they, like the Thames Embankment, are really worthy of London ; but as yet we do not seem to have moved a step towards the establishment of a garden-market worthy of the town.   Were this done with as broad an aim as has been shown in the other markets just named, we should have a feature added to London which would assuredly be of the greatest utility and benefit to the public at large.   We should also have an exhibition of the garden-produce of the country around London, presenting new objects of interest every day as the seasons changed.   A market fitted to accommodate, from the point of view of buyers and the public as well as the trade, the produce of the market- and fruit-gardens, would be one of the greatest improvements that could be effected in London.

In the Paris market, in addition to ample provision for wholesale trade, there are streets of stalls containing everything the purchaser requires, classified so that the market-women who vend the same sorts of produce are brought into proximity and competition with one another.   The advantages gained by the public are obvious—the housewife has not only the opportunity of purchasing everything good and at its fair price; she also has a great variety to choose from. But it is needless to enumerate all the advantages that a good retail and wholesale market confers upon its neighbourhood. In those little avenues of neatly-arranged stalls in all the Paris markets the name and number of the occupant is plainly printed; there is usually a free passage between each two rows, along which the purchaser can walk free from such crowding as must occur in badly-arranged markets. In fact there is every convenience for both purchaser and seller. The adoption of the same system of stalls in the new fruit and vegetable market, to which we may look forward, would be a great improvement. London is, however, now so vast in extent that little less than a series of well-managed markets will ever supply its population so well as Paris is supplied. Nevertheless one large central well-ordered market to begin with, would be a great boon to Londoners.

The history of the Halles Centrales illustrates to some extent the essentially-practical turn changes and improvements have taken in Paris of recent years. At one time the site was occupied by a vast graveyard, where the greater portion of the dead of Paris were gathered for centuries. At one time it lay outside the walls, but it gradually became surrounded by narrow streets, and eventually the place became a horrible nuisance. Then the government caused the vast accumulation of human remains to be removed by night in covered carts, escorted by chanting, torch-bearing priests, to the subterranean quarries that lie under Paris, and which, now filled with the piled bones of millions of men, are known as the Catacombs.

The most noticeable and admirable features of this great covered market are the neat stalls for retail dealers before alluded to, the lightness of design and good ventilation, and the roomy, airy character of the whole. It is constructed so as to be a protection against extremes of weather at all seasons; it is cool and shady in summer, the system of cellars underneath roomy and good, and with many useful arrangements for storing away the provisions, both alive and dead. The roof is of zinc, the flooring partly asphalte, partly flags, and, like every new building, or avenue, or wide street in Paris, trees adorn the margin of the wide footways around it, shading the scene of almost ceaseless animation beneath. There are many other markets in Paris, but

all of them are smaller than the Halles, which offer most interest
to the stranger.   A good deal of the choicer produce is, however,
taken to the Marché St. Honoré, after having been sold wholesale
in the central market.

There are thousands of Parisians whose garden is the window,
or a basket mossed over in the room, or a glazed case, and to most
of them the flower-market is a nursery ; an excellent nursery too,

*A Flower-market and City-square in one.   The new Central Flower-market, with Plantation of
Paulownias for shade :—(early morning view.)*

for there they can get numerous pretty plants in the best of
health for a trifling sum.   Considering that a few miles of sea
have for ages separated many marked customs of both peoples,
and that thousands of miles of sea have not prevented English
habits, that have never crossed the Channel, from spreading to
the Antipodes, it is perhaps vain to hope for the adoption of such
a feature as the flower-markets of Paris in our great towns ; yet
few could be more agreeable and useful.   In Paris the larger

flower-markets are not in permanent buildings, but occupy spaces which may be compared to that in Trafalgar-square—the plants being placed in groups on the gravel or flags, and the flowers and choicer plants under temporary tents. When the market is over, the space is cleared. In the great central market and in the minor markets there are also rows of stalls for flowers; shops vending them are numerous, and occasionally a solitary stand with abundance of them is seen here and there in the streets.

To the already well-known flower-markets, that against the new Hôtel Dieu is an important addition made since the war. It is well worth the attention of all interested in city-markets, from its simplicity of plan and fitness for the end in view. Beneath a young and healthy plantation of Paulownia-trees are arranged neat, permanent stands with cast-iron supports and zinc roofs; the paths and roads between are of asphalte and perfectly clean. In spring and summer, when the weather will permit, quantities of flowers are exposed in the uncovered spaces, and the roads and quays near are on market-days covered with whole nurseries of plants, shrubs, and young trees. As the market is a large and well-supplied one, the scene is a pleasant one on market-mornings. When it is over, the market-place forms a desirable open space kept in perfect order, and as it is cooled in summer by the shade of the large leaves of the Paulownia, it is probably as useful to the surrounding inhabitants as a square would be. The regular flower-markets are held at the Place de la Madeleine, the Château d'Eau, the Quai aux Fleurs, and in the Place St. Sulpice —twice weekly in each place.

THE CLIMATES OF PARIS AND LONDON COMPARED.—Devoted to his institutions, the Briton is generally very hard on his climate. If anything remarkable in the way of vegetable-produce comes out of other lands, the merit is not sought in the system or the cultivator, but in the fine climate, while all our own shortcomings are accounted for by climate, so that even those who heap most abuse upon it should be grateful to it for settling so many questions. But those who have lived in Paris during the winter or spring will not be under any such illusion, and will probably begin to suspect that there is at least one other climate in the world as little like that of Paradise as is our own. Even of those who have visited Paris many are under the impression that for clearness, salubrity, dryness, and heat, the climate of that city is incomparably superior to that of London.   The idea has no doubt arisen from the fact that most visitors to the French capital choose either summer or autumn for their trip.   At these periods even our own smoky metropolis is at its best; but the Londoner who for the first time finds himself walking down the boulevards or the Rue Royale upon a lovely June or August afternoon, sees the Paris climate in its fullest perfection.   The air is free from smoke, the buildings and houses are either dazzlingly white or of a delicate cream colour, and even the mud itself is of a clearer and brighter hue than the greasy, metallic-looking paste with which we are so familiar here.   Let him, however, choose November or December for his excursion, and he will soon discover that Paris can be as cold and cloudy, and even as foggy, as our own city.   A few figures from various unimpeachable sources, both French and English, will perhaps do something to dispel the prevailing notion of the great superiority of the climate of Paris over that of London.

The climate of Paris may be taken as being typical of that of the whole of the north-west of France, its changeableness, however, being somewhat less than that of the districts bordering on the sea.   In general characteristics it may be said to stand midway between the climates of the north-eastern portions of the country and the channel-shores.   It is less cold in winter than the former, being warmed by the breezes from the Atlantic Ocean, but is colder than the south and west.   In summer it is more temperate than the south and east, but hotter than the extréme west.   The mean temperature of Paris, taken from a series of official and private observations running over thirty-six years, may be taken at 51·55° F.   The lowest temperature observed during fifty-two years was 2° below zero F.; the highest during the same time was within a fraction of 99° F.

These figures deserve a little consideration.   For a similar period the averages of the observations taken in London by the officers of the Royal Society are as follows: Mean temperature 50·50° F.; highest temperature, 97° F.; the lowest, 5° below zero F.   The mean temperature of Paris is therefore one-twentieth of a degree over 1° F. higher than our own, while the highest temperature only exceeds ours by something less than 2° F.

It will also be instructive to compare the mean temperature of the four seasons in both places.

		Paris. Fahr.	London. Fahr.
Mean Temperature,	Spring	50·0	49·0
„	Summer	64·8	62·5
	Autumn	52·0	51·0
„	Winter	39·5	39·0

It must, however, be borne in mind that in the suburbs of London the mean temperature is 2° F. below that of the city, and that on winter nights, when Jack Frost is striving his hardest to destroy all the vegetation within his reach, there is often as much as 4° F. between the thermometers of the city and the suburbs. The cause of this variation is twofold. In the summer a large quantity of heat is radiated by the masses of brickwork in the city, to say nothing of the amount of solar heat absorbed by day and given off again during the night; while in the winter the city is obviously warmer than the suburbs during both day and night, on account of the extra heat caused by the numerous fires, both industrial and domestic. Paris, as a city, being under precisely similar conditions, we may feel safe in assuming that the same difference exists between the mean temperature of the Observatory and Montreuil as between that of Somerset House and Tottenham for instance. Luke Howard, one of our most acute British meteorologists, on the strength of many thousands of observations made at Plaistow, Stratford, and Tottenham, gives the difference between the mean temperature of London and the country as 2° F. exactly, and a careful examination of his data has proved his figures to be correct within a fraction. This difference sinks to less than half a degree in spring; it increases in summer and autumn, and often rises on winter nights to as much as $4\frac{1}{2}°$ F. It is a singular fact that towards the end of spring, when the fires are being discontinued, and the sun has not yet reached his full power, it sometimes happens that the day temperature is somewhat greater in the country. This is doubtless to be attributed to the veil of smoke and cloud that is hanging over the metropolis which intercepts the action of the sun. The effects of the higher mean winter-temperature in the city are singularly apparent in the earlier budding and blooming of the trees, which frequently begin their spring life several days

before their suburban cousins—a fact which may easily be verified
by a walk from the suburbs into the city, just as the Elms are
beginning to bud, or when the Pear-trees are putting on their
early spring livery.

The amount of annual rainfall in London only slightly exceeds
that of Paris, although any unprejudiced person would feel
inclined to give it as his opinion that the number of rainy days
in London greatly exceeded those in Paris. The French authorities
who have been consulted differ somewhat in their calculations,
owing possibly to having collected the rain with dissimilar instru-
ments. The English figures are from Luke Howard, the French
from Gasparin and Bouvard.

	Gasparin. Inches.	Bouvard. Inches.	Howard. Inches.
Rainfall in Spring	5·6	4·0	5·0
„ Summer	6·8	6·0	6·5
„ Autumn	5·3	6·4	7·5
„ Winter	4·6	4·8	6·0
	22·3	21·2	25·0

INDEX.

LONDON: PRINTED BY WILLIAM CLOWES AND SONS, STAMFORD STREET
AND CHARING CROSS.

4250